A STEIN READER

A Stein Reader

GERTRUDE STEIN

EDITED AND WITH AN INTRODUCTION BY ULLA E. DYDO

NORTHWESTERN UNIVERSITY PRESS *Evanston, Illinois*

Northwestern University Press
Evanston, Illinois 60208-4210

Printed in the United States of America

ISBN: cloth 0-8101-1058-x
paper 0-8101-1083-0

Library of Congress
Cataloging-in-Publication Data
Stein, Gertrude, 1874–1946.
[Selections. 1993]
A Stein reader / edited by Ulla E. Dydo.
p. cm.
Includes bibliographical references.
ISBN 0-8101-1058-x (alk. paper). — ISBN 0-8101-1083-0 (pbk. : alk. paper)
I. Dydo, Ulla E. II. Title.
PS3537.T323A6 1993
818′.5209—dc20 93-29181
CIP

The paper used in this publication meets the minimum requirements of the American National Standard for Information Sciences—Permanence of Paper for Printed Library Materials, ANSI Z39.48-1984.

CONTENTS

The Table of Contents includes for each selection the date of composition; information on the first publication (usually in a magazine) and, if applicable, the first book publication; and the Yale Catalogue (Haas-Gallup) number. For full titles and bibliographical information, see the List of Abbreviations.

Abbreviations of Stein Works xi

Acknowledgments xiii

Introduction 1

A Note on the Texts 11

THE MAKING OF AMERICANS. BEING A HISTORY OF A FAMILY'S PROGRESS (Selections)
1903–11. *Transatlantic Review* 1, nos. 4, 5, 6; 2, nos. 1, 2, 3, 4 (1924). Dijon: Contact Editions, Maurice Darantière, 1925. H-G 2. 17

ADA
December 1910. *G & P,* 1922. H-G 13. 100

TWO WOMEN
1911(?). *Contact Collection of Contemporary Writers,* Paris, 1925. H-G 5. 104

ORTA OR ONE DANCING
1911–12. *TWO,* 1951. H-G 7. 120

MATISSE
1911. *Camera Work,* August 1912. *P & P,* 1934. H-G 28.

PICASSO
1911. *Camera Work,* August 1912. *P & P,* 1934. H-G 29. 137

NADELMAN
1911. *Larus* 1, no. 4 (July 1927). *P & P,* 1934. H-G 37. 144

PLAY
1911(?). *P & P,* 1934. H-G 31. 147

BON MARCHE WEATHER
Spring 1911. *TWO*, 1951. H-G 25. 149

A LONG GAY BOOK
1911–12. *GMP*, 1933. H-G 32. 151

MISS FURR AND MISS SKEENE
1911. *G & P*, 1922. H-G 27. 254

PORTRAIT OF CONSTANCE FLETCHER
1911 and 1912. *G & P*, 1922. H-G 23. 260

WHAT HAPPENED
A FIVE ACT PLAY
April 1913. *G & P*, 1922. H-G 52. 268

ONE
CARL VAN VECHTEN
June 1913. *G & P*, 1922. H-G 53. 273

ARTICLE
1913. H-G 54. 276

GUILLAUME APPOLLINAIRE
1913. *DP*, 1930. *P & P*, 1934. H-G 72. 278

PINK MELON JOY
1915. *G & P*, 1922. H-G 105. 280

LADIES' VOICES
CURTAIN RAISER
1916. *G & P*, 1922. H-G 129. 306

MARRY NETTIE
ALRIGHT MAKE IT A SERIES AND CALL IT MARRY NETTIE
1917. *PL*, 1955. H-G 155. 308

ACCENTS IN ALSACE
A REASONABLE TRAGEDY
Spring 1919. *G & P*, 1922. H-G 189. 314

TOURTY OR TOURTEBATTRE
A STORY OF THE GREAT WAR
1919. *G & P*, 1922. H-G 207. 322

A CIRCULAR PLAY

A PLAY IN CIRCLES

May–June 1920. *LO & P*, 1949. H-G 228. 326

PHOTOGRAPH

A PLAY IN FIVE ACTS

July 1920. *LO & P*, 1949. H-G 222. 343

REREAD ANOTHER

A PLAY

TO BE PLAYED INDOORS OR OUT

I WISH TO BE A SCHOOL.

1921. *O & P*, 1932. H-G 257. 347

MILDRED'S THOUGHTS

1922. *American Caravan*, 1927. *RAB*, 1973, incomplete; 3rd printing, 1975, complete. H-G 261. 356

IDEM THE SAME

A VALENTINE TO SHERWOOD ANDERSON

December 1922. *Little Review* 9 (Spring 1923). *UK*, 1928. H-G 277. 376

SAINTS AND SINGING

A PLAY

November/December 1922. *O & P*, 1932. H-G 264.

A LIST

1923. *O & P*, 1932. H-G 286. 381

CAPITAL CAPITALS

1923. *This Quarter* 1, no. 1 (Summer 1925). *New Music* 20, no. 3 (April 1947). H-G 287. 415

CEZANNE

1923. *P & P*, 1934. H-G 283. 427

AN ELUCIDATION

1923. *transition*, no. 1 (April 1927). *P & P*, 1934. H-G 289. 429

PRACTICE OF ORATORY

1923. *PL*, 1955. H-G 291. 443

HE AND THEY, HEMINGWAY
July or early August 1923. *Ex Libris* 1, no. 6 (December 1923). *P & P,* 1934. H-G 294. 449

A BOOK CONCLUDING WITH AS A WIFE HAS A COW
A LOVE STORY
September 1923. Paris: Editions de la Galerie Simon, 1926. *transition,* no. 3 (June 1927), incomplete. H-G 295.
VAN OR TWENTY YEARS AFTER
A SECOND PORTRAIT OF CARL VAN VECHTEN.
September 1923. *UK,* 1928. *P & P,* 1934. H-G 296.
IF I TOLD HIM
A COMPLETED PORTRAIT OF PICASSO
September 1923. *Vanity Fair* 21, no. 8 (April 1924). *DP,* 1930. *P & P,* 1934. H-G 299. 451

GEOGRAPHY
September 1923. *PL,* 1955. H-G 300. 467

DESCRIPTIONS OF LITERATURE
1924. *ASP,* 1926. *transition,* no. 13 (Summer 1928). H-G 322. 471

SITWELL EDITH SITWELL
1925. In *Composition as Explanation* [and other pieces], 1926. *P & P,* 1934. H-G 330. 475

BUSINESS IN BALTIMORE
1925. *UK,* 1928. H-G 333. 479

LIPCHITZ
Late 1925. *Ray Art Miscellany,* no. 2 (June 1927). *P & P,* 1934. H-G 344. 491

COMPOSITION AS EXPLANATION
January 1926. *Dial* 81, no. 4, (October 1926). London: Hogarth Press, 1926. H-G 339. 493

AN ACQUAINTANCE WITH DESCRIPTION
Summer 1926. London: Seizin Press, 1929. H-G 342. 504

THE LIFE OF JUAN GRIS
THE LIFE AND DEATH OF JUAN GRIS
May 1927. *transition,* no. 4 (July 1927). *P & P,* 1934. H-G 361. 535

GEORGE HUGNET
Late summer 1928. *Blues*, no. 6 (July 1929). *DP*, 1930. *P & P*, 1934. H-G 373. 538

EVIDENCE
Autumn 1929. *Blues*, no. 8 (Spring 1930), incomplete. *Modern Things*, 1934, incomplete. H-G 392. 541

MORE GRAMMAR FOR A SENTENCE
Summer 1930. *AFAM*, 1954. H-G 399. 547

HOW SHE BOWED TO HER BROTHER
Fall 1931(?). *transition*, no. 21 (March 1932). *P & P*, 1934. H-G 431. 564

STANZAS IN MEDITATION (Selections)
Summer/Fall 1932. *SIM*, 1956. H-G 451. 568

IDENTITY A POEM
Summer 1935. *Masterpieces*, 1940. Rpt. in *PGU*, 1971. H-G 486. 588

DOCTOR FAUSTUS LIGHTS THE LIGHTS
February–June 1938. *LO & P*, 1949. H-G 515. 595

ABBREVIATIONS OF STEIN WORKS

AFAM — *As Fine As Melanctha (1914–1930)*. Vol. 4 of the Yale Edition, 1954.

ASP — *As Stable Pamphlet*. Englewood, N.J. 1926.

DP — *Dix Portraits* (in French and English). Paris: Editions de la Montagne, 1930.

G & P — *Geography and Plays*. Boston: Four Seas Company, 1922.

GMP — *Matisse Picasso and Gertrude Stein With Two Shorter Stories*. Paris: Plain Edition, 1933.

LO & P — *Last Operas and Plays*. New York: Rinehart & Co., 1949.

WAM — *What Are Masterpieces*. Los Angeles, Calif.: The Conference Press, 1940.

O & P — *Operas and Plays*. Paris: Plain Edition, 1932.

PL — *Painted Lace and Other Pieces (1914–1937)*. Vol. 5 of the Yale Edition, 1955.

P & P — *Portraits and Prayers*. New York: Random House, 1934.

PGU — *A Primer for the Gradual Understanding of Gertrude Stein*. Santa Barbara, Calif.: Black Sparrow Press, 1971.

RAB — *Reflection on the Atomic Bomb*. Los Angeles, Calif.: Black Sparrow Press, 1973.

SIM — *Stanzas in Meditation and Other Poems (1929–1933)*. Vol. 6 of the Yale Edition, 1956.

TWO — *Two: Gertrude Stein and Her Brother and Other Early Portraits (1908–1912)*. Vol. 1 of the Yale Edition, 1951.

UK *Useful Knowledge.* New York: Payson & Clarke, Ltd., 1928.

The Yale Edition of the Unpublished Writings of Gertrude Stein. 8 vols. New Haven, Conn.: Yale University Press, 1951–58. Posthumous.

The Yale Catalogue is a bibliographical listing: Robert Bartlett Haas and Donald Clifford Gallup, *A Catalogue of the Published and Unpublished Writings of Gertrude Stein* (New Haven, Conn.: Yale University Press, 1941). Its last (fourth) section, "A Chronological List of Published and Unpublished Writings of Gertrude Stein," lists each piece with a chronological H[aas]-G[allup] number. This numbering system organizes the papers in the Stein Archive. The listing has many problems with dates, as the numbers in the Table of Contents in the *Reader* suggest.

ACKNOWLEDGMENTS

This volume was initiated by Marjorie Perloff, whose familiarity with the progress of my work on Gertrude Stein led her to propose to Jonathan Brent, the former director of Northwestern University Press, a collection of Stein texts. Without their commitment *A Stein Reader* could not have been undertaken. Under the guidance of Susan Harris and her staff at Northwestern University Press texts were prepared and the volume completed in exemplary collaboration.

Research on Gertrude Stein for my study of her work from 1923 to 1932 was supported in 1981–82 by a Fellowship for College Teachers from the National Endowment for the Humanities and in the summer of 1980 by a grant from the P.S.C. - C.U.N.Y. Research Award Program. The work these awards allowed me to do became in effect support also for *A Stein Reader* and they are gratefully acknowledged.

I cannot here name all my friends and colleagues or the acquaintances of Gertrude Stein who aided my research. I confine acknowledgments to those who gave direct help for the *Reader.* Donald Gallup, retired Curator of the Yale Collection of American Literature, answered questions and critically reviewed my headnotes. Leon Katz, whose headnotes and selections from *The Making of Americans* are a part of this book, gave unstinting help on Stein's early work. Anne Lindbeck offered me years of hospitality that made my work possible. I thank others without whose faith the texts printed here could not have become a book: Stan Brakhage, Edward Burns, Bruce Kellner, Richard Morrison, Peter Quartermain, Robert A. Wilson.

The center of this book, the texts of Gertrude Stein, are printed with the permission of Calman A. Levin for the Estate of Gertrude Stein. For the actual review of texts I thank Patricia Willis, Curator of the Yale Collection of American Literature, and the staff of the Beinecke Rare Book and Manuscript Library, Yale University: Patricia Middleton, Stephen Jones, Daria Ague, Richard Hart, Lori Misura, Catherine Sharp. They not only made available to myself and my collaborators, Rosalind Moad and William Rice, manuscripts, typescripts and other papers needed for this edition but tolerated and supported our murmuring presence in the lower hall of the library where for eight weeks in the summer of 1990 we read aloud every word, every spelling and punctuation mark of every text in this book. A publication grant to Northwestern University Press from the National Endowment for the Humanities made that textual work possible.

Rosalind Moad and William Rice brought to our task their deep knowledge of Stein's language, which allowed us to collaborate on true readings of the texts in this collection. Without William Rice's unfailing ear for Stein's voice and mine the headnotes for this book could not have been written.

A STEIN READER: INTRODUCTION

On sheets of unbound copies of the 1855 edition of *Leaves of Grass,* Walt Whitman jotted down notes for *An American Primer,* a lecture he never delivered. It declared speech in America free of the rules of the English mother tongue, and claimed "liberty to carry out the spirit of the laws [of language], even by violating them, if necessary.—The English language is grandly lawless like the race who use it—or, rather, breaks out of the little laws to enter truly the higher ones." "I have heard it said that when the spirit arises that does not brook submission and imitation, it will throw off the ultramarine names.—That Spirit already walks the streets of the cities of These States—I, and others, illustrate it."

. . .

After World War II, Gertrude Stein spoke of educating the Germans,

> I said there is only one thing to be done and that is to teach them disobedience. . . . Teach them disobedience, I said, . . . confuse their minds, get their minds confused and perhaps then they will be disobedient and the world will be at peace. The obedient peoples go to war, disobedient peoples like peace. . . .

. . .

In a notebook for *The Making of Americans,* Stein wrote of the respect for authority in East Coast institutions,

> Eastern colleges too dam anxious to be safe. They needn't be so afraid it ain't so easy to be hurt as they seem to think least at least not by getting hit hard on the head. They needn't be so scared of any of us got any chance of real stuff in us just because we are made different. . . . They needn't be so afraid of their damn culture, it'd take more than a man like me to hurt it.

. . .

At Stein's talk of 31 March 1935 in Pasadena, Hal Levy, a graduate student, took notes for a term paper. "The great thing about language is that we should forget it and begin over again." And later, "American literature one long struggle without changing language to make it do what it has never done before."

. . .

Among the Stein papers is a review of *Finnegans Wake* by Oliver St. John Gogarty from *The Observer* of 7 May 1939. A marked passage insists that Joyce's style began in resentment at feeling driven out as an artist. "Thus the style had its beginnings in resentment, and its precedents in Lewis Carroll and Gertrude Stein, who was first, so far as I know, in her 'Portrait of Mabel Dodge,' to strive for a new effect from the contortions of grammar and syntax." Did Stein feel driven out of America, as Joyce felt driven out of Ireland, by language gone stiff and dead—what she called associative language, used from unthinking habit? She declined to observe rules and composed each piece as a new experiment in how to write. Like a child with a primer, she played a word or two until they became a new construction.

...

She followed Cézanne, refusing to subordinate all elements to a compositional center. As he had done with brush strokes and daubs of color, so she patterned sensation into composition with each letter, syllable, and word, each space and line. One of the poet Mina Loy's "Aphorisms on Futurism" of 1914 described modern perception, "Consciousness has no climax." Stein also reminds herself, "Climax no climax is necessary." Each word is an increment, none a digression, from the verbal and visual design.

...

When she set a text, she said what she meant and she meant what she said. She knew that paraphrase withdrew the words from the text rather than elucidating them: "You must not think that you do not understand it because you cannot say it . . . in other words," she said in an interview in New York in November 1934. bpNichol understood perfectly in his own words of her: "i am these words / these words say so" ("song: for saint ein," 1983). Stein followed her sense of words, not the rules of grammar and word order that editors, printers, and proofreaders observed. She worked to subvert the authority of language—as did Joyce later. Many called her, as they also called Joyce, illiterate or mad. Since neither adhered to conventional standards, their phrasing was thought arbitrary and textual accuracy did not seem to matter. Both ended up in print with countless errors.

...

On the inside cover of a notebook for *Sentences* (1929), Stein played with two words, two names—or perhaps it is one:

Caesar Onestone
Mr. Einesteine

Imperial singularity? Einstein Englished? Stein herself, an Einstein with a feminine -e added to the masculine Mister (half-rhyming with Caesar)? A stoneware stein for beer? A stone's weight? And in the year of the formulation of the unified field theory, Einstein's thought in relation to Newton's, "where before, if all things were emptied from the world, time and space were left—time and space would now disappear with the things" (Louis Zukofsky, *Bottom; On Shakespeare* [Berkeley and Los Angeles: University of California Press, 1963], 163).

. . .

No time, no space, no center, standard, or authority. Stein wrote in a world changed by Einstein and even more by Heisenberg and Schrödinger. She knew she was one of them, constructing for words what they had constructed for quantum mechanics. On 25 May 1928 Dorothy Dudley Harvey wrote to Stein from New York, where in the new issue of the *Saturday Review of Literature* Bertrand Russell's "Physics and Metaphysics" had just appeared. Harvey described Stein with a quotation from Russell as a visionary in the world of the new physics,

> "Nowadays, physicists, the most hard-headed of mankind . . . have embodied in their technique this insubstantiality which some of the metaphysicians have so long urged in vain."
>
> In connection with grammar I thought at once of you, and wondered, knowing little about them, if you have not been one of the metaphysicians as an artist, with whom the physicists have just caught up.

• • • • •

These passages describe the subversive experimental work of Gertrude Stein, which changed language and writing for us all. *A Stein Reader* is an introduction to her language experiments. Not only that. Since each piece she wrote was a new beginning that questioned language, writing, and reading, this *Reader* also becomes a primer. It returns us to the schoolroom where Stein asks what the three Rs are and teaches us to read in ways more fundamental than we had thought possible, more literal than we had known. One of her descriptions speaks of literature as "[a] book which asks questions of everyone." Questions, not answers, may make it "[a] book more than ever read."

From early to late years she listened to people expressing themselves by repeating themselves. She learned how words joined for the ear to hear, the eye to see, the mind to know, and she made them move in composition. An inventor of new ways, she wanted desperately to be read. She submitted everything for publication, but most of it was returned because it did not represent a familiar world and could not be read in familiar ways. Stein, who knew attack and resistance in human relations, did not know how much resistance her work provoked by refusing the accepted ways. "Listen to me," she said over and over, but most editors would not listen and would not print her. In the manuscript of *Identity A Poem* she made a personal comment about her frustration in a sentence that she rightly eliminated. "I know now why when one is [xd creating] writing and nothing has been printed and therefore there is no audience every single word every scrap of writing is important because there being no audience." In the deleted sentence she had already revised "creating" to "writing." Near the end of her life, in *The Mother Of Us All,* she had Susan B. Anthony speak for her: "They themselves will they deny that they listen to me but let them deny it, all the same they do listen to me . . . they cannot either see or hear unless I tell them so. . . . Yes said Susan B. yes they always listen to me."

The *Reader* represents many new Stein ways, but it differs from other widely used collections in print. Chief among these is *Selected Writings of Gertrude Stein,* edited by Carl Van Vechten (New York: Random House, 1946), with a "Message" Stein wrote a month before she died. This collection was first discussed with Bennett Cerf of Random House in the summer of 1936 but not published until October 1946. Its history from 1936 to 1946 is documented in *The Letters of Gertrude Stein and Carl Van Vechten,* ed. Edward Burns (New York: Columbia University Press, 1986). *Selected Writings* was planned from the start to include both late "public" works in conventional English and a limited number of experimental pieces, especially from the early period. The volume begins with the popular *Autobiography of Alice B. Toklas;* goes on to the lecture *The Gradual Making of* The Making of Americans, to lead into a section of that long novel; and continues with a variety of other works, some excerpted, some complete. This order followed the personality publicized and familiar from the American lecture tour. Published soon after the war, the volume ends with wartime work. Notes are confined to matters of publication.

Also well known is *The Yale Gertrude Stein,* a selection by Richard Kostelanetz from the eight posthumous volumes published by Yale between 1951 and 1958. The works selected are described by such phrases as "an extended abstraction" (*Stanzas in Meditation*); "a mixture of poetry and prose" (*Patriarchal Poetry*); "a lesbian classic" (*Lifting Belly*); and as "major long poems," "minimal poetry," and "sound poetry," categories that Stein resisted. The order of the pieces is not explained, and errors in dates are not corrected. Printed in 1980 from the plates of the posthumous volumes, *The Yale Gertrude Stein* reprints their errors.

Another collection was planned but never realized by Robert Bartlett

Haas, who had Stein's approval to assemble a "primer" consisting of selected Stein pieces as touchstones for reading and understanding her work. The primer was never printed in this form. However, Haas issued three collections of Stein work with brief comments: *A Primer for the Gradual Understanding of Gertrude Stein,* 1971, the closest to his original aim; *Reflection on the Atomic Bomb,* 1973; and *How Writing Is Written,* 1974 (all published by Black Sparrow Press).

A Stein Reader has larger aims. First, it represents Stein the modernist innovator, not the personality. It concentrates on experimental work written "from inside" and excludes her late public works written "from outside" in conventional English. These later works, such as *The Autobiography of Alice B. Toklas, Everybody's Autobiography,* and the book *Picasso,* involve few textual problems and are available in separate editions. The *Reader* includes a more substantial group of innovative works than *Selected Writings* and is more broadly representative than *The Yale Gertrude Stein.* The works in the *Reader* are largely, though not completely, from the years before she achieved popular success with *The Autobiography of Alice B. Toklas,* written in 1932 and published in 1933. The *Reader* does not rely on explanations of work written with hindsight, such as *Lectures in America.* The only lecture included is her first, *Composition as Explanation* of 1926.

The *Reader* changes the balance of Stein work in print, including as it does pieces that are almost unknown and omitting others that are well known. For example, *Three Lives* and *Tender Buttons,* each available in paperback, are not included, but the dramatic change in style that resulted in *Tender Buttons* can instead be followed in *A Long Gay Book.* Likewise, while such a widely anthologized play as *Four Saints in Three Acts* is not included, *Reread Another, Saints and Singing,* and *A List* draw attention to her many unknown plays. *Pink Melon Joy* is a sensuous riot less familiar than the much discussed *Lifting Belly.* The *Reader* offers variety and interest precisely because it includes work hardly known or long out of print.

Second, following Stein's conviction that each word is essential to the design of a piece, the *Reader,* with two exceptions, prints only complete works, including some printed incompletely in earlier publications. The main exception is *The Making of Americans,* always the most important work to Stein. The selection from the long novel published in 1934—the same as the French *Américains d'Amérique* of 1933—shows how unsatisfactory it is to abridge a book whose center is not a narrative of plot and character. The *Reader* includes extracts that make no attempt to summarize the book but show the stages through which the novel and Stein herself developed in the nine years of writing and rewriting. The extracts were selected by Leon Katz, whose research on the first works and early notebooks, which he reviewed with Alice Toklas, laid the foundation for understanding Stein. The second exception, *Stanzas in Meditation* of 1932, is also a work of large scope. It was written alongside *The Autobiography of Alice B. Toklas,* which by 1933 brought Stein fame and publicity. The untitled stanzas are not held together by a narrative thread that a selection would break. The poems included in the *Reader* reveal the context that governed their writing and should allow the same reader whom the excerpts from *The Making of Americans* prepare for the full novel to enter the text of the complete *Stanzas.*

Third, the *Reader* prints all pieces in chronological order of composition, not publication. The dates of composition reflect Stein's development as dates of publication cannot, since her difficulties with publishers and readers, voiced over and over in the phrase "Listen to me," were such that she could never count on speedy printing of new work though she always submitted it. The pieces in the *Reader* have been dated or redated as accurately as possible, to supplement and correct the *Yale Catalogue,* reprinted in Richard Bridgman's *Gertrude Stein in Pieces* (New York: Oxford University Press, 1970).

With every element—every letter, syllable, sound, even white space—essential to composition, and no distinction between important and unimportant words to guide reading, accurate texts become indispensable. Where authority is in question, conventional usage does not help us. Many printed Stein pieces show errors overlooked by proofreaders and even Stein herself. *A Stein Reader* is the first collection that has received textual attention such as is now being given to Joyce and others whose writings deviate from the conventions of English.

To check texts would appear to be a simple task of proofreading print against manuscript. However, textual authority is often a puzzle of interpretation far beyond proofreading. Changes that are not in manuscript but are penned by Stein into the typescript and appear in print must be considered revisions, not corrections. When several different typescripts survive, which is the authoritative text? Some published versions show that in setting type the printer relied on a different manuscript from the one preserved; which text is then authoritative, and why? When two printed versions of a piece differ, what is the reason, which is more reliable, and why? Are changes that we see errors? revisions? late additions? corrections? Authority maddeningly changes from piece to piece. To explore the nature of the texts as fully as possible for *A Stein Reader,* not only manuscripts but also early and late typescripts of Toklas as well as printed versions and their sources have been compared. We have retained Stein's use of *s* rather than *z* in words like *realise, authorise,* and *emphasise.*

Stein took pride in the orderliness of her work and paid attention to how it was typed, but she never regularized mechanically, for she did not value consistency for itself. *More Grammar For A Sentence* opens without indentation, breaking the rule we are taught about beginning a piece. Why? Because her opening is merely a sentence, not a paragraph. A reading of the manuscript of *Doctor Faustus Lights The Lights* shows Stein marking character transformation by a change in name from Doctor Faustus to Faust, depending on the dramatic action. She was interested in more than consistent nomenclature.

Following an author's deliberate variations is exciting. However, we are only beginning to see in certain bodies of work not only the words but the process of composing. For Stein and others—one thinks of the poet Susan Howe's variant readings of the poems of Emily Dickinson—the word *text* includes that process. The energy of a piece comes in part from the act of writing, which enters it as value that can be read, just as hues and brush strokes can be read in a painting. A text must be transcribed with attention to the evidence of its making. Print, while it cannot always reproduce that process, need not wipe it out. Inside a text are the lines that carry the words, the hand moving on paper, line breaks and spaces dictated by notebook or leaf, size and folds of paper, pen or pencil forming words, the shape of a draft visible in the way it is copied into a notebook, and even the effort to end a work in the space of one notebook.

Manuscripts sometimes show what print wipes out. The title *Five Words In A Line* (not included in the *Reader*) simply describes itself. Stein must have noticed that about five of her handwritten words filled a line in her French notebooks. Print cannot reproduce this fact except in the title, and a title is not a line. Knowing the nature of a line, consider the variant, "Four words in a line." The manuscript still *shows* five words in the line but says "four words in a line." The tension between the two originates in a tiny visual observation, as a headnote can explain. The portrait *Lipchitz* (Stein and Toklas followed the original spelling, Lipschitz, silently corrected in the *Reader*) in manuscript and typescript shows Stein's handwritten signature on the last line, flushed right, as in a letter. In the printed text in *Portraits and Prayers,* her name is omitted, presumably because the editors did not realize that it was a part of the text. The *Reader* restores the name. Immediately after *Lipchitz* Stein wrote a portrait of Cocteau, not included in the *Reader,* signed also as a letter, "G. Stein." This name, printed as it is in *Portraits and Prayers* at the top center of a new page, looks like a subtitle, which destroys it as signature. Where words appear on the page determines how they speak.

Who would ever think about the ampersand, that odd symbol that is also a word. It is a corruption of *and per se and,* equivalent to the symbol &, made by combining the Latin letters *e* and *t.* Literature uses words, not symbols, but Stein did not worry about propriety and used both. The play *A List* shows Marius, Maryas, Mary, Martha, and Mabel, the names of the characters, in rows that make lists down the left margin. Some have single lines after their names. Others are joined with "and" as couples or groups of three, four, or five. But some couples in this farcical game of lovers, hidden letters, initials, and names are joined instead with an ampersand that is not reproduced in *Operas and Plays.* Yet symbols and words regulate relationships differently. The *Reader* restores the ampersand. Another unliterary word is Latin *idem,* which appears with its translation, "the same," as if in a class recitation. *Idem the same* precedes *A Valentine for Sherwood Anderson,* which was already a valentine for Alice Toklas. One valentine served both, and all may be the same—or not the same. The smallest words and even symbols have been explored.

Reviewing texts for the *Reader* has included attention to design. *Pink Melon Joy* consists of many sections varying in length and written in variable lines. Each section is introduced by a short phrase or sentence that becomes a heading for what follows. In the typescript and in print in *Geography and Plays,* these headings are centered on the page, followed by a small space. But in the manuscript notebook Stein entered the headings diagonally across the left page, with the text in regular horizontal lines across the right page or pages. All sections follow this spacious design, which creates a balance of blocks and directions of text. The printer followed the typescript, which had regularized the text. Only a costly facsimile edition could print the piece as Stein wrote it, but a page can be designed that preserves her balance. At the least, a headnote can describe the design, which she liked enough to use again in the next piece, *Study Nature.*

The *Reader* prints texts in the most correct form the editorial team has been able to trace. Where the process of composition becomes apparent, an effort has been made to open it. At the same time, this book is a reader, not a full scholarly edition, which must wait until a complete *Works* is undertaken. The *Reader* does not include the superscripts and footnotes that go with variants, for they clutter reading. Though not exhaustively annotated, it includes responsible texts and headnotes about context and text to lead into reading.

Every piece in this book is about taking language apart. Every part of every word is turned, examined, and tossed about in composition. To follow Gertrude Stein is to discover the world in words we had never known until she used them:

> To be using a new word in my writing is to me a very difficult thing. Every word I am ever using in writing has for me very existing being. . . . I am feeling many ways of using one word in writing.

The texts in this book teach lessons of the schoolroom for the twentieth century and for modernism. In the *Sixth Eclectic Reader* of 1857 William Holmes McGuffey answered the question of language, "Which shall yield, the poet or established usage? Certainly not the latter." In the fragmented worlds of Whitman and Stein, usage lost its authority. Whitman's *Primer* spoke the language of the new world: "What a history is folded, folded inward again, in the single word I." Stein knew the price of disobedience. "You know you will be laughed at or pitied by every one and you have a queer feeling and you are not certain and you go on writing."

A NOTE ON THE TEXTS

The introduction to the *Reader* speaks of puzzling out textual authority for writing made of words as things rather than words as signs. In the absence of a consistent set of principles informing authority for all Stein pieces, texts had to be verified individually. While reading them, however, we came to see that the process of writing is at the very center of Stein's work. Her words often speak of this process. Yet when the words are frozen in print, a large part of the creative process itself is lost.

That process can be read, however, in how the words appear on the handwritten pages of the manuscripts, which make Stein's intentions visible. We see the intentions in the way the hand formed the words and moved them on the page; in notebooks chosen; pen or pencil used; in fast, slow, tight, or loose writing; in lines, breaks, spacing, excisions.

To discover intentions and authority, we together read each selection aloud against available sources—handwritten, typed, and printed. We consulted the typescripts, discovering quickly that the late ones prepared by Toklas for Carl Van Vechten in 1937 were far less reliable than the ones done at or near the time of writing. We checked publications in which Stein participated, which gave them authority. Finally, we reviewed the eight posthumous Yale volumes of the Unpublished Writings of Gertrude Stein. Our obligation became not only to print the words accurately but also, as far as possible, to give access to the process of composition. Starting with print and going on to manuscript, this Note on the Texts summarizes how we worked, how we learned to read texts, how we made decisions.

Different printed texts have different authority. For work in whose publications Stein was involved, we have usually given greater weight to the printed text in evaluating authority than for works in which she was not involved. However, in the case of *Geography and Plays* the printed pieces so often do not correspond to the manuscript texts and typescripts that we came to distrust this book. We could not assume that the typescripts at Yale were the same as those sent to the publisher, the Four Seas Company in Boston, unless revisions were inked in before mailing. We assumed Stein forwarded a second typescript, not preserved, with changes in texts, including phrasing, punctuation, and arrangement of titles. But none of this is entirely clear.

Since the beautifully printed and designed Random House *Portraits and*

Prayers of 1934 included serious errors, we did not trust it. It was not proofread by Stein. We do not know what setting typescripts Random House received, but they cannot have included errors such as are identified in the headnotes for *Lipchitz,* the elegy for Juan Gris, and *How She Bowed to Her Brother.* The seductive design of this book overrode text rather than serving it.

The Plain Edition, Stein's own venture for printing her unpublished work, should have produced reliable texts, but they are beset by problems. Stein was not experienced in printing. Publishing her own work may have been fraught with anxiety, and she may have saved money at cost to the texts. We do not know the arrangements for payment for errors and revisions. As setting typescripts do not survive, we do not know whether changes were authorized that were not entered in the manuscripts. For *Capital Capitals,* for example, we had to discover her intention by returning to the manuscript from the text confusingly set on the pages of the Plain Edition volume *Operas and Plays.* As the play is printed in the *Reader,* the intentions of the manuscript are followed in spacing, indenting, and separating spoken lines from the "characters," the capitals. For accurate texts, the authority of each of these publications requires evaluation.

The Making of Americans created the most serious problems. For some sections there is a first draft; a second draft, sometimes with further revisions; and a typescript. For others there is only one of these. We followed the printed text as far as possible, since we considered it to have authority as a result of being proofread by Stein and Toklas in contact with the printer. Because changes could have been made in the course of printing or in a typescript that does not survive, we decided that we had no authority to remove printed text. On the other hand, major long sections were excised, but it is often unclear on whose authority. In the first paragraph of selection A, Stein excised a full paragraph between "singled themselves out from the crowd" and "it was all new, strange and dangerous. . . ." As a result two sentences that do not go together ended up run together with a comma, without textual adjustment. To show that there is no error but a writer failing to adjust the result of revision, the excision must be identified. We debated some editorial decisions at length. In the first part of the H selection of *The Making of Americans* (pp. 725–30) we restored a major paragraph, beginning "Some are glad that the other one is dead . . ." in accordance with the manuscript. This paragraph was not printed in the novel, possibly because it was very personal. There is no typescript for this section, but the paragraph remains in the manuscript, unlike others that are clearly lined through in the process of excision. We have included it in the *Reader.* A note inserted in the manuscript illustrates the complexities. It reads "Commas dictated." Unless we know to what passages such a note applies, it cannot become evidence.

Authority was a problem for *An Elucidation,* where spacing, line breaks, and setting on the page are especially important because of varied long and short lines and sections, subsections, and offset passages. A printer's mix-up of pages caused the piece in the first issue of *transition* (1927) to be printed cut up in the wrong order. Subscribers received a corrected reprint with the following issue. We expected the reprint to have been done with special care, but it shows serious errors in spacing. As a result, the text in the *Reader* relies on the authority of the manuscript. Yet the manuscript is copied over from various drafts written at different times in different notebooks, which made verification an additional puzzle.

Unexpectedly, *An Acquaintance With Description* raised a question of authority. The text is identical in manuscript and typescript, but the printed book shows differences that are not typesetter's errors or proofreader's oversight. We concluded that the Seizin Press received a setting typescript, not located, that differed from the typescript and manuscript at Yale. We followed the authority of the book rather than restoring the manuscript text.

Printing errors, which often look like spelling errors, are common in texts that do not follow the conventions of writing but explore irregularities. Some look like but are not errors. Yet actual errors occur in print and even in typescripts. We silently corrected obvious spelling errors in order not to add *sic* and to prevent them from being interpreted as printing errors. For example, we did not print the word "somethings" that is in the manuscript of *Two Women* but followed the Contact Edition, which printed "some things," presumably with Stein's approval. We removed hyphens not used today, for example, we printed "grandparent" for "grand-parent." Toklas, with Stein's approval, corrected Stein's spelling errors. However, Toklas typed words like color with *ou,* as some American publishers as late as the early thirties still advised. Stein never used the *ou,* and the *Reader* follows her spelling. Stein omitted accents from French words. Yet in the manuscript of *Accents in Alsace,* though not in print in *Geography and Plays,* the name René has its accent. We did not restore it, but Stein's spelling is a tiny comment on the French thrust of the play. The last of the *Stanzas in Meditation* includes the word "therefor" five times insistently in close succession.

Spelling it "therefore" would have destroyed a dimension of meaning the reader cannot afford to lose.

The plays raise innumerable questions, for ambiguities constantly appear in their formats. Stein plays do not look like regular plays. Even her titles do not follow a standard form but inconsistently add details in subtitles or parentheses. How is a director to come to conclusions about lists of characters, characterization, spoken words, and stage directions that are all parts of a continuous text? We know from *Four Saints in Three Acts* that stage directions are a part of the text of that play and can become spoken or sung lines, but exactly how this is to be done is not always clear. In *A List,* names are grouped and given lines, but are they to be spoken in unison, singly, broken up, or is a director meant to be free? Stein described *Doctor Faustus Lights The Lights* accurately as a "dramatic narrative." What is to be done with the narrative sections in performance? Contrary to the original plans of 1938, the libretto was not set to music. A contemporary score, which would carry a degree of authority, might show her intentions, but without it, we do not know whether Stein meant narrative sections to be set to music. *The Geographical History of America* includes subsections that are plays. It is perfectly possible to include plays in a narrative. But are such plays meant for performance? *Identity A Poem* is made of plays culled from the *Geographical History;* is it one play or several, and how do they relate? Is the line "I wish to be a school" in *Reread Another* a part of the performance? Experimenting with formatting plays, Stein never used the same method twice, perhaps because she was not sure about the conventions but perhaps also because she was exploring the play form. Clear setting of text on a page becomes a crucial way of opening it for reader or performer.

A great, unexpected pleasure was to watch the young Stein learning in the revisions of *The Making of Americans.* With a sure hand she eliminated adjectives, removed words that interfered with rhythm, depersonalized details. The German name Herman was made to fit better into the prose of her American book as Henry. Shifting spoken words into different positions, she tried out how to make the immigrants' locutions ring right in their English. She amended the original opening, "Stop John," removing with the "John" an element of address to the reader in the fictional convention of her first manner that in revision she gradually gave up.

From piece to piece we made new discoveries as we watched Stein composing. Often we felt we were in a hard school, each attempt to gain access to a text returning us to new uncertainties of reading and writing. One lesson of our shared work was that in refusing to be pinned down to single meanings, Stein texts refuse to shut out readings that are new.

28 August 1991

Ulla E. Dydo
Rosalind Moad
William Rice

THE MAKING OF AMERICANS.

BEING A HISTORY OF A FAMILY'S PROGRESS

(SELECTIONS)

Stein began *The Making of Americans* early in 1903 during a brief residence in New York, but put it aside before the summer, when she left for Paris to stay with her brother Leo at his new home at 27, rue de Fleurus. The novel remained dormant for the next three years, during which time she wrote two short novels (*Q. E. D.*, 1903, and *Fernhurst*, 1904–5) and the three stories published as *Three Lives* (finished in the spring of 1906). After completing *Three Lives*, she returned to "the long novel," and for two years worked at what appears to be the draft of a fairly conventional nineteenth-century family novel. But in 1908 she discarded this version and for the next three years wrote a completely new text, which incorporated a few of the passages and most of the story material of the discarded draft. One of the substantial remnants of the earlier text was inserted in revised form into the new, final version in 1909 and appears in the chapter "Martha Hersland."

Completed in 1911, the book that Stein always called her main work suffered rejection after rejection by publishers and did not appear until fourteen years later, in 1925, as the first Contact Edition printed by Maurice Darantière in Dijon. Copies of this edition were used by Albert and Charles Boni in New York to make the first American edition in 1926, and two photo-offset editions were printed by Something Else Press in the United States in 1966 and by Peter Owen in England in 1968. Page numbers in the headings of the following selections refer uniformly to these editions.

The first version of the novel, and the early pages of the final version, begin as a chronicle of the Dehning family of German-Jewish immigrant stock aspiring through wealth, education, and marriage to rise in the new world. Their story was based on the New York branch of the Stein family. It was to include a lesson about the dangers of an ill-judged marriage such as that of Julia Dehning, Stein's cousin Bird Stein, to a worthless bounder. Stein planned to contrast this marriage with that of Julia's younger sister Bertha, not modeled on a family member. A work of realistic fiction, it was also to recount the familiar story of an *haute bourgeoisie*, successful in acquiring wealth, aspiring to a "singularity" and culture for which it had small gift.

When she returned to this material of limited promise, Stein introduced another family, from California. This "western" family, the Herslands, was based on her own and included three offspring: Martha, the oldest; Alfred, Julia's suitor; and David, the youngest and most "singular." It was planned as an instructive contrast to the rich New

York Dehnings, whose cultural and spiritual narrowness would be brought into moral conflict with the greater potential for being of westerners with their "out-of-doors-living." But theme, plot, and moral were soon displaced. As Stein began her scrutiny of father and mother Hersland and their three children, in the process of exploring in almost excruciating detail the "fundamental natures" of her mother and father and of their relations with their children, their servants, and the world around them, the novel took partial flight from its story moorings and became overwhelmingly an examination of character and character relations as such, burgeoning rapidly into an exploration of the nature of human being itself.

The direction of her flight from narrative convention had in a sense been predetermined. It had involved a series of moral and intellectual struggles for which the novel provided interim resolution. Her view of personality and of the mathematics of psychological relationships had already been honed during her painful love affair with May Bookstaver, and had been explored in purely fictional terms in *Q. E. D.*, *Fernhurst*, and *Melanctha*. And the radical shifts in form and technique in the work of Cézanne, Matisse, and Picasso and the Paris school, with which she became familiar during her first three years in Paris, provided role models, if not precise aesthetic models, for her reconsiderations of personality, knowledge, and writing itself.

Increasingly, the story initially planned became lost to sight as the novel advanced, though it remained, sometimes invisibly, the guiding principle of the book's progression. But the elaborate unfolding of the landscape of human personality and of the relation of all the kinds of human personality to one another was inevitably in sharp conflict with the assumptions of traditional narrative. Moving out of narrative's constraints, Stein attempted a total, systematic description of all the elements of human being, an ambition possible to entertain but ultimately impossible to realize fully.

The struggle to realize this impossibility led to a third turn in the novel's focus. Stein came to view the struggle itself, both toward a total grasp of the human landscape and toward a style that could embody the very feel of her understanding of it, as part of the subject matter of the book itself. Her recording of this struggle within the pages of the book provides some of its most profoundly moving passages.

In a sense, then, *The Making of Americans* is several books compounded into one. The modifications of its initial conception in the course of nine years, from the first notes for writing through final rewriting, record the evolution of a unique aesthetic sensibility and the maturing of a major American writer.

During the writing of the book, Stein kept notebooks, preserved among her papers at Yale, detailing plans for the book's narrative, analyses of friends and associates who were to be used for her developing psychological typology, and plans for the structuring of this typology and for miscellaneous personal matters. It is from the notebooks that the sense of the originally planned novel could be recovered. The following selections from the final version were made and are introduced in headnotes by Leon Katz, who first studied Stein's notebooks for *The Making of Americans* and in 1952–53 reviewed them with Alice Toklas, who generously clarified elusive references and their relevance. The selections make no attempt to offer a short version of the novel's continuity. They provide instead a chronological account of the significant changes in the novel's matter and style. Substantive restorations are bracketed.

A. 432–41

So far as we know, these are the only remaining pages from the earliest version of the novel (1903). Stein inserted them in revised form in a much later section of the final version of the book, the chapter entitled "Martha Hersland." These pages illustrate Stein's apprenticeship in the conventions of the novel. Described in broad strokes by an omniscient narrator, Martha is contrasted with the seductive, chivalrous Philip Redfern, whom she eventually marries. The episode is based on events at Bryn Mawr College, renamed here Farnham College; on Alfred Hodder, renamed Philip Redfern; and on the dean and an instructor at the college, Helen Carey Thomas and Mary Gwinn, renamed Miss Hannah Charles and Miss Cora Dounor. In what she later called young writing, Stein awkwardly editorialized, "An observer would have found it difficult to tell . . . ," "It happens often about the twenty-ninth year . . ." (Stein's age when she first wrote this section), "It is the french habit in thinking. . . ."

In the last two paragraphs Stein acknowledges with embarrassment the failure of language to render what she is trying to say. Her words ("categories") have lost meaning; she must look for new ways to express meaning and does so in incantatory shaping of repetitions that eventually allow her to devise a descriptive language.

B. 3–8, 28

The opening pages of the novel, in the voice of an omniscient narrator, prepare the reader for a prototypical American epic. They introduce the migration of Europeans to America, from those who will succeed to those who will fail in making family history. Setting is introduced and immigrant characters are delineated, including their faulty English and foreign grammar.

The description moves to the house of Henry Dehning in Bridgepoint (Baltimore). Now that he has everything, Dehning can no longer identify with the man who came from nothing. To his children he preaches over and over what has become the family myth of his rise in the world and the lesson of the evils of luxury.

Stein in direct address asks her reader to journey through the novel with her. Not until the last chapter of the book does she discard reliance on the reader's collaborative presence.

C. 35–36, 40

Stein introduces the theme of "western" living close to nature in California, in Gossols (Oakland; the name derives from Gosol, in the Pyrenees, where Picasso spent the summer of 1906). The sections on the family's journey from Europe to America and on western living mark the first break in the novel's style, which now relies less on narrative statement and more on onomatopoetic, lyrical evocation. Stein works intensively with rhythm and sound to convey the hot, tired walking of the family leaving Germany and the luxuriant sense of western living.

D. 62–63

The passage on the death of Grandfather Hissen in his daughter's house marks the height of Stein's lyrical and evocative style. The rhythm of his personality is created in the rhythm of his meeting his death, wrapped in the solitary consciousness of his religion while cut off from his family and from his daughter, who has no sense of herself and no religion. The lyricism of the section builds toward resolution in the last four words, "living," "dying," "being," "religion."

E. 79, 115, 137, 149, 150–54

In these pages an entirely new vision of character emerges. While we know that the notebooks of this period are the source for her vision, what is remarkable is how Stein is able to convert the dry system of the typology she is developing into language that constantly renews itself as she considers how "they are there repeating themselves around one" (115).

We know from the notebooks that during these years Stein systematically studied friends, relatives, and acquaintances for the repetition of characteristic behavior that would allow her to place them in her typology. We have in these pages the beginnings of her capacity to transmute into language we recognize as uniquely her own the vision of multitudes of human types—"many millions made of each kind of them" (115).

In the repetitions of behavior, Stein studied the discerned elements shared in common. She speaks of the "bottom level," which generally controls behavior, and of the complicating factor in "the important feeling of himself to himself inside him" (149), a sense of self that is an essential motif of self-classification in personalities acting themselves out. She attempts to discern this element intuitively in the process of repeating behavior.

F. 162–63, 165, 169–70, 178–80

Whereas the foregoing pages considered men and focused on David Hersland, Stein now concentrates on women, on Mrs. Hersland and her relations to husband, children, servants, and governesses. We know from the notebooks that the following pages are indebted to Stein's reading in 1908 of *Sex and Character* by the Viennese psychologist Otto Weininger, whose violent antifeminism and rigid categorizations of types by degree of maleness and femaleness affected Stein's schematization.

Here we see conflict between her desire to describe Mrs. Hersland and her relations and at the same time to elaborate a system of character types and to pursue her goal of "a history of every one who ever can or is or was or will be living, . . . a history of every one . . . [to] the last touch of being . . ." (179–80). She realizes here that writing a novel is not the same as devising a universal characterology. Nevertheless, for another one hundred pages, to the end of the chapter on Mrs. Hersland, she doggedly pursues the typology.

G. 289–300, 347–51, 388, 458, 459–60, 483–85, 520–21, 539–40, 611

Stein's dissatisfaction with the progress of the novel leads to another displacement of its central subject and another change of "style." The new chapter on Martha Hersland, ostensibly beginning with Martha's childhood, rapidly goes beyond her planned subject and type categorizations to examine what will now gradually become her true subject: the scrutiny of herself in relation to her ongoing perceptions and formulations—the writer in the act of writing. Embracing the reader as though in a private, collaborative enterprise ("I write for myself and strangers"), she now focuses on one element of her previous styles, "aiming again and again."

This notion requires explanation. In a pivotal entry in her notebooks, Stein rejects her brother Leo's characteristic way of theorizing by building an initial perception into a series of increasingly abstract conclusions that end up emptied of the original perception. "Real thinking," she notes, "is aiming again and again, always going back to the beginning and aiming again." The conclusion must carry the weight and force of the first perception as well as the long series of formulations that have developed out of it.

"Beginning again and again" becomes Stein's principal mode of structuring discourse. With each beginning she takes fresh aim to find the language that is exactly consonant with her thought as she aims at and finally reaches finished formulations in the struggle of "winning sentences."

But formulations of what? Three separate aims are being pursued: the novel's plot, now so attenuated as to be almost lost to notice; the typological descriptions of characters, now so fraught with ambiguities and uncertainties as to bring the characterization itself into question; and Stein observing herself in the act of writing the novel. The last of these, from the early pages of the Martha Hersland chapter (289–300), becomes the major focus of her "aiming again and again." She invites the reader into the writer's workshop as she struggles for exact perception and exact expression. Her work becomes a diary of the mind in the act of thinking a book. The record of this triple pursuit, from moments of despair to renewal to fatigue, may be followed in the passages of this section.

H. 723–30, 757–59, 782, 805–7, 853, 864, 882, 900–904

In the course of some months before Stein began the "David Hersland" chapter (723–904), she temporarily stopped work on the novel to produce a series of portraits. These short pieces were written without the theoretical scaffolding, without the worry that characters were remaining "in pieces" and were no longer coming out "whole," and without the despair about failure that had brought her last completed chapter ("Alfred Hersland") to an impasse.

The portraits are simpler in their context than the descriptions of personality in the novel. She speaks of the subject and no longer addresses the reader. She abandons the typological framework, aiming only at essence and the character's inner motion ("the being inside him"). Her technique of "aiming again and again" adds in smaller increments to simpler initial statements, with the effect of flattening her conceptual structures.

The effect of this work on her language in the novel is radical. She abandons all attempts to enlist the reader's collaboration in the transaction between her object and herself. The final chapter, "David Hersland," relies on a reduced vocabulary and the same few words in familiar grammatical contexts to suggest a wider range of meanings than they would normally bear. From the perspective of the reader, they effectively veil the complex object, but from the perspective of the writer, their ordered progress and their rhythmic patterning carry a greater range of meaning. Here we see Stein unhinging language, redefining its function, and changing the world of modern writing.

• • • • •

A. 432–41

Among the many vigorous young women in the place there was then Martha Hersland. She was a blond good-looking young woman full of moral purpose and educational desires. She had an eager earnest intelligence, fixed convictions and principles by then, and restless energy. She and Redfern were students in the same studies in the same class and soon singled themselves out from the crowd, it was all new, strange and dangerous for the south-western man and all perfectly simple and matter of course for the western girl. They had long talks on the meanings of things, he discoursing of his life and aims, she listening, understanding and sympathising. This intercourse steadily grew more constant and familiar. Redfern's instincts were dangerous was always there as a conviction in him, his ideals simple and pure was almost always real inside him, slowly he realised in this constant companion the existence of instincts as simple and pure as his ideals.

They were going through the country one wintry day, plunging vigorously through the snow and liking the cold air and rapid walking and excited with their own health and their youth and the freedom. "You are a comrade and a woman," he cried out in his pleasure, "It is the new world." "Surely, there is no difference our being together only it is pleasanter and we go faster," was her eager answer. "I know it." said Redfern, "I know it, it is the new world." This comradeship continued through the three years. They spent much time in explaining to each other what neither quite understood. He never quite felt the reality of her simple convictions, she never quite realised what it was he did not understand.

One spring day a boy friend came to see her a younger brother of John Davidson who used to play duets with her and all three went out in the country. It was a soft warm day, the ground was warm and wet and they were healthy and they did not mind that. They found a fairly dry hill-side and sat down all three too indolent to wander further. The young fellow, a boy of eighteen, threw himself on the ground and rested his head on Martha Hersland's lap. Redfern did not stop a start of surprise and Martha Hersland smiled. The next day Redfern frankly came to her with his perplexity. "I don't understand," he said. "Was it alright for Davidson to do so yesterday. I almost believed it was my duty to knock him off." "Yes I saw you were surprised," she said and she looked uneasy and then she resolutely tried to make him see. "Do you know that to me a western woman it seems very strange that any one should see any wrong in his action. Yes I will say it, I have never understood before why you always seemed on guard." She ended pretty steadily, he flushed and looked uneasy. He looked at her earnestly, whatever was there, he certainly could not doubt her honesty. It could not be a new form of deliberate enticement even though it made a new danger.

After two years of marriage Redfern's realisation of her was almost complete. Martha was all that she had promised him to be, all that he had thought her, but that all proved sufficiently inadequate to his needs. She was moral, strenuous and pure and sought earnestly after higher things in life and art but her mind was narrow and in its way insistent, her intelligence quick but without grace and harsh and Redfern loved a gentle intelligence. Redfern was a hard man to hold, he had no tender fibre to make him gentle to discordant suffering and when once he was certain that this woman had no message for him there was no way in which she could make to him an appeal. Her narrow eager mind was helpless.

It was part of him elaborate chivalry and she though harsh and crude should never cease to receive from him this respect. He knew she must suffer but what could he do. They were man and wife, their minds and natures were separated by great gulfs, it must be again an armed neutrality but this time it was not as with his parents an armed neutrality between equals but with an inferior who could not learn the rules of the game. It was just so much the more unhappy.

Mrs. Redfern never understood what had happened to her. In a dazed blind way she tried all ways of breaking through the walls that confined her. She threw herself against them with impatient energy and again she tried to destroy them piece by piece. She was always thrown back bruised and dazed and never quite certain whence came the blow, how it was dealt or why. It was a long agony, she never became wiser or more indifferent, she struggled on always in the same dazed eager way.

Such was the relation between Redfern and his wife when Redfern having made some reputation for himself in philosophy was called to Farnham college to fill the chair of philosophy there.

There was then a dean presiding over the college of Farnham who in common with many of her generation believed wholly in the essential sameness of sex and who had devoted her life to the development of this doctrine. The Dean of Farnham had had great influence in the lives of many women. She was possessed of a strong purpose and vast energy. She had an extraordinary instinct for the qualities of men and rarely failed to choose the best of the young teachers as they came from the universities. She rarely kept them many years for either they attained such distinction that the great universities claimed them or they were dismissed as not being able enough to be called away.

Phillip Redfern had taken his doctor's degree in philosophy, had married and presently then he came to hold the chair of philosophy at Farnham college. Two very interesting personalities in the place were the dean Miss Charles and her friend Miss Dounor.

Redfern had previously had no experience of women's colleges, he knew some thing of the character of the dean but had heard nothing of any other member of the institution and went to make his bow to his fellow instructors in some wonder of anticipation and excitement of mind.

The new professor of philosophy was invited by the dean to meet the assembled faculty at a tea at her house two days after his arrival in the place. He entered alone and was met by the dean who was then just about beginning the ending of her middle living. She was a dignified figure with a noble head and a preoccupied abrupt manner. She was a member of a family which was proud of having had in three successive generations three remarkable women.

The first of these three was not known beyond her own community among whom she had great influence by reason of her strength of will, her powerful intellect, her strong common sense and her deep religious feeling. She carried to its utmost the then woman's life with its keen worldly sense, its power of emotion and prayer and its devout practical morality.

The daughter of this vigorous woman was known to a wider circle and sought for truth in all varieties of ecstatic experience. She mingled with her genuine mystic exaltation a basal common sense and though spending the greater part of her life in examining and actively taking part in all the exaggerated religious enthusiasms of her time she never lost her sense of criticism and judgement and though convinced again and again of the folly and hypocrisy of successive saints never doubted the validity of mystic religious experience.

In the third generation the niece of this woman, the dean Hannah Charles, found her expression in still wider experience. She did not expect her regeneration from religious experience and found her exaltation in resisting.

Through her influence she was enabled to keep the college in a flourishing state and to keep the control of all things entirely in her own hands but she was anxious that in the teaching staff there should be some one who would be permanent, who would have great parts and a scholarly mind and would have no influence to trouble hers and before many years she found Miss Dounor who ideally fulfilled these conditions.

Miss Dounor was a graduate of an eastern college and had made some reputation. She was utterly unattached, being an only child whose parents died just before she entered college and was equally detached by her nature from all affairs of the world and was always quite content to remain where she was so long as some took from her all management of practical affairs and left her in peace with her work and her dreams. She was possessed of a sort of transfigured innocence which made a deep impression on the vigorous practical mind of Miss Charles who while keeping her completely under her control was nevertheless in awe of her blindness of worldly things and of the intellectual power of her clear sensitive mind.

Though Miss Dounor was detached by the quality of her nature from worldly affairs it was not because she loved best dreams and abstract thought, for her deepest interest was in the varieties of human experience and her constant desire was to partake of all human relations but by some quality of her nature she never succeeded in really touching any human creature she knew. Her transfigured innocence, too, was not an ignorance of the facts of life nor a puritan's instinct indeed her desire was to experience the extreme forms of sensuous life and to make even immoral experiences her own. Her detachment was due to an abstracted spirit that could not do what it would and which was evident in her reserved body, her shy eyes and gentle face.

As I was saying Phillip Redfern had been invited by the dean to meet the assembled faculty at a tea at her house. He entered in some wonder of anticipation and excitement of mind and was met by the dean Miss Charles, "You must meet Miss Dounor" she said to him breaking abruptly through the politeness of the new instructor who was as I said south-western. Redfern looked with interest at this new presentment of gentleness and intelligence who greeted him with awkward shyness. Her talk was serious pleasant and intense, her point of view clear, her arguments just, and her opinions sensitive. Her self-consciousness disappeared during this eager discussion but her manner did not lose its awkward restraint, her voice its gentleness or her eyes their shyness.

While the two were still in the height of the discussion there came up to them a blond, eager, good-looking young woman whom Redfern observing presented as his wife to his new acquaintance. Miss Dounor checked in her talk was thrown into even more than her original shy awkwardness and looking with distress at this new arrival after several efforts to bring her mind to understand said "Mrs. Redfern yes yes, of course, your wife I had forgotten." She made another attempt to begin to speak and then suddenly giving it up gazed at them quite helpless.

"Pray go on as I am very anxious to hear what you think," said Mrs. Redfern nervously and Redfern bowing to his wife turned again to Miss Dounor and went on with the talk.

An observer would have found it difficult to tell from the mere appearance of these three what their relation toward each other was. Miss Dounor was absorbed in her talk and thought and oblivious of everything except the discussion, her shy eyes fixed on Redfern's face and her tall constrained body filled with eagerness, Redfern was listening and answering showing the same degree of courteous deference to both his companions, turned first toward one and then toward the other one with impartial attention and Mrs. Redfern her blond good-looking face filled with eager anxiety to understand listened to one and then the other with the same anxious care.

Later Redfern wandered to a window where Miss Hannah Charles, Miss Dounor and Mrs. Redfern were standing looking out at a fine prospect of sunset and a long line of elms defining a road that led back through the town of Farnham to the wooded hills behind. Redfern stood with them looking out at the scene. Mrs. Redfern was listening intently to each one's thinking. "Ah of course you know Greek," she said with eager admiration to Miss Dounor who made no reply.

It happens often about the twenty-ninth year of a life that all the forces that have been engaged through the years of childhood, adolescence and youth in confused and sometimes angry combat range themselves in ordered ranks, one is uncertain of one's aims, meaning and power during these years of tumultuous growth when aspiration has no relation to fulfillment and one plunges here and there with energy and misdirection during the strain and stress of the making of a personality until at last we reach the twenty-ninth year, the straight and narrow gateway of maturity and life which was all uproar and confusion narrows down to form and purpose and we exchange a dim possibility for a big or small reality.

Also in our american life where there is no coercion in custom and it is our right to change our vocation as often as we have desire and opportunity, it is a common experience that our youth extends through the whole first twenty-nine years of our life and it is not till we reach thirty that we find at last that vocation for which we feel ourselves fit and to which we willingly devote continued labor. It must be owned that while much labor is lost to the world in these efforts to secure one's true vocation, nevertheless it makes more completeness in individual life and perhaps in the end will prove as useful to the world, and if we believe that there is more meaning in the choice of love than plain propinquity so we may well believe that there is more meaning in vocations than that it is the thing we can first learn about and win an income with.

Redfern had now come to this fateful twenty-ninth year. He had been a public preacher for women's rights, he had been a mathematician, a psychologist and a philosopher, he had married and earned a living and yet the world was to him without worth or meaning and he longed for a more vital human life than to be an instructor of youth, his theme was humanity, his desire was to be in the great world and of it, he wished for active life among his equals not to pass his days as a guide to the immature and he preferred the criticism of life in fiction to the analysis of the mind in philosophy and now the time was come in this his twenty-ninth year for the decisive influence in his career.

Cora Dounor had on her side too her ideals which in this world she had not found complete. She too longed for the real world while wrapped away from it by the perverse reserve of her mind and the awkward shyness of her body. Such friendship as she had yet realised she felt for the dean Miss Hannah Charles but it was not a nearness of affection, it was a recognition of the power of doing and working, and a deference to the representative of effective action and the habitual dependence of years of protection. What ever Miss Charles advised or undertook seemed always to Miss Dounor the best that could be done or affected. She sustained her end of the relation in being a learned mind, a brilliant teacher and a docile subject. She pursued her way expounding philosophy, imbibing beauty, desiring life, never questioning the things nearest her, interested only in abstract ideas and concrete desire and all her life was arranged to leave her untouched and unattached but in this shy abstracted, learned creature there was a desire for sordid life and the common lot.

It was interesting to see what every one but the dean did see, the slow growth of interest to admiration and then to love in this awkward reserved woman, unconscious of her meanings and the world's attention and who made no attempt to disguise or conceal the strength of her feeling.

Redfern's life experience had been to learn that where there was woman there was for him danger not through his own affections but by the demand that this sex made upon him. By this extreme chivalry he was always bound to more than fulfill the expectations he gave rise to in the mind of his companion. Indeed this man loved the problem of woman so much that he willingly endured all pain to seek and find the ideal that filled him with such deep unrest and he never tired of meeting and knowing and devoting himself to any woman who promised to fulfill for him his desire and here in Cora Dounor he had found a spirit so delicate so free so gentle and intelligent that no severity of suffering could deter him from seeking the exquisite knowledge that this companionship could give him. And he knew that she too would willingly pay high for the fresh vision that he brought her.

It is the french habit in thinking to consider that in the grouping of two and an extra it is the two that get something from it all who are of importance and whose claim should be considered; the american mind accustomed to waste happiness and be reckless of joy finds morality more important than ecstacy and the lonely extra of more value than the happy two. To our new world feeling the sadness of pain has more dignity than the beauty of joy. It takes time to learn the value of happiness. Truly a single moment snatched out of a distracted existence is hardly worth the trouble it takes to seize it and to obtain such it is wasteful to inflict pain, it is only the cultivators of leisure who have time to feel the gentle approach the slow rise, the deep ecstacy and the full flow of joy and for these pain is of little value, a thing not to be remembered, and it is only the lack of joy that counts.

Martha Redfern eager, anxious and moral had little understanding of the sanctity of joy and hardly a realisation of the misery of pain. She understood little now what it was that had come upon her and she tried to arrange and explain it by her western morality and her new world humanity. She could not escape the knowledge that something stronger than community of interest bound her husband and Miss Dounor together. She tried resolutely to interpret it all in terms of comradeship and great equality of intellectual interests never admitting to herself for a moment the conception of a possible marital disloyalty. But in spite of these standards and convictions she was filled with a vague uneasiness that had a different meaning than the habitual struggle against the hard wall of courtesy that Redfern had erected before her.

This struggle in her mind showed itself clearly when she was in the company of her husband and Miss Dounor. She would sit conscientiously bending her mind to her self-imposed task of understanding and development, when in the immediate circle of talkers that included her husband and Miss Dounor she gave anxious and impartial attention to the words of one and the other occasionally joining in the talk by an earnest inquiry and receiving always from Redfern the courteous deference that he extended to every one, to everything, to all women. She listened with admiring attention particularly to Miss Dounor who genuinely unconscious of all this nervous misery paid her in return scant attention. When she was not in the immediate group of talkers with these two she kept her attention on the person with whom she was talking and showed the burden of her feeling only in the anxious care with which she listened and talked.

She was not to be left much longer to work out her own conclusions. One afternoon in the late fall in the second year of their life at Farnham, Miss Charles came to the room where she was sitting alone and in her abrupt way spoke directly of the object of her visit. "Mrs. Redfern," she began "you probably know something of the gossip that is at present going on, I want you to keep Mr. Redfern in order, I cannot allow him to make Miss Dounor the subject of scandalous talk." She stopped and looked steadily at the uneasy woman who was dazed by this sudden statement of her own suspicion, "I, I don't understand," she stammered. "I think you understand quite well. I depend upon you to speak to him about it," and with this the dean departed.

This action on Miss Charles' part showed her wisdom. She knew very well the small power that Mrs. Redfern had over her husband and she took this method of attack only because it was the only one open to her. Mrs. Redfern could not accomplish anything by any action but she was a woman and jealous and there was little doubt, so the dean thought, that before long she would effect some change.

Martha Redfern's mind was now in a confusion. Miss Charles had added nothing to her facts, nevertheless her statement had made a certainty of what Mrs. Redfern had resolutely regarded as an impossibility. She sat there long and long thinking over again and again the same weary round of thoughts and terrors. She knew she was powerless to change him, she could only try to get the evidence to condemn him. Did she want it, if she had it she must act on it, she dreaded to obtain it and could not longer exist without it. She must watch him and find it all out without questioning, must learn it by seeing and hearing and she felt dimly a terror of the things she might be caught doing to obtain it, she dreaded the condemnation of Redfern's chivalrous honor. She did not doubt his disloyalty she was convinced of that and she still feared to lose his respect for her sense of honor. "He is dishonorable, all his action is deceit," she said to herself again and again but she found no comfort in this thought, she knew there was a difference and that she respected his standard more than her own justification.

In the long weary days that followed she was torn by these desires, she must watch him always and secretly, she must gain the knowledge she dreaded to possess and she must be deeply ashamed of the ways she must pursue. She was no longer able to listen to others when her husband and Miss Dounor were in her presence, she dared not keep an open watch but her observation was unceasing.

Redfern was not wholly unconscious of this change in his wife's manner perhaps more in the relief that she ceased her eager efforts to please him than in the annoyance of her suspicious watching. Redfern was a man too much on guard to fear surprise and with all his experience too ignorant of women's ways to see danger where danger really lay.

It was the end of May and one late afternoon Mrs. Redfern filled with her sad past and sadder future, sat in her room watching the young leaves shining brilliantly green in the warm sunshine on the long row of elms that stretched away through the village toward the green hills that rose beyond. Mrs. Redfern knew very well the feel of that earth warm with young life and wet with spring rains, knew it as part of her dreary life that seemed to have lasted always. As she sat there in sadness, the restless eagerness of her blond good-looking face was gone and her hands lay clasped quietly without straining, time and sadness had become stronger in her than desire.

Redfern came into the house and passed into his own study. He remained there a short while and then was called away. As soon as he was out of sight Mrs. Redfern arose and went into his room. She walked up to his desk and opening his portfolio saw a letter in his writing. She scarcely hesitated so eager was she to read it. She read it to the end, she had her evidence.

Categories that once to some one had real meaning can later to that same one be all empty. It is queer that words that meant something in our thinking and our feeling can later come to have in them in us not at all any meaning. This is happening always to every one really feeling meaning in words they are saying. This is happening very often to almost every one having any realisation in them in their feeling, in their thinking, in their imagining of the words they are always using. This is common then to many having in them any real realisation of the meaning of the words they are using. As I was saying categories that once to some one had real meaning come later to that same one not to have any meaning at all then for that one. Sometimes one reads a letter that they have been keeping with other letters, and one is not very old then and so it is not that they are old then and forgetting, they are not very old then and they come in cleaning something to reading this letter and it is all full of hot feeling and the one, reading the letter then, has not in them any memory of the person who once wrote that letter to them. This is different, very different from the changing of the feeling and the thinking in many who have in them real realisation of the meaning of words when they are using them but there is in each case so complete a changing of experiencing in feeling and thinking, or in time or in something, that something, some one once alive to some one is then completely a stranger to that one, the meaning in a word to that one the meaning in a way of feeling and thinking that is a category to some one, some one whom some one was knowing, these then come to be all lost to that one sometime later in the living of that one.

This is very true then, this is very true then of the feeling and the thinking that makes the meaning in the words one is using, this is very true then that to many of them having in them strongly a sense of realising the meaning of the words they are using that some words they once were using, later have not any meaning and some then have a little shame in them when they are copying an old piece of writing where they were using words that sometime had real meaning for them and now have not any real meaning in them to the feeling and the thinking and the imagining of such a one. Often this is in me in my feeling, often then I have to lose words I have once been using, now I commence again with words that have meaning, a little perhaps I had forgotten when it came to copying the meaning in some of the words I have just been writing. Now to begin again with what I know of the being in Phillip Redfern, now to begin again a description of Phillip Redfern and always now I will be using words having in my feeling, thinking, imagining very real meaning.

B. 3–8, 28

Once an angry man dragged his father along the ground through his own orchard. "Stop!" cried the groaning old man at last, "Stop! I did not drag my father beyond this tree."

It is hard living down the tempers we are born with. We all begin well, for in our youth there is nothing we are more intolerant of than our own sins writ large in others and we fight them fiercely in ourselves; but we grow old and we see that these our sins are of all sins the really harmless ones to own, nay that they give a charm to any character, and so our struggle with them dies away.

It has always seemed to me a rare privilege, this, of being an American, a real American, one whose tradition it has taken scarcely sixty years to create. We need only realise our parents, remember our grandparents and know ourselves and our history is complete.

The old people in a new world, the new people made out of the old, that is the story that I mean to tell, for that is what really is and what I really know.

Some of the fathers we must realise so that we can tell our story really, were little boys then, and they came across the water with their parents, the grandparents we need only just remember. Some of these our fathers and our mothers, were not even made then, and the women, the young mothers, our grandmothers we perhaps just have seen once, carried these our fathers and our mothers into the new world inside them, those women of the old world strong to bear them. Some looked very weak and little women, but even these, so weak and little, were strong always, to bear many children.

These certain men and women, our grandfathers and grandmothers, with their children born and unborn with them, some whose children were gone ahead to prepare a home to give them; all countries were full of women who brought with them many children; but only certain men and women and the children they had in them, to make many generations for them, will fill up this history for us of a family and its progress.

Many kinds of all these women were strong to bear many children.

One was very strong to bear them and then always she was very strong to lead them.

One was strong to bear them and then always she was strong to suffer with them.

One, a little gentle weary woman was strong to bear many children, and then always after she would sadly suffer for them, weeping for the sadness of all sinning, wearying for the rest she knew her death would bring them.

And then there was one sweet good woman, strong just to bear many children, and then she died away and left them, for that was all she knew then to do for them.

And these four women and the husbands they had with them and the children born and unborn in them will make up the history for us of a family and its progress.

Other kinds of men and women and the children they had with them, came at different times to know them; some, poor things, who never found how they could make a living, some who dreamed while others fought a way to help them, some whose children went to pieces with them, some who thought and thought and then their children rose to greatness through them, and some of all these kinds of men and women and the children they had in them will help to make the history for us of this family and its progress.

These first four women, the grandmothers we need only just remember, mostly never saw each other. It was their children and grandchildren who, later, wandering over the new land, where they were seeking first, just to make a living, and then later, either to grow rich or to gain wisdom, met with one another and were married, and so together they made a family whose progress we are now soon to be watching.

We, living now, are always to ourselves young men and women. When we, living always in such feeling, think back to them who make for us a beginning, it is always as grown and old men and women or as little children that we feel them, these whose lives we have just been thinking. We sometimes talk it long, but really, it is only very little time we feel ourselves ever to have being as old men and women or as children. Such parts of our living are little ever really there to us as present in our feeling. Yes; we, who are always all our lives, to ourselves grown young men and women, when we think back to them who make for us a beginning, it is always as grown old men and women or as little children that we feel them, such as them whose lives we have just been thinking.

Yes it is easy to think ourselves and our friends, all our lives as young grown men and women, indeed it is hard for us to feel even when we talk it long, that we are old like old men and women or little as a baby or as children. Such parts of our living are never really there to us as present, to our feeling.

Yes we are very little children when we first begin to be to ourselves grown men and women. We say then, yes we are children, but we know then, way inside us, we are not to ourselves real as children, we are grown to ourselves, as young grown men and women. Nay we never know ourselves as other than young and grown men and women. When we know we are no longer to ourselves as children. Very little things we are then and very full of such feeling. No, to be feeling ourselves to be as children is like the state between when we are asleep and when we are just waking, it is never really there to us as present to our feeling.

And so it is to be really old to ourselves in our feeling; we are weary and are old, and we know it in our working and our thinking, and we talk it long, and we can see it just by looking, and yet we are a very little time really old to ourselves in our feeling, old as old men and old women once were and still are to our feeling. No, no one can be old like that to himself in his feeling. No it must be always as grown and young men and women that we know ourselves and our friends in our feeling. We know it is not so, by our saying, but it must be so always to our feeling. To be old to ourselves in our feeling is a losing of ourselves like just dropping off into sleeping. To be awake, we must have it that we are to ourselves young and grown men and women.

To be ourself like an old man or an old woman to our feeling must be a horrid losing-self sense to be having. It must be a horrid feeling, like the hard leaving of our sense when we are forced into sleeping or the coming to it when we are just waking. It must be a horrid feeling to have such a strong sense of losing, such a feeling as being to ourselves like children or like grown old men and women. Perhaps to some it is a gentle sense of losing, some who like themselves to be without a self sense feeling, but certainly it must be always a sense of self losing in each one who finds himself really having a very young or very old self feeling.

Our mothers, fathers, grandmothers and grandfathers, in the histories, and the stories, all the others, they all are always little babies grown old men and women or as children for us. No, old generations and past ages never have grown young men and women in them. So long ago they were, why they must be old grown men and women or as babies or as children. No, them we never can feel as young grown men and women. Such only are ourselves and our friends with whom we have been living.

And so since there is no other way to do with our kind of thinking, we will make our elders to be for us the grown old men and women in our stories, or the babies or the children. We will be always, in ourselves, the young grown men and women.

And so now we begin, and with such men and women as we have old or as very little, in us, to our thinking.

One of these four women, the grandmothers old always to us the generation of grandchildren, was a sweet good woman, strong just to bear many children and then she died away and left them for that was all she knew then to do for them.

Like all good older women she had all her life born many children and she had made herself a faithful working woman to her husband who was a good enough ordinary older man.

Her husband lived some years after his wife had died away and left him.

He was just a decent well-meaning faithful good-enough ordinary man. He was honest, and he left that very strongly to his children and he worked hard, but he never came to very much with all his faithful working.

He was just a decent honest good-enough man to do ordinary working. He always was good to his wife and always liked her to be with him, and to have good children, and to help him with her working. He always liked all of his children and he always did all that he could to help them, but they were all soon strong enough to leave him, and now that his wife had died away and left him, he was not really needed much by the world or by his children.

They were good daughters and sons to him, but his sayings and his old ordinary ways of doing had not much importance for them. They were strong, all of them, in their work and in their new way of feeling and full always of their new ways of living. It was alright, he always said it to them, and he thought it so really in him, but it was all too new, it could never be any comfort to him. He had been left out of all life while he was still living. It was all too new for his feeling and his wife was no longer there to stay beside him. He felt it always in him and he sighed and at last he just slowly left off living. "Yes," he would say of his son Henry who was the one who took most care and trouble for him, "Yes, Henry, he is a good man and he knows how to make a living. Yes he is a good boy to me always but he never does anything like I tell him. It aint wrong in him, never I don't say so like that ever for him, only I don't need it any more just to go on like I was living. My wife she did always like I told her, she never knew any way to do it different, and now she is gone peace be with her, and it is all now like it was all over, and I, I got no right now to say do so to my children. I don't ever say it now ever no more to them. What have I got to do with living? I've got no place to go on now like I was really living. I got nobody now always by me to do things like I tell them. I got nothing to say now anymore to my children. I got all done with what I got to say to them. Well young folks always knows things different, and they got it right not to listen, I got nothing now really to do with their new kinds of ways of living. Anyhow Henry, he knows good how to make a living. He makes money such a way I got no right to say it different to him. He makes money and I never can see how his way he can make it and he is honest and a good man always, with all his making such a good living. And he has got right always to do like he wants it, and he is good to me always, I can't ever say it any different. He always is good to me, and the others, they come to see me always only now it is all different. My wife she stayed right by me always and the children they always got some new place where they got to go and do it different." And then the old man sighed and then soon too he died away and left them.

Henry Dehning was a grown man and for his day a rich one when his father died away and left them. Truly he had made everything for himself very different; but it is not as a young man making himself rich that we are now to feel him, he is for us an old grown man telling it all over to his children.

He is a middle aged man now when he talks about it all to his children, middle aged as perhaps sometimes we ourselves are now to our talking, but he, he is an old grown man to our thinking.

Yes truly this Henry Dehning had made everything for himself to be very different. His ways and his needs and how much money it took now to live to be decent, and all the habits of his daily life, they were all now for him very different.

And it is strange how all forget when they have once made things for themselves to be very different. A man like Dehning never can feel it real to himself, things as they were in his early manhood, now that he has made his life and habits and his feelings all so different. He says it often, as we all do childhood and old age and pain and sleeping, but it can never anymore be really present to his feeling.

Now the common needs in his life are very different. No, not he, nor they all who have made it for themselves to be so different, can remember meekness, nor poor ways, nor self attendance, nor no comforts, all such things are to all of them as indifferent as if they in their own life time themselves had not made it different. It is not their not wanting to remember these things that were so different. Nay they love to remember, and to tell it over, and most often to their children, what they have been and what they have done and how they themselves have made it all to be so different and how well it is for these children that they have had a strong father who knew how to do it so that youngsters could so have it.

Yes, they say, it long and often and yet it is never real to them while they are thus talking. No it is not as really present to their thinking as it is to the young ones who never really had the feeling. These have it through their fear, which makes it for them a really present feeling. The old ones have not such a fear and they have it all only like a dim beginning, like the being as babies or as children or as grown old men and women.

And this father Dehning was always very full of such talking. He had made everything for himself and for his children. He was a good and honest man was Henry Dehning. He was strong and rich and good-tempered and respected and he showed it in his look, that look that makes young people think older ones are very aged, and he loved to tell it over to his children, how he had made it all for them so they could have it and not have to work to make it different.

"Yes," he would often say to his children, looking at them with that sharp, side-long, shrewd glance that makes fathers so fearful and so aged to their children. Not that he, Dehning, was ever very dreadful to his children, but there is a burr in a man's voice that always makes for terror in his children and there is a sharp, narrow, outward, shut off glance from an old man that will always fill with dread young grown men and women. No it is only by long equal living that their wives know that there is no terror in them, but the young never can be equal enough with them to really rid themselves of such feeling. No, they only really can get rid of such a feeling when they have found in an old man a complete pathetic falling away into a hapless failing. But mostly for all children and young grown men and women there is much terror in an old man's looking.

Not, we repeat, that the Dehnings had much of such a feeling. Their mother had learnt, by perhaps more than equal living that there really was no terror in him and through her they had lost much of such feeling. But always they had something of that dread in them when he would begin talking to them of what had been and what he had done for them. Then it was that he always became very aged to them and he would strongly hold them with his sharp narrow outward kind of looking that, closing him, went very straight into them.

"Yes," he would often say to his children, "Yes I say to you children, you have an easy time of it nowadays doing nothing. Well! What! yes, you think you always have to have everything you can ever think of wanting. Well I guess yes, you have to have your horses and your teachers and your music and your tutors and all kinds of modern improvements and you can't ever do things for yourself, you always have to have somebody there to do it for you; well, yes you children have an easy time of it nowadays doing nothing.

The home the rich and self-made merchant makes to hold his family and himself is always like the city where his fortune has been made. In London it is like that rich and endless dark and gloomy place, in Paris it is filled with pleasant toys, cheery and light and made of gilded decoration and white paint, and in Bridgepoint it was neither gloomy nor yet joyous but like a large and splendid canvas completely painted over but painted full of empty space.

The Dehning city house was of this sort. A nervous restlessness of luxury was through it all. Often the father would complain of the unreasoning extravagance to which his family was addicted but these upbraidings had not much result for the rebuke came from conviction and not from any habit of his own.

It was good solid riches in the Dehning house, a parlor full of ornate marbles placed on yellow onyx stands, chairs gold and white of various size and shape, a delicate blue silk brocaded covering on the walls and a ceiling painted pink with angels and cupids all about, a dining room all dark and gold, a living room all rich and gold and red with built-in-couches, glass-covered book-cases and paintings of well-washed peasants of the german school, and large and dressed up bedrooms all light and blue and white. (All this was twenty years ago in the dark age, you know, before the passion for the simple line and the toned burlap on the wall and wooden panelling all classic and severe.) Marbles and bronzes and crystal chandeliers and gas logs finished out each room. And always everywhere there were complicated ways to wash, and dressing tables filled full of brushes, sponges, instruments, and ways to make one clean, and to help out all the special doctors in their work.

It was good riches in this house and here it was that Julia Dehning dreamed of other worlds and here each day she grew more firm in her resolve for that free wide and cultured life to which for her young Hersland had the key.

c. 35–36, 40

This house they had always lived in was not in the part of Gossols where the other rich people mostly were living. It was an old place left over from the days when Gossols was just beginning. It was grounds about ten acres large, fenced in with just ordinary kind of rail fencing, it had a not very large wooden house standing on the rising ground in the center with a winding avenue of eucalyptus, blue gum, leading from it to the gateway. There was, just around the house, a pleasant garden, in front were green lawns not very carefully attended and with large trees in the center whose roots always sucked up for themselves almost all the moisture, water in this dry western country could not be used just to keep things green and pretty and so, often, the grass was very dry in summer, but it was very pleasant then lying there watching the birds, black in the bright sunlight and sailing, and the firm white summer clouds breaking away from the horizon and slowly moving. It was very wonderful there in the summer with the dry heat, and the sun burning, and the hot earth for sleeping; and then in the winter with the rain, and the north wind blowing that would bend the trees and often break them, and the owls in the walls scaring you with their tumbling.

All the rest of the ten acres was for hay and a little vegetable gardening and an orchard with all the kinds of fruit trees that could be got there to do any growing.

In the summer it was good for generous sweating to help the men make the hay into bails for its preserving and it was well for ones growing to eat radishes pulled with the black earth sticking to them and to chew the mustard and find roots with all kinds of funny flavors in them, and to fill one's hat with fruit and sit on the dry ploughed ground and eat and think and sleep and read and dream and never hear them when they would all be calling; and then when the quail came it was fun to go shooting, and then when the wind and the rain and the ground were ready to help seeds in their growing, it was good fun to help plant them, and the wind would be so strong it would blow the leaves and branches of the trees down around them and you could shout and work and get wet and be all soaking and run out full into the strong wind and let it dry you, in between the gusts of rain that left you soaking. It was fun all the things that happened all the year there then.

And all around the whole fence that shut these joys in was a hedge of roses, not wild, they had been planted, but now they were very sweet and small and abundant and all the people from that part of Gossols came to pick the leaves to make sweet scented jars and pillows, and always all the Herslands were indignant and they would let loose the dogs to bark and scare them but still the roses grew and always all the people came and took them. And altogether the Herslands always loved it there in their old home in Gossols.

All, the wagon and the driver and the horses and the children, had waited for them to come up to it. Now they went on again, slowly and creaking, as is the way always when a whole family do it. Moving through a country is never done very quickly when a whole family do it.

They had not gone very far yet. They had not been going many hours. They were all having now just coming in them their first tired, the first hot sense of being very tired. This is the hardest time in a day's walking to press through and get over being tired until it comes to the last tired, that last dead tired sense that is so tired. Then you cannot press through to a new strength and to get another tired, you just keep on, that is you keep on when you have learned how you can do it, then you just get hardened to it and know there is no pressing through it, there is no way to win out beyond it, it is just a dreary dull dead tired, and you must learn to know it, and it is always and you must learn to bear it, the dull drag of being almost dead with being tired.

In between these first and last are many little times of tired, many ways of being very tired, but never any like the first hot tired when you begin to learn how to press through it and never any like the last dead tired with no beyond ever to it.

It was this first hot tired they all had in them now just in its beginning, and they were all in their various ways trying to press themselves to go through it, and they were mostly very good about it and not impatient or complaining. They were all now beginning with the dull tired sense of hot trudging when every step has its conscious meaning and all the movement is as if one were lifting each muscle and every part of the skin as a separate action. All the springiness had left them, it was a weary conscious moving the way it always is before one presses through it to the time of steady walking that comes when one does not any longer do it with a conscious sense with each movement. It is not until one has settled to it, the steady walk where one is not conscious of the movement, that you have become really strong to do it, and the whole family were now just coming to it, they were just pressing through their first hot tired.

D. 62–63

Later in the old man's living, when his wife had died away and left him, he came to live with a daughter who had not any kind of an important feeling to herself inside her, neither from a religion to be all her nor from a constant rising up inside her as the dreary mother had it in her to have an almost important feeling to be inside her from the constant trickling of her, the father later came to live with this daughter who had a gentle dignity and good ways in her from the sweet nature of her not from any important feeling in her, and she and the man who was married to her, both, though they had respect in them for the father, and goodness and a delicate feeling to consider all who ever had to do with them, though they were glad to do for him everything he wanted them to be doing yet they had together very different ways of thinking, of feeling, and of living than he had known it to be right to have all his life in his necessary living.

The old father, strong as he always had been in his nature, firm in being for himself all there was of religion, knowing to his dying that religion was all there was of living, yet never in any way was he ever interfering in the living and the feeling and the thinking of his daughter or her husband or any of their children or any of his own children who were there in the same house with him. Now, for him who was no longer leading in a house with others shut up with him, with him who was all there was of religion, for him, now, that they were apart from him being grown men and women to him, even though they were all together every minute with him, although he was up to the last moment of dying as strong as ever in the faith of him, to be himself and to be all there was of religion, yet now it was not for him to ever in any way interfere with any one of them. He never found out anything that was happening, anything that he would not wish to know that any one of them was doing. What a man does not know can never be a worry to him. This was his answer to his children whenever any one of them wanted to explain anything to him or to get him to agree to any new thing in their living.

And so he went on to the last minute of his living, never having had any power in him over any one who was not shut up with him and a necessary part of his living, strong always in his being to himself all that were was of religion, strong in knowing that religion was all there was of being. And so he went on with his living, now never interfering with anybody's living, now that he was himself for himself all there was of living, all there was of religion, and religion always was all there was of living. And so he went on to his dying and through his being so all himself all there was of living and of religion, he was in his old age full of toleration, and slowly in his dying it was a great death that met him. He was himself all there was of him, all there was of religion, and religion was all there was of living for him, and so the dying from old age that came slowly to him all came together to be him. He was religion, death could not rob him, he could lose nothing in his dying, he was all that there was of him, all there was of religion, and religion was all there was of living, and so he, dying of old age, without struggling, met himself by himself in his dying, for religion was everlasting, and so for him there could be no ending, he and religion and living and dying were all one and everything and every one and it was for himself that he was all one, living, dying, being, and religion.

E. 79, 115, 137, 149, 150–54

It is a queer feeling that one has in them and perhaps it is, that they have something queer in them something that gives to one a strange uncertain feeling with them for their heads are on them as puling babies heads are always on them and it gives to one a queer uncertain feeling to see heads on big women that look loose and wobbly on them.

Old Mrs. Shilling was such a one. It was uncertain always even after a long knowing of her whether the wobbly head on her was all that made a strange thing of her or whether there was something queer inside in her, different from the others of them, different from all of them who always give to one a strange uncertain feeling, all the many fat ones who are made just like her. Perhaps that was all that was queer in her, that which is always queer in all the many fat ones who are made just like her.

The fat daughter Sophie Shilling in the ways one mostly felt her has many millions who are made just like her. The fat daughter Sophie Shilling was a little like her mother but her head was not yet wobbly on her. Sometimes there was something about her that perhaps came from something queer inside her. Mostly she was just an ordinary rather fat young woman and there are many millions made just like her.

There are many kinds of men. Some kinds of them have it in them to feel themselves as big as all the world around them. Some have such a sense in them only when a new thing begins in them, soon they lose it out of them.

There are many ways of being a man, there are many millions of each kind of them, more and more in ones living they are there repeating themselves around one, every one of them in his own way being the kind of man he has in him, and there are always many millions made just like each one of them.

There are many ways of being a man and sometime one gets to know almost all of them, some sometime get to know all of them, there are many millions made of each kind of them, each one of them is different from all the other millions made just like him, this makes of him an individual, this in some of them makes in him an individual feeling to have inside in him, in some of some kinds of them there is almost nothing of such an individual being, perhaps always in every one in some way there is something of such an individual being, in all men, in women, and in the children of them.

There are many kinds of men then and there are always many millions made of each kind of them. There is a kind of them that have it in them to be as big as all the world in their feeling, to be strong in beginning, and that is their kind of men. For such a kind of men the world around them is all in a beginning, for each of them beginning is the strongest thing in them. There are many millions of such a kind of men and they have it in all of them to be strong in beginning. In some of them, and they are mostly weaker in all their living, weaker than some of the other millions made of that kind of them, some of them keep on to their last minute with beginning, they are always a little weaker in their living, they are always to their last ending busy with beginning, some of such a kind of them have a great kind of bigness in them but they are weaker in their living than others of that kind of men, some of such ones of that kind of men have a great kind of feeling in them but it is in them only great in its beginning, it goes out into little things later in them, they must then have it in them to commence a new beginning to be big again inside them, they go on to their last ending in beginning, they are always a little weaker in living, they are always to their last ending busy with beginning. Some of this part of that kind of men have it in them to be big in their beginning, to have then a kind of greatness in them in the feeling they have inside them with beginning, and then it turns into an empty nothing in them, sometimes it turns into a blown up feeling in them, sometimes into a full emptiness that is then all there is of them then and keeps on so inside them to their ending. They are some then who keep on to their last minute with beginning, they are always a little weaker in their living, they are always to their last ending busy with beginning. There are some of the kind of men, the kind that have beginning as the strongest thing inside them, there are many of them many of the many millions of them, there are many of them who sometime keep on going keep on going a little time with some one thing they have had in them as beginning; there are some who sometime keep on going with something they sometime had as a beginning, keep on going with it then to their ending. These are some of the many millions of such a kind of men who have it in them to be as big in their feeling as all the world around them. There are some of such a kind of men who have it in them to push some one thing through to an ending something they have sometime had as a beginning, there are some of the many millions of this kind of men who have it in them to push several things through to an ending several things that they have had as a beginning in them.

A man in his living has many things inside him, he has in him his important feeling of himself to himself inside him, he has in him the kind of important feeling of himself to himself that makes his kind of man; this comes sometimes from a mixture in him of all the kinds of natures in him, this comes sometimes from the bottom nature in him, this comes sometimes from the natures in him that are in him that are sometime in him mixed up with the bottom nature in him, sometimes in some men this other nature or natures in him are not mixed with the bottom nature in him they are never mixed with the bottom nature in him at any time in his living many of such men have the important feeling of themselves inside them coming from the other nature or natures in them not from the bottom nature of them.

Many men have sometime in their living the important feeling of themselves to themselves inside them, some men have always this feeling inside them, most men have such a feeling more or less in them, perhaps all men and mostly all women have sometime in them a feeling of themselves to themselves inside them; this comes sometimes from a mixture in them of the kind of natures in them, this comes sometimes from the bottom nature of them, this comes sometimes from the natures in them that are mixed up with the bottom natures of them, sometimes in some of them the other nature or natures in them are not mixed with the bottom nature in them, many of such of them have the important feeling of themselves inside them coming from the other natures not from the bottom nature of them.

Mostly all men in their living have many things inside them. As I have just been saying the feeling of themselves inside them can come in different ways from the inside of them, can come in different ways in some of the many millions of one kind of men from the other millions of that same kind of them.

A man in his living has many things inside him. He has in him his feeling himself important to himself inside him, he has in him his way of beginning; this can come too from a mixture in him, from the bottom nature of him, from the nature or natures in him more or less mixed up with the bottom in him, in some, though mostly in all of them the bottom nature in them makes for them their way of beginning, in some of each kind of men the other nature or natures in them makes for them their way of beginning.

Men in their living have many things inside them, they have in them, each one of them has it in him, his own way of feeling himself important inside in him, they have in them all of them their own way of beginning, their own way of ending, their own way of working, their own way of having loving inside them and loving come out from them, their own way of having anger inside them and letting their anger come out from inside them, their own way of eating, their own way of drinking, their own way of sleeping, their own way of doctoring. They have each one of them their own way of fighting, they have in them all of them their own way of having fear in them. They have all of them in them their own way of believing, their own way of being important inside them, their own way of showing to others around them the important feeling inside in them.

In all of them in all the things that are in them in their daily living, in all of them in all the things that are in them from their beginning to their ending, some of the things always in them are stronger in them than the other things too always in them. In all of them then there are always all these things in them, ways of being are in all of them, in some of the many millions of each kind of them some of the things in them are stronger in them than others of them in them.

In all of them then in all the things that are in them in their daily living, in all of them in all the things that are in them from their beginning to their ending—in all of them then there are always all these things in them—

in some of the many millions of each kind of them some of the things are stronger in them than others of them.

There are then many kinds of men and many millions of each kind of them. In many men there is a mixture in them, there is in them the bottom nature in them of their kind of men the nature that makes their kind of thinking, their kind of eating, of drinking and of loving, their kind of beginning and ending, there is then in many men this bottom nature in them of their kind of men and there is mixed up in them the nature of other kinds of men, natures that are a bottom nature in other men and makes of such men that kind of man.

In many men there is a mixture in them, there is in them the bottom nature in them the nature of their kind of men and there is mixed up in each one of them the nature or natures of other kind of men, natures that are each one of them a bottom nature in some of the many millions that there are of men and make of such men that kind of man.

In all the things that are in all men in all of their living from their beginning to their ending there can be as the impulse of them the bottom nature in them, the mixture in them of other nature or natures with the bottom nature, the nature or other natures in them which in some men of the many millions of each kind of men never really mix up with the bottom nature in them. Some of the things all men have in them in their daily living have it to come, in more men, only from the bottom nature in them than other things in them. Nothing of all the things all men have in them in their daily living comes in all men from the bottom nature of them. Eating, drinking, loving, anger in them, beginning and ending in them, come more from many men from the bottom nature of most of them than other things in them but always there are some men of all the millions of each kind of them who have it in them not to have even eating and drinking and doctoring and loving and anger in them and beginning and ending in them come from the bottom nature of them.

David Hersland had a mixture in him. He had as I was saying a big beginning in him a feeling of himself to himself of being as big as all the world around him. As I was saying he had a big beginning feeling in him all through his living to his ending. As I was saying his wife knew it about him in her feeling. She did not have it as a conscious thing in her in him but she felt it about him even before his children felt it in him, how far the nature in him would carry him.

As I was saying, in ways of eating, in ways of drinking, in ways of loving, in ways of letting anger come out from them about little things in their daily living, in ways of sleeping, in ways of doctoring, there is more, in strong middle living, of simple repeating than in other things in the middle living of vigorous active men and women. At the beginning of the ending of the middle living of vigorous active men and women, ways of thinking, ways of working, ways of beginning, ways of ending, ways of believing come to be in them as simple repeating.

In all men as I have been saying there are their own ways of being, in them. In some men some of their ways of being that more and more in their later living settle down into simple repeating some of their ways of being come from the bottom nature of them. There are some men of all the millions always being made of men there are some men who have only in them a bottom nature to them. From such men, and in all the millions of every kind of men some of the millions of each kind of them are such a kind of men they have in them only a bottom nature to them, all their ways of being come in such men, some of the millions of each kind of men, come all from the nature that makes their kind of men that makes the kind of men that have all of them in them as bottom nature in them their way of thinking, of eating, of drinking, of sleeping, of loving, of having angry feeling in them, their way of beginning and of ending. Every man has in him his own way of feeling about it inside him about his ways of doing the things that make for him his daily living; that is the individual feeling in him, that is the feeling of being to himself inside him, that is in many the feeling of being important to themselves inside them, that is in some men a feeling of being important to every one around them, that is in some men a feeling of being as big as all the world around them.

David Hersland was of such a kind of men, men who have sometime in them a feeling of being as big as all the world around them. David Hersland had a mixture in him. He mostly came all together from the bottom nature in him but there was in him too a mixture in him, and this made him, in his later living, full up with impatient feeling. There was in him a mixture in him but with him it made a whole of him.

As I was saying some men have it in them to be made altogether of the bottom nature that makes their kind of men. Some have it in them to have other nature or natures in them, natures that are the bottom nature to make other kinds of men, and this nature or natures in them mixes up well with the bottom nature of them to make a whole of them as when things are cooked to make a whole dish that is together then. Some have other nature or natures only as a flavor to them, the bottom nature is mostly the whole of them, some have other nature or natures in them that never mix with the bottom nature in them and in such ones the impulse in them comes from the bottom nature or from the other natures separate from each other and from the bottom nature in them, in some of them there is in them so little of the bottom nature in them that mostly everything that comes out from inside them comes out from the other nature or natures in them not from the bottom nature in them.

There are many things in every man in his living from his beginning to his ending. Some of the things in men have it in them to come more from the bottom nature of them than the other things in them but there are some men of the millions of every kind of men that have it in them to have almost nothing coming from the bottom nature of them. Some of the things in men have it to come from the bottom nature of men but there are some men of the many millions of every kind of men that have it in them to have nothing coming from the bottom nature of them. Some of the things in men have it in them to come more from the bottom nature of them, some of the things in men have it in them to come in more men not from the bottom nature of them. Some of the things in men have it in them to come more from the bottom nature of them but there are some men of the many millions of every kind of men that have it in them to have almost nothing coming from the bottom nature of them. There is from this on every kind of mixing in men. There is from that every kind of mixing and every kind of keeping separate of the natures in men; in some of the millions of every kind of men there is almost nothing in them in their living of the bottom nature of them, from that there is every kind of keeping separate and every kind of mixing of the natures in men to those millions of every kind of men who have in them only the bottom nature of their kind of men and have almost nothing in them of other kind of nature or natures in them. There is in men every kind of mixing and every kind of keeping separate of the natures in them. There are men who have nothing in them in their living of the bottom nature of them that makes their kind of men, there are men who have in them nothing of any nature in them excepting the bottom nature of them. There is from that every kind of mixing and every kind of keeping separate of the natures in men, from some men some of the millions of every kind of men with nothing in them in their living of the bottom nature of them to those millions of every kind of men who have in them only the bottom nature of their kind of men and have almost nothing in them of other kinds of nature or natures in them.

As I was saying men have in them their individual feeling in their way of feeling it in them about themselves to themselves inside them about the ways of being they have in them. Some have almost nothing of such a feeling in them, some have it a little in them, some have it in them always as a conscious feeling, some have it as a feeling of themselves inside them, some have it as a feeling of themselves inside them as important to them, some have it as a feeling of being important to themselves inside them as being always in them, some have it as being important to the others around them, some have it as being inside them that there is nothing existing except their kind of living, some have it that they feel themselves inside them as big as all the world around them, some have it that they are themselves the only important existing in the world then and in some of them for forever in them—these have in them the complete thing of being important to themselves inside them.

As I was saying in his middle living a man is more simple in his repeating of it in him of his ways of eating, ways of drinking, ways of doctoring, ways of loving, ways of sleeping, ways of walking, ways of having anger inside him than in his ways of having other things in him. A man in his middle living has in him already then simple repeating. It comes then that in his daily living often his wife has it earlier in her feeling how far the nature in him will carry him than anybody around him, not in her conscious feeling, not when she is talking about him, but in her feeling in her living with him.

F. 162–63, 165, 169–70, 178–80

Mrs. Hersland had in her then in her middle living a real feeling of being important to herself inside her in her feeling. If she had gone on in the living that was the natural way of being for her this never would have come to be real inside her, this would have been in her a real important feeling from the living that was natural to her but never a really important feeling of herself to herself inside her. She always would have had in her a feeling inside her that in her mother came out in the dreary trickling that was, almost all her later living, all that was of her. A little of such a feeling there would have always been in the daughter if she had gone on living the life that was the natural way of living for her but such a feeling would never come to be in her as it never came to be in her mother a feeling of herself to herself inside her, a feeling of herself to herself as important inside her. Some of her sisters and one brother had a little of the important feeling of the father, he had had a being that in any kind of living would have given a feeling of himself to himself as a religion. Mrs. Hersland had not in her any such a thing inside her, she had in her only the feeling that gave to her mother the dreary trickling that made all her, this in the daughter never had in it sadness and sorrow inside her it was in her a gentle pleasant timid sometimes an angry sometimes hurt feeling in her, in the living that was not the natural way of living for her it came to be inside her a feeling of herself to herself as important in her.

She had then in her, in her middle living it was strongest inside her, a feeling of herself to herself inside her. Once this came to be in her almost a lonesome feeling inside her but it really was not real enough in her, it did not come enough of itself from inside her, it never came to be altogether really a lonesome feeling in her.

There are very many ways for women to have loving in them, some have loving in them for any one or anything that needs them, some have loving in them from the need in them for some other one or for something they see around them, some have a mixture in them. There are some who have really not any loving in them. The kinds of loving women have in them and the way it comes out from them makes for them the bottom nature in them, makes them their kind of women and there are always many millions made of each kind of them.

Mrs. Hersland like almost all women had different things in her for loving. For her her children when they were little things around her it was not to her that they had need of her they were to her a part of her as if they were inside her, as they grew bigger and had their individual living in the house with her as they did not then need her to fight out their daily living with their father they did not feel any importance in her, they were for her then no longer a part of her, she had then weakening in her, she was a little thing then and they were so large around her, they were then struggling with themselves and with their living and with their father, she was weakening then and more and more they were not a part of her, she had not loved them because they had need of her, they were a part of her, then they were all struggling around her, she was a little thing then with weakening in her, more and more then they forgot about her, they were all struggling then around her, they were all of them having in them their individual living, they were all big then and she was a little gentle thing and lost among them and then she died away and left them. For her then with her children she was not of them who love those who have need of them nor of those who love any one near them because they have need of them. Some women have it in them to have children as part of them as if they were part of their own body all the time of their living. Such never have in them an important feeling of themselves inside them from the children that have come out of them, some of such of them can have it in them an important feeling from their children as it makes of them a larger thing being all one themselves and their children. Mrs. Hersland was of such of them of those who have in them not any important feeling of themselves inside them from their children. She was of such of them, the important feeling she had in her living came a little from her husband and more from the governesses and servants and dependents living in the house with them. She could not have in her a feeling of herself inside her from the children around her, they were to her like rich right living, they were a natural part of her, they could never give to her a feeling of herself to herself as important inside her. They were to her of her as her family living in Bridgepoint had been of her, important to her because they were her they were never cut off from her as she was never to her cut off from her the way of living that was the natural way of living for her.

Some women have it in them to love others because they need them, many of such ones subdue the ones they need for loving, they subdue them and they own them; some women have it in them to love only those who need them; some women have it in them only to have power when others love them, others loving them gives to them strength in domination as their needing those who love them keeps them from subduing others before those others love them. This will come clearer when this kind of women comes into this history of many kinds of men and women.

Mrs. Hersland was not of these two kinds then, she had a gentle little bounty in her, she had a sense in her of superior strength in her from the way of living that was the natural way of being to her, she had a larger being from the children who were always to her a part of her. She had in her a little power from the beauty feeling she had for her husband in his living with her; she was for him then a tender feeling in him, she was for him then a pleasant little joke to him resisting to him, she was to him a woman for his using as she was to herself part of her children, that was the simple sense in her that never gave to her a sense of being important to herself inside her.

There are then two kinds of women, those who have dependent independence in them, those who have in them independent dependence inside them; the ones of the first of them always somehow own the ones they need to love them, the second kind of them have it in them to love only those who need them, such of them have it in them to have power in them over others only when these others have begun already a little to love them, others loving them give to such of them strength in domination. There are then these two ways of loving there are these two ways of being when women have loving in them, as a bottom nature to them, there are then many kinds of mixing, there are many kinds of each kind of them, some women have it in them to have a bottom nature in them of one of these two kinds of loving and then this is mixed up in them with the other kind of loving as another nature in them but all this will come clear in the history of all kinds of women and some kinds of men as it will now be written of them.

There are then two kinds of women, there are those who have in them resisting and attacking, and a bottom weakness in them, women with independent dependence in them, women who are strong in attacking, women who sometimes have not bottom weakness in them, some who have in them bottom weakness in them and this inside is a strength in them when they have children when they have strong loving in them when it is in them in such of them a fine sensitive weakness inside them, there are then such ones of them women who need others around to love them before they have any power in them from the weakness in them, in such of them attacking is a power in them but not when they meet with real resisting, the bottom weakness in them is only a power in them when those around them love them, so only can these have any power in them; all these then all these women have not it in them mostly to believe that it never can come to them the last end of a bad thing to destroy them. All these then make one kind of the two kinds there are of women, the two kinds too there are then of men, and there are many kinds of such of them many strengths in them of this strength and weakness in them, many mixtures in them of the independence and dependence in them, many mixings and sometimes a mixing in the top of them with the other kind of nature of some men and women the dependent independent kind in men and women but more or less it is in them in all of this one kind of them it is in them to have independent dependence in them, it is in them to have attacking in them, to have aggressive optimism in them, to not believe the last end of a bad thing can come to them and destroy them, and then to have weakness as the bottom of them; and in many of them this weakness is all there is to them, in some of them attacking is all there is of them.

The other kind of women and there are many kinds of such of them in the many millions always of women, this other kind of them need to own the people around them when this nature is strong in them; they have many of them, a dependent patient way of living, but with the dependent nature in them they have never such of them, a feeling of themselves inside them, this comes out in them only with the bottom independence in them, when they feel themselves resisting, when they own some one around them, when it comes to them to own themselves inside them, some of such of them never have such a moment in their living, some of such of them never feel themselves inside them; there are then always many women living, there are then these two kinds of them, this is now a history of some of each kind of them, sometime there will be a history of all of each kind of them and that will then be a history of all women who are living, of all the many millions who ever were or will be living and then there will begin a history of all the men and the two kinds of them for there are in men the same two kinds of them like with women and it works out differently a little in them for they are men and have themselves mostly more inside them in their living, there are then these two kinds in women and in men and always every one is of one kind or the other kind of them.

It is hard to tell it about them, to describe it how each one is of the kind of them that is in that one. It is hard to tell it about them because the same words can describe all of them the one and the other kind of them, they are very different the one from the other kind of them, more and more perhaps it will come out clearly about them. It is hard to describe it in them the kind of being each one has in them, it is hard to describe it in them it is hard to know it in them, it is only slowly the two kinds of them come to be clear to every one who listens to the repeating that comes out of them, who sees the repeating that is in them the repeating of the bottom nature of them. Sometimes resisting comes like attacking, sometimes attacking seems like resisting, slowly it comes out from each one the kind of nature in them. So then this makes always a pair of them and this is always true in successful loving and this will soon then be a history of every kind of loving and how it comes from every one the nature of them.

Mrs. Hersland had dependent independent being, she could sometime in her have resisting. This is now a history of her and the servants and governesses and dependents who had to do with her. Mr. Hersland had attacking in him, mostly he was in his feeling as big as all the world in all of his beginning and all of his living was beginning, he never knew it inside him until his children told it to him when they were angry with him when impatient feeling filled him, he never knew that he did not go on to the last end of fighting that he had in him such a weakness in him; this is now a history of him and of how the servants and the governesses and the dependents and his wife and children felt all these things in him.

All kinds of men and women have impatient feeling and sometime this will be a history of every kind of impatient feeling and of every kind of men and women who have impatient feeling. Now this is a history of servant living, of servants who have in them servant girl being, of servants who have in them servant being, of servants who have in them not any real servant being, of servants who have in them a mixing of some or all of these kinds of nature in them, of how it works out through them the two kinds of nature in all men and women the independent dependent and the dependent independent natures in all of them, this will be too a history of servant queerness and how it works in such of them as have this in them.

As I was saying Mrs. Hersland had mostly in her middle living in Gossols in that part where no other rich people were living older foreign or foreign american women as servants in the house with them. Sometimes she had a young one to train, Mrs. Hersland never knew it in her that she never really liked to do such training. They always then had german or german american older women as servants in the house with them, but sometimes Mrs. Hersland could not get any of them, once she had an Irish woman to do the cooking, twice Italian women and once a Mexican, the Irish woman had servant queerness in her and she left all of a sudden, one Italian woman had servant queerness in her and she had to be sent away quickly without any warning, Mrs. Hersland never liked to have queer people near her she wanted her servants to be of the same kind of nature that was natural to her in the living at Bridgepoint the good living that was natural to her, she needed a servant around her that she Mrs. Hersland in her feeling could be of her and above her, she never wanted any servant to have servant queerness in her.

Some time then there will be every kind of a history of every one who ever can or is or was or will be living. Some time then there will be a history of every one from their beginning to their ending. Sometime then there will be a history of all of them, of every kind of them, of every one, of every bit of living they ever have in them, of them when there is never more than a beginning to them, of every kind of them, of every one when there is very little beginning and then there is an ending, there will then sometime be a history of every one there will be a history of everything that ever was or is or will be them, of everything that was or is or will be all of any one or all of all of them. Sometime then there will be a history of every one, of everything or anything that is all them or any part of them and sometime then there will be a history of how anything or everything comes out from every one, comes out from every one or any one from the beginning to the ending of the being in them. Sometime then there must be a history of every one who ever was or is or will be living. As one sees every one in their living, in their loving, sitting, eating, drinking, sleeping, walking, working, thinking, laughing, as any one sees all of them from their beginning to their ending, sees them when they are little babies or children or young grown men and women or growing older men and women or old men and women then one knows it in them that sometime there will be a history of all of them, that sometime all of them will have the last touch of being a history of them can give to them, sometime then there will be a history of each one, of all the kinds of them, of all the ways any one can know them, of all the ways each one is inside her or inside him, of all the ways anything of them comes out from them. Sometime then there will be a history of every one and so then every one will have in them the last touch of being a history of any one can give to them.

G. 289–300, 347–51, 388, 458, 459–60, 483–85, 520–21, 539–40, 611

I am writing for myself and strangers. This is the only way that I can do it. Everybody is a real one to me, everybody is like some one else too to me. No one of them that I know can want to know it and so I write for myself and strangers.

Every one is always busy with it, no one of them then ever want to know it that every one looks like some one else and they see it. Mostly every one dislikes to hear it. It is very important to me to always know it, to always see it which one looks like others and to tell it. I write for myself and strangers. I do this for my own sake and for the sake of those who know I know it that they look like other ones, that they are separate and yet always repeated. There are some who like it that I know they are like many others and repeat it, there are many who never can really like it.

There are many that I know and they know it. They are all of them repeating and I hear it. I love it and I tell it, I love it and now I will write it. This is now the history of the way some of them are it.

I write for myself and strangers. No one who knows me can like it. At least they mostly do not like it that every one is of a kind of men and women and I see it. I love it and I write it.

I want readers so strangers must do it. Mostly no one knowing me can like it that I love it that every one is of a kind of men and women, that always I am looking and comparing and classifying of them, always I am seeing their repeating. Always more and more I love repeating, it may be irritating to hear from them but always more and more I love it of them. More and more I love it of them, the being in them, the mixing in them, the repeating in them, the deciding the kind of them every one is who has human being.

This is now a little of what I love and how I write it. Later there will be much more of it.

There are many ways of making kinds of men and women. Now there will be descriptions of every kind of way every one can be a kind of men and women.

This is now a history of Martha Hersland. This is now a history of Martha and of every one who came to be of her living.

There will then be soon much description of every way one can think of men and women, in their beginning, in their middle living, and their ending.

Every one then is an individual being. Every one then is like many others always living, there are many ways of thinking of every one, this is now a description of all of them. There must then be a whole history of each one of them. There must then now be a description of all repeating. Now I will tell all the meaning to me in repeating, the loving there is in me for repeating.

Every one is one inside them, every one reminds some one of some other one who is or was or will be living. Every one has it to say of each one he is like such a one I see it in him, every one has it to say of each one she is like some one else I can tell by remembering. So it goes on always in living, every one is always remembering some one who is resembling to the one at whom they are then looking. So they go on repeating, every one is themselves inside them and every one is resembling to others, and that is always interesting. There are many ways of making kinds of men and women. In each way of making kinds of them there is a different system of finding them resembling. Sometime there will be here every way there can be of seeing kinds of men and women. Sometime there will be then a complete history of each one. Every one always is repeating the whole of them and so sometime some one who sees them will have a complete history of every one. Sometime some one will know all the ways there are for people to be resembling, some one sometime then will have a completed history of every one.

Soon now there will be a history of the way repeating comes out of them comes out of men and women when they are young, when they are children, they have then their own system of being resembling; this will soon be a description of the men and women in beginning, the being young in them, the being children.

There is then now and here the loving repetition, this is then, now and here, a description of the loving of repetition and then there will be a description of all the kinds of ways there can be seen to be kinds of men and women. Then there will be realised the complete history of every one, the fundamental character of every one, the bottom nature in them, the mixtures in them, the strength and weakness of everything they have inside them, the flavor of them, the meaning in them, the being in them, and then you have a whole history then of each one. Everything then they do in living is clear to the completed understanding, their living, loving, eating, pleasing, smoking, thinking, scolding, drinking, working, dancing, walking, talking, laughing, sleeping, everything in them. There are whole beings then, they are themselves inside them, repeating coming out of them makes a history of each one of them.

Always from the beginning there was to me all living as repeating. This is now a description of my feeling. As I was saying listening to repeating is often irritating, always repeating is all of living, everything in a being is always repeating, more and more listening to repeating gives to me completed understanding. Each one slowly comes to be a whole one to me. Each one slowly comes to be a whole one in me. Soon then it commences to sound through my ears and eyes and feelings the repeating that is always coming out from each one, that is them, that makes then slowly of each one of them a whole one. Repeating then comes slowly then to be to one who has it to have loving repeating as natural being comes to be a full sound telling all the being in each one such a one is ever knowing. Sometimes it takes many years of knowing some one before the repeating that is that one gets to be a steady sounding to the hearing of one who has it as a natural being to love repeating that slowly comes out from every one. Sometimes it takes many years of knowing some one before the repeating in that one comes to be a clear history of such a one. Natures sometimes are so mixed up in some one that steady repeating in them is mixed up with changing. Soon then there will be a completed history of each one. Sometimes it is difficult to know it in some, for what these are saying is repeating in them is not the real repeating of them, is not the complete repeating for them. Sometimes many years of knowing some one pass before repeating of all being in them comes out clearly from them. As I was saying it is often irritating to listen to the repeating they are doing, always then that one that has it as being to love repeating that is the whole history of each one, such a one has it then that this irritation passes over into patient completed understanding. Loving repeating is one way of being. This is now a description of such feeling.

There are many that I know and they know it. They are all of them repeating and I hear it. I love it and I tell it. I love it and now I will write it. This is now a history of my love of it. I hear it and I love it and I write it. They repeat it. They live it and I see it and I hear it. They live it and I hear it and I see it and I love it and now and always I will write it. There are many kinds of men and women and I know it. They repeat it and I hear it and I love it. This is now a history of the way they do it. This is now a history of the way I love it.

Now I will tell of the meaning to me in repeating, of the loving there is in me for repeating.

Sometime every one becomes a whole one to me. Sometime every one has a completed history for me. Slowly each one is a whole one to me, with some, all their living is passing before they are a whole one to me. There is a completed history of them to me then when there is of them a completed understanding of the bottom nature in them of the nature or natures mixed up in them with the bottom nature of them or separated in them. There is then a history of the things they say and do and feel, and happen to them. There is then a history of the living in them. Repeating is always in all of them. Repeating in them comes out of them, slowly making clear to any one that looks closely at them the nature and the natures mixed up in them. This sometime comes to be clear in every one.

Often as I was saying repeating is very irritating to listen to from them and then slowly it settles into a completed history of them. Repeating is a wonderful thing in living being. Sometime then the nature of every one comes to be clear to some one listening to the repeating coming out of each one.

This is then now to be a little description of the loving feeling for understanding of the completed history of each one that comes to one who listens always steadily to all repeating. This is the history then of the loving feeling in me of repeating, the loving feeling in me for completed understanding of the completed history of every one as it slowly comes out in every one as patiently and steadily I hear it and see it as repeating in them. This is now a little a description of this loving feeling. This is now a little a history of it from the beginning.

Always then I listen and come back again and again to listen to every one. Always then I am thinking and feeling the repeating in every one. Sometime then there will be for me a completed history of every one. Every one is separate then and a kind of men and women.

Sometime it takes many years of knowing some one before the repeating in that one comes to be a clear history of such a one. Sometimes many years of knowing some one pass before repeating of all being in such a one comes out clearly from them, makes a completed understanding of them by some one listening, watching, hearing all the repeating coming out from such a one.

As I was saying loving listening, hearing always all repeating, coming to completed understanding of each one is to some a natural way of being. This is now more description of the feeling such a one has in them, this is now more description of the way listening to repeating comes to make completed understanding. This is now more description of the way repeating slowly comes to make in each one a completed history of them.

There are many that I know and always more and more I know it. They are all of them repeating and I hear it. More and more I understand it. Always more and more I hear it, always more and more it has completed history in it.

Every one has their own being in them. Every one is of a kind of men and women. Many have mixed up in them some kind of many kinds of men and women. Slowly this comes clearly out from them in the repeating that is always in all living. Slowly it comes out from them to the most delicate gradation, to the gentlest flavor of them. Always it comes out as repeating from them. Always it comes out as repeating, out of them. Then to the complete understanding they keep on repeating this, the whole of them and any one seeing them then can understand them. This is a joy to any one loving repeating when in any one repeating steadily tells over and over again the history of the complete being in them. This is a solid happy satisfaction to any one who has it in them to love repeating and completed understanding.

As I was saying often for many years some one is baffling. The repeated hearing of them does not make the completed being they have in them to any one. Sometimes many years pass in listening to repeating in such a one and the being of them is not a completed history to any one then listening to them. Sometimes then it comes out of them a louder repeating that before was not clear to anybody's hearing and then it is a completed being to some one listening to the repeating coming out of such a one.

This is then now a description of loving repeating being in some. This is then now a description of loving repeating being in one.

There are many that I know and they know it. They are all of them repeating and I hear it. More and more I understand it. I love it and I tell it. I love it and always I will tell it. They live it and I see it and I hear it. They repeat it and I hear it and I see it, sometime then always I understand it, sometime then always there is a completed history of each one by it, sometime then I will tell the completed history of each one as by repeating I come to know it.

Every one always is repeating the whole of them. Every one is repeating the whole of them, such repeating is then always in them and so sometime some one who sees them will have a complete understanding of the whole of each one of them, will have a completed history of every man and every woman they ever come to know in their living, every man and every woman who were or are or will be living whom such a one can come to know in living.

This then is a history of many men and women, sometime there will be a history of every one.

As I was saying every one always is repeating the whole of them. As I was saying sometimes it takes many years of hearing the repeating in one before the whole being is clear to the understanding of one who has it as a being to love repeating, to know that always every one is repeating the whole of them.

This is then the way such a one, one who has it as a being to love repeating, to know that always every one is repeating the whole of them comes to a completed understanding of any one. This is now a description of such a way of hearing repeating.

Every one always is repeating the whole of them. Many always listen to all repeating that comes to them in their living. Some have it as being to love the repeating that is always in every one coming out from them as a whole of them. This is now a description of such a one and the completed understanding of each one who is repeating in such a one's living.

Every one always is repeating the whole of them. Always, one having loving repeating to getting completed understanding must have in them an open feeling, a sense for all the slightest variations in repeating, must never lose themselves so in the solid steadiness of all repeating that they do not hear the slightest variation. If they get deadened by the steady pounding of repeating they will not learn from each one even though each one always is repeating the whole of them they will not learn the completed history of them, they will not know the being really in them.

As I was saying every one always is repeating the whole of them. As I was saying sometimes it takes many years of listening, seeing, living, feeling, loving the repeating there is in some before one comes to a completed understanding. This is now a description of such a way of hearing, seeing, feeling, living, loving, repetition.

Mostly every one loves some one's repeating. Mostly every one then, comes to know then the being of some one by loving the repeating in them, the repeating coming out of them. There are some who love everybody's repeating, this is now a description of such loving in one.

Mostly every one loves some one's repeating. Every one always is repeating the whole of them. This is now a history of getting completed understanding by loving repeating in every one the repeating that always is coming out of them as a complete history of them. This is now a description of learning to listen to all repeating that every one always is making of the whole of them.

Now I will tell of the meaning to me in repeating, of the loving there is in me for repeating.

Always from the beginning there was to me all living as repeating. This is now a description of loving repeating as a being. This is now a history of learning to listen to repeating to come to a completed understanding.

To go on now giving all of the description of how repeating comes to have meaning, how it forms itself, how one must distinguish the different meanings in repeating. Sometimes it is very hard to understand the meaning of repeating. Sometime there will be a complete history of some one having loving repeating as being, to a completed understanding. Now there will be a little description of such a one.

Sometime then there will be a complete history of all repeating to completed understanding. Sometime then there will be a complete history of every one who ever was or is or will be living.

Sometime there will be a complete history of some one having loving repeating to a completed understanding as being. Sometime then there will be a complete history of many women and many men.

Now there is to be some description of some one having loving repeating to a completed understanding as being. Then there will be a complete history of some.

More and more then there will be a history of many men and many women from their beginning to their ending, as being babies and children and growing young men and growing young women and young grown men and young grown women and men and women in their middle living and growing old men and growing old women and old men and old women.

More and more then there will be histories of all the kinds there are of men and women.

This is now a little description of having loving repeating as being. This is now a little description of one having loving repeating as being.

Loving repeating is one way of being. This is now a description of such being. Loving repeating is always in children. Loving repeating is in a way earth feeling. Some children have loving repeating for little things and story-telling, some have it as a more bottom being. Slowly this comes out in them in all their children being, in their eating, playing, crying, and laughing. Loving repeating is then in a way earth feeling. This is very strong in some. This is very strong in many, in children and in old age being. This is very strong in many in all ways of humorous being, this is very strong in some from their beginning to their ending. This is now some description of such being in one.

As I was saying loving repeating being is in a way earthy being. In some it is repeating that gives to them always a solid feeling of being. In some children there is more feeling in repeating eating and playing, in some in story-telling and their feeling. More and more in living as growing young men and women and grown young men and women and men and women in their middle living, more and more there comes to be in them differences in loving repeating in different kinds of men and women, there comes to be in some more and in some less loving repeating. Loving repeating in some is a going on always in them of earthy being, in some it is the way to completed understanding. Loving repeating then in some is their natural way of complete being. This is now some description of one.

There is then always repeating in all living. There is then in each one always repeating their whole being, the whole nature in them. Much loving repeating has to be in a being so that that one can listen to all the repeating in every one. Almost every one loves all repeating in some one. This is now some description of loving repeating, all repeating, in every one.

To begin again with the children. To begin again with the repeating being in them. To begin again with the loving repeating being in them. As I was saying some children have it in them to love repeating in them of eating, of angry feeling in them, many of them have loving repeating for storytelling in them, many of them have loving repeating being in them for any kind of being funny, in making jokes or teasing, many of them have loving repeating being in them in all kinds of playing. Mostly every one when they are children, mostly every one has then loving repeating being strongly in them, some have it more some have it less in them and this comes out more and more in them as they come to be young adolescents in their being and then grown young men and grown young women

To begin again then with children in their having loving repeating being. Mostly all children have loving repeating as being in them but some have it much more and some have it much less in them. [Loving repeating being is earth being, it gives to them that have it in them more and more solid sense of being. Mostly those who have in them dependent independent being have it in them to have loving repeating more in them than the independent dependent kind of men and women.] Loving repeating being is more of that kind of being that has resisting as its natural way of fighting than of that kind of being that has attacking as its natural way of winning. But this is a very complicated question. I know very much about these ways of being in men and women. I know it and can say it, it is a very complex question and I do not know yet the whole of it, so I can not yet say all I know of it.

As I was saying all little children have in them mostly very much loving repeating being. As they grow into bigger children some have it more some have it less in them. Some have it in them more and more as a conscious feeling. Many of them do not have it in them more and more as a conscious feeling. Mostly when they are growing to be young men and women they have not it in them to have loving repeating being in them as a conscious feeling.

Mostly every one has not it in them as a conscious feeling as a young grown man or young grown woman. Some have it in them, loving repeating feeling as steadily developing, this is now a history of one.

Many men and many women never have it in them the conscious feeling of loving repeating. Many men and many women never have it in them until old age weakening is in them, a consciousness of repeating. Many have it in them all their living as a conscious feeling as a humorous way of being in them. Some have it in them, the consciousness of always repeating the whole of them as a serious obligation. There are many many ways then of having repeating as conscious feeling, of having loving repeating as a bottom being, of having loving repeating being as a conscious feeling.

As I was saying mostly all children have in them loving repeating being as important in them to them and to every one around them. Mostly growing young men and growing young women have to themselves very little loving repeating being, they do not have it to each other then most of them, they have it to older ones then as older ones have it to them loving repeating being, not loving repeating being but repeating as the way of being in them, repeating of the whole of them as coming every minute from them.

In the middle living of men and women there are very different ways of feeling to repeating, some have more and more in them loving repeating as a conscious feeling, some have less and less liking in them for the repeating in, to them, of mostly every one. Mostly every one has a loving feeling for repeating in some one. Some have not any such loving even in the repeating going on inside themselves then, not even for any one they are loving.

Some then have always growing in them more and more loving feeling for the repeating in every one. Many have not any loving for repeating in many of those around them.

There are then many ways of feeling in one about repeating. There are many ways of knowing repeating when one sees and hears and feels it in every one.

Loving repeating then is important being in some. This is now some description of the importance of loving repeating being in one.

Some find it interesting to find inside them repeating in them of some one they have known or some relation to them coming out in them, some never have any such feeling in them, some have not any liking for such being in them. Some like to see such being in others around them but not in themselves inside them. There are many ways of feeling in one about all these kinds of repeating. Sometime there will be written the history of all of them.

[To begin again then with loving repeating in children.] To begin again then with some description of the meaning of loving repeating being when it is strongly in a man or in a woman, when it is in them their way of understanding everything in living and there are very many always living of such being. This is now again a beginning of a little description of it in one.

Repeating of the whole of them is then always in every one. There are different stages in being, there is being babies and children and then growing young men or women and grown young men or women and men or women in middle living and in growing old and in ending. There are many kinds of men and women and soon now there will be a beginning of a history of all of them who ever were or are or will be living. There will be then here written a history of some of them. To begin again then with loving repeating being as a bottom nature in some. To begin again with the developing of it in one.

As I was saying children have it in them to have strongly loving repeating being as a conscious feeling in so far as they can be said to have such a thing in them. It gives to them a solid feeling of knowing they are safe in living. With growing it comes to be more in some, it comes to be less in others of them. Mostly there is very little conscious loving repeating feeling in growing young men and women.

In the beginning then, in remembering, repeating was strongly in the feeling of one, in the feeling of many, in the feeling of most of them who have it to have strongly in them their earthy feeling of being part of the solid dirt around them. This is one kind of being. This is mostly of one kind of being, of slow-minded resisting fighting being. This is now a little a description of one.

Slowly then some go on living, they may be fairly quick in learning, some of such of them seem very quick and impetuous in learning and in acting but such learning has for such of them very little meaning, it is the slow repeating resisting inside them that has meaning for them. Now there will be a little a description of loving repeating being in one of such of them.

The kinds and ways of repeating, of attacking and resisting in different kinds of men and women, the practical, the emotional, the sensitive, the every kind of being in every one who ever was or is or will be living, I know so much about all of them, many of them are very clear in kinds of men and women, in individual men and women, I know them so well inside them, repeating in them has so much meaning to knowing, more and more I know all there is of all being, more and more I know it in all the ways it is in them and comes out of them, sometime there will be a history of every one, sometime all history of all men and women will be inside some one.

Now there will be a little description of the coming to be history of all men and women, in some one. This is then to be a little history of such a one. This is then now to be a little description of loving repeating being in one.

Almost every one has it in them in their beginning to have loving repeating being strongly in them. Some of them have attacking being as the bottom nature in them, some of them have resisting being as the bottom nature in them. Some of both these kinds of them have more or less in all their living loving repeating being in them, it works differently in them to come out of them in these two kinds of them. Later there will be much description of the way it comes out from them and is in them in the different kinds of them. Now there is to be a little description of it in one having resisting as the way of winning fighting. This is now some description of such a one having loving repeating being developing into completed understanding. Now to slowly begin.

The relation of learning to being, of thinking to feeling, of realisation to emotion, all these and many others are very complicated questions. Sometimes there will be much description of them with the kinds of men and women with being in them, with mixtures in them, that complicates them. There will sometime be a history of every one. This is a sure thing.

Now again to begin. The relation of learning and thinking to being, of feeling to realising is a complicated question. There will now be very little talking of such way of being. As I was saying some have it in them to have slowly resisting as their natural way of being can have learning and thinking come quickly enough in them. This is then not bottom being in them. It is bottom being in some of such of them. This is very clear now in my knowing. Now to begin again with it as telling.

Some then who are of that kind of being who have slow resisting being as their way to wisdom have it in them to be quick in learning and in thinking and in acting. As I was saying in some this is not of the bottom nature in them, in some it is bottom nature in them for the slow resisting winning bottom to them was not put in in the making of them, in some it is in them but dull and not mixing in their living, in some it is not sensitive to action in their living, it is there in them going on inside them not connecting on with the rest of them. This is not just talking, this all has real meaning. These are all then of a kind of men and women who have resisting being as the real wisdom in them. In some of such of them they seem to be winning by acting by attacking they live so very successfully in living but nevertheless they are of the kind of them that have resisting winning as their real way of fighting although never in their living does this act in them. Careful listening to the whole of them always repeating shows this in them, what kind they are of men and women.

To begin again. This is now some description of one having loving repeating as a way to wisdom, having slowly resisting winning as the bottom being. As I was saying learning in such a one and thinking about everything can be quick enough in the beginning.

The important thing then in knowing the bottom nature in any one is the way their real being slowly comes to be them, the whole of them comes to be repeating in them.

As I was saying some can have quick learning and nervous attacking or one or the other in them with slow resisting being in them as their natural way of winning. There is every kind of mixing. There is every degree of intensification. There is every degree of hastening the resisting into more rapid realisation. There is every degree of hurrying. In short there are all degrees of intensification and rapidity in motion and mixing and disguising and yet the kind he is each one, the kind she is each one, comes to be clear in the repeating that more and more steadily makes them clear to any one looking hard at them. These kinds then are existing, the independent dependent, the dependent independent, the one with attacking as the way of winning, the other with resisting as the way of wisdom for them. I know then this is true of every one that each one is of one or the other kind of these two kinds of them. I know it is in them, I know many more things about these two kinds of them. Slowly they come to be clearer in every one, sometime perhaps it will be clear to every one. Sometime perhaps some one will have completely in them the history of every one of everything in every one and the degree and kind and way of being of everything in each one in them from their beginning to their ending and coming out of them.

This is then a beginning of the way of knowing everything in every one, of knowing the complete history of each one who ever is or was or will be living. This is then a little description of the winning of so much wisdom.

As I was saying the important thing is having loving repeating being, that is the beginning of learning the complete history of every one. That being must always be in such a one, one who has it in them sometime to have in them the completed history of every one they ever can hear of as having being.

There are so many ways of beginning this description, and now once more to make a beginning.

The resisting kind of being in men and women and how I feel it, how I know it in them. They are it, they live it, they repeat it, sometime I know it in them, this is now some description of the way I realise it.

The bottom nature in many then is of the dependent independent kind of being there can be in men and women, these have resisting fighting as their natural way of winning. In such of them reaction is not quick and poignant in them, in such of them emotion has not the poignancy of a sensation. I know it in them, always sometime I know it in them, often it is hard to know it in them from the mixing of the other kinds of nature in them. Perhaps now I will give just a little description of it, later I will give more description of it. I understand it and I can tell it. I will wait a little longer before I tell very much about it. Now there will be only a little description of it. Slowly there will be a complete description of it coming out of me and sometime there will be written all any one knows of it. I know it and now I will tell a little of it.

Resisting being in men and women. This is now then a little a description of my realising resisting being in men and women. This is then now a little description of my realising resisting being in some.

There are many that have resisting being in them as a bottom nature to them, sometimes I know it in them. There are many then that have it, I know it and sometime I tell it, they are all of them showing it in the repeating they are all of them doing all their living, sometime I know it in each one of them, sometime I know it and sometime I tell it. There are many that have it, that makes all of them one kind of men and women. I know it in them in each one of them of men and women I am ever knowing who have it and sometimes I understand it, I know it and understand the action of it in each one of them that have it, in each one of them that I come to know of that kind of men and women. There are many then that have it, about half of all men and women are of the kind of men and women having resisting being as a bottom nature in them, the rest of them mostly have attacking being in them. This is a general division. I understand a good deal of it, I can tell more and less than I understand of it. I am now going to tell less and more than I understand of resisting being as a bottom nature in many men and women who have it.

Resisting being then as I was saying is to me a kind of being, one kind of men and women have it as being that emotion is not as poignant in them as sensation. This is my meaning, this is resisting being. Generally speaking then resisting being is a kind of being where, taking bottom nature to be a substance like earth to some one's feeling, this needs time for penetrating to get reaction. Those having attacking being their substance is more vibrant in them, these can have reaction as emotion as quick and poignant and complete as a sensation. Generally speaking, those having resisting being in them have a slow way of responding, they may be nervous and quick and all that but it is in them, nervousness is in them as the effect of slow-moving going too fast and so having nervous being, nervous being in them is not the natural means of expression to such of them, some have quick response in them by the steadily training of themselves to quicker and quicker reaction and some of them in the end come to seem to have quick reaction as their natural way of being, mostly in such of them this is a late development in them and that is natural from the kind of being in them. Attacking being often has nervousness as energy as a natural way of active being in them, often these then lose the power of attacking with the loss of nervousness in them. There are so very many ways of knowing these two kinds in men and women. I know so very many of them, I will not now tell of very many of them. Mostly the resisting being when they have conservative being in them have it from not having the activity of changing, the attacking kind of being have conservative sense in them from convictions, traditions, they are attackingly defending. Mostly those having in them resisting being have more feeling of objects as real things to them, objects have to them more earthy meaning than to those who have attacking as their natural way of being. Mostly then objects to those having attacking being as their natural way of being have for them meaning as emotion, as practically to be using, as beauty, as symbolism, that is to many of them their natural way of seeing anything they are knowing, to those who have resisting being as their natural way of being an object is it itself to them, the meaning, the use, the emotion about it, the beauty, the symbolising of it is to such of them a secondary reaction, not altogether at once as in those having in them attacking as their natural way of being. So then those having resisting being have also in them passive adaptability strongly in them when they are not really resisting while those who have attacking being are generally more active in adapting, they may have yielding in them or stubbornness or sensitive responsiveness in them when not attacking they have not generally speaking passive adaptability in them. They are very different then the attacking and the resisting kind in men and women. This division has real meaning. Sometime when I am all through all my writing, when all my meaning, all my understanding, all my knowing, all my learning has been written, sometime then some will understand the being in all men and women.

I am all unhappy in this writing. I know very much of the meaning of the being in men and women. I know it and feel it and I am always learning more of it and now I am telling it and I am nervous and driving and unhappy in it. Sometimes I will be all happy in it.

I know it and now I begin again with telling it, the way I feel resisting being in men and women. It is like a substance and in some it is as I was saying solid and sensitive all through it to stimulation, in some almost wooden, in some muddy and engulfing, in some thin almost like gruel, in some solid in some parts and in other parts all liquid, in some with holes like air-holes in it, in some a thin layer of it, in some hardened and cracked all through it, in some double layers of it with no connections between the layers of it. This and many many other ways there are of feeling it as the bottom being in different ones of them; different men and women have resisting being as their natural way of being, always I am looking hard at each one, feeling, seeing, hearing the repeating coming out of each one and so slowly I know of each one the way the bottom in them is existing and so then that is the foundation of the history of each one of them and always it is coming out of each one of them.

This then this bottom nature in them, the way it is made in them makes the bottom history of them, makes their way of being stupid, wise, active, lazy, continuous, disjointed, is always there in them, in some their kind of them is more, is less, is the same all through their living, is more or less affected by the other nature or natures in them if they have other nature or natures in them, can be stimulated or hurried or slowed but never really changed in them, can come very nearly to be changed in them, can never really be changed in them, really not ever to my knowing, really not ever really changed in them. This then is very certain and now to speak again of attacking being. Attacking being as I was saying has it to be that emotion can be as quick, as poignant, as profound in meaning as a sensation. This is my meaning. I am thinking of attacking being not as an earthy kind of substance but as a pulpy not dust not dirt but a more mixed up substance, it can be slimy, gelatinous, gluey, white opaquey kind of thing and it can be white and vibrant, and clear and heated and this is all not very clear to me and I will now tell more about it.

This is the way I am thinking of it. In the one in which I first learned to know it it was like this to me. It was like this to me in the first one I came to know it, the substance attacking being is, in its various shaping. In this one it was so dull, so thick, so gluey that it was so slow in action one almost could think of it as resisting but it was not resisting earthy dependent independent being, it was attacking, stupid, slow-moving, it was independent dependent being, it was a different substance in its way of acting, reacting, of being penetrated, of feeling, of thinking than any slow resisting dependent independent being and now there is to be here a very little explaining of how I know this as a kind of being.

In this one then, as I was saying it was attacking being but very slowly getting into motion but not because it the stimulation was lost into it and had to be remade out of it but because it being shaken it was a slow mass getting into action. I know this distinction, it has real meaning, I am saying it again and again and now I begin again with a description.

This then the attacking being was first clear to me in one having it as a slow, stupid, gelatinous being that when it got moving went on repeating action, never could get going any faster, had a nervous anaemic feeling that was part of its getting moving and keeping going. The resisting medium has a different kind of action as I was explaining. Now this attacking being when it is vibrant can be nervous and poignant and quicker than chain-lightning, there can be to it a profound complete reaction having the intensity of a sensation. Its sensitiveness is different in kind from that of the resisting kind of being, its sensitiveness is quivering into action not a sensitiveness just existing, but this is all too much to be now explaining, wait and I can tell it, clearer, always it has to be told as it has been learned by me very slowly, each one only slowly can know it, each one must wait for little pieces of it, always there will be coming more and more of it, always there will be a telling of every way the two kinds of being are different in everything and always it is hard to say it the differences between them, always more and more I know it, always more and more I know it, always more I come back to begin again the knowing of it, always I will tell it as I learned it, sometime I will have told all of it, always I am telling pieces of it, more and more I will know it, more and more I will tell it, sometime it will be clear to some one and I will be then glad of it.

This then is attacking being to me, this then was the way it came first to be clear in me, in one in whom it was slow moving, and in others then I knew it when it was quick and poignant and complete and I saw it, and I knew it as the same substance as this slow moving mass and in all its forms of acting more and more then I knew it. In some as I was saying it is as emotion, in some it is as passion, in some it is as sensitive responding; it has a way of thinking, loving, acting, different in kind from that of resisting being and some time, and it is a very long time too I know it now I am beginning telling all I know all I am always learning, sometime there will have been a complete description of these two kinds of being.

In some then this quick and poignant and profound reaction has to break through a resisting being lying on it and then it is very interesting in the changing in the action it takes to get through the covering, sometimes it is in some more quivering vibrant at the bottom than through the rest of it and then it is lighted and set in motion the rest that of itself never has more activity than quivering by the more vibrant part at the bottom, sometimes all of it is not more active ever than quivering, this is true in some, in some it is all vibrant and completely poignantly passionately acting, in some its nervousness is its most vigorous action, in some it is a big mass always slowly moving but would like to stop acting and a resolute will, a mind, a conviction, education in such a one keeps it moving, sometimes it stops moving, there are so many ways, there are such a various kind of mixing that can be in any one, sometime there will be a history of each one, sometime there will be a description of all the ways resisting being can be in any one, all the ways attacking being can be in any one.

[More and more then as there are being told now histories of women and of men it will be clearer to every one the kind of being that is a bottom being in them, the other natures or nature in them, some time every one will understand the action and interaction of bottom nature and other nature and natures in them. This is the fundamental way of knowing kinds in men and women, all other ways of knowing kinds in men and women can be with this knowing of them, there are many ways of seeing kinds in men and women, all of them are interesting, this then of the bottom nature in them is one way of knowing kinds in men and women. This will be now soon more descriptions of it in each one, this will be now soon more description of kinds of these two kinds of them, resisting and attacking being.]

This then is then one way I have been seeing kinds in men and women, the way I see the bottom natures and other natures in them. Always I see them as kinds, always as kinds of substance and ways of that substance being in them as bottom nature. Sometime all this will be clearer. This is then the way I see kinds in men and women. This then makes every one sometime a clear one, a whole one to me, this is now soon to be more description of such learning by me, of such understanding of the being in men and women.

As I was saying often for many years some one is baffling, the repeated seeing, hearing, feeling of the being in them does not make clear the nature of the bottom being in them. Sometimes for many years some one is baffling and then it is clear in that one and then by resemblances between that one and other ones many are clear then. This is now some description of such learning.

This one, and the one I am now beginning describing is Martha Hersland and this is a little story of the acting in her of her being in her very young living, this one was a very little one then and she was running and she was in the street and it was a muddy one and she had an umbrella that she was dragging and she was crying. "I will throw the umbrella in the mud," she was saying, she was very little then, she was just beginning her schooling, "I will throw the umbrella in the mud" she said and no one was near her and she was dragging the umbrella and bitterness possessed her, "I will throw the umbrella in the mud" she was saying and nobody heard her, the others had run ahead to get home and they had left her, "I will throw the umbrella in the mud," and there was desperate anger in her; "I have throwed the umbrella in the mud" burst from her, she had thrown the umbrella in the mud and that was the end of it all in her. She had thrown the umbrella in the mud and no one heard her as it burst from her, "I have throwed the umbrella in the mud," it was the end of all that to her.

It is very hard telling from any incident in any one's living what kind of being they have in them. Kinds in being is a subject that is very puzzling. Martha Hersland had independent dependent being but this that I have just been telling might have been in the living of a little one having independent dependent being, might have been in the living of a little one having dependent independent being, might have been in the living of a little one having a mixture in its being. This then was in the living of Martha Hersland when she was a little one but as I was saying it is very hard to know from anything in any one's living the kind of being in them. Slowly some one comes to know the being in some one. Slowly then now every one reading will know all the being in Martha Hersland. This is then a beginning.

Sometimes I am almost despairing. Yes it is very hard, almost impossible I am feeling now in my despairing feeling to have completely a realising of the being in any one, when they are telling it when they are not telling it, it is so very very hard to know it completely in one the being in one. I know the being in Miss Dounor that I am beginning describing, I know the being in Miss Charles that I am soon going to be beginning describing, I know the being in Mrs. Redfern, I have been describing the being in that one. I know the being in each one of these three of them and I am almost despairing for I am doubting if I am knowing it poignantly enough to be really knowing it, to be really knowing the being in any one of the three of them. Always now I am despairing. It is a very melancholy feeling I have in me now I am despairing about really knowing the complete being of any one of each one of these three of them Miss Dounor and Miss Charles and Mrs. Redfern.

It is so very confusing that I am beginning to have in me despairing melancholy feeling. Mrs. Redfern as I was saying was of the independent dependent kind of them and being in her was never really attacking, it was mostly never active into forward movement it was incessantly in action as being in a state of most continual nervous agitation. They were then very different in their being the three of them Miss Dounor and Miss Charles and Mrs. Redfern and they had each one of them their own way of hurting the other ones in their then living, of having in them sensitiveness to something.

It is hard to know it of any one whether they are enjoying anything, whether they are feeling something, whether they are knowing they are giving pain to some one, whether they were planning that thing. It is a very difficult thing to know such things in any one any one is knowing, very difficult even when they are telling that one all the feeling they have in them, a very difficult thing when they are not telling anything. It is a very difficult thing to tell it of any one whether they are enjoying a thing, whether they know that they are hurting some one, whether they have been planning the acting they have been doing. It is a very difficult thing to know anything of the being in any one, it is a very difficult thing to know the being in any one if they tell you all that they themselves know of it as they live it, if they themselves tell you nothing at all about it. It is a very difficult thing to know the being in any one. It is a very difficult thing to know whether any one is feeling a thing, enjoying a thing, knowing that they are hurting some one, planning that thing, planning anything they are doing in their living. It is a difficult thing to know the being in any one if that one tells to any one completely all that that one has in them of telling, it is a very difficult thing to know the being in any one if they are not telling any one anything that they can have as telling in them. It is a very difficult thing to know it of any one the being in them, it is a very difficult thing to tell it of any one what they are feeling, whether they are enjoying, whether they are knowing that they are hurting some one, whether they had been planning doing that thing. It is a very difficult thing to know these things in anyone, it is a difficult thing if that one is telling everything they can be telling, if that one is telling nothing. It is certainly a difficult thing to know it of any one whether they have in them a kind of feeling, whether they have in them at some time any realisation that they are hurting some one, whether they had planned doing that thing.

Disillusionment in living is finding that no one can really ever be agreeing with you completely in anything. Disillusionment then in living that gives to very many then melancholy feeling, some despairing feeling, some resignation, some fairly cheerful beginning and some a forgetting and continuing and some a dreary trickling weeping and some violent attacking and some a letting themselves do anything, disillusion then is really finding, really realising, really being certain that no one really can completely agree with you in anything, that, as is very certain, not, those fighting beside you or living completely with you or anybody, really, can really be believing anything completely that you are believing. Really realising this thing, completely realising this thing is the disillusionment in living is the beginning of being an old man or an old woman is being no longer a young one no longer a young man or a young woman no longer a growing older young man or growing older young woman. This is then what every one always has been meaning by living bringing disillusion. This is the real thing of disillusion that no one, not any one really is believing, seeing, understanding, thinking anything as you are thinking, believing, seeing, understanding such a thing. This is then what disillusion is from living and slowly then after failing again and again in changing some one, after finding that some one that has been fighting for something, that every one that has been fighting something beside you for a long time that each one of them splits off from you somewhere and you must join on with new ones or go on all alone then or be a disillusioned one who is not any longer then a young one. This is then disillusionment in living and sometime in the history of David Hersland the younger son in the Hersland family living then in a part of Gossols where they alone of rich people were living there will be completely a history of the disillusionment of such a realising and the dying then of that one, of young David Hersland then.

This is then complete disillusionment in living, the complete realisation that no one can believe as you do about anything, so not really any single one and to some as I am saying this is a sad thing, to mostly every one it is sometime a shocking thing, sometimes a shocking thing, sometime a real shock to them, to mostly every one a thing that only very slowly with constant repetition is really a complete certain thing inside to give to them the being that is no longer in them really young being. This is then the real meaning of not being any longer a young one in living, the complete realising that not any one really can believe what any other one is believing and some there are, enough of them, who never have completely such a realisation, they are always hoping to find her or him, they are always changing her or him to fit them, they are always looking, they are always forgetting failing or explaining it by something, they are always going on and on in trying. There are a very great many of them who are this way to their ending. There are a very great many who are this way almost to their very ending, there are a great many men and women who have sometime in them in their living complete disillusion.

There is then as I am saying complete disillusion in living, the realising, completely realising that not any one, not one fighting for the same thinking and believing as the other, not any one has the same believing in her or in him that any other one has in them and it comes then sometime to most every one to be realising with feeling this thing and then they often stop having friendly feeling and then often they begin again but it is then a different thing between them, they are old then and not young then in their feeling.

Young ones sometimes think they have it in them, this thing, some young ones kill themselves then, stop living then, this is often happening, young ones sometimes, very often even, think they have in them this thing but they do not have it in them, mostly not any young one, as a complete realisation, this thing, they have it in them and it is sometimes, very often then an agony to them, some of them kill themselves or are killed then, but really mostly not any of them have really realised the thing, they may be dead from this thing, they have not realised the thing, it has been an awful agony in them, they have not really grasped the thing as having general human meaning, it has been a shock to them, it may perhaps even have killed completely very completely some of them, mostly then a young one has not really such a thing in them, this is pretty nearly certain, later there will be much description of disillusionment in the being of David Hersland who was always in his living as I was saying trying to be certain from day to day in his living what there was in living that could make it for him a completely necessary thing.

This is then a very little description of feeling disillusionment in living. There is this thing then there is the moment and a very complete moment to those that have had it when something they have bought or made or loved or are is a thing that they are afraid, almost certain, very tearful that no one will think it a nice thing and then some one likes that thing and this then is a very wonderful feeling to know that some one really appreciates the thing. This is a very wonderful thing, this is a thing which I will now be illustrating.

Disillusionment in living is the finding out nobody agrees with you not those that are and were fighting with you. Disillusionment in living is the finding out nobody agrees with you not those that are fighting for you. Complete disillusionment is when you realise that no one can for they can't change. The amount they agree is important to you until the amount they do not agree with you is completely realised by you. Then you say you will write for yourself and strangers, you will be for yourself and strangers and this then makes an old man or an old woman of you.

Every one to me just now is in pieces to me. That is to say every one is to me just now as pieces to me. That is to say that each complete one is only as a piece to me, that all there is of each one at anytime in them gives to me a feeling of pieces not of a whole thing, that is to say I am having just now with each one I am knowing or remembering a feeling an emotion from them as if they were each one not a whole thing. I have this perhaps not altogether with every one but I have it just now with a good many of them a good many that I am knowing, knowing now or remembering now and most of the time now I have such a feeling. A little it comes to me I am certain from my realisation that many of them are not completely thinking or feeling the way a complete one of their kind of them would be thinking or feeling. They are thinking and feeling in pieces then now to me to my feeling just now in my emotion and that makes of them to me pieces of being, makes all there is of them of each one, not whole ones, this is very strongly in me just now in my feeling, very very strongly in me, men and women very many of them those I am knowing those I am remembering, not all of them, I do not say that it is true of all of them even just now in my feeling but very many a great many of them are to me just now in pieces to me. There are pieces then and that is whole being, there is a piece then and that is the whole being of some one, they may be, such a one may be completely of one kind of being, but it is only a piece of such a kind of being as that one is in being. It is not such a very joyous feeling, having the emotion of having every one as a piece to one, it does make of everything a thing without ending and all the time then there is not any use of anything keeping on going. Why should anything any one keep on going if not ever at any time anything any one will be a whole one, what is the use of anything or everything keeping on going if not at any time I will not be having a sensation that any one anything will be a whole one, once every one sometime was a whole one, now mostly every one is a piece of a one, not all the being as a complete one and yet every one has their own being in them and putting all of each kind of them together to make a whole one can not be to me a satisfaction, cannot give to me any real satisfaction can not be a satisfactory way in my feeling of having completion of having anything or any one a whole one cannot give to me any reason why the world should keep on being, there is not any reason if in repeating nothing is giving to me a sensation of a completed one, I have then this in me now and mostly every one I am knowing or remembering is to me just now a piece of a kind of being and every one is themselves inside them, that is always to my feeling certain and so then feeling each one is a piece of a kind of being and always then feeling each one is entirely existing so that each one is not a part of any whole thing I cannot to myself have any very real satisfaction from getting together all the ones there are of a kind of them, to make a whole one, that is, not to my feeling, that cannot give to me an emotion of satisfaction, that is not to my feeling satisfying and so then I am not feeling each one is sometime to me a whole one, no then no, I am now feeling that mostly all of them every one I am knowing every one I am remembering is to me a piece of being and so then there is not any use in the world going on existing so that every one can keep on with repeating a piece of being, not any use at all then to me to my feeling, not any use then really to any one and this is now then the real state of feeling I am now having.

To be using a new word in my writing is to me a very difficult thing. Every word I am ever using in writing has for me very existing being. Using a word I have not yet been using in my writing is to me very difficult and a peculiar feeling. Sometimes I am using a new one sometimes I feel new meanings in an old one, sometimes I like one I am very fond of that one one that has many meanings many ways of being used to make different meanings to every one. Sometimes I like it, almost always I like it when I am feeling many ways of using one word in writing. Sometimes I like it that different ways of emphasising can make very different meanings in a phrase or sentence I have made and am rereading. Always in writing it, it is in me only one thing, a little I like it sometimes that there can be very different ways of reading the thing I have been writing with only one feeling of a meaning. This is a pleasant thing, sometimes I am very well pleased with this thing, very often then I am liking a word that can have many ways of feeling in it, it is really a very difficult thing to me to be using a word I have not yet been using in writing. I may know very well the meaning of a word and yet it has not for me completely weight and form and really existing being. There are only a few words and with these mostly always I am writing that have for me completely entirely existing being, in talking I use many more of them of words I am not living but talking is another thing, in talking one can be saying mostly anything, often then I am using many words I never could be using in writing. In writing a word must be for me really an existing thing, it has a place for me as living, this is the way I feel about me writing. I have been mentioning this thing for I am just now feeling a learning in me for some words I have just been beginning using in my writing.

Yes it is certainly true of them of very many men and very many women I have not been hearing more than a part of the repeating coming out of them. They are each one always repeating all the being in them. I am certain. I am hearing always very much repeating coming out of each one I am ever knowing. I am not hearing anywhere nearly all the repeating coming out of them each one I am ever knowing. I am always hearing, seeing, feeling repeating coming out of each one I am ever knowing. I am knowing kinds in men and women. I am not hearing a wonderful amount of repeating always coming, I am now quite certain. I could be so happy knowing everything. I could be enjoying so much having curious feeling about every one if always more and more I could certainly be hearing, feeling seeing all every bit of repeating coming in any way out of every one. I am enjoying having curious feeling about every one, I like every bit of repeating I am hearing, I get an awful sinking feeling when I find out by an accidental hearing, feeling, seeing repeating from some one what I have not been hearing, feeling, seeing as repeating in this one and then I am saying if it had not been for this little accidental thing I would not have known this repeating in this one and it is so easy not to have such an accidental happening. Alas, I say then, alas, I will perhaps not really ever be knowing all the repeating coming out of each one. I know some of the repeating coming out of Alfred Hersland and Julia Dehning and some others whom they knew and some others who knew them and I will now be describing what I am desolately feeling is all being in them. I am desolate because I am not certainly hearing all repeating, I am almost sulking. I am beginning now to go on with my history of the Dehning family and of Julia Dehning and of her marrying and of the Hersland family and of Alfred Hersland and of every one they any of them came to know in their living. To begin again then from pretty nearly the beginning. I am remembering everything I have been telling. I am always loving all repeating. I am realising kinds in men and women. I am realising Alfred Hersland and Julia Dehning. That is I am certainly somewhere near to a fairly complete realisation of them and of some whom they knew each one and who came to know them either of them. I am a little tired now with all this beginning again. I am hoping that I am going on again.

H. 723–30, 757–59, 782, 805–7, 853, 864, 882, 900–904

I do ask some, I would ask every one, I do not ask some because I am quite certain that they would not like me to ask it, I do ask some if they would mind it if they found out that they did have the name they had then and had been having been born not in the family living they are then living in, if they had been born illegitimate. I ask some and I would ask every one only I am quite certain very many would not like to have me ask it if they would like it, if they would very much dislike it, if they would make a tragedy of it, if they would make a joke of it if they found they had in them blood of some kind of a being that was a low kind to them. I would like to know how every one can be feeling about such a thing, if they have any feeling about any such thing. David Hersland was the younger son of Mr. David Hersland and Mrs. Hersland. In his younger living he never thought about any such thing as that about which I have just been telling. In his later living he liked thinking about feeling such things, thinking such things being in men and women. Some when they are quite young ones are thinking then about such things. He was never at all when he was a young one thinking about any such thing. This is to be now a history of him.

What am I believing about living. I am believing that I am not certain when I am saying something from being one being then being loving that I am meaning anything by what I am then saying, I am not certain that I am not then having being in being one being loving that is being that is having the meaning as being of what I am then saying. I am believing that I am not certain about being being in one meaning what one being in being loving is saying. I am believing that I am not certain being being loving in one is in one then meaning what that one is then saying. I am believing that I am not certain that being is not in one meaning what that one being then being loving is saying. What is it I am knowing about living, I certainly am not knowing that I am not knowing everything about being in living. I am not certain that I am knowing everything about being living. I am not certain that I am not knowing everything about being living. I am not certain that I am knowing everything about being living.

I know I am not certain about what I would do for some one what I would not do for some one. Not any one is certain so that acting by them shows it to any one what they would do for some one, what they would not do for some one. Each one then would do something for some one, would not do something for some one, would do something for any one would not do something for any one. Some are quite certain about themselves in this thing. Some are quite not certain about themselves in this thing. Not any one is rightly certain about themselves about this thing. Perhaps not any one is really certain about themselves about this thing. Perhaps one is certain about that one about this thing. I know I am not certain about what I would do for some one, what I would not do for some one.

Some one having some one who was with them become a dead one could be saying, when some one was saying something, that one does not know he is a dead one, he will never know that thing. He does not know he is a dead one, some one said of some one who was a dead one. Some one could be certain that some one who is a dead one would not know he was a dead one, some one could not know that some other one who was a dead one would not know that that one was a dead one. Some one then has been quite certain that some one who was with them when that one was a dead one did not know then that that one was a dead one. Some have been certain that every one who is a dead one does not then know that that one is a dead one.

It is a surprising thing sometimes to be learning which ones of some one has been knowing are quite certain and say the thing then as a very simple thing that anybody can be knowing that some one who has been with them being a dead one is not knowing that that one is a dead one.

It is certainly something that some are saying when some one who was with them is a dead one that that one is not knowing then that that one is a dead one. Some like very well to be hearing some one say this thing that some one is a dead one and is certainly not then knowing this thing. Some like very well hearing this thing. Some are not wanting ever to be hearing any thing about any one ever being a dead one. This will soon now be the beginning of a description of living that David Hersland did before he came to be a dead one.

Some are satisfied with having been living when they are come to be a dead one with not having had in them any very sick feeling, any very bad thing to be doing, any very hard work for them in them, not any queer feeling of not having had their head quite right inside them. Some are satisfied then with having been living ones when they have come to be a dead one, some are not satisfied then with having come to be then a dead one. Some are satisfied, some are not satisfied with having been one being living. Some are quite satisfied with having been one having living in them, some are not satisfied at all with this thing. Some are very well satisfied with having come to be a dead one, some are not at all satisfied with this thing.

Some one gives to another one a stubborn feeling when that one could be convincing that other one if that other one would then continue listening. Some are certain that sometimes they can be convinced by some one. Some are certain they are sometimes convinced by some one. Some are certain that they could be convinced sometimes by some one but that they will not be letting themselves ever have any such a thing happen to them. Some like being convinced of some things by some, by some one.

Some one and I certainly never did think that one ever could do such a thing has it to be so strongly repeating the facts that one is remembering that almost always I am always convinced that I have been wrong in my feeling. I certainly am not certain whether I ever can be certain whether

I ever am when I am feeling something justified from my way of feeling anything in having such a feeling when this one is repeating the way that one is remembering everything. Some one said about some one who was saying something that seemed a very foolish thing to some one about how some one did something, but that one was not saying foolish things, she was judging from the feeling of being convenienced and inconvenienced that she would be having and that was all that concerned her in her judging. [I had a shock in hearing this thing.] It was not a foolish thing then that that one had been saying. No, there are many ways of not being a foolish one in being living. There are certainly lots and lots of them of ways of not being a foolish one in being in living. So then some certainly could be convincing me of many things if I go on listening. I am quite certain that this is certain.

David Hersland was a dead one before he was a middle aged one. He was then never in his living an old one. He was dead before he came to the middle of his middle living.

I am coming to know some whom I have known as middle aged ones, as young ones. This is a pleasing thing.

David Hersland was a dead one before he was a middle aged one. He was then never in his living a middle aged one. He was dead before he came to the middle of his middle living.

I have come to know some as being young whom I have been knowing as middle aged ones as coming to be old ones, I know now what ones being young ones will come to be middle aged ones like some I have been knowing as middle aged ones. This seems an easy thing. It is a very difficult thing.

It is hard to be certain to one's feeling that some one one has been knowing is a dead one, will not be a growing older one. Some one was saying that his grandfather had been a dead one before his grandfather was finished being a young one. That is a queer thing that a grandfather was never in his own middle living.

I am coming to know now more and more of a group of them in men and women what kind they are when they are young ones, when they are middle aged ones, when they are old ones. To-night I came to be certain about one group of them what kind they are when they are young men when they are young women. I am not yet certain about some groups of them what they are when they are old ones, I am not certain about some groups of them what they are when they are middle aged ones, I am not certain about some groups of them what they are when they are young men when they are young women, I am not certain about some groups of them what they are when they are young ones younger than young women and young men. I am certain I am not yet knowing all the kinds there are in men and women.

David Hersland was come to being one not being living before he could come to be a middle aged one. He was not ever then an older one, an old one, a middle aged one. He came to be a dead one after a considerable beginning of his middle living.

I know now how quite a number of groups that there are of men and women are ones existing when they are young ones, that is young women and young men, that is just ending their beginning living, just beginning their middle living. I am beginning to know of some groups in men and women, what they have as hands and faces and ears and bodies to them and being in them, and ways of acting in them when they are young men and young women, older young men and young women, middle aged men and women, old men and women. I do not know yet very much about what any group of them are when they are young children. I am slowly spreading very slowly spreading to them, I have not yet spread to them, not at all reached to them yet in spreading out in knowing being in groups of men and women.

As I was saying David Hersland was a dead one before he was a middle aged one. He was dead before he came to the middle of his middle living. He was then never a middle aged one, he was then never an old one. He was one of a kind in men and women. Certainly each one is one of a kind in men and women. I am knowing more about being in each group of them when every one of a group of them is a young one, and an older one, an old one. I am knowing then being in some groups of men and women as it is in them when they are young men or women, older men or women, old men or women.

[Some are glad that the other one is dead if one of the two of them had then to come to be a dead one. Some are saying then, and are saying it to themselves and some other ones that the other one having that being the matter inside that one could not have been going on living through the seeing the other one a dead one, and then there would have been two dead then and now that other one being the dead one there is only one being then a dead one. Sometimes the other one, the one not being dead then is worried about being then an old one and sometime soon then, that one cannot be certain whether soon or very soon or not for a long time, a dead one. There are many reasons in men and in women for wanting the other one of the two of them to be a dead one, if one of them is then to be a dead one, before that one. There are many reasons in men and women for this thing. I have been lately hearing some of them I have been lately listening and talking about this thing. I have been lately doing very much talking I have been lately doing very much listening. I will be doing more and more ever always of this thing, of that thing until I am not any more doing either thing, until I am not doing so much of these two things in being one being living.]

No one will listen while I am talking. Some have very much such a trouble in being one being living. Some have not at all any of such trouble in them. Some will listen when I am talking. Some will not listen when I am talking. Some will listen while they are fat ones, they do not listen when after dieting they have become thin ones. These then listen to other ones and some of these other ones could not get any listening from them before the dieting that made these come to be thin ones from having been fat ones. Some are listening to me now and before they were always listening every evening to another one. They are listening to me now, I like them to be listening. Some who are young men and young women are listening to me now very often. Some who are now young men are listening to me now very often, they listen to me and I am talking very much now quite often to them. Some are very faithful in being ones listening and these are not listening very often. I know very well one such a one. Some quite older ones are listening but then really I am not talking very much when they are listening. Some have it to be certain that not any one ever is listening when they are talking. Some of these are mistaken, some of these are not mistaken. Some of these come to know it in them that they are not listening being so certain in them that there can not ever be conversation in any living for them. This will be soon a description of being in David Hersland and how men and how women listened to him, how some listened to him, how others listened to him, how some heard him doing talking but never listened to him, how some did not ever hear him doing any talking, how some forgot about him, how some remembered him, how some talked to him, how some said they would prefer not having ever to talk to him, how some had to talk to him, how some stopped talking with him, how some being with him liked what they were then doing, how some being with him sometimes did not at all like that thing, how some told him everything that they could think of telling and how some were sorry they had told him and how some were not sorry they had told him and how some wanted to go on telling him more and how some forgot they had told him anything. This is then to be a description of David Hersland of being and listening and talking and being liked and disliked and remembered and forgotten and going on being living and dying and being a dead one.

Some are listening to me and I tell them then the being they have in them. I tell them what they have what they have not in them, how it comes together, how it does not come together in them, how the being they have in them is important to them, how it is not important to them, how it can be active in them, how it can be not active in them, why they like having their being in them, why they do not like having their being in them. Mostly every one has listened some when I have been telling them about being in them. Some have listened and I have thought that they were believing what I was telling them and then many years after they have been telling that they were certain then that I was lying, that I was telling them what I had not any reason to believe was true of them. And sometimes then later when they tell me such a thing they find it that I am not certain that I was not then doing this thing. Some make of themselves a new one by my telling them about the being in them and to very many then they are quite a new one and to some then they are not at all a new one, they are quite an old one. Some like listening and later then they have a frightened feeling that I will influence them to be another one, they do not like very well some of them what they are in living, they do like some of them what they are in living, they are quite certain they do not want me to be influencing them. Some are listening and I am talking and I am talking and then they ask a question and then I say to myself that words can have a meaning to some one and a meaning to some other one and that I was talking and that that one was intelligently listening and that that one has then asked this question. I have told so many so much about the being in them. I will tell I am quite certain some more about the being in them. This will be now much history of talking and listening. I talk one way and listen one way and talk other ways and listen other ways and so probably does every one. This is to be now very much description of talking and listening, of a number of young men and young women talking and of a number of older men and older women talking and of each one of them the young men and young women and the older men and the older women listening.

Some are certain that sometime some could be different ones in being in being living, some are certain that sometime every one will be a different one in being in being living, some are hoping that sometime some one will be a different one, some are certain that they are believing that something can be different in living sometime for some, some are certain that they are believing that something can be different in each one, some are believing this thing about men some are believing this thing about women, some are believing this thing about men and women, some are thinking they are believing this thing, some are not believing that they are believing this thing, some are always believing this thing, some are not always believing this thing, I am not believing this thing, another one is not believing this thing, another one is not believing this thing, another one is believing this thing, another one is believing this thing, another one is believing this thing, another one is believing this thing, another one is not believing this thing, another one is not believing this thing, another one is not believing this thing, another one is believing this thing, another one is believing this thing.

This is to be a history of David Hersland and of his coming in his living to be thinking again and again and very often of coming to be a dead one. This is to be a history of him and of his coming to be thinking of coming to be a dead one and of his thinking about coming to be a dead one and about being a dead one and about his coming to be a dead one.

This then is to be now a history of David Hersland and of talking and of listening and of thinking about being dead ones in men and women being in being living. This then is to be now a history of David Hersland and of his talking and of his hearing talking and of his listening and of other ones doing listening and of very much talking and of thinking and feeling and of everything that ever was or is or will be being in some men and some women doing living. This then is to be now commencing being a history of David Hersland being in living and being talking and being listening and being talking and listening and being talking and being talking and being talking and being listening and being listening. This is then to be now a history of him.

Every one has experiencing in being one being living. I am saddening with not feeling each one being experiencing as each one is having that thing. I am saddening with this thing. There are so many being in living and there are so many that I am knowing by seeing and hearing being in living and each one of these is experiencing in being living and I I cannot be feeling what way each one is experiencing, I who am suffering and suffering because of this thing, I am in desolation and my eyes are large with needing weeping and I have a flush from feverish feeling and I am not knowing what way each one is experiencing in being living and about some I am knowing in a general way and I could be knowing in a more complete way if I could be living more with that one and I never will live more with every one, I certainly cannot ever live with each one in their being one being living, in my being one being living. I tell you I cannot bear it this thing that I cannot be realising experiencing in each one being living, I say it again and again I cannot let myself be really resting in believing this thing, it is in me now as when I am realising being a dead one, a one being dying and I can do this thing and I do this thing and I am filled then with complete desolation and I am doing this thing again and again and I am now again and again certain that I will not ever be realising experiencing in each one of very many men and very many women, I can realise something of experiencing in some of them, in them as kinds of them but I am needing to have it in me as a complete thing of each one ever living and I I know I will not, and I am one knowing being a dead one and not being a living one, I who am not believing that I will be realising each one's experiencing. I do not want to realise each thing they are experiencing, I do not care anything about such a thing, all that I am needing to be one being living is to be realising completely how each one is experiencing, with what feeling, thinking, believing, creating and I I am very certain that I will not ever be completely with each one doing such a thing, I will be doing something in such a thing with kinds in men and women, with some of some kinds of them but not with each one not with every one, no certainly not with every one. No certainly not with every one, completely, certainly not, and more and more knowing some one experiencing and completely knowing that one makes it certain that if I could live with each one I could realise the experiencing in each one and I cannot ever live with each one, I certainly never will be living a good deal with each one ever having been living.

Some are wanting to be needing in their living to have some one have some angry feeling. Some are needing it in their living to have some one have some angry feeling. Some are needing angry feeling being existing, some are wanting to be needing angry feeling being existing. David Hersland was one sometime in his living wanting to be needing having angry feeling being existing he was sometime in his living needing angry feeling to be existing, he was sometime in his living not wanting any angry feeling to be existing, he was sometime in his living completely wanting not angry feeling being existing, he was sometime in his living having an angry feeling about angry feeling being existing, he was sometime in his living completely needing having angry feeling really being existing, he was one wanting sometime in his living that not any angry feeling should be existing.

Some are needing angry feeling being in some one existing, some are needing angry feeling being inside them being existing, some are wanting to be needing angry feeling being in some existing, some are wanting to be needing angry feeling being sometimes existing inside them, some are wanting to be needing that angry feeling be not existing in any one, not in themselves inside them, some are having angry feeling and they are never certain whether they are needing whether they are not needing that thing, some are having some one having angry feeling and they are not certain whether they are liking whether they are not liking that thing, some are having angry feeling inside them and they are not certain whether they are liking whether they are not liking that thing, some are having some having angry feeling some one having angry feeling and they are not certain whether they are needing or whether they are not needing that thing. Certainly very many are sometimes having angry feeling in them, certainly very many are having others having angry feeling for them, certainly very many are having some one having angry feeling for them, certainly very many are having some often having angry feeling against them, certainly very many have some to have angry feeling about them, certainly a very great many have some one having angry feeling about them, have some one having angry feeling against them, have some one having angry feeling with them.

To some it is extraordinary that any one having angry feeling can then come to be convincing. Some having angry feeling come then to be convincing about something to some one. Some came to be very convincing to David Hersland when they had angry feeling in them sometime in his living. Some did not come to be convincing to him about anything when they had angry feeling in them, sometimes in his living not any one having angry feeling was convincing to him about anything, sometimes in his living almost any one having angry feeling in them were convincing to him then about something they were saying then, certainly for sometime while he was being living some certainly some one was mostly always convincing about something when those, when that one, were angry ones, was an angry one. Certainly very many living are changing in their feeling about any one being an angry one about some one being an angry one, about they themselves that one being an angry one. Some certainly are very different in different times in their living in their feeling about angry feeling being existing. Some are not changing very much in the time of their being living in their feeling about angry feeling being existing. Each one certainly has in them their own way of feeling, of changing in feeling about angry feeling being existing. Very many come to know in being living quite a number who are then existing. Some come to know of some they are then knowing how they have angry feeling in them, some do not come to know of very many they are knowing how they have angry feeling in them, some come to know of quite a number they are knowing how they have angry feeling in them. Alfred Hersland came to know of some he was knowing how they come to have angry feeling in them. David Hersland came in some way to know of quite a number he came to know in being living how they came to have angry feeling, what they do when they have angry feeling. As I was saying sometimes when he was living he was one wanting to be needing that not any one was having angry feeling, as I was saying sometimes in his living he was needing, to be one going on being living with any meaning in that thing, that not any one having angry feeling in being in living that not any angry feeling was being existing, sometimes in his being living he was wanting to be needing that there was angry feeling quite a good deal of angry feeling existing, sometimes while he was living as I was saying of him he was quite needing that angry feeling was really existing, as I was saying he was in his living one changing about ones having angry feeling being ones being convincing about something. This is to be in a way a history of him and of every one that he ever knew and of every one who ever came to know him or of him.

Certainly some are pretty certain that there is not enough connection to make it interesting, in very many, between what they are meaning, they are thinking, they are feeling, they are saying, they are certain is something existing.

I mean, I mean and that is not what I mean, I mean that not any one is saying what they are meaning, I mean that I am feeling something, I mean that I mean something and I mean that not any one is thinking, is feeling, is saying, is certain of that thing, I mean that not any one can be saying, thinking, feeling, not any one can be certain of that thing, I mean I am not certain of that thing, I am not ever saying, thinking, feeling, being certain of this thing, I mean, I mean, I know what I mean.

And certainly some one is right in saying such a thing, such a one some of such of them certainly are right in saying such a thing. Some of such of them have it that the moment of sensibility, emotion and expression and origin is all in a state of completion and then it is a finished thing and certainly then that one was meaning something and he was saying I mean, I mean, and it was all finished and then there was another something and this one certainly very often said I mean. That one said that very often in being one being living.

There are some when they are being living and when they are beginning being living are ones completely being living and are ones completely being living to themselves then and to mostly every one and are ones being completely being living doing many things and doing them, most of them, very often. There certainly are some being living who are ones certainly being ones completely being living and are such ones and any one can be completely certain of this thing being one knowing such a one, being one knowing any one knowing such a one. Certainly there are very many being completely living in being living and are such to any one and are ones doing some thing and another and another thing and doing one again and again and again and doing the other thing again and again and doing the other thing again and again and again. Certainly there are some being ones completely being living in being living and doing something and doing it again and again and doing another thing of the same kind of thing and doing it again and being one being completely living in being one being living. Certainly some are ones completely being living in being living and are such ones to any one, to every one and certainly there are ones being living not being ones completely living that is not to some knowing them knowing of them and some of such of them are ones certainly doing something and certainly doing another thing of the same kind and another one of the same kind and doing each one of them very much and very often and again and again and again and again. Certainly some are ones being ones completely being living to themselves in being living and some knowing them are certain that this is not being in them in some of such of them that they are ones being completely living in being living. There certainly are ones who are ones not being completely living in being living to themselves then and some are certainly certain that some of such of them are ones being completely being living in being living and some are certainly certain that some of such of them are not ones being completely living in being living. Certainly each one being living is beginning being living and some are then knowing this thing and some are not then knowing this thing, those being in being beginning being living. Some who are beginning being living are then knowing that thing. Some who are beginning being living are then not knowing that thing. Some beginning being living are almost then knowing that thing. Certainly some beginning being living are quite certainly not knowing anything at all of any such thing being in being living. Certainly there are many ways of being ones being completely living in being living, being ones not completely living in being living. There are certainly many ways of being ones completely being living in being young ones, there are certainly many ways of being ones not completely being living in being young ones.

When one is a young one one is a young one. Certainly when one is a young one one is then a young one. In a way one is knowing then that one is not then a young one, in a way one is knowing it then that one is then a young one. When one is a middle aged one one is then a middle aged one. In a way one is knowing then that one is then a middle aged one, in a way one is knowing then that one is not then a middle aged one. When one is an old one one is then an old one. In a way one is knowing then that one is then an old one, in a way one is knowing then that one is not then an old one.

When one is a young one one is a young one. Certainly when one is a young one one is then a young one. In a way one is knowing then that one is then a young one, in a way one is knowing then that one is not then a young one. When one is an older one one is then an older one. One is then in a way knowing then that one is then an older one, one is then in a way knowing then that one is not then an older one.

When one is a young one one is a young one. When one is a young one one is certainly then in a way a young one. When one is a young one one is certainly in a way then not a young one.

When one is a young one one is a young one. One is a young one and is then in some ways then not a young one. One is a young one and is in some ways then a young one.

One is a young one and one is knowing in some way that one is a young one. One is a young one and one is knowing in some way that one is not a young one.

One is a young one and is knowing that one is not a young one and is knowing that one is a young one. One is an older one and is knowing that one is an older one and is knowing that one is not an older one. One is a middle aged one and is knowing that one is a middle aged one and is knowing that one is not a middle aged one. One is an older one and is knowing that one is a middle aged one and is knowing that one is not a middle aged one. One is an older one and is knowing that one is not an older one and is knowing that one is an old one. One is an old one and is knowing one is an old one and is knowing that one is not an old one. One is an older one and is not knowing one is an older one and is knowing one is an older one. One is a very old one and one is knowing one is a very old one and is not knowing one is a very old one. One is an older one and is knowing one is an older one and is not knowing one is an older one. One is a young one and one is and one is not knowing one is a young one. One is a young one and one is knowing one is not a young one and one is knowing that one is a young one. One is a young one and is then knowing that one is a young one and is then knowing that one is not a young one.

One is a young one and is knowing and is not knowing then that that one is then a young one. One is a young one and is knowing then that that one is not a young one, is knowing then that that one is then a young one.

David Hersland was a young one, he was knowing he was then a young one, he was knowing that he was then not a young one. He knew some who were young ones then. Some of them were knowing then that they were young ones then and knowing then that they were not young ones then.

She says go, go and I go, she says come, come and I come. She says come, come, and I come, she says go, go, and I go. David Hersland was almost wanting to be needing to be such a one, one coming and one going. When he was not any longer a completely young one he was one wanting to be needing to be such a one. He was not really waiting to be such a one, he was really not waiting, he was almost completely wanting to be such a one, one needing to be going and coming, one needing to be coming and going. He was one almost completely clearly thinking, he was one quite clearly feeling, he was one not waiting to be such a one, one going and coming, one coming and going. He was almost completely wanting to be needing being such a one. In a way he was not ever coming and going, going and coming, in a way he was almost doing this thing, coming and going, going and coming. He was one clearly feeling in being living. He was one almost completely clearly thinking. He was one almost completely waiting to be needing being one coming and going, going and coming. He was one almost completely waiting to be needing this thing. He was not needing this thing, he was almost completely wanting to be needing this thing. He was one clearly feeling in being living, he was one almost completely clearly thinking. He was not completely liking being living. He was clearly feeling in being living. He was quite completely clearly thinking in being one being living.

He was being living every day. He was knowing every day that he was being living on that day. He was knowing every day that he was being living. He would know that he was meaning being one being living every day. He would be one being living every day and knowing every day he was being living that day and would be knowing every day the meaning in being living that day. He was being living every day. He was, every day, knowing he was being living. He was, every day knowing he was knowing the meaning of being living that day. He was not succeeding. He was being living. He was being living and that was being existing by knowing the meaning of being existing on that day. He was being living until the end of the beginning of middle living. He was succeeding in being living until the end of the beginning of being in middle living. He was being living every day. He was knowing every day that he was being living that day.

He was being living every day. He was knowing every day that he was being living that day. He was being living every day when he was in the beginning of being living. He was knowing then every day that he was being living that day. He was living every day when he was at the ending of the beginning of being living. He was knowing then every day that he was being living that day. He was being living every day when he was in the middle of the beginning of being living. He was knowing then every day that he was living that day.

He was living every day, all of his being living. He was knowing every day that he was being living that day, every day all of his being living. He was being living every day all of the beginning of being living. He was knowing every day that he was being living that day all of his beginning being living. He was being living every day all of his being living. He was knowing every day that he was being living, all of his living. He was being living every day through the beginning of the middle of being living. He was knowing then every day that he was being living that day. He was being living every day, all of his being living. He was knowing he was being living every day, all of his being living.

He was quietly enough doing that thing, being one being living. He was quietly enough being one being living. It was astonishing that he was so quietly doing that thing, being one being living.

He was quite quietly doing that thing, being one being living. Certainly not every one was certain of this thing that he was quietly doing that thing, being one being living. Not every one was certain that he was one quietly doing being one being living. Some were certain that he was not so quietly doing this thing, being one being living. Some were certain that he was not quietly doing this thing, being one being living.

He was quietly doing this thing, quietly being one being living. This was a thing that might have been astonishing. That he was quietly doing the thing, quietly being one being living is a thing that might be astonishing to any one. Any one might be certain that he was not quietly doing that, not quietly being one being living. Some were certain that he was quietly doing this thing, doing being one being living.

A quite gentle one, a quite quiet one, any one was certain of this thing that this one was a quite quiet one, a quite gentle one, this one who was a quite quiet one was one whom he was knowing some and he was always being one, needing to be completely wanting to be certain that this one, that some one, that almost any one was one who was being existing and making something then be a thing leading to something which was then a thing feeling being a complete thing, a whole one then and then not needing being anything not having been a beautiful thing.

He was a quietly enough one being one being living and he was then teaching any one any other thing. He was teaching some then. He was very nearly completely teaching some. He was being one then whom some who were quite quietly being living then were following then and all of them, any one of them were very quietly being one being living then, almost being one being living.

He was not really needing anything. He was not needing being certain that being living is existing. He was not needing being one going on being living. He was needing understanding that he was being living. He was almost completely needing being one completely clearly thinking. He was almost completely wanting to be feeling needing that any woman he was seeing was completely beautifully something. He was almost wanting to be giving advice strongly enough to some. He was almost being one coming to be beginning succeeding in living. He was completely clearly expressing something. He was completely understanding any one's understanding anything of that thing.

He was not really needing anything. He was not needing being one going on being living. He was almost completely needing being one completely clearly thinking. He was not needing being one remembering that any one can come to be a dead one. He was not needing being certain that being living is something that is existing. He was not needing to be remembering anything. He was not needing to be forgetting something. He was understanding that he was being living. He was almost needing to be one almost only eating one thing. He was being living. He was understanding that thing. He was clearly expressing something. He was not forgetting anything. He was not forgetting everything. He was not needing to be one remembering anything. He was not needing to be one remembering everything.

He was completely clearly expressing something. He could mention this thing, mention that he was completely clearly expressing something. He did sometimes mention that he was completely clearly expressing something. He was completely clearly expressing that thing, the thing he was clearly expressing. He could have been one being one clearly, completely clearly expressing that thing. He was such a one, he was one being one completely clearly expressing that thing the thing he was expressing. He was not completely filling anything in completely clearly expressing the thing he was completely clearly expressing. He could have been one completely filling something in being one completely clearly expressing what he was completely clearly expressing. He was completely clearly expressing something. He was completely clearly thinking. He was almost completely clearly feeling. He was almost completely being one eating only one thing. He was being living and he was not beginning that thing beginning being living. He was not ever beginning again and again.

He was completely clearly expressing one thing. He was understanding any one's understanding of that thing. He was understanding anything of any one's understanding of that thing. He was sometimes mentioning something of some one's understanding of that thing. He could go on mentioning some one's understanding of that thing. He was completely clearly expressing something. He was not being one going on being living. He was one being living. He was understanding that thing. He did sometimes mention that thing mention understanding being living. He did not mention anything again and again. He did not really mention anything again and again. He did completely clearly express something. He was being one who was completely clearly thinking. He did do that thing. He did completely clearly think about something. He did completely clearly think about anything. He did almost completely clearly think about everything. He did think completely clearly. He did completely clearly express something. He was being living. He did understand being one being living. He did understand any one else's understanding the thing he was completely clearly expressing.

He was not feeling being one being completely a different one from any other one. He was knowing something of this thing. He was knowing something of being one who was one who was completely a different one from any other one. He was feeling something and there was something in him to be feeling of being one who was completely a different one from any other one. He was feeling something. There was in him something to be feeling. There was in him knowing something of being one who was completely a different one from any other one. He was not feeling that thing feeling his being one being completely different from any other one. He came to be a dead one at the ending of the beginning of middle living. He was not feeling anything in being one being completely different from any other one. He was being this one one who was completely different from any other one. He was not feeling anything in being such a one. He was not living after the ending of the beginning of being living.

He was not completely forgetting knowing something of such a thing of being one being completely different from any other one. He was being living. He was understanding being one being living. He was not living after the ending of the beginning of middle living. He came to be a dead one. He was completely forgetting something of being one knowing that he was a different one from any other one.

He was not feeling being one being a completely different one from any other one. He was knowing that he was being a completely different one from any other one. He was not forgetting knowing that he was a different one from any other one. He was not feeling being a different one from any other one.

He was not living after the ending of the beginning of middle living. He had come to be a dead one. He had been almost completely eating only one thing. He had been understanding being living. He had not been feeling being a different one from any other one. He had been understanding being one being living. He had been giving advice strongly enough to some. He had not been needing being one going on being living. He had not been needing being certain that being living is something existing. He had been coming and had then not come to be beginning succeeding in living. He had been knowing being a different one from any other one. He had been understanding something and understanding any one understanding that thing. He had been completely clearly expressing something. He had been almost completely clearly feeling. He had been completely clearly thinking.

He had come to be a dead one and he was then at the ending of beginning living. He had come to be a dead one and some then were knowing that thing knowing then that he was not any longer being living. Some were then knowing that he was a dead one.

He was not one who had been one being fighting. He had been one who had been completely eating only one thing. He was not one who had been one being fighting. He had been one coming to be beginning succeeding in living. He had not been one being fighting. He had been one choosing something and not then being one coming to be receiving any other thing to go with the thing he had been choosing. He had not been one being fighting. He had been one not doing another thing than the thing he had been choosing. He had been one coming to be beginning to be succeeding in living. He had been one who could be one completely urging that he was not one needing doing some other thing. He was completely clearly thinking. He was not coming to be one going on beginning to be succeeding in living and he was then not fighting and he was then almost urging being one not needing choosing some other thing and he was then completely clearly expressing something, and he was then going on being one almost completely eating only one thing and he was then one understanding any one's understanding something he was completely understanding.

He was not going on being living in being living. He was a dead one at the ending of the beginning of middle living. He was being living. He was understanding being living. He was not beginning being living. He was not beginning again and again in being living. He was almost needing being one coming to be beginning to be succeeding in living.

He was knowing he was understanding being one being living. He was almost completely knowing this thing. He was not completely knowing that he was not completely needing being certain that being living is something existing. He was almost completely clearly expressing being one not needing being one receiving doing some other thing. He was almost completely clearly expressing this thing. He was not completely clearly expressing being one almost needing to be coming to be beginning succeeding in living. He was not being one succeeding in living. He was not one failing in living. He was one not being living when he was at the end of the beginning of middle living. He was then a dead one. He was then not needing that thing not needing being then a dead one not at all needing that thing. He was then being eating only one thing. He came then to be a dead one. He had not been completely needing that thing needing being a dead one. He had not been one needing that thing really at all needing that thing needing being a dead one. He was then understanding something and understanding any one else who was understanding something of that thing. He was then eating only one thing. He was then not needing to be a dead one. He was then not living then when he was at the end of the beginning of middle living. He was then one who came to be a dead one and some were not knowing that thing before he was completely buried there where he had come to be a dead one. He had come to be a dead one. He certainly then had been eating only one thing. He certainly then had not been needing not really needing not at all needing being a dead one. He was a dead one and he had been then one being living and understanding that thing understanding being living in being one being then being living.

He came to be a dead one and not any one had been needing that thing had been at all needing that thing, had been wanting to be needing that he was a dead one. Not any one had been wanting to be needing that thing that he had come to be a dead one. Some did not know he had come to be a dead one before he had come to be buried there to be a buried one there where he had been a dead one.

He had come to be a dead one. He had not come to at all beginning this thing, beginning being a dead one. He had come to be a dead one. He had come to be a buried one and some then were coming to know this thing that he had come to be a dead and buried one.

Some knew he was a dead one after he had been buried there where he had come to be a dead one. Some knew it then and were earnest then in being certain that he could not have come to be a dead one and some of such of them were saying it again and again. Some knew it then knew that he was a dead one after he had been buried there where he had come to be a dead one and they regretted that he had come to be a dead one, they regretted that thing. Some of such of them were interested in any one's regretting that thing. Some of such of them could come to be wondering if he might have been one coming to be beginning succeeding in living. Some who regretted that he had come to be a dead one were wondering if any one would come to know anything about his being a dead one, some of such of them were interested in that thing in some one coming to know something about him as being a dead one.

Some did not know anything of his having come to be a dead one for sometime after he had come to be a dead one. Some of such of them were feeling it to be a strange thing that he had come to be a dead one. Some of such of them were hearing something about his being a dead one a long time after he had come to be a dead one.

He was not living after the ending of the beginning of middle living. He came to be a dead one and was buried there where he had come to be a dead one. This was a surprising thing to some that he had come to be buried there where he had come to be a dead one. Not any one was needing this thing that he should have come to be a dead one and to be buried there where he had come to be a dead one.

Not any one needed to be one expecting that he should come to be a dead one and be buried there where he had come to be a dead one. Not any one needed this thing, he had not needed this thing, it was not a needed thing. He had come to be a dead one and had come to be buried there where he had come to be a dead one. Some were indignant about this thing that he had come to be a dead one. Some were wondering about this thing that he had come to be a dead one. Some were remembering this thing, that he had come to be a dead one. Some were regretting this thing, that he had come to be a dead one. Some were hoping that there was not this thing, his having come to be a dead one. Some were vague about this thing about his having come to be a dead one and having been buried there where he had come to be a dead one. Some were interested in this thing, in his having come to be a dead one and some of such of them were wondering about coming to be knowing something about him as being then a dead one. Some were not remembering that he had come to be a dead one. Some were not certain that he would have been one coming to be beginning succeeding in living. Some were certain that he might then not have come to be a dead one. Some were quite certain about this thing. Some were not certain that there was any difference in anything in his being then a dead one. Some were certain that he was then a dead one and were certain that it was an important thing. Some were certain that he was then a dead one and were not certain that it was an important thing that he was then one not being a living one. Any one could be one not very constantly remembering his being a dead one, his having been a living one. Any one could remember this thing, his having been a dead one, his having been a living one.

ADA

This piece about Alice Toklas may have been the very first portrait Stein wrote, in December 1910, with *Matisse* and *Picasso* following soon after. Writing these became not only telling about the three figures but defining herself personally and artistically. *Ada* appears to begin as a conventional narrative, with the first third given to family background about Toklas' father, Ferdinand, and her young brother, Clarence, under the pseudonyms Abram and Barnes Colhard. Instead of conveying information by copious descriptive detail as traditional narratives do, Stein's sentences are stripped of facts to bare essence, suggesting quality of personality and relationships and setting themes.

The minimal information is entirely accurate, as Stein points out near the beginning of *The Autobiography of Alice B. Toklas* to certify her reliability. The portrait records the subservient position of Alice Babette Toklas, who at twenty lost the only person to whom she could relate when her mother died of cancer. She ended up keeping house for the men in her family—her father, her grandfather, and her brother, whom she advises to marry. For the first two-thirds of the portrait, she appears only as daughter and sister, with no name and no life of her own. At age thirty, in 1907, she left San Francisco for Paris, where she met Gertrude Stein. In 1910, the year of the portrait, she joined Stein in what was to become a permanent union. Only then do we hear of her becoming "happier than anybody else who was living then."

From Paris Toklas maintained intermittent and uncertain contact with her father by letter until 1924, when he died in a nursing home. No letters from him or other relatives survive, only a few from California friends whom Toklas and Stein each knew before they themselves met. Once Toklas joined Stein, she virtually gave up her own separate life. She kept almost no possessions or papers and became a part of Stein's life and Stein's story.

Storytelling, or talking, which leads to writing, is the central theme of *Ada*. It is an early way for mother and daughter and then for women to relate. Men like to hear Ada talking, but for her, talking with men and listening to their stories is uncomfortable and turns into something "not nice." Storytelling appears also in *The Autobiography of Alice B. Toklas* (139), where Stein tells the anecdote of taking the completed portrait to Toklas in the kitchen to read as a surprise. If this story is true—the *Autobiography* is replete with charming invented stories that cannot be relied on as history—Stein read the new portrait to Toklas from her draft in "the little tiny pages" of her preliminary pocket notebook. In the manuscript of *Ada* Stein and Toklas joined hands by sharing the labor of copying the text from the pocket notebook. Transcribed in both hands, the manuscript of *Ada* links Toklas' inspiring storytelling with Stein's story writing in a testament to a symbiotic relationship in which living and writing become one.

Storytelling is about the intimate interaction between Toklas and Stein. Endless telling and listening to stories is the perfect writer's situation and the perfect lovers' situation, each enabling the other. *Ada* is in a sense about audience—finding a you who listens to me. It is about speaking and hearing, writing and reading, making love in words and making words of love.

The name Ada appears in two connections that must have been familiar to Stein. One is Byron's daughter, Augusta Ada Lovelace. Another occurs in the second chapter of *Alice in Wonderland*, "The Pool of Tears." Alice has grown enormously tall and, radically changed, wonders whether her smaller self is the same person as her former self. "I'm sure I'm not Ada for her hair goes in such long ringlets, and mine doesn't go in ringlets at all."

• • • • •

Barnes Colhard did not say he would not do it but he did not do it. He did at it and then he did not do at it, he did not ever think about it. He just thought some time he might do something.

His father Mr. Abram Colhard spoke about it to every one and very many of them spoke to Barnes Colhard about it and he always listened to them.

Then Barnes fell in love with a very nice girl and she would not marry him. He cried then, his father Mr. Abram Colhard comforted him and they took a trip and Barnes promised he would do what his father wanted him to be doing. He did not do the thing, he thought he would do another thing, he did not do the other thing, his father Mr. Colhard did not want him to do the other thing. He really did not do anything then. When he was a good deal older he married a very rich girl. He had thought perhaps he would not propose to her but his sister wrote to him that it would be a good thing. He married the rich girl and she thought he was the most wonderful man and one who knew everything. Barnes never spent more than the income of the fortune he and his wife had then, that is to say they did not spend more than the income and this was a surprise to very many who knew about him and about his marrying the girl who had such a large fortune. He had a happy life while he was living and after he was dead his wife and children remembered him.

He had a sister who also was successful enough in being one being living. His sister was one who came to be happier than most people come to be in living. She came to be a completely happy one. She was twice as old as her brother. She had been a very good daughter to her mother. She and her mother had always told very pretty stories to each other. Many old men loved to hear her tell these stories to her mother. Every one who ever knew her mother liked her mother. Many were sorry later that not every one liked the daughter. Many did like the daughter but not every one as every one had liked the mother. The daughter was charming inside in her, it did not show outside in her to every one, it certainly did to some. She did sometimes think her mother would be pleased with a story that did not please her mother. When her mother later was sicker the daughter knew that there were some stories she could tell her that would not please her mother. Her mother died and really mostly altogether the mother and the daughter had told each other stories very happily together.

The daughter then kept house for her father and took care of her brother. There were many relations who lived with them. The daughter did not like them to live with them and she did not like them to die with them. The daughter, Ada they had called her after her grandmother who had delightful ways of smelling flowers and eating dates and sugar, did not like it at all then as she did not like so much dying and she did not like any of the living she was doing then. Every now and then some old gentlemen told delightful stories to her. Mostly then there were not nice stories told by any one then in her living. She told her father Mr. Abram Colhard that she did not like it at all being one being living then. He never said anything. She was afraid then, she was one needing charming stories and happy telling of them and not having that thing she was always trembling. Then every one who could live with them were dead and there were then the father and the son a young man then and the daughter coming to be that one then. Her grandfather had left some money to them each one of them. Ada said she was going to use it to go away from them. The father said nothing then, then he said something and she said nothing then, then they both said nothing and then it was that she went away from them. The father was quite tender then, she was his daughter then. He wrote her tender letters then, she wrote him tender letters then, she never went back to live with him. He wanted her to come and she wrote him tender letters then. He liked the tender letters she wrote to him. He wanted her to live with him. She answered him by writing tender letters to him and telling very nice stories indeed in them. He wrote nothing and then he wrote again and there was some waiting and then he wrote tender letters again and again.

She came to be happier than anybody else who was living then. It is easy to believe this thing. She was telling some one, who was loving every story that was charming. Some one who was living was almost always listening. Some one who was loving was almost always listening. That one who was loving was almost always listening. That one who was loving was telling about being one then listening. That one being loving was then telling stories having a beginning and a middle and an ending. That one was then one always completely listening. Ada was then one and all her living then one completely telling stories that were charming, completely listening to stories having a beginning and a middle and an ending. Trembling was all living, living was all loving, some one was then the other one. Certainly this one was loving this Ada then. And certainly Ada all her living then was happier in living than any one else who ever could, who was, who is, who ever will be living.

TWO WOMEN

The portrait of the Cone sisters, Claribel and Etta, is one of a number of double and even group portraits of personality types as they emerge by contrast in relationships among friends, lovers, artists, and family members. In *The Making of Americans* Stein first explored and systematized types and pairs. Other group portraits appear in *A Long Gay Book,* which began as studies of pairs of women, men, and women and men; in *Miss Furr and Miss Skeene,* about the changing relationship of two painter friends who were lovers; and even in *Bon Marche Weather,* which may be read as a kind of anonymous group portrait generated by forms of colloquial response to the weather. The spinster sisters Claribel Cone (1864–1929) and Etta Cone (1870–1949) are considered in a power relationship—dominant and submissive, leader and follower.

Stein knew the Cones from Baltimore, where the immigrant Steins had settled and where, after her father's death in Oakland, she was sent to live with an aunt. A large Jewish family like the Steins, the Cones had also started modestly and become wealthy and successful. Of the two spinster sisters, Claribel, ten years older than Stein, became a doctor and was doing research and teaching when Stein entered the Johns Hopkins Medical School. Etta, the youngest, remained bound to home and family. By the turn of the century, Etta and Claribel began to use their wealth to travel extensively in Europe, meeting Gertrude, Michael, Sarah, and especially Leo Stein, who acted as a guide and teacher of art. Through the Steins, the sisters also met Matisse, Picasso, and other artists, purchasing and commissioning work. The great collection of modern paintings they acquired became an important addition to the Baltimore Museum. Stein was friendly with Etta Cone, who typed the manuscript of *Three Lives* before Alice Toklas came to Paris. As Stein sharply told the story in *The Autobiography of Alice B. Toklas,* Etta typed without reading the book. By the time this was written, the once warm friendship had cooled, possibly with the assistance of Alice Toklas.

Stein probably wrote the portrait of the Cone sisters early in 1912, after finishing *The Making of Americans* in the fall of 1911. In *Two Women* she gives Claribel, whose own name is never used, names that bear personal associations. One name is Bertha, which may recall Stein's older sister, Bertha Stein Raffel; or Bertha Cone, the widow of the senior Cone brother. Both are older sister types who are disliked and who bring into the portrait associations of wicked figures that go back to the nursery. Another name used for Claribel, reinforcing Bertha by rhyme but contrasting by associations, is Martha, recalling Martha Hersland in *The Making of Americans,* who in turn stands for Gertrude Stein. On the other hand, for Etta she substitutes Ada, the name for Alice Toklas in the portrait *Ada,* which creates an imperfect feminine rhyme with Etta in the mind. Not mentioned in Stein's portrait but in her working notes is the name Ida

(Gutman), Etta Cone's companion, whose name also fits into the transposition of Etta to Ada. The names in *Two Women* hint at intricate personal relations and overtones of tender feeling and subdued hostility, loving, liking, listening, and remembering.

The text in the *Reader* relies on the authority of the manuscript and the first printing of the portrait in the *Contact Collection of Contemporary Writers*, Contact Editions (Paris: Three Mountains Press, 1925). Wording and spelling of "everything," "anything," "something," and "some things" follow these authorities. Hyphenated words such as "good-looking" are retained only where both the manuscript and the *Contact Collection* agree.

• • • • •

There are often two of them, both women. There were two of them, two women. There were two of them, both women. There were two of them. They were both women. There were two women and they were sisters. They both went on living. They were very often together then when they were living. They were very often not together when they were living. One was the elder and one was the younger. They always knew this thing, they always knew that one was the elder and one was the younger. They were both living and they both went on living. They were together and they were then both living. They were then both going on living. They were not together and they were both living then and they both went on living then. They sometimes were together, they sometimes were not together. One was older and one was younger.

When they were together they said to each other that they were together and that each one of them was being living then and was going on then being living. When they were together they called each other sister. When they were together they knew they were together. When they were together, they were together and they were not changing then, they were together then.

There were two of them, they were both women, they were sisters, they were together and they were being living then and they were going on being living then and they were knowing then that they were together. They were not together and they were living then and they were each of them going on being living then and they were knowing then that they were not together.

Each of them were being living. Each of them were going on being living. Each of them was one of the two of them. One of them was older. One of them was younger. They were sometimes together. They were sometimes not together. The younger called the older, sister Martha. The older called the younger Ada. They each one knew that the other one needed being one being living. They each one knew that the other one was going on being living. They each one knew that that one needed to be one being living. They each one knew that that one was going on being living. The younger knew that the older was going on being living. The older did not know that the younger was going on being living. The older knew that the younger would be going on living. They both were going on being living. They were both needing being one being living.

They were together and they spoke of each other as their sister. Each one was certain that the other one was a sister. They were together and they were both then being living. The younger one called the older, sister Martha. The older called the younger Ada. They were together and they were then both of them going on being living.

The older one was more something than the younger one. The younger one was not so much something as the older one. The older one was more something than the younger one. The younger one was receiving everything in being one going on being living. The older one was more something than the younger one. The older one was going on being living, the older one was telling about this thing about being more something than the younger one. The older one was telling about this thing about the younger one being more something than any other one. The younger one was telling about being more something than any other one. The younger one was not telling about the older one being more something than any other one. The younger one was telling about both of them being more something than any other one.

They were together and they knew it then, knew that they were together. They were not together and they knew it then, knew that they were not together. They both went on being living. Later they were not together. They knew it then both of them that they were not then together. Later then they were together. They knew it then, both of them, that they were then together.

They did some things. The elder did some things. The older one went on being living. She did some things. She went on being living. She did this thing, she went on being living. She did some things. She did go on being living. She was more something than any other one. She did some things. She went on being living. She did this thing, she went on being living.

The younger one did some things. She was receiving some things more than any other one. She went on receiving them. She went on being living. She received this thing, she went on being living. She had this thing more than any other one, receiving going on being living. She received this thing, she went on being living. She received going on being living. She received this more than any other one. She went on being living. She was receiving this thing, she was receiving it more than any other one. She was receiving it some from her sister Martha, she received it more from every one. She received this thing, she received going on being living.

They were together and they knew that then, the two of them, both of them knew it then, knew that they were together. They were not together and they knew it then, both of them knew it then, each one of the two of them knew it then, knew that they were not together then.

There were others connected with them, connected with each of them, connected with both of them. There were some connected with both of them. There had been a father and there had been a mother and there were brothers and quite enough of them. They each of them had certainly duties toward those connected with them. They had, each one of them, what they wanted, Martha when she wanted it, Ada when she was going to want it. They had brothers and a mother and a father. They were quite rich, all of them. They were sometimes together, the two of them, they were sometimes travelling. They were sometimes alone together then. They knew it then. They were sometimes not alone together then. They knew that then. They were, the two of them, ones travelling and they were then ones buying some things and they were then ones living in a way and they were then ones sometimes living in another way. They were very different the one from the other of them. They were certainly very different.

They each of them knew some who were knowing them. They each of them pleased some who were knowing them. They each of them were pleased by some who were knowing them. They were large women, both of them, anybody could see them. They were large women either of them. Very many saw them. Very many saw each one of them. Some saw them. Really not very many saw them, saw both of them. They were large women. Really not very many saw both of them. And that was a natural thing. There were two of them. They were together and they knew it then. They were not together and they knew it then. They were both large women and they were very different the one from the other of them, very different, and one, Ada, was younger and called her sister, sister Martha, and one, Martha was older and called her sister Ada.

There were two of them. They were each one of them rich. They each one of them had what they wanted, Martha when she was wanting, Ada when she was going to be wanting. And they both had not what they were wanting. The older Martha because she was not wanting it and the younger Ada because she could not come to want it. They both of them were spending money that they had and they were both of them very different one from the other of them. They were both of them doing what they were doing that is to say Martha was doing what she was doing that is to say she was not changing in doing what she was doing, that is to say she was going on and that was something that she was saying was a curious thing, that she was doing what she was doing and not changing and not doing that thing. Ada was doing what she was doing that is to say she needed to be doing what she was doing, that is to say she was having what she was having to do and she was doing what she was doing, that is to say she was doing what she was doing and any one could be certain that she was doing what she would be doing, that is to say she was doing what she would be coming to be doing and certainly then sister Martha was with her then and certainly then Ada was not doing that thing, certainly then Ada was doing something, certainly then she had something to do and certainly then she was doing something and certainly then her sister Martha was not then changing and certainly then they were rich ones and buying things and living in a way and sometimes then they were living in another way and buying some things and sometimes then they were not together and then they did not know it then that they were not any longer travelling together. They were each of them rich then. There were some whom they pleased then, each one of them, that is to say there were some who knew each one of them, there were some who knew both of them. There were two of them, they were sisters. There was an older one and she pleased some and she was interesting to some and some pleased her. There was a younger one and she was pleasing some and she was feeling something about this thing and feeling something about some pleasing her some. There were two of them, they were sisters, they were large women, they were rich, they were very different one from the other one, they had brothers enough of them, the older one had what she wanted when she wanted it, that is to say she did not have what she wanted because she did not want it. The younger had what she wanted when she was coming to want it, that is to say she did not have what she wanted as she could not come to want it. They were living together in a way and then they were living together in another way and then they were not living together.

The older one was one who did with distinction telling about being one being living. She was one who was being living. She was one telling about this thing and many people were not listening. She was telling about this thing about being one being living, telling about this thing with some distinction and some were knowing this thing were knowing that she was telling this thing, telling about being living and telling it with distinction and they were not listening, were not listening to her telling about this thing, telling about being living, telling with distinction about being living. She was one being living and she was telling about this thing telling about it very often, beginning and going on then and certainly very many then were not listening.

The younger one was one being living and she was telling about this thing, telling again and again about this thing about being living and she was telling this thing and some were listening, certainly some were listening, and she was telling again and again about being one being living and certainly some were listening and certainly she did this thing again and again, she told about being one being living and certainly anybody might not be going on being listening and certainly some were listening and certainly some went on listening. And certainly sometime not any one was really listening, certainly some time pretty nearly not any one was really listening and certainly sometime she was to herself not telling about this thing not telling about being living and certainly in a way she was always telling about this thing telling about being living and certainly then in a way the older one was listening, and certainly then in a way not any one was listening.

The older one went on living, the younger went on living, they both went on living. The older one went on living. Certainly she went on living and certainly some were enjoying this thing enjoying that she was going on living, some who were not then listening, some who certainly would not be listening and she certainly would be telling and telling with distinction of being one being living. Some were certainly enjoying this thing that she was one being living. Anybody could be pleasant with this thing that she was being living. Mostly every one could not be listening to her telling this thing telling of being one being living and certainly all of living in her was being one telling with distinction of being one being living. She was being living, any one could remember this thing, any one could be pleasant in this thing, some could be tired of this thing, not really tired of this thing, any one could be pleasant with this thing, some were very pleasant in this thing in her being one being living.

The younger one was one being living, any one could be tired of this thing of this one being one being living, any one could come to be tired of this thing of this one being one being living. Any one could be careful of this thing of this one going on being living, almost any one could be pretty careful of this thing of this one being one being living. This one was one being one being living. Very many were quite careful of this thing of this one being one being living.

These two were being ones who were being living. They had been for some time ones being living. They had been living each one of them, they were living, each one of them, they were going on living each one of them. They were, each one of them, being living, they had been being living, they were going on being living. Each of them was a different one from the other one in having been living, in being living, in going on being living.

The older was one and any one could know this thing for certainly if she was not such a one she was not anything and every one knew she was something, the older one was one who had distinction and certainly she said that she did not do anything to be any one and certainly she did everything and certainly not anything was anything and would not be anything if she were not one having distinction. And certainly she was one having distinction and certainly some were interested in this thing and certainly she was doing nothing and certainly she was doing everything and certainly very many were very tired of this thing of her not doing anything, of her doing something, and certainly any one could know she was a person of distinction. She certainly did not do anything, that is to say she certainly never had done anything. She certainly did anything, that is to say she certainly was always going on doing something. She told about such a thing, she told about going on doing something, she told about never having done anything. She certainly never had done anything. She certainly was always really going on doing something.

She was a person of some distinction. She was not ever changing in this thing. She was not ever changing in anything. She was not changing in being one being living. She was not changing in being one not having done anything. She was not changing in being one going on doing something. She was not changing about anything. She was not changing in telling about this thing. She was not changing and certainly any one could come to be certain of this thing. She was certain of this thing, any one could be certain of this thing, any one could come to hear her be certain of this thing. She was a person of distinction. She was not changing in this thing. She had not ever done anything. She was not changing in this thing. She was going on in doing something. She was not changing in this thing. She was needing that any one was knowing any of these things. She was always needing this thing needing that any one was knowing any of these things, was knowing that she was not changing, that she had distinction, that she had not done anything, that she was going on doing something. She was needing that any one was knowing some of these things. Some were knowing some of these things, she needed that thing. Certainly her sister knew some of these things and certainly in a way that was not any satisfaction, certainly that was in a way considerable satisfaction, and certainly there was in a way considerable satisfaction in their being two being living who were, the one sister Martha and the other Ada, considerable satisfaction to almost any one. They talked to each other about some things, they did not talk to each other about everything and certainly they both were needing this thing that some one was knowing that they were being ones being living and not being then two of them, being then each of them.

The older, sister Martha, talked some and certainly she wanted to hear talking, and certainly some do want to talk some and want to hear talking and it is about something, something which they have not ever been doing and certainly some of such of them will not in any way really be doing any such thing, not in any way really be doing anything of any such thing. The older, sister Martha certainly was willing, was needing to be willing to be talking, to be listening to talking about something and certainly she would not ever in any way be doing anything of any such thing. Certainly she was one, if she had been one who was more of the kind she was in being living would have been needing to be really doing some such thing again and again. And certainly she was not ever really doing anything of any such thing and that was because she was one not needing to be willing to be doing any such thing and she was one needing to be telling and listening to telling about doing such a thing. Certainly she was one quite completely needing to be telling and to be listening to telling about doing some such thing. Certainly she was not one ever needing to be willing to be in any way doing any such thing. And this would be puzzling if it were not completely a certain thing and it is completely this thing. She was one being one of a kind of them that when they are that kind of them are ones completely needing to be doing some thing, some one thing. She was of that kind of them. She was of a kind of them and that kind of them when they are that kind of them are ones needing to be willing to be doing, really doing one thing and she was of that kind of them and she was not needing to be willing to be doing that thing. She was of a kind of them and some of that kind of them are ones needing to be telling and to be listening to telling about doing a thing and she was of that kind of them and more and more she was completely needing to be listening and to be telling and to be asking and to be answering about doing that thing. There are some and they are of this kind of them and they certainly are not telling or not talking about this thing, are not listening, are not asking, are not needing to be willing to be hearing, to be telling anything about any such a thing. Sister Martha then was of a kind of them of ones being existing.

Ada, the younger, certainly was of a kind of them of a kind being existing. She was one certainly hearing, certainly talking, she and sister Martha certainly were listening and were talking and about something they certainly were needing to be willing to be talking about and listening about. Ada, the younger, was one not willing to be needing to be doing that thing and certainly she was completely needing doing that thing and certainly she was not ever completely needing to be willing to be doing that thing. And this then was soon not completely interesting to any one but her sister Martha who certainly was interested in any such thing.

Ada, the younger, was one being living and certainly she was one being living in needing anything that was in her being living to be being living. She certainly was using anything in being living. That is to say she needed to be one being living and certainly she was needing to be using anything that could be something being living for her to be one being living. That is she was one needing being one being living, that is she was one needing to be one going on being living. She certainly was needing this thing, needing being one going on being living, and she was one not easily feeding to be one going on being living. Feeding on being living to be one going on being living was a thing that she was not easily doing. She certainly was needing to be one going on being living. She certainly was not one easily being living to be one going on being living. She certainly was needing to be one going on being living. She certainly was not easily feeding on being living, on anything being living, she certainly was needing being one going on being living. She was feeding some on something being living, on some things being existing, on being living being existing and she was going on being living. She was needing going on being living. She did go on being living.

She was sometimes together with sister Martha, she was sometimes not together with her. She was one being living. She was needing going on being living. She was going on being living.

Any one being living can be one having been something. Not any one, some being living, can be one having been something. Some being living have been one being something. Certainly having been doing something and then not doing that thing and having been something and certainly then being something is something that has been making a living that is almost a family living in some one. Certainly sister Martha and Ada had been ones having family living and certainly they were ones having family living and certainly they were ones going to be having family living and certainly family living is something that is not existing in a family living together in any daily living. And certainly each one of them, each one of the two of them were living and had been living and certainly very many were certain of this thing and certainly such a family living was a thing to be remembering and certainly some could be certain that such a family living made any one have a finer feeling, and sometimes some one was quite certain that fine feeling was not then existing and certainly this thing was interesting to sister Martha and not convincing and certainly this thing was not interesting to Ada and sister Martha was not repeating this thing any too often and Ada was quite certain of any such thing, of fine feeling in a way being existing and sister Martha was pretty nearly certain of some such thing.

They were both of them certain that there was some connection between loving and listening between liking and listening and certainly some listened to each one of them and certainly there were some who were listening and liking the one to whom they were listening and certainly there were some who were listening and were having some tender feeling for the one to whom they were listening.

The older one, sister Martha, was one in a way needing that there should be some connection between liking and listening between liking her and listening to her and she was not in any way suffering in this thing, through this thing, she was not suffering for certainly some were listening and really then listening being existing certainly something was then being existing, listening was being existing, and certainly in a way there being some connection between liking and listening something was certainly in a way being existing. The older one then was one being living in something being existing and listening being existing, something was being existing, and there being some connection between liking and listening, certainly something was being existing.

The younger one was certain that there was completely a connection between tender feeling and listening, between liking and listening and she certainly was completely suffering in this thing, suffering from this thing. She was completely suffering and there certainly was connection between tender feeling and listening and liking and listening. She was almost completely suffering and certainly some were listening, quite a number were quite listening and certainly there is some connection between tender feeling and listening, and liking and listening. She had been suffering and she was suffering in there being a connection between tender feeling and listening, and between liking and listening. Quite a number were listening, certainly quite a number were listening and in a way she was quite certain of this thing, quite certain that quite a number were listening and she was quite certain, she was completely certain that there was connection between listening and tender feeling, and listening and liking. She certainly had been, she certainly was going on suffering from this thing, she certainly was suffering in this thing. She was certain that some were listening and she went on being certain of this thing that quite a number were listening and certainly quite a number were listening to her and certainly that was going on being existing. She certainly was suffering in this thing in their being existing a connection between listening and liking, and listening and tender feeling.

They were together and they were very often then not together. Certainly each one of them was sometimes then not with any other one. That is to say the older one was sometimes then not with any other one, she was very often not with any one and always then some one, some were in a way doing something and certainly then were meeting this one who was then being living. This one the older one in a way was very often not with any one. She was quite often not with any one. She certainly was not needing this thing. She certainly was not certain that she was not needing this thing. She was being living and certainly then very often she was not with any one.

She was not needing anything and she was needing being living and she was needing anything that she was needing for this thing for being living. She could be needing very much for this thing for being living. She was having something to be doing this thing to be being living, she was using a good deal for this thing for being living and in a way she was not needing anything and she was needing to be living and she was using quite enough for this thing for being living.

She was using some for this thing, for being living, that is to say if not any one were living she would not be living and really then she was not using them very much, she was not using any one very much, she was using them and really she was not needing that they should be any one. She was not using women and men and not at all children to be one being living. She was not using any one of any of them. She was needing being living and a good deal was being existing in this thing, she was not using very much of anything for this thing, a good deal had to be existing for this thing.

She was very often not with any one, quite often not with any one and she was being living and enough had to be being existing for this thing, quite a good deal had to be existing for this thing. She was one not needing to be very often with not any one. She was one not needing anything, not needing any one, she was one needing, pretty well needing being living and she was one needing that enough things be existing and in a way she was not using any of them anything being existing.

The younger one was sometimes not with any one and certainly this was not what this one was needing she certainly was needing being with some one and certainly she was sometimes with her sister Martha and in a way she was not ever really needing this thing needing being with the older one. She certainly was needing that the older one, that sister Martha had been and was being existing. She the younger one was certainly needing using something and some one and very often any one and certainly very often she was not doing this thing she was not using anything she was not using any one and certainly then she was with some one for she was one who certainly was needing going on being living. She certainly was needing that she was going on being living and certainly she was completely needing for this thing to be using some to be using some things and certainly sometimes she was almost completely not using anything not using any one and certainly then she was still with some one, still with something for certainly she was one going on being living.

Certainly each one of them were ones that might have been better looking, might have been very good-looking when they were younger ones and this had not been, they had not been as good-looking when they were younger ones as they were when they were older ones neither the one nor the other of them. They were quite good-looking when they were older ones, they were quite big enough then for this thing for being good-looking and quite old enough then for being good-looking, they were big then and old enough then and they certainly were quite good-looking then. When they were older ones they were ones saying again and again and again, and some one always was listening, what they had had as pretty nearly feeling when they were younger ones. When they were younger ones they certainly were feeling something and certainly then they were not ever completely saying that thing saying what they were feeling and they were certainly not then saying it again and again and they certainly were then not completely feeling that thing the thing they were later in being older ones saying completely and again and again and again. They were, each one of them, saying something when they were young ones and saying it again and again and they were feeling that thing and they were really feeling something and more and more they were ones completely feeling that thing and completely saying it again and again and again and again and again. They were, each one of them completely feeling a different thing from the other one of them and completely saying that completely different thing. Each one of them was completely saying a complete thing and saying it again and again and again and again and again and again and again.

Martha was quite young once and that was never of any interest to herself or any one. She did some things then, that was a natural thing. She was not ever completely interested in having done any of them. She was quite young then a completely young one and not any one then was very proud of this thing that she was a young one then. Some one may have been then a little proud of this thing that she was a young one then, it was not an interesting thing her being, her having been a young one.

She had been a quite young one, there were many others in the family then, some being very young ones then some being a little older ones then, there were always many others in the family and that was certainly a thing that was quite interesting.

Martha then was not any longer such a quite young one. She certainly then was doing something. Any one could then have been proud of that thing that she was certainly then doing something. Enough were then proud of that thing that she was doing something. She was interested enough in that thing that she was doing something. All her life then, all the rest of her living, she was doing that thing she was interested enough in doing that thing, some were proud enough of that thing that she was doing that thing. And certainly she was interested enough in doing that thing and certainly what she had done and was doing was not in any way completely interesting and it was almost completely interesting as being something that she had been all her living doing and finding interesting to be one being doing that thing. So then Martha was not any longer quite a young one and certainly then there were a good many of them and they were all of them being ones any one could be remembering as being in the family living. There were many of them and all of them were proud enough and interested enough in this thing and certainly Martha was one of them and certainly not any one of them was completely anything excepting that any one of them and all of them were being living.

Martha was then one being living. She was then not such a young one, she was almost then an older one and certainly then she was being living and so were all of them and so was any one of them. Certainly any one of them might have it come that something would stop in going on and then that one would not be any longer living. Certainly this could, certainly this did happen to some of them and certainly then all of them were remembering this thing that something could be stopping in them and they would then not be being living. And this could sometime happen to Martha and she could sometimes be remembering to think about this thing and this then was not an interesting thing as happening to any one of them, it was an interesting thing as being something happening to each of them and certainly it was not a thing going to happen to each of them but it was as such an interesting thing to Martha and as such she was completely remembering it and certainly she was almost remembering that perhaps it would not be happening to herself ever and certainly it could be happening to herself.

Ada the younger one was always completely remembering such a thing could be happening to herself, she was always completely remembering this thing. She was always completely remembering that there were very many of them. She was not always completely remembering that this thing could be happening to every one of them. She was very often remembering this thing that that could be happening to all of them, she was always completely remembering that it could be happening to herself, she was not ever completely remembering that that thing could be happening to any one of them, she was remembering this thing after it had happened to one of them and she was completely remembering this thing after it had happened to another one of them, and she completely remembered this thing after it had happened to another one of them. Certainly this thing did not happen to her in her being living and certainly she completely remembered all her being living that it would happen to her in her being living.

She had been a young one a quite young one and this had been completely enough interesting to her then so that she was completely certain that having been a quite young one was a thing that any one could be remembering. She had been a completely young one and certainly then she had been then not doing anything and certainly she completely remembered this thing and some other ones could remember this thing. Even her sister Martha could remember this thing and certainly she did not remember this thing. Certainly some did remember this thing. Ada was then not such a quite young one and certainly then she did not do anything and certainly then it was an important thing to any of them that she was then being one who was one remembering that each one was being living then and needing this thing needing being living. She was one then who was not completely interested in that thing in herself then, in being one being living, she was certainly then being completely interested in being one going on being living. She always went on being living.

Surely Ada would like to have been one going on living and she was remembering that she had been going on living and she was remembering that she had been liking going to be enjoying something then. She certainly, then when she had been going on being living, she had been certain that she could be coming to be enjoying something that sometime she would be having. She certainly was needing then to be going to be enjoying something. She certainly was then going to be enjoying some one and she certainly knew this thing then and could tell any one this thing then that she would be enjoying some one and certainly then she was going on being living.

She certainly could remember this thing, in a way she could remember anything, and certainly in a way she did remember everything. She always could remember that she would enjoy some, that she would enjoy some things. She always did remember that she had been going on being living. She always could remember this thing. She always did remember this thing. She always could remember that she would enjoy some, that she could enjoy some thing, that she needed this thing to be one going on being living and she always could remember that she had always been going on being living. She could remember everything. She was remembering everything. She was remembering that she had been going on being living. She remembered that she could enjoy some, that she could enjoy some things, that she had needed this to be one going on being living. She could remember everything. She did remember everything. She remembered again and again that she had gone on being living. She remembered again and again that she could remember this thing that she could remember, that she did remember that she had gone on being living. She did remember this thing. She remembered some other things. She remembered everything. She remembered that anything might happen and that certainly she was not needing that thing that anything was happening. She remembered and remembered it again and again that not any one was remembering any such thing that anything might be happening and that she was completely remembering this thing. She remembered this thing and she remembered that she had been going on being living.

She was not, to every one, remembering everything, and certainly she did remember this thing, she did remember that, to some, she did not remember everything, she did remember that some did not remember everything, that they did not remember that she could remember everything. She could certainly not forget this thing that some did not remember everything.

She certainly was one needing going on being living. She certainly was being living. She certainly had been going on being living. She certainly was going on being living. She certainly went on being living. She certainly remembered everything of this thing of going on being living. She certainly remembered everything. She certainly remembered about some remembering everything. She certainly remembered about some not remembering everything. She certainly could remember everything. She certainly remembered again and again this thing remembered that she could remember everything.

She was younger than her sister. Her sister was older. She called her sister, sister Martha, her sister called her Ada. When they were together they were each one of them certainly being living, the older was then certainly being living, she was knowing that thing, her sister was knowing that thing, the younger was then going on being living, the younger then knew that thing, the older one then knew that thing.

They were together and they were both being living then. They were not together and they were both being living then. The older was being living then. The younger was going on being living then.

The younger one was always remembering that they were both being living. The older was not ever forgetting that they were both being living. The younger was knowing that the older was being living, was knowing that she herself was needing going on being living. The older was knowing that the younger was going on being living, that she was needing this thing, she was knowing that she herself was being living.

ORTA OR ONE DANCING

Stein wrote a portrait of the American dancer Isadora Duncan (1878–1927) as a great artist while she was grappling with the nature of the creative personality in *Two,* a long double portrait of her brother Leo and her sister-in-law Sarah Stein. *Two* contrasted the excessive intellectuality that removed Leo from direct experience with the greater sensitivity to experience of Sarah, whose intellect, however, remained undeveloped. The recognition of their limitations led Stein to the idea of the integrated artistic personality as a step in reaching for self-definition. Isadora Duncan came to represent fluid, creative expression of complete physical experience that included thought. Her free, expressionist dancing is shaped into the rhythmic repetitions and permutations of the portrait, which embodies what it says in what the language does. It also incorporates motherhood and children into the portrait rather than omitting them and implying that they conflict with her art. The words encircle Duncan as "one being one" in a verbal dance of great rhythmic skill.

In her early notes for this portrait Stein compared Duncan to friends and acquaintances who yielded the elements of her typology of personality, and carefully delineated Duncan's characteristics. Isadora is what she does—dance—just as Stein is what she does—write. At the center of the portrait is Duncan's firm belief, in spite of initial adversity, in what she was doing as a founder of modern dance and a free spirit, who wanted, like Whitman, to "see America dancing": "This one is one going on thinking in believing in meanings." Isadora dances and thinks, but her thinking, never stiff and sterile, is never apart from dancing.

In the manuscript one phrase near the center spells out Stein's identification with Duncan as an artist. The paragraph beginning "She went on being one" asserts that "[s]he was then resembling some one, one who was not dancing, one who was writing," and continues the description of the dancer's stance and movement that now implies her own emotional and intellectual attitude. In the typescript that Stein retained but not in the manuscript and not in a typescript she sent to Carl Van Vechten, she lined out the phrase about herself in ink in a revision that shows her care with the single focus of the portrait. The phrase has been retained in the *Reader* as it is also retained in the posthumous volume *Two and Other Early Portraits,* where the portrait was first published. It shows Stein's struggle to define herself in the very being of another artist, the first portrait of a woman artist that Stein wrote.

Stein's working notes contrast Duncan's temperament with that of the sculptor Elie Nadelman. The name Orta in the title aligns Duncan as an artist through Horta de Ebro, now Horta de San Juan, with Picasso and Spain. Picasso first went to Horta in the summer of 1898, spending eight months with his friend Pallares, and returned there

for the summer of 1909 to do the first work defining analytic cubism. By the winter of 1912, Picasso was working on the "Ma Jolie" paintings.

• • • • •

Even if one was one she might be like some other one. She was like one and then was like another one and then was like another one and then was like another one and then was one who was one having been one and being one who was one then, one being like some.

Even if she was one and she was one, even if she was one she was changing. She was one and was then like some one. She was one and she had then come to be like some other one. She was then one and she had come then to be like some other one. She was then one and she had come then to be like some other one. She was then one and she had come then to be like a kind of a one.

Even if she was one being one, and she was one being one, she was one being one and even if she was one being one she was one who was then being a kind of a one.

Even if she was one being one and she was being one being one, even if she was one being one she was one having come to be one of another kind of a one.

Even if she was then being one and she was then one being one, even if she was then being the one she was one being, she was one who had come to be one being of another kind of a one.

Even if she was one being one and she was one being one, even if she was one being the one she was one being she was then another kind of a one, she was then being another kind of a one.

Even if she was one being one, even if she was one being one and being that one in being one, even if she was being the one she was being in being that one, even if she was being that one she was being a kind of a one she was come to be of a kind of a one, she was coming to be quite of a kind of a one.

Even if she was one being the one she was being, even if she was being that one the one she was being, the one she had been being, even if she was being that one, that one she was being, even if in being that one the one she was being she was being that one, being the one she was being, even if she was being the one she was being, even if she was being that one, even if she was being that one she was one coming to be of a kind of a one, coming to be and being of a kind of a one, quite coming to be of a kind of a one, of another kind of a one, of that kind of a one.

She was one being one. She was one having been that one. She was one going on being that one. She was one being one. She was one being of one kind of a one. She was one being that kind of a one. She was one being another kind of a one. She was one being another kind of a one. She was one being another kind of a one. She was one being another kind of a one.

She was one being one. She was one going on being that one. She was one being that one.

She was one being one. She was one always being that one. She was one always having being that one. She was one always going on being that one. She was one being one.

She was one being one and that thing, being that one was a thing that had come to be something. She was one being one and that thing, being that one was a thing that did then go on being existing. She was one being that one. She was being one.

She was one believing that thing, believing being the one she was being. She was one always believing that thing, always believing being the one she was being.

She was one who had been believing being the one she was being. She had been one believing being the one she was being. She is believing being the one she is believing. She has been believing this thing. She always has been, she always is believing being the one she is being.

She is one doing that thing, doing believing being the one she is being. She is one being the one she is being. She is one being one. She is one being that one.

She is one being the one she is being. She is one doing something. She is one being the one she is being. She is one being that one.

In doing something that one is being the one doing that thing. In doing something, the one doing the thing is the one being one doing that thing. This one is one doing something. This one is being the one doing the thing. That one is doing the thing. That one has been doing the thing. That one is dancing.

Meaning that thing, meaning being the one doing that thing is something the one doing that thing is doing. Meaning doing dancing is the thing this one is doing. This one is doing dancing. This one is the one meaning to be doing that thing meaning to be doing dancing.

This one is one having been doing dancing. This one is one doing dancing. This one is one. This one is one doing that thing. This one is one doing dancing. This one is one having been meaning to be doing dancing. This one is one meaning to be doing dancing.

This one being one meaning to be doing dancing, this one being one dancing, this one is one, this one is being that one. This one is one. This one is one being one. This one is being one and has been one being one having a kind of way of being one believing anything, this one is being one and has been one being one having a kind of way of meaning anything. This one is one being one having a way of being one thinking of anything. This one is one having a kind of way of meaning everything.

This one is one being that one. This one is one and is that one and is one having had and having a way of being one believing something and meaning something and dancing. This is one being one having a way of dancing. This is one being that one.

This is one being one and having been one who is one being one showing being that one in being one changing and being that one, that kind of a one, the one that is the kind of a one that is meaning and believing the way this one is meaning and believing. This one is not changing. This one is changing, that is to say this one is looking like different ones of them who are ones who are believing and feeling and meaning the way this one is meaning and feeling and believing. This one is one who has been, who is meaning and feeling and believing. This one is one who is meaning. This one is one who has been meaning. This one is one who has a way of meaning. This one is one who has been one who is one meaning in the kind of way that some looking like this one are meaning. This one has a way of believing, this one has a way of feeling. This one has a way of feeling, this one has a way of believing and that is a way of feeling, and that is a way of believing that some have who sometimes look very much like this one looks some of the time. This one is one being one. This one is one dancing. This one has a way of believing and feeling and meaning. This one has a way of feeling, believing and meaning in dancing.

Being one having meaning, being one believing, being one dancing, being that one is what this one is one doing. This one is one who has meaning, this one is one who is dancing and is one having meaning in that thing in dancing. This one is one meaning to be having meaning in dancing. This one is one believing in having meaning. This one is one thinking in believing in having meaning.

This one is the one being dancing. This one is the one thinking in believing in dancing having meaning. This one is one believing in thinking. This one is one thinking in dancing having meaning. This one is one believing in dancing having meaning. This one is one dancing. This one is one being that one. This one is one being in being one being dancing. This one is one being in being one who is dancing. This one is one being one. This one is one being in being one.

This one is one changing. This one is one who has been, who always has been one being living in being that one. This one was one quite living in being that one. This one is one finishing living in being that one. This one is that one. This one has been that one. This one is one having been in the beginning been that one. This one has been going on being that one. This one is quite finishing being living in being that one.

This one is one who has been one being dancing. This one has been one beginning in being one being dancing. This one has been going on being living in being one being dancing. This one has been ending in being one going to be dancing. This one is finishing living in being one dancing.

This one is one not changing. This one is one coming to be one completely believing in thinking. This one is one beginning in being one coming to be believing. This one is going on in being one believing in meaning. [This one is one going on thinking in believing in meaning.] This one is going on believing in thinking in having meaning. This one is going on in believing, this one is one going on in believing in thinking, this one is one going on in believing in having meaning. This one is one going on. This one is one finishing in thinking in believing having meaning in dancing. This one is finishing in being one thinking in believing in meaning. This one is finishing in believing in thinking. This one is finishing in believing in having meaning. This one is finishing in believing. This one is finishing in thinking in believing. This one is finishing in believing.

This one is one who is that one, who is one dancing, who is one being one doing that thing, who is one being one believing in meaning. This one is one being one believing in thinking having meaning. This one is one being one believing that meaning is existing. This one is one meaning to be thinking in believing. This one is one believing in meaning.

She was not needing to be one believing in meaning being existing. She was not one needing this thing, needing being such a one. Needing being such a one, needing that meaning is existing is something, needing that meaning is existing is something that some one being one is having. Very many being one one having that thing, are having that needing of meaning being existing. Very many are being one having it that being that one they are the one the one that is needing that meaning is existing. This one is one being one having it that being that one she is one the one needing that meaning is existing.

She was one beginning being living and there were then others who were ones doing that thing, being living. Her mother was being living and was living then with four children. The mother was one having been married to some one and she was one then not needing that thing enough not needing that thing so that the one to whom she had been married could then marry another one.

She was living then with four children and all of them all the four children were being living then, were quite commencing then being ones being living. There were four children. The oldest one was a son, the second one was not a son, the third one was this one, the fourth one was a boy and all four of them were living then and the mother was living then and all five of them were living together then.

The mother came to be one believing that meaning was something that could be exciting to any one. She had come to be one knowing that meaning was completely interesting to her youngest one and to the one who was a little older than her youngest one. She had come to be forgetting that her oldest son had not any meaning, was not remembering that he was the oldest one, was not forgetting that he was being one having been in the family living. She had come to be remembering that her daughter, the one who had not been a son was one who could be supporting that meaning is existing, could be quite supporting some. She went on then being living and she was finishing in being one fading in meaning, fading and meaning and greeting meaning and fading and being then anything being faded and having meaning. She was then one not completely fading, she was then knowing that every one could be greeting meaning being existing. She was then still not yet being come to be a dead one.

She was fading then and asking any one to be one greeting meaning being existing. She was asking any one to do this thing. She was fading enough then. She was a dead one sometime.

She was not living with any children then when she was greeting meaning being existing. She was then not living with any child she had been having. All four were being living then. All four of them were being living and any one of them might be one being dancing. Any one of the four of them might then be one being dancing. The oldest one of them was not then being one dancing. He was not doing that thing, he was not dancing. The second one was one not then dancing, she was then completely knowing everything about all dancing. She was then being one living in dancing being existing. She was then living in this thing.

The third one was one dancing. She was quite doing that thing quite dancing. She was one dancing.

The fourth was one who in a way was one dancing. He was in a way being one doing that thing. He was one in a way completely meaning that thing completely meaning being one being dancing. He was in a way then dancing. He was one being one asking and answering in dancing being asking. He was one asking in dancing being existing. He was one answering in dancing being existing. He was one in a way dancing that is he was one coming to be one asking and answering. He was one asking. Dancing was existing. He was one answering. Dancing was existing. He was one asking and answering. He was one meaning that thing meaning that dancing had come to be existing. He was one not dancing. He certainly was not dancing. Any one could be one dancing. He was not then dancing. He was then meaning the thing meaning that something is existing and that something is one thing. In a way he was doing nothing that was not something that was meaning that something had been existing, that dancing had been existing. He could be one dancing. Dancing was existing.

She, Orta Davray, was one being of a kind of a one. That is to say she was one looking like some. She was changing. In the beginning she was one and then she was one having the same look as some other one and that one is of a kind of a one. Then she was changing and she was looking as another one was looking and that one was of a kind of a one. Then she was changing and she was looking as another one was looking and that one was of a kind of a one. Then she was changing and she was looking like another one who was of a kind of a one. All four of them were quite different kinds of ones all four whom she was resembling. All four were in a way of a kind of a one. All four could be ones being ones needing believing that meaning is existing. All four could be ones expecting something from some such thing. All four of them could be ones expecting something in meaning being existing. They were quite different ones these four of them.

She was one beginning being living and then she was one being that one being dancing. She was beginning then being one being existing. She was then being one and every one in her family living was needing then needing being completing that thing, completing her being one being dancing. She was then beginning being living. She was then one being like some and she was then one being existing, being one who was a young one and family living was being existing and she was then one completing that thing completing family living in being one being dancing and being the one each one was then completing as being one being dancing. She was being then quite like some. She was then feeling anything in any one being one completing her being one being dancing. She was then being one feeling anything in being one completing the family living in being one being dancing. She was then being one feeling anything in being one needing being that one, the one she was then.

She was then an older one, she was then like some. She was then dancing. She was then creating family living being existing. She was then completely creating that thing. She was then one of them one of all of them who were all ones who had been ones completing her being one being dancing.

She was then one being dancing. She was then being one exceeding in being that one. She was then being one who was being dominated by being one dominating anything. She was dancing then. She was exceeding everything. She was one dancing.

She was one who would be contradicting any one if she had not been one exceeding in affirming everything. She was one not contradicting every one. She was one contradicting. She could contradict any one. She was dancing. She was not contradicting she was dancing. She was exceedingly dancing. She was not contradicting every one. She was one dancing.

She was one meaning something in being one not contradicting every one. She was one meaning something in being one contradicting any one. She was one being one meaning in being one not contradicting any one. She was one having meaning in being one who was contradicting any one. She was one having meaning in being one who was not contradicting every one. She was one having meaning in dancing. She was one having meaning in exceeding in being the one being one dancing. She was having meaning in being that one the one contradicting every one. She was having meaning in being that one the one not contradicting every one. She was having meaning in being the one contradicting any one. She was having meaning in being the one not contradicting any one. Contradicting every one was existing. She was affirming dancing. She was exceeding in not contradicting every one. She was exceeding in not contradicting any one.

Dancing was what she was doing then. She was doing dancing. She was doing dancing and she was that one she was the one dancing. She was doing dancing and she was then one having meaning in being that one. She was then one being that one, she was then one being dancing, she was then one having meaning, she was then one dancing in being that one, she was then one being one dancing in being that one the one having meaning. She was dancing then. She was being that one. She was meaning that thing quite meaning being that one. She was dancing.

She was being that one. She was dancing. She was one needing meaning being existing. She was not then showing needing meaning being existing. Not anything then was showing anything in her being one then needing that meaning is existing.

She was thinking then. She was not then meaning everything in thinking. She was thinking then. She was dancing. She was thinking then and dancing had been existing. She was dancing then, she was thinking then, she was meaning everything, she was completely then being dancing, she was exceeding then exceeding in being that one the one then dancing.

She was dancing then. She certainly was thinking then. She had been thinking some. She was meaning everything then. She was completely then meaning everything then and thinking then thinking that meaning is existing and she was dancing then, quite dancing then. She was dancing then, she was meaning that thing, meaning dancing, she was dancing then, she was meaning thinking then, she was thinking then, she was meaning everything, she was dancing.

She went on then dancing. She was dancing again and again. She went on then being one being dancing. She went on then being that one. She went on then being one being dancing. She went on then being that one being that one being dancing. She went on dancing.

She was then one looking like some one. She was then one looking like some. She was then one looking like some one who was one needing to be thinking in meaning being existing. She was then one looking like some one and that one was one living in believing in thinking in meaning being existing. She was then one looking like some one and that one was one moving in every direction in believing meaning is existing. She was then one looking like one and that one was straining in being one thinking in believing that meaning is existing. She was looking like this one and she was dancing then, she was quite dancing then.

She was dancing then she was being strained then quite strained then by meaning being existing. She was strained then quite strained then in believing in thinking in meaning being existing. She was quite strained then. She was dancing then. She was quite moving in every direction in meaning being existing.

She was dancing, she was answering, she was carelessly domineering, she was domineering, she was dancing, she was answering.

She was dancing, she was that one then, the one dancing and answering, the one domineering and answering, the one having meaning in believing in thinking in meaning having the condition of being in a direction. She was one dancing, she was one answering. She was that one the one dancing. She was that one the one dancing, the one answering. She was that one the one answering and dancing. She was that one the one dancing and answering. She was worn some then, she was not quite at all worn then, she was dancing then, she was answering then, she was moving in every direction in being one being worn some then. She was believing in thinking having meaning in meaning being existing.

She was thinking, she was believing, she was dancing, she was meaning. She was thinking, she was believing in thinking, she was thinking in believing, she was believing in dancing, she was thinking in believing in dancing. She was thinking in believing in dancing having meaning. She was believing in thinking in dancing having meaning. She was dancing in having meaning, she was having meaning in dancing, she was dancing, she was believing, she was thinking, she was answering, she was domineering, she was going on answering, she was worn with believing, she was careless in domineering, she was energetic in answering, she was believing in going in any direction, she went on in changing, she was simple in not going on questioning, she was moving changing, she was changing in connecting, she was seeing feeling in connecting dancing, she was feeling in careless domineering, she was needing dancing in believing.

She would be dancing in being that one the one having been dancing. She was that one the one having been dancing. She was dancing. She was dancing in being that one the one dancing. She was dancing.

She was dancing in being that one believing that thinking in having meaning in meaning being existing. She was dancing in this thing. She was dancing. She was dancing in moving in every direction being something having meaning. She was dancing in this thing. She was dancing. She was dancing, she was using then being one believing in meaning being existing. She was dancing in being one having feeling of anything being cheering. She was dancing in feeling that something had been coming. She was dancing in feeling that something having been coming is having meaning. She was dancing in feeling that feeling has a meaning. She was dancing in feeling that any one coming to be one being asked something would be one answering that meaning is existing. She was one dancing in feeling certain that some doing something are ones being certain that meaning is existing. She was one dancing in being one being that one being the one dancing then.

Being that one being the one dancing then was then being something, was then being some one. She was that one, she was the one dancing, she was the one being that one that is being something, she was the one being that one that is being some one.

Being that one being that one dancing was then being one quite completing that thing quite completing being that one, that one dancing. Being that one, the one dancing, being that one was being some one, was being something. Being that one dancing was then being that one. She was that one, she was completely being that one being the one dancing. She was quite being that one, quite completely being that one, the one dancing, the one meaning everything, the one moving in that direction, the one thinking in believing in meaning being existing, the one moving in every direction, the one feeling in thinking in meaning having existence, the dancing, the one being that one.

Remembering being dancing is something. Completely remembering being dancing is something. Completely remembering being dancing is what she was doing in being that one the one dancing. She completely remembered something of being one being dancing.

She completely remembered dancing. She was that one, she was one dancing, she was dancing, she was that one the one dancing.

She went on being that one, the one dancing. She went on being that one. She went on being that one, the one dancing.

She was that one, the one dancing. She went on being that one, the one having been dancing, the one dancing, the one being that one the one having been dancing and being dancing, the one being the one that one was.

She went on being one. She was one. She was then resembling some one, one who was not dancing, one who was writing, she was then resembling some all of whom were ones believing in thinking, believing in meaning being existing, believing in worrying, believing in not worrying, believing in not needing remembering that some meaning has been existing, believing in moving in any direction, feeling in thinking in meaning being existing, feeling in believing in thinking being existing, feeling in moving in every direction, believing in being one thinking, believing in being one moving in a direction, feeling in being any one, feeling in being that one the one the one is being, believing in feeling in being that one the one each one has been and is being.

She was one dancing and she was one not dancing. She was one not dancing. She was one dancing. She was one believing in meaning being existing. She was dancing.

She had been dancing. She was dancing. She could be dancing. Being dancing was something every one was needing and she was being one dancing. Being dancing was what every one expressing meaning being existing was assisting to be existing, she was dancing, any one expressing meaning being existing was one needing to be one understanding anything of assisting to dancing being existing.

She had been dancing. She was dancing. She could be dancing. She could remember that she could be dancing. She did remember something of that thing. She did remember anything of that thing. She did remember everything of being one who could be dancing.

She was dancing. She had been dancing. She could be dancing. She could remember everything of dancing. She could remember everything of having been dancing. She could remember everything of being one who could be dancing.

She was dancing. She was remembering this thing. She was dancing. She was asking any one who had been one expressing that meaning is existing to be one assisting dancing to be existing. She was dancing. Any one was then assisting that dancing be existing. Some were then assisting so that dancing could be existing. She could be dancing. She was remembering then everything of being one who could be dancing. She was dancing then. She was remembering then, remembering everything of being dancing. She had been dancing then. She was remembering everything of dancing then. She was dancing then.

In being that one, one dancing, she was one who was one being that one the one seeing thinking in meaning being existing. In being that one the one dancing then she was such a one, one believing in thinking being in meaning being existing.

In being one then being dancing she was being then one who might be one worrying to be exerting thinking being in meaning being existing. In being one then being dancing she would be one worrying to winning thinking being existing in meaning being existing if she had not been one winning some to be ones expressing meaning being existing who were ones having been ones feeling in believing in meaning being existing. She might have been one worrying in continuing thinking in feeling in believing in meaning being existing if she had not been one remembering something of having been one being dancing. She might have been one being worrying in feeling in believing that meaning is existing if she had not been one believing that sometime any one could be learning what she might have been one teaching. She might have been one worrying in thinking in feeling in meaning being existing if she had not been one who could be one teaching anything of meaning being existing. She might have been worrying if she had not been one remembering anything of what she had been one doing in being living in dancing being existing, in meaning being existing. She might have been one worrying if she had not been one forgetting something of thinking in believing in meaning being existing. She might have been one worrying if she had not been one not completing coming to be worrying. She might have been one worrying if she had not been one who had been dancing. She might have come to be one worrying if she had not been one being one dancing. She was dancing. She had been dancing. She could be dancing.

In being dancing she was dancing, she was remembering having been dancing, she was believing in thinking in meaning being existing, she was being one being one going to be moving in any direction, she was being one being one who had not been dancing, she was being one being one leading and following every moving in any direction, she was being one being one dancing.

In being one dancing she was being one dancing. In dancing she was doing that thing she was doing dancing. In doing dancing she was dancing.

In being one dancing she was being that one being one dancing. In being dancing she was dancing. In dancing she was quite being that one the one being dancing. In being dancing she was dancing. She was dancing.

In having been dancing she had been one dancing. In having been dancing she had been being that one the one being dancing. In having been dancing she had been dancing.

She had been dancing. She had been one dancing. She was dancing then. She had been doing dancing. When she had been doing dancing she had been dancing. She had been dancing when she had been dancing. She had been dancing.

She was always being one who was one who was dancing. She was dancing then. She was always dancing some. She was always dancing in being one being dancing. She always would be one dancing some. She always would be one dancing some when she was one being one being dancing. She always would be that one, one having been one being dancing. She always would be one who was one dancing. She always would be one dancing when she was one being one being dancing. She always would be one being dancing. She always would be one being that one.

She always would be one remembering everything about dancing. She always would be that one. She always would be remembering anything about dancing. She always would be such a one. She always would be thinking in believing in meaning being existing. She always would be that one. She always would be moving in a direction and almost then would be one moving in a direction in being one dancing, in having been one dancing.

In being one remembering everything of dancing she was one coming to be one who was one who was of a kind of them a kind of them remembering everything of something and expressing then that every one is believing in thinking in meaning being existing. In being one remembering that dancing is existing, in being one remembering anything of dancing being existing in meaning being existing she was being one being that one one expressing that thinking in meaning is being existing in dancing being existing. She was then that one. She was then one dancing. She was then one moving in any direction. She was then being that one, the one dancing.

In being that one the one dancing she was being one who was not then one coming to be changing. In being that one the one dancing she was being then one who had not been changing. In being one who had not been changing, in being the one who was not one changing she was being dancing. She was one dancing.

She was one dancing and if she had not been one changing she would always have been one being a young one. She was not always being one being a quite young one.

In being one changing she was one who would be one showing something of being one who was an older one, one doing a little dancing.

She was one not changing. She was one dancing. She was one showing everything of this thing, of being one dancing.

In being one going on being that one the one dancing she was one who would have been one going on dancing if she had not come to be one showing some that every one could be needing to be understanding the meaning of believing that dancing is existing in thinking in meaning being existing. She would have been one going on being one dancing if she were not being that one the one dancing. She would have been one going on being dancing if she had not been that one the one who had been dancing.

Being one dancing and being one remembering everything of that thing is something. Being one dancing and being one going on being one dancing is something. Being one dancing and being one believing in feeling in thinking in meaning being existing is something. Being one dancing is something. In being one dancing this one the one dancing is one doing that thing doing dancing. In being one dancing this one is being that one the one dancing.

This one in being dancing is one being dancing. In being one being dancing this one is one who in being dancing is one expressing that thing expressing being one dancing. In dancing this one is one expressing that dancing is existing. In being one dancing this one is expressing that dancing is existing. In dancing this one is expressing anything. In dancing this one is one feeling the expressing everything. In dancing this one is dancing. In dancing this one is being one dancing. In dancing this one is being that one the one dancing.

In being one dancing this one is one being one remembering anything in dancing. In being one dancing this one is one remembering something in dancing. In being one dancing this one was dancing and dancing being that thing being dancing this one was doing that thing was doing dancing. In being one dancing this one was one being dancing. In being dancing this one was dancing. In dancing this one was dancing.

In dancing she was dancing. She was dancing and dancing and in being that one the one dancing and dancing she was dancing and dancing. In dancing, dancing being existing, she was dancing, and in being one dancing dancing was being existing.

She was one and being one she was one in a way being one, she was one dancing. She was one she was one dancing. She was one dancing, she was being one, she was in a way one, she was one, she was one dancing.

In being one, in being in a way one, she was one dancing. In being one dancing, she was in a way one. She was in a way one. She was one dancing, she was one remembering anything of dancing, she was in a way one. She was one dancing. In being one who was one dancing she was in a way one. She was in a way one, that is, she was one and being one she was one dancing and being one dancing she was one being that one the one dancing, and being that one the one dancing she was one. She was one, that is, she was one being one dancing. She was one and she was being dancing, that is in a way she was one. In being dancing, she was one, that is, she was in a way one.

She was in a way one, that is she was dancing, that is she was in a way one, that is she was dancing, and she was one dancing and being that one the one dancing, being that one she was in a way one. She was one, she was in a way one, she was dancing.

She was believing in thinking in meaning being existing, she was in a way one. She was thinking in feeling in believing in meaning being existing. She was in a way one. She was one, she was moving in some directions, she was moving, she was thinking in feeling in meaning being existing. She was that one. She was dancing. She was in a way one. She was that one, she was one. She was in a way one.

In being in a way one she was one being one being the one she was. She was in a way one, she was one dancing. She was that one, she was in a way one. She was in a way one, she was one dancing and dancing was being existing and she was one dancing. She certainly was one dancing. Dancing being existing is something. She was in a way one. She was one dancing. She was that one, she was one dancing. She was dancing. Dancing is being existing. She was in a way one.

In being one she was one completing that thing. In being one she was not completing that thing again and again. She was not completing again and again being that one. In being that one she was not completing that, she was not completing being that one. She was not completing being that one, the one she was.

In not completing being that one, the one she was, she was one doing anything. In not completing being that one, the one she was, she was one moving in some direction. She was one not completing being one, being that one, she was not completing that thing. In not completing that thing, she was being that one, she was being the one she was. She was one being one who being one not being completing being the one she was, was one who was completing something again and again, who was completing being one she was, who was not completing being that one, being one, being the one she was.

She was one resembling some. She was one resembling some and being one resembling some she was one not resembling one kind of a one. She was resembling some and they were one kind of a one, they were a kind of a one not completing being one, not completing being that one, not completing being the kind of a one completing being that one. She was resembling some and each one of them were not resembling the other ones in being ones being the one they were being.

In being one she was being one who being one resembling some was one being one not completing being that one, the one being one. In being one not completing being one she was resembling some.

In being one she was one and in being that one she was one some one was knowing was that one. In some knowing she was that one she was one who would be completing being one and she was completing being one and she was one and she was one who was resembling some and these were ones who were ones who were a kind of one which is a kind which is completing being one who are not completing being one, they being ones being one and not being ones being completed then and being ones then not any one has been completing.

She was one. She was one and knowing one, that one was being one she was knowing and it might be that they were going on knowing one another if they went on knowing one another and going on knowing one another she might be one not going on knowing that one and not going on knowing that one she would come to be knowing some whom she would be knowing and who would not come to be ones being the same ones and they would be ones expressing something for some being ones listening and looking. She would be one telling something and she would be one being one. She was one. She was dancing. She was one. She had been one. She was one. She was being that one. She would be that one.

In being one dancing she was being one and being one who was resembling some and these were of a kind of a one being ones thinking in feeling in meaning being existing she was one who had been, who was dancing and dancing could be, had been existing.

In being one in being that one, she was one. She was one and being that one she was that one. She was that one and being that one and being one feeling in believing completing being existing, and being one thinking in feeling in meaning being existing and being one being of a kind of a one and being of that kind of them and they being of a kind of them and complete connection being existing in her being one dancing between dancing being existing and her being one not being one completing being one, she was one dancing and being that one she was that one and being that one she was that one the one dancing and being the one dancing being that one she was the one going on being that one the one dancing. She was dancing. She had been dancing. She would be dancing.

MATISSE

PICASSO

The portraits of the two great painters, Stein's contemporaries, probably composed in close succession very soon after *Ada*, contrast their personalities as they are reflected in their work. Although they were not written as joint studies, it is useful to consider them together, for they provided opportunities for Stein to observe the artists and their work, to clarify her own direction, and to develop a language of decentered composition that would embrace her emerging vision of artistic capacity.

That vision came out of direct contact with the painters and their work. In the autumn of 1905 Leo and Gertrude Stein acquired Matisse's controversial *Woman with a Hat*, which marked them as collectors to be reckoned with. The Matisses became regular visitors to the studio of Leo and Gertrude and the apartment of Michael and Sarah Stein. Sarah became a devoted disciple, a student in his school, and a collector of his work. Leo greatly admired Matisse's intelligence, his conscientiousness, and his subordination of everything, including personal relations, to his work. Gertrude Stein always maintained that he was a painter of genius but gradually came to reject him as a person, to reject his theories of art, and to reject what she considered his decorative, two-dimensional work after *La Joie de Vivre* of 1905–6.

Between 1906 and 1911, while developing her system of characterology to support and organize *The Making of Americans,* Stein included in her notes descriptions of the painters she encountered. These portraits helped her gradually to define her view of painting as an art and her own emerging art. She had difficulty placing Matisse as a personality but little by little, while maintaining respect for his genius, came to describe him as a person blinded by his own "unreasonable tenacity" and "brutal egotism."

Her growing admiration for Picasso as an artist during the heroic years leading to analytic cubism from 1907 to 1911—at the same time that she was struggling with her novel *The Making of Americans*—came to balance her rejection of Matisse. She saw Picasso as a talent less solemn and infinitely more fecund in creativity than Matisse, a genius capable of an effortless outpouring of great work in steadily new forms that appeared ugly until their beauty was gradually perceived.

The effort Stein put into her attempts to seize the personalities and evaluate the art of the painters is evident in her early notebooks of these years. The notebooks also show her groping for solutions to the problem of representation and portraiture in her own writing. The portraits of artists that resulted from her efforts are concentrated word compositions. Stein's notes are not required for reading the self-contained portraits, although they document and amplify her conscious, painstaking search.

Both Matisse and Picasso, who met at the Steins' in 1906, are portrayed as individual artists but also as leaders of the avant-garde whose efforts are being watched by others and who command a following. They are considered separately, but the implication of the two portraits is also that each challenges the leadership of the other.

Matisse begins with negative, laborious, and complex sentence constructions in the service of the painter's struggle to achieve "certainty"—one of the key words of the portrait. The sentences are surrounded by statements emphasizing the controversial critical reception of his work, his own sensitivity to his audience, and the many competing certainties that beset his futile search for true certainty about "expressing something." Two further key words are "struggling" and "suffering," in gerundive forms describing the process of difficult personal discovery embodied in the work.

As the portrait continues with assertions of this one being a great one struggling, his greatness appears to turn in upon itself, annulling itself in its very affirmation until "very many were not listening" and many of his followers defected. The portrait ends with two perfectly balanced sentences of certainty and uncertainty about the value of Matisse's work.

Picasso, on the other hand, begins with four assertions of the artist's charm. Instead of the struggle and suffering in *Matisse, Picasso* shows the artist constantly working, "bringing out of himself" in a steady, procreative act "coming out of him," almost effortlessly, an art intellectually incoherent but enormously various. It is first shown as "heavy," "solid," and "complete." Later Stein describes it in all its abundant, confusing diversity—"lovely," "perplexing," "disconcerting," "simple," "clear," "complicated," "interesting," "disturbing," "repellent," "pretty," but always with "a real meaning." The birth imagery associated with Picasso is repeated in a series of singing, irregularly rhythmical figures radically different from the single-minded formulations of *Matisse.*

She perceived character weaknesses in Picasso, one "not always completely working." She watched him all her life with anxiety, for she feared that his susceptibility to sexual temptation might interfere with his art, a problem she also noted in *Matisse Picasso and Gertrude Stein,* or *G. M. P.,* of 1911–12. Her notebook entries speak of his lack of continuity and his quick facility accompanied by insufficient "resistance" to temptation. Her very praise implies her uneasiness when she says, "Pablo is never dragged [by lack of courage], he walks in the light, and a little ahead of himself like Raphael, therefore his things often lack a base. Do him." And immediately she begins, "One whom some were certainly following. . . ."

• • • • •

One was quite certain that for a long part of his being one being living he had been trying to be certain that he was wrong in doing what he was doing and then when he could not come to be certain that he had been wrong in doing what he had been doing, when he had completely convinced himself that he would not come to be certain that he had been wrong in doing what he had been doing he was really certain then that he was a great one and he certainly was a great one. Certainly every one could be certain of this thing that this one is a great one.

Some said of him, when anybody believed in him they did not then believe in any other one. Certainly some said this of him.

He certainly very clearly expressed something. Some said that he did not clearly express anything. Some were certain that he expressed something very clearly and some of such of them said that he would have been a greater one if he had not been one so clearly expressing what he was expressing. Some said he was not clearly expressing what he was expressing and some of such of them said that the greatness of struggling which was not clear expression made of him one being a completely great one.

Some said of him that he was greatly expressing something struggling. Some said of him that he was not greatly expressing something struggling.

He certainly was clearly expressing something, certainly sometime any one might come to know that of him. Very many did come to know it of him that he was clearly expressing what he was expressing. He was a great one. Any one might come to know that of him. Very many did come to know that of him. Some who came to know that of him, that he was a great one, that he was clearly expressing something, came then to be certain that he was not greatly expressing something being struggling. Certainly he was expressing something being struggling. Any one could be certain that he was expressing something being struggling. Some were certain that he was greatly expressing this thing. Some were certain that he was not greatly expressing this thing. Every one could come to be certain that he was a great man. Any one could come to be certain that he was clearly expressing something.

Some certainly were wanting to be needing to be doing what he was doing, that is clearly expressing something. Certainly they were willing to be wanting to be a great one. They were, that is some of them, were not wanting to be needing expressing anything being struggling. And certainly he was one not greatly expressing something being struggling, he was a great one, he was clearly expressing something. Some were wanting to be doing what he was doing that is clearly expressing something. Very many were doing what he was doing, not greatly expressing something being struggling. Very many were wanting to be doing what he was doing were not wanting to be expressing anything being struggling.

There were very many wanting to be doing what he was doing that is to be one clearly expressing something. He was certainly a great man, any one could be really certain of this thing, every one could be certain of this thing. There were very many who were wanting to be ones doing what he was doing that is to be ones clearly expressing something and then very many of them were not wanting to be being ones doing that thing, that is clearly expressing something, they wanted to be ones expressing something being struggling, something being going to be some other thing, something being going to be something some one sometime would be clearly expressing and that would be something that would be a thing then that would then be greatly expressing some other thing than that thing, certainly very many were then not wanting to be doing what this one was doing clearly expressing something and some of them had been ones wanting to be doing that thing wanting to be ones clearly expressing something. Some were wanting to be ones doing what this one was doing wanted to be ones clearly expressing something. Some of such of them were ones certainly clearly expressing something, that was in them a thing not really interesting then any other one. Some of such of them went on being all their living ones wanting to be clearly expressing something and some of them were clearly expressing something.

This one was one very many were knowing some and very many were glad to meet him, very many sometimes listened to him, some listened to him very often, there were some who listened to him, and he talked then and he told them then that certainly he had been one suffering and he was then being one trying to be certain that he was wrong in doing what he was doing and he had come then to be certain that he never would be certain that he was doing what it was wrong for him to be doing then and he was suffering then and he was certain that he would be one doing what he was doing and he was certain that he should be one doing what he was doing and he was certain that he would always be one suffering and this then made him certain this, that he would always be one being suffering, this made him certain that he was expressing something being struggling and certainly very many were quite certain that he was greatly expressing something being struggling. This one was one knowing some who were listening to him and he was telling very often about being one suffering and this was not a dreary thing to any one hearing that then, it was not a saddening thing to any one hearing it again and again, to some it was quite an interesting thing hearing it again and again, to some it was an exciting thing hearing it again and again, some knowing this one and being certain that this one was a great man and was one clearly expressing something were ones hearing this one telling about being one being living were hearing this one telling this thing again and again. Some who were ones knowing this one and were ones certain that this one was one who was clearly telling something, was a great man, were not listening very often to this one telling again and again about being one being living. Certainly some who were certain that this one was a great man and one clearly expressing something and greatly expressing something being struggling were listening to this one telling about being living telling about this again and again and again. Certainly very many knowing this one and being certain that this one was a great man and that this one was clearly telling something were not listening to this one telling about being living, were not listening to this one telling this again and again.

This one was certainly a great man, this one was certainly clearly expressing something. Some were certain that this one was clearly expressing something being struggling, some were certain that this one was not greatly expressing something being struggling.

Very many were not listening again and again to this one telling about being one being living. Some were listening again and again to this one telling about this one being one being in living.

Some were certainly wanting to be doing what this one was doing that is were wanting to be ones clearly expressing something. Some of such of them did not go on in being ones wanting to be doing what this one was doing that is in being ones clearly expressing something. Some went on being ones wanting to be doing what this one was doing that is, being ones clearly expressing something. Certainly this one was one who was a great man. Any one could be certain of this thing. Every one would come to be certain of this thing. This one was one certainly clearly expressing something. Any one could come to be certain of this thing. Every one would come to be certain of this thing. This one was one, some were quite certain, one greatly expressing something being struggling. This one was one, some were quite certain, one not greatly expressing something being struggling.

One whom some were certainly following was one who was completely charming. One whom some were certainly following was one who was charming. One whom some were following was one who was completely charming. One whom some were following was one who was certainly completely charming.

Some were certainly following and were certain that the one they were then following was one working and was one bringing out of himself then something. Some were certainly following and were certain that the one they were then following was one bringing out of himself then something that was coming to be a heavy thing, a solid thing and a complete thing.

One whom some were certainly following was one working and certainly was one bringing something out of himself then and was one who had been all his living had been one having something coming out of him.

Something had been coming out of him, certainly it had been coming out of him, certainly it was something, certainly it had been coming out of him and it had meaning, a charming meaning, a solid meaning, a struggling meaning, a clear meaning.

One whom some were certainly following and some were certainly following him, one whom some were certainly following was one certainly working.

One whom some were certainly following was one having something coming out of him something having meaning and this one was certainly working then.

This one was working and something was coming then, something was coming out of this one then. This one was one and always there was something coming out of this one and always there had been something coming out of this one. This one had never been one not having something coming out of this one. This one was one having something coming out of this one. This one had been one whom some were following. This one was one whom some were following. This one was being one whom some were following. This one was one who was working.

This one was one who was working. This one was one being one having something being coming out of him. This one was one going on having something come out of him. This one was one going on working. This one was one whom some were following. This one was one who was working.

This one always had something being coming out of this one. This one was working. This one always had been working. This one was always having something that was coming out of this one that was a solid thing, a charming thing, a lovely thing, a perplexing thing, a disconcerting thing, a simple thing, a clear thing, a complicated thing, an interesting thing, a disturbing thing, a repellent thing, a very pretty thing. This one was one certainly being one having something coming out of him. This one was one whom some were following. This one was one who was working.

This one was one who was working and certainly this one was needing to be working so as to be one being working. This one was one having something coming out of him. This one would be one all his living having something coming out of him. This one was working and then this one was working and this one was needing to be working, not to be one having something coming out of him something having meaning, but was needing to be working so as to be one working.

This one was certainly working and working was something this one was certain this one would be doing and this one was doing that thing, this one was working. This one was not one completely working. This one was not ever completely working. This one certainly was not completely working.

This one was one having always something being coming out of him, something having completely a real meaning. This one was one whom some were following. This one was one who was working. This one was one who was working and he was one needing this thing needing to be working so as to be one having some way of being one having some way of working. This one was one who was working. This one was one having something come out of him something having meaning. This one was one always having something come out of him and this thing the thing coming out of him always had real meaning. This one was one who was working. This one was one who was almost always working. This one was not one completely working. This one was one not ever completely working. This one was not one working to have anything come out of him. This one did have something having meaning that did come out of him. He always did have something come out of him. He was working, he was not ever completely working. He did have some following. They were always following him. Some were certainly following him. He was one who was working. He was one having something coming out of him something having meaning. He was not ever completely working.

NADELMAN

The Polish sculptor Elie Nadelman (1882–1946), who executed highly polished sculptured forms that tended increasingly toward geometric reduction, is another subject Stein used to define creativity in 1911, when she also worked on the portraits of Picasso and Matisse. The portrait opens with Nadelman's capacity for thinking, separate from his capacity for feeling, which is associated with loving women. Thinking and feeling are placed in the context of his central artistic preoccupation with light and its full expression, which can be attained only by an artist whose feeling merges with his thinking, as she sees Nadelman's finally failing to do. Stein said of Picasso also that he walked in the light. What in her working notes she called Nadelman's "steady brilliant inside flame" is unable to realize itself in perfected art because his feeling and thinking do not merge. As in all the early portraits, it is important not only to see but to hear such key words and the ways they are composed into the dramatic fabric of an evolving piece.

• • • • •

There was one who was a great man and his head showed this thing showed he did thinking. There was one who was a great man and his face showed this thing showed sensitive feeling. There was one who looked like the one the one who was a great one. This one looked like the other one the other one who was a great one. There was one who looked like both of them. He did look like that one the one who was a great one the one who did thinking. He did look like the other one the one who was a great one the one whose face showed this thing showed sensitive feeling. There was one and he looked like both of them, like both of the men who were great men. He did look like one. He did look like the other one. He did look like both of them.

He was one of a family in which there were seven children and he was the seventh one. He was one who had very much light coming out of him, it came out of him and it was a wonderful thing when he had been one working and then was one discovering himself being one being living.

He was one certainly doing thinking. He was one looking like one who was a great one and that one that great one had been one greatly thinking and his head did show that thing did show that he had been one greatly thinking.

The one looking like this one was one feeling light being something being existing. He was one looking like some one who was a great man and who had been one showing this thing in his face which was one showing sensitive feeling.

There was then one looking like one man who was a great man, and looking like another man who was a great man. He was one looking like both of them.

He was one feeling light being existing. He was one completely thinking about expressing light being existing. He was one completely working. He was one needing to be one completely loving women.

He was one feeling light being existing. He was completely thinking about expressing light being existing. He was one needing to be one completely loving women. He was one completely thinking about expressing loving women being completely in him. He was one who was working. He was one who was completely working when he was working. He was one looking like one man who had been a great man and greatly thinking. He was one looking like one man who had been a great man and greatly feeling light being existing. He was one looking like both of them.

Light was coming out of this one. This one was needing to be one completely loving women. This one was one who was completely working. This one was one who was completely thinking about expressing light being existing. This one was one who was completely thinking about expressing being one completely loving women.

This one was one being sometimes completely convincing as being one expressing light being existing, as expressing completely loving women, as expressing completely thinking about expressing something.

This one was one being sometime completely convincing as being one expressing light being existing, as expressing completely loving women, as expressing completely thinking about expressing something. This one was then completely convincing as one not being one realising light being existing, as completely loving women. This was one completely being convincing as being one not expressing light being existing, not expressing completely loving women.

This one was one having light coming out of him. This one was not expressing light being existing. This one was one loving women. This one was not expressing needing loving women. This one was not expressing completely loving women.

This one was one completely working. This one was one expressing thinking. This one was one completely working. This one was one completely expressing completely working. This one was one expressing thinking. This one was one having light coming out of him. This one was not one expressing light being existing. This one was one expressing thinking, this one was one expressing complete working. This one was one not expressing completely loving women. This one was one having some light coming out of him. This one was one not expressing light being existing.

PLAY

Like many of the early portraits, including *Picasso, Orta Or One Dancing,* and *Nadelman,* this piece is an exercise in disciplined writing with a reductive vocabulary—here, a motif that is a single word. The piece, which Stein in a tiny hand at the top of the first manuscript leaf marked "Story," is the most extreme example of insistent design, built on the word *play,* repeated and modulated as noun and verb in narrowly shifting grammatical forms. By this means the "story" becomes not a narrative of characters, events, and objects that might be identified but a grammatical and musical happening of one word. The word *play* must be read in all its meanings, from game to performed amusement, with the pronounced musical character ranging from children's ditties to ballet or dance. What appears to be a simple, childish procedure becomes a sophisticated redefinition of composition, a portrait of a word.

• • • • •

Play, play every day, play and play and play away, and then play the play you played to-day, the play you play every day, play it and play it. Play it and remember it and ask to play it. Play it, and play it and play away. Certainly every one wants you to play, every one wants you to play away, to play every day, to play and play, to play the play you play every day, to play and remember it and ask to play it and play it and to play away and to play every day and to-day and all day. That's the way to play, to play every day and all day, to play away, to play and play and play, to play and to remember what you play and to play it the next day and to ask to play it another day and to play it and to play it every day, to play it to-day, to play it all day.

This is the way to play, every one wants them to play all day, to play away, to play to-day, to play all day, to play every day, always to play. Every one is very glad to have them play, to have them play all day, to have them play every day, to have them play and play and play.

Every one is certain that some of them are playing, playing and playing and playing every day and all day and to-day. Every one is certain that some of them are playing and remembering and playing again again what they were playing. Some of them are certainly playing, playing, playing. Every one is wanting some of them to be playing and playing and playing, to be playing to-day, to be playing all day, to be playing every day, to be playing away.

Some are certain that playing is good for them, good for some of them, playing all day, every day is good for them, good for some of them.

Some are going to be playing all day, playing every day. Some are going to be playing to-day, going to be playing away, going to be remembering to play and going to play every day, all day, going to play and play and play.

Some play every day, play all day, play every day and all day, play all day every day. Some play and play and play and play all day and play every day.

Some play and remember what they play and ask to play that again the next day and they play it again the next day and play it all day and play and play.

Some play every day. Some play all day. Some play to-day. Some play and play. Some play and play and play. Some play every day and all day. Some play away. Some play and play and play.

BON MARCHE WEATHER

A few pieces of the spring of 1911 bear as titles the names of locations in central Paris—*Rue de Rennes*, a busy shopping street; *Galeries Lafayette*, a department store—and one, *Mi-Careme*, refers to Mid-Lent. Other pieces directly portray individuals or groups, most often artists. Au Bon Marché, literally, "at the well-priced market or store," is a department store in Paris (the adjective *bon marché* means "reasonably priced, a good buy"). *Bon Marche Weather* (Stein never used accents when writing French) shows how shopping and weather connect.

This piece is a study of a common phrase we use in talking. It begins with the weather, that eternal topic of conversation that helps us keep our days from silence and emptiness. "Very pleasant weather we are having." This oddly constructed but common colloquial phrase leads to others that employ the same phrasing about different topics—eating, traveling, the season, and above all shopping. The phrase triggers this study of how one staid conversational comment leads to another, one observation to another, one purchase to another and another in one place and another.

• • • • •

Very pleasant weather we are having. Very pleasant weather I am having. Very nice weather everybody is having. Very nice weather you are having.

Very nice eating everybody is having. Very nice eating I am having. Very nice eating they are having. Very nice eating you are having.

Very comfortable travelling they are having. Very comfortable travelling you are having. Very comfortable travelling I am having. Very comfortable travelling everybody is having.

A very bad season everybody is having. A very bad season pretty nearly everybody has been having. A very bad season they have been having. A very bad season I have been having. A very bad season you have been having. A very bad season you are having. A very bad season they are having. A very bad season almost everybody is having. A very bad season I am having.

There are a very great many things everybody is buying. There are a very great many things you are buying. There are a great many things they are buying. There are a great many things I am buying.

There are a great many things not any one is buying. There are a great many things I am not buying. There are a great many things you are not buying. There are a great many things some are not buying.

There are a great many things a great many are buying. There are a great many things a very great many are buying.

There are a great many things a great many are buying very often. There are a great many things a great many are not buying very often. There are a great many things a good many are buying very often.

Very many are being living. A very great many are being living. Some are not going to be any bigger than they are and they are going to be different in their proportions. Very many are going to be bigger than they are and are not going to change much in proportions. Very many are not going to be any taller and their proportions will later be like those of their mother. Very many are not going to be any taller and later their proportions will be different they will be like those of their father. Some are not going to be any taller and they are as tall now as their mother and their proportions will not be like those of their mother later when they are older. Some are not going to be any taller and they are as tall now as their father and their proportions will not be like those of their father.

Some are later going to be taller, some are later going to be fatter. Some are quite tall, some are quite small, some are quite fat, some are not so fat, some are quite thin, some are not so thin.

Some are ones needing to go very often to buy something they are not then buying. Some are ones not needing to go so often to buy something they are not then buying. Some buy something and it is something they might have been buying somewhere else than where they were buying that thing. Some buy something and they certainly would be buying that thing where they were buying that thing.

Certainly a very great many are buying something where they would be buying that thing. Certainly a very great many are buying something and they might not have been buying that thing. Certainly a very great many are buying something and they might have been buying that thing in some other place than where they did buy that thing.

A LONG GAY BOOK

A Long Gay Book remained unpublished until Stein herself printed it in 1933, in a volume with two other early pieces, *GMP* (*Matisse, Picasso and Gertrude Stein*) and *Many Many Women*. Stein no doubt thought of all three as books, expecting the long book to become even longer than *The Making of Americans* and adding "gay" to show that twos and threes moved faster and became livelier—gayer—than one alone. Early raw material for *A Long Gay Book*, as for *The Making of Americans*, is in the early notebooks.

Late in the composition of *The Making of Americans*, when Stein reached an impasse between systematizing personality and writing realistic stories about people in the "Alfred Hersland" chapter, she wrote into the novel a plan for a new work. She felt discouraged by the "excessively complicated questions" of personality types, "and sometime I am going to write a book and it will be a very long one and it will be all full up, completely filled up with pairs of them twos of them, sometimes threes and fours and fives but mostly with twos of men, of women, of women and men, of men and women" (549). She probably began the new book soon after writing this note and apparently finished it in the early spring of 1913.

Among the Stein papers is a list that names the real-life counterparts of the people who appear under pseudonyms in *A Long Gay Book*. Among them are relatives, friends, college classmates, and members of the Paris crowd—all known to Stein but few known to us. Among them are some people of whom Stein also wrote portraits: Paul (Picasso), Larr (Leo Stein, Gertrude's brother), Claudel (Matisse), and Eugenia (Etta Cone). The list is a simplified representation of types whose complex elements she had tried to diagram and tabulate in her notebooks. The first part of *A Long Gay Book* portrays characteristic behavior of individuals and pairs from the list and continues the study of paradigms of personality begun in *The Making of Americans*.

Stein begins the book, however, with a celebrated passage about why people have children. She considers the multitudes of kinds of human beings in the world and the realization to which they come that they were once powerless, helpless nothings. That realization makes them lose what sense of their own power they have—what Stein calls the sense of "everlasting." Some compensate for the loss by making babies, which creates "a new everlasting feeling" and empowers them to be adults. For Stein making babies is not the answer. Nor, as she continues her book, does the sense of everlasting remain central. Her struggle becomes to "see clear" and say what she sees in the immediate world. If personality is about how we see things, then writing is about how we say what we see. Stein went as far as she could in her effort to see and say with exactitude.

That new effort is in the last third of the book. Within some ten pages the manner, the matter, and the very nature of Stein's enterprise change radically. The shift looks swifter and more sudden on the few pages of text than it actually was, for a lengthy hiatus intervened before Stein wrote the final section in the style often associated with *Tender Buttons.* The shift in style—from abstract, patterned, rhythmical repetitions to a vocabulary of short, concrete, and even broken words and brief, sharp, declarative sentences that do not follow habitual grammatical order and paragraphing—represents her new way of looking at the world.

On a trip to Spain with Toklas from May until the late summer of 1912, Stein discovered the concrete, sensual world in sexual fulfillment. In the last section she speaks of love, marriage, and the whispering talk of love that is already hinted at in the continuing exchange of "stories" in *Ada,* the 1910 portrait of Toklas. Here, however, the lines sing in sexual, lyrical joy of concrete sensuality. "A private life is the long thick tree and the private life is the life for me. . . . All the times that come are the times I sing. . . ." The new way requires living and doing, not defining. "The way to be loving is to do that and not to say that something is something. . . . The only way to say what is the meaning of anything is to say that thing . . . every morning and evening."

The last third of *A Long Gay Book* records the discovery of the new reality. She confronts a world of magnificent, joyous chaos where no connections are given, no relations taken for granted, and everything is perceived anew every day in all its heterogeneity. There is no need for a totalizing system to explain the world. The old "language [is] segregating" and a new way of saying is needed, which in turn becomes a powerful way of creating the new reality. *A Long Gay Book* shows the drama of this new way happening.

• • • • •

When they are very little just only a baby you can never tell which one is to be a lady.

There are some when they feel it inside them that it has been with them that there was once so very little of them, that they were a baby, helpless and no conscious feeling in them, that they knew nothing then when they were kissed and dandled and fixed by others who knew them when they could know nothing inside them or around them, some get from all this that once surely happened to them to that which was then every bit that was then them, there are some when they feel it later inside them that they were such once and that was all that there was then of them, there are some who have from such a knowing an uncertain curious kind of feeling in them that their having been so little once and knowing nothing makes it all a broken world for them that they have inside them, kills for them the everlasting feeling; and they spend their life in many ways, and always they are trying to make for themselves a new everlasting feeling.

One way perhaps of winning is to make a little one to come through them, little like the baby that once was all them and lost them their everlasting feeling. Some can win from just the feeling, the little one need not come, to give it to them.

And so always there is beginning and to some then a losing of the everlasting feeling. Then they make a baby to make for themselves a new beginning and so win for themselves a new everlasting feeling.

It is never very much to be a baby, to be such a very little thing and knowing nothing. It certainly is a very little thing and almost nothing to be a baby and without a conscious feeling. It is nothing, to be, without anything to know inside them or around them, just a baby and that was all there was once of them and so it is a broken world around them when they think of this beginning and then they lose their everlasting feeling.

Then they make a baby or they have the feeling and so they win what once a baby lost them.

It is not very much to be a baby. It certainly is nothing just to be one, to be without a conscious feeling. It is something to have a baby come into the world by way of them but it certainly is not very much to have been the little thing that was once all them.

It is something to have a baby come into the world through them. It is nothing just to be one.

First then they make a baby. No it is never very much just to be a baby. Later in life when one is proud as a man or as a lady it is not right that they ever could have dandled and kissed and fixed them, helpless, just a baby. Such ones never can want to feel themselves ever to have been a baby.

No it is not very much to be a baby It is not right to one to begin them until a little they can resist to them who would hold them helpless, kiss and dandle and fix them as they were then, such a very little thing, just nothing inside to them. I say it is not right to many of them then to begin them, but it is not all of them who would resist them. There are some who do not feel it to be bad inside them to have been a baby without any conscious feeling of themselves inside them, to have been a little thing and that was all there was then of them, they are some who have not any proud kind of feeling in them.

They are some who like it in their later living that they were then such a very little thing and that was then all there was of them and then others kissed and dandled and fixed them. They are those who are within them weak or tender as the strongest thing inside them and to them it is very much to have been a baby and to have had others to feel gently toward them, who kissed and dandled and fixed the helpless bundle they were then. With them being proud is not strong inside them.

Some, and we can know them, have a curious uncertain kind of feeling when they think of themselves as they were then and some so lose the feeling of continuous life inside them.

It is a very different feeling each kind of man and woman has inside in them about the baby the very little thing that was once all them, and the little thing that comes into the world by them, and the very little things that all about fill the world every moment with beginning.

There are many kinds of men and many kinds of women and each kind of them have a different feeling in them about the baby that was once all them. There are many kinds of men and many kinds of women and there are many millions made of each kind of them. Each one of the many millions of each kind of them have it in them a little to be different from all the other millions of their kind of them, but all of each kind of them have it in them to have the same kind of feeling about the little thing that was once all them, about the little things that come to a beginning through them, about the little things beginning all around them. There are many kinds of men and many kinds of women and this will be a history of all the kinds of them and of pairs of them.

As I was saying every man and every woman was a little baby once and knowing nothing. I am saying there are many ways of feeling it inside them in the many kinds of men and women that they were little things once then and that was then all there was of them and they were dandled and fixed and kissed then, little things then and knowing nothing.

I am saying that there are many kinds of men and women and many millions made of each kind of them. Each one of the many millions of them has it in him to be different from all the millions of his kind of them. I am saying that all the millions of one kind of men or one kind of women have it in them to have the same kind of feeling inside them about the little thing that was all them, the baby that once was all there was of them then. One kind then of men and women have it in them when they know this was once all of them a little baby then and knowing nothing, one kind of men and one kind of women have it in them then to lose inside them their everlasting feeling, the world is then a broken world inside them, more broken for them then than death breaks it for them, ending is less of a breaking to such kind of them than beginning, they have then when they think it inside them that they were a baby then and knowing nothing they have then inside a loss of the everlasting feeling, to such a one such a beginning, being a baby and knowing nothing, breaks the everlasting feeling breaks it as dying as ending never can break it for them.

There are many ways for men and women to have it in them that they were little babies once and knowing nothing, that they were little babies once and full of life and kicking, that they were little babies once and others kissed them and dandled them and fixed them, that they were little babies once and they had loving all around and in them, that they had earthy love inside them.

Some people in their later living have pride in them, some never have anything of such a thing in them. There are many kinds of men and women and many millions of each kind of them and there is this history of all the kinds of them.

Every one has in them a fundamental nature to them with a kind of way of thinking that goes with this nature in them in all the many millions made of that kind of them. Every one then has it in them to be one of the many kinds of men or many kinds of women. There are many kinds of men and many kinds of women and of each kind of them there are always many millions in the world and any one can know by watching the many kinds there are of them and this is to be a history of all the kinds of them.

Every one of the kinds of them has a fundamental nature common to each one of the many millions of that kind of them a fundamental nature that has with it a certain way of thinking, a way of loving, a way of having or not having pride inside them, a way of suffering, a way of eating, a way of drinking, a way of learning, a way of working, a way of beginning, a way of ending. There are many kinds of them but everywhere in all living any one who keeps on looking can find all the kinds of them.

There are many kinds of them then many kinds of fundamental nature in men and in women. Sometimes it takes long to know it in them which kind of fundamental nature is inside them. Sometimes it takes long to know it in them, always there is mixed up with them other kinds of nature with the kind of fundamental nature of them, giving a flavor to them, sometimes giving many flavors to them, sometimes giving many contradictions to them, sometimes keeping a confusion in them and some of them never make it come right inside them. Mostly all of them in their later living come to the repeating that old age gives almost always to every one and then the fundamental nature of them comes out more and more in them and more and more we get to know it in them the fundamental nature in each one of them.

Always all the men and women all around have in them some one of the many kinds of men and women that have each one of them many millions made like them, always all the men and women all around have it in them to have one fundamental nature in them and other kinds of nature are mixed up in them with this kind of nature in them so it takes all the knowing one can learn with all the living to ever know it about any one around them the fundamental nature of them and how everything is mixed up in them.

As I was saying the mixture in them of other kinds of nature to them gives a flavor to some kinds of them to some kinds of men and some kinds of women, makes a group of them that have to them flavor as more important in them than the fundamental nature in them and the kind of thinking and feeling that goes with the fundamental nature in them. The flavor in them is real inside them more real to them than the fundamental nature in them, the flavor the other kinds of nature mixed up in them give to them. To many of such a kind of them the flavor is to them the reallest thing in them, the reallest thing about them, and this is a history of many of such of them.

In this book there will be discussion of pairs of people and their relation, short sketches of innumerable ones, Ollie, Paul; Paul, Fernande; Larr and me, Jane and me, Hattie and Ollie, Margaret and Phillip, Claudel and Mrs. Claudel, Claudel and Martin, Maurice and Jane, Helen and John, everybody I know, Murdock and Elise, Larr and Elise, Larr and Marie, Jenny Fox and me, Sadie and Julia, everybody I can think of ever, narrative after narrative of pairs of people, Martin and Mrs. Herford, Bremer and Hattie, Jane and Nellie, Henrietta and Jane and some one and another one, everybody Michael and us and Victor Herbert, Farmert and us, Bessie Hessel and me.

Some one if they dreamed that their mother was dead when they woke up would not put on mourning. Some if they believed in dreams as much as the one who dreamed that their mother was dead and did not put on mourning would if they had dreamed that their mother was dead would put on mourning. Hattie if she dreamed that her mother was dead would not put on mourning. Mrs. Claudel if she believed in dreams as much as Hattie and had dreamed that her mother was dead would put on mourning.

Some would be surprised that some could dream that their mother was dead and then not put on mourning. Some would be surprised that any one having dreamed that their mother was dead could think about then putting on mourning.

Some people know other ones. This is being a history of kinds of men and women, when they were babies and then children and then grown men and women and then old ones and the one and the ones they were in relation with at any time, at some time.

This is a general leading up to a description of Olive who is an exception in being one being living. Then there can be a description of the Pauline group and of the Pauline quality in Ollie and then there can be a complete description of the Pauline group and there can be a description of ones who could be ones who are not at all married ones a whole group of them of hundreds of them, and they grade from Eugenia to Mabel Arbor who is not like them in being one who could have been one not being a married one. Then once more one can begin with the Pauline group and Sophie among them, and then one can go through whole groups of women to Jane Sands and her relation to men and so to a group of men and ending up with Paul. Then one can take a fresh start and begin with Fanny and Helen and run through servants and adolescents to Lucy and so again to women and to men and how they love, how women love and how they do not love, how men do not love, how men do love, how women and men do and do not love and so on to men and women in detail and so on to Simon as a type of man.

Then going completely in to the flavor question how persons have the flavor they do there can be given short sketches of Farmert, Alden, of Henderson and any other man one can get having very much flavor and describing the complications in them one can branch off into women, Myrtle, Constance, Nina Beckworth and others to Ollie and then say of them that it is hard to combine their flavor with other feelings in them but it has been done and is being done and then describe Pauline and from Pauline go on to all kinds of women that come out of her, and then go on to Jane, and her group and then come back to describe Mabel Arbor and her group, then Eugenia's group always coming back to flavor idea and Pauline type, then go on to adolescents, mixing and mingling and contrasting. Then start afresh with Grace's group, practical, pseudo masculine. Then start afresh with Fanny and Helen and business women, earthy type, and kind of intellect. Enlarge on this and then go back to flavor, to pseudo flavor, Mildred's group, and then to the concentrated groups.

From then on complicate and complete giving all kinds of pictures and start in again with the men. Here begin with Victor Herbert group and ramify from that. Simon is bottom of Alden and Bremer and the rest. Go on then to how one would love and be loved as a man or as a woman by each kind that could or would love any one.

Any one being started in doing something is going on completely doing that thing, a little doing that thing, doing something that is that thing. Any one not knowing anything of any one being one starting that one in doing that thing is one doing that thing completing doing that thing and being then one living in some such thing.

Some are ones being certain that any one doing a thing and having been started in doing that thing are ones not having been taught to do that thing, are ones who have come to do that thing. Some are certain that not any one has been taught to do a thing if that one is doing a thing and not any one is remembering that that thing is something that has just been done.

Doing something is interesting to some if not any one is remembering that that thing has just been done. Doing something is interesting to some if not any one is remembering that any one was one beginning doing some such thing. Doing something is interesting to some when those are remembering that every one has been doing that thing in having been shown that thing. Doing something is interesting to some when they are certain that all having been doing that thing have been completely dead and have not been forgotten. Doing something is interesting to some when they are certain that very many being dead were ones completely doing that thing. Doing things are interesting to some when some one is beginning to be finishing having done that thing. Doing something is interesting to some when they are remembering that every one could be doing that thing. Doing something is interesting to some when they are certain that every one should do that thing.

When some are very little ones they very completely do some thing. Some are certain that every one when they are very little ones are ones who could very completely do some thing. Some when they are very little ones very completely then do something. Some then find in this thing that beginning and ending is not at all something being existing. Some find in this thing that beginning and ending is not at all interesting. Some are finding in this thing that nothing is satisfying. Some are finding in this thing that some other thing is interesting. Some are finding in this thing that any one is being one being living. Some are finding in this thing that every one is one being existing. Some are finding in this thing that very many are being existing and are not completing then anything.

Some are certain that when any one is a very little one they are not then beginning anything. Some are finding in this thing that beginning and ending is being existing. Some are finding in this thing that beginning and ending are not being existing. Some are not finding anything in this thing. Some are finding in this thing that any one is being existing. Some are finding in this thing that some are being existing. Some are finding in this thing that not any one is being existing.

Any one being one being a little one is being then one having some, having some one knowing something of that thing. Some being a little one are asking then how some other one could have been one being a little one. Some being a little one are then not needing anything of asking anything. Some being a little one are forgetting then having been asking anything. Some being a very little one are not then needing being one being existing.

Some are not needing that any one being a little one is then being existing. Some are not needing any one being a little one. Some are not needing any one having been a little one. Some are not needing that any one has been one being existing. Some are needing that every one is being one being existing.

Being a little one is what any one being existing is being one knowing is existing. Being a little one is then existing enough for every one to be knowing something of some such thing.

Any one loving any one is being one in some way loving some one. There can be complete lists of ones loving. There can be complete lists of ones loving again and again.

If there is a thin thing and some one is seeing through that thing if there is a thin thing, very many are telling about seeing through that thing. If there is a thin thing some are saying that it is like some other thing. If there is a thin thing some are denying that it is a thin thing. If there is a thin thing some are not hearing what some one has been saying who has been saying that the thin thing is a thin thing.

There are thin things and some of them are hanging in front of something. There are thin things and they are nicely thin things, things nicely being thin enough and letting then all the light in. If there are thin things they are thin enough to hang and let light in. If there are thin things it is certain that they are like some other things. There are thin things and any one not having seen them is not completely certain that they are thin things. They are thin things the things that are thin things and some have seen them and have said then that those things are thin things.

A man in his living has many things inside him. He has in him his being certain that he is being one seeing what he is looking at just then, he has in him the kind of certain feeling of seeing what he is looking at just then that makes a kind of them of which a list will be made in making out a list of every one. This feeling of being certain of seeing what he is looking at just then comes from the being in him that is being then in him, comes from the mixing in him of being then one being living and being one then being certain of that thing.

In all of the men being living some are more certain than other ones who are very much like them are more certain of seeing the thing at which they are looking.

In all men in their daily living, in every moment they are living, in all of them, in all the time they are being living, in the times they are doing, in the times they are not doing something, in all of them there is always something in them of being certain of seeing the thing at which they are looking. In all of them in all the millions of men being living there is some feeling of being certain of seeing the thing at which they are looking. Some of the many millions of men being living have stronger the feeling of being certain of seeing the thing at which they are looking than others of them.

There are many millions of men being living and many millions are very certain that they are seeing the thing at which they are looking. In many men there is a mixture in them of being strongly certain of seeing the thing at which they are looking and just being certain that they are seeing the thing at which they are looking. In some men there is a mixture in them of being certain of being strongly certain, of not being strongly certain, of being quite certain, of being uncertain that they are seeing the thing at which they are all looking. In all the men who are being living there is something of being certain of seeing the thing at which they are looking. In all the men who are being living there is a kind of feeling about being certain of seeing that at which they are looking.

Loving is loving and being a baby is something. Loving is loving. Being a baby is something. Having been a baby is something. Not having been a baby is something that comes not to be anything and that is a thing that is beginning. Having been a baby is something having been going on being existing. Not having been a baby is something not being existing. Loving is loving. Not having been a baby could be everything. Having been a baby is something. Being a baby is something. Loving is something. Loving is loving. Not being a baby is something.

Any one has been a baby and has then been something. Any one is not a baby and is then something. Not coming to be a baby is not anything.

Not coming to be loving is something. Coming to be loving is something. Loving is something. Babies have been existing. Babies are existing. Babies are something being existing. Not being babies is something being existing.

Loving is something. Anything is something. Babies are something. Being a baby is something. Not being a baby is something.

Coming to be anything is something. Not coming to be anything is something. Loving is something. Not loving is something. Loving is loving. Something is something. Anything is something.

Anything is something. Not coming to anything is something. Loving is something. Needing coming to something is something. Not needing to coming to something is something. Loving is something. Anything is something.

How can any one be one any one is loving when every one is a fat one or a thin one or in between. How can any one be one loving any one when every one is one not loving some. Every one loving any one is a thin one or a fat one or in between. Any one loving any one is one loving in being a fat one or a thin one or in between. Being a fat one and loving is something. Being a thin one and loving is something. Being in between being a thin one and being a fat one and loving is something. Being a fat one or being a thin one or being in between is being one being that one. Loving is something. Being a fat one is something. Being a thin one is something. Being in between being a fat one and a thin one is something. Being loving is something. Being not loving is something. Being believing in loving is something. Being not believing in loving is something. Being certain that not being a baby is something is something. Being certain that being a baby is something is something. Why is any one being something? Any one is being something because any one is being one being a fat one or a thin one or in between.

Loving is being existing. Loving has been being existing. Loving being existing and some being ones being loving and some having been ones being loving loving is being existing. Loving is being existing and some are ones being loving. Loving is being existing and some are ones some are loving. Loving is being existing and some are believing that loving is being existing. Loving is being existing and some are believing that babies are being existing. Babies are being existing and some are believing that loving is being existing. Babies are being existing. Loving is being existing. Some are believing that loving and babies are being existing. Any one can come to believe that babies have been existing. Some can come to believe that loving has been existing. Some babies are being living. Any one can come to believe that some babies are being living. Believing something is what some are doing. Not believing something is what some are doing. Loving is what some are doing. Not loving are what some are doing. Being one being that one is something. Any one being that one is being that one. Loving is existing. Believing is existing. Any one is existing. Babies are existing. Anything any one has been beginning is something. Any one begun is something. Not any one is certain of being begun when they are babies. Not any one is then certain of that thing that anything is something. Some loving is existing. Some babies are existing. Loving being existing is something. Some being existing is something. Any one being existing is something. Not every one being existing is something. Everything is something. Any one can be certain that not anything is anything. Any one can be certain that loving is not existing. Any one can be certain that babies are existing. Any one can be certain of something. Some can be certain that loving is existing. Some can be certain of anything. Some can be certain that loving is existing. Some can be certain of anything. Some can be certain that babies are existing. Some can be certain of that thing.

Some can be certain of something. Some can be certain that babies are existing. Some can be certain of anything. Some can be certain that babies are existing. Some can not be certain of something. Some can not be certain that babies are existing. Some can not be certain of anything, they cannot be certain that babies are existing. Some cannot be certain of everything, some of such of them can be certain that babies are existing, some of such of them can not be certain of babies being existing.

Every one being some one, every one is like some other one. Every one is like some is like some other one. Each one is a kind of a one. Each one is of a kind of a one and of that kind of them some one is a very bright one, some one is a stupid one, some one is a pretty one, some one is an ugly one, some one is a certain one, some one is an uncertain one, some one is in between being a bright one and a stupid one, some one is in between being a pretty one and an ugly one, some one is in between being a certain one and an uncertain one.

There are kinds of them that is to say there are some who look like others quite look like others. All of them are of that kind of them, all who are ones who look like some, all of them are together that kind of them. There can be lists and lists of kinds of them. There can be very many lists of kinds of them. There can be diagrams of kinds of them, there can be diagrams showing kinds of them and other kinds of them looking a little like another kind of them. There can be lists and diagrams, some diagrams and many lists. There can be lists and diagrams. There can be lists.

It is a simple thing to be quite certain that there are kinds in men and women. It is a simple thing and then not any one has any worrying to be doing about any one being any one. It is a simple thing to be quite certain that each one is one being a kind of them and in being that kind of a one is one being, doing, thinking, feeling, remembering and forgetting, loving, disliking, being angry, laughing, eating, drinking, talking, sleeping, waking like all of them of that kind of them. There are enough kinds in men and women so that any one can be interested in that thing that there are kinds in men and women.

It is a very simple thing to be knowing that there are kinds in men and women. It is a simple thing to be knowing that being born in a religion, in a country, in a position is a thing that is not disturbing anything. It is a different thing to the one being that one, quite a different thing. It is quite a different thing and each one is of a kind of them is completely quite of a kind of them and it is an interesting thing to some to make groups of them, to diagram kinds of them, to have lists of them, of kinds in men and women. Some are not worrying are not at all worrying about men and women. Some of such of them are knowing that there are kinds of them. Some of such of them have some lists of them. Some of such of them have diagrams of the kinds there are of them.

Any one being one being of a kind of one is doing something. Every one is doing something. That is an interesting thing to some. Some are having lists of ones doing anything. Some are having diagrams of that thing.

Any one is one doing something. Any one is one being of a kind of one and is one doing something in the way the ones looking like that one are doing something.

Being a dead one is something. Being a dead one is something that is happening. Being a dead one being something that is happening, some are completely knowing that thing knowing that being a dead one is something that is happening. Being loving is something that is happening. Being loving is happening. Being a dead one is happening.

Being loving is happening. Being a dead one is happening. Completely loving is something that is happening. Being a dead one is something that is happening. Some are knowing all that thing, are quite knowing all that thing.

Being completely loving is something that is happening. Being completely loving is something that is completely happening. Being a dead one is something that is happening. Being completely loving is something that is happening. Being completely loving is something that is happening and some then are completely knowing that thing, are knowing that completely loving is happening. Being a dead one is certainly happening. Some are knowing all of that thing, of being a dead one being happening. Some are knowing all of completely loving being happening and are completely using that thing completely using loving being completely happening. Being a dead one is completely happening. There is then not any way of using any such thing of being a dead one being happening. Any one can know something of being a dead one being happening. Some can know completely such a thing. Some of such of them are not needing to be using such a thing. Some of such of them are completely using loving being completely happening.

Loving can be completely happening. Some can then be using that thing and needing then that everything is beginning. Loving can be completely happening. Some can then be completely using that thing and can be then not be beginning, not be ending anything. Loving can be completely happening. Some can use something then in knowing that thing. Being a dead one is completely happening. Some can completely use that thing.

Any one knowing anything is repeating that thing and being one repeating that thing makes of that one one coming to be one knowing something of some being ones beginning some other thing, beginning that thing. Any one having been doing anything and repeating the thing and not repeating the thing can come to be one knowing something of some being ones not saying anything in any way about that thing. Any one buying something and then not going on buying that thing can be one knowing something of some not saying anything to that one, saying very little to that one.

Being a young one and an older one and a middle aged one and an older one and an almost old one and an old one is something that any one can know by remembering reading. Remembering reading is something any one is needing to be one knowing that one is being a young one, an older one, a middle aged one, an almost old one, an old one.

When they are very little just a baby they cannot know that thing. When they are a little bigger they can know that other ones are older and younger. When they are a little bigger they can remember that they were littler. When they are a little older they can know that they are then not what any one is describing, they are knowing then that they are older than the description, than every description of the age they are then. When they are older they are beginning to remember their reading, they are beginning to believe a description of them. When they are a little older they are knowing then that they just have been younger. When they are a little older they are beginning to know they will be older. When they are a little older they know they are old enough to know that age is a different thing than it has been. When they are a little older they are knowing they are beginning then to be young to some who are much older and they are beginning to be old to some who are much younger. When they are a little older they know they are beginning to be afraid of changing thinking about ageing, they are beginning then to know something of being uncertain about what is being young and what is being old, they are beginning then to be afraid of everything. When they are a little older they are coming to be certain that they have been younger. When they are a little older they are beginning to be certain that age has no meaning. When they are coming to be a little older they are coming to be saying that they are beginning to be wondering if age has not some meaning. When they are a little older they are certainly beginning to be believing what they remembered reading about being young and older and middle aged and older and almost old and old. When they are a little older they are commencing to be certain that ageing has meaning. When they are a little older they are certain that they can be older and that being older will sometime be coming. When they are a little older they are commencing mentioning ageing to prepare any one for some such thing being something that will be showing in them. When they are a little older they are commencing mentioning that they are expecting anything. When they are a little older they are commencing mentioning any such thing quite often. When they are a little older they are not mentioning being an older one, they are then mentioning that many are existing who are being young ones. When they are a little older they are mentioning anything and mentioning it quite often. When they are a little older any one is mentioning that thing and not mentioning everything and they are mentioning being a little older and they are mentioning everything. When they are a little older it depends then on how much longer they will be being living just how long they will be mentioning anything again and again. They are then completely old ones and not any one is knowing everything of that thing.

Knowing everything is something. Knowing everything and telling all of that thing is something. Knowing everything and not meaning anything in knowing everything is something.

Meaning something is something. Meaning something and telling that thing is something.

Knowing something is something. Knowing something and not meaning anything is something. Knowing something and not meaning anything and telling that thing is something.

Any one having finished needing being that one is one who might finish then in some way being that one. Any one having finished needing being that one is one going on being that one. Any one being finished with needing being that one is one who might then come to almost finish being that one. Any one coming to be finished with needing being that one might come then to finish being one.

Any one meeting any one who might come to finish being that one is believing is not believing that one will come then to finish being one. Some do then finish being one. Some do then not finish being any one. Any one can believe of any one who is finished being that one that that one will finish being one.

Any one can be finished with some one. Any one can be finished with some. Some can be finished with some. Some can be finished with some one.

Any one can be finished with some. Any one can be finished with some one. Some one is one some one can be finished with and that one is then one who is not finished with another one.

Finishing with one finishing with another one is something any one doing that thing is doing. Finishing with any one is what any one doing that thing is doing. Finishing with one, finishing with some, finishing with some other one is something any one doing any such thing is doing. Finishing with one is one thing. Finishing with some is one thing. Finishing with another one is another thing. Finishing with some other ones is another thing. Finishing with the same ones is another thing.

Finishing with some one is what any one is doing who is one finishing with some one. Finishing with some is what any one is doing who is one finishing with some.

Finishing with some and remembering that thing is what some are doing who are remembering everything. Finishing with some one and remembering that thing is what some are doing when they are finishing with some one. Finishing with some and not remembering that thing is what some are doing who are remembering anything. Finishing with some one and not remembering that thing is what some are doing who have finished with some one.

Some one is finished with some one and that one is one who was one not any one needed to be finished with as that one was one being one not coming to any finishing. Finishing with such a one is what some one is doing and that one then is knowing that thing and not any one then is finishing any such thing. Being finished with some one is what has happened to some one and that one is then one being one not having finished anything as that thing is something that not any one can be beginning to be finishing. Finishing with some one is something and that finishing then is done. Finishing with some one is something some one is beginning and that thing then is begun.

Liking something and being then one offering something is what some are doing. Liking something and paying something then and not forgetting anything then is what some are doing.

Some one is wanting to have some one come again. That one is not coming again. Some are then remembering everything. Some are then wanting to be certain that the one will perhaps come again.

Being one feeling that some one has come is what some are doing. Being one feeling that that has been happening that some one has come and has been looking is what some are doing.

Being finished with one and with another one and with another one is what some are doing. Being finished with one is something. Being finished with one and with another one and with another one and with another one is something. Being finished with one, that is, being finished with having been liking being needing one is something. Being finished with one, that is, being finished with having been liking one is something. Being finished with knowing one is something. Being finished with one is something. Being finished with one and with another one and with another one is something.

Being listening when some one is telling something one is liking is something. Being finished with being listening when some one is telling something one is liking is something. Being listening is something. Having been listening is something. Having not been listening when some one has not come to be talking is something. Having been listening when some one has not come to be talking is something.

Some one, Sloan, listened and was hearing something. He went on then beginning anything. Sloan had heard something. He did not hear that thing again. He asked then, he asked if he would hear something like that thing. He asked it again. He listened then. He did not hear that thing. He began anything. He had expected to hear something. He did hear something. He began anything.

Some one, Gibbons, did hear something. He almost always heard something. He did say everything. He did know that he almost always heard something. He did know that he said everything. He did know that it almost sounded like something when he said everything. He did know that thing.

He did know he almost always heard something. He did know that was something.

Johnson did not tell any one that he told everything. He told some that he told something. He did tell something and he told any one that he had told something, that he would tell something, that he was telling something. He did tell some one that he could tell something. He did tell some that he was telling something. He did listen, he did not tell everything to any one of having been doing such a thing of having been listening.

Hobart did not expect anything in being one listening. He was then doing that thing and then he was regretting completely politely regretting not having been able just then to quite complete that thing to quite complete listening. He had been listening, he had not been hearing everything, he had been hearing something, he was completely pleased with that thing, with having then quite heard something. He was completely polite then, completely pleasant then, completely then satisfying any feeling of understanding being the one having heard something then.

Carmine had quite listened then and remembered then something that was not then something that was completely needing such remembering. He had listened some, he had heard everything, he had remembered something and that was not a thing to completely satisfy any desire for remembering he could have been having. He remembered something. He quite remembered that thing.

Watts looked in listening, he completely looked then. He listened and he was looking, he was completing looking, he had completely looked then. He could go on then completely looking.

Arthurs always listened and if he could then have remembered anything he would then have been one being quite charming. He was pleasant, he had charm, he was listening, he was expecting to be coming to be one listening and hearing and remembering.

To be finished with any one is something. Some one is finished with some one. Some one is finished with one.

Vrais is some one with whom some one is almost finished and that is not surprising and that is not exciting although the one finished with him is one who has said of him said of Vrais that he was a faithful one. Vrais was a faithful one that is to say he was not always coming when he might have been pleasantly coming to be being that one being a faithful one but he was one who had come and had been then a faithful one and had come again sometime and had been then a faithful one. The one who was finishing then with him was one who had said that Vrais was a faithful man.

That one was finished with Vrais that is to say Vrais was not needing then to be one coming sometime to be then a faithful one. Vrais was not needing then to be a faithful one for that one who had been one who had said that Vrais was a faithful one. There were some then who were coming and any one then coming was a faithful one and the one who had said that Vrais was a faithful one was one then not finishing but finished with him with his having been one sometimes coming and having been then a faithful one. He had been one sometimes coming and had been a faithful one and not one was finished with that thing. There were enough then coming, all of them were enough then to be any one coming sometimes and being a faithful one. Vrais was then one with whom some one was finished then and not needing anything, not needing any one being a faithful one in being coming sometimes, in being completely a faithful one in having been coming sometimes.

Some one was finished with Jane Sands. Several were finished with Jane Sands. Any one could come to be certain that she had not ever been a dangerous person. Any one could come to be certain that she had not gone on doing something. Any one could come to be certain that she had not been meaning what she was living in meaning. Any one could come to be certain that she had not been understanding anything. Any one could be certain that she had not begun anything. Any one could come to be certain that she was not feeling what she was one completely resonating. Any one could be certain that she had been completely born and been a stupid one. Any one could come to be enough finished with her to be quite finished then quite finished then with her. Any one could come not to be paying any attention to having been finished with, when they had been for a little time finished with her. Any one then could be one being finished with her. Any one could be such a one. Any one was some time some such a one. Any one was one who was finished with her when they were certain of anything of her everything.

Larr was one, almost any one could be certain not any one would be one being completely finished with him. Not any one was completely finished with him that is to say he was one who could be one with whom not any one had been completely finished. One could be completely finished with him and one was completely finished and he was one with whom not any one was completely finished that is to say he was one who might be one with whom not any one was finished. He was one with whom some were more finished than they might have been if he had been one being more completely one with whom not any one was completely finished. Some were quite nearly enough finished with him so that for them they were finished enough with him.

Mrs. Gaston was one who if she had been one not beginning being one not going on being the one she had been would have been one whom not any one would have been one feeling anything about finishing with her being existing. She was beginning being one and that one was one repeating what was not succeeding and some were certain that very many had come to be remembering that finishing with her was existing. Any one could come to remember something of finishing with her being something being existing.

George Clifton said himself that any one wanting to know that he was one some had come to be finished with should come to him, he could tell them something of some such thing. He could tell them that not every one could be finished with him, that he was finished with himself and that was a thing that could have been something that was not happening and certainly then he had been a healthy one and not needing everything and having everything was something he had been having and he could be having everything and he was not having everything and he was finished enough with having everything and he was finished enough for any one who was not wanting to be having him to be finished with him.

Loving is certain if one is going on loving. Loving then in a way is certain. Loving is certain when one is going on loving.

Loving is certain. Going on loving is something when loving is certain. Loving is certain and going on loving is something.

Some one being loving is going on loving. Some one being certain that loving is something is going on loving. Some one going on loving is certain that loving is something.

Some one loving is certain that that one is going on loving. Any loving is certain and any one being certain is going on loving. Some one loving is certain that going on loving is something.

Some are certain of going on loving as being existing. Some are completely certain of going on loving being existing. Some are certain about loving being about loving not being existing. Some are not certain about loving being, about loving not being existing. Some are certain about loving going on about loving not going on. Some are not certain about loving going on, about loving, not going on.

Any one looking is loving, that is sometimes quite certain. Sometimes any one looking and looking again is loving. Sometimes any one looking is loving. That is something.

Any one looking is loving. Any one remembering that thing is remembering anything. Any one looking is loving. Any one not remembering that thing is not remembering that thing.

Any one remembering about looking and loving is mentioning anything and resenting something. Any one looking is loving and any one is mentioning anything, and any one is resenting something.

Any one resenting something is remembering that any one looking and loving is looking and loving. Any one resenting something is mentioning something. Any one mentioning anything is looking and loving.

Looking and loving is something. Remembering anything is something. Mentioning anything is something. Resenting something is something.

Remembering that looking is loving is something. Remembering that any one looking has been loving is something. Remembering that looking is loving and not then mentioning that thing is something. Remembering that looking is loving and being then mentioning that thing is something.

Having been one being one who had been looking is anything. Having been one who had been looking and any one had then been mentioning that looking is loving is anything. Having been one who had been looking and having been then one being one not mentioning that looking is loving is anything.

Having been one looking and being one then having mentioned that thing and some one then having mentioned that looking is loving is anything. Having been one looking and having been then one having been mentioning looking and any one then mentioning that looking is loving is then anything.

Having been looking and not loving, having been not looking and not loving is everything. Having been not looking and not loving and having been looking and not loving and having been looking and loving is everything. Having been not looking and not loving is everything.

Having been looking and loving, and not looking and loving, and loving and looking, and loving and remembering having been looking is something. Having been not looking and loving is something. Having been loving and not looking is something. Having been loving and looking is something.

Each one is one. Each one looking is that one the one then looking. Each one looking and loving is then that one the one looking then and loving. Looking and loving is anything.

Some one, that one was one who was married to some one and he was one whose name was Claudel and he was married to one and she and he knew that thing knew that he was looking and loving. They were married the two of them. They had been married and they had three children. They were married and he had come to be looking and in a way then he was loving. Mrs. Claudel knew then that he had been looking and in a way then was loving. He was looking at one whom he had naturally been looking at. He went on looking at her and some had been doing that thing had been looking at her. She had been looking at any one and touching every one and certainly then she was one not loving, not looking, she was one touching any one and not looking and not loving. She was one touching any one and telling every one that she was not looking and not loving, that she was touching any one, that she was not looking at any one, that she was not loving any one, and it was this thing that she was doing, she was not looking, she was not loving, she might be touching any one. He looked then and in some way then he was looking and loving some then. She was not looking then, she was all loving then, she was then being one who had not been looking, who was loving then, who was quite touching any one then. She was then one going on loving and leaving then. Mrs. Claudel then was continuing in being one married to Mr. Claudel then. They were married then. They had been quite married, they were quite married then.

Paymen knew all of them. He knew others too then. He knew that any one looking and loving might be one refusing to be marrying.

Looking and loving and refusing to be marrying is something. Mayman was being one knowing that looking and loving and refusing to be marrying is something. He was looking and loving and refusing to be marrying.

He was looking and not loving. He was looking and seeing one, he was looking and seeing Miss Hendry and he was not loving. He was looking and he went on then looking and he was looking then. He was not loving, he was not then refusing to be marrying. He was then looking and looking then. He was not then looking and loving and refusing to be marrying. He was looking then, he was looking at Miss Hendry then.

He was looking and loving he was looking and loving and he was loving and he was looking and he was not then beginning to be refusing to be marrying. He was looking then at Miss Damien. He was looking and loving. He was looking. He was loving and looking. He was not being then being one looking and loving and refusing to be marrying. He was loving then and looking. He was loving then and not looking. He was looking then. He was looking and loving then. He was not looking then. He was not looking and loving then. He was not looking then at Miss Damien.

He was looking at Miss Lane then. He was not looking and loving then.

He was looking then. He was not looking at Miss Lane and loving her then. He was not loving Miss Lane. He had been looking at Miss Lane.

He had been refusing to be marrying Miss Walting. He had been hoping to be refusing to be marrying Miss Walting. He had not been needing to be quite deciding to do that thing to be refusing to marry Miss Walting.

He had been looking at and not refusing to marry Minnie Claudel. He had been looking at Minnie Claudel. He had not been refusing to marry Minnie. He married Miss Walting.

He knew that Mr. Claudel had been looking and loving. He knew that Mr. Claudel had come to doing that thing. He knew that looking and loving is not anything. He quite knew that thing. He knew that Mrs. Claudel knew that thing that looking and loving is not anything. Mr. Claudel had been looking and loving. Any one could be one suffering.

Any one being one suffering can be one having been mentioning something of some such thing. Any one being one suffering is one being one going on then having been one mentioning something of some such thing. One, Marie, had been mentioning that suffering was existing. She had been one who had been mentioning that suffering is being existing.

In mentioning that suffering is being existing Marie was beginning the completing of being one mentioning something. She was mentioning that suffering is being existing. She was mentioning this thing. She had not mentioned any such thing to Haick, she was not mentioning any such thing to him. She had mentioned that suffering is being existing. He was not one asking any one to remember being one mentioning that suffering is being existing. He was not one mentioning to any one to mention to any one that suffering is being existing. He was not mentioning to any one to not mention to any one that suffering is being existing. He was not mentioning to any one that suffering is being existing. He was not mentioning to any one that any one was mentioning that suffering is being existing. He was asking some one to tell him to whom Marie was coming soon to marrying. That one was then not mentioning any one. He and Marie then mentioned that he and she were going to marry each other very soon and very soon then they did marry and they did have two children, and Marie was married to him and he was married to Marie and each of them were ones who were succeeding in being the ones they were being in living, they were ones being married ones who were a family then, a family succeeding quite succeeding in living.

Any one repeating that any one can come again is one repeating something. Any one repeating that every one does come again is one repeating anything.

One repeating that some one coming again is one who always will be welcome is one repeating everything. One repeating that when some one comes that one will be welcome is one repeating everything. One repeating that any one coming is one being welcome is one repeating that thing. One repeating that any one coming and saying that he has come then is one who can be welcome, is one repeating being one who has been saying that thing. One repeating that some one has said something and was then one who was not welcome is one who is repeating everything.

One who has been coming and is one then not going on being one who is welcome is one who is then not remembering that he would have been coming if he had not been welcome if he had not then come to not coming. This one was one who was not then welcome. This one was then one who had not been coming.

One who had been telling something was then repeating that thing, the thing he had been telling and when he was doing that thing repeating the thing he had been telling he was being one who would be one remembering that some one had been very sorry for him and that he had been completely sorry then for that one and had completely been giving himself to that one.

One who had been telling one who was married to him that she was something was one who was telling some one who was married to another one that he should be one going on being that one being one who was needing something of being married to be one being living. The one telling that thing was telling the wife of the other man that she was one who was not needing anything to be one having been married to the one to whom she was married. They were then not welcome the one and his wife to the wife of the other one.

One who was married to some one was one who would be one married to some other one. This was one who was one who came to be married to the other one. Any one would be one then married to some other one.

When one is born and not remembering any one can be one having been one who would have been one bathing that one if the one who was born then and not remembering had not come to be one knowing that some one who had been a very little one then was the one who had been bathing that one. Knowing something and telling it again and again is a happy thing if the two of them are then completely knowing that thing that knowing a thing and telling it again and again is a very happy thing.

In beginning going on living any one is beginning, any one is not beginning. In beginning going on living any one is going on living.

Any one is going on living. Any one in going on living is going on living. Any one in going on living is certainly going on living. In going on living any one is doing something, is doing going on living. In going on living any one is going on beginning going on living. In beginning going on living any one is going on doing that thing.

Going on living is what any one is doing. In going on living any one is doing that thing is going on living.

One in going on living is doing that thing and in doing that thing is one remembering that any one is going on living and is doing that thing.

In going on living, in doing that thing one is one doing something that is happening so that going on living is continuing. In going on living each one is doing enough to be one going on and be one going on living.

Each day is every day, that is to say, any day is that day. Any day is that day that is to say if any day has been a day there will be another day and that day will be that day.

Each day is a day. Any day is a day. Each day is a day. Each day and each day is every day. Every day is a day.

Every day is a day and some day some will know that that day is the day that is that day. Every day is a day and some are thinking what each one is doing if a day is a day, if any day is a day, if every day is a day. Some one is thinking about any one doing something, about every one doing something, and about any day being a day. Some one is thinking something of some doing something and any day being a day and every day being a day.

If every day is a day and every one does something every day, every one can be certain that each day is a day and some can be thinking about what some are doing every day.

In each day being a day and in every day being a day and any day being a day, in every day being a day any one being one going on being living in each day being a day any one being one is being one doing that thing being one having been one going on being living. In each day being a day and any day is a day, any day being a day, in each day any one coming to be one continuing being living is one having been one being living, having been one going on being living.

Any day being a day, each one every day is being that one the one being that one. In each day any one is being one. In each day any one being one is being that one.

Any day being a day one being that one is one being that one then. Any day being a day any one being then one and going on being that one is one going on being that one.

Any day one being that one is one being that one. Any day is a day. Any one being one is being that one. Any one going on being one is being that one. Any day is a day. Every day is a day. Each day is a day. Each one is one. Any one is one. Any one is the one that one is.

Each day being a day Nettie was telling that thing, was telling that any day is a day, that every day is a day. Nettie telling that any day is a day is telling that any day is a day. Nettie telling that again and again is telling often that any day is a day.

Nettie telling that any day is a day is telling that any day being a day, any day is a day. Nettie telling again and again that any day being a day any day is a day is telling that again and telling it, telling it that any day is a day.

George Clifton telling that a day is a day is telling it every day. George telling that a day is a day is telling it every day, is telling every day that a day is a day. George telling that any day is a day is telling that every day has been a day. George telling every day that a day is a day is telling every day that each day was a day. George telling that each day was a day is telling it any day. George telling that each day was a day is telling it every day, is telling it any day. George is telling every day that each day was a day. George is telling any day that any day is a day.

Any day is a day and a day, a day that is any day is a day. A day that is a day is a day. Any day is a day and Elise was one being one and every day was a day. Every day was a day, every day being a day every day was a day Elise was being one. Elise being one every day, being that one every day, Elise being that one any day was one, every day, doing everything of being that one. Every day she was doing everything of being that one.

In doing everything every day of being that one she was one every day doing everything of being that one.

In doing everything every day, in doing everything of being that one she was one running, that is she was one running when she was just coming to be doing something of doing everything of being that one. She was every day doing everything of being that one. She was one running any day, she was one running every day. She was one running when she was just coming to be doing something of everything and she was doing everything of being that one every day, she was doing everything of being that one any day.

Any day is a day. Every day is a day and any one not needing that day just then is one not needing that any day is a day. Some one not needing that every day is a day is one not needing that every day is a day. Some one not coming to be wanting some day to be a day and having every day being a day is some one coming sometime to be one remembering that every day is a day, is one remembering any day that any day is a day. Madeleine is one remembering any day that any day is a day. She is one having been remembering any day that any day is a day.

In remembering that any day is a day, in remembering that thing some are remembering that they are not going on being living. In remembering that every day is a day some are remembering that they have been going on living.

In remembering that a day is a day some are being one kind of a one. In not remembering that a day is a day they are being that kind of a one.

Some are not remembering, some are remembering something about any day being a day. Some are remembering that they have been remembering that any day is a day.

In a day being a day, that is in each day being a day, that is in there being one day and then being another day any one is one being one and any one being one is one being that one. Any one being that one is one who has been one going on being one all that day if that one has not come sometime in that day to be a dead one.

Any one being one and any one is one, any one going on being one every day is one being that one and any one being one is one being that one.

One being one and being living every day is one who would be one deciding that going on being living another day would be a different thing from being living that day if it were not the same thing. She was one being one and every day in being that one she was not expecting to be a different one. She was one and being that one she would be one being one not liking the day as well as she had been liking some other day if she had not been one who had not been one needing liking that day. She was liking any day, that is to say she was not needing to be not liking any day. She was liking any day, that is to say any day was a day, every day would be a day, any day was a day, a day was a day, any day was that day.

Some being certain that a day is a day and any one not being certain of some thing about a day not being a day are certain that a day is a day, any one being certain that a day is a day are certain that they will be ones going on doing that thing, being certain that a day is a day.

One day, one man is saying to another man that they will go where they have come from. Any day they can say, they do go where they were going. Any day is a day. Any day they have been all day where they were all day. Every day is a day. They can be certain that any day is a day. They can be certain that a day is a day.

Mr. Peter was knowing that being one being of a kind who are ones knowing that in a day, in any day they are winning some and losing a little and sitting in doing this thing and inventing a little different ways of going on sitting and telling some of being ones not needing anything just then, Mr. Peter knowing a little of being one being such a one is one knowing that in being that kind of a one he is one who could be refusing what he might be buying if he was completely inventing buying everything. Mr. Peter is one understanding that he is not inventing each day buying everything. Mr. Peter is one understanding that he is one inventing each day buying something. He is knowing he is of a kind of a one not knowing he is that kind of a one. He is knowing that he is that kind of a one. He is knowing that if any one wants any one being that kind of a one, being that kind of a one is quite a good thing.

Every day he is being that one and knowing that thing he is saying that anything is a good thing and in a way being that kind of a one is a good thing. He is saying this thing any day. He is believing some little thing any day. He is inventing some little thing any day. He is sitting and playing something every day.

Mrs. Peter is one remembering that being one being living where any one who is polite is not mentioning everything they are seeing, Mrs. Peter being one laughing and being one remembering having been laughing where any one being a polite enough one is not remembering anything they were seeing, Mrs. Peter being one having been one living where she had been living was remembering that every day then she was laughing and was remembering that any day then was a day she would not be living there if she could come to be living elsewhere. She came to be living elsewhere. Every day there she was one laughing and remembering. Every day there she was one meeting some and remembering that she could come to remembering everything she was seeing. Every day she was laughing and any day some one was mentioning that she had not come to be remembering everything she was seeing. Every day she was being that one.

Any day Flint could be one saying that he had said what he had been saying. Any day Flint could be such a one. In diagramming anything Flint could come to be certain that he had been a slow one. He was one and being that one he was one seeing something. He was one and being that one every day he was not seeing something. He was one and being that one every day he was describing what he hoped he would not come to be seeing. He was one and he was seeing something. He was one and he was demanding that he could be mentioning what he was seeing. Every day he was mentioning something he was seeing which was the thing he was deciding not to be seeing. Every day he was mentioning that seeing everything was something. Every day he was telling that he had been seeing something and in being one seeing that thing he was one needing to be one seeing some other thing. Every day he was seeing something. Every day he was mentioning seeing something. Every day he was seeing something and seeing that thing he was seeing that that thing was a heavy thing, a dreary thing, a sad thing. Every day he was seeing something. Every day he was seeing something and every day he was mentioning that he was seeing something and it was a delicate, a graceful, an impressive, a tender thing, the thing he was seeing. Every day he was seeing something. Any day he was telling that he might come to be seeing something and to be going on being one seeing that thing and any day he was one being uncertain being uncertain of his being one going to be seeing that thing.

Martin if he had not been one not coming very often would have been one always asking if he might be one saying anything. He was one asking if he might be one saying that he was going to be saying something. Supposing every day was a day and every day he was asking very often if he might be saying anything, supposing he was such a one and supposing that he went on being that one, would he then be one not coming to be one any one would want to be one saying something. If he was one asking any day and very often if he might do something he would be the one who had come to being one who might have known that he could do something if he did not come to be one who was going on being one not coming to be where he could do anything.

He was one and being one who every day was using all day in having that day be that day, he was one and having come to be one he was one having come to use every day to be a day and in doing that thing in making a day be a day he was using up all of a day and he was then that one. He was one then knowing all of that thing, knowing all of a day being a day. He was then knowing something. He was then doing something. He was then being that one.

George was one and being one and not polishing that thing because it being a quite full thing and a fairly dull thing and a quite delicate thing, polishing would be brightening, George being that one he was one and any part of any day was a day to him and a day to him was a day and in being that thing it was something and something was done and again and again it would be finished and something could then be begun that would be finished any day which was a part of a day for any part of a day was a day when that part of a day was being there and being then a day.

Maddalena had every day for being one being living and being one having been using something for such a thing she was using any part of a day that was needing using and she went on being one who had been one keeping going being living. Every day then in a way was a day. Every day was a day and many days were many days and all the days she had been living were all the days she had been living. She was living every day and being living every day that day was a day coming after the other day. Any day was a day and she was doing that thing she was doing every day to be a day and every day coming to be a day she had been living that day. She lived every day, that is the day was a day and she was living the next day and that day was a day. Any day was a day and anything hurting any one that day was something hurting that day. Any day was a day and any being sick that day was the being sick that day. Any day was a day. Every day was a day. There were enough days as every day was enough of a day.

Eugenia knowing that she was one needing to be one enjoying that she was not exhausting having been living was one needing not to be completely working, not completely not working every day. She was one arranging having been that one. She was one being that one. She was one working, she was one not working every day. She was one working, she was one not working any day. Every day was a day.

She was one completing that each day she was quite showing that she was one working and not working. She was completing every day quite neatly every day that she was working, that she was not working every day.

She was arranging any day that every day was all of that day. She was completing arranging every day that every day is a day. Every day is a day. Any day is a day.

Being one remembering what being that one is meaning is something. Being one intending to be completing being that one is something. Being one conceiving that that one is that one is something. Completing remembering that one has been conceiving that that one is that one is something.

Any one being any one is being one that that one could be conceiving to be that one. Any one being one is being one remembering that that one could have been conceiving that that one could be that one.

If in having been one one was one then that one the one that one was was one having come to be that one. In having been one one who was one was one and in having been that one that one was one having come to be that one. In having come to be that one one having come to be that one was one coming to be that one.

One being one, being that one, is one and being one, having come to be one, having come to be that one, is one and being that one is one and in being that one is one keeping that thing keeping being that one. Any one being one and keeping being that one is that one. Any one keeping to be one is one and being that one is that one.

Minnie Harn was one, she had come to be that one. Miss Furr was one, she had come to be that one, she was keeping being that one. Anne Helbing had come to be one, to be keeping being that one. Minna had been coming to be one. She was one. She had been keeping being that one.

Each one being one and coming to completing that thing is in being that one remembering something of beginning completing that thing. Any one is one completing being that one.

Paul was one and in being that one he was one being one remembering having been coming to be that one and being one not needing doing that thing not needing remembering coming to be that one because being that one very many were expecting to be remembering his coming to be that one. He was remembering coming to be that one and in remembering coming to be that one he was choosing quite choosing to have been remembering everything and having everything being having been what he was remembering in remembering everything. He was one remembering everything in having everything being having been what he was remembering as having been in his coming to be being that one. Any one could remember that thing could remember that he was one who had come to be that one. He was the one remembering everything in having everything having been and he being the one having come to be that one.

Having come to be that one he was one come to be one and some came to be ones knowing that thing that he was one having come to be one not having come to be that one.

He was one. In being that one he had been one. In having been one he was one who had been one. In being one he was not one coming to be one. He had not come to be one. He was not coming to be one. He had been one. He was that one. He was one and he had been one. He had been one. In being one he was one. He had been one. In having been one he had been one.

In being one he was one and in being one he was one and in being one he was one. In being one he was one.

In having been one he had been one. He had been one. He was one. He had been one. In being one he was one.

In being one he was one and in being one he was one. He had been one. In having been one he had been one. In having been one he had been one.

In being one he was one. In being one he was one and in being one, in being one he was one. He was one. He had been one. He had been one.

He was one. In being one he was one. He was one. He was one.

Arranging being one and any one not arranging being one is one not arranging being one, in arranging being one any one arranging being one is feeling something coming. In arranging being one any one is feeling something doing. In arranging being one any one is having a piece of them spreading. In arranging being one any one is beginning completing something. In arranging being one any one is existing. In arranging being one one is almost completing that thing.

In arranging being one one was completing that thing. In completing being that one that one was one coming to be one having to remember that he had arranged that thing. He came to be one not needing anything to be that one but complete remembering that he had arranged that thing.

Mr. Hurr, it is natural that being one he is arranging that thing. It is natural that arranging that thing and going on being that one and being one who could be selling anything it is natural that he being that one that Mrs. Hurr speaking to, speaking of him should speak of him as Mr. Hurr and say then that that is a natural thing.

It was a natural thing that he being that one and satisfying that thing it was a natural thing that in helping any one he was helping very many and in helping very many he was helping some who had already been succeeding and he was helping some who might not have been succeeding if he had not been helping then and who were then ones a little succeeding then. It was a natural thing that he being one he was not helping some who were coming to be ones quite succeeding. He being one and being one who could be selling anything, it was a natural thing that he was one arranging to be one coming to be one working to have been one working and feeling. He being one it was a natural thing that he was one and being married then it was a natural thing that he and she were then ones spending and economizing. They being ones being married then it was a natural thing that he was understanding that some living that was a living was a living having meaning. He being one feeling understanding that some living being living having meaning it was a natural thing that he was a man expressing dignity in suffering, he was a man expressing women dreaming, he was a man expressing dim awakening, he was a man expressing dim disappearing.

Any one arranging telling something was arranging something for that thing, was arranging anything for that thing. Any one arranging anything is arranging something.

In arranging anything, in arranging hoping to be one coming to expect arranging to be existing, in arranging anything some one arranging something is arranging that an arrangement is not completely existing.

Some one arranging something is arranging that having arranged that thing it is necessary to arrange that that thing is something that being arranged is not completing anything.

Some one arranging everything is arranging that something that will not then come to be arranged is something that will be arranged when that thing which is arranged is something that has been completely arranged and completely begun being arranged.

Arranging something so that in disarranging that thing something will be arranged is something. Arranging something so that some one arranging something is arranging that thing is something.

Arranging anything and then arranging something in that arrangement and then completing the arranging of some other thing is something. Arranging something and then arranging that in arranging another thing any arrangement is an arrangement is something.

Arranging something and then having something and then losing anything and then arranging everything is something. Any one arranging is arranging. Every one arranging is arranging. Any one believing that arranging is something is believing that arranging is something.

Clay was arranging that he would be worrying if arranging everything would be what he was needing. He was arranging that he would not be worrying if in going on being living he would be losing being one needing to be arranging everything.

He could be arranging that he would not arrange everything and he almost did arrange this thing. He arranged almost everything. He went on almost arranging everything.

Henns in arranging that he would go on arranging what he wanted to go on arranging was arranging that he would begin to arrange something.

He began arranging that thing and then some one and he had asked him to arrange with him came to arranging the thing with him. They arranged the thing the two of them. They arranged it and then Henns was completely having it that he was one who had come to be one who would arrange what any one telling many to arrange things was telling him to arrange. He came to arrange things then. He went on arranging some such things.

Arranging being one having a feeling of being one is something. Arranging being one having a feeling of not being an important one is something. Arranging being one having a feeling of being one admiring being one succeeding is something. Arranging being one completely being that one is something. Arranging being one continuing is something. Arranging being one needing being one dreaming is something.

Dear Anne Helbing, she was that one, she remembered that thing, she remembered having been that one. She remembered something, she remembered that she had remembered being that one, she remembered that thing, she remembered something.

Dear Anne Helbing, she was being that one, she was remembering everything, she was remembering that thing. She had been that one and that thing was something she was not wanting to be using, it was something she was not needing, it was something she was not remembering, it was something, she had been that one she was one, she was Anne Helbing.

She was Anne Helbing, she was that one, she was working, she was remembering that thing, she was learning anything, she was forgetting everything, she was remembering nothing, she was Anne Helbing.

She was Anne Helbing and she was arranging that thing, she was arranging being working, she was arranging hoping everything, she was arranging doing something, she did something, she did something and her mother was doing everything and her mother did anything and Anne Helbing was working and she was remembering everything.

Minna was one and she married sometime and she had arranged to be one not needing doing that thing, she had arranged to be one and she was that one she had arranged to be one being a quiet one.

She had arranged to be one taking very much time to be a quiet one. She had arranged that she should be one having everything and she arranged to be one being a quiet one. In being a quiet one she was arranging to be one coming to be a married one. In being a quiet one she was arranging being one having everything in having time to be one being a quiet one.

She was arranging something she was arranging that a very long time she would be arranging to be a married one. She was arranging something she was arranging that all the time she would be a quiet one. She was arranging something she was arranging that being a quiet one she would be one having what she was needing to be that one.

Any one having been coming and having been coming once and some one having been remembering that thing, any one being one coming and being one listening and being one coming to be quite old enough to be one having been coming and having been is one being one coming again and coming again is one telling that coming again is a pleasant thing, a profitable thing and a thing that that one will be doing again. That one will then be doing that thing again if that one has not come before then to be a quite older one.

Thomas Whitehead is one and being one is one who sometime will be a quite old one and having come then to be a quite old one will be one who has been one coming and telling that coming again would be a pleasant thing and then have come again and have been telling that it was a pleasant, a profitable thing to have come and that he will be one coming again and he would be one coming again if he came again before he became a quite quite old one.

Any one listening and hearing anything is one having been saying something. Any one listening and telling that thing is one needing something. Any one listening and hearing everything is one having been one not needing telling anything. Any one listening and telling everything is one being one who has been hearing something. Any one being one having been hearing something is one being one not having been needing all of that thing. Any one being one going on hearing something is one who has come to be one telling something of that thing. Any one hearing what he has been hearing is one telling what he has been telling.

Clellan telling and Clellan hearing is Clellan not having been one needing to be hearing and telling. Clellan telling is Clellan not completing needing to be telling. Clellan hearing is Clellan not completing needing to be hearing.

Clellan being is being not needing to be hearing. Clellan being in being not needing to be telling, Clellan hearing is Clellan being hearing. Clellan telling is Clellan being telling. Clellan hearing is Clellan. Clellan telling is Clellan.

Clellan being is being not completely needing to be being. Clellan being is being one completely going on being. Clellan being is being in being one being Clellan. Being Clellan is being being one. Being Clellan is being being that one. Being Clellan is one completely going on being being one. Being Clellan is being one hearing, telling completely going on being, being one telling and hearing and being Clellan. Being Clellan is being Clellan. Being Clellan is being one.

Being Clellan and being one, being Clellan and being hearing, being Clellan and being telling, being Clellan and going on being, being Clellan and not being one not being Clellan, being Clellan and quite being Clellan, being Clellan and being Clellan and completely quite going on being Clellan is being Clellan.

Being Clellan and being and doing and hearing and telling and being quite completing needing and being Clellan and being that Clellan and being going on being that Clellan is being Clellan.

Being Clellan is being that Clellan. Being that Clellan is being Clellan.

Little ones being ones any one is being one. Little ones having been ones every one is being one. A little one being one any one is needing then that every one is any one. A little one being one any one is needing then that any one is every one. A little one being one some one is some one being one coming later. A little one being one some are ones being ones coming to not coming often. A little one being one some are ones deciding everything. A little one being one that one is one and that one being one every one is one and every one being one some one is some one and some one being some one some one is going. Some one going some other one is coming. Some other one coming every one is changing. Every one changing any one is directing. Any one directing every one is mentioning everything. Every one mentioning everything any one is coming again. Any one coming again, some one has been coming. Some one having been coming every one is leaving. Every one leaving every one will come again. Every one coming again, some one will have been. Some one having been, some one will be coming. Some one coming, every one is staying. Every one staying each one is explaining. Each one explaining, every one is listening. Every one listening, each one is being.

Murdock being one is one who if he were one explaining would be explaining that he was not doing what he would be doing if he were doing what he would be doing if he were one doing what he was being one being doing. Murdock might be one explaining. Murdock was one being one.

Nantine if he were a sadder one would be a lonely one in explaining that thing. Nantine in being a sad enough one was almost a lonely one in telling anything. Nantine in being a lonely one was being one not completing that thing in explaining that being that one was being one having been keeping going living.

He was being one and seeing any one, and seeing any one he was putting down something, and putting down something he was reproducing anything, and reproducing anything it was looking like that one, and looking like that one it was being something that some one being one seeing what was being was putting down in being one who was one not being a lonely one because he was being one seeing what was what any one was seeing.

He was being one not being a lonely one because he was putting down what every one was seeing. He was one almost being a lonely one because he was seeing what he was putting down. He was one being a sad one because he was one being almost a lonely one. He was one being a sad one and he was one not being a sad enough one to be one not going on being one asking any one to be one asking him to be one going on being living.

In putting down anything any one putting down something is that one, one putting down something. In putting down something if something is put down then that which is put down is something. If that which is put down is something then that thing is what it is and being what it is it is something and being something any one being any one is being one and being one is one and any one is one and then any one is one and anything having been put down is a thing and that thing is a thing and anything is something.

Anything having been put down and being down and any one being one and anything having been put down being something and any one being one being one, then anything being put down and being something and any one being one being one then, anything being something is something and any one being one is one. Any one being one is one. Anything being put down is something. Anything being put down being something and anything that is something is being that thing, then that thing is a thing and any one is any one. Any one being one being one then any one is one being one and being one anything that is put down is something.

Any one being one is one. Anything put down is something. Anything being down is something and being that thing it is something and being something it is a thing and being a thing it is not anything and not being anything it is everything and being that thing it is a thing and being that thing it is that thing. Being that thing it is that thing and being that thing it is coming to be a thing having been that thing and coming to be a thing having been that thing it is a thing being a thing it is a thing being that thing.

A thing being a thing that is that thing, a thing being a thing, a thing having been put down a thing being something and putting down a thing is a thing that is happening and then the thing put down being then that thing, a thing being that thing, a thing is something and a thing being something, a thing being that thing is then that thing and being then that thing it is a thing and being a thing it is that thing and it is then that thing, it is then that thing.

A thing being that thing, they are many things. There are many things. Each thing is that thing.

Any one being one is that one. One being one and being that one and going on being is going on being that one. In going on being that one he is one going on being one.

Lamson is one. He is one. He is that one. He is one going on being that one. He is that one in going on being one. In going on being one he is being that one. He is that one.

Lamson is being one. He is one. He is one and he is one who is one. He is one. He is experiencing something. He has not been experiencing everything. He has not been experiencing being that one. He has been experiencing being that one. He has not been experiencing everything.

He is one who is one. He is one being one. He is one going on being one. He is one going on being that one.

In going on being that one he is going on experiencing being that one. He is not experiencing being that one. Being that one is something that he is not going on experiencing. He is not experiencing being that one. Experiencing being that one is not existing.

Experiencing being that one not being existing he is not experiencing being that one. He is going on being that one. Experiencing being that one is not coming to be something being existing.

In not experiencing being that one that one is one being that one and being one going on being that one and being one being that one in being that one. In being that one, in experiencing being that one not being existing that one is one being one is one going on being one, is one being that one is one going on being that one, is one being in being one.

If, and if not then it is not, if something is and some one being certain is denying it then, if something is and some one being certain is not telling that the other one is not seeing what is in denying that it is, if some one being certain is not certain then something that is is what it is and if it is what it is then being what it is is what is interesting to some one interested in that thing. If some one hearing something is not saying anything and hearing that thing is certain that something is not anything then if that thing is something that one is one who is certain that that thing is not anything. If that one is quite certain that that thing is not anything and is going on being certain and if that thing is something then that one being certain that that thing is not anything is one who would be an important one if that thing is something. That one being an important one and being certain that that thing is not anything he is one going on being an important one and going on being an important one he is one coming to be certain that if that thing is anything then it is something.

Being certain that something is something is an important thing to some one. Being certain that something is not anything is an important thing. Being certain that it is an important thing to be certain that something is not something is an important thing.

Something being something and some one seeing everything and some one seeing anything and any one knowing that it is an important thing that something being something some one is seeing every thing, some one is seeing anything, some one is an important one. Some one being an important one anything is something. Anything being something some one is seeing anything.

Some one seeing anything some other one is seeing anything. That one seeing everything is always right in judging. That one always being right in judging some one is always believing something.

Something and anything being what is being then anything coming is what some one has been intending and some one having been intending something something that is something is what any one is seeing. Any one seeing is saying something unless they are not saying anything. If they are saying something they are saying that something is not anything, if they are not saying anything they are not saying anything. If they are saying that something is not anything they are then saying that anything is something.

One feels something about depression. One feels something. That one feels something and that one feels something about some one's liking about some one's not liking something that one has been continuing. Some one feels something about something that one knows about and has been neglecting.

What is that one feeling that one who is feeling something in feeling something about that one being a sad one. That one is feeling something in feeling that being a sad one is what that one is then. That one being one and feeling something is feeling something about any one feeling something about what that one has been doing. That one who is one and feeling something is feeling something about something that one knew and has been neglecting.

That one feeling something, that one hearing something is knowing that

that one has been knowing something and having been neglecting that thing something that one has been knowing is something that that one in telling everything has not been using.

In telling everything and any one telling everything is doing something, in telling everything any one neglecting something is knowing that in feeling everything they are needing that thing. In feeling everything any one feeling everything is doing something. In feeling everything every one explaining everything is knowing something that that one has been neglecting.

Every one explaining everything is doing something. Every one feeling everything is doing something. Every one telling everything is doing something.

Any one doing something is knowing that they are knowing something they are neglecting. Every one knowing something they are neglecting is doing something.

Miss Harvey admiring Wilbur is doing that thing quite doing that thing quite admiring Wilbur. In admiring Wilbur she is not knowing anything she is neglecting. In admiring Wilbur she is telling that Wilbur is not knowing anything he is neglecting. In admiring Wilbur she is doing that thing she is admiring Wilbur. In admiring Wilbur she is admiring some one and in admiring some one she is admiring Wilbur. In admiring Wilbur who is a young one she is not knowing anything she is neglecting, she is knowing Wilbur is a young one she is not neglecting that thing. In not neglecting knowing that Wilbur is a young one she is admiring Wilbur and in admiring Wilbur she is telling everything, she is telling that Wilbur is knowing what he is knowing and not neglecting that thing. In admiring Wilbur she is not neglecting anything she is knowing, she is knowing that Wilbur having been a young one and coming to be knowing something was not neglecting coming to be knowing that thing. In admiring Wilbur she was not neglecting anything she was knowing, she was knowing that having been admiring Wilbur she had been admiring Wilbur.

In admiring Wilbur she was being one completing knowing everything and not neglecting anything. In knowing Wilbur she was telling anything of that thing anything of knowing everything and not neglecting anything. In admiring Wilbur she was admiring every thing of knowing every thing and not neglecting anything.

If Clellan had been impatient and any one being one who is one not being considerate might be one being impatient if Clellan had been one being impatient he would have been quite an impatient one. He was not an impatient one. He was not at all such a one. Being one and not being an impatient one is being one who is not an impatient one.

One not being an impatient one may be one who is feeling something about something that one is doing in being one doing something. It is certain, certainly it is certain that being one doing something in being one one may be one who is an impatient one, one may be one who is not an impatient one. If one is one who is not an impatient one in being that one one may be one going on not being an impatient one. If one is an impatient one in being one being one doing something one may be one going on being one being an impatient one.

Any one being one and being one doing something in being one is one and being one that one might be one who was one who in doing something was doing that thing with a feeling that if he went on being one he would come to be one expecting some to be accepting that he was one doing something. Any one who might be such a one might come to not going on being one. Any one being one and feeling something about being one doing something is one who if that one were one going on doing something might be one coming to be feeling something about any one accepting about any one not accepting that he was one doing something. Any one being one and very many are being ones, any one being one and feeling anything and expecting to be feeling something is one who might come to be one feeling that that one had been feeling something.

A big one a very big one and a little one being together another one an appreciative one one looking to be accepting enjoying entering into admiring, the three of them being every day all three of them telling anything some one meeting one of them is remembering that any one doing anything could be discouraging in laughing at every one and being discouraging any one being a nervous one would be one being a depressed one when that one was one having been sitting listening.

Some who would be ones succeeding would be ones failing if some one who would have been one succeeding if he had been the one to be succeeding had not been one deciding to be going on and being then succeeding. Some who are ones succeeding are ones succeeding and being ones succeeding they are the ones the very ones the ones succeeding.

Some who having been ones the ones succeeding, being ones are ones and they are the ones who were the ones succeeding. They are the ones who were the ones succeeding, they are the ones and they are succeeding in seeing each other one being the one the one succeeding. They are the ones the ones who were succeeding. They are the ones the ones seeing each other one and looking each other one coming is succeeding and succeeding they are the ones who were succeeding.

One being one not asking because if he were asking he would be wanting to hear the answer that he was hearing, one being one not asking is one asking some one what some were answering to asking he would have been asking if he had been one being asking. He being one not asking he was one being one who being one freeing what he was completing he being that one and controlling that thing controlling having been one who was completing something that one was one who in freeing everything was one needing to be asking and asking he was one being one going on being a very nervous one. He being one being that one and going on remembering that he was being one he was one who if he went on being one would go on being one who had been freeing what every one would be freeing if freeing was not something that they freeing that thing were not freeing. He was one and he was that one and being that one he was sitting and sitting he was not resting and not resting he was changing and changing he was struggling and struggling he was being lost and being lost he was asking if some one finding him would be remembering that he had been found.

Vrais says good good, excellent. Vrais listens and when he listens he says good good, excellent. Vrais listens and he being Vrais when he has listened he says good good, excellent.

Vrais listens, he being Vrais, he listens.

Anything is two things. Vrais was nicely faithful. He had been nicely faithful. Anything is two things.

He had been nicely faithful. In being one he was one who had he been one continuing would not have been one continuing being nicely faithful. He was one continuing, he was not continuing to be nicely faithful. In continuing he was being one being the one who was saying good good, excellent but in continuing he was needing that he was believing that he was aspiring to be one continuing to be able to be saying good good, excellent. He had been one saying good good, excellent. He had been that one.

Boncinelli in being one was the one explaining that he knew what he was saying. He did know what he was saying. He did know that knowing what one is saying is something having meaning.

Boncinelli in feeling was feeling that he was living. He was living. He was feeling.

He was feeling, being feeling he could be one making something, and having completely arranged that thing the thing he was making he was one knowing that knowing that he was arranging what he had been making is something. Knowing that knowing he was arranging what he is arranging is something he was one knowing that he was living. In knowing that he was living he was knowing that he was feeling. He was feeling and knowing that he was feeling he was knowing that he was arranging what he was feeling in what he had arranged in making the thing he knew he had been arranging. He was feeling.

Why do you mind if you heard one thing and told something once and did not believe anything and denied everything, why do you mind if you continue something and admit everything and upset something and remember everything, why do you mind if you repeat something. Why do you mind if you destroy nothing, if you arrange everything, if you continue anything, why do you mind if you admit something. Why do you mind if you believe anything, if you admit everything, if you hear something why do you mind if you do not remember everything. Why do you mind if you remember something, if you like anything, if you resist something, why do you mind if you do not forget everything. Why do you mind if you do not resist anything, if you believe something, if you do not forget anything, if you like everything, why do you mind if you remember something.

Mr. Peter in saying something was saying that he was understanding something by knowing that he had heard before what he was then hearing. Mr. Peter was often hearing what he had not heard before. Mr. Peter was not always understanding something. Mr. Peter was saying that he being one who was hearing was one who was saying that if he could have been one suffering he would have been one suffering in having been hearing what he was not understanding. Mr. Peter was saying that he was one who could be suffering. Mr. Peter was saying that he was one who was not suffering. Mr. Peter was hearing what he would not have been understanding even if he had heard it before and he had not heard it before. Mr. Peter was saying that he was not understanding it because he had not heard it before but he would not be understanding it if he had heard it before. Mr. Peter was saying that he might not come to be understanding what he was hearing. Mr. Peter was saying that he was not suffering.

Mrs. Peter was saying that having gone where she had gone she would not go again. Mrs. Peter was saying that in not going again she was deciding that going again was a foolish thing when one did not like it when one had been. Mrs. Peter might go again if she went with some one and Mrs. Peter said she might go with some one but Mrs. Peter said that she would very likely not go again as she very likely would not be going there with any one. Mrs. Peter had been. Mrs. Peter was not going again.

If in going on there is beginning and if in beginning any one is certain and if in being certain one is certainly needing to be able to believe anything in order to believe what certainly is certain, if there is continuing then certainly there has been enough said when in arranging to be certain one has said very often that which it is certain that one is believing.

One was, not certain, but one was, not believing, but one was having what was existing. In having what was existing one was being enjoying agreeing with the one who was saying who was saying often, often saying somethings. In that one saying somethings if these things were the things that were certain then in that one saying those things some one enjoying living in agreeing in saying those things was saying things that were certain. That one then being one coming to be certain was certain about those things having been, having not been certain. Any one being such a one and feeling anything is one feeling something. In one feeling something there is certain to be something that in being discouraging is not saddening. In not being saddening that thing having been something is something but some other thing which is something is everything and being everything is something. In being something that thing is then encouraging.

Why if some one is enough that thing to be that one why is that one, in being one being inside in that one, completely that one, why is that one then being one who in being one is being so little that one that that one is then another kind of a one. Why is that one being one who in being one is one who would be expressing being that one if that one were not one who in expressing being one is not expressing being that one. Clellan is being one. Any one being one is being one. Clellan is being one. In being one he is one, he certainly is one and in certainly being one he is doing something and in doing something he is expressing being one and in expressing being one he is not expressing being that one. In not expressing being that one he is one expressing being completely something. In expressing being completely something he is not expressing being that one. In expressing being completely one he is hardly expressing anything. In hardly expressing anything he is being one. In being that one he is one who is not being the one he is being. In not being the one he is being he is being what he would not be being if he were being anything and he is being something he is being something that would be something if it were anything but not being something it is not anything. Clellan is one, when he is that one he is one. When he is not that one he is completely expressing something. When he is completely expressing something he is not expressing being that one. When he is not expressing being that one he is not expressing anything. He is that one. Clellan is one.

In doing anything if ones are knowing that if they are telling that they have not a reason for doing the thing some will be knowing that they are ones not deeply thinking, then they can say anything. In being ones who can say anything they can be ones knowing that they are deeply thinking. In being ones knowing that they are deeply thinking they can be ones being certain that thinking deeply is not meaning anything.

In being ones who can say anything they are ones who are knowing that if giving a reason is meaning something they are ones who have not given a reason. In being ones who have not given a reason they are ones knowing that some who have given a reason are ones who can be certain that they certainly have it to be ones deeply thinking.

In doing anything and giving a reason one can be doing the two things and one can be deeply thinking. In being one deeply thinking one can be one giving a reason. In being one giving a reason one can be one doing something. In doing something one can be one deeply thinking. In deeply thinking one can be one hearing that some are not giving any reason.

Expect to be right and you are right if you complete everything. That is something that any one reasoning is expecting and any one reasoning is one being one not needing expectation.

In not needing expectation one is being one completing something and completing anything is anything.

This is something. This and everything is something and all of everything is what any one deciding everything is expecting. In expecting all of that thing that one not needing expectation is beginning again completing everything. In completing everything beginning and ending has no meaning and why should beginning and ending have meaning if everything is something. Why should they have meaning if deciding anything is what any one is doing.

Some are deciding something. In deciding they are not expecting and in not expecting they are attending to being ones arranging everything if everything being arranged anything is happening. But nothing is happening because if anything were happening beginning and ending would be having meaning and if beginning and ending did have meaning then not anything would be something any one was deciding and if not any one was deciding anything then every one would be expecting something and if every one were being ones being expecting then not any one would be one doing reasoning and if not any one was one reasoning then not any one would be one completing everything. This is that thing.

Hearing and not answering, hearing and answering something, telling little things and telling too much then, making suggestions and not making the whole of any one of them, changing before completely beginning to tell that something is like some other thing, remembering that if one were telling something some one would be answering, forgetting that laughing is annoying, remembering that forgetting is annoying, explaining that beginning anything is what is not happening, denying that every one said something, telling some little thing that some one might have said, explaining that if anything was said it was a thing that being something was something that not any one could have said, all this is something. When all this is something and all this is always something, when all this is something then some one being certain that something is existing is certain that all this is existing. When that one is certain that all this is existing then that one explaining everything will be explaining that all this being something anything is something and anything being something something is existing and something being existing anything is existing and anything being existing everything is expressing that thing.

Some are some who being some and remembering something of that thing come to be some who are existing in being some who are being remembering that having been and being something they are being and being something. They are some and going on they can tell everything they can tell that telling everything is telling what they are in being some who are being some who are something. Yes they are telling that thing. Certainly they are telling that thing. Why should they not tell that thing when they are ones being ones who being existing in being ones who are something are ones who in telling that thing are telling everything. They are then they are telling everything, they are telling that they are some who are something. They are some and they are coming to be the ones who being existing are the ones any one listening will be hearing telling everything. In telling that they are some they are telling everything. In telling everything they are ones having it continuing that every thing is existing. They are all some who are something. They are telling that thing. That is everything.

Any one remembering something is one who might not have been doing that thing doing the thing that one is remembering having been doing. Any one doing anything is one who may be one not remembering the thing that one was doing. In being one tumbling some one may be one who might have been tumbling if that one had been one who was running. That one was tumbling that one had been one who commenced to be one commencing to run. In being that one that one was one tumbling. In being one tumbling any one could be one picking up that one. In any one picking up that one some were certain that that one could have been one tumbling. In picking up that one some were certain that that one was one who would not be tumbling. In picking up that one some were remembering that picking up some one was something that they might not be doing. In picking up that one some were expecting that if they were picking up any one again it would not be that one.

In doing something some who could be ones being gay ones are ones remembering that they are then being ones who are not gay ones. In doing something some who are ones who could be ones doing that thing are remembering that they are not ones to do that thing they certainly are not ones to do that thing then. In being ones who certainly are not ones to do that thing then they are ones coming to be knowing that any one who comes to be one doing that thing comes to be one who can be doing that thing. Any one doing anything can come to be one who can be doing that thing. A person who is visiting and who is uncomfortable can be more uncomfortable before that visiting is over. A person who is visiting and is not comfortable can go on being not comfortable through the whole of the visit and can then visit again and not be comfortable again. One who is visiting is one who if any one is asking that one to visit them is one who visiting is not comfortable and will be more uncomfortable. Any one being visited is one doing something and being one doing something is one doing anything. Doing anything is doing everything. Doing everything is something.

Any one took some one somewhere and having taken them they left them. Any one going anywhere is one going and being going any one who is knowing that thing knowing that some one is going is one who is one knowing something.

Some came in. Some were there. Two came in. Two had been there. The two who had been there were there. The two who came in were there. There were four there.

The four there the two who came in and the two who had been there the four there were all then there and being there they did not stay there. The two who came in did not stay there, they left and the two who had been there were the two who were there.

The two who were there were angry there and being angry they were left there. Being left there one of them was angry, the other one was not angry. The one that was angry was sitting. The one that was not angry was resting. The two were there, one was angry and the other could have known that, if that one had not been resting. The one that was angry was angry because if being that one was something then being angry was nothing. The one that was angry was angry and being angry was not suffering and not being suffering was not having that being angry was being what that one was being in being that one when being that one was nothing.

That one was one who had been one being one who was not an angry one. In being that one in being one who had been one not being an angry one that one was not being one. That one was that one, that one was being then one who was resting and there being then two of them and both resting they were not being then there the two of them. One of them was there then. That one was resting.

In a thing being one way and having come to be another way, in a thing having come to be another way some one can be one trying to be telling something. In trying to be telling something that one can come to be saying something and some one asking something then that one is one then wishing anything. In being one then wishing anything and that one then is one wishing anything, in being one then wishing anything that one is not then one wishing that the thing that is a changed thing is the thing it was before that was a changed thing. That one is one wishing anything, in wishing anything that one is not wishing that thing. And why is that one in wishing anything not wishing that thing. That one in wishing anything is not wishing that thing because that one in wishing anything is wishing that some other one would be one knowing that the thing is a changed thing. In wishing that the other one were one knowing that the thing is a changed thing that one is one wishing anything rather than that the other should be one being one knowing that thing knowing that the thing is a changed thing. The one wishing would be one wishing if that one were not one quite knowing everything of what would be happening if the other one were knowing that the thing is a changed thing. Wishing anything is wishing anything. Knowing everything that will be happening is knowing everything that will be happening. Some one who is knowing everything that will be happening is wishing anything.

You agree, I agree, we agree. If we agree and we do not agree, if we agree and both say something then I say I do not agree and you say you do not agree. If we both say something and you say I agree and I say I do not agree then if we agree we agree that you agree and if you agree that you agree then I agree that I then do not agree. Some agree, some do not agree. That is something that any one saying any other thing is saying is not happening. We agree, that is something that some say is not happening. We agree that is something you are saying. In saying that thing you are saying that thing and I am not saying anything. In not saying anything I am saying that agreeing is nothing, any one saying anything is agreeing, any one saying anything is not agreeing.

Some when they are talking are saying that they are not only saying that thing, they are saying anything and in saying anything they are saying that everything is nothing. In saying that thing they are saying that they are hoping that if any one is answering them they will then not need to answer again and they do answer again and then they are hoping again that they will not need to be answering if any one says anything. Any one answering can be one hoping that they will not be one expecting to be answering again. Any one answering can be such a one.

If very many who come and say yes had come and said no, not any one who was liking that many come and say yes would have been liking what was happening. Very many who would not have been liking what was happening if very many had come and said no did like what was happening as very many came and said yes.

All who came and said yes said that they said yes and some of them said that they had intended to say no and they would have said no if they had not said yes. Having said yes they said that having said yes they would say yes again if they did not say no.

One being one who had said no said that having said no he was saying yes and saying yes he was saying that he would come to say no if he would not come to say yes. This one was saying that he was not waiting to say no. This one was saying that he was not waiting to say yes. This one was saying that he would come to say no if he came to say no. This one was saying that he would come to say yes if he came to say yes. This one was asking if some one who had said yes had not said no. This one was saying that one who had said no had said no.

This one was waiting and waiting was not waiting to say no was not waiting to say yes. He was not waiting for any one to say no for any one to say yes. He was not waiting for every one to say no, for every one to say yes, this one was waiting and in waiting he said that he had said yes if he had not said no. This one was waiting and in waiting he asked any one what they had said whether they had said no, whether they had said yes.

In talking and any one who was not listening was talking, in talking every one who was not remembering what they were saying and not any one can be one remembering that thing remembering what they were saying, in talking every one in saying something is saying that something is not anything and in saying that something is not anything is saying that something might be something. Any one talking and any one who is not talking and listening is talking, any one talking is remembering that something that was said was something that being said was meaning that something is something. Any one talking is one remembering something of something. Any one talking is telling that something having been something, something is something.

In being one not expecting that one will be taking what one will not be taking, in being such a one one is one and one being one one can be that one and when one can be that one and is that one then that one is the one who can be that one and is that one and being that one then one is being that one and being that one reducing and increasing is existing and reducing and increasing being existing that one is that one and that one being that one reducing is reducing and increasing is increasing.

Reducing being reducing and increasing being increasing everything is something and everything being something anything is the thing that will not be some other thing. This is all of that thing and this being all of that thing something is all of something and something being all of something reducing and increasing are being existing.

Continuing and having been destroyed then and continuing and not having been destroyed then are two things that are happening. These two things being things that are happening enough is happening to encourage any one who is being encouraged then and to discourage any one who is being discouraged then. In continuing and some continuing are telling that that thing has been happening, in continuing some are destroyed and some are telling that that thing has been happening. Some in telling that thing are telling everything and in telling everything are telling that travelling is not fatiguing, that travelling has been a dangerous thing, that travelling is happening.

In bringing back inside in one what one can not have again inside in one one can be one being certain that if one could have again inside in one what one is not having again inside in one one would believe anything and in believing everything would not be telling any one anything. Alright, tell it again and tell it again and again and again and tell something, why not tell something if in telling any one is telling it again and again and again.

Wente was one who could remember that he was small enough to tell a thing he would not be telling again and again and again if he were bigger. He knew he was not bigger and being smaller he was not small enough to forget that he was one who was not so small that anything could worry him that did not worry him. Almost anything that worried him worried him enough so that in telling that he was worrying he was telling it again and again. In telling that he was worrying he was telling that being the one he was he would not be telling any more of anything that was worrying than that that worrying him he was one who was worrying. In being that one and he was worrying, in being that one he was one who would certainly be frightened if he worried enough and not at all frightened if he was having worry him anything that was worrying him.

He said that thing, he said that he said anything in saying that thing and he did say anything in saying that thing and he said that again to any one.

He said a little thing and he said he would be worrying if he were not the one who was one worrying. He said he was not worrying again. He said that he could say all of that thing. He said he did say that thing and he would say another thing and he did say that other thing and he said he was not worrying, and he was not worrying, he was not worrying again. He was worrying and in being worrying he came again and again in being that one to that thing the thing he had not been telling again and again. He was not smaller than he had been, he was the size he had been, he was not worrying about any such thing.

If every one was not believing that every one was believing that living is continuing and any one can come to be a dead one, if every one was not believing enough of this thing then any one doing anything would be doing something of what they are doing. In doing something of what they are doing any one doing something is doing what that one is doing.

Any one can be one telling something of some such a thing of any one doing something in not believing anything of living being continuing.

Enough being done by any one doing something, doing something of that thing so that any one believing that any one can be a dead one is believing that every one could be believing that living is not continuing. Living is continuing if any one who can come to be a dead one can come to be a dead one. Living can be continuing if every one believing that every one is not believing that living is continuing, is believing that any one can come to be a dead one.

It is not a thing that is comforting to be certain that any one listening is one who can not be convinced that the one talking is really explaining what is being really explained by that one. The one talking is explaining what is really being explained by that one. The one listening can not be certain that the one talking is really explaining what is being explained by that one. It is not comforting to be one being living. It is not comforting to be one not being living. Nothing is comforting if one is being comforted by something. Nothing is comforting if one could be comforted by anything. Nothing is comforting. Not any thing is comforting and anybody being living can be being living and anybody not being living can be not being living.

He said something and understood that any one understanding that thing could say something of that thing. He said something and understood that any one understanding that thing could say that he had not said what he had said when he had said that thing. This is something.

If some one wants something and not having that thing is not getting that thing and not getting that thing might be certain that that one could not have that thing and being certain that that one could not have that thing is certain to need that thing if that one does not get that thing and that one can not get that thing if that one does not get that thing and that one is certain that it is a thing that one could have if that one had that thing then that one will want that thing and that one wanting that thing will be certain that when that one gets that thing there will not be any reason why that one has not got that thing and that one will have that thing if that one gets that thing and that one will get that thing if that one can get that thing. That is enough to make some certain of something. That is enough to make any one say anything. Any one saying anything and every one saying something is saying anything, any one saying anything about that thing is saying anything.

Any one being born and born a baby if they are not a man will be a woman and if they are not a woman will be a man unless they are dead before they come to be grown.

Any one born and saying something is saying anything and saying anything is saying something about being born and coming to be a man and being born and coming to be a woman. There are many being living. Any one of them can say anything. Any one can say something. Each one of them saying anything is saying in the way of being a man or being a woman and any one saying anything is saying something and any one saying something is saying anything.

There are enough being living to be very many being living and there are enough of all of them saying something and they are each one of them saying anything.

Altogether some of them were there where if a noise were made all of them said something. All of them saying something any of them said anything and any of them saying anything some were certain that some of them were saying something. Some of them being certain, any of them were saying anything.

Any of them saying anything so could be continuing and all of them being continuing one could be saying that all of them had been saying anything and not any of them had been saying something and if one of them had been saying something, they all of them having been saying anything, not any of them had been saying something. One of them saying something all of them were saying anything. All of them saying anything any one of them was saying that they would not have been saying something. They were altogether and then they were not altogether and they were not again all together and they were not again all together because all of them having been all together and any of them having been saying they were not saying something in saying that they could have been saying anything.

One was one and being that one and telling that having been that one that one had been that one when that one had been that one, that one being that one that one had been that one in having been that one when that one had been the one that had been that one.

This one was one and could, remembering that thing and remembering that thing, could not remember any other thing and not remembering any other thing was remembering remembering having been and being that one and not having been and not being remembering any other thing. That one being that one remembered having been saying anything so that that one would be the one saying something when any other one being one saying something every one would have said something. That one was one then having been one saying anything so that that one could be the one saying something and every one would be one saying anything and not any one would be one saying something. That one remembered having been that one. That one was that one. That one remembered that that one was that one when that one was remembering that that one being that one that one was to be that one.

Some forget something. Some forget anything. Some are being the one they are being when they are forgetting anything. Some can come to be one having what they might have had if they had not forgotten something. Some of such of them will forget something. Some of such of them have conviction.

One who is a pleasant one in being one finding what he has been finding, one who is a continuous one in feeling what he can be seeing is one who is liking what he is liking and in liking what he is liking is not mentioning that he is being that one and not mentioning that thing that thing is not everything, that thing is something that may not be anything.

Having been complaining is something. Having been explaining is something. Having been withdrawing is something. Having been emphasising is something. Some one is one and being that one that one is not that one and that one can be certain of anything in being one being one. That one is one being one who can be certain of anything in being the one being that one.

One knowing everything is knowing that sometime knowing something is something but not everything. One knowing everything is knowing that some one knowing something is one and being that one is the one knowing what that one is knowing. One knowing everything is knowing that sometime one will know some things some are knowing and one knowing everything is knowing that knowing some things is something but not everything as one knowing everything might be one always having been knowing those things.

One knowing everything is one knowing that anything is exciting. One knowing everything is knowing that knowing some things one might come to know more things and one might have known everything and if one had known everything then one could have decided to know everything and having decided to know everything then one knowing everything would be knowing that everything is exciting.

Believing anything is believing that something is something. Believing that something is something is beginning not to be exciting. Doing anything is doing something. Doing anything is exciting if doing that thing excites some one.

Believe that something is something. Believe that believing that something is something every one can believe something. That is beginning not to be exciting.

Believe that any one is the one that one is and believe that any one doing the thing that one is doing is doing that thing and doing that thing is being that one and being that one is doing that thing. Believe that and any one can believe something. Believe that believe any one can believe something and that can begin not to be exciting.

Bremer is doing what he is doing that is he is doing what he would be doing if he were believing that he was doing what Paul is doing. He is not believing that he is doing what Paul is doing. He is believing that Paul is doing what Paul is doing. Bremer is doing what Bremer is doing. Bremer is believing that Paul is doing what Paul is doing. Bremer is doing what Bremer is doing. Bremer is doing what he would be doing if he were believing that he was doing what Paul is doing. Bremer is believing that Paul is doing something. Bremer is believing that he is doing something. He is doing something. He is believing something, this can begin not to be exciting.

Herford is doing something. He is believing that not any one is believing anything. He is believing that he is doing what he would be doing if not any one was believing that he was doing anything. Any one can be believing that he is doing something. Any one can believe that doing something is not anything. He can believe that not any one is believing anything. He can believe he is not believing anything. He can believe that he is doing what he would be doing if he were not believing anything. He is believing that doing anything can begin not to be exciting.

Clellan will believe what he can believe not any one can believe who is doing what he will be doing if he does what he is going to be doing. Clellan believes that he can believe what he will believe if he does what he will do. Clellan does what he does. Clellan will do what he will do. Clellan will believe what he does believe he can believe if he can do what he will do. Clellan does what he does. Clellan believes that doing what he does can be exciting. Clellan believes that believing what he believes he can believe will begin not to be exciting.

Cheyne was answering and answering he was doing something and doing something he was not believing anything and not believing anything he was saying something and saying something he was irritating and irritating he was pleasing and pleasing he was dying and dying he was burning.

Helen was hoping to be laughing. She was saying she was going to keep on laughing. In going to be laughing she was beginning and in beginning she was continuing. She was continuing, she was believing anything, she was believing that she had been laughing, she was believing that she had been continuing. She went on believing. She was believing something. Believing something she was believing everything and believing everything she was believing just what she was believing. Believing just what she was believing she was believing and believing she was completing continuing and completing continuing she was being believing and being believing she was astonishing and being astonishing she was not being astonished then.

Paul was one believing and being one believing he was saying what he was not saying, he was saying that he was one believing and not saying what he was not saying. Paul was one and being one was feeling that doing something might come again and again to be exciting and coming to be exciting he would have been one believing that he had been saying what he had not been saying. Doing something being exciting so that some one doing it is doing it again, doing something being exciting and believing being existing he was not saying what he was saying, he was saying what he was not saying.

Dethom was saying that he was believing in saying what he was saying. Dethom was saying that he was believing that doing something that is exciting is exciting. Dethom was doing what he was saying he was doing. Dethom was believing what he was saying he was believing.

Dethom was winning. Dethom was remembering all of any one being one winning. Dethom was a decided one. Dethom was expecting enough to be receiving what any one winning could be receiving. Dethom was winning. Dethom liked something. Dethom was not convincing as being one losing what he would be winning. Dethom was hoping when he was hoping. Dethom was hoping when he was winning. Dethom was winning. Dethom was liking that this would be continuing. Dethom was hoping when he was hoping. Dethom was liking something. Dethom was winning. Dethom was expecting what he was expecting when he was winning. Dethom was winning. Dethom was hoping that this would be continuing. Dethom was hoping all he was hoping. Dethom was winning.

Dethom was enlarging what he was enlarging. Dethom was filling what he was filling. Dethom was feeling what he was feeling. Dethom was improving what he was winning.

Dethom was expecting what could be coming. Dethom was hoping what he was hoping. Dethom was feeling what he was feeling. Dethom was filling what he was filling.

Dethom was arranging what he was arranging. Dethom was not arranging what he was destroying. Dethom was not destroying what he was arranging. Dethom was hoping what he was hoping.

Any one being one and remembering that being one is everything of that thing is being one remembering that that thing is something that that one could be remembering if that one had not been then being one forgetting what that one could be remembering. Being one being all of that one is not anything if one is not remembering everything of that thing. Being one being all of that one is something that that one is willing to be arranging when that one is remembering all of that thing.

Clellan, why should Clellan remember all that he is remembering when he is remembering everything that he can remember if he is not being one forgetting that being one is all of being that one. Clellan is remembering all he does remember. Clellan is remembering that being one is all of being that one. Clellan is forgetting what he is forgetting. Clellan is arranging what he is remembering, Clellan is arranging what he is forgetting. Clellan is determining that being one is being all of that one and that remembering and forgetting is not everything. Clellan is arranging that he is being one being all of that one. Clellan is arranging what he is arranging. Clellan is expecting that arranging is everything.

Clellan is forgetting what he is forgetting. Clellan is remembering what he is remembering. Clellan is deciding that forgetting is something, that remembering is something, that arranging is something. Clellan is feeling that he is deciding. Clellan is deciding what he is deciding. Clellan is feeling that being that one is being that one. Clellan is deciding to be arranging that being that one is being that one.

If his contentment had been greater, if Larr's contentment had been greater he would not have been content and he would not have been content because of reasons he could know if he could know that he was not content. His contentment would not be greater if he knew that he was not content because he would then know something of what he did not invent. He did not invent all that he came to tell that he had invented. No he had not invented those things, he had not done any of the things he came to understand in inventing them, in doing them. He did think. He thought very well and in thinking very well he did invent thoughts and in inventing thoughts he told all of them and having told all the thoughts he had invented he told what those thoughts would invent and had invented and he had not invented what he told that he had invented, and they had not been invented those things, they would have been invented if he had had thoughts that would invent them and they were things that were invented and he told how he would have invented them if he had told all that he had told and he invented all the thoughts he said he invented. He did invent all the thoughts he said he invented. Larr did invent many thoughts and he told all the thoughts he invented.

If any one were one being such a one such a one as any one is then that one would be one expressing all of that thing and expressing all of that thing would be what that one expressing is expressing. Each one is one. That is enough to satisfy some, each one being one is enough to satisfy some. One being one is one that many are certain is a different one from the ones others are who are not like that one. That one is a different one and being a different one he is the one knowing everything of there being very many who are just like him. That is enough to satisfy him.

He is one and being one and being afraid enough and being not afraid enough he comes to be one expressing enough of being that one to be the one being that one to any one and every one is satisfied enough that he is that one.

If he said anything and he did say anything, if he said anything he said that he was satisfied enough in being that one to be enjoying something and enjoying something he was losing what he was not keeping and getting what he was having and trying what he was expecting. He was losing enough and keeping enough and getting enough and having enough and trying enough and expecting enough to be that one being that one. Being that one being that one was continuing and continuing he was saying anything of that thing, of being that one and saying anything he was saying that he was saying enough to satisfy himself of something of being that one. He was that one. He was satisfying any one enough that he was that one. He was satisfying himself of something of being that one.

When every one comes not to hear what they hear and see what they see and feel what they feel and mean what they mean, when every one is changing and eating and drinking and dying and when every one is using what they are using and are having what they are having then every one being one every one is being the one every one is being and that being anything and anything being something then something being something and anything being anything and everything being everything every one will be saying what each one of them is saying and each one of them is saying what each one is saying and each one is saying what each one saying is saying.

If Clellan asks a question he will ask if some one knowing something must not be knowing that that can be something to be known. Clellan asking that question is saying that he has learnt quite learnt that knowing something one does not know that that is something that can be known. Clellan is continuing to be working and he will be working when he continues to be working. Clellan is one asking and answering in asking and answering.

If everything is altogether and everything is not altogether, if everything is altogether and everything is altogether, if everything is altogether then everything is something if everything being altogether is anything. Everything being altogether is this thing.

When you see it so clear it is certainly all there. If it is all there then every where is every where. If every where is every where then any one seeing anything clear is seeing it there. Anywhere is anywhere.

Seeing clear is something. Seeing clear is everything. Seeing clear is seeing what any one seeing is seeing and any one seeing is seeing and any one seeing and seeing clear is seeing and seeing clear. Seeing clear is seeing here, seeing clear is seeing there, seeing clear is seeing anywhere. Seeing is seeing. Seeing clear is seeing clear.

If he were seeing clear if Gibbons were seeing clearly he would clearly see that he was describing what he was seeing. Gibbons was describing. Gibbons could describe what he was seeing and wearing and what any one was wearing that he was seeing. If he were seeing clearly he would be seeing that he was describing what he was seeing. He would be seeing clearly if he were seeing clearly and he would be seeing clearly when he saw clearly that he had been describing what some are wearing.

That is what some are doing, some are wearing what they are wearing and are describing what they are wearing.

Lilyman was wearing what he was wearing and in wearing what he was wearing he was clearly seeing that being what he was being he was wearing what he was wearing and was describing what he was describing. He was being the one being all of that one and doing all of that thing and doing all of that thing he was clearly seeing all he was seeing and he was clearly seeing that he was wearing what he was wearing and he was wearing that he was clearly describing what he was wearing, what he was describing. He was describing that if he was clearly seeing he would be wearing all that he could be wearing and he was clearly seeing that he was clearly describing that he was wearing what he was wearing.

Fabefin was not flourishing and not flourishing he was regretting that he was continuing. He was regretting that he had been wearing what he could not be describing. He was seeing what he would not be wearing and seeing what he would not be wearing he was improving in aspiring. He did wear something and he did change the way of wearing that thing and he did then clearly describe that he was wearing what he was wearing in the way he wore what he wore. He did wear something and wearing something he was attacking what he would be wearing if he wore what he could wear. He was not attacking when he was winning. He was not attacking when he was winning and he was not winning. He was wearing what he was describing he was wearing. He was describing that he was wearing what he would wear if he wore what he wore.

Watts did not continue to wear what he would continue to wear. He did not continue to wear that and he did not continue to wear that when he wore what he wore. He was wearing what he did wear.

If anybody wished that they saw what they meant to see then they would see that anything is something. If anything is something then explaining is explaining and explaining being explaining explaining is that thing. Explaining being that thing, anything being something, then wishing to be seeing what they are meaning to be seeing is something and that being something deciding is something. Deciding being something, saying something is saying something.

If some one said something he said that thing, if some one answered something he answered that thing, if they both were then being living any one could be hearing what any one would be hearing. Being finishing and being beginning are being meeting and leaving.

He says that he has said what he said and that changing he is not repeating what he has been saying.

She says that she has said what she said and that changing she is repeating what she has said.

A new thing having come it is a new thing and being a new thing and repeating being existing it is a new thing.

One if he is talking is saying that he is feeling all that he is feeling. He is saying that he is feeling all that he is feeling.

He is saying that feeling all that he is feeling he is saying that he is feeling all that he is feeling.

Donger was not quicker than he would have been if he did not say all that he did say. He was not slower, he was not quicker.

If every one said something and every one is saying anything if any one said something every one would be certain that any one could be tired enough to say what any one says. Saying what any one says is saying everything and any one can be certain that any one can be tired enough to say everything.

Saying everything is what any one saying that they are saying what is being said is saying they can be saying and saying they can be saying everything they can be tired enough in having been saying everything.

Murdock did say that if one were very tired one could come to be completely tired. Murdock did say that being completely tired one was not so tired but that one could look for a way to find what one wanted to find so that one could have a way of saying what one would be saying if one were saying everything. Murdock in not being tired was not troubled that he was quite tired. He was troubled that being tired is being tired and being tired is being certain that everything is everything.

Murdock is not tired. Murdock is not tired because he does not tire when he is hoping that he will not be completing not finding that which he is not persisting in expecting. Murdock is not tired.

There is a way of not being tired. There is a way of coming to know that having a way of doing what one is doing one can do what one does do. Clellan is saying, and he would be tired if one could be tired in saying what he is saying, that having a way of doing what one does one can do what one does. He is saying this thing. He is saying that any one can be tired and every one is tired and not being tired one can do what one does do when one has a way of doing what one does. He is saying that that is all that thing.

He is saying that going to be doing what one is doing is making the doing of that thing a thing to complete tiring the one doing that thing. He is saying that going to be doing what one is doing is what he is not going to be doing again. He is going to do what he does in the way he does what he does. He says that all of that thing is all of that thing.

Enough come so that somebody hears something. Enough go so that hardly anybody is left. Enough are left so that some hear what they hear. Some come where they did not hear and some go where they will see what was seen.

If many come then many are here and if few come then a few are here and if they are here often they come again and coming again they hear what they hear.

One having come and heard is asking if he has heard all that he heard. That one going is not coming again if hearing all he has heard he is not asked to come again. He does come again and asks why he has not heard what he intended to hear. He comes again and hearing what he could hear he asks what it was that he has not heard. Coming again he does not look at what he has not seen because he has seen all of not looking at that and he has asked that that is what he is to hear again. He is that one.

No not all that all can hear is enough to change what all are changing. In changing it all and all is changing in changing it all it is determined that any one who is convinced is convinced. This is why in having what each one is having all are having what all have come to be having. This is enough to determine every one to continue and every one being determined some remain where they did not like to stay and staying there they are determined, quite determined.

Starting in is not beginning because starting in has come when not any one has told all that they have to tell and beginning is beginning telling something. This is all that each one learning is explaining to some one who has or who refuses something.

If the one having what he has keeps what he has he can say that he had what he had but did not expect to keep it.

If one coming to remember all that has been happening knows that he can not lose everything he can decide to give up keeping anything and in that way he can resolve quite completely resolve what he has known he could not resolve. This is all of what has been happening and very much has been happening and very much is happening.

The joy of having a little thing when all of that little thing has disappeared is what is interesting some who are having something of what they have been having. That is not enough to complete quite everything. That is enough to help arrange something.

Having all of something is not useful when all of that thing is lacking what it is lacking. This is not annoying. This is not discouraging. This needs all there is of explanation.

Clellan came to where if he had not come he would have been deciding that not any one going anywhere could come. He did not like everything.

It is in a way what Clellan is doing doing what he has been liking. It is in a way what Clellan is not expecting not doing what he is doing. Clellan is feeling that he has not been arranging everything. Clellan is quite feeling this thing.

All and enough of them have come all have gone away. Some look again. Some do not look again. It is not a sad thing. Always it is not a frightening thing. That is quite enough.

If Antliss had continued to win he would have been astonishing because he could astonish any one by believing what he did believe. He believed what could astonish any one that he was one believing. If he said that he expected all he expected any one could come to be certain that he was not knowing that expecting is what not any one having what he is having is doing. And he was not expecting what he, having what he was having, could be saying that he was expecting without astonishing every one if any one could believe that he was saying what he was saying. Antliss was not peculiar, he was not strange, he was not really frightened, he was not careful, he was not quite stupid, he was not at all lazy, he was not complicated, he was clearly saying what he was saying in the way that not any one is clearly saying that thing. He did feel that something would not be coming and he was not expecting anything of its coming. He was not expecting to be having what he would not be having.

Enough of all who know that they have read something say that reading that thing is quite exciting. Some say that they have come to a conclusion. Some say that there should be more reading before there comes concluding. Any one can say anything.

There comes then to be everything. Very many being mentioned some are remembering something of all of them and are saying that saying what they are saying is saying what is being said.

To begin. There is one. There being one there have been some. There having been some there have been a number but not a great many. Remembering all of them is remembering what any one saying anything is saying. That is enough to arrange something. That is all that has not been mentioned.

Not nicely having what all are having is to be nicely having what all are having. This could be satisfying and being satisfying every one can be remembering something.

Not enough can be enough and being enough quite enough is enough and being enough enough is enough and being enough it is that. Quite all that can be what it is and all of it being that, quite all of it is all there is of it.

Doing it again is not finishing everything. Doing it again and again is not finishing everything. Doing it again and again and again is not finishing everything. Doing it again and again and again and again is not finishing everything. Doing it again and again and again and again and again is not finishing everything. Doing it again and again and again is not finishing everything. Doing it again is not finishing everything.

After Clellan said that he knew that he was not feeling that expression is needing that it is determined he was not feeling all the hope he had been feeling and he had felt more hope when he was not saying what he was saying when he was understanding all he was hearing. Clellan did not deny that he had heard something. Clellan did not deny that he felt something.

Donger liked what he found when he looked for that for which he was looking. Donger did not like all the searching he was doing. Donger did not like all he found when he was tired of looking for that for which he was looking. Donger did not have what he said that he needed and Donger did not begin again. He certainly did not begin again in having been finding everything. Donger said all that.

If it was a long time being living, coming and leaving, it was quite happening very often. It came and it went and sometimes Clellan stayed and sometimes Clellan did not stay.

Clellan not staying was something. Clellan staying was something. That did happen. That did not happen.

All who have a way of not completing, and any one having a way of not completing is any one, all having a way of not completing some time being long enough is long enough and being long enough any one coming and going is, is not staying.

Donger asked if he could go where some one went and he did not get an answer then and he did not need answering enough to complete being living to get any answer later. He came to get what he asked and he did not ask anything he might have asked and he did not because he was not asking. He was not asking and he did not need remembering that thing remembering that he was not asking. He remembered enough.

He talked when he talked very much and he talked when he did not talk very much and he talked.

All that there was if some said what they said was what they all did if they did what they did.

In the beginning one saying something and doing something was remembering that not having been admitting anything that one was one convincing and being convincing was admitting something and admitting something and saying something and doing something was not admitting what was not being convincing. That one was older and being older was doing was saying what that one had been doing and saying.

If any one can determine that they are saying what they are saying and doing what they are doing they are determining that they are hearing what they are hearing and seeing what they are seeing. This is not exciting, this can be annoying, this can be common, this can be convincing, this can be perplexing, this can be repeating.

One and he was one and any one can be one and any one is one and any one being one being one is being one, one was saying what he was saying and doing what he was doing and he was determining what he was saying and determining what he was doing and he was hearing what he was hearing and seeing what he was seeing.

If some one came and another one came and some one said and another one said and some one heard and another one heard and some one saw and another one saw then there would be enough who were dead if everybody came to be dead and there would be enough being living if every one were living and certainly some did not see everything and some did not do everything and some did not hear everything and some did not see everything and one said what another said and one saw what another saw and one did what another did and one heard what another heard and one came and another came and one left and another left and if everybody did what they did and anybody came and if they did not see what they saw and if they heard what they heard then certainly something had happened and something having happened some said what they said.

It was a happy way the way he stayed all day any day and he said, what did he say, he said that he had gone and he had seen and that he would do what he liked to do and he liked to do what he had arranged to feel he would do when he saw all there was to see.

In looking for everything and finding everything and asking any one to leave all that they had and to give all they had some are seeing that they are seeing all that there is to be seen.

It was not satisfying, not upsetting, not amusing, not perplexing to say all that is being said about any one having been feeling what that one was feeling.

Polly and she was not using all she had bought Polly was offering and forgetting to give what she would give if she had had packed what she had taken up to pack. Polly did not remember everything.

Anne Helbing is standing. Anne Helbing in standing was wearing what some would not be needing to be wearing if they could stand without wearing them. Anne Helbing had them on and she was standing, Anne Helbing was sitting, Anne had them on and was sitting. Anne told some one that she had them on. Anne did not come back again and she was not suffering and she was working. Anne was standing and sitting and was wearing the things she needed for standing.

George did not come when he had not had all that he would have had if he had gone everywhere where he could go. He found a thing that he gave every one. He did not take what he intended to take.

Henns was prospering that is to say he had a wife and a baby and he had been sick. This was not all he had in being living and he thought about it and he did all that he did in getting what he got.

Henns had a father and a brother. His father was prospering that is to say he married again and he need not have done it then and he did not keep all that he kept when he continued in not being annoying. The brother, Henns had a brother, the brother was prospering. He was directing everything he was directing and he was accidentally dying. Henns did not come back when he was where he was and he did not continue when he did what he did and he was prospering when he received what he received and when he did not expect to have any more children. He did not have very many children.

Antliss was not successful in urging every one to be the one hearing what every one could be hearing. Antliss was not successful. Antliss expected that some who were not successful would be continuing feeling what they were feeling. They were feeling what they were feeling. Antliss was not successful, he was holding all he was expecting to be able to hold. He was urging all he could urge in explaining the way he was explaining that he was feeling what every one is feeling.

Some are dead and if they had heard that said they would not repeat that they were dead.

Sender came and he said that those who were not dead had not said what some said they said. Sender did not stay long. Sender intended to come again. He would come again. When he came again he would say something of what some who were not dead had not said.

All who are tired and are hearing what they are hearing are expecting to be hearing that some one who is waiting is going to ask if he will be visited. It is a very difficult thing being tired and hearing what one is hearing when some are not asking what they might be asking.

It is easy to begin again if repeating is anything and repeating being existing it is a difficult thing to commence answering something and commencing answering is all of that easy thing and that easy thing is existing.

All who have left have not come again and coming again they are saying that it is an easy thing not to hear what they are hearing, not to repeat what they are repeating.

It is kindly to be friendly, it is pleasant to be repeating, it is agreeable to be returning having been answering, it is charming that some one says something, it is pleasing that some one has heard something, it is disturbing that some one has not been expecting something, it is astonishing that some one has forgotten something, it is disappointing that some one is not saying that he has not seen what he has seen, it is saddening that some one has put something back and has gone then and has come to leave nothing that he had when he came. It is enough to please any one that every one who has come has not said all that they say when they come again. It is not amusing when two who have come have gone. It is not disturbing when three who have come and gone have asked a question. It is not interesting when some one who is pleasing has pleasantly explained everything.

If in having told a thing one has been appreciated then one can want not to tell it again and one can tell it again and one can be interesting then and one can be not very interesting then. It is exciting to be tired and to tell all that has been told. It is exciting to be tired and to be not expecting anything. It is exciting to be tired and to sit and tell all about everything any one is doing. It is exciting to be tired.

If it were pleasing to be enjoying one could enjoy something and one could say that they had heard all that they heard. If it is not pleasing to be enjoying and if it is not pleasing is it continuing, if it is not pleasing to be enjoying and one is hearing what one is hearing then certainly if there is any purpose in enjoying being pleasing then it is easy enough not to be enjoying.

Is it or isn't it pleasing not to be enjoying and if it is is it continuing and if it is not is it continuing. If it is what it is then it is easy enough for it to stay where it stays and if it stays where it says is it what it has been. Donger saw what he said meant something and he said that if it meant something he was doing what he did not intend to do and he did not intend to finish everything he began. Donger said that he saw what he said meant something and he did know that when he asked if something was something he did know that an answer would come and if it came it might not come again. If it came again and an answer that came might come again it might be the thing that would determine him to ask something that he had just asked. Donger said that he knew that what he said had that meaning.

Donger knew enough to remember that if something is something he could ask what he would ask if, he knew what he knew. Donger knew and asked and he said perhaps it is perhaps it isn't and he said that if he asked and something is something it was very well for him to have asked what he hoped to ask.

They all liked asking that any one who decides what is decided decides, when it is to be decided that that which is to be decided is to be decided. They all ask and they all do not refuse and they all do not hear and they all stay and they all stand and they all open what has been open when anything that is open is open. If they do not like it they will ask so that they can not like it and when they can not like it it is enough that they have seen enough to have seen what they have seen. It is not very likely that any of them felt that it would be finished in the way it came to be finished. It is not very likely.

Enough of them who walk walk quickly and so there are very many. There being very many and very many not walking there are very many.

If he told each one what each one wanted to know who asked him who had come he would have to tell each one what he told the one who had just asked him. And he did this thing.

Any one talking and every one talking and any one laughing and every one laughing might be meaning that they were feeling that some one was a funny one. This is not certain.

Not like that is the other way and like that is the same way and all are not doing again, walking. Walking is sounding and talking is existing.

Pulling and going is regularly sounding and answering is intermittently continuing. Running and disappearing and gesticulating and waiting is happening.

Being proud and easily pleased and surprised and amused and quiet and quickly walking and sufficiently eating is regularly sounding.

Talking and not turning and answering and not seeing is quietly continuing. Waving and showing what is imitating is copying some one.

A little one preparing is a little one expressing and a little one expressing is a little one discovering and discovering is saying what is truly efficiently existing and saying what is truly efficiently existing is describing what everything badly chosen is lacking.

He was pleased to hear that we ate all we ate. He was pleased to hear that we left what we left. He was pleased to hear that we had been where we had been. He was pleased to hear that we asked what we asked. He was pleased to hear that we knew what we knew. He was pleased to hear that all had looked at what they had looked.

He who made a motion to call some one made a noise and then he said that he had been misunderstood and he said that he would repeat what he had said and then he said that he had not been understood and that he would not ask what he had asked. He said that he knew what he would not hear and that he would not ask again.

If all did what they turned to do they would all stay wherever they went and all staying any one going away would notice something. That is enough to make any one remember all of the thing that was seen when some did not do so quickly as some one else would do something that one had come to do.

If the one saying all was saying then saying all would be the thing that not every one who was saying all would then say. Enough is said if every one is saying all.

If every one is saying all and every one is saying after waiting is saying we are coming, we are going, we are meeting then every one is saying what each one is saying and each one is saying everything that each one is saying.

If they are all not alike that is enough to arrange being certain that expressing what expressing is expressing is not expressing what expressing is not expressing and anyway a pie that each one is putting where each one is putting the pie each one is putting anywhere, in putting the pie where each one putting a pie anywhere is putting a pie each one is not putting the pie where in putting the pie he might be putting the pie and each one is putting the pie where each one putting the pie anywhere might be putting the pie in putting the pie where each one is putting the pie that is anywhere. Each one putting the pie anywhere is putting the pie anywhere. This is enough to please all and all are not pleased when all are pleased. All are pleased and nicely pleased and completely pleased when all are all pleased and all are not pleased not quite pleased when each one doing what each one is doing each one is not seeing that any one doing what any one is doing is doing and a nice house where some have come and a house not so nice where some have come, all of it and any of it is what is not annoying and each one has eaten what has left in them all that has come out of them if they face a way which is the other way they were facing when they were facing the way they were facing when they were facing the other way.

One not being running was not being deserted. One not being waiting was not being deserted. One not interfering was receiving what the other one had who had what she naturally had and she would have what she naturally had if she could have what she would naturally have.

If refusing is easily done then it is to be done as it is done when it has come to be done so that some one will say to all, do not do so.

It is very high up and yet to be so high is not to say that that is likely to be heavy if it is built lightly enough so that falling is not easy.

Falling is not easy and it is not easy when there is a river that is bigger than it is where it is smaller and it is not easy when there are ways of hearing enough sounds that make all the little things come together who were scattered until they were called. Falling is not easy.

It is impossible to disturb every one and yet it is done when anything which is walking is appearing. It is done and then that is not ended not at all ended. It is done and some little thing is not completed when it is done. Not enough is left then to remain where any one had been.

Not any of all who were not wrong were right and that could have been what some were saying if all were not saying what they saw when they looked where they fell.

They did not fall all over the pleasant sound that was being sung. They did not fall and they did not sit and they walked pretty well and in walking they had not all the sizes they would have. They had sizes that were larger and they had sizes that were smaller.

The ones who clap when they laugh and laugh when they look mean that that they clap when they laugh and laugh when they look.

They all, all who saw while they heard what they heard, all were there and remained until they were not to stay where they were any longer.

There was enough of all that had been done again to start all those who were started to come again. They all came again. They came again and they sat while they heard what they heard and saw all of some of what they saw.

If some one was not liking doing something more it was not because that one was feeling all of more being more it was because that one had not had what she had not had when she had wanted what she had wanted.

Finishing not wasting any little thing is beginning not wasting any little thing. It is enough that all who are finishing not wasting any little thing are bowing when what has been living has come to be dead by rolling over after kneeling. It is enough that some who are finishing not wasting any little thing are waiting and doing very little moving when what is dying has not been dead enough to be rolling.

They have something growing those who are finishing wasting any little thing and if that which is growing is showing it is a completing thing, a strangely completing thing.

If one has a thing that on the front of him is browning and he is proceeding and meaning is existing, that is if he is the one and any one is proceeding then he is the one and he is proceeding.

If they did not like it they would do it and this was not lightly why there were three of them sitting and this was not uneasily why three were standing and this was not suddenly why five of them were coming and this was not entirely why all of them were waiting.

They who had a house and had all of it were the ones who had enough of it to come out and in and to do it often. If there were three of them three houses there were all of them all of the three houses three houses.

If making a little movement such as nodding is done then it is a custom that any one meeting any one is not talking if they have not met that one. If they look if every one looks and has not said that he is feeling then all of them are doing what they are doing because they have not come to say what they could say if they had come to say what they would say. This is in a way a pleasant way of walking and disappearing. This is in a way a way of feeling that what is happening is surprising. This is in a way a way of not regretting everything.

If in leaving some one is leaving then in having been disappearing some one has been disappearing and has not been saying that he has said what he said he would say if he saw what he would have seen if there had been what there would have been if there was what there was as there was not.

A tiny violent noise is a yellow happy thing. A yellow happy thing is a gentle little tinkle that goes in all the way it has everything to say. It is not what there was when it was not where it is. It is all that it is when it is all that there is.

If she who was lifting the thing that lifting was lifting she was arranging putting anything where she was arranging putting what she was arranging. If putting a thing that can be cutting where some one is jumping is disconcerting it is a neat thing that not any one is being quite cut then. It is a delicate thing that hanging down something is a gentle thing. It is a lively thing that moving and clapping is a measured thing. It is a queer thing that singing is a common thing. It is an amusing thing that two are where they are when they were not where they were.

If they are what they are and they intend what they do and they offer what you use and they wear what they wear then it is naturally all that they mean when they do not say that they are strange every day. They move the way they go as they do not stay together in not at all leaving one another. They do not manage it then when they are standing and mounting anything they are riding. They need not be the last of it all and they need not have been an irregular thing a thing not regularly living.

If saying that being is existing is meaning that feeling is existing, then talking when talking is happening is telling what is being told by telling. Any sound that is louder or not so loud is one that is happening when that sound is coming.

It is not necessary that a light that is changing is coming and going. It is necessary that a sound that is continuing is coming from the two who are sighing.

Likely to be familiar and not likely to be strange, very likely to be the same and quite likely to be dark, likely enough to have it light and very likely to have it strong, any way that is likely is very likely to be old and every way that is likely is quite likely to be curling and all that is likely is that it will not be different.

In turning a little thing into a little little thing and rolling what was walking, it is not enough to be certain that it happening is not anything, it is necessary to do it, quite do it again.

Multiplying is not adding, that is to say it is adding and adding is not marking, adding is not bowing, adding is not laughing, adding is that which walking comes to be sitting and not expecting all of any attention. Adding is not complicating. Adding is teasing. Adding is a division of three and one and that would make four if all of adding was subtracting.

A little way is longer than waiting to bow. Not bowing is longer than waiting longer. It would sadly distress some powder if looking out was continual and sitting first was happening and leaving first was persisting. It would not change the color, it would not harmonise with yellow, it would not necessitate reddening, it would not destroy smiling, it would not enlarge stepping, it would not widen a chair or arrange a cup or conclude a sailing, it would not disappoint a brown or a pink or a golden anticipation, it would not deter a third one from looking, it would not help a second one to fasten a straighter collar or a first one to dress with less decision, it would not distress Emma or stop her from temperately waiting, it would not bring reasoning to have less meaning, it would not make telling more exciting, it would not make leaving necessitate losing what would be missing, it would though always mean that three and one are not always all that remain if ten remain and eight are coming.

They always thought that they did all eat what was said to be what was given to them. They did not fail themselves then.

If the color is not dark and it is dark but is not predestined, if the color is dark and the passing away of walking is not too quick then all that was expected from asking was that what had been done had not had any way of laughing. That was what was left when there had been all that was not meaning that what was dark had come to be dark as it was dark as it had been dark. It was not lighter.

The only feeling that is she is the way she did not see and she did lean she did quite lean alone. She did not desert the reward and she had it all and she did bow and there was there where she went there was there certainly all of not needing to be refusing having her relieve saying good evening. She did not have it all on and there could be more and often when she was there she wore that which was where she was and it was not all cut from the same place and that was not ceasing to be intending to be completing being leaning and she was leaning and she was not refusing needing to be keeping addressing bowing. She magnified repeating being existing in repeating. She did not repeat speaking. She did not deny good evening. She did not repeat leaning alone in leaning where she was not without not leaning being existing.

All who stayed long enough and talked said what they said. He who talked did not say what he said because he had been the one who had come to stay away. And this was not anything. He liked having it and he liked asking to leave it.

All of them were not alone. The way to be alone, the way to stand and walk, the way to sit and look, the way to talk, all of it is not beguiling and passing away is a way to complain.

Very likely they did not have a little more those who had and have what they have. Very likely the ones they know are the ones they know. Very likely it would not do any harm to say what they say as they do say what they say. Very likely they can laugh when they laugh and very likely they like what they like when they like what they like.

It is always a way to say that going away is a way in going away.

If stumbling is continuing then a side-walk is restoring. If a side-walk is restoring then eating is satisfying. If eating is satisfying then undertaking is beguiling. If undertaking is beguiling then shooing is concentrating. If shooing is concentrating then resounding is destroying. That is the way to sleep.

If a piece that is longer is longer and stirring is wetting then surely no one need know anything.

To refuse is the way to refuse all the way and there is enough and to spare when in being asked to take what is given not being there is all there is of not having had anything. Quantities are not lost when there is satisfaction and yet there is the whole way of counting and there is some way of retiring. Nevertheless it cannot be seen that the way to remove what is not seen is not the way that washing makes plain. It is slightly difficult to have what is being had and to say that sleeping is sleeping a little any day. It is not thoughtful to think that the way to make a sound is by hearing a roaring that may be a mingling and certainly is existing.

All the perplexity of congratulation is removed when two are talking and are saying that they are not where they were. They have been moving and they saw one and pleasantly took something and they did not see one and this had to do with eating. Particularly undertaking refusing everything is a means that is wholesome when health and wealth is not deteriorating. All that can be included is not all that is withheld and rashly enough the water that came all flowed away. There was then a happy ending.

If two talking together are saying that they have not been together when each one saw something then they are not always listening, they are sometimes tired. This is enough so so that two can be married.

One is the one who came and looked down and did not frown and could walk longer if the way which is long is harder. This one who did walk went back again and said that that which was seen was peculiar. The one who did not walk would walk longer and did walk and did see that thing and did say that perhaps it was peculiar but it did not matter as it would not be seen again and certainly not longer. They were not opposing listening neither the one or the other who was talking. They were not asking it again as much and this was the way of arranging that there was not to be all there was of future. They took a walk together and they came oftener and they were not hidden by the light that made a flicker. They had undertaken enough.

It was a lovely way and the man who stood was slow and the hidden thing that was clearly seen was climbing in between. If either was together and the two were all then it was not only lightly but delicately and completely and astonishment never can be expressive.

Altogether to look and pronounce that conversation is not pleasing is the way to accept responsibility and to have children. This is not alarming. It is happening every day when the dining room is changing.

If the child is bigger and the noise comes quicker then the part that is standing is lifted and the noise is not continuing. When the way to remove what is lying has been seen then a little one that has an apron ties a string and lying on anything is sleeping. This is not occupying all of anything. Actually there has been a condition. Actually there is a condition. Actually all of them are together. They are there and are there where they stand and sit and look often. They are continuing.

If the accumulation of inexpediency produces the withdrawing of the afternoon greeting then in the evening there is more preparation and this will take away the paper that has been lying where it could be seen. All the way that has the aging of a younger generation is part of the way that resembles anything that is not disappearing. It is not alright as colors are existing in being accommodating. They have a way that is identical.

Charging the admission is not the only way of doing. Opening the falling and seeing the illuminating is not the only way of whitening. The oily half of the higher place is the hard things that do not get in and remain. They change what is darker and they make louder what is regular. They keep together and separate later. That is all of the rest. The half that sleep are opening what is receiving. The two parts are enough together to be closer. They are not seeking anything that is muddier. Something is running and the sound is not increasing. It is loud enough to wet the thing that is beginning. It is not undertaking to see what is seen. Sleeping is continuing. Joining is quite soothing. All ways are remarking something. It is again. It is where it has been. One again and one again and that is everything as that is something. All of the eating is beginning. One two has it. That is often. There is no remaining that there is complaining. It is filling.

Standing and expressing, opening and holding, turning and meaning, closing and folding, holding and meaning, standing and fanning, joining and remaining, opening and holding.

It is a way the way to say that being finished is all of waking, it is a way to say that not doing again what is being done again is a way of intending to assist an only one. It is not too distracting to be there where closing is coming before opening. It is the only way to know everything. It can be done. All of the way is that way. Hardly ever is there more perfection. All perfection is increasing. This is stimulating and causing sleeping. One is there in the beginning and is finding interrupting to be decreasing. That one is recommending saluting. That one is not disappointed. That one is obliging. That one is remaining the complete expression of knowing everything. That one is there and there is that one.

A heavy way to pass that way is not the last way to pass that way. Passing that way is passing away. It is being done again.

When the twin is not one and there has been a fat one the thin one is not losing delicate existing. Singing is everything.

A far away place is near the place that is having the carriage standing. Any one driving is bumping. That is the only way of returning excepting walking.

A simple way of remaining away is not to say that the only way of passing the day is waiting for what has come to stay. It is not so very long and then any one can join. They do join, that one is the one used to beginning and she is not moving where the light is not shining. This is not a habit it is the way that changes some day when any change is repeating what each one has been saying.

Which did she put in and take out again and which did she put in and leave in and what did she say when she did put everything away and what did she say when everything was not put away. She said that she was not suffering. She said it was fatiguing. She said she was not worrying. She said she would not ever do it again. She said she would not leave anything. She said she would finish something in the morning. She said she did not mean to begin again. She said she was not satisfied with everything. She said she did not care to repeat what she had said. She said she would be obliging. She said that that was not surprising. She said that she did not have any such feeling. She did do everything. She was succeeding. She was pleasing.

She could not be saying that authorising something was believing that she was not having what she was having. Now I have it. Now I see. This is the way. Not that way. The other way is not the way.

A lively way to call is to run and call and a lively way to stand is to stand. A very lively way to say what is to say is to say that a happy way to go away is to pay when there is something that can come to be there where there will not be any way to say that there will not be pay. He came back and offered enough so that when he heard what there was he could advise that they had a precious thing. He did scold some. He was not too neglectful when he went where there was not any smiling. He adjoined where there was no indication of the meaning of acquisition. He was all the same not tormented. He did not tolerate the rest. He did not refuse that. He chose where he would leave what he had hoped to choose. He did say everything. He told all that.

If there is not a duplicate when there is every way of telling that the time is changing then it is very satisfying. There is the most complete way of moving when some one disappearing has been calling. The sound that is left is not so loud as the sound that would be left if all the rest of the way was open. This is not enough to make any one really unhappy.

If the little way was that way and the smell remained it would be nice to smell tobacco. This is not the only mixture. Something else is pleasing.

Half of all that which is the matter is the part that is the rest of the disturbance and it is not a bother, not at all, it does not matter and that is a simple matter, it is very simple, it comes to be that when there is enough left and there is enough left when everything is there and when everything is there that causes all that kind of pleasure and all that kind of pleasure means it all. He was not very much afraid and this was not the way he meant to say that he was prettily drawn this is the way he meant to say that he agreed to follow and discover all that often. He was a medium sized but not like that in saying enough. He was the best of all. He was there and he did not dispute that he saw all he saw. He was not obliging. There were there the same. They satisfied that. They were equitable. They were not lenient. They were there. They placed that. This is the same.

Water did not make all the best curves, it did some curving, it used to make a noise, that is not the only way of washing, soap and some kinds that smell are not the same as the best perfume. This is not the best way to be loving. There is a way to be loving. The way to be loving is to do that and not to say that something is something. That is not the only way of having a feeling of having to sit where the sun is shining. The only way to say what is the meaning of anything is to say that thing and say it every morning and evening and in between and in between there will be the whole day and a day is a kind of a day and a kind of a day comes when there will not be again such a one. It is very likely that the raising of the beginning is the saddest thing to keep continuing. It is very likely that all the better will be coming. It is certainly establishing that which will be succeeding. The water will be sweeter and the soap has some intention. There is a lively winning of establishing completely that which is continuing when one and that one is the one who says what is said and that one will do that will say it all, will be deciding something and something being anything, anything is everything. It is the best way that way which is that way and that way is establishing everything. All is alike. That is not decided. All being alike control is the arrangement. One can say the same. One sees all that.

The card said that the whole thing was the right size, and it was disappointing that it was not there. The card did not say everything.

All holy and walking and all the rest not passing the two were certainly saying that the whole evening was ending. They did not dispute that. They had the principle of not being astounding. They were not wonderful. They admired half of what was all there was. There was enough. They did not leave it all. They were the only ones to say that they saw the little things that did not eat any little piece. It was undertaken. It was not done. They saw some looking. They did not change their expression.

Pocketing by the pocket having in it what is in it is the illustrious way of seeing the lights that are lit and seeing the spots that are black. All the sun and the moon and the clouds and the lights together can not help all the people who are living some where else where it is comfortable for some who say that they like to see what they see. They did not change the heavy horses and the quick carriages and the whistling train and the lights that are lit, they did not change the best flowers and fruits and cake, they did not dislike the kind of stones that were shown where they were shown. They did not. They mentioned everything. This is the way to say that they are not saying anything to-day.

Leading the rain through the thing that is open and making it wet where the smell has been smelling is the hardest way to kill the whole bull that is charging in and running. It is not losing everything in losing all the blood that is oozing. It is goring. It is not distressing. That is one way to delay what is happening when it happens that day. They all waved something. That was not everything. They did the rest. They remained, they had all the noise. They did not disturb him and he was one who was exciting and he was excited then. He held all that open. He went telling that he was always willing. He did not repeat being winning. He received all the sum and he said all that made him sad. He did not advise anything. He was not there to be the only one. He said he knew that. He did not leave the ring. He was obliging. He did not do anything. He said he did not do anything. It was not a test. He knew all the rest. He had done the same. It had been startling. He was not subdued. He did not come distinguishing any one from every other one. He was between some one and some other one. He did move away. He said that that was all there was to do. He showed what he held up so that any one could see what there was there. He was not refusing it. He did not say all there was to say. He was not tired.

If the reason that the way that is the leaning in the writing is the time when the little that is all that is four is the most that there is and there can be all which is the most then the best which is the one is the thing that is the four those four and there will be more. A hundred and the hall and the rest and a ball and a little one who is not staring, and the sound that is there where there is not too much air is the pretty sound that comes when the only one says what is said about air and sounds and heads. This is the best way and so there is the time and there is all that and there is more and more is enough and there is what will be wanted and it will be all the same and not any more is gone when more is there where everywhere everything is all there. That is enough and so much, such a thing, why the way it is made is the way it is and really there can be all that. In the time there is that time which is all of the whole of it where there is not anything that is not where there is one and one is that one and one. A loud sound is louder than any other way a sound is loud.

Alarming looking at each one has begun. That is not the only way to stay away. The rest of the way is gone when there is none who are pleasing to some one who is one of the two of them and they are both agreeing. The necessity of not using everything is what keeps them staying.

They did come. They came and it was the way they said they had stayed that made the little one who sat where there was a seat eat what he ate. He ate that and it was not the only way to ask for a pencil, it was almost the best half of the whole that made them answer that the one who had changed had been fatter. They said he had looked as if he were fat when he was fatter, they said they were altogether. They meant that her name was Lucy. They did not remember to say it. It was not complicated. Everybody was not tired.

Half of the little piece was enough and if there was a quick movement there would not be any change as the four who came would not come often. That was the very friendliest thing to do to have a little pew and not to sit in it and not to keep still a minute and to have a bed and to have it said that the bed is not the best bed that was made when there were not left any beds that had marble that was not colder than some other that was not marble when it was where they saw it. It was not the only bone the piece that was left when the day passed and in the evening it was late, it was not the only piece there was when the little one said that he would not stay to eat if he was to be taken away to go to bed. They all ate something and they knew it was wet. Yesterday had not been away. That was not easy not to say. They did say that they had not been away.

All across the best of the wall space there is the place that is where the pretty thing is and not alone is it there not alone, it is not there. This is not what he said. He came to say that he knew that all that that meant was that he had done very well to keep all those he kept because if it did happen that he meant to keep away he would not have all that which he said he had and he did not mean to refuse everything he meant to finish very nicely. He did say that. He had been agreeable. This was not the last time that he had the place finished. Certainly not.

Able to answer he said that he was looking as he had to stay where there was what he saw, he said that he liked flowers, he said that if he whom he did not like to have living was rich, anything was awful. He did not hesitate then. He came alone. That was nicer then, he did not say that he had written the rest. If there was shown a piece that took up all that space he would not part with it. He would not part with any of it. Any day that was yesterday would keep bringing what he needed. He knew that he had that little way. He said that he did not hear anything. He came to remember a country that had been seen.

He was not the only one to have the meaning that a cold day that is darker is darker. He did not underestimate the last of production. He did say that he did not get any pleasure when one was showing what there was. He did not wish to go. It was not the rest. He did not refuse to repeat everything.

It was a likely day to hear the music play the day when the little one was not any larger. She did decide the very wide street to avoid and she did not say how prettily they play. She did not hesitate any. She was not the tallest who sat there. She was the distinct expression of the only decision. She was the leader of the exercise that expressed that the way to do is not the only way to stay. She was remarkable.

How sweetly the tune that is written is saying that obeying is meaning that apologising is not beautifying. How sweetly the tune that is winning is expressing that regretting is not necessitating repetition. How nicely there is agreeing when leaning is not forbidden. How sweetly is repeating expressing that feeling is pleasing. How tenderly is the expression expressing that all of it is saluting the whole of that which is the same as that which is what is when changing is not dividing. It is nicely done.

Not to ask the way when there is nothing else to say is the only way to stay away. A longer one is not shorter. He can have a beard.

A lovely decision is the marvelous hope when the refusal is sullen and the fire is going, a better piece of light is going when there has been admiration for a piece that has been showing. Then turning away is the way to give all the rest of the description of the reason that the whole piece is together and has that meaning. I did not like her. She was not unpleasant. She was not the only one to say that she did not know that I did that. It was not a reputation. She was not antagonistic.

If there is no time to have the predestination, there can be half of all that there is when there is all they have. They like living. They say they are not hot. They say that the way to smell is to have the same thing stay that is touched when touching is not diminishing. They need the bath-room. They are not healthy. They have light and heat.

A remarkable exhibition was the one that showed that an aptitude for delineation is the same as adjustment. It was admitted that having explained that there would be undertaken a readjustment. The end was outlined. The completion was distinguished. The relative actuality was not detailed. There was precedence. There was not lingering. There was the article that was not destroying. There was that meaning. There was the description. These did have what there was no need to occupy. There came to be that.

If the potatoe was there and the light were bright then it would be sweet to be clean and to have the same seat. It is always necessary to carry the same piece of bread and butter. It is nicely brown and yellow and prettily sticking together that with what it is when it is where it is and it is where it is as it is only where it is. It is the particular attraction by which it is the piece that is eating and being eaten. It is mentionable. It is not deceptive. It is the practice of everything. It is what is necessary.

If the travelling has a way of stopping the staying where there is continuation then certainly there has been that there is what is when there is that time and condition. This is enough to begin that satisfaction and commence that finishing.

In the part of the gold piece that has a bright center there is the little place that hurts. It is the sweetest way to be any way.

The article that in sitting is slowly telling that starting is not happily achieving the blameworthy criterion of arresting all abomination, the particle there is when there is diminishing the precipitation there is when the parting is not nearing, all the exchange which is not returning is affording that illusion. It is not darkened.

Kindly let the person who in the pleasure is not accepting repudiating anything, kindly let the one who is not anticipating accompany herself then, kindly say something. She who is not destroyed is not obliging to be refusing to reform what she is offering. She is not urgent. She has not that participation. It is not altered when the time is increased and the balancing is not upsetting when there is all that disagreement. There is not compensation. She who is likely is possibly likely.

If he who threw it gaily was sitting he changed some position when he gave some direction. He was younger.

There is the piece that is open and there is what there is commencing and there is not any obstacle and there will not be any disposal.

If there is a high way and the pleasure of it is there when the lower is sounding then the evening is not finishing and standing is passing. It is not silent.

The grammar that is used is that which has that same way and it darkens that piece which is every piece. It is not the penetration that brings it all about. It is the loneliness that is what is the only way to say that the blue eyes are the same and when there is not any change from any name. It is possible.

The bargaining that is not coming when there is not that decision is what has been suppressed. It will not happen.

The evening when the light piece is blacker and the darkness has not come to engage anything is the satisfying shining. It is lying and there it is the best when there is not that prediction. It is not a position.

If there are two and there is one there and another in the other direction then slightly being pleased is to be happy. There is that reason for not using the light that is to be burning. There is such a simple way to say that breathing is that satisfaction. There is some pleasure. This is the nature. That is the sound. There is the place.

If the particular objection is that there is a long time to keep that ready which has to be used when there is that waiting then the whole situation is the same when the garden is full and the objects are separated by a piece of paper. The rain does not hurt everything. It can be cold.

It is a steady bargain that which takes every one away. It is not the only place to praise.

All the appetite that makes that little pain is not so far ahead when the change is imminent. The one had that abandonment. It took all that concentration.

He did not leave enough to establish the whole fire-place. This was bragging. He had all that to authorise.

Evading and then relaxing and then stipulating and then hearing that there is a protection is not the whole way to have it said that there has been laughing.

There where the voice is parting it is not changing the meaning. It is the same. It has that elongation.

The president who has that definition is the one who has that decoration. He is not placid. He is not discourteous. He is not robust.

He who wondered heard the listening and he was not distracted. He had that intimate progression. It was not a party.

A best feeling is that which if that one has not been adding is what that one is hoping to be smiling. He was not tender. If he was simple he saw the way to ask not to have that which would be paid be paid away. He did not come to get that pay. He used it all. He had not that hope. He was begetting bargaining. He had that intention. He was predicting succeeding.

A lot of dark ways are cheerful. They predict assuagement. It is not past the time when all that has been sent has bought a loud sound. A loud sound is not artificial. There can be enjoying satisfaction.

Let him see that in leading he has the sound that he is hearing. Let him do that and the time he says he takes away is what he says needs tender breathing. He is the best of all the poor and he is the most startling when he is not alone. He describes everything.

The far help that teaching is not deceiving is urging him to repeat that Isadore is money. He does not deny that of Lisa. He does not pass away.

A little piece cut off is not added if the piece of grain is using that emotion. There is not that way to stay.

If we go away we say that we go away because if we stay we stay away from there where we would be if we were where we were as we are when we are there. We are not there. We do not say that we do not stay.

A way to say the way to go is the way to say that she is there. That is the place that is not occupied. What dexterously indicate the augmentation. It is not a precipice. Please the practice and the sight remains restless. That is not the discomfort of every name. It is almost enough to destroy a place. It is enormous. It is not rushing.

If the banner which is not hung waves gently that does not mean that the only way to say that there must come to be a drum is the best way to put all the pages in the paper. It is harder to hit the sitting position than to stand up the way to stand up in being tried. This does not mean that all that is mixed has the salt taste that pepper has.

The whole meeting has that noise and the noise not following some one is talking.

There Harriet has come. She did that so well that enough sitting was so wholesome that Jane did not go away. She did not have that idea.

Emma was not that one who said that she had been looking for some one. She was the one that had the same warm cloak that was hers when she bought her clothing and she had enough money that did not mean that if William were waiting he would not stand on the end of his ulster. He did not have that diagram. All the cabs were open. This did not make the night colder. This did not show the Lutetia.

A practical lesson is one that is given.

Come to the edge of the border and there with enough crocheting any one who is hard of hearing can come to have a subdued voice. A little iron comes to take that place and that is not a discovery. A sign is enough to destroy that invention.

He and she were sitting there and he and she were not comforting everywhere where there is a chair. They did not put a little piece there where there was a chair. They did not feel what they did when the name that had used all of the time was mentioned. They were not employed in looking.

Let the best way of saying how do you do occupy the morning and the evening. This will not fill all the time. Happy day.

Ask the two to look at the table. One is not always looking. The other has that astonishment. Something has changed. That is what would be the defence if any one saw that she was flatter. She had the smile and it was not lightening all her evenings. They were not always too hot. They closed the heater.

Come and see the baking that does not trouble the oven and the kitchen. There is not time to have the whole of all that glass and yet surely the day is not darker than the rest of the evening. To open the door is not to lose that look of there being some change and surely there is enough to worry any one. She is anywhere.

He had not that plan and he was quite young. That did not make him speak french. He spoke it quicker. In that way he was attracting having all of the feeling that passing being a worker was giving to him.

She who was not resplendent was so honest that if she gave it all away she made it cleaner. She did not look that way. She was using that attraction and she was not so orderly that she did not own everything. She could go away any way.

A longer brown when there is a chair there is what gives that long meaning to that extreme extension. If it happens and there is any way than certainly to stay is to stay away and that is the plan when any certain one is the certain one that says he says he has all that there can have been and is of that which is some plan. There is not that defeat.

The sight that is the same as that hearing is the one that takes enough of all that evening and so the whole which is what there is when ten have that leaning is the weight and the height and the volume and there is all there is of ten who are enough there.

They are there and the entrance is there where there is that air. They have not come in to fill the time together they have the same invention and that is all there is of that distraction.

Passing that expression they have all there is of what there is in some indication. They have not that which is the same expression. This is that position.

A lame way to say that the day is not that time and to stay away is that intention is to repeat one question, to repeat that extension. He said that he could not go to bed and he would not stay away because any day is a cold day. He said all he said and then he came in. He was in and he said that he said that same and that different thing. He did not accuse that of being all of that thing. He said he was distributing that extinction.

Pull it there and sit on that chair that is to say put out the hand and walk forward and not push away what is not there where there is that decoration. A longer stay and later going away and giving the attention where the hand is extending that thing is not filling every one with anything.

Separate them and do not put between them that which while not waiting is paying attention to that thing.

Place the laughing where the smile is lending what there is of expecting that attention. It is not expecting something. It is obeying all of that consideration.

A place to stay when sitting and standing are so increasing that that which is exciting is spreading is the continuing of engaging the whole of that expression. It is rising and pervading. It has that to hear.

Waste not want not have a piece of carpet, use the laugh when longer use it any time you go away. That is to say a heavy way to leave it all alone is to use the time in every way.

A parcel. A parcel is the thing that when there is a heavy one is the one that every one eating is not receiving. They were all there. They each had that diversion. They came to have the time when they were not accepting that string which was not there when the paper was not there. They all had some of that intention.

Powdering a little pepper and neglecting that in the morning paper is one way to begin the day. They were not all using either. They did not have a lovely time.

Banking in the hope of a tradition and so there is no sound. A little place to have a shoulder. A particle of eye and that which is there to meet another is talking and telling what is not hushing. Any one can sit down. There are not many chairs.

Pale pet, red pet, pink pet, blue pet, white pet, dark pet, real pet, fresh pet, all the tingling is the weeding, the close pressing is the tasting.

Have the hand browner. It is that color. It is not holding that dimension. It is not changing in holding a black thing that is used for anything.

Faithful and constant, never budge from her side. If there is a direction there is not that clouding. A clearer and then the same that made that picture makes a picture and there has been that change. There is no use for that. A place is plain.

Kindly clean the whole surface when there is enough time and then when the whole surface is clean, it does not shine because if shining were anything that which is clean would not be shining. That is to say that that which is clean is so clean.

The best place for all that which is warm is where there is enough to give all.

A whole one is not so small when it is little. It sees all that beaming. A target is all in the middle and it receives it most. That is a Sunday.

If the little that is not bigger has gone away it has not been there. That is the way to complete pleasure. It is alright.

A touch of too much was not what was intended. It was intended to pay that day. A different ending is not coming. The happiness is regarding the little fitting that is not made for that and yet is on it nicely. That is one hope.

That is in the side place and is not there to stay. It is to come here which is where there is the place underneath a non-conductor.

The same thing is not changed and if he won't he will. That will be enough and anyway all that will not be sent away where there is no room. Certainly not.

The plainer the little letter that finishes a word is put where it is seen, even if it is much smaller, has that meaning that a memory is not forgotten and a progression comes to happen. That is that decision.

Anyway two are not the same, they have a way of hoping that if they are there they are not disturbing. They do disturb if it is all the same. That is hopeful. It is not a bitter day when the taste is sweet.

Largely additional and then completely exploding is one way to deny authorisation. It is not the easiest way to get excited. The easier way is to say that a decision has been changed. That is one way to make some of that precise pleasure.

It is not alarming to be together if all that is in a little look is what was what was expected and there is disappointment. Then there can be that same particular repetition and surely any picture is pleasing.

It was not tranquil, that was not what made that little moisture, that was not the change, there was not any change, there was walking. And if there had come to be a place where there was enough use there would not have been later that time and surely there will be so much that there is not any distraction.

There is that and what there is is what is everywhere and there is always the most.

All the part that was cold has the warm feeling and the least that is pink is not purple and the presence of that relief is that all together are not sorry. There could recommence but there will not be any feeling. This is certain. There is all of a guaranty.

The presence of that shape in that head makes the act of passing some hair there a great pleasure. It is so understood and the whole of the pleasure is the same and there is a place that is thinner that is where the hair is a beginner. It is a dark subject and the discussion makes it blonder. The best way to feel the future is the celebration of the evening. Every morning comes after. A disappointment is not foretold.

All the evening and the walking, all the passing of the living, all the knowing of the living of the ones who are prospering, all the tender pressing of the complete expression, all the exaggerating in examination, all the actual decision, nothing is more than too much then, there is all of that waiting and there is that one sleeping.

The rattle that is not in the room can talk some of the language that rises. When it is pleasant to be important a question is as good as answered.

A wave of the white and the black and all the precious substance that which is the whole resemblance is so keen that it is the not in between, it is the whole and there is laughing. The happy way is the way to color the grey.

To put it there where there is no time to wait is the time that is not chosen, it has been refused and given. All the result will be different and all the satisfaction will be expressed.

The size that is wide and the length that is short and the gloves that have stitching and the slippers that are where there is that position, all this and there is curling when the hearing is in the earring, all this and the outlining which is ermine, all this and the buckles showing, all this is that intention and some expectation. The success is recurring. All the pleasure is more.

What the time makes is no noise, what the time makes is that event. The spread of the land is not skirted and the order is not shirted. The harmless way is all day and the use of that change is that the voices have that deadening. Any place has that symptom.

The littlest use is the cane that has no gold ball, it is all made of the same and it is curving where there is a beginning. This does not make beauty black, this makes beauty a beautiful color.

This is the time to say that a bath is not so clean when there is no soap to be seen. A bath is clean when the bather has the wish to state and is fulfilling everything.

A way to spend the day is to give away the time to say that is not the day that is to be used that way. Every day is to be used that way. That is that installation.

Be the same complainer and then quarrel nicely, agree to arrange speaking first and then dismiss the visitor, accept the late arrival of the one who is there to say that he is welcome, disturb the time by not coming to say good-by, that is one way of changing a dismal way.

To relieve the heat by saying that some one is neat is the way to have winter come earlier and not stay later. All the pleasure of having been telling what is the laughter when there is no spelling has come to be drowned by the experience of one who has earned some changing of the house she had been engaging. The pleasure of conquest is the same when distraction has no limit. The quick way to say that beauty is not in the way is the way that the one receiving the offering of adjusting all the pleasure has all the sweetness of decision. Beauty is the thing to see when beauty is there. Any little way is all that and the question is answered. There is no choice.

To lift a plant and see it green this does mean that there is a plant and green is more color than any other. A time to dress is the time it takes after some one is frightened. Not at all, there will not be any more and most directions are the directions to use in deciding to obey. To obey nicely is something.

There are except the ribbon more than before, they are all there. Blending is not a rose and pink is a color. The use of a pen that makes ink show is the seasonable way to show pleasure. The union is perfect and the border is expressing kissing. There is no more than that touch. That comes altogether. To satisfy a message there needed to be a dwindling and then altogether the horizon was met. The window is there. The door is no more. The object is this.

Pardon the fretful autocrat who voices discontent. Pardon the colored water-color which is burnt. Pardon the intoning of the heavy way. Pardon the aristocrat who has not come to stay. Pardon the abuse which was begun. Pardon the yellow egg which has run. Pardon nothing yet, pardon what is wet, forget the opening now, and close the door again.

Say more and tell the use there is in listening. Exchange that and receive a little spoon which is one of seven.

The occupation which makes the reason clear is so absorbing that a night which is not any longer is discovered.

To please while there is no attention is one way when there is a way to be older. This has many little interruptions and a kiss on both cheeks is not in disorder.

A goose-girl is not a girl that geese regard and explain, a goose girl is a real wonder. To sustain a breath is not so dignified as to laugh longer and to do that with that wail is the principal task of more plucking.

A card of time means that all that is shown sparkles. There is no way to have it more than satin. The black and the white and the mixture which is ermine is enchanting when there is more dress than linen. There is no lining when the form is slender. There is every graceful date when the hair is washed and there is no hairpin tickling. A little rubber would not make it neater.

A lovely love is sitting and she sits there now she is in bed, she is in bed. A lovely love is cleaner when she is so clean, she is so clean, she is all mine. A lovely love does not use any way to say all day she is to say that all the day is all there is to say. A lovely love is something and there is no handwriting, it is that there is no printing. A lovely love is there to be the rest of all there is to put into that which is what there is there.

When there is no astonishment there is that happening. To choose looking at the appetising ending is not a sign of predisposition. It does not defy accomplishment. It lingers there.

Not to rub away is to let it stay and surely that is neat and sweet. The two which makes enough is what is that and the question is that it comes in the morning.

A little expression of marrying means that and it succeeds in saluting. This means something.

Why does that the one being there see that see that reflection, why, because there is no separation and there is no talking when the time has come for all more and there is that result of definite cooking which is not to be forgotten while eating is that necessity in establishing not drinking.

The celebration of the evening is not in settling an extraction that will come out after walking. That is that necessity and using that is the best proof. There is none.

Carpet sweeping is so timely and a comb would be useful if there was poverty.

If the wading is so sweet and there is day-light then the time which turned black grey and the earrings longer were the months that had that time. All the pepper which has a color is the color that is so articulate. There is the increase of more.

Astonishing is when there is no ring. Not astonishing this which is no adaptation. All the color that is there shows that the company is smaller. They see that and they put in some salt and some butter. This is not to cause a quarrel. This is not to keep eating away.

Tail pieces and a doll, a covering that is blue and white, a cup and not a mixture in it, darkness and sympathy, this does not mean that some one has been afraid to stay away.

If the road-bed has no saw-dust and the water has no flour, if the money has no butter and the conversation is successful then in some way we will have a room and a bath and more. That is the way.

Please the spoons, the ones that are silver and have sugar and do not make mischief later, do not ever say more than listening can explain.

Winter and the wet is on the apple, that means more handkerchief of any color, the size is the same when the pillow is little. That is the way to be conscious. A perfume is not neater.

All the size which is so slower when the figs are dry make the change which is obtained with walking have the size which is that production. The surface is not covered and a lighter brown is yellower. Any day can be that. Singing is in vegetation. There is more green than potatoe. That produces that result. Red is not needed but more helps than another. Any little piece of fig is left.

Dark and slow and the little court is wrong as is the way when there are so many and not a few are left. To bespeak that affection is to declare no more.

All right away and so much where there is nothing empty, so much and such a pretty color to shine often, there is no praise where the pleasure is so precise and more than that there can be and the most is black and another color.

A pen held by a pen holder does show more of that than most. It has been some preparation and the talk is so interwoven.

A pale policeman has some contract and the nice way is to say that the darkness is in the cape. All the particle of peril is shown in that gleam.

A cushion has no pretty color. A white surface has that meaning and two are seen and the present is the same.

Charming the messenger and kissing the footstool, seasoning the grape-juice and coloring the rose stalk, the danger to the minute is the time of day.

Wednesday, the sender who wants no coins away, Tuesday the use of a push that does not paralyse the rubbing, all day, the resemblance to no blame, Sunday a movement of a little water. Persons with a face and no spitting. Alluding to a fresh man shows no signs of wear. That is the meaning of a measure. There is every remains of a trace.

Climbing the same division with a haughty lady does seem no more monstrous than the return of a colored hat. There is no choice when the head is everywhere, none whatever and the same thing would be so changeable if the hair were made of that silk. If the little one were that size and she is then the round spot would be alike and it was not. So there must be some regret. There was.

Say the difference, say it in the brook, say it in the perpendicular horizon, say it in the retreat from St. Petersburg.

The tame coffee is not so stern as the singing of swinging. The brown complete has a tall leader and the distance is seen and is not safer. There is no loss of mud and the collar is lower.

Little lingering and lantern lighting is the pleasant sing song and sing song is singing and the wish is more than any father it is the whole pressure of the little and the big which comes the way singing has whispering and so and the blanket is not so regular as every sheet and not more neat not any more neat.

Peas and green peas and surely cooked, there was a difference, a simple sample did cause that description. So then we conclude that if there is food there is no higher place and nothing deranged and the necessity the whole necessity is there, there is material.

Little leg of mutton always still and true, little long potatoe is so like the green, little celery eaten, shows the time of day, little rhubarb is all red and still there is a last time to discuss a matter, little piece of pudding is not very red, little piece of fish fried is the same as bread, little pieces of it are the bread there is, each one is all happy and there is no time for pears. Pears are often eaten, figs have such a way, all the time is better and this shows in that way, all the best is certain and there is that use, when there is no time to stay there will be no abuse. All the time is there then, there is time to stay, all the best is mentioned most and there is more to say, all the length is thickness, all the length is breadth, talking is a pleasant way and there is not enough, more is not permitted, there is meaning there, all is in that particular time there is the meaning clear.

Leave the peculiar people here who have the love of any day, leave them stay and sit and have the open seat filled up with fire, this makes merriment and an afternoon.

Marking the smiling of a beer does show the happy cloth that is here, asking the time of opening doors does make the noise grow louder.

Bake the little stay away, and choose the apple every day, place the thing with it and sing it well and nicely there will come all that. This means that there is all that there and there is more than is obliged, choosing that is the way all is best and light in color is the most.

All the dearest children say that they may, they do not say all the words any day, they say they hear that it is where there is no happening that the conviction is deepening. They say it.

To begin the hymn there is a word there, four makes the whole completer. An excess is refined. That is so likely.

Biting a piece of a sample and refusing a piece of a laugh and learning a longer refusal and soiling every seat is not the way to follow a preceder.

The whole is so much that there is a half, there is more than a house there is a larger room. This gave the whole thing a beginning.

Taming more that is large and shouting minus a sight is not a disappointment not at all when breathing has no temperature.

All the pudding has the same flow and the sauce is painful, the tunes are played, the crinkling paper is burning, the pot has a cover and the standard is excellence. So the pig is painful and the red is never white. A little lamb is not more than every sheep and any flavor. The order is so filled with hope that there is no distress.

So kindly and so shiningly and with a special temperature, so far and here and always there and all interpretation holding the place of all decision. There is no use in saying Madame. An open face has hair, it can have it so.

In more winding there is glass and in a sound there is a swing. Any time to do it different means a change in every second, the seconds are the same.

Pleasure in onions means that gambling has no milk. That is what has come to remain away. The time of the pansy is so original.

The spoon, the spoon, that weight, a closet, a plate and all of the chase that makes silver so killing, a whole temper is sustained and the noon has more place than daylight. All the happy day is that way. A question is answer.

A lamp and trimming and the description of the children and the certain indigestion when the reason is not thrilling. So then the time comes when some one has to stay.

All the temper which shows that there must not be that meaning shows no more than is forgotten. Hoping anything is hoping that that is a lesson. Not hoping does not show more memory than there is fact. There is no fact.

More mining than pedestrianism and more hot water bottling does mean that cheapness is something and nothing is subdued. More shows the place and feathers are neglected for more winter and surely steam is something, it surely has no way to make a house change the river, really not any way.

Please the locksmith and the price and throw the cushion on the floor and make a little piece of butter show more strength than any orange. All of it together make the sun and the change is delightful. There is no moon. Cats see that. They can misuse a piece of surrounding moss.

Pale and paling, all the octoroon has some color. A chocolate is not sweet if it is not vanilla. It is a sweet taste and the mouth is bigger. It eats more. It is not annoyed with pink powder. It is not annoyed any more. Containing contradictions makes a melon sour. A melon has no use for such a color. It has no unrest.

To climb and shine and to decline, to sink and save and have the water pour, all this and more, there is no sight that has not every vestige sold in pieces. There is no interval between mentioning. There is a tropical misuse. There is the same. There are many there more.

The two shouting are not about. They have the coil in their hair. All hair is idle. There is no medicine.

Like no sheep and like a lamb, there is no meat, there is a sheet. Like a church and like a tape there are circles there, there is a hidden chair.

All the day that the print discloses is that which causes the circle. A feeling is nice.

By the little piece of string, by the ocean travel, by the whole thing dwindling, by the recitation, by the actual counting there are things to doubt, there are more exaggerations there than there is a twinkling bucket. So the decision has that vellum syncopation. A blind bed bite is thunder struck.

Please tell the artichoke to underestimate valor. Change is made in the book-trade.

Lay the end left and put the tooth next, spice the same handkerchief and season the tomato, it is no use to be silly and if there is spoiling why should an atlas show that. It does, that is what makes it a journey.

To mention that the sound a piece is all in the same bosom. So then.

Present the time and section the sailing of a coat. Show no theory. Show the satisfaction and see the window. All the gentleness is mixing. There is a dream.

All the rest is burned. There is no auction.

Then the singing is dirty and silence is louder. Then there is a dwelling. There is mingling in a cushion. The pet is particular. It sees silkiness in sulking. It is so delighted. It is a wonder.

Aim to please and tend to save, show the honor of the tripe, squeeze the whole pen wiper close, show the arc light where to choose, see the cable leave the ton, show it the face merrily, there is rousing in the cake there is a bite in the plain pin, there is no more disgrace than there is. There certainly is not.

Alright, show more, show it broadly, show it so that if there is a dispute, if there is any reason to fear more than the most there will be the time to say more and to say it very nicely. This is the reason given for shaken a cream pitcher. Surely there is that much certainly.

A dirty bath is so clean that there is eyesight. A sponge, a crack in soap, all that makes nails longer. It does and yet if there is no change of name there is an example. Names are mingling.

Names are mingling and the surprise is not official. It is recorded and a nightingale is a song. A song is pretty nearly more. It is singing.

Please utter that change three times and then what happens, it happens and the whole little taste is so winking that there is no light. There is night. There is night light, there is pink light, there is midnight. All the chief occupations are in the checked dress. This is made of curtains and calico and rhodedendrons and kindling wood and even of some gauze. This is so soon summer. All of it is in a hat. A hat is yellow. If a hat is that color why should sleeves be shorter. If sleeves are shorter why is a dress yellow. There is an answer.

A blade and a setting that has the colors of a simple sample of right resolution is so sweet that there is a precious saying.

I and y and a d and a letter makes a change. The obligation is mutual. Will the pieces widen. If they do then thickness is increasing. A caution, that makes midnight. A cake, that makes squeezing. If there is reading and recollection is tall and the time that has light has made the night, if there is reading and a recollection makes arithmetic, then a memory has no choice, it remembers nothing, it remembers more, it enlarges satisfaction. Is satisfaction suspicion, it is there, it is in peace. All the time is sweeping. All that and more. No use is more hindered than a smelling cover. That is so neat and particular. All the same there is no answer.

Smell is not a wall. So small and so drunk from a well. A wink is not somber. So fine and there is no time. Patience means curls.

A patent is not the same thing as no place to lay down in a room. This does show that something is bought. The means to station a chair in a place is so made that the feet are covered. A little of feet does not make any difference. There is no interpretation.

Light as a spoon and no duller and some silver and a spilling of a whole assortment of cheese this does make the suggestion that not touching is not everything.

Candy is lively. The kindness of smelling. That last scent is lingering. If the precious thing is ripe it has been washed. Smelling is not patient. It is reduced and remembered.

The sign, the left and the laugh, all the tangle, the length of light, piece the pressing, to be near and that graciously makes hindering gracious in sleeping. The sent hindering is attacking clinging. The closeness is thin request.

Wipe no more and pillow the time to rise, wipe in and have no shutter, weigh and rest more in the middle, protect the top, hold all principally.

Dimmer than a demand of a dance in the surrounding depreciation. And then than whom is the pleasure. A life was sardine to play. A land was thinner. Than which side was tacit. The noise was a pimple. A convex is not hurtled.

So the same solid slice shows the use of that. It was not right. If there was the occasion then surely there should be the sanction. And why if there is no chance should there be no refusal. Because if the place is there, there are the times. More does not make that difference. There will not be.

A turn in the place and smelling is sticking, the section that is is not unsatisfactory. To begin to be plain. To begin to be plain is a plain duty. The right to be plain is a plain right. The resumption of being plain is the resuming being plain. There is a conviction and a satisfaction and a resemblance between blue houses and blue horizon.

A private life is the long thick tree and the private life is the life for me. A tree which is thick is a tree which is thick. A life which is private is not what there is. All the times that come are the times I sing, all the singing I sing are the tunes I sing. I sing and I sing and the tunes I sing are what are tunes if they come and I sing. I sing I sing.

A lovely night to stay awake and smell the cake and masticate. A lovely night and no need of surprises, that is what makes it so free of noises.

He came and said he had fried it hard and he had and we smelled it and it was as he did not say it was, it was chewy and it was made as it was made and if there was no hesitation there was no refusal. Could it be true that there was meaning in there being no refusal. Very likely it was not true that there was meaning in there not being refusal.

A curious little thing is that a substantial piece of cauliflower shows in the nose and shows so well that there is no smell. A very curious thing is that a whole name means no more than if there is success, not a bit more place is used by those using more than by those receiving company. It makes every one glad to see the genius and the energy and the simple way that a thing is put down. Why is there any reason that there should be hesitation. Is it necessary that one seeing the time not wasted should arrange that there is no more fatigue. Is it singular that the afternoon and the evening follow the morning. Does follow mean coming after and why if it does, why is there no reason. It is not especial that no more reason is curious than a large picture. A single moment and no catastrophe does show that care makes any one nervous. There is no time to use speed. The promise will be kept and sometime any little word will be the one written.

Once upon a time when there was a word which went there once upon a time there was a pillow. A pillow is not whiter when there is a moon than it is when there is paper. Once when there was more extravagance than there is blaming once there was a door and that was made of white lining. This had under it what did not disappoint a chicken. This is not industry it is regularity.

Four sses are not singular. Four sses are not at all singular and the fashion which is changing shows itself then, it shows in there being four and many more, it shows itself in blame, in expectation, in direct appeal, in singular ways of establishing a result, in certain very particular investigations and hopes and determinations and even it does even sometimes show itself in audacity and in endearments. All the time that this is happening there is result and anticipation.

The faithful prosecution of an intermediate expression between obligation and restraint and reverberation is such that the mornings could be used.

To go into the mud and spill potatoes, to go into the water and pick up water, to go everywhere and wash a petunia, this is a disgrace, it is such a disgrace that there is no meaning in closing and yet, why forget, when to forget is one thing, which to forget is something, the simple time to select a new example is in the same way. This happened and the end of it all was that any way there was no reason why any establishment should have a way to pray. This did not mean that there was any reason in eye sight, this means simply that the whole thing is not any of the appurtenance of the register. The time when that is mentioned. The time how, that is mentioned. All the time there is mentioned that the list is long.

A dot in the center and that which is proportioned if it is made of lead, if it is easily made is so impressionable. There is no greater satisfaction than in everything.

A baker had a basket and a basket was bigger, there is no baker and a basket is bigger, there is no wax and there is an impression and certainly very certainly there is proportion.

A beggar who begs and a print which prints, a surface which heats and a smoke which smokes, all this makes silver and gold is not cheaper not so much cheaper that there is no clatter. All the conscience which tells that little tongue to tickle is the one that does not refer to teeth. To remember, to forget, to silence all the mistakes, to cause perfection and indignation and to be sweet smelling, to fasten a splendid ulster and to reduce expenses, all this makes no charge, it does not even make wine, it makes the whole thing incontestable. The doctrine which changed language was this, this is the dentition, the doctrine which changed that language was this, it was the language segregating. This which is an indication of more than anything else does not prove it. There is no passion. A little tiny piece of stamp, a little search for whiting, a little search for more and more does not disturb the resting.

A liking that has teeth that show it are the same as a smile and the candle is clean, it is clean if there is obedience, it is clean if there is hot water and no soap, it is clean, it is so clean that there is no open top, this does not make wind, it does not make china, it does not even make a remainder and then the deplorable difficulty, why is there no deplorable difficulty, there is and there is an excuse, there is the best fence in the water, this does make no distress, surely there is no reason why it should, surely it does and then there would be a center, in all ways there is a resemblance.

Why does a little one like a middle sized one, why does a little one mention everything. A little one mentions everything because in mentioning a middle sized one the little one is mentioning everything.

When does a middle sized one mention mentioning anything, a middle sized one mentions mentioning everything when a middle sized one mentions anything. A middle sized one is mentioning mentioning everything. A middle sized one does not sin, that means that a middle sized one mentions anything and mentions mentioning everything in mentioning anything. Anything is everything. Middle size is mentioning everything.

A quiet thought in a lively example shows that chalk, any chalk makes a mark and it also shows that the middle is the same distance between two birds. How dark all this shows in green and brown and yet white real white is cream.

A curve, a curve is that angle which determines the recognition of the center in relation to the gathering extension, a curve is that result which is disturbing the roundness that is not redder. The center the whole center is a flower and being a flaming flower does not mean that there is a shadow, it means just watering and winking and wading and rearranging, it means just that exactly.

Life on the Mississippi and in Missouri, life is that which when undertaken is not bashful. Why should it be bashful. Suppose there comes the time which shows that there was a difference, is this any disgrace, does this make pride, it does not make pride but it does make secretion, and what is secretion, secretion is that amusement which every little mark shows as merit. A mark is very necessary. Suppose there is a mark well then there is a mark.

All the mark comes, all the mark is, all there is is a mark, all there comes

comes to mark, a mark has that character and that price, a likely price a completely likely price.

Not seasoning a turnip, this does make a story, it makes this story, it tells how what is just alike has no difference. The patience for that is not denied.

Daylight is measured by there being a dinner a staple sobriety and a wise widow. Day-light is not meant by the evening and too much repetition.

A feather, what is a feather, a feather is restraint, and this shows in yellow, it does not show in every color.

Why is there white which is creamy, there is white which is creamy because it is necessary.

The whole cabinet shows that uselessness is not tearful. No excitement is necessary, it is sadness that is eaten.

A window and a wife, a chair and a stable, all very likely to be in the habit of extracting precise results. This is so manifest, it is so precious and perfect.

A plain light, what is a plain light a plain light is twinkling. Is there any credit given when there is a frog, there is not. All the same it is very good to be busy, to be gracious and to be religious, it is very good to be grand and disturbed and exchanging, a sign of energy is in a soup, is there no sign of energy. There is a little joke in all the mice, there is a little tenderness in soup, there is a plant, there is a coat, there are seven dresses to see, there is no doubt any choice in that, there is certainly a single obligation for a hat, there is no doubt that there is no curve, no curve, at all to a shape, there is no doubt that something has that way.

Climate is not a color. A little thing is a color. When to discover and when to disturb and when to lead a rock away all this is known and no disgrace.

Can a question be clear. Can a pin be a shape. Can a length be different.

Two, two are not more than one when there is a dress. This is no obstacle. To begin the dress, supposing there is that and there is a process, the thing to do is to determine who is the one that shows it all. This is not determined because there is activity. There being activity there is beauty. There being beauty all the pins are changed. So late there can be no beginning and yet it was all done. How was it done, it was done by one.

Half a sausage, a whole sausage, two sausages, more sausages, four sausages, this with a little mixed sour, this and the rest and the corn which is grain, this and the best and certainly no kind of way of saying that it was unexpected, this completed the single selection of a curtain of repetition. This was such a security.

Argue the earnest cake and the dirty inside blotter, argue it and sign the best way of standing. Supposing fifty are nineteenthirteen, supposing they are is that the reason that the trimmings are shorter. Why any wonder when the color of the sand is so dark and raisins are fig trees and apples are smarter.

Why is the illusion correct, it is correct because it is black and gold.

Why are little squares neater, they are neat because if they are obstructed there is a result that is pretty, very pretty and very likely there is the color.

Pin a little pin inside each muff, show the slant that should expose a foot, serve the same thing that has seen enough, love the moment best which is all bliss. A mighty circle and a clean retreat, a master piece and any fist you please, all this and collusion, was there ever a sign. There was it showed that the back like the front has a middle. It does not deceive plaster, it does not arouse a rose.

Cease carpeting, cease carpeting and what happens, the same thing happens and there is silence and there is water and there is a rush of the same fire that showed in the other stove.

If the white which is white and the green which is green mixed with the brown which is brown shows no sign of the expectation that does not disappoint expectation, if it does not then is there news, there is news. A lamb has no neigh, a chicken has breeding, a circus has an object and the best is to be done. The very best is to be done, it is to be done and the example the very example shows no steel, it shows no steel and it shows no selfishness and success, it shows just what there is which is all that necessarily.

The darkness does not mean light ways and single noises it just means that there certainly will be success and a serious remedy, it means that pins any pins are a quantity, it means that a whole proceeding is necessary and outlined and that a list a whole list means no more disturbance than a masterpiece.

An argument is seen in a hurry, why is there no danger in advice, and in a point and in a single exchange of generosity, why is there even no danger in a return and an investment and in electing a single side of clock making, why is there no more danger in a curtain and a silence and a hasty spilling of the milk and maple sugar and the rest of it all. Why is there no danger and why when there is a cottage why is there anything hasty in asking for nothing and not staying longer. Why is there no danger in an attitude and in the certainty of tea and bread and butter. Why is there no danger.

Lecture, lecture a hat and say it is a cat, say it is a lively description, say that there is collusion, to say this and say it sweetly, to say this and make alike service and a platter, to do this is horrid and yet when does kindness fail.

An alarm a study and dragged alarm is splendid. It is shocking and a disgrace. It is a garment in disposition.

Boiling what is boiling, currants are boiling and india rubber and more negligence and certainly a dress too and more likely a coat and a head dress and a sight of shoes. Very likely all of this is boiling and very likely there is nothing hot, nothing is so hot that there is any way to choose.

If there is a piece to part is there any lighter part is there when the fat is thinner, is there when the moths are slimmer, is there any way no table when there is and where there is. This is not in the interest of the pins nor really in the interest of white thread nor indeed in the interest of the afternoon or the morning, it is not in any interest, it will cause slippers. This is cute.

Explain a curve, a curve is that angle which placing a line there shows a regular chance to be fitting. This is so boastful.

A little occasion shows no twisting and real politeness, politeness shows credit and earrings and even large feet, it even shows a sample. This is so much more like what it is.

Once upon a time there was a reverence for bleeding, at this time there was no search for what came. That which was winsome was unwinding and a clutter a single clutter showed the black white. It was so cautious and the reason why was that it was clear there had been here. All this was mightily stirring and littleness any littleness was engaged in spilling. Was there enough there was. Who was the shadow.

The rest was left and all the language of thirty was in the truth. This made it choose just that establishment. Consume apples and there is no cider. Drink beer and be ready later. Snug and warm is the chin and arm, struggle and sneeze is the nose and the cheese, silent and grey is the dress near the bay, wet and close is the sash they chose. A likeness and no vacation. A regularity and obedience. Congratulations.

There is no truth in the decision which is in the center. When the center is not in a line but in a circle a tub, a whole tub is necessary. The sorrow is not satisfied by the moon and motion, it is urged to be strong and to save a specimen.

A single noise, reddening is distressing, a single noise, blue is no mystery, a single noise, loving dissimulating, a single noise, completely correcting.

A practice, no practice is careless, a loud practice, no practice is silent, a wild practice, no practice is perfect.

She said that she did not do it and she did do it, she did it so that the same page was not copied and the same book was not lost and the same sayer would be spoken.

A line is the presence of a particular sugar that is not sugary but splendid and so bland, so little and so rich, so learned and so particular, so perfectly sanguine and so reared.

To indicate more wall flowers than there is paper, to indicate more houses than there are houses, to indicate nothing more is not an urgent and particular privilege, it is selected and if it is not wanted is there any reason for losing anything. There is what there is by the raking of the felt hats.

Does anybody think so, does anybody think so. Does anybody think so in the future. Does anybody think so. Does anybody think so.

Does anybody think that the turn and the break and the lavender and the currants and the hot cocoanut altogether is a wonderful mixture. Does anybody think so.

Tune, a tune is in the hurt way there is no mountain. There comes to be, there comes to be, there is an exchange of that taste. Sweetness is no reason. Results are strained.

If a length and it is there is not covered by where there is a section then is there no use in a foot. There is, there is.

An addition, suppose it is more on the beach is that the time to reach more and is there any more likely. If there is there is no can late.

A real red intoxication and no perspiring blaze not even a silk hat, is there no stranger showing, is there not a selection. The pleasantest elegance is in a collar, it is and there is the red exactness that shows color and no such light.

Which is in the dish there is yellow and the white and all the sleep, all the variegation lying makes the best as in the grate. Sound the goose and if in shining ees are all the wealth between, if there is a right and roaming, if the left has all that team, if it has and roaming roaming lectures all that and makes mines, why is silentsses inner when there is the seldom roar. All the use is humorous.

A bird is birdie. A little bird and a little blight and a little balance to a best button. A little bright bitten bucking anything.

Cunning to eat, circular to baste, splendid to chew, solemn to drink, surprising to assemble and more opportunely.

Bud what is a bud, a bud is not busted. What is a bud. A bud is a sample.

A bud is not that piece of room and more, a bud is ancient.

Class a plain white suit as a fairy turtle, class an amazing black cup as an hour glass, class a single relief as a nut cracker, show the best table as a piece of statuary.

Suppose it did, suppose it did with a sheet and a shadow and a silver set of water, suppose it did.

Beef yet, beef and beef and beef. Beef yet, beef yet.

Water crowd and sugar paint, water and the paint.

Wet weather, wet pen, a black old tiger skin, a shut in shout and a negro coin and the best behind and the sun to shine.

A whole cow and a little piece of cheese, a whole cow openly.

A cousin to a cow, a real cow has wheels, it has turns it has eruptions, it has the place to sit.

A wedding glance is satisfactory. Was the little thing a goat.

A, open, Open.

Leaves of hair which pretty prune makes a plate of care which sees seas leave perfect set. A politeness.

Call me ellis, call me it in a little speech and never say it is all polled, do not say so.

Does it does it weigh. Ten and then. Leave off grass. A little butter closer. Hopes hat.

Listen to say that tooth which narrow and lean makes it so best that dainty is delicate and least mouth is in between, what, sue sense.

Little beef, little beef sticking, hair please, hair please.

No but no but butter.

Coo cow, coo coo coo.

Coo cow leaves of grips nicely.

It is no change. It is ordinary. Not yesterday. Needless, needless to call extra. Coo Coo Coo Cow.

Leave love, leave love let.

No no, not it a line not it tailing, tailing in, not it in.

Hear it, hear it, hear it.

Notes. Notes change hay, change hey day. Notes change a least apt apple, apt hill, all hill, a screen table, sofa, sophia.

Ba but, I promise, I promise that that what what is chased is chased big and cannily and little little is big too big best.

No price list, no price list, a price-list, a price and list and so collected, so collected pipe, all one cooler, a little apple needs a hose a little nose is colored, a little apple and a chest, a pig is in the sneezing, no blotter, raised ahead.

I promise that there is that.

The hour when the seal up shows slobber. Does this mean goat. It does yes.

Be a cool purpose and a less collection and more smell more smell.

Leave smell well.

Leaves in oats and carrots and curve pets and leaves and pick it ferns and never necessary belts.

Little b and a a coat, little b and a a cat, little b and a coat cat, little be cat, little be coat little be and cat and cut and hat, little be and hat and a pear and a pear, little b and a pear and a coat, little be and a coat and grape cat grape cat, little b and a coat grape cat, little be and a cat pear coat hat grape, little grape and a coat grape cat, little coat and a pear and a hat grape coat, little pear and a be at hat, pear.

Leaves, that is leave, that is look in 6 pieces, six pieces and a kitchen, a kitchen when, in guarding, in guarding what, a kitchen. All I say is begin.

A lake particular salad.

Wet cress has points in a plant when new sand is a particular.

Frank, frank quay.

Set of keys was, was.

Lead kind in soap, lead kind in soap sew up. Lead kind in so up. Lead kind in so up.

Leaves a mass, so mean. No shows. Leaves a mass cool will. Leaves a mass puddle.

Etching. Etching a chief, none plush.

MISS FURR AND MISS SKEENE

Here is not only a double portrait but a complete narrative—a love story, which makes this piece especially accessible. Helen Furr and Georgine Skeene are suggestive tactile pseudonyms for Miss Ethel Mars and Miss Maud Hunt Squire, two midwestern American women who came to Paris to take up painting and live a lesbian relationship. Stein writes of them in a limited neutral vocabulary, using repetitions and permutations to tell of their falling in love, living together, and separating.

Themes that preoccupied Stein in her early work return here. One theme, as Stein phrases it in the *Portrait of Constance Fletcher,* is stifling confinement in "family living," which Stein knew well. Every time Helen Furr's home and her parents are described as "pleasant," they become less so, until Helen leaves to join Georgine Skeene. The two lead as conventional a life as any heterosexual couple, being gay and regularly visiting their own families as a matter of unquestioned propriety.

Another theme is "cultivating something" which turns out to be a voice. This self-conscious, theatrical phrase describes their learning lesbian behavior and speech, cultivated code for the unnameable something. It describes their learning the language of lovers, similar to the telling of stories in *Ada.* Miss Furr and Miss Skeene are also learning forms of intimacy essential between women, not only lesbians, of which we also hear in *Ada.* Their voices are less lyrical and more self-conscious than the storytelling voices in *Ada.* They may reach for intimacy, but their range is narrow, their voices affected, and they fail. Their relationship peters out.

A third theme derives from the second. Once Miss Skeene leaves to visit her brother and fails to return—we do not know why and it does not matter—Miss Furr maintains her cultivated voice, but speaks less. Without a lover, without an echo, her stories lose life, her manner rigidifies, and the voice that the two had so carefully cultivated speaks in shrill hysterical repetitions, alone.

When Miss Furr and Miss Skeene turn to sit with the dark and heavy men, we do not know whether the men are homosexual or heterosexual. We do not hear them talk. There is no exchange. The men seem southern, foreign, older, and rather sinister. Are they shadows of the old Jewish men in the family from whom Toklas fled in early years and that Stein put into *Ada?*

The word *gay* nowadays means homosexual, but in 1911 it did not. It must first be read literally. It includes the French adjective *gai,* "pleasant, cheerful," as well as bright, gaudy colors as in the dyed hair of Miss Mars and the heavy makeup of both women. Stein works intensively with this word. "Regularly gay" by repetition becomes demonstrative and sexual but by further repetition ends up not gay anymore, just as

the pleasant Mr. and Mrs. Furr and their house turned out not to be pleasant. By the end, Helen Furr's cultivated gay voice and manner float in a nowhere of pure pathos that is no longer even lonesome.

In 1924 Ernest Hemingway wrote *Mr. and Mrs. Elliot.* It followed *Miss Furr and Miss Skeene* as a model. His story appeared in the *Little Review* in 1924 and was included in *In Our Time* the following year.

• • • • •

Helen Furr had quite a pleasant home. Mrs. Furr was quite a pleasant woman. Mr. Furr was quite a pleasant man. Helen Furr had quite a pleasant voice a voice quite worth cultivating. She did not mind working. She worked to cultivate her voice. She did not find it gay living in the same place where she had always been living. She went to a place where some were cultivating something, voices and other things needing cultivating. She met Georgine Skeene there who was cultivating her voice which some thought was quite a pleasant one. Helen Furr and Georgine Skeene lived together then. Georgine Skeene liked travelling. Helen Furr did not care about travelling, she liked to stay in one place and be gay there. They were together then and travelled to another place and stayed there and were gay there.

They stayed there and were gay there, not very gay there, just gay there. They were both gay there, they were regularly working there both of them cultivating their voices there, they were both gay there. Georgine Skeene was gay there and she was regular, regular in being gay, regular in not being gay, regular in being a gay one who was one not being gay longer than was needed to be one being quite a gay one. They were both gay then there and both working there then.

They were in a way both gay there where there were many cultivating something. They were both regular in being gay there. Helen Furr was gay there, she was gayer and gayer there and really she was just gay there, she was gayer and gayer there, that is to say she found ways of being gay there that she was using in being gay there. She was gay there, not gayer and gayer, just gay there, that is to say she was not gayer by using the things she found there that were gay things, she was gay there, always she was gay there.

They were quite regularly gay there, Helen Furr and Georgine Skeene, they were regularly gay there where they were gay. They were very regularly gay.

To be regularly gay was to do every day the gay thing that they did every day. To be regularly gay was to end every day at the same time after they had been regularly gay. They were regularly gay. They were gay every day. They ended every day in the same way, at the same time, and they had been every day regularly gay.

The voice Helen Furr was cultivating was quite a pleasant one. The voice Georgine Skeene was cultivating was, some said, a better one. The voice Helen Furr was cultivating she cultivated and it was quite completely a pleasant enough one then, a cultivated enough one then. The voice Georgine Skeene was cultivating she did not cultivate too much. She cultivated it quite some. She cultivated and she would sometime go on cultivating it and it was not then an unpleasant one, it would not be then an unpleasant one, it would be a quite richly enough cultivated one, it would be quite richly enough to be a pleasant enough one.

They were gay where there were many cultivating something. The two were gay there, were regularly gay there. Georgine Skeene would have liked to do more travelling. They did some travelling, not very much travelling, Georgine Skeene would have liked to do more travelling, Helen Furr did not care about doing travelling, she liked to stay in a place and be gay there.

They stayed in a place and were gay there, both of them stayed there, they stayed together there, they were gay there, they were regularly gay there.

They went quite often, not very often, but they did go back to where Helen Furr had a pleasant enough home and then Georgine Skeene went to a place where her brother had quite some distinction. They both went, every few years, went visiting to where Helen Furr had quite a pleasant home. Certainly Helen Furr would not find it gay to stay, she did not find it gay, she said she would not stay, she said she did not find it gay, she said she would not stay where she did not find it gay, she said she found it gay where she did stay and she did stay there where very many were cultivating something. She did stay there. She always did find it gay there.

She went to see them where she had always been living and where she did not find it gay. She had a pleasant home there, Mrs. Furr was a pleasant enough woman, Mr. Furr was a pleasant enough man, Helen told them and they were not worrying, that she did not find it gay living where she had always been living.

Georgine Skeene and Helen Furr were living where they were both cultivating their voices and they were gay there. They visited where Helen Furr had come from and then they went to where they were living where they were then regularly living.

There were some dark and heavy men there then. There were some who were not so heavy and some who were not so dark. Helen Furr and Georgine Skeene sat regularly with them. They sat regularly with the ones who were dark and heavy. They sat regularly with the ones who were not so dark. They sat regularly with the ones that were not so heavy. They sat with them regularly, sat with some of them. They went with them regularly went with them. They were regular then, they were gay then, they were where they wanted to be then where it was gay to be then, they were regularly gay then. There were men there then who were dark and heavy and they sat with them with Helen Furr and Georgine Skeene and they went with them with Miss Furr and Miss Skeene, and they went with the heavy and dark men Miss Furr and Miss Skeene went with them, and they sat with them, Miss Furr and Miss Skeene sat with them, and there were other men, some were not heavy men and they sat with Miss Furr and Miss Skeene and Miss Furr and Miss Skeene sat with them, and there were other men who were not dark men and they sat with Miss Furr and Miss Skeene and Miss Furr and Miss Skeene sat with them. Miss Furr and Miss Skeene went with them and they went with Miss Furr and Miss Skeene, some who were not heavy men, some who were not dark men. Miss Furr and Miss Skeene sat regularly, they sat with some men. Miss Furr and Miss Skeene went and there were some men with them. There were men and Miss Furr and Miss Skeene went with them, went somewhere with them, went with some of them.

Helen Furr and Georgine Skeene were regularly living where very many were living and cultivating in themselves something. Helen Furr and Georgine Skeene were living very regularly then, being very regular then in being gay then. They did then learn many ways to be gay and they were then being gay being quite regular in being gay, being gay and they were learning little things, little things in ways of being gay, they were very regular then, they were learning very many little things in ways of being gay, they were being gay and using these little things they were learning to have to be gay with regularly gay with then, and they were gay the same amount they had been gay. They were quite gay, they were quite regular, they were learning little things, gay little things, they were gay inside them the same amount they had been gay, they were gay the same length of time they had been gay every day.

They were regular in being gay, they learned little things that are things in being gay, they learned many little things that are things in being gay, they were gay every day, they were regular, they were gay, they were gay the same length of time every day, they were gay, they were quite regularly gay.

Georgine Skeene went away to stay two months with her brother. Helen Furr did not go then to stay with her father and her mother. Helen Furr stayed there where they had been regularly living the two of them and she would then certainly not be lonesome, she would go on being gay. She did go on being gay. She was not any more gay but she was gay longer every day than they had been being gay when they were together being gay. She was gay then quite exactly the same way. She learned a few more little ways of being in being gay. She was quite gay and in the same way, the same way she had been gay and she was gay a little longer in the day, more of each day she was gay. She was gay longer every day than when the two of them had been being gay. She was gay quite in the way they had been gay, quite in the same way.

She was not lonesome then, she was not at all feeling any need of having Georgine Skeene. She was not astonished at this thing. She would have been a little astonished by this thing but she knew she was not astonished at anything and so she was not astonished at this thing not astonished at not feeling any need of having Georgine Skeene.

Helen Furr had quite a completely pleasant voice and it was quite well enough cultivated and she could use it and she did use it but then there was not any way of working at cultivating a completely pleasant voice when it has become a quite completely well enough cultivated one, and there was not much use in using it when one was not wanting it to be helping to make one a gay one. Helen Furr was not needing using her voice to be a gay one. She was gay then and sometimes she used her voice and she was not using it very often. It was quite completely enough cultivated and it was quite completely a pleasant one and she did not use it very often. She was then, she was quite exactly as gay as she had been, she was gay a little longer in the day than she had been.

She was gay exactly the same way. She was never tired of being gay that way. She had learned very many little ways to use in being gay. Very many were telling about using other ways in being gay. She was gay enough, she was always gay exactly the same way, she was always learning little things to use in being gay, she was telling about using other ways in being gay, she was telling about learning other ways in being gay, she was learning other ways in being gay, she would be using other ways in being gay, she would always be gay in the same way, when Georgine Skeene was there not so long each day as when Georgine Skeene was away.

She came to using many ways in being gay, she came to use every way in being gay. She went on living where many were cultivating something and she was gay, she had used every way to be gay.

They did not live together then Helen Furr and Georgine Skeene. Helen Furr lived there the longer where they had been living regularly together. Then neither of them were living there any longer. Helen Furr was living somewhere else then and telling some about being gay and she was gay then and she was living quite regularly then. She was regularly gay then. She was quite regular in being gay then. She remembered all the little ways of being gay. She used all the little ways of being gay. She was quite regularly gay. She told many then the way of being gay, she taught very many then little ways they could use in being gay. She was living very well, she was gay then, she went on living then, she was regular in being gay, she always was living very well and was gay very well and was telling about little ways one could be learning to use in being gay, and later was telling them quite often, telling them again and again.

PORTRAIT OF CONSTANCE FLETCHER

Printed in *Geography and Plays* in 1922 and, incomprehensibly, not reprinted since, the *Portrait of Constance Fletcher* is almost unknown. Yet it is of extraordinary interest. Twice Stein's style changes radically in this portrait. The three sections were written at different times and in separate manuscript notebooks, a most unusual step for Stein, who was not given to revisions and additions. In the typescript though not in print, the additions are offset by spaces, restored in the *Reader,* to mark the separate writing.

Stein probably first met Julia Constance Fletcher (1858?–1938), fat and almost blind, at Mabel Dodge's Villa Curonia in Arcetri near Florence in 1911. She may have written what later became the first section of the three-part portrait during or immediately after her visit. The second and third sections were probably done in the late summer of 1912 or after, upon another visit by Stein to Mabel Dodge. It is not clear whether Stein and Fletcher met again in 1912.

The way to enter a Stein portrait is through the words, not through what we know of the subject. Stein's work is almost invariably grounded in details of place, time, person, but it is not always possible to see on which facts she relies. As a result, we resist the temptation to read information from the life and times of a subject into her text. Constance Fletcher is a particularly puzzling subject for a portrait. *Article* and its connection with Picabia is another example of a problematic relation of subject and text.

The three different sections of *Constance Fletcher* are more than variations and continuations of one piece. Is Stein doing three different portraits of Fletcher? Who is Fletcher to merit this extraordinary treatment in installments? The questions become more and more compelling, especially since Fletcher, a writer of many connections with the world in which Stein lived, has hardly been studied.

When the editors of the *Reader* reviewed the portrait, they became fascinated with Constance Fletcher both in her own right and in relation to Stein. Layer upon layer of interesting detail peeled off the sources consulted to create a compelling subject and endless questions. After divorcing her husband, an American missionary, Fletcher's mother, along with Constance and her brother, left America with the painter Eugene Benson and moved to Venice. Constance apparently had a brief romantic relationship that she never forgot with Lord Lovelace, the son of Byron's daughter, Ada. Under the pen name George Fleming, Fletcher began early to write as a journalist and novelist. *Kismet,* dramatized by Edward Knoblock, brother-in-law of Mary Knoblauch, is one of her many works. She met Oscar Wilde, whose likeness she included in her novel *Mirage,* and he dedicated a poem to her. She knew Henry James and the novelist Constance Fenimore Woolson, in whose house in Venice James began *The Aspern Papers*.

None of these few bare facts, a tiny sampling of absorbing concatenations, are visible in Stein's portrait. But that Stein knew many of them is beyond doubt.

The first thirteen paragraphs rely on repetitions and permutations of phrases in a reduced vocabulary to characterize Fletcher as filled—fulfilled—with "family living." She experiences herself as absorbed in family living and family love, not as a person in her own right. The description shows her as a vessel filled or enveloped by family living—the two are the same. The paragraphs formulate and reformulate the family situation until we wonder whether Constance Fletcher has a sense of who she is.

But suddenly the new section begins and the old woman who lived in a shoe appears from the nursery rhyme. "They do not move in the shoe." Is it a shoe of constricting family living?

The second part continues in the new style, with flowers, colors, bells, light and dark, an arabesque, statuary—perhaps elements of a garden. There appear to be comments on art, sculpture, and writing. Stein sounds personal, serious, at times didactic. We hear the tone of *A Long Gay Book* and of the plenitude recorded in Spain in "[A] reception . . . not filled with more than all every day."

After some pages, the language changes again, as does the organization, with long paragraphs alternating with short words that change the rhythm. The piece moves in deliberate, declarative clauses toward its ambiguous ending, where the "shadow which is larger is not flickering."

And of course Constance Fletcher returns as a character in *The Mother Of Us All*. "Dear dear me if he had not been an Adams he would have kneeled at my feet and he would have kissed my hand."

• • • • •

When she was quite a young one she knew she had been in a family living and that that family living was one that any one could be one not have been having if they were to be one being one not thinking about being one having been having family living. She was one then when she was a young one thinking about having, about having been having family living. She was one thinking about this thing, she was one feeling thinking about this thing, she was one feeling being one who could completely have feeling in thinking about being one who had had, who was having family living.

She was one having, she was one who had had family living. When she was a young one she was one having, she was one having had family living.

She was one thinking about having family living, about having had family living. When she was a young one she was thinking about having family living, she was thinking about having had family living.

She was feeling having had family living, she was feeling having family living. When she was a young one she was feeling having had family living, she was feeling having family living.

She was knowing, when she was a young one, that she could be completely feeling in having family living, in having had family living. She was knowing, when she was a young one, she was knowing that she was thinking, she was knowing that she was feeling in having family living, in having had family living. She was thinking and feeling having had, having family living.

She could be completely feeling having, having had family living. She was thinking in being one who could be completely feeling having had, having family living. She was feeling in being one who could be completely feeling having had, who could be completely feeling having family living.

She was living in feeling, in thinking having had, having family living. She had had family living. She was having family living. She could be completely feeling having family living, having had family living.

She was then a young one, she was then quite a young one, she was later a little an older one. She was then feeling in being one loving, she was then thinking in being one loving. She was then living in being one loving. She could be then one being completely loving. She was filled then, completely filled then, she was then feeling in being loving, she was then thinking in being loving. She was completely filled then. She was feeling, she was thinking, she was feeling and thinking then in being one loving.

She could be then one being completely loving, she was thinking and feeling in being one who could be completely loving. She was coming then to be a full one, she was coming then to be thinking and feeling in this thing in being one being a completely filled one. She was full then, she was filling in then in being one living in loving, in living in thinking in being loving, in living in feeling being one being loving.

She was full then and was not then losing anything. She was thinking then, she was feeling then, she was thinking then and feeling then in being full then. She was thinking and feeling then in being one not losing anything of any such thing as being one being full then.

She could be one being completely full. She was thinking in being one who could be completely full. She was feeling in being one who could be completely full. She was always living in being one feeling and thinking in being one who could be completely full.

She was full then and she was thinking and feeling, thinking in this thing, feeling in this thing. She was thinking and feeling and being full then. She was thinking and feeling in being one who could be completely full.

She was filling in in all her living to be a full one. She was thinking and feeling in all her living in being a full one. She was thinking and feeling all her living in being one who could be a completely full one. She was all her living a full one. She was completely filling in to be a full one and she always was a full one. She was thinking in being a full one. She was feeling in being a full one. She was thinking in feeling in being a full one. She was feeling in thinking in being a full one.

If they move in the shoe there is everything to do. They do not move in the shoe.

The language of education is not replacing the special position that is the expression of the emanation of evil. There is an expression when contemplation is not connecting the object that is in position with the forehead that is returning looking. It is not overpowering. That is a cruel description. The memory is the same and surely the one who is not older is not dead yet although if he has been blind he is seeing. This has not any meaning.

Oh the bells that are the same are not stirring and the languid grace is not out of place and the older fur is disappearing. There is not such an end.

If it had happened that the little flower was larger and the white color was deeper and the silent light was darker and the passage was rougher it would have been as it was and the triumph was in the place where the light was bright and the beauty was not losing having that possession. That was not what was tenderly. This was the piece of the health that was strange when there was the disappearance that had not any origin. The darkness was not the same. There was the writing and the preparation that was pleasing and succeeding and being enterprising. It was not subdued when there was discussion, it was done where there was the room that was not a dream.

This is all to prepare the way that is not the way to like anything that in speaking is telling what has come that like a swelling is inside when there is yellowing.

There is that liking. That does not shape the way to say that there is not anywhere anything that is resembling. Perfection is not adulteration. There is the substance that has not any defect.

If the program is not despondent and it has that substance then certainly the beginning is the tender blessing that unfolding is not subduing. There is that presentment and the quiet is not so sound but that there can be a change of origin. There can be that elevation. This is not an argument. There is the work that has that place and there is a garden. A little taller bending does not hasten the erection of the grotto that has a fountain. That is so soon.

To pardon, that is to have seen that there was a long way to stare when the heat was the same as there was when the voices were together. This was the temptation and so solidly was there when there was there that the whole reception was not filled with more than all every day who had come anywhere and had heard that there was. This did not mean more than all. It meant all and the result of the precious and precise way was that there was that preparation and not the disintegration when there was that distinct evolution. There could be the same if any one was certain that there is not any evolution. This does not make the tedium that is eternal so particular that listening is a blessing. This does not disguise a flower.

Come in and that expression is not that one of waiting. To use a name is not the time that seeing has not been. This is discussion. This is obligation. This is the composition.

Oh sadly has the oak-tree not that sadness. It has not the particular reason. It has not that digression. It has not that penetration. It has that piece that is there where there is all that remains when everything remains. Nothing is all old. That is not the redoubtable repudiation. That has that precious meaning when the hindrance has not that little pain which is not the same as the passing out of what is not about when it is there where there is no care to say that anything is better. Everything has that description. That is not reorganization. The way to say that they went away is the way that the passage has come to be adhered. This is not the token that shows the steering that is not broken. The plea is not that the arabesque has that meaning when the whole thing is exposed. The meaning is that the precious picture is the bargain that has not met the ancient day when there is everything to say. The light is finer. That is not that discrimination. That is the way to have that to keep where there is not any interdiction. She had that name. That was the origin of the penguin. That was not that bird. And because the strong man is the warder when the little ones are sounder so the particular ticket is not limited when there is not the best establishment where all the black and white show that. It is a blessing when there has been falling the heavy way to stay where the regard is what is not all that distance. The breaking of the tame show is not the way to glow because the waste is not there. It is not any where.

Mark the data that tells the merit of having that time to state that not to wait is to say that the door has not been entered. If to wait marks the place where the entrance if it is made comes to be approached then to do what is not done is to do all that and carefully that which is solid does not fill the space. That is not a disclosure. That is not the way for all of them who are looking to refuse to see. That is not at all any such way. It is not a pleasure to be the one when there is the whole of it all and when there where there is no separation there is weeping, quite ostentation, completion, not any compensation, where there is the softening of the published soap. This is not that decree. There is no failure. There is no condition of incision.

Particle of all the color is that which is not white and the black which is open is not older when the time has come back for black to be younger.

The meaning of this is that why the difference is always louder is that that which is above that which is all there is and there is much is that there is all that there has that reason to be which is the reason that is all certain and this which is not mentioned and which does not make that which is lost is the same and has the detail which does not make any escaping remain separate. This does adjoin all and all is enough so that the whole which is not parted has not the place where sticking makes anything that is wet dry. This has not that mistake when softness is union.

The first time.

Winning distinction is discretion and all who are going are the three who have not that distraction. They have not all the hardihood. They are not separated. The two who are not older are not remaining to be interesting. They are not undertaking any beginning. Excellent is the same union. Breathless is not the shade when the opening is not limiting. They did not seem in that place. That was any end.

She.

If three are eager and plainer and having a full temper and if all of them unite in that happy way that makes a garden give the way to be there where there is a way, if there is the last time and a young time is a stolen beauty then the way it has been said that the white flower has not been bled is the way to remember that decision is not the same as crumpling a parting. She did not animate what was mechanical. She has not this to do.

They.

They were the three and they were not employed in looking. They had not every union when they had that education.

To be they and then not be away is not the time and place that makes the whole expression because after all when there is the time and the place and when they are they they are not away and that does not make any more. If they were there they had the time to see which way was older and when they did not feel that stain they had the time to address what they did address when they would address one another. They did not all listen.

No silence.

There was not that hesitation and this was not all there was when the sounds were not so loud but that they might be hearing. They had the quiet and surely if they taught that they were each one not all of any other. This was not the half of all the time. It took a separate ticket.

All the time that there was all the winning of all the wonder that was not under the weather was not passing as the exchange was not lessening. The older was not newer. They had the same description. This does not mean that if there are all three to learn that not any one is there but they have any way to say that not to go away is to stay. They were equal to enough so that all the separation made them remain. They had so much excess.

It was not the only smile the smile that did not come to face the pleasure of there being three and the three were not there to gather together.

One.

If the way to learn is to have that presence then certainly the changes did not balance the description. She had that which was not alarming.

Two.

If the habit of saying all the education is the development of that expression then certainly if there is being pleasant all can be there to not expect that measure of all who are together.

Three.

The one who is a sun is the last flower that is not open when all the petals falling feel the whole of all intention.

So there are then what is not what will not have been when all the seeing that is and is not seen is had and has been having having and having had and meaning. That is some intention and all is enough to complete all the whole.

The delay was not that which separated that separation from the time when all the ones who said something said everything. It was not so in place.

The change.

There was not any time and all there was was reason. There was all that and if there were all there were there were the ones there were.

That which was pleasing was not all there was if there was all there was of that consideration. Certainly the time was not the present and past flavor and the time was not the future and the present presentation. There was all there and sincerely did the biting that was not bit fill out the strength and explanation. It did not furnish the intention. It did not succeed when there was all that care.

This which did not escape was not the narrow connection that can make a larger blossom and make it take the sea where the ocean is larger and the ships are quicker. The pleasure is the same.

To face that way.

To face the way that each one does say that they have any day which is clearly not away is to say that the time is not there when the color is not lighter and the hair is not redder. This does not make all there is of any invitation. There is not anything of any such suggestion.

If the practice of the present and the practice of the past and there is any practice and the practice of the future then latterly there is not any change. If the way to say the turn is the turn the way that is the way to turn that way then all of the thing is in that thing. There has been all of that painstaking.

Awhile while there is no band, awhile while the train is late, awhile while the town is full, awhile while the sounds have the tone, awhile there is a settled waste and this is not to say that anything that is given away is given away, nothing is wasted that is not given away and anything that is given away is wasted. The appearance is not the only way to say that what is given away is wasted and nothing is given away. It is so remained.

That which is not tiring and that which is not aiding any of that which is not needing tiring, that was the sampler and there was not the sewing which was using any corner. That did not need the same width as all that is solid is using which is not wider. That which is solid is all that is wider and the rest is not that which has that passing odor which is not passing. It does not pass anything. It is not the only primrose. It has the sentence that in placing what is not that care has all that is which is all there where any more care is most care. There where the time is not cruel is the place where the time is what is filling the half and the whole and no passage that has that intention can be intended when that which is solid is not building every house. All houses are open that is to say a door and a window and a table and the waiter make the shadow smaller and the shadow which is larger is not flickering.

WHAT HAPPENED

A FIVE ACT PLAY

"What happened?" we ask anyone who returns from doing something. What happened at the theater? The answer is tautological, "a play." Stein uses the exchange to ask what a play really is.

This play, which Stein claimed to be her first, responds to an equivalent question about what happened at a dinner party for the birthday of the painter Harry Phelan Gibb (1870–1948) on 8 April 1913. Gibb, about whom not enough is known, was close to Braque and Picasso in the early years of cubism in Paris and later returned to England. What happened was a dinner party, including a leopard coat . . . food . . . cake . . . speeches . . . photographs . . . , but hardly what we think of as a five-act play. What actually happened—the essence of a party—was random talk or conversation, whose patterns and atmosphere Stein's play reproduces.

Conversation at a dinner party follows no plot and moves toward no climax or conclusion. The five short acts of Stein's play poke fun at the rigid form of five-act plays. There are no stage directions. We do not know how many characters there are, who they are, or which words are spoken by whom. As in the following portrait of Carl Van Vechten, also "a kind of a play," Stein uses centered numbers followed by equivalent numbers of paragraphs of what may be conversation. "One" paragraph might be spoken by one character, "five" by five different characters. The word "One," centered on the page as it is in the manuscript, indicates a character. But the arrangement of elements of conversation is left open. She offers no directions for how to stage the play or how to arrange characters and lines. Indeed, much of the talk may be simultaneous rather than sequential.

The din of superimposed or simultaneous utterance blurs the outlines of words, and makes us mishear or double hear. The play fills up with puns: shutter carries over to shooting, fury to flurry, windowful to wonderful, cake to keg, bread is heard as breathing, sorrow becomes borrowing, eraser, razor, left, lift, always with both meanings fitting and audible. Involuntary rhymes and half-rhymes add to the din.

Boundaries of phrases and sentences blur, and idiom falls apart so that one sentence or phrase wipes out the next or superimposes itself on the preceding one to make new combinations, often apparent but never complete nonsense. The language appears to move from speech to commentary, placing us both inside the play and outside as observers.

At the end, after a photograph of the party, we move with regrets into the doorway that narrows the view to departure. We leave with a picture of what happened framed in the mind. Long before color photography, it is a permanent vivid image filled with the color that fills the play.

• • • • •

ACT ONE

One.

Loud and no cataract. Not any nuisance is depressing.

Five.

A single sum four and five together and one, not any sun a clear signal and an exchange.

Silence is in blessing and chasing and coincidences being ripe. A simple melancholy clearly precious and on the surface and surrounded and mixed strangely. A vegetable window and clearly most clearly an exchange in parts and complete.

A tiger a rapt and surrounded overcoat securely arranged with spots old enough to be thought useful and witty quite witty in a secret and in a blinding flurry.

Length what is length when silence is so windowful. What is the use of a sore if there is no joint and no toady and no tag and not even an eraser. What is the commonest exchange between more laughing and most. Carelessness is carelessness and a cake well a cake is a powder, it is very likely to be powder, it is very likely to be much worse.

A shutter and only shutter and Christmas, quite Christmas, an only shutter and a target a whole color in every center and shooting real shooting and what can hear, that can hear that which makes such an establishment provided with what is provisionary.

Two.

Urgent action is not in graciousness it is not in clocks it is not in water wheels. It is the same so essentially, it is a worry a real worry.

A silence a whole waste of a desert spoon, a whole waste of any little shaving, a whole waste altogether open.

Two.

Paralysis why is paralysis a syllable why is it not more lively.
A special sense a very special sense is ludicrous.

Three.

Suggesting a sage brush with a turkey and also something abominable is not the only pain there is in so much provoking. There is even more. To begin a lecture is a strange way of taking dirty apple blossoms and is there more use in water, certainly there is if there is going to be fishing, enough water would make desert and even prunes, it would make nothing throw any shade because after all is there not more practical humor in a series of photographs and also in a treacherous sculpture.

Any hurry any little hurry has so much subsistence, it has and choosing, it has.

ACT TWO

Three.

Four and nobody wounded, five and nobody flourishing, six and nobody talkative, eight and nobody sensible.

One and a left hand lift that is so heavy that there is no way of pronouncing perfectly.

A point of accuracy, a point of a strange stove, a point that is so sober that the reason left is all the chance of swelling.

The same three.

A wide oak a wide enough oak, a very wide cake, a lightning cooky, a single wide open and exchanged box filled with the same little sac that shines.

The best the only better and more left footed stranger.

The very kindness there is in all lemons oranges apples pears and potatoes.

The same three.

A same frame a sadder portal, a singular gate and a bracketed mischance.

A rich market where there is no memory of more moon than there is everywhere and yet where strangely there is apparel and a whole set.

A connection, a clam cup connection, a survey, a ticket and a return to laying over.

ACT THREE

Two.

A cut, a cut is not a slice, what is the occasion for representing a cut and a slice. What is the occasion for all that.

A cut is a slice, a cut is the same slice. The reason that a cut is a slice is that if there is no hurry any time is just as useful.

Four.

A cut and a slice is there any question when a cut and a slice are just the same.

A cut and a slice has no particular exchange it has such a strange exception to all that which is different.

A cut and only slice, only a cut and only a slice, the remains of a taste may remain and tasting is accurate.

A cut and an occasion, a slice and a substitute a single hurry and a circumstance that shows that, all this is so reasonable when everything is clear.

One.

All alone with the best reception, all alone with more than the best reception, all alone with a paragraph and something that is worth something, worth almost anything, worth the best example there is of a little occasional archbishop. This which is so clean is precious little when there is no bath water. A long time a very long time there is no use in an obstacle that is original and has a source.

ACT FOUR

Four and four more.

A birthday, what is a birthday, a birthday is a speech, it is a second time when there is tobacco, it is only one time when there is poison. It is more than one time when the occasion which shows an occasional sharp separation is unanimous.

A blanket, what is a blanket, a blanket is so speedy that heat much heat is hotter and cooler, very much cooler almost more nearly cooler than at any other time often.

A blame what is a blame, a blame is what arises and cautions each one to be calm and an ocean and a masterpiece.

A clever saucer, what is a clever saucer, a clever saucer is very likely practiced and even has toes, it has tiny things to shake and really if it were not for a delicate blue color would there be any reason for every one to differ.

The objection and the perfect central table, the sorrow in borrowing and the hurry in a nervous feeling, the question is it really a plague, is it really an oleander, is it really saffron in color, the surmountable appetite which shows inclination to be warmer, the safety in a match and the safety in a little piece of splinter, the real reason why cocoa is cheaper, the same use for bread as for any breathing that is softer, the lecture and the surrounding large white soft unequal and spread out sale of more and still less is no better, all this makes one regard in a season, one hat in a curtain that is rising higher, one landing and many many more, and many more many more many many more.

ACT FIVE

Two.

A regret a single regret makes a door way. What is a door way, a door way is a photograph.

What is a photograph a photograph is a sight and a sight is always a sight of something. Very likely there is a photograph that gives color if there is then there is that color that does not change any more than it did when there was much more use for photography.

ONE

CARL VAN VECHTEN

"One" instead of a name for the title or the person portrayed appears more than once in Stein's work, always to depersonalize a subject and remove it from anecdote and incident. Here, however, she plays a game, following "one" with "two," omitting "three," but adding "four" and even "five" until we wonder whether to think of five characters or five acts that might make "[a]lmost a play." This phrase is played with as a subtitle in the manuscript, where an alternative also appears, "A kind of play." The reference to a play and other details here might also connect with Stravinsky's ballet *Le Sacre du Printemps,* whose second performance on 2 June 1913 Stein, Toklas, the actress Florence Bradley, her sister Alixe, and Carl Van Vechten attended, sitting in the same box. Van Vechten's pleated silk shirt is in the portrait, which is altogether theatrical with gold, boxes, scenes, costumes, colors, and coaches punning with coats. It is punctuated with irregular rhythmic beats, repeated motifs, and the numbers, prominently centered in the manuscript and thus printed in the *Reader.*

Carl Van Vechten (1880–1964) arrived in Paris on 29 May 1913 with a letter of introduction to Stein from Mabel Dodge. He knew Stein's *Portrait of Mabel Dodge at the Villa Curonia* and had heard of her at the International Exhibition of Modern Art—the Armory Show—of February–March 1913. Stein responded to the introduction by inviting Van Vechten to dinner on Saturday, 31 May. Her account in *The Autobiography of Alice B. Toklas* of the events that became the beginning of one of the most important friendships of her life is not historical but fictionalized to dramatize the meeting, as is Van Vechten's own account. They did not meet for the first time as strangers at the Stravinsky ballet but had met three nights earlier at her studio for dinner.

By the time Stein met Van Vechten, Alice Toklas and Pablo Picasso were already established as her two most important friends. Van Vechten, whose faith in her work and whose efforts to publish her never flagged, became Stein's third lifelong friend. Their correspondence documents their lives, Stein's problems with publication, and the cultural history of Paris and New York. Stein returned to these three friends in 1923, in Nice, with three second portraits, included in the *Reader,* written in short succession to mark their great importance to her and her devotion to them.

• • • • •

One.

In the ample checked fur in the back and in the house, in the by next cloth and inner, in the chest, in mean wind.

One.

In the best most silk and water much, in the best most silk.

One.

In the best might last and wind that. In the best might last and wind in the best might last.

Ages, ages, all what sat.

One.

In the gold presently, in the gold presently unsuddenly and decapsized and dewalking.

In the gold coming in.

ONE.

One.

None in stable, none at ghosts, none in the latter spot.

ONE.

One.

An oil in a can, an oil and a vial with a thousand stems. An oil in a cup and a steel sofa.

One.

An oil in a cup and a woolen coin, a woolen card and a best satin.

A water house and a hut to speak, a water house and entirely water, water and water.

TWO.

Two.

A touching white shining sash and a touching white green undercoat and a touching white colored orange and a touching piece of elastic. A touching piece of elastic suddenly.

A touching white inlined ruddy hurry, a touching research in all may day. A touching research is an over show.

A touching expartition is in an example of work, a touching beat is in the best way.

A touching box is in a coach seat so that a touching box is on a coach seat so a touching box is on a coach seat, a touching box is on a coat seat, a touching box is on a coat seat.

A touching box is on the touching so helping held.

Two.

Any left in the touch is a scene, a scene. Any left in is left somehow.

FOUR.

Four.

Four between, four between and hacking. Four between and hacking.

Five.

Four between and a saddle, a kind of dim judge and a great big so colored dog.

ARTICLE

Unpublished until now, *Article* was apparently written in the spring or early summer of 1913, soon after *What Happened* but before the portrait of Apollinaire. On a single short list of early pieces, the title *Article* is followed by the name Picabia in parentheses. In every other listing of work, the title is only *Article*. If the parentheses mean that it is not exactly a portrait, how does Picabia (1879–1970) relate to the piece?

The first way to enter such a text is by careful reading. Following words and sentences yields almost no meaning. We instead follow visually and phonetically syllables, letters, phrases—phonemes and morphemes—in English and non-English configurations to assemble readings. The second way is to follow Picabia's activities in 1913 as they relate to Stein, in the hope that text and context, what the piece says and what we know, may merge. We know that Picabia exhibited in the Armory Show and that Alfred Stieglitz gave him a successful one-man exhibition at his Little Gallery of the Photo-Secession ("291") in March–April 1913. In New York for both exhibits, Picabia wrote, gave interviews and took part, with Mabel Dodge, in the many discussions of Stein and modernism. These in turn led him to visit Stein after his return to Paris.

Picabia sometimes claimed he made not art but things—articles. Though this may suggest a relation to Stein's piece, it is too tentative to allow us to enter the text, and we return to reading. The title that refuses to name a subject forces us to attend to words. An article may be an essay or newspaper piece, or an object such as an article of clothing; the text allows both, and a wavering reading results. It relies on the language that Stein, in *A Long Gay Book,* defined as "segregating." Words cease to be stable, unchanging elements of language. Punning makes them audible and visible in pieces, broken into other words and phrases, even crossing from English to French. Homonyms and homophones separate until meanings pile one on top of another. "A cute blessing" becomes an "acute" blessing or, in French, an acute *blessure* or "wound." Flounders in buckets sounds like a fishmonger's scene and indeed, there is a fish course—but of salmon, not flounder. The buckets are bouquets of flowers. Words refuse to behave according to expectation as nouns, verbs, adjectives, even conjunctions in making sentences. Every word we add makes a sentence new. The sections of *Article* separated by indentation, including the one beginning with "Cousin" that is set flush left by Stein, leave us struggling to assemble the whole article.

It is as if Stein, remembering the family dry-goods business, was cutting out, seamstress fashion, paper patterns for articles of clothing. She puts together a verbal collage from a "cut out kind of apron" and a man's formal cutaway coat. As in *Tender Buttons,* she composes into still lifes domestic detail that women might observe at an elegant birthday party—clothes, food, flowers, all in decorative formality.

• • • • •

In the cut out kind of apron, in the best demander, the pudding the reasoning and the humbleness and the cut away, the cut away in the way that there is besides.

Climate and any number of two.

Bertha in a birthday and so what is there to show it, this that the same time is wounded and winked at in waylaying customs apiece.

Climate and any number of two. Buckets, in buckets there is more order ordered in. In buckets flounders have any ache intentionally.

Any way and a blank with a birthday a cute blessing instead of entirely.

Best exchange best do it best and most. A climate.

Winding in and way in best.

Cousin, a course in that which shows that no kind of salmon is fiendish, none is and so that is. The best and the best.

A gin case handsomely. A spoilt not a spot, a spoilt and the peas not those barring the eggs in and the cuts out.

Waving not wintergreen not cucumber not a soiled ointment, waving and not winding, waving that there. The son place the soon place, the sun.

The suck and the suck and that in the suck. The suck.

GUILLAUME APOLLINAIRE

The opening four-word sentence appears to make no sense. Singly or grammatically, the words refer to nothing in the world that we recognize. So we return to the words as words or even to the letters that make them up. Reading aloud, we gradually begin to hear not the words we see in print but others immediately behind them. Eventually the two sets of spoken words collapse into one: "Give known or pin ware" sounds "Guillaume Apollinaire." The four English-looking words turn into two French-sounding words, a name written as Stein heard it, transliterating and translating it separately into English sounds and words. As if she had never seen the name in writing, she put down the foreign sounds in the nearest English equivalent. Yet she knew Apollinaire, as her original title in manuscript, "Guillaume," shows in its familiar first-name form. It all sounds like a baby learning to talk.

Of course, Guillaume Apollinaire is not even the real name but the pen name of Wilhelm Apollinaris Albertus de Kostrowitzky (1880–1918), a Pole, not a Frenchman. In 1913, when this portrait was written, anyone hearing the Wilhelm behind Guillaume might also have heard the name of the German Kaiser Wilhelm, which now also enters this strange scenario of French and English word formations. The poet's and the kaiser's foreign name is transcribed by a foreigner into a foreign language that puts before the reader the subject-as-name, or the subject-as-words. Most of us say who we are by jumping from our name to a reference—a picture, a description, a photo, an anecdote. But Stein repeats the name as homophone until it puns and plays in the ear. Referentiality is back in a transcription more literal than we thought possible and more essential to the art of writing than visual appearances. The piece is a portrait of a word that is a name. The anecdotes in the *Autobiography* will not help us read it.

The portrait becomes a bilingual eye lesson that is also an ear lesson in new reading. Deceptively brief, it must be heard and seen over and over for verbal possibilities, English and French, grammatical and semantic, auditory and visual. Stein wrote in English, but around her was French, which she spoke, as she also spoke German. Her work, even in erroneous formations and misspellings, always includes possibilities of French and even German play extending the verbal world. The words "lesson," "leave," *leçon, laissons* are examples. Other French words perhaps segregating into English ones are *surtout,* an adverb meaning "chiefly" but also a noun meaning "overcoat"; *pour,* a preposition meaning "for" but also becoming the adjective or noun "poor," which translates into *pauvre.* Both these groups are behind "sour stout pore, pore caesar." That "pore caesar, pour state at" echoes *pour l'état* is easy to hear. And behind Caesar marches kaiser.

Grammar also determines understanding. The second line as printed in the *Reader,* relying on the manuscript rather than the typescript, reads "teethe," not "teeth." Did Stein want the verb or did she misspell the noun with a final -e? Did she revise, forget, or carelessly proofread her original word? Did Toklas in typing err or correct Stein's spelling? We cannot know. But if the word is "teethe," then "fancy teethe" becomes not an adjective and a noun but two verbs, unless it becomes the sentence "infants (or Fr. *enfants*) teethe." The readings we adopt here—perhaps more than one—affect the next syntactic configuration, "gas strips." Stein plays endlessly, but always with a purpose and always with her subject in her eye and ear.

• • • • •

Give known or pin ware.
Fancy teethe, gas strips.
Elbow elect, sour stout pore, pore caesar, pour state at.
Leave eye lessons I. Leave I. Lessons. I. Leave I lessons, I.

PINK MELON JOY

When World War I broke out at the end of July 1914, Stein and Toklas were in England. "The air was thick," Stein wrote. Advised not to return to France until it was safe to travel, they stayed with Alfred North and Evelyn Whitehead in Wiltshire. Stein worked to absorb into the continuity of her writing the discontinuities of the world of war. Until she began relief work in 1917, she observed the war as a civilian, from England until October 1914, from Paris until March 1915, and from Mallorca until May 1916. Where she was in part determined how she perceived the war.

The first part of *Pink Melon Joy* of the summer of 1914 was written in England, but before the end of the second part she was apparently back in Paris, where she finished the piece. It is the most lighthearted, humorous, and erotic work of this time, exuberant with pleasure in what words can make of the difficult here and now. Could the friendship with Whitehead have added to its joys? It sings the hymns of hospitality, notes flowers and fruits in the garden, attends to English speech and voices and to the rhetoric of war. The freedom of this piece shows also in play with long and short lines, in sections of varied length and tone, and in the many funny headings.

Pink Melon Joy absorbs events and objects into its verbal process. What she does and sees is barely identified in referential details. It is easy to forget in reading such a piece that Stein's verbal games are not fictions but always start from facts. For example, in London Stein and Toklas purchased furniture and household goods for the Paris apartment, depleted by the removal of her brother Leo's property to Florence. In *Pink Melon Joy* only tiny, momentary details—large plates, the height of the table—hint at purchases that in other London pieces stand solidly and heavily, pulling us from the words to the objects. Such details, however, are behind the domestic joys of the piece. Names also come from actuality. Alfy in the third section is Alfred Maurer, the painter, who, as Stein tells in the *Autobiography,* returned to safety in America. A different hint turns up late in the second section with "James is nervous," which may refer to the refusal by Henry James in 1914 of a visit by Alvin Langdon Coburn offering to introduce Stein. Yet this sentence returns in *I Can Feel the Beauty* of early 1918 and in the summer of 1918 becomes the title of a piece. Stein's astonishing verbal memory echoes in words and phrases that reappear, never by accident, across the years.

• • • • •

My dear what is meat.
I certainly regret visiting.

My dear what does it matter.
Leaning.
Maintaining maintaining checkers.
I left a leaf and I meant it.
Splintering and hams.
I caught a cold.

Bessie.

They are dirty.
Not polite.
Not steel.
Not fireless.
Not bewildered.
Not a present.
Why do I give old boats.
Theresa.

Exchange in bicycles.

It happened that in the aggregate and they did not hear then, it happened in the aggregate that they were alone.

It is funny. When examples are borrowing and little pleasures are seeking after not exactly a box then comes the time for drilling. Left left or left. Not up. Really believe me it is sheltered oaks that matter. It is they who are sighing. It really is.

Not when I hear it.

I go on.

This is not a dear noise. It is so distressing. Why was he angry. Did he mean to be laughing.

I was astonished besides. Oh do go on.

He was a ruffian.

Especially made. Why does she satisfy it.

It was a beautiful hat anyway it looked like that or by the way what was the handkerchief. Good.

Now I neglected him.

I made mention of an occasion. I made mention of a syllable. I mentioned that. I was reasonably considerate. I undertook nothing.

Why were birds.

When I decided not to look twice I felt that all three were made of the only distinct changeable brown. I did not mean foxes. This is why I shall not visit. Do go gladly. Do be willing.

What an accident.

What a horrid thought.

What a decent ribbon.

That is why I answered.

No please don't be wakened. Do think it over. Do mind what I say. Do breathe when you can. Explain whites for eggs. Examine every time. Do not deceive a brother. What is perfect instigation. I make I go across.

Instances.

Violences.

Not any whirl.

Not by all means.

Don't you think so.

Fourteen days.

I meant to be closeted.

I should have been thin.

I was aching.

I saw all the rose. I do mostly think that there is politeness. All of it on leather. Not it. I shall speak of it. I so mean to be dried. In the retracting glory there is more choice. There is what was threaded. I don't mean permitting.

Webster.

Little reinforced Susan.

Actual.

Actual believe me.

I see it all.

Why shouldn't I.

Lizzie Make Us.

I believe it.

Why shall I polite it. Pilot it.

Eleven o'clock.

Pillow.

I meant to say.

Saturday.

Not polite.

Do satisfy me.

This is to say that baby is all well. That baby is baby. That baby is all well. That there is a piano. That baby is all well. This is to say that baby is all well. This is to say that baby is all well.

Selling.

She has always said she was comfortable.

Was the water hot.

Hymns.

Look here let us think about hospitality. There is more said and kindness. There are words of praise. There is a wonderful salad. There can be excellent excellent arrangements. There can be excellent arrangements. Suddenly I saw that. I rushed in. I was wise.

We were right. We meant pale. We were wonderfully shattered. Why are we shattered. Only by an arrest of thought. I don't make it out. Hope there. Hope not. I didn't mean it. Please do be silly. I have forgotten the height of the table.

That was a good answer.

I have been going on in a little while.

I am going to take it along. Lena says that there is a chance.

I don't mean to deny it.

That's right.

I shall be very tired I shall be extraordinarily pleased, I shall settle it all presently.

Very likely.

I have to look at her all the time. I never see fruit now unless I pick it in my garden. Put it in my garden. Don't put too many. Because it's so much looser. All right. Oh no. I haven't. Chalk. Great Portland Street. I'll mention it. I have resisted. I have resisted that excellently well. I have resisted that I have resisted that excellently. Not a disappointment.

I don't understand, why hasn't she been there before. I know why. I will not have a selection again. It is too many horribly. Is it any use.

I do want to meet pearly. Now I am forgetting I will begin. She had a jewel. She was in that set.

It meant so much.

I wish I had a little celebration.

It meant so much.

The wise presentation comes from saying north, the best one comes a little way, it comes because she wanted to try breads. Why are pansies so stringy, why do they have heaps of resemblance. I said she was anaemic. I meant to coincide. I did certainly. It was so. Not in Paris.

Not in Paris very likely.

I do not mention that for a name. I mention it for a place. I mention it for a please do not consider me. I mention it for that.

Did she mind my saying that I was disappointed. I was not in that way out in that way. I was not in that way a circumstance which counted for it. She did not meet me. She did not observe clouds. She did not say that we were in the window. She did not like it before it was mentioned.

Come in.

I don't mean to antagonize the present aged parent. That is a strong present leaf.

Line.

Line line line away.

Line.

Lining.

I don't care what she mentions.

It will be very funny when I don't mean to say it.

I can forgive that is to say chopping.

Not any more.

Will I be surprised with Jane Singleton. I will not if I meet her. I will say not yet. I will say that. I am determined. It is so much. Good bye.

I did do it then.

Come back to me Fanny.

Oh dear.

Come back to me Fanny.

That's a picture.

When I remembered how surprised I was at certain places which were nearly in the way I cannot doubt that more accumulation is needed. I cannot doubt it.

All recovering.

James Death is a nice name.

I am breaking down I suppose he said when he arrived.

Forbade any communication with him.

He did say when he arrived I suppose.

It was a bright warm spring Sunday morning.

This egg for instance.

She was dressed in dark blue set off by red ribbons.

Except that of custom perhaps.

If you prefer it I will go.

The only lady who had been saved.

He was not hungry and he knew that there would be nothing to eat.

He was aware of a desire to eat and drink now that it was quite impossible for him to obtain anything.

Thanks I chew.

Jakins thinks me a fool I know sometime maybe I'll be able to prove I'm not.

You're busy.

His excitement was gone.

With mouth and muscle.

When used for male voices substitute bless for kiss.

Shall rest.

Shall rest more.

Shall in horror.

Shall rest.

Shall rest more then.

This is it mentioning.

Why do richness make the best heights.

Why do richness make the best heights.

Enough to leave him for ever and to live in another country

I don't see anything any more do I. Yes you do.

Are you pleased with them darling.

I meant to guess later.

I do not please.

Thanks so much.

Yes.

Yes.

Yes.

Please remember that I have said I will not be patient. Please remember that which I have said.

Do not put in a hot water bottle. Thanks so much.

Feeling mounting.

What did she do. She did not sit she was standing. She was standing and filling with a pepper thing and she had a collar not on her head but because she was shining. She was shining with gloves. This is a new destination. I never was surprised before.

What is the matter with it.

Nothing is the matter with it.

I mean to cough.

She said it was a wish.

You are not angry with me.

It's infamous. To put a cold water bottle in a bed. It is steering.

I meant to mention it and it is astonishing that there is a sentence.

Silence is southern.

I will not especially engage to be sick. I will not especially engage to be sick.

Why is Ellen so attractive.

Willing.

Willing, willing.

Willing willing, I met a kind of a clock. It was deepened.

I am not pleased. I am not satisfied and pleased. I am not pleased and certainly I am not more pleased. I am so repressed and I can state it. I can say. It was bitter.

I do not like her.

Fancy a miserable person. Repeat flowers.

A section.

Breathing.

Polite.

Politeness.

Absolutely.

Not a curl.

I come to say.

Winding.
Place.
Wheat.
Or not.

Come in.

Splashes splashes of jelly splashes of jelly.

Weather.

Whether he was presented.

I meant to stay.

Easy or blocks.
Do not be held by the enemy.
All the time.

Now line or them.

That's an established belt or tooth. Really not. I didn't mean to bellow. I won't be a table. I regret it. I shall be very likely to be walking. I shall introduce myself fairly. I do mind it.

Not again.

I do say not again.
I mean to be heavy.
It stands up against as much as it stands up for. That's what I object to. I don't want to be unflattering to us but I think it has been entirely forgotten.

Furs.

Perhaps you will. Then she wrote a very warm letter and sent these furs.

Shall ill.

I don't like it and in neglecting cherishing songs I am so pleased with all and by settling chalk. I am satisfied. We are neglected immensely. Not resting.

Shall it be continuous the liberty of sobriety. The dear thing. Little tremors. I ask the question.

With a wide piano.

Come.

Neglecting cherishing says shall I mistake pleases. In mistakes there is a salutary secretion. What. I said it.

Now and then.

War is Saturday and let us have peace.

Peace is refreshing, let us bear let us be or not by that mine.

Mended.

Now I come to stay away.

Answer.

I shook a darling.

Not eating Oh it was so timely.

Why should pitchers be triumphant. Does it proclaim that eleven, eleven, eleven, come across, speak it, satisfy a man, be neat, leave off oxes, shine flies, call spoken shouting call it back call it by little dotted voices and do be sweet, do be sweet, remember the accoutrement. No I will not pay away.

What a system in voices, what a system in voices.

I met a regular believe me it is not for the pleasure in it that I do it. I met a regular army. I was not certain of that, I was not certain of paper. I knew I was safe. And so he was. Shall I believe it.

I can't help mentioning that I was earnest. In that way there was a reason. I can destroy wetter wetter soaps. I can destroy wetter soaps.

I do.

I do not.

Leave it in there for me.

Leave it in an especial place. Do not make that face. Show it by the indication. I do mean to spell. I am. Believe me.

Pink Melon Joy.

II.

It pleases me very much.

Little swimming on the water.

I meant to mention pugilism. Pugilism leaning. Leaning and thinking. Thinking.

I meant to mention pugilism. Pugilism and leaning.

Leaning and thinking. I think.

I meant to mention that it was a resemblance that was not by way of exceeding the kind thought.

Pugilism. Pugilism and leaning.

I saw a door not that exactly, I saw a lamp shade. Certainly that. I will not stir. Pugilism and leaning.

Leaning.

Pugilism and leaning.

The reason I mention what is happening is not by way of concealing that I have babies. I don't mean to leave so and I shall speak in silence.

What is a baby.

Now I know what I say.

I had loads of stationary.

Not pink melon joy. Pink melon joy. Pink melon joy.

I had loads of stationary.

Pugilism and leaning.

The little keys trembling. Why do they spoil a part. They were noisy.

Go to Mudie's first.

Go slowly and carefully and love your dearest.

That's a good idea.

Reconcile is a plain case of wretched pencils.

I cannot see what I shall a bit.

My one idea is to place cloth where there is cloth and to paper where I have hotter water, to place paper where I have hotter water.

I don't determine selfishness. I point it so that always I can always I do, I do always mean to get about.

Shall I be splendid.

Baby mine baby mine I am learning letters I am learning that to be sent baby mine baby mine I arranged it fairly early.

Complete cause for handles.

Complete cause for not tightening that.

I won't say it again.

This is the place to water horses.

I like to be excellently seized.

I made a mistake.

I like to be excellently seizing.

North north I went around and went in that minute.

I like to be excellently searching.

I like to be excellently chimes.

Chiming.

It isn't very good.

Deep set trustworthy eyes dark like his hair.

Lips close fitting and without flew.

Blue should have dark eyes.

Light brown flesh color amber shades black nose, ears, legs, good sized feet rather.

Color dark blue, blue and tan, tan and liver, sandy, sandy and tan.

Height about fifteen to sixteen inches.

He wondered if she had ever thought of him as she sat in the chair or walked on the floor.

Islands.

I came to say that I like some things better.

Actual likenesses.

Of course I need large plates.

Standing alone.

She doesn't like it.

She likes to walk on the floor.

She might as well be pretty.

I don't blame Carrie.

No.

What do I see when I like to be tall.

I see when there is a platter.

I was not mistaken with violets.

It was no pleasure.

Can you believe me.

Can you not be thoughtful.

Can you be aghast.

I mention most things regularly.

I do not wish whispers.

This makes mining such a loud noise.

I do not forget a war.

It isn't easy to please everybody.
Teeth are perfect.

No.

There is no influence.

Scattered.

Nine times twenty.
Crowded.
Crowded in.
Cups white.
I am solemn.
All taste.
Do you excuse me.
It was a stir.
Please state it please deny it please mean to be right. I am intending.

Able to mingle pennies.

A penny is not a cent.

Why do I see sisters.

It's rice.

Wheat.

I couldn't imagine gladder or more perfect shapes, I couldn't imagine others.
He was really interested in the fluttering deftness of her twinkling hands.
I don't care too.
Likely.
I meant pearls.
Shall I be pleased.
Wire cakes.

In time or.

Not so far back.

Please.

When I came to stay.
Old places.

When a girl speaks.
Shall you.

Not pleasing.

It is a time for that.
Formidable.
Amiable.
Amiable baby.
Fan.

Fanning.

There is no way of stretching.

Plan.

It is a good pitcher it is a good pitcher and a black pitcher.

It is a circle.

It is a circular.

I beg of you not to.

Bring in the fruit.

She was very comforting.

I wonder what he is doing. If he saw, well he couldn't see him because he is not here, if he saw him he would not ask him any questions, he would beg him to give him all the pictures and in any case he would ask him to arrange it.

What is a splendid horse. A splendid horse is one that is spread and really makes a lot of noise really makes an agreeable sound and a hoarse. This is not an interchange of rapid places by means of tubs.

I know you don't know what the pins are. I know you suspect much more. I know that anything is a great pleasure. I know esquimaux babies, that is to say tender.

I know what I am hearing. I am hearing accents. Not by any means placarded. Not by any means placarded. So that I met everybody.

What is the meaning of photographs.

Yes I mean it.

I believe that when there is a collection and tall pieces are missed and guided, I could have said it.

Let us take boats.

Boats are ships.

We will not take ships.

Ships are doors.

That's the way to be perfect.

I sell hats.

That's a kindness.

Please powder faces.

I have little chickens.

That doesn't mean anything.

When I said water I meant Sunday. Dear me it was Monday. No Tuesday. I don't care I shall please neatness. Then I calculated I did not see arithmetic I saw feathers, any two of them are thicker. What was the principle coughing, it went by way of dishes.

To be binding is to mean Sunday Saturday and eight o'clock. To be eight o'clock oh how heavenly singing. Leave Leave Leave oh my leaving and say why say, say I say say say go away go away I say. I say yes.

Plans.

I was able to state that I believed that if targets if targets not if targets.

Shall I be restless.

I could not eat buttons. I could not eat bundles. I couldn't, I might be why was I seen to be determined. I was surprising. Wasn't I silly.

Please miss me.

Not spider.

I saw a spider there.

Where.

I saw another.

Where.

I saw another and there I saw a pleasing sight.

I saw a waiter.

A spider.

Yes.

Not by left out.

Will you be faithful, will you be so glad that I left any way. Will you be delighted Saturday. Do you understand colors. It was my sister.

Why.

I cannot mention what I have.

I have.

Guess it.
I have a real sight. This is so critical.
Alice.

Put it in.

Put it in.
Nestles.
I wish I was a flower.
Were.
Were when.
Towers.

That is.

That is astonishing.

Mother.

I meant it.
When the moon.
I don't like it.
A million and ten.
Ten million and ten.
Ten and ten million.
Oh leave it to me.

Brutes.

I said whisper.

Anyway pink melon or joy.

Is that the same.
Pink melon and enjoy.
Pink melon by joy.
Is that in him.
Is that in.
Positive.

At night.

Please be cautious and recalcitrant and determined to be steady. Please be neglectful. Please be ordered out.

Please be ordered out.

Franz Joseph was Emperor of Austria before gold had been discovered in California.

I do not.

Their thoughts were of one another.

The maid a very pretty girl somewhat showily dressed in a costume composed of the royal colors fixed curious eyes down a long passage and a short one. Presently the girl in blue returned.

Blue and white.

Returned.

Food and wine.

How could it be how could it be.

Blue and white, not an especial pinching.

I wish I was may be I am.

This isn't good.

Short erect ears and bold intelligent faces.

He seemed to like it.

Who are you.

Safety in comfort.

A flower should never lack an admirer in its namesake.

Unfortunately.

Unfortunately our weeks in London were full up so that I did not get a felt hat.

Unfortunately before.

Oh dear what did I do with them.

Here is a key for the house painters.

Glove stretchers.

Not any more begging.

Please have it ready.

She did not move.

She was not going to move.

It guards the life the health and the well-being of each user.

Parents encourage its use.

You can be the subject of wild admiration in ten days if you care to.

The skin has the tint of purity.

Very pleasant to use.
A freshly blown rose.
I can't be feeling badly.
I prefer water.
I like no I don't like it.
I fill a free uniform black instantly.
These features are peculiar to a construction.

Please be dark.

Straws.
Please be straws.
I wish yes.
Plates.
And plates.
When do you gather together.
By ways of extra pages which mean colored places.
I read about the war.
I said that I didn't know Geoffrey Young. I said I believed in boys. I said I was enthusiastic.
I said little more.
To be able to spread water.
To be able to spread water.
There is a difference between kitchen coal and bedrooms.
What pleases you.

What Eugene said.

Eugene said that she would have a different expression from her sister. He did not say anything about her hair. She mentioned a wedding. Oh it was sinful.

Eugene said that there were straits. He did not stop for plates. She said she could cook. He was violent. He never was moved by birthdays. He liked Saturday. He was clean. He was not annoyed.

Consider a pleasant time.
All the time that there is commotion there is powerful autocracy.
Nicely said.
I do mean to win.
Pages and pages.
I don't care about lists.
I don't care about lists.

Pointed or why do you.

When I used that expression I was nervous. Don't take it too seriously James is nervous.

Plans.

Six fires.
Two lights.
Four lights.
Eight lights.
Eighty days.
I wish I was restless.

Out of four.

Out of four.
Six.
Sixty.
Little cats not all gone.
Little dove little love I am loving you with much more love. Parlor.
I saw an extraordinary mixture.
By nearly leaving out gloves and washing them.

By nearly leaving out gloves and washing them and towels, by nearly leaving out towels and all of it by way of reminding every one of every time, by leaving out invitations, by passing some day, let us say Tuesday, by passing Tuesday together and eating, by leaving out all the powder, by leaving out all the powder, Nellie made a mistake. Was it a week Monday. Not with the carelessness. It was carelessness. I meant to do it.

Pink Melon Joy.

III.

Thanks so much.
Do not repeat the miracle.
Thanks so much.

War.

I wish I was in the time when all the blame was feelingly added to mercies. I wish I could ask what's the matter now.

By believing in forms by believing in sheds by more stationing by really swimming as usual, no shell or fish. Pray.

I can hear extra rabbits, I can hear them and I mean beats. What is it.

It is not any use. It's no use. I do believe it. I shall select. I relieve officers. I sell potatoes. That is what clergymen sing.

Singing. What is singing quietly. We are singing quietly. I wish chimneys were old. They sound alike. They bother me.

All the day.

I was disappointed.

Going up.

Good night Mildred.

Good night dear.

They bother one so.

The cause of receding the cause of receding more, the cause of receding is in me. In me by me, for the rest. All of it organ. Take out a name. He did it.

Anything.

Anything to drink.

Anything to think.

Anything.

Very resistant

I meant to spell teeth.

This is the way to pay.

Why should old people be vivacious. Thumbs do it.

They poison everything. They manage six.

I wish anger.

I wish religion.

I wish bursts.

I do wish fancies.

Fancy balls.

Blue dresses.

Other color cushions.

Points.

Disappoints.

Why should eating be agreeing.

Why should darkness turn colors.

Why should peddling be honorable.

Why should another be mother.

Mother to all.

Mother to some.

I say.
I say it.

He laughed.

He laughed believe me.
I do believe you.
He did not bother to sob.
I do not relegate that to the reverberation.
Please me.

It's not polite.

Cleaning silver.

Colored sack.

If I meant weather and I do mean to be obeyed, if I meant whether I was better I would not say bitter I would speak to every one.

Public character.

Stems.
Stems are caught by better seats they need watches.

I don't mean to be so finished.

Let us consider the french nation, let us watch its growth its order its humanity its care, its elaboration its thought its celebrated singing and nearly best nearly best with it. Let us consider why we are in authority, let us consider distribution, let us consider forget me nots.

Pensive.

By land.
By land.
By land.
By land.

I mentioned gayety.

I mentioned gayety.
No.
Not willing.
By pleasure.
Leading songs.

The moon is as round as a button.
All buttons aren't round said Alfy.

Plated onions.

I wish matches.
I wish all right.
I wish coal.
I do wish.
I wish I may.
I wish not a bird.
I wish when I make it.
I wish again.
I wish more than that.

Carving.

I didn't complain Susie.

If I really believed it I wouldn't be able to know.

But why the sitting was not the bed room he could never understand.

I am just gradually beginning to get to look around.

We were using the end that is by the fire and now that we have good coal I am beginning to separate expenses. I do see shell fish. It is a mistake to recollect all of it very nearly. I had better undertake to measure out a real wood and to borrow little pieces. It was chosen by me. I spoke to a man. He said he would come at once. I said no wait until you finish dinner. He mentioned that the soup was so hot he would prefer that it should cool. I said I would not allow it, that I would be uncomfortable and that there was no hurry I left no one. I never see fire, Mr. Matisse, Mr. Julian, Mr. Meininger, Mrs. Walter and Miss Howard without thinking of it. By nearly wishing for a country by nearly wishing for a country, by this you will spoil her. Do you. Do you ask for Greek. Do you deny Spain. Do you not praise England. Do you prize England. I said that I believed in the country and that I was silent in the city. I said I was silent about the city, I said I believed in the country. He asked me why I reigned. I said I did not deny rain. I said he could promise his mother. When the whole arrangement was mentioned leaving out pieces of plaster, when the whole thing was mentioned and he did not recommend oil, he did not say that he had not made an attempt, he said it was useless at this time to ask a minister to serve an individual.

He said they were too busy. He said he would not speak to one another. He said I will ask.

I am trying a new one.

Believe two names.

I am really surprised.

In my surprise I shall stammer.

I do not stammer ordinarily.

Widening putty is not lonesome. It makes a door. I was wondering if the door was wide enough and if not whether the double door would be broken. It certainly would be and now if it were there would be no reparation. Not by reason of not inclining to mend it but because of the time that is only shown by the absence of women. It is astonishing. Really it is astonishing and it's true. We have found it out. The day that we asked we heard it. We were surprised. If I wanted the door there is yet to be found the man who makes plaster. Plaster, cement. We say cement.

I am disappointed in women. No I cannot say that. There are ten days. I will be so pleased. I am so pleased. Do you credit me with hearing. I am so pleased.

It's been a success, it's been a perfect success.

Harnessing on or another. Harnessing another.

Harnessing on or another. Harnessing on or another is a great success. I offer. I offer. I offer. I do need it. Please be careful. Harnessing another is a great success. I was surprised when I looked at the picture to see that I could recognise everybody. I had been perfectly right in saying that they were stupid. It is chance. An accident. A resemblance. An offspring. An intuition. A result. A repetition. Repeat. I knew I wanted four hundred. I forgot to ask if he had seen an electrician. If he had was he at Versailles. A silver designer that is a name, Emile. I wanted to laugh. The voice was loud. I did not understand English. I am beautifully rich.

Once when I was fastening a drawing, I fastened it with decision. I did not like it there. We have decided not to have an umbrella stand. I don't think either that we will put everything away. I think what we will decide is this, to meet the train, to insist on paying, to give four eggs, bread, butter, water, meat and pears. Then we will go away and after that I don't think there is any need to notice noise. It is so silvery. I mentioned a fork. We were astonished by all languages. I meant to be told.

This is the light. I can not see plainly. I make a difference.
When are brothers.
By times.
Do old age missions sing.
They do choose choirs.
Why are mistakes late. Because they pleased us and we shall be late.
Render yourselves further. This means servants.
Render yourselves together.
Render together.
I saw a team running. I saw plenty of lamps.
It was lighter than London.
Do you think so.
To be dangerous mother.
We were so tired from sheer pity.
I wish we had loaned another.
Please be a buyer.
I shall spoil.
Not he.
Not he or hurry.
Not he. Not she. For her. Not very good.

The rebellion of Esther.

In a rebellion of Esther or with a study of a sheepdog. What is a police dog.

There may come a pause.

His task accomplished he may feed. It was seldom that increase or decrease in accordance with the one who welcomes first of all the incoming ill-natured purpose showed lightly conscienced boys bribed for the purpose. These exclaim. Do not for a moment fall into the error of considering them as to what becomes of them after they are fifty years of age. Had they been they would have succumbed to earlier opportunities. The sun set upon a curious scene.

I went faster.

The infant's face being uncovered the helpless little thing opened its eyes. Although this separation was unavoidable it is I who am never permitted who have never permitted any one to ask me to interfere.

Pears.

Leave me leave me by way of pointing.

Believe me see me by way of dealing out plans.

Believe me believe me be careless, lead it by permission. Is Henner going to Paris.

By me I see sounds of dirt. I can hear something. I listen best. I am willing.

With no plan.

Have you said yes. I think it would be best to ask a baker. He sent her. He meant to hear me. He was loud. He had an unexpected spelling.

Hear me hear me I do.

Plainly.

If I carry you. If you carry, what will you carry.

Carrie.

Carrie.

If you carry me.

Seating.

Little manners.

When I asked everybody to sit down they were annoyed.

Please be at wax matches.

Please beat.

Please beat.

I cannot express emotion.

Any house is a home.

Two hands.

I heard today that it was appalling. I believe what is said and why it is said. I believe that lights are normal. I believe that separate stones coming together count as forty. I believe in two horses. I believe that.

When I heard the description of mud and shouting when I saw him and it was a surprise then I said I would stand. It was pleasant. It was not gentle. It was black and hopeful. It was principally very shapely. Anything can astonish a citizen. I was cautious. I believe in the best.

Not a mile.

When I say that introductions mean that, when I feel that I have met them, when I am out aloud and by spacing I separate letters when I do this and I am melancholy I remember that rivers, only rivers have suppressed sounds. All the rest overflow. Piles are driven. Ice is free. Changes are by little spools, and toys are iron. Toys are iron whether or not they are Italian.

This is so far. Please be at rest. I shall. I shall not speak for anybody. I shall do my duty. I shall establish that mile. I shall choose wonder. Be blest.

When she said six and meant seven I made her leave it more than she chose to revise. I made her please me. Do be careful.

I cannot help it. I cannot expect places. I can see that there is some obligation in deciding on straps and in lessening tails. I can see what I come to mention. But do not deceive anybody, do not be churlish. Do place exercises in a book. To be excellently winning, to be exclaiming and really I don't see any use in leaving yet when really there is no moon. I do believe in some. I shall suggest it. Very likely there is cause. I don't say I neglect to mention it. I forgot to place any of it higher. I meant to relieve eyes. I saw wealthy boys. I shall judge then. Do not go away. This is this call. I edged it. I mean to say goodness. Don't be a worry. Don't resemble mother. I saw the oldest boy sneeze. It is a calamitous poison. Not when it is old. Not by nearly so much as yesterday. I do believe I hear whether I do see knives. Indeed I do.

What was she going to do Monday morning.

There are plenty of rubber wheels of a kind. The mischief lies in getting the wrong ones. They are remarkable in many shapes and when you ask for hurrying see that you get it.

I think this will be enough.

Closets are cleaner.

We came to be rosy.

Prayers.

I mentioned it satisfactorily.

Do not be careful.

Do not be careful.

She said she would not have displeased her by herself. I will mention it to another. Be quick.

Quickly.

I don't know why emigration has been stopped.

Maps.

I am thinking.

I will not say that.

This is the way I feel about it. He said that. He did not say he was reluctant. He went to the place in front of the same thing. Any one is not tired.

To believe me it is necessary to have a resumption. To resume is war. I say it in the morning. I don't say it in the morning. This is not mischief. I do not believe in fancies in respect to bread. This was mentioned with coal. But not with the same authority.

He goes and he does not believe in draughts. He is invited.

It seems a splendid day.

I said he knew this thing. I said everybody knows something. I was winding stockings. This is the day to pray.

Please be restless.

I cannot count.

I looked for the address.

There was plenty of time in softening.

He said he was surprised and he said laughing is coughing.

There is one such in my company. I am impatient. I believe in crops.

I do not care about the same thing in another way.

Would you have another.

What.

Kiss.

LADIES' VOICES

CURTAIN RAISER

This tiny playlet explores the world of spoken words, as do many Stein works. Sound, rhythm, tone, manner and phrasing make its auditory life, which also recalls the story-telling in *Ada,* the voices in *What Happened,* and the various studies of conversation. Stein wrote this play of overheard fragments spoken by women in 1916 in Mallorca, probably at carnival time. The location is relevant in part because it explains details, for example, Mahón, the capital, harbor, and fortress of Minorca, a name joined with Christ and Lazarus to produce a biblical ring though it is not itself biblical; and the Hotel Victoria, the main hotel of Mallorca. More important, Mallorca, a resort with a large Anglo-Saxon clientele, in wartime attracts an international set of expatriates from all sorts of places speaking all sorts of languages. A masked ball compounds the mingling of persons and languages and words that seem, as she says, English, though they may not be so.

• • • • •

Ladies' voices give pleasure.

The acting two is easily lead. Leading is not in winter. Here the winter is sunny.

Does that surprise you.

Ladies voices together and then she came in.

Very well good night.

Very well good night Mrs. Cardillac.

That's silver.

You mean the sound.

Yes the sound.

ACT II.

Honest to God Miss Williams I don't mean to say that I was older.

But you were.

Yes I was. I do not excuse myself. I feel that there is no reason for passing an archduke.

You like the word.

You know very well that they all call it their house.

As Christ was to Lazarus so was the founder of the hill to Mahon.

You really mean it.

I do.

ACT III.

Yes Genevieve does not know it. What. That we are seeing Caesar.

Caesar kisses.

Kisses today.

Caesar kisses every day.

Genevieve does not know that it is only in this country that she could speak as she does.

She does speak very well doesn't she. She told them that there was not the slightest intention on the part of her countrymen to eat the fish that was not caught in their country.

In this she was mistaken.

ACT IV.

What are ladies voices.

Do you mean to believe me.

Have you caught the sun.

Dear me have you caught the sun.

SCENE II.

Did you say they were different. I said it made no difference.

Where does it. Yes.

Mr. Richard Sutherland. This is a name I know.

Yes.

The Hotel Victoria.

Many words spoken to me have seemed English.

Yes we do hear one another and yet what are called voices the best decision in telling of balls.

Masked balls.

Yes masked balls.

Poor Augustine.

MARRY NETTIE

ALRIGHT MAKE IT A SERIES AND CALL IT

MARRY NETTIE.

The Italian futurist Marinetti is not the subject of *Marry Nettie*. Rather, the name offered Stein the pun. In this piece done in Mallorca, there is no futurism and no serial composition.

Why a series? In late March 1916 Carl Van Vechten wrote that if Stein came to America she would be received like Jenny Lind, the famous Swedish soprano. On 18 April Stein answered that she was making "so much absorbing literature with such attractive titles and even if I could be as popular as Jenny Lind where oh where is the man to publish me in series" (*The Letters of Gertrude Stein and Carl Van Vechten,* 53). She wanted a publisher to take her on and print her seriatim.

The spoken subtitle sounds as impatient and abrupt as the whole piece and much of the work done in Mallorca. Many details are illogical and ill fitting. A cane falls out of a window, is apparently stolen, and is difficult to get back. A Miss Thaddeus with an androgynous name helps to retrieve it by indirection. It is not non sequiturs in writing that exasperate us but sequences in events that seem to go wrong.

Marriage appears in many of the Mallorcan pieces, but it is an empty designation for couples about whom there is little to say. On the island of Mallorca, where nothing happens, there are couples, some single people, and Stein and Toklas, impatient in their unacknowledged marriage. The wartime mood of Mallorca is not pleasant.

Stein and Toklas compensate for the discomfort of their situation and the war by attending to domestic life and private intimacy. They go shopping for souvenirs. They enjoy new vegetables, flowers and fruits, fish, shoes or sandals of rope and rubber, pens and pencils, tuberoses. The war, far from the island, enters her writing through newspapers, creating irritation and tension precisely by its distance. Nervousness occurs again, filled with contradictions in a carefully wrought series of denials, "She said I was nervous. I said I knew she wasn't nervous. The dear of course I wasn't nervous. I said I wasn't nervous."

Marry Nettie ends suddenly, impatient with everything, with "Shut up," like *Painted Lace* of the beginning of the war. It is hot. Summer may be coming. "We wish to go now." The piece may have been written shortly before the return to Paris in May 1916.

• • • • •

Principle calling.
They don't marry.
Land or storm.
This is a chance.
A Negress.
Nurse.
Three years.
For three years.
By the time.
He had heard.
He didn't eat.
Well.
What does it cost to sew much.

A cane dropped out of the window. It was sometime before it was searched for. In the meantime the Negress had gotten it. It had no value. It was one that did bend. We asked every one. No one would be intended or contented. We gave no peace. At last the day before we left I passed the door. I saw a bamboo cane but I thought the joints were closer together. I said this. Miss Thaddeus looked in. It was my cane. We told the woman who was serving. She said she would get it. She waited and was reasonable. She asked if they found it below as it was the cane of Miss Thaddeus. It was and plain. So there. We leave.

There is no such thing as being good to your wife.

She asked for tissue paper. She wanted to use it as a respirator. I don't understand how so many people can stand the mosquitoes.

It seems unnecessary to have it last two years. We would be so pleased.

We are good.

We are energetic.

We will get the little bowls we saw to-day.

The little bowls we saw to-day are quite pretty.

They will do nicely.

We will also get a fan. We will have an electric one. Everything is so reasonable.

It was very interesting to find a sugar bowl with the United States seal on one side and the emblem of liberty on the other.

If you care to talk to the servant do not talk to her while she is serving at table. This does not make me angry nor annoy me. I like salad. I am losing my individuality.

It is a noise.

Plan.

All languages.

By means of swimming.

They see English spoken.

They are dark to-day very easily by the sun.

We will go out in the morning. We will go and bring home fish. We will also bring note-books and also three cups. We will see Palma. Shoes are necessary. Shoes with cord at the bottom are white. How can I plan everything.

Sometimes I don't mind putting on iodine and sometimes I do.

This is not the way to be pleasant. I am very careful.

To describe tube-roses.

This is the day.

Pressing.

John.

Eating garlic. Do be careful. Do be careful in eating garlic particularly on an island. There is a fish a devil fish an ink fish which is good to eat. It is prepared with pepper and sauce and we eat it nicely. It is very edible.

How did we please her. A bottle of wine not that doesn't do it.

Oil.

Oil.

To make her shine.

We entwine.

So that.

How do you do.

We don't think highly of Jenny.

SPANISH NEWSPAPER.

A spanish newspaper says that the king went to a place and addressed the artillery officer who was there and told him, artillery is very important in war.

THE COUNT.

Somebody does sleep next door.

The count went to bathe, the little boy had amber beads around him. He went.

I made a mistake.
That's it.
He wanted the towel dried.
They refused.
Towels do not dry down here.
They do up at my place, said the Count.

SHE WAS.
NOT ASTONISHING.

She came upstairs having been sick. It was the effect of the crab.

Was I lost in the market or was she lost in the market.

We were not. We thought that thirty nine was a case of say it. Please try. I could find her. A large piece. Beets. Figs. Egg plants. Fish. We walked up and down. They sold pencils. The soldier what is a soldier. A soldier is readily given a paper. He does not like that pencil. He does not try another. We were so happy. She ought to be a very happy woman. Now we are able to recognise a photograph. We are able to get what we want.

A NEW SUGAR BOWL WITH A CROSS ON TOP.

We said we had it. We will take it to Paris. Please let us take everything.

The sugar bowl with a cross on top now has sugar in it. Not soft sugar but the sugar used in coffee. It is put on the table for that.

It is very pretty. We have not seen many things. We want to be careful. We don't really have to bother about it.

ANOTHER CHANCE.

That's it. Beds. How glad I am. What was I worried about. Was it the weather, was it the sun, was it fatigue was it being tired. It was none of these. It was that wood was used and we did not know.

We blamed each other.

WE BLAMED EACH OTHER.

She said I was nervous. I said I knew she wasn't nervous. The dear of course I wasn't nervous. I said I wasn't nervous. We were sure that steam was coming out of the water. It makes that noise. Our neighbours have a small telescope. They can see the water with it. They can not see the names of ships. They can tell that their little boy is lonesome which he is. He stands there and calls out once in a while to the others. I am so annoyed.

Do we believe the germans.
We do not.

SPANISH PENS.

Spanish pens are falling. They fall there. That makes it rich. That makes Spain richer than ever. Spanish pens are in places. They are in the places which we see. We read about everything. This is by no means an ordeal. A charity is true.

WHY ARE WE PLEASED.

We are pleased because we have an electrical fan.
May the gods of Moses and of Mars help the allies. They do they will.

WE WILL WALK AFTER SUPPER.

We will not have tea. We will rest all day with the electric fan. We will have supper. We can perspire. After supper. This is so humorous.

WE HAD AN EXCITING DAY.

We took a fan out of a man's hand. We complained to the mother of Richard. Not knowing her we went there. They all said it. It was useful. We went to the ball room where there was billiard playing and reading. Then we accepted it. He said it was changed from five to seven and a half.

NOT VERY LIKELY.

We were frightened. We are so brave and we never allow it. We do not allow anything at last. That's the way to say we like ours best.

PAPERS.

Buy me some cheese even if we must throw it away. Buy me some beets. Do not ask them to save any of these things. There will be plenty of them. One reason why we are careful is that carrots are indifferent. They are so and we forgot to say Tuesday. How do you do. Will you give me some of the fruit. It is thoughtless of me to be displeased.

HOT WEATHER.

I don't care for it. Why not. Because it makes me careless. Careless of what. Of the example of church. What is church. Church is not a question. So there is strength and truth and rocking.

PLEASE BE QUICK.

Why do they unload at night. Or is it that one hears it then. Perhaps it has just come. I am not suspicious.

WHY DO YOU LIKE IT.

Because it is all about you. Whom do you marry. Nettie.

WHOM DO YOU SAY YOU SEE.

You see plenty of french people. You see some foolish people. You hear one boasting. What is he saying. He says it takes a hundred men to make a steam boat landing. I am going to say you missed it. Do be still. We are awkward. Not in swimming. We are very strong. We have small touches and we do see our pride. We have earned plates. We are looking for a bell.

YOU LIKE THIS BEST.

Lock me in neatly.
Unlock me sweetly.
I love my baby with a rush rushingly.

SOMETIMES THEY CAN FINISH A BUGLE CALL.

Sometimes they can finish a bugle call when they know it. They have a very good ear. They are not quick to learn. They do not have application.

MARRY NETTIE.

Marry who. Marry Nettie. Which Nettie. My Nettie. Marry whom. Marry Nettie. Marry my Nettie.

I was distinguished by knowing about the flower pot. It was one that had tube-roses. I put the others down below. That one will be fixed.

I was also credited with having partiality for the sun. I am not particular. I do not like to have it said that it is so necessary to hear the next letter. We all wish to go now. Do be certain that we are cool.

Oh shut up.

ACCENTS IN ALSACE

A REASONABLE TRAGEDY

SCENE MULHOUSE

In Alsace-Lorraine accents change and names change each time the region passes from France to Germany and back to France. Stein played with the changing language, accent, pronunciation, and spelling that come with changes of political and social order. She wrote this play after the end of World War I, when Alsace, freed of German rule, had reverted back to France. At the same time, in the spring of 1919, near the end of six months of work for war relief in Mulhouse, she also wrote it as a gift to Alice Toklas for her birthday, on 30 April. The piece is filled with spring love ditties for Toklas whose language carries the double entendres of private intimacy.

The play opens with a kind of moral exemplum about the Schimmel family. Their name makes a double rhyme with *Himmel,* "heaven," and its several German meanings and spellings ask for wordplay; one alternate spelling, Schemil, even echoes the Yiddish schlemiel. The son of this family escapes German conscription by joining the French Foreign Legion, which leads to harrassment, bribes, payoffs. War breeds trouble, cover-ups, lies.

Verses and phrases alternately reveal and conceal identity and cover up misdeeds of mixed kinds in the no-man's-land that had been German but with the end of World War I had become French again. Each change of order calls for a switch in language, pronunciation, accent, that may be serious in public life but is known to lovers anywhere as a light game. The ditties allow Stein to play across English, French, and German words, spellings, accents, and rhymes. (Here for once she even includes a word butchered of its wordness to make possible the dreadful rhyme "trois/wha.") The songs are cover-ups or giveaways that become protective cloaks around individuals in sensitive positions. It is a language familiar to those, like Ada, Miss Furr and Miss Skeene, who know private understanding, public misunderstanding, and the need for coded speech.

Germany and the German language take Stein to her own German-Jewish antecedents, which she rejects. The first line of the play admonishes the Schimmel son—perhaps any son or brother—for his own good "to go away and stay" away from the Germans, who will kill him. Stein resists any rigid order because it breeds intolerance, whether it is that of Germany, of the patriarchal family, or of heterosexual society. She had seen distressing instability in the region but in a sense placed a positive value on it. To her, by the end of World War I, a rigid, intolerant, inflexible world had broken open.

Edith Sitwell read this play when she prepared to review *Geography and Plays* in 1923. She later said that her "Jodelling Song" was founded on "The Watch on the Rhine," the concluding section of *Accents in Alsace*.

• • • • •

ACT I. THE SCHEMILS.

Brother brother go away and stay.
Sister mother believe me I say.
They will never get me as I run away.

He runs away and stays away and strange to say he passes the lines and goes all the way and they do not find him but hear that he is there in the foreign legion in distant Algier.

And what happens to the family.

The family manages to get along and then some one of his comrades in writing a letter which is gotten hold of by the Boche find he is a soldier whom they cannot touch, so what do they do they decide to embrew his mother and sister and father too. And how did they escape by paying somebody money.

That is what you did with the Boche. You always paid some money to some one it might be a colonel or it might be a sergeant but anyway you did it and it was neccesary so then what happened.

THE SCHEMMELS.

Sing so la douse so la dim.
Un deux trois
Can you tell me wha
Is it indeed.
What you call a Petide.
And then what do I say to thee
Let me kiss thee willingly.
Not a mountain not a goat not a door.
Not a whisper not a curl not a gore
In me meeney miney mo.
You are my love and I tell you so.
  In the daylight

And the night
Baby winks and holds me tight.
In the morning and the day and the evening and alway.
I hold my baby as I say.
Completely.
And what is an accent of my wife.
And accent and the present life.
Oh sweet oh my oh sweet oh my
I love you love you and I try
I try not to be nasty and hasty and good
I am my little baby's daily food.

ALSATIA.

In the exercise of greatness there is charm.
Believe me I mean to do you harm.
And except you have a stomach to alarm.
I mean to scatter so you are to arm.
Let me go.
And the Alsatians say.
What has another prince a birthday.

Now we come back to the Schimmels.
Schimmel Schimmel Gott in Himmel
Gott in Himmel There comes Shimmel.
Schimmel is an Alsatian name.

ACT II.

It is a little thing to expect nobody to sell what you give them.
It is a little thing to be a minister.
It is a little thing to manufacture articles.
All this is modest.

THE BROTHER.

Brother brother here is mother.
We are all very well.

SCENE.

Listen to thee sweet cheerie
Is the pleasure of me.

In the way of being hungry and tired
That is what a depot makes you
A depot is not for trains
Its for us.

What are baby carriages
Household goods
And not the dears.
But dears.

ANOTHER ACT.

Clouds do not fatten with teaching.
They do not fatten at all.
We wonder if it is influence
By this way I guess.
She said. I like it better than Eggland.
What do you mean.
We never asked how many children over eleven.
You cannot imagine what I think about the country.
Any civilians killed.

ACT II.

See the swimmer. He don't swim.
See the swimmer.
My wife is angry when she sees a swimmer.

OPENING II.

We like Hirsing.

III.

We like the mayor of Guebwiller.

IV.

We like the road between Cernay and the railroad.
We go everywhere by automobile.

ACT II.

This is a particular old winter.
Everybody goes back.

Back.
I can clean.
I can clean.
I cannot clean without a change in birds.
I am so pleased that they cheat.

ACT 54.

In silver stars and red crosses.
In paper money and water.
We know a french wine.
Alsatian wine is dearer.
They are not particularly old.
Old men are old.
There are plenty to hear of Schemmel having appendicitis.

SCENE II.

Can you mix with another
Can you be a Christian and a Swiss.
Mr. Zumsteg. Do I hear a saint.
Louisa. They call me Lisela.
Mrs. Zumsteg. Are you going to hear me.
Young Mr. Zumsteg. I was looking at the snow.
All of them. Like flowers. They like flowers.

SCENE III.

It is an occasion.
When you see a Hussar.
A Zouave.
A soldier
An antiquary.
Perhaps it is another.
We were surprised with the history of Marguerite's father and step-father and the American Civil War.

Joseph. Three three six, six, fifty, six fifty, fifty, seven.

Reading french.
Reading french.
Reading french singing.

Any one can look at pictures.
They explain pictures.
The little children have old birds.
They wish they were women.
Any one can hate a Prussian.
Alphonse what is your name.
Henri what is your name.
Madeleine what is your name.
Louise what is your name.
René what is your name.
Berthe what is your name.
Charles what is your name.
Marguerite what is your name.
Jeanne what is your name.

ACT 425.

We see a river and we are glad to say that that is in a way in the way today.

We see all the windows and we see a souvenir and we see the best flower. The flower of the truth.

AN INTERLUDE.

Thirty days in April gave a chance to sing at a wedding.
Three days in February gave reality to life.
Fifty days every year do not make subtraction.
The Alsatians sing anyway.
Forty days in September.
Forty days in September we know what it is to spring.

ACT IN AMERICA.

Alsatians living in America.

FEBRUARY XIV.

On this day the troops who had been at Mulhouse came again.
They came in the spring.
The spring is late in Alsace.

Water was good and hot anyway.

What are you doing.

Making music and burning the surface of marble.
When the surface of marble is burned it is not much discolored.
No but there is a discussion.
And then the Swiss.
What is amiss.
The Swiss are the origin of Mulhouse.

ALSACE OR ALSATIANS.

We have been deeply interested in the words of the song.
The Alsatians do not sing as well as their storks.
Their storks are their statuettes.
The rule is that angels and food and eggs are all sold by the dozen.
We were astonished.
And potatoes
Potatoes are eaten dry.
This reminds me of another thing I said. A woman likes to use money.
And if not.
She feels it really is her birthday.
Is it her birthday.
God bless it is her birthday.
Please carry me to Danemarie.
And what does Herbstadt say.
The names of cities are the names of all.
And pronouncing villages is more of a test than umbrella.
This was the first thing we heard in Alsatia.
Canary, roses, violets and curtains and bags and churches and rubber tires and an examination.
All the leaves are green and babyish.
How many children make a family.

THE WATCH ON THE RHINE.

Sweeter than water or cream or ice. Sweeter than bells of roses. Sweeter than winter or summer or spring. Sweeter than pretty posies. Sweeter than anything is my queen and loving is her nature.

Loving and good and delighted and best is her little King and Sire whose devotion is entire who has but one desire to express the love which is hers to inspire.

In the photograph the Rhine hardly showed

In what way do chimes remind you of singing. In what way do birds sing. In what way are forests black or white.

We saw them blue.

With for get me nots.

In the midst of our happiness we were very pleased.

TOURTY OR TOURTEBATTRE

A STORY OF THE GREAT WAR

The title of this "Story of the Great War" comes from Tourtebatte, a *filleul de guerre* or war *protégé,* whose name lends itself to punning (*tour de bataille; tous se battre, pour te battre*). Stein and Toklas met Georges Tourtebatte, who suffered from a hand injury, in Perpignan in June 1918. He remained in touch with Toklas by letter for several years. The letters, neat, formal, stiff, subservient, and uninformative, are preserved among the Stein papers at Yale. After Stein and Toklas left Perpignan, he was transferred to Montpellier for further treatment and eventually recovered. To pass the time in the hospital, he made pictures out of paper, ribbons, and beads in part supplied by Stein and Toklas. These included images of the two women, which he sent to them, as Stein says in the piece. They are not preserved.

None of this is worth telling about. It leads Stein to question what, especially but not only in wartime, is worth telling or can be told. What is worth telling about Tourtebatte turns out to be a series of complications that concern his wife, M[arguerite?], who was in Paris with a young son. We know about her only because Alice Toklas got involved in helping her, found her a room at rue Madame, around the corner from Stein's apartment at 27, rue de Fleurus, but the wife suddenly left, then asked for more help, which she did not receive; she may have stolen and have had a relationship with another man. She was not in touch with her family. There was trouble, but the facts are not clear.

The piece becomes a series of "reflections" or meditations on what we can say about relations when they are disrupted by war. "Can we reflect one for another." It becomes a dialogue with strong narrative features between Stein and Toklas, who remember different things about Tourty, on how to tell stories, how to get at the facts, how to find reasons, how to make literature. "Can we say it. We cannot." "What did he ask for. / Why I don't know. / Why don't you know."

• • • • •

Tourtebattre came to visit us in the court he said he heard Americans were in town and he came to see us and we said what is your name and what americans have you known and we said we would go to see him and we did not and we did not give him anything.

Then when we went out to see the hospital we did not take him anything. We asked to see him. Then when the new things came we did take a package to him and we did not see him but he came and called on us to thank us and we were out.

REFLECTIONS.

If I must reflect I reflect upon Ann Veronica. This is not what is intended. Mrs. Tourtebattre. Of this we know nothing.

Can we reflect one for another.

Profit and loss is three twenty five never two seventy five.

Yes that is the very easy force, decidedly not.

Then Tourtebattre used to come all the time and then he used to tell us how old he was when he was asked and he took sugar in his coffee as it was given to him. He was not too old to be a father he was thirty seven and he had three children and he told us that he liked to turn a phrase.

China. Whenever he went to the colonies his sister was hurt in an automobile accident. This did not mean that she suffered.

Some one thought she was killed. Will you please put that in.

His father's watch, his wife gave all his most precious belongings to a man who did not belong to the town he said he belonged to. We did not know the truth of this.

REFLECTIONS.

We should not color our hero with his wife's misdeeds. Because you see he may be a religion instead of a talker. Little bones have to come out of his hand for action this was after his wound. A good deal.

He was wounded in the attack in April right near where he was always going to visit his wife and he saw the church tower and then he was immediately evacuated to an american hospital where every one was very American and very kind and Miss Bell tried to talk french to him and amuse him but overcome with her difficulties with the french language she retired which made him say she was very nice and these stories that he told to us you told to Sister Cecile which did not please her and she said we must come and hear from every one else the stories they all told of the kindness they had received in the American hospital before they came to her and she said to them what did the major do, and they said he played ball. He did. And you too and all of them said, no sister but you were wounded in an attack. We were both wounded, said the soldier.

REFLECTIONS.

Reflections on Sister Cecile lead us to believe that she did not reflect about Friday but about the book in which she often wrote. We were curious. She wrote this note. This is it. Name life, wife, deed, wound, weather, food, devotion, and expression.

What did he ask for.

Why I don't know.

Why don't you know.

I don't call that making literature at all.

What has he asked for.

I call literature telling a story as it happens.

Facts of life make literature.

I can always feel rightly about that.

We obtained beads for him and our own pictures in it.

Dear pictures of us.

We can tell anything over.

We gave him colored beads and he made them with paper that he bought himself of two different colors into frames that we sent with our pictures to our cousins and our papas in America.

Can we say it.

We cannot.

Now.

Then he told us about his wife and his child.

He does not say anything about them now.

Some immediate provision was necessary.

We said in English these are the facts which we are bringing to your memory.

What is capitol.

He told us of bead buttons and black and white. He answered her back very brightly.

He is a man.

REFLECTIONS.

What were the reflections.

Have we undertaken too much.

What is the name of his wife.

They were lost. We did not look forward. We did not think much. How long would he stay. Our reflections really came later.

The first thing we heard from her was that the woman was not staying and had left her new address.

How do you do.

We did not look her up.

Her mother and her mother.

Can you think why Marguerite did not wish Jenny Picard to remain longer.

Because she stole.

Not really.

Yes indeed. Little things.

This will never do.

And then.

I said we must go to see her.

And you said we will see.

One night, no one day she called with her mother.

Who was very good looking.

She was very good looking.

And the little boy.

Can you think of the little boy.

They both said that they were not polite.

But they were.

Reflections can come already.

We believed her reasons were real reasons.

Who is always right.

Not she nor her eleven sisters.

No one knew who was kind to her.

What is kindness.

Kindness is being soft or good and has nothing to do with amiable. Albert is kind and good.

And their wives.

Can you tell the difference between wives and children.

Queen Victoria and Queen Victoria.

They made you jump.

And I said the mother you said the mother. I did not remember the mother was in Paris but you did.

IRCULAR PLAY

'LAY IN CIRCLES

This light and playful piece, a choreographed ballet of verbal circles, opens most undramatically with a sleepy "Papa dozes mama blows her noses." As papa and mama drowse, things begin to go around in circles of baby talk. Whether sleep yields to dreams of sexual joy or to reawakening in desire, the result is the same: "A miss and bliss. / We came together. / Then suddenly there was an army. / In my room." The army is not only that of Napoleon Bonaparte but also that of Napoléon Cailloux, the great nineteenth-century lexicographer and grammarian, whose dictionary Stein must have known. A double army that is here either to stop or to join the goings-on, it is asked by the ambivalent lovers both to leave and to stay. But both Napoleons are dead. There is no imperial, sexual, or grammatical authority. Sexuality and language surge in play about the creative process.

The occasion appears to be a birthday, probably a Fourth of July celebration or its aftermath. There are gifts, songs, dances, colors, flags, party hats, a band. From the slow and sleepy dozes/blows/noses of the beginning, circles arise spontaneously in the eye and the ear. Songs go around, rounds are danced or sung, rhymes and puns and repetitions echo back and forth and around as they do in *Photograph*. Through the opening doors pass the guests at the party celebrating in circles that the reader needs no further introduction to join.

A Circular Play is only one of many Stein pieces built on circles, rounds, cycles. The texts of circles appear in innumerable guises, each time a new charm, a new ring, an oval, an eye, an orifice, a mouth. The linear printed shape of "Rose is a rose is a rose is a rose" in "Sacred Emily" curls into the magic circle of her seal, which turns into a cauliflower, centered and sacred, a new form of the essence of a rose. Like the Möbius strip, the world of Stein's work has no beginning, middle, or end, and her perceptions back in upon themselves in a continuous process that makes inside and outside indistinguishable, one, complete only in its continuing. A Stein reader is wise to remember that like stones dropped into a quiet pool, her word ideas make circles upon new and unexpected circles in her work.

• • • • •

First in a circle.

Papa dozes mamma blows her noses.
We cannot say this the other way.
Exactly.
Passably.

Second in circles.

A citroen and a citizen
A miss and bliss.
We came together.
Then suddenly there was an army.
In my room.
We asked them to go away
We asked them very kindly to stay.
How can Cailloux be dead again.
Napoleon is dead.
Not again.
A morning celebration.
And a surprising birthday.
A room is full of odd bits of disturbing furniture.
Guess again.

The third circle.

Round as around as my apple.
An apple is out of season
So are raisins.
We rise above it.
A circle is contained in there.

Four times three.

Canned fruit and sugar
Plates at Toys

Coal and wood.
Hat blocked.
He is blocked by a driver.
I forget.
Little silver clasp for necklace.
Circles.
We can be won to believe that the President saw through the trick.
Miss Mildred Aldrich is isolated. Is isolated with the President.
A circular play.
Cut wood cut wood.
I hear a sore.
Stop being thundering.
I meant wondering.
He meant blundering.
I have been mistaken.
No one is so certain.
She is certain.
Certainly right.
Can I be so sorry.
How can I turn around. I will leave it to her to decide how to arrange it.

Circle Hats.

My color.
Their color.
Two
One
Two won.
I can think so quickly.

Silent and thoughtful. Crimson rambler and a legion post legion, a poor post legion. Crimson rambler or star.

Circles.

It is a good idea to stare. We had our photographs taken, not intentionally but we happened to have seats in the front row near the arena and so when a photograph was taken we were in it.

In a circle.

The Inner circle is one in which we hope to engage places.
We were so sorry.
A great many people realise this better.
In the morning.
Good night.

Encircle.

A dog with a rabbit.
How can you tell a treasure.
We can tell by the reaction. And after that. And after that we are pleased.

The idea of circle.

I bind myself to exercise myself only in one way.

Beauty in a circle.

A beauty is not suddenly in a circle. It comes with rapture. A great deal of beauty is rapture. A circle is a necessity. Otherwise you would see no one. We each have our circle. How old is America. Very old.

The Circle.

The work can you work.
An meat
Can you meet
And flour
Can you flower
Calligraphy. Writing to a girl.
A great many say we have wives and children to-day.
Can you be angry at women.

Another circle.

I believe that they are pleased with us.

For a circle.

Prizes.
When you win prizes.
Explain winning prizes.
A growing plant is given to us.
Mrs. de Monzy has adopted a child.

A mildred circle.

The balcony is airy. You can put five persons on it. Do little children have hernia. Are they born with it. Babies smile. Have a care of a vermillion.

A circle higher.

Jennie dance to Marguerite. Vera dance alone. And what can you say about tuberculosis.

It was not a circle. Amelia and Susan were not scared. They said we are refreshed by the news. I can never forget the slaughter.

Eggs and eggs.

A dog stares.

Mrs. Whitney before her door.

Circular saws.

Did you speak of offering, did you speak of offering me.
Offer is a word used.
Oil well is a well.
Try fish exclusively.
Jessie Jessie said.
Do have a line.

Or go ahead.
Go ahead of him.
Discharge blessing.
Mrs. Wells lives in Palma da Mallorca.
We are going to dinner Thursday.
She is the first to profit here.
Circle sings.
At first in circles.
Jessie Jessie is not messy. She has her old earrings.

I knew that bird. I was deceived by the star-light. The morning makes mention of the sun and the dirt of Lockey and all of that of Caesar. Dear Caesar I am always willing to wear Caesars. Not down or away but stay.

An inner circle.

And inner circle again. Do tease me. Nose kisses and thirds. I have been deceived. No you have been refused. I have refused ten spots as one. But not as ten. As ten. But not as too. Dear thought and receipt.

A climbing entrance.
This is a circle.
Legally a circle.
When the Russians speak.
When did you hear from me last.
This is the way we settle.

Circle one.

Has he been rude.
Did he touch me.

Circle two.

Can you be careful of money. Can you believe in roses. Can you make mint like lilacs that is the leaves.

Nelly can.

Circle Three.

Red on it.

It is strange to distribute it to the women. They can see around it. It makes them young.

Does it around.

Round they are.

Circle Four.

She can admire me always. She can always admire me.

Do not try circles exclusively.

Four circles.

He was a disappointment to me. I could not understand the reason for the waiting. Do we prefer seven or fourteen. Do we like sixteen times fifty. We are all agreed that we like the letters of Henry James.

Consider a circle.

In the car there are four three if you like and outside two, four if you like. Four necessarily more than. Two necessarily more than two.

Four if you like.

Expressly a circle.

Were we at home. In messages, in sending messages, in quarreling, in shooting, in endangering, in resolving and in destroying there is a course of events. Honeysuckle grows and peas. Can you sing together.

Not a circular saw.

I saw what I saw.

Believe me to be an offender. Offend me and I do not wish to hear from Ollie. Can you explain that contraction.

A mystery.
Sing in a circle.
Messages are received all the time. Frank says. Mildred. An afternoon.

Leave a circle.

Leaves in or circle.
In travelling to California what do you say to me. I say oh have you been thin.

Leaves or a circle.

I leave you there.
Do not despair.
I recollect that there is no hurry. Why do the Indians make China. They make Indo china.
Leaves for to-day.
A circle in royalty.
Royal circles are distinguished by their color.
Remain in a circle.
A distinction. Have they changed their minds. He looks very well. We were surprised that he did not resemble Mr. Mirrlees. You meant the Frenchman.
A Neapolitan noble is a neapolitan noble. And women are that. Do you know the brother. Poor brother he is dead. He was killed in the army.

Let us circle.

We circle around.
Not a fragrance not a common gift not an address. A change of scene.
She was glad to come to Paris.
A little boy in a large circle.
An island is not round by much.
Commence again to encircle water.
Sleep a credit to me or.

Or what did I say.

A circle stretches. From San Francisco to the sun. From Tangier to the moon. From London to the water.

From Bird to lessens.

Can a circle enlist.

Can a circle exist.

Can we be all tall.

50 pounds and 40 pounds makes 80 pounds. We paid for thirty pounds. I paid for it all.

Crushed circle.

Red or cranberries.

Strawberries or meat.

Sugar or potatoes.

Roast beef or water.

Melon or rehearsed.

Take a street.

One does not run around in a circle to make a circular play.

Do not run around in a circle and make a circular play.

It is not necessary to run around in a circle to get ready to write a circular play.

I used to be able to do this very nicely.

Once more I think about conversations.

Conversations conversions, Hindustani and remorse.

I necessarily gather a circle.

I gather in a circle.

And now to play.

Play for a circle.

Do stand proudly.

Do faint well.

Do call hearers.

Do believe in roads.

Do have dark currants.

In a circle.

They gathered to say.
Figs.
Butter.
Pine apple cloth.
Hurt oranges.
And melons.
In July we are in the midst of summer.
Will be happy to-day.

Inner circle.

How can I finish.
Now think.
I think of a reason.
Often soften.
A negro.
A splendid custom and a splendid interest.
I believe in whirrs.
Fourth of July.
Strawberries.
Flags strawberries and yellow flowers.
Now we really circle.
Action.
When we first see Sylvia we ask where have you been.
When we first recall them we say and your mother.
We expect them soon.
Early in July.
With tobacco.
But no dream.
This is the way we act.
Come in.
How do you like Morocco.
Very well and the weight is splendid.
In a circle.
A father and mother and a son.
Mother father son and daughter.

Can I recall nations.
Around the grass.

Relieved for a circle.

Cause an excitement.

The cause of an excitement is this, the language is not the same, the door is not the same the bed is the same the door is the same the window is nearly the same and the pencil is of silver.

In bringing a thing into the country can we ask is it of gold. A country is not in a circle it is near and in the distance.

Let me amuse you.

Round circles.

Realise that you have to write a letter.
And teeth
Teeth are sincerely regretted.
I want to urge winter.

Encircle Alice.

I have not met their wife.
And how can Alice pay.
She makes Herbert work like a Turk.

Sing fifty.

A circle of her children.
Can you be sorry he went.
Can you be sorry that she went away.

Now we come to the circle.

Frederick.
A Palm.
Jacky.
Leaves.
George
A diary.
Marion
Wishes.
Mabel
Reckless.
And Harriet,
Dear Harriet.

Sing circles.

Can you believe that Mary Ethel has plans.
Indeed I do and I respect her husband.
Do you dislike her children.
I have not always had a prejudice against twins.
To be catholic to be african to be Eastern.
Have you always had a prejudice against twins.
Tomorrow we go.
If you say so.

Circular watches.

Methods.
How do you recognise hats.
How do you marry.

Circular glasses.

Indeed indeed we speed.
And what do you feel now.

How wonderfully charming are the appearances.

And then you are satisfied.

And even rested.

Circular eye glasses.

Swing into the circle.

See it comes to-day.

Make a swing on Monday.

We made ours Thursday.

In an hour.

The singing bird is singing in the cuckoo tree. Singing to me oh singing to me.

Circular sets.

Glass candlesticks and glass mandolins and perhaps glass candles and roads.

In circles.

Do they make you sad or sympathetic or more nearly ruddy.

Repeat north.
More circles.

The action of a circular play consists in reasonably enlarging doors. Doors can be made circularly.

Also we can go to Saint Cloud.

We can also have prejudices against voices.

How many more wish to come in.

Circles circle to-day.

Now I want to tell about whimsies.

Whimsies consist in pleasing a wife in instantaneous reference, in pleasure, in fatigue and in resolution. Also it means no errors nor indeed any disturbance. Principally a peculiarity is no peculiarity.

And how do I neglect circles.

I consider whether I tie or whether I neglect to tie.

Dogs are contagious.
And I mean cats.
Not freely.

Circular addresses.

Mrs. Persons was hurt because we said she had not left her address.

She was also embarrassed by the mention of the date in addition to the name of the week.

Can you imagine addresses.

I know nothing more difficult than to imagine addresses.

How old can you be.

You can be very old and very well preserved.

And addresses.

Dresses and addresses.

Circular dresses.

Rescue.

Let us breathe in matches.

And really lilacs.

And most of all we are religious.

Can you think of a Jew.

Please be a religious circle.

A religious circle earnestly pleases those who protest those who attach that meaning and even those who regather fowl. How can you say they were killed. In my country we do this we leave it there and in a way a rabbit is not necessarily there.

Oh how you love to Knead.

Bread.

Think of the brown bread.

Think of tigers.

Think more of Indians

And think how easily we can finish.

What

The white flour.

Of course the white flour.

There is white flour.

Conceive that as a circle.

Do you mean to please.

I reason like this. A proceeding which necessitates that recollection perfection selection and protection rhyme and that stupefaction action satisfaction and subtraction rhyme and that dearer clearer freer and nearer follow one another a proceeding which not any one dislikes stamps a play as a wonderful beginning.

Tea.

Before tea.

Let me express about the noise let me say that he is easily dissatisfied.

Listen to me.

Circles are cheery.

We have no noon.

Indeed we draw two pictures one with glasses one without. Every time they shake the table cloth near the window a glass falls out.

How can you be surprised by news.

Suppose one tells you he was furiously angry at his son. Another says it was his wife who was his pride and yet another assures you that after all he was born in Paris. Only a mercenary would work so hard.

News of circles.

Where is she where is she where is she.

Wish she.

She wishes for Robert Dole and William Heynse.

Where is she.

She is not readily mistaken.

Mabel Stern can she burn.

I can break a pear.

Clamor for me.

I reminded her that I need not give her flowers. Them flowers. I need not give them flowers. Give flowers to them I need not give flowers to them. I need not have given flowers to them.

Circular dancing.

Dole keeps a dancing club. He is an American from the United States of America. He was never in Europe before the European war. Since then he has remained. He has prospered he has seemingly prospered. William Heynse acts as his orchestra. He plays the piano. They do not have a mechanical piano. William earned a great deal more money before they put a tax on music not in music halls but in restaurants. He is fond of Pepper.

And Mr. Lambert.

Mr. Lambert appears.

Sing a song of sight.

Circulating songs.

How bright are Frank and Nellie.

Very bright.

And Lou Flower. Not so at night. Not so very bitter at sight. Not so monstrous for the height. Not irregular at all.

Let us encircle let us encircle graciously.

Can you see the moon can you see it seen can you see a boy of sixteen.

And if I answer yes can you guess how many candles out of six make a mess.

None of ours.

Oh yes they do in cooking.

Electricity we say makes it very light to-day. To-day the sun is shining tenderly. Y. D.

A circlet of kisses.

Can you kiss to see.

Some see.

Can you kiss me.

I see.

Can you hear of kissing me.

Yes I see where you can be.

Do I sound like Alice.

Any voice is resembling.

By this I mean when I am accustomed to them their voices sound in my ears.

Can you say the page to-day can you say the pages. Sleeping in the day is like Klim backwards.

Klim backwards is milk just like silk.

Is milk a can.
Circles are candy.
Irregular circles.
Can you think with me.
I can hear Alice.
So can a great many people.
In Terra Cotta Town.
I named roses wild flowers.

Circles.

Fourteen circles.
Fifteen circles.
I wonder if I have heard about those circles.

PHOTOGRAPH

A PLAY IN FIVE ACTS

After the long period of relief work, Stein was in Paris again by May 1919 and gradually returned to her life as a writer. American artists began to come to Europe. Possibilities of publication opened as editors of magazines like the *Little Review* came to Paris and new journals like *Broom* began to appear in Europe. In 1920 Stein wrote her last war pieces and moved into new verbal inventions.

The occasion for *Photograph* appears to be a picture taken at a birthday party, perhaps for new twins. Whether the guests line up along a wall for a party picture, or a photograph is to be hung on a wall, the wall becomes a set that makes her "sigh for a play."

From the start, the play fills with doubling. Photographs copy subjects. They can be enlarged and printed in many copies. People enlarge and reproduce themselves in babies or even as one-egg or two-egg twins, which lead to twin rooms, a twins' room, twin houses. The ladies at the party—most appear to be pregnant—are all the same, Americans born in America, but to say so merely uses tired language to repeat irrelevancies of birth and nationality, what we fall back on when we have nothing to say except the old story of reproduction and twinning, endlessly repeated. Doubling carries over to writing. Title leads to subtitle, original to translation and doubled authorship. Linguistic twinning of a different sort makes rhymes, puns, refrains, and other repeated lines.

In the second line appears star gazing, perhaps astrological predictions for the twins. The French word for twin in its masculine form is *jumeau*. The French word for the zodiac sign for the Twins, Gemini, is *Gémeaux*. Surely the two French words doubled in Stein's ear as she played with them. She may have composed the play under the sign of Gemini, between 21 May and 21 June 1920.

She comments, "one comes in more frequently than another and yet they always come together. This is not exactly so. They do come together but some come more frequently than others and we like to see them all." Who are they? Stein does not tell, and we do not pin them down, but they start as people, including babies, perhaps tourists and relatives visiting, then perhaps become characters in plays, words that double and reproduce faster than you can keep up with—from reality to copy, theater to life. In short, language may be free, as Marinetti's "parole in libertà" claims, but Stein shows it to be tired and endlessly reduplicative.

Twinning in this play is both visual and auditory. We hear and see, look and listen to a play whose verbal twinnings change quickly from the seen to the heard to the

thought. It sings and jokes with duplicates and copies, crying twins, cooing mothers, and hymn-singing guests smiling.

• • • • •

For a photograph we need a wall.
Star gazing.
Photographs are small. They reproduce well.
I enlarge better.
Don't say that practically.
And so we resist.
We miss stones.
Now we sing.
St. Cloud and you.
Saint Cloud and loud.
I sing you sing, birthday songs tulip belongs to red cream and green and crimson so that the house chosen has a soft wall.
Oh come and believe me oh come and believe me to-day oh come and believe me oh come just for one minute
Age makes no difference.
Neither does the Vieux Colombier.
Why do you think of that at all.
I describe a different house.
So does Gabriella.
Twins.
There is a prejudice about twins.
Twins are one. Does this mean as they separate as they are separate or together.
Let me hear the story of the twin. So we begin.

PHOTOGRAPH.

The sub title. Twin.
Two a twin.—Step in.
Margot.—Not a twin.
Lilacs.—For a twin.
Forget me nots.—By a twin.
Twin houses.

We are considering twin houses. I say.
Have I read all about twins.
And now to walk as twins walk.
Two twins have two doors.
One twin is a bore.
I exercise more. I walk before the twins door.
Dozens above the eggs dozens above.
Afternoons seen.
Mrs. Roberts.
Mrs. Lord
Mr. Andrew Reding.
Miss Nuttall
Mrs. Reading
Come in and be lame.
Come in together Alsatian.
A language tires.
A language tries to be.
A language tries to be free.
This can be called Twinny.
She had one god-daughter
Burning.
We are very bitter.
We are bitter.
Railroads are mistaken
They insult us.
Now I can occasion remonstrance.
Miss Nuttall was born in America.
Mrs. Roberts was also born there.
Mr. Andrew Reding went to America.
Mrs. Reading was born in America.
Mrs. Lord was born on the boat

Now indeed this is not what I meant to say for this does not describe my feeling.

My feeling is that one comes in more frequently than another and yet they always come together. This is not exactly so. They do come together but some come more frequently than others and we like to see them all.

I can sigh to play.
I can sigh for a play.
A play means more.

ACT SECOND

Two authors. Rabbits are eaten.
Dogs eat rabbits.
Snails eat leaves.
Expression falters.
Wild flowers drink.
The Star Spangled banner.
Read the notices.

ACT III

A photograph. A photograph of a number of people if each one of them is reproduced if two have a baby if both the babies are boys what is the name of the street.

Madame.

ACT IV

We say we were warm. Guess McAdam.

We say we talked about them.

Joseph moan, Edith atone, the bird belongs to the throne.

Birdie sing about an intention.

Did you intend to depress me. Certainly not I asked for a translation. Do not compromise my father. Zero.

Baby was so interested in one part of the story. And I, I was interested. And what can pearls mean. Pearls can mean some sort of reason. It is very reasonable. I am very sleepy and burned.

Burned by the sun to-day.

Stand up to sing.

ACT V

I make a sentence in Vincennes. It is this. I will never reason away George.

REREAD ANOTHER

A PLAY

TO BE PLAYED INDOORS OR OUT

I WISH TO BE A SCHOOL.

"Reread," the odd title commands, though we have not read anything. Read what? "Another," but we do not even know what the first is. Or are we to reread the *word* "another"? Look at Stein making a play out of reading, the last thing we think of for performance. But she turns it into a light and funny school play full of word and reading games.

The world of this play becomes a book and we become schoolchildren reading it or perhaps reading things that are more interesting than any schoolbook. As warm weather sets in, school disbands, the world becomes larger and reading goes outdoors, where there are birds' nests and shotguns and mountains.

The play is full of words for people and personified things. Nearly all of these appear more than once, most an orderly four times. Pearls, reunions, dirigibles in French spelling, as well as grocers, sculptors, and record breakers come alive as they are named, enumerated, and named again. The First Mountain, Second Mountain, Third Mountain line up as in a landscape. Or look at the pound, "First pound. I have fallen. / Second pound. I have not fallen. / Third pound. I am falling. / And fourth pound. Pound sterling." That just about describes what can happen to the pound sterling, and it also gives practice in verb forms. Another plays with word forms: "I hate sentences. I sentence him to have a little rebellion." Bankers are characterized in phrases with the key word *cousin,* "I am my cousin's cousin," "And who is your cousin." Bankers may do business through family connections, but Stein is also speaking of her own banker cousins and disowning them. In their stead she claims, "My cousin is Henry James." A little later, another of her cousins is Macbeth, who appears from a play like her own but for a moment casts a dark mood over her family. In this world of puns, readings become mutable. That is one reason everything demands rereading one way and another.

Interspersed with the little readings are love verses to Alice Toklas, the wife, the leader, the little Jew, the queen. These are varied over and over and become new with each repetition, as love verses always do. They use spoken language and are a part of the performance that is this play. Many pick up the tone and themes of the long love poem *A Sonatina Followed By Another* of the spring of 1921. *Reread Another* appears in the Yale Catalogue as the last piece of 1921, presumably written late in the year.

But it asks, as does *A Sonatina,* who will win the heavyweight fight between [Georges] Carpentier and Jack Dempsey. That fight took place on 2 July 1921 and was won by Jack Dempsey. *Reread Another* was probably composed before that date, in the summer of 1921, while the women were in southwestern France. As for winning, it is possible to win on a foul. "And we said the winner will have won but who will win. And he said. The winner." In World War II, that phrase returned to echo in a title, *The Winner Loses.*

• • • • •

When wings, when teeth and wings, when birds and shots, shot tower, how easily we describe mellow.

Don't think a shot tower means war, it only means shot guns, or shooting.

Now we breed.

First Mountain. You're a chinaman.
Second Mountain. Please yourself.
Third Mountain. I like warm weather.

Then there are no schools. No nothing but birds nests. What a happy May.

I have followed I have been followed I am followed by another.

She is a dirigeable.

Four dirigeables

The first. Have a lesson.
The second. And a mission.
The third. And a prison.
The fourth. And a meal soon.

Twenty eight, I ate what my master. Twenty eight I hate what to be led but to be wed. Twenty eight I wait, to be led. To be wed, I was wed, I am wed. I said I am led. Twenty eight, I wait to be led. By she who is all to me.

Can Christians touch much.

First soldier. I am not a christian.
Second soldier. I have no wife.
Third soldier. I am not a christian and I have no wife.

Do be hot to-day.

First Mountain. I am told that words are used in the sense in which they are felt.

I am persuaded of nothing else.

Can you effect trees. Yes by gasoline and what is the result. The leaves fall. A great many people are married.

How can flowers sweat.

The dear little thing it just gets hot.

First pound. I have fallen.

Second pound. I have not fallen.

Third pound. I am falling.

And fourth pound. Pound sterling.

A great many riches are riches.

In quiet squares in quiet squares and circles.

How well they love squares and circles.

How can you love squares and circles.

Can you be a witness I am a witness.

SCENE II

In a room where is a stove and in summer it is not necessary to keep it lighted as with a glass roof a room with the sun shining upon it is very warm.

Any man who is in the country is a sailor.

First sailor. How often do you wear my coat.

Not very often.

How often do I take off my hat.

It blows off.

The first sailor is remarkable for the strength of his hands. He hands heavy weights to the men. He is a splendid example of the strength a man has in his hands.

The second sailor is remarkable for the violence with which he remains at home in the mountains. He loves the mountains and he never leaves them.

We are not miserable.

I do hate sentences. I sentence him to have a little rebellion. Why should the public rebel. Why should a stove be known. A stove is known by its name.

SCENE III

A mother and a child. How can you tell that a mother has a child.

Let us be in earnest.

A mother has a child. How can you be certain that a mother has her child.

The first chauffer. How do you do I forgive you everything and there is nothing to forgive.

Do not repeat yourself.

The first singer. I take lessons.

And what do you do in between.

I mean to be strong and well but really I am not very well.

A Swiss Italian.   I am leaving for France. And there.

And there I will be apprenticed to my uncle who is a house painter and is color blind.

What a tragedy.

Not at all he always has some one to assist him.

Georgiana and Louise.

I remember Louise and Georgiana.

SCENE IV

It is strange that all the Americans want Carpentier to win and all the Frenchmen want Dempsey to win. Carpentier can win on a foul. That means that Dempsey fouls. Dempsey can win. How.

First Banker.   Whose cousins are you.

Second Banker.   I am my cousin's cousin.

Third Banker.   And who is your cousin.

Fourth Banker.   And who is your cousin.

Second Banker.   My cousin is Henry James.

Diamonds are not scarce, pearls will not be scarce, no one is interested in coal and gold is virgin. All people rush together.

Be easy.

Be easy be easy.

Mr. Thorndyke was impressive. He said I know who will win. And we all said. Who will win. And he said the winner. And we said the winner will have won but who will win. And he said. The winner.

I can be as stupid as I like because my wife is always right. And my cousin. I have several who are my cousin. Clamor and clamor. No one knew that his name was Macbeth.

SCENE III

The Portuguee.

First ribbon maker.   I am making ribbons for Mrs. C.

Second ribbon maker.   In what color.

Third ribbon maker.   Black shot with gold.

Fourth ribbon maker.   I have meant to love silk.

All silk and a yard wide. We almost think in meters.

SCENE IX

I regret nothing.

Titles make a rejoinder.

First grocer.	I am sincere.
Second grocer.	I believe in service.
Third grocer.	I love my mother.
Fourth grocer.	I am rich.

The fifth day they all came together and said. How many worlds have men who can fly.

We do not think there is another.

SCENE X

Reader I wish you to understand how to speak and return every day. If anybody returns every day we don't want to hear them.

Reader I wish you to understand how to speak and return every day. If every one returns every day we do want to hear them.

Markets are full of greens. Beauty is full of green. There are a great many who do not like green. I remember very well some one being asked if they liked a room full of pictures replied quite simply. But you see I don't like green.

My neck is not thick.

My face is not fat.

My nose is not large.

My mouth is not quiet.

And I have my hair.

My best wishes for your success.

SCENE XI

A brilliant Susan.

How can you be elfish.

Enthusiasm and daughters. I am the daughter of enthusiasm.

First record breaker.	How do you date your skies.
Second record breaker.	I wish to rest.
Third record breaker.	I have a brother.
Fourth record breaker.	I am fatigued.

And why do you cherish copper. Or gold. Or silver. Because I love to sell.

Very well.

SCENE XII

A horse shoe soothes a Jew.

What can a horse shoe do.

It can ease jealousy.

First sculptor.	How I wish to be read.
Second sculptor.	Reading made easy.
Third sculptor.	Marriage means a daughter.
Fourth sculptor.	I love my father.

THE MARKET.

A street. Nobody in New York is sweet. A street leads to a girl. How old is Holly.

SCENE XIII

I improvise.

The first negro.	It is raining and the sky is blue.
The second negro.	I do not like blue.
The third negro.	And I don't like yellow.
The fourth negro.	I am very fond of colors.

A little nose and a tired eye and a broad yellow face and thin Jewish hair, and lovely hands and a strong physique and sensitive ears and a shortish chin, and a heavy head and a curly neck, and no reason to sin. He does not win a gold watch nor a torch but he is a print and I say that much. He is not a print. He carries what he carries. He loves grammar and sadness. He is a reproach to grammar and sadness. I do not despair. Read me easily.

The first author.	I am.
The second author.	I am too.
The third author.	I was very happily finished.

The fourth author was a painter.

Miss Constant Lounsberry present me.

Can you love all of the painting, can you love a little Christ. Can you love the roar of weasels can you love the little wife. I do see what makes me thunder when the words are not repressed. I do love the little Jesus I do really love him best. You mean of all the pictures. Yes I mean of all the pictures.

SCENE XIV

Little words of a queen.

The american army.

I will be ordered like the American army and I will like it.

Say yes.

First boy. I am awake.

Second boy. I am awake nicely.

Third boy. I am waking up very nicely.

Thank you very much. I seem to be pleased.

False smile. False smiler.

SCENE XV

Why does a tail curl.

First girl. I see the hair.

Second girl. I see the greek.

Third girl. I see fishes.

SCENE XVI

How does French make French. How do French make french.

The first imitation imitates very well.

The second imitation is very well imitated. The third imitation is not useless. The fourth imitation urges you to be exact.

SCENE XVII

I recognise a bust.

Do you.

I recognise a crust.

Do you.

I recognise that I must.

Do you always.

I recognise animals.

Birds and mouse a mouse. We have so carefully forgotten mice.

Will we ever remember birds.

It is astonishing how suddenly we are pleased.

And so many people may marry for pleasure and for words because really religiously speaking words are nearly always spoken.

SCENE XVIII

Everytime I mention a number I am lightened. And a great many numbers are nodded.

First reunion. A message to Anne.

Second reunion. A message to Emma.

Third reunion.	A message to Mary.
Fourth reunion.	A message to please.

Please enlighten me about how dark the room is at midnight. In these days it is not very dark. In these nights it is not very dark.

SCENE XIX

How can you.
How can you.
Let me lead you gently.
Where to.
Anywhere I want to.
The battle reader.
How many pictures are sold.
Do you know what a discussion is.
Do you know whom a discussion is with.
I am very happy here.
I am so much happier than to-day.
Than yesterday.
Than every day.

SCENE XX

Don't you like to make it.
Do you not like to make it.
A continued story is one that continues when it is begun.
This is very nearly done.

SCENE XXI

A door and a man.
He says a woman inspires him more.

SCENE XXII

I love my love with a z because she is exact.
I love him with a z because he is candid.
How very funny you are.

The first pearl.	I am from the country of rivers and factories.
The second pearl.	Are the factories near the rivers.
The third pearl.	Almost always.
The fourth pearl.	They are not in big cities but in large villages.

That must be very pleasant.

I have almost meant to be kind.

I like that kind.

Now I can tell you about another man.

She does not say I have left my purse she always says I have left my gold purse. And she often had.

SCENE XXIII

Catherine of Russia.

Hildegarde of Prussia.

Gertrude of Roanne.

And Michael of Bavaria.

And Alice of England.

And Henry of Armenia.

And Rupert of Bologna.

And Richard of Savoy.

Which is your toy.

I do not care for places.

The first building put in America was larger than a house.

SCENE XXIV

My memory does not tell me how and what to remember and so what do I do. I remember everything. How kind you are.

I do very nearly love you. So do the friends of France.

END

MILDRED'S THOUGHTS

The Mildred of these thoughts is Mildred Aldrich (1859–1928), an American journalist, critic, and author older than Stein, who lived in a farmhouse overlooking the Marne River. Her account of the battle of the Marne in *A Hilltop on the Marne* (1915) was serialized in the *Atlantic Monthly* and its success led to further books which helped Americans identify with the French cause. In late August 1922, after long efforts by French and American friends, including Stein, the French légion d'honneur was awarded to Aldrich. "Lend me oceans of trophies. . . ." Stein well understood the need for recognition. She had met Aldrich, an educated, intelligent, and courageous woman with ties to Boston, in her early years in Paris; Stein and Toklas came to share a deep American friendship with her. They visited regularly and exchanged letters, magazines, and news about the seasons, people, and books. It was one of the early, pre–World War I friendships with Americans in France, quite different from Stein's relations with painters and with young writers of the postwar years.

In July 1922 Stein entered Mildred's mind and let tumble into words this low-keyed portrait of her merry thoughts. A summer meditation, it asks to be read and reread slowly and aloud. Out of long intimacy Stein's writing touches the flow of Mildred's thought, reading her mind better perhaps than the admirers who want to "see the room" where she "compose[d] the charming books [they] so much admire" and better also than the public statements honoring Aldrich.

Stein locates the thoughts in the lightest of frames, made of a visit to Aldrich, from arrival by car on a dusty road in the heat of July, through a day to an overnight, another day, and departure. The thoughts arise and move in the domain of Mildred's mind and house, her garden and the surrounding farmers' fields, where flowers, memories, and vegetables are in the air and the land luxuriates in new growth after the war, even as the people of the region remain diminished. Thoughts come in words, the staff of life. To compose them, Stein explores phrases about thought: my thoughts are elsewhere, give them my thoughts, it came to my mind, a penny for your thought, give it a thought, second thought, I had a thought.

Whether the pronouns I, you, we, that appear throughout are heard in the mind or spoken by those around her, Mildred's thoughts arise from exchange with others. Innumerable people appear in the thoughts that become characters moving about in plays. The piece can be read as a series of plays of thoughts, with the scene wherever Mildred's thoughts may be. The piece moves from these plays of thoughts to the process of her thinking.

Finishing the meditation on thoughts is difficult. Stein ends abruptly with advice about money. Aldrich made money with her book but managed it poorly and was often broke. "Please buy a clock." Time is money. The clock measures it. Thoughts may not be worth money. But Stein is completing proofs for *Geography and Plays*, whose publication she is financing. She hopes to get her money back. "Get your money back. Please buy me a clock."

• • • • •

Pigeons cooing only open cards and cases.

And when does grain yellow and the vegetables.

How horribly we crowned the evergreens. We always used to say that we lived in an aquarium. And now how silently the sun shines with a warm wind and cherished water. How livelily we chalk the earth and it opens. How can opening be feeble.

Caroline do not be religious do not be religiously free. Do not love hopes and pearls. I know you don't.

I think, I think, I think that it is a victory a victory of force over intelligence and I I do not agree, I think it is a victory a victory.

Can you hope for the rest.

And now let us tell how it affects me.

Can you tumble out.

I suppose I pose I expose, I repose, I close the door when the sun shines so, I close the door when the wind is so strong and the dust is not there but there is a glare, how tenderly I sun. The fuchsia how can you enclose a fuchsia, the fuchsia has learned this that Caroline loves her sister and will neglect the fuchsia for her sister. I mention this not to displease Henrietta because in all things I obey Henrietta.

How did she weaken Ireland. Give a thought to them, and give them my thoughts. Tell them to remember that every eleven years the sun shines hotly and also bid them remember that a farmer's life is a hard hard life a farmer's life for me.

Establish curls and swelling places. Did you mention me all day. How can I think in between. Henry McBride and Susan's pride. And plenty of chickens in every day. Oh how clean are lots of places.

I have thought very much about heat. When it is really hot one does not go about in the day-time. It is just as well to drink water and even to buy water if it is necessary. So many people diminish. And flowers oh how can flowers be north. They are in the air. How often do we air everything. Seem to me sing to me seem to me all safe. Seem to me sit for me sit to me all Wednesday. I do not mind July. I do not mind Thursday or Friday or Saturday. I do not mind breath of horses. We know what we think.

Give pleasure girls give pleasure to me and how do we know them in their turn. Because they do not turn away restlessly. We have imagined so much.

Amelia move Amelia move I can be recognised as that.

I can be seen by the light of the moon moonlight. I can be bright by my nephew's light, nephew contrite.

The nephew says, a marquise, a marquise if you please, she can read and write, and a willing, and willing to, willing to alight. Do not delude me by a beautiful word.

Can it be easily seen that country life makes us realise women giants and little negresses and the color of curtains and almost always worth.

Can a planet please. Mildred is not pleased with the heat of the sun.

Johnny get your gun get your gun get your gun Johnny get your gun get your gun right off.

Johnny get your gun get your gun get your gun Johnny get your gun get your gun right off.

Mildred's thoughts are where. There with pear, with the pears and the stairs Mildred's thoughts are there with the pear with the stairs and the pears. Mildred be satisfied with tomatoes, apples, apricots, plums, and peaches, beets and ever greens, peas and potatoes. Mildred cares for us and Kitty Buss, what a fuss what a happy surprise. We only expected you last night and you have come again. When. It is very hot and no one knows what is the reason.

Can you think. Of me.

I have a sweet place full of air and of space. It is represented for me by idolatry. I idolise in this wise. When I am seated I am easily disturbed. When I am hungry I am easily disturbed. When I love riches I am easily disturbed. And when I am remembered how I am led I am easily disturbed. I am not easily disturbed. I can see the very smallest of lady-bugs. And how eminently I resemble you.

Can you run quickly, and fly. Do not crush me and do not sigh. I sigh and when I sigh, when do I sigh. I am so religious. Religiously speaking five people sleep in one room. Every room has its gloom. And fire-places. No we prefer heat in summer and cold in winter. No we prefer coolth in summer and warmth in winter.

Let us think Mildred thinks. What do you think. Read me read for me read in me, read my notes. I said in it that I was both good and happy and that you know it.

I count him as negligent. A great many come away.

How have you meant to talk with me.

Now we will credit Mildred with this thought.

Words have often replaced me. Wishes have often replaced me. And courage has often replaced me. I replace blue glasses by white, blue crystals by white, the restoration of Louise Sixteenth. How many Louis make a hundred. How hungry are you in Saint John. Saint John and Saint Louis and Saint Ignatius. How loyally they support Saint Ignatius. Mildred has thought a great deal. She thinks once at a time and without difficulty. She thinks twice. I have called her away. How pleased I am with passages.

And now to introduce a play.

Mildred's Thoughts.

We find ourselves in Mildred's house. We have many ways of expressing our pleasure. We arrange ourselves so that we are never pleading. We plead with each other to be rich. And then we begin to learn. A new name is mentioned. I have already mentioned it. It is Katie Buss. You would imagine that I would reason about this that I would say come together come together and what really makes me feel happy is that I know very well that I have no authority. I reverence her to whom I delegate authority. And indeed I cannot say that the authority is delegated. Indeed no.

How often do we swell. Very well. We will sell very well. And you know what I mean.

I continue to play.

Have you seen a man in there.

Why do you care.

He was looking at me.

Did he know you.

He knew who I was.

Did you know who he was. I didn't then but I did afterwards. When do you expect to meet him. I am not certain that I will meet him at all. Do you think he was pleased with you. My impression was that he was not. Your impression may not be correct. No certainly I may be wrong I often am and what I expect is not what happens.

And if something else happens will you be pleased. It depends upon what that something else is. Lend me a light. Lend me a lighter. Lend me a pleasant curtain. Lend me boys. Lend me oceans of trophies and lend me my hat lend me what you have given me and let me lend you my land. All land is hot in the afternoon.

Can you be careless and cut hair. Can you be careful of grain. Can you wonder about tomatoes and can you believe it of her.

Come and kindly smile.

I remember a play.

A play, can you say, say can you play.

Dinner.

Dinner.

A dinner.

A cold dinner.

And how we can be able to tell them. We told them regularly.

Four doors and a bed. We find some beds very comfortable but when it is as hot as it is just now I find it easier to make a diagram. I will invite well. The first picture is a picture of pears, pears and grapes and a dog and and all that we need when we are happy. How are we happy.

In that case can we preserve quinces.

I have decided that in any case I will love islands. Islands are to the main land what poetry is to plays. I play to you. I play favorably.

In the first play I say, can we pray. Can we pray to her to be kind and good. Can we pray to her to favor us with her company. Can we pray to her to be regarded. In the second play we play that Spaniards may that Spaniards and how easily I prefer french tunes. I can not tell them that that fate is recognised in islands. Please catch a match.

After that play I came together that is we came together reading the rest of it. I can so easily remember misspelling funny. How useful to be another mother.

In spite of a day a day lost in the heat a day lost in the heat of the hall, in spite of the day lost in the heat of all the heat that we know, in spite of words of surprise in spite of mats and strawberries, strawberries in the woods, how prettily I have taught you to say, the woods the poor man's overcoat, and really this year, how many years were victorious. This year the heat has been intense.

I can easily surrender a play, I yield and you yield, and I yield to you.

I continue to be merciless and I am wretchedly hot. You do not really mean that I would mean it if it were possible to express this.

In a play, I repeat in a play we must say that we hesitate to lose a day.

And how gladly I would give you activities. Please me in the morning. Yes. And I will please you at night.

Can you confess to me why the Irish and they why they and the pens why the whole republic and records, why records and researches and why most of all why we can relish melons. I find melons with tomatoes. And oil. I find melons with tomatoes and oil. Do be ashamed of it all and let me tell you what to say. Let me tell you what to say about instincts. Instincts relieve me and so do grapes and so do parched plants. Parched plants apart how are you selfish. Parched plants apart connect me with them. Connect with them here in tender ways. I tenderly speak flowingly.

And new glances. Repeat new glances to the moisture. How pleasing is a whole hill and we know how quickly we know how steeply we know best. We know best we say.

A half measure makes a hundred weight. Why do islands perish. Islands perish in poetry. I repeat. Islands perish in poetry. And now for this much.

Come in.

He said it.

Come in this evening.

She said it.

Come in this evening anyway. He said it. That makes it contemporary. Compatriots and contemporary are not the same words.

I feel the wind on the barometer and the thermometer and the compass. I feel the barometer the thermometer and the compass. When we feel neglected we are ready to be searched. I search you for sins. Sins have spoons and knives and candles. Spoons have silver. And silver is clean. Silver can shine.

Dance and sing.

Dance and sing to him

Dance and sing.

She can dance and I can sing.

I find so few feathers that fall.

Relieve me of all the tenderness and the respect and the repetition and the upshot and the winter. How easily the sun is hot in the winter. How easily the sun is hot in the summer. How easily the sun is hot in the summer and in the winter. How easily the winter and how in the summer, how easily in the winter is the sun hot.

How can you drive me by inches. Inches and measures. Ladies and colors. Not sadly pairs. How can pears be sad.

He does and he does and he does. Does he. She does. How can you read about Susanne. Susanne read to me. I do not know how to read. That does not surprise me. Susanne how tall are you. I do not know but I am very tall, I bend my head to enter. Indeed you do, you are very tall. And every one else is every one else as tall. No indeed I am the tallest here. You are including every one. No indeed I am not including every one. Susanne I find you very difficult to instruct. This does not surprise but indeed I have no need of instruction. Thank you very much. I like to be paid, I like to save money and I adore searches. I search everywhere for water and salt. But there is a great deal of salt in this country. There is more chalk than salt. A great many people admire me.

I quote from my note.

I have told that I meet the train.

Backers.

I read it he reads it she reads it, she has heard it. I remember very well the story of his wife.

I know that New York is not Boston and I thank god for it. Do not mistake me I do not wish New York to be Boston, I wish Boston to be as it is to continue to be as it is. I do not wish that Boston should change. I don't care if I never hear the word New York mentioned in Boston I feel that I know exactly how I feel. I do feel very well.

A voice mixed with me. Do listen to Barney. He was called Barney before he was born. And weddings how many weddings have been meant to happen. Indeed we eat easily.

And now.

Splendid addresses. When we met together and we very frequently met together a child could imitate us. When we were often mistaken and we were often mistaken we selected them over and over again. Indeed we are not accustomed to contradictions. But that is because we so often agreed. Words agree and hay and vegetables. We often agree about hostages. How can we guarantee anything and worst of all how can we beguile how can we beguile the brother. In every day life we often think of a nephew. It is natural to be anxious. We are anxious. She is not anxious to please. She is not anxious to please me. Please do not be too tired. I will try not to. And you will succeed. I mean to see to that. You will let me. Oh yes. But do you really mean it. Oh yes. Please do not be too tired. I will see to that.

Have come back to my note. Note, boat, goat, float, dote, mote. I wrote you that I was anxious to please. She is not anxious to please me.

Sweet, feet, treat, meat, and bleat.

Complete.

I feel completely how she completes me.

How could you confuse her. Myra or Myra does screen her. She is not Myra to her. She is not breakfast to her. Myra or Myra to confuse her.

We amuse her.

Do you love boys.

How have you been happily willing.

Come, repeat to me just what you have heard.

I can continue to write.

I can continue to write to her.

I can continue to write to him.

I can continue to write, and I can not be defeated. Do not blame at all, do not at all blame them. Do not blame them because of their understanding of their misunderstanding do not blame them because of their misunderstanding me. In so far Mildred says and thinks Mildred thinks and says yes. To do so is a pleasure. Here we repeat a day.

In the morning not at all in the morning. In the morning we are very well.

Very well.

Later in the day we ask may we stay please.

Very well.

We can very easily understand any languages. Any language but that. Any language but that. We can very easily understand any language. And very well pleased. We are easily very well pleased. We understand what we say.

What a beautiful day.

We prefer the train.

Not we.

We prefer rain.

Not we.

We prefer cartridges.

Not we.

We prefer delusions.

Not we.

We prefer allusions.

Not we.

We prefer rough water.

We prefer rain water.

We prefer vegetables.

We prefer flowers.

We prefer lawns.

We prefer it all.

Do not be worried about me.

Do not be worried at all.

Be cautious be Emil.

Be cautious be a meal. Dear me how useful it all is.

And may I go on with Mildred's thoughts.

And I am to continue the honeymoon. A sonatina followed by another is a honeymoon.

A honeymoon is a full moon a quarter moon a new moon a large moon a twin moon and a sleepy moon. A honeymoon is a moon. We are not restless on a honeymoon. We are not nervous on a honeymoon, we are not impatient on a honeymoon. We are reasonable on a honeymoon. A honeymoon is a honey moon.

Go right on calling it Mildred's thoughts. Mildred thinks quite quickly.

And now what do we say.

We begin.

We bow.

We bow to the right and to the left.

We advance and we look at the noon. At noon the guests leave and so does Peter the waiter. After that we feel neglected. Then we sing together.

Sing to me sing to me sing to me I see. I see you sing to me. I see I see I see. I see that you sing to me. Sing to me together. We sing to you together. We sing to you together. We sing to you I sing to you. We sing to you together. And Myra was not a disappointment.

Leave me the peaches, the pears and the currants. It is really astonishing how many fruits have double meanings. I have often been astonished by it. Mildred thinks to me. Mildred's thoughts. How pleasant. And now let us think singly. You know very well how I feel about that.

Maps many maps are maps on weddings. Weddings are so cheery. And they have made ways of being Mrs. Beffa.

Lost. What was lost. I lost the name of the gate which opens except that it is never shut. One speaks of it as a gate and is a gate a gate. I feel that necessarily we must change our light. They felt so also. They felt about it exactly in the same way that we did. We had a most efficient honey-moon. Mildred Mildred say to me we both belong to the land of the free.

And now we have a correspondence with Mr. Willetts.

We find that he answered too promptly that he tells us exactly what we wanted to know that he means to annoy us, that he has a pleasant way of having a superior. A thousand people write letters.

How do you do I have been meaning to swim.

How do you do a great many people ask for a thousand pounds.

How do you do Katie Buss has not answered for the autobus.

We are eighty miles away from an autobus.

And now houses are not made of wood.

Will you come and spend days with me.

Will you come and spend the days with me.

How often do I read hand writing.

Come again.

It was a very exciting story.

Katie Buss, Frank, Louise, and Ernestine went together to serve the queen.

Spain still has a queen.

Katie Buss, Frank, Louise and Ernestine went together and religiously ask for a brother. Brothers and fathers. How can women be religious with candles.

Candles are expensive in some countries.

Katie Buss, Frank Louise and Ernestine meant to escape consequences. They had pleasure in their own astonishment, they knew that republics breed republics they were equally certain of this about kingdoms. How would it be if a statement were made about that being sufficient.

Can we suffer by necessity.

Katie Buss, Frank Louise, and Ernest were famous for their love of mosses. Mosses really only exist in a moist climate.

And Mildred wishes for rain.

I have frequently told the story of Mildred and the three stories.

Mildred is not easily pleased with Susan. Henrietta is not easily pleased with Caroline. Nelly is not easily pleased with Henry. And Kate Buss is not easily pleased with Dorothy. Jane is easily pleased. Yvonne is not very easily pleased. Marjory is not easily displeased. And William is an excellent citizen. How can you be uproarious. We have earnestly prayed for Katie Buss, Frank, Louis and Ernestine and they have as readily rented as their farm. I too will tell all about it.

Mildred says that water, wells and washing are secondary only to letters. She writes letters. And so do we. Many thousands write letters.

Domestic scenes. Different in domesticity.

I find a domestic scene created by two and without pets. They can be found in various situations. For instance. If one is leaning out of a window and another is seeing that one and expecting that one to descend the stairs it constitutes a domestic scene. Again if unexpectedly one is awakened and another has been likewise awakened and there is then no doubt that morning has come, this also constitutes a domestic scene. If asking reasonably that one discharges one's duty with consideration for the eagerness for change on the part of the other this too constitutes a domestic scene. And most reasonable of all, when one serves the other and the other serves the one and both remove the coverings that conceal titles then indeed we may speak of it as of the genuine character of a domestic scene.

How easily are we entitled to more.

Come again.

I do know that I am recognised. I do know that rain and dust and sun and travelling and gratitude expressed in letters leads me to remain sleepy. And then what.

I come to cherish me and heat water. Cherish me and let us dream. We dream of the martyr. How can a season pass. How can pink indicate martyrdom. How can feelings resolve themselves. He has resolved to love me the day after to-morrow.

I think the silver ones are prettier than the gold ones, thank you so much for giving them to me. You have been I have been you have been seen. You have been you are being you are my queen.

I think the silver ones are far prettier than the gold ones. Thank you so very much for giving them to me.

And a domestic scene. I mention my name. I mention that my name is Herbert and that I feel very well. And then I am very pleased with everything and naturally I am cheerful and gay.

How can pearls please. Pearls please me because they are accompanied by a drawing I draw merrily and I win, I win. I win I win. Pearls please me and I draw carefully and I do win. And I do wish to be that fairy. How many fairies are fair to me. One fairy is fair to me. One very fairy is fair to me.

How easily I raise glasses. Am I apt too. Am I apt to raise glasses. And everything makes me happy. We are so ready.

Do earrings, do earrings tell sex. Do earrings feel very well. Do earrings alarm. Do earrings tease. Do earrings please. Do be especially grateful to the little man who rings the bell.

Connect one with him.

Now I sing.

Sing a song of utterance. I mutter to you. Sing a song of expression. I express the meaning. Sing a song of reading. I read of the adventures of Mrs. Whitney.

Sing a song of pleasure. I please her.

And now mix up Frank with meat.

I do not care to eat so much and now I say. Baby is all well baby is all well baby is all well baby is all well.

Very well.

How much is money. Money is very funny.

In play.

Baby I am happily married Baby. To whom am I happily married.

Baby I am happily married to my husband. Baby. And to whom is my husband married. Baby. My husband is married to me. Baby. And to whom is my husband happily married. Baby. My husband is happily married to me.

Baby. When was I married.

Baby. I was married like a queen before I was seen.

Baby. And how was I seen.

Baby. As a baby queen. Baby. And so I was married as a baby it would seem.

Baby. Yes I was married as a baby queen.

Baby. You mean as a happy queen.

Baby. Yes I was married before I was seen.

I understand you very well.

How long is our street. Long enough to be paved in Italian. And how small is the man. As small as the pump. And can he use it. He can use it all day. And can he be a man although he does not look as if he could say anything. Yes indeed. He never tires.

Now we make mischief.

Frank, Lyman, William and Genevieve. How often they call them by their name. And Constance pleads.

Please plead.

Now be in earnest.

Baby is all well baby is all well baby is all well I say. Baby is all well baby is all well baby is all well all day, and all night too.

Baby how can you speak of wishes.

Kitty Buss is silent when she wakes. Thank you Kitty Buss.

Baby how can you manage to stare. I stare at the chair and I say baby is all well all day, and all night too.

How can you drink water. How can you drink water too.

I am very sleepy when I say how do you do Mrs. Addis.

Call me a buss sir. There is a buss. How often were words misspelled mispronounced and misquoted.

I have a feeling that earls, that there are no more earls.

How can you be so happy.

She is a dear.

She is here.

Read me to sleep Arthuro, Arthur in Spanish. The major likes chintz. Do eyeglasses go with earrings. All this and more was mentioned just before they sailed.

Sailing.

How many have ingenuity in making a plot. How many have ingenuity for mathematics. How many have ingenuity enough to find new prints for old. Old prints are valuable. New prints are valuable too. And cone chickens are lovelier than bread birds. Birds and bread may marry, chickens and birds and ducks too. How we do like cooler weather. Have a farm. Do have a farm with me. As for me I prefer a garden. This is true in English. We talk English determinedly. We speak English loudly. We control English serenely. Did you say secretly. I did not.

Do you believe in Gaul. All Gaul is divided into many parts. Each one is a department. Beffa is going away to another. And the Caesars. God bless the Caesars.

And now for the reasons.

The reason we have for succeeding is that an eraser made from finely spun glass an eraser made of rubber and an eraser made of other things all have their usefulness. And Mrs. Whitney. I cannot despise Mrs. Whitney.

I am so glad that Louise's cold is no worse.

And now for detail. The first detail we find it necessary to mention is a tailor. The second a shirt maker, the third a dressmaker, a fourth a retailer and the fifth a milliner. Hats we don't quite know why hats have such a strange name. Startle me.

And a door.

A door finds itself an outlet.

And the windows. We have been alarmed by windows.

And the noise of the street.

And the noises of the street.

How easily he changes from one workman to the other from one electric current to another. I am afraid that his diagnosis is incorrect. I am inclined to believe that I have been right.

Did I hear everything correctly. We sweetly sleep. This never tempts me to say, hush until to-morrow morning. Good-night and remember the cow. You know we promised to speak of farming.

Can you be afraid of crackers.

I am now going to tell a long story of the speculations concerning Cabot Lord. He is named that because he was born in England and came to America in infancy. He was named that because he was the son of a converted Presbyterian, converted from atheism to presbyterianism. He was named that because he was converted from Presbyterianism to Catholicism. He was named that because he was willing to save men and women and went to very many an early wedding. He was named that because he fought for freedom for saving everything from predestination. He was willing to be engaged for needing the soldier and civilian. He was a gentleman when he was selecting, he was reluctant when he was bewildering and he was admired by those who selected him to admire him because of his wisdom. How can a jew be an atheist or a farmer a civilian. Do please speak to me as well as bow.

These are a collection of purchased roses. I use my cases in case of need.

This is my collection.

Now and again.

How soon do we steal away E. A. We do not steal any one away. She can stay. He can stay. Do they stay any way. Please call them to the steamer. The steamer and calling. E. A. can pack everything away.

I guess that he is illustrious.

I feel very much the need of universal rows. Rows and rows of windows and they change, the exchange, what is the difference between the cotton exchange and money in exchange. My cousins visited me. And I did not find them cautious. How old have I been this year.

And now the annual. How can the annual being two be the dial. And how can the desert being two be the broom. Broom grows in Spain. Therefor it is called Spanish broom.

And now think.

Think all together.

How can we think such thoughts.

Another description of summer. Summer is very hot and this summer, it has been exceptionally hot. And I have enjoyed meeting Merry thoughts. How can you be determined to arise. He arises and I arose.

Thank you for the meaning of reading. Read aloud. How can training make two cities have the same name. It is extraordinary how often this happens.

Another lad.

Are you using the ladder.

He had forgotten the mildew but we haven't. We remember Waterloo and Louise Haynes and repetitions and Emil and extra riches. We remember our word. We give our word. And have we been faithful to our friends. Have we been loyal to our enthusiasm and have we been nervous specialists. I mean to please Demuth and his father. You can not please his father. His father knows Arnold very well. I hate you Kate he does not hate Kate. She hates we hate they can hate us. We hate you hate now hate Kitty Buss. We hate they hate they shall hate plus, plus winning a town. A village a town a tree all of it looks better with water. A swimming school has plenty of exuberance. And what do you think of balls. Hush dont mention. The nineteen year old Beatty wife did. Call me a brother. You are not that brother.

Caesars I trust you, to be true and to have come through a cow for my jew. Caesars I trust you to have come through, for you are true a cow for my jew, Caesars I trust you to have come through a cow from my jew because you are so true. Caesars you are so true that I trust you to have come through a cow for my jew.

How can you be pale at Christmas how can you be tall so soon, how can you be splendid and gracious and call Follette at noon. And are they going away. My wife says no not to-day. How can they be young and strengthened and earnest and splendid too. That is what I think of them. And they think that they are staying longer.

Chick chick chick chick chick. Chicken made of glass. How happily I pass the rolling fields of brass with the balls that say not so.

We have won.

What.

The war.

And how many can say so.

How many can say so.

Belle and Babcock both begin with b. B is beautiful for a foundation. How can you be surprised. I was surprised to find that he was mentioned.

Katie Buss is tall and fair. Fair to me. Katie Buss is tall and fair to me. You mean to use fair in the sense of just. Yes indeed. Chicken made of glass. Alas.

Chicken made of glass. Alas.

I am very pleased with the chicken. Thank you so much my dear wife for having presented it to me and for having been so careful in bringing it back.

Chicken made of glass.

Plots.

Come and dream of stealing a table from Harriet.

Stories.

Come and be generous. Let me tell the story of Henrietta, Henrietta did not think that she had been well treated. She cried hysterically in the garden.

Thoughts.

I think very well of my mother.

Mildred's thoughts. How well we finish the water.

While she was talking she found what she was needing. Jennie did that.

She went upstairs quickly. She went upstairs very quickly. And how could she laugh. She laughed this afternoon. The chicken made of glass is comparable to an ass made of wood and a fig made of bread is comparable to a cow made of pudding. Do you see me. Yes I see.

A plot.

The janitor the janitor has not left. He and his wife linger. The janitor has come. He and his wife have installed themselves.

The visitors have enjoyed themselves. Do not laugh too heartily. Nor sing too merrily.

I can call Eugene Eugene. And can you call many men. I can call many men. Eugene and Norman and Morgan and Henry and Elizabeth and Genevieve and Constance and Ermentrude. I can also call on all of you to get fatter. And in climbing who leads the way. A hillock leads the way. Hay there has been an extraordinarily large yield of wheat here this year. Vegetables are not abundant, fruit is good but not plentiful.

Read this for me. The first novel. I wonder how they happened to think that I knew them when they came again. They came again and said, do you remember me. And I said very well. They said very well then may I bring a friend. And I said certainly. And then I explained. I said Norman remember that I dont need your wife. I have friends of my own. I am not married to my husband. He has no one but me and the money is mine. My father's name was Jepthah and there were four of us. Four children and we have all married. That is to say the women have had husbands and the men wives. And yet are we married. Can you reason with me. I cannot repeat what I hear. We are all very wealthy and we are all fond of our money and keep control of it absolutely. We sign our checks with our maiden names because we are not married. And now I listen to them and I do not feel angry at all except when there is a question of belonging to a secret organisation. It is natural that in union there is strength. Have you seen this embroidered. I remember you wished to buy it and it was for sale.

Mildred's thoughts. I think strongly. And riches how often are there different ways of re-editing worlds. Do you think that I would wish it if Frank I call him Frank.

Mildred's regard. How have you spelled your name.

And handkerchiefs are neat on heads in hands and around necks. Handkerchiefs are neat and feet, feet are splendidly ambidexterous. And now I have repeated what I have said that a great many expressions are such that they cannot be sudden. We have lost our servant but she was no paragon. A daughter of the armistice is not necessarily young and beautiful. She is not necessarily happy and rich. She is not necessarily faithful and strong. She is not necessarily winnowed. If there has been a good crop and there has been a good crop if there has been a good crop, of wheat not vegetables if there has been a good crop what can sisters say to one another.

Mildred I think. Mildred I do think that you have been rich that is to say wealthy.

She never thinks about them.

Mildred never thinks about Marsden Hartley or Marcel Duchamp or Martin Dehmuth. Mildred never thinks about Marsden Hartley or Marcel Duchamp or Martin Dehmuth presently.

Presently we manage to influence her, we say come come come to Myra's husband. Myra with an i Mira.

Come come Mira's comes, come come.

We were splendid about extravagance. We said Mildred how can Ferdinand deceive you.

We were splendid about the Literary Digest. We said I get all the foolish novels for Alice. We were splendid about friendship. We said listen to me and prepare yourself for San Tropez or Frejus or Italy or Mallorca. We said how can you imagine I wonder. I wonder if you can imagine what I mean.

Mildred thinks of them. She thinks of George, Marsden, Marcel, Martin and Lee Master. She thinks of busy ways and mistakes. She thinks of relief. It is a relief to her to stand still. And this does sound like one another. High in her hands she held the chasuble of her life and she measured by a measure. How sweetly, flowers, how sweetly flowers need water.

And now to be able to tell a story.

Marsden Hartley knows what he worships he worships a dome. Marcel Duchamp knows what he worships. He worships that thought. Martin Dehmuth knows what he worships. He worships the end. And Mr. van Aymand van Burgh worships letters. How pleasingly we all see George.

George was in love with a blond. He sang a song I love a brunette. George was in love with fables and he said Josie Josie I am not in love with thee. George was in love with Frejus and he said things are as they were. George was not neglected by wireless. He said I have no fear of winter in summer nor in winter. And in this way no one knew that anything had happened.

He held his life in his hands and he wished to be reasonable. He was very reasonable and he said Josephine you are not my queen we have the same origin, we love the south in winter and the North in the North they speak of Spaniards as poor Spaniards. They love only Poles and Armenians. And even this many change.

Have you been in earnest about me. Have you understood leaves. Leaves of salad. Hundreds of salads.

Have you been in earnest about me. Have you understood the means by which I have planted. Have you understood my needs and have you wept. Have you swept the paths since Barney left and have you put out the fires the little fires. Have you been in earnest about me and now to change.

You repeat I repeat they repeat this. We repeat they repeat that we will miss. They repeat you repeat that I do please. They repeat you repeat that they will please me. They repeat you repeat that they will please me too.

How can you thunder past.

They said that there was a strain. They said that was a strain in attempting to cajole me. And laborers. How can laborers be rich and sell something. How can we be disappointed with the price. Pray for me for tea. How can you refuse to accuse me. How can you accuse me of wishing to avoid expense. How can you avoid excusing me when I say that I was prepared to stay. But did they ask what is the best reason, did they ask me to tell it to them all again. Did they tell me that Nellie, did they tell me that Nellie was winsome. Oh Mildred dear we certainly are here.

How can the words mean Joseph. And how can Joseph be the patron saint of what. Do convents teach that. Oh dear me no. Do convents teach that.

How can Joseph be that. How can he be the patron saint of husbands who have been deceived. Can convents teach that or do we learn this thing in time. Time and time again. And she sleeps very quietly, and words are said that serve as bread. That is to say they are indigestible. Bread is the staff of life and so are words.

I cannot neglect women. A woman is best when spoken to as if there was no reproach. She does not reproach me nor I she. We do not mount in the same silence. A mountain of joy. What is the difference between S.O.S. and L.O.L.

I cannot see the necessity of having authority in the kitchen or in the room. Pray for me.

A prayer.

May we see the room. We have heard that it is extremely beautiful, that the objects in it are of great interest and that every one has a feeling of restfulness when seated there. We also understood that it is there that you compose the charming books which we so much admire. May we come and see the room. May we.

Clandestine correspondence.

How do you do.
I forgive you everything.
And there is nothing to forgive.

An interchange of obligations.

If I supply you with salad will you supply me with cheese.
If I supply you with apples will you supply me with fish.

The result of a separation.

She writes letters to me about the boys. He tells me about the boys. They tell me about the boys. She says that the boys need America. He says that the boys need France. They say that the boys need sweetness. And the boys are prepared to swim.

And Barney.

A song of Barney.

Barney looks like Julia. Barney is not small. Barney hopes to be an Irishman and to play cricket when he grows tall. Barney is like the boy on the stage. Barney is as sweet as he can be. Barney is a favourite with Mildred, Miss French, Alice and me. Barney is the son of Joseph Hone.

Mildred's thoughts when Susan has deserted her and when Alfred has sent her his book.

I resent it particularly as it is a thing to which I am completely unaccustomed. I did not enjoy it inordinately because he has forgotten the spiritual side. I have been able to understand his mathematics but many people will be unable to interest themselves in it.

She was glad the dance was over.

How much is told. I can see the subject of a diary.

Yesterday I was nervous.

To-day I am feeling better.

To-morrow I am going to be successful. And Thursday I am selfish.

How can you please Mrs.

You say yes ma'm in America.

In England, you say yes.

In Italy you say I am very pleased that you are of that nationality and in Brazil you cross the street slowly.

Give a thought to Cuba.

How pleasantly I dwell upon that.

Mildred thinks that chicken made of glass a horseshoe made of glass, a king's messenger made of glass, she feels that we have taught the working-man to feel what he feels. And I, I please myself. I teach myself to feel what I feel. I beg your pardon. I did not mean. I meant that I am taught to feel what I feel and I feel what I feel when I am taught to feel what I feel. I feel for them. They feel for me. Frank feels very well. And Katherine Buss. She certainly has reasons for saying that she and New England, that Mildred and New England that they and New England she has reason in saying she has reasons for saying that they and New England love France.

Mildred thinks that the world has accepted its manhood its womanhood and its age and its childhood. She thinks that she herself so feels no effort is necessary. Please buy a clock. Mildred is still thinking.

Please buy a clock. Please buy a clock. Please buy a clock. Please buy a clock. Money is back. Get your money back.

Money is back. Get your money back. Please buy a clock for me.

IDEM THE SAME

A VALENTINE TO SHERWOOD ANDERSON

The valentine was written in St.-Rémy, not for Valentine's Day, which is hardly the only occasion for a love poem. For Stein, the occasion was the publication of *Geography and Plays* in December 1922. She was indebted to Sherwood Anderson for the foreword, which added to her book a prominent name likely to make for sales and critical attention, as the publisher acknowledged. The "valentine" is an appreciation, an offering of thanks to Anderson. At the same time, most of the sections of the valentine are a love poem to Toklas, though she is not named. Without her inspiration and practical help neither *Geography and Plays* nor any other book could have been produced. She was the moving force behind Stein.

The text and title of this piece went through changes. It is not known whether the sections were composed in the order in which they are printed, nor is the order or time of revisions of the title clear. Given the hints of Christmas and the late 1922 date of composition, the piece cannot have been written for Valentine's Day. The title "A Valentine," without a name, inscribes it to an unnamed recipient, plainly Toklas. Another title is *Idem the Same*. The piece later became "A Portrait of Sherwood Anderson," revised to *A Valentine to Sherwood Anderson. Idem the Same* appears in the form in which students memorize it, the Latin word followed immediately by its English translation, which makes the phrase redundant since it twice says what it means. But what is "the same" as what else is not stated. It may be one valentine written for or about two people, or two people who are both valentines of the writer. However, the valentine is a text inscribed to Anderson, with a subtext for or about Toklas, not named.

On the back of the notebook for this piece are tiny private love verses to Toklas. Some become sections of the text. In the notes, details of "A Very Valentine" appear in more personal form than in typescript and in print. The original line "Very Stein is my valentine very Stein and very fine" becomes in print "Very mine is my valentine very mine and very fine." Stein and Toklas are each other's valentines, two lovers who are one, idem the same.

The valentine has a pastoral, religious tone and a formal, processional feeling, with counting and lists of diverse detail in order of size, such as pervade much of Stein's writing in St.-Rémy. "A very little snail. / A medium sized turkey. / . . . / A fair orange tree. / . . . / Listen to them from here." Alice Toklas said that as Stein wrote "A History Of Giving Bundles" she inserted into it, presumably at the hotel in St.-Rémy, the figures and gifts from a procession to the Christmas crèche on the mantle. Never heavy and systematic, the poem plays lyrically and lightly, as if ringing changes or offering blessings to creatures, to nature, to and in words.

• • • • •

I knew too that through them I knew too that he was through, I knew too that he threw them. I knew too that they were through, I knew too I knew too, I knew I knew them.

I knew to them.

If they tear a hunter through, if they tear through a hunter, if they tear through a hunt and a hunter, if they tear through the different sizes of the six, the different sizes of the six which are these, a woman with a white package under one arm and a black package under the other arm and dressed in brown with a white blouse, the second Saint Joseph the third a hunter in a blue coat and black garters and a plaid cap, a fourth a knife grinder who is full faced and a very little woman with black hair and a yellow hat and an excellently smiling appropriate soldier. All these as you please.

In the meantime examples of the same lily. In this way please have you rung.

WHAT DO I SEE.

A very little snail.
A medium sized turkey.
A small band of sheep.
A fair orange tree.
All nice wives are like that.
Listen to them from here.
Oh.
You did not have an answer.
Here.
Yes.

A VERY VALENTINE.

Very fine is my valentine.
Very fine and very mine.
Very mine is my valentine very mine and very fine.
Very fine is my valentine and mine, very fine very mine and mine is my valentine.

WHY DO YOU FEEL DIFFERENTLY.

Why do you feel differently about a very little snail and a big one.

Why do you feel differently about a medium sized turkey and a very large one.

Why do you feel differently about a small band of sheep and several sheep that are riding.

Why do you feel differently about a fair orange tree and one that has blossoms as well.

Oh very well.

All nice wives are like that.

To Be
No Please.
To Be
They can please
Not to be
Do they please.
Not to be
Do they not please
Yes please.
Do they please
No please.
Do they not please
No please.
Do they please.
Please.
If you please.
And if you please.
And if they please
And they please.
To be pleased
Not to be pleased.
Not to be displeased.
To be pleased and to please.

KNEELING

One two three four five six seven eight nine and ten.

The tenth is a little one kneeling and giving away a rooster with this feeling.

I have mentioned one, four five seven eight and nine.

Two is also giving away an animal.

Three is changed as to disposition.

Six is in question if we mean mother and daughter, black and black caught her, and she offers to be three she offers it to me.

That is very right and should come out below and just so.

BUNDLES FOR THEM.

A HISTORY OF GIVING BUNDLES.

We were able to notice that each one in a way carried a bundle, they were not a trouble to them nor were they all bundles as some of them were chickens some of them pheasants some of them sheep and some of them bundles, they were not a trouble to them and then indeed we learned that it was the principal recreation and they were so arranged that they were not given away, and to-day they were given away.

I will not look at them again.

They will not look for them again.

They have not seen them here again.

They are in there and we hear them again.

In which way are stars brighter than they are. When we have come to this decision. We mention many thousands of buds. And when I close my eyes I see them.

If you hear her snore
It is not before you love her
You love her so that to be her beau is very lovely
She is sweetly there and her curly hair is very lovely
She is sweetly here and I am very near and that is very lovely.
She is my tender sweet and her little feet are stretched out well which is a treat and very lovely
Her little tender nose is between her little eyes which close and are very lovely.
She is very lovely and mine which is very lovely.

ON HER WAY.

If you can see why she feels that she kneels if you can see why he knows that he shows what he bestows, if you can see why they share what they share, need we question that there is no doubt that by this time if they had intended to come they would have sent some notice of such intention. She and they and indeed the decision itself is not early dissatisfaction.

IN THIS WAY.

Keys please, it is useless to alarm any one it is useless to alarm some one it is useless to be alarming and to get fertility in gardens in salads in heliotrope and in dishes. Dishes and wishes are mentioned and dishes and wishes are not capable of darkness. We like sheep. And so does he.

LET US DESCRIBE.

Let us describe how they went. It was a very windy night and the road although in excellent condition and extremely well graded has many turnings and although the curves are not sharp the rise is considerable. It was a very windy night and some of the larger vehicles found it more prudent not to venture. In consequence some of those who had planned to go were unable to do so. Many others did go and there was a sacrifice, of what shall we, a sheep, a hen, a cock, a village, a ruin, and all that and then that having been blessed let us bless it.

SAINTS AND SINGING

A PLAY

A LIST

These two very different plays are introduced together because both came out of Stein's acquaintance with Avery Hopwood (1882–1928), the American playwright of successful Broadway farces and melodramas. For *Saints and Singing* the connection with him is documented in a note Stein wrote in the manuscript, and for *A List* in a letter to Edmund Wilson. While the Yale Catalogue dates the plays late 1922 and mid 1923, biographical and textual details suggest that both were written before February 1923.

The title *Saints and Singing* is followed in manuscript and typescript by a note in Stein's hand, "[A Play] To be called Saints and Singing as a Protest against Demi Virgins." Hopwood, who must have seen Stein in Provence, apparently lent her a copy of *The Demi-Virgin,* his adaptation of *Les Demi-Vierges* (1895) by Marcel Prévost. The demi-virgins of Hopwood's farce are Hollywood starlets. *Saints and Singing* joins nuns, saints, and virgins with the demimonde of farce.

The play begins with the rituals of holy season in Provence—choir practice, refurbishing of the church, intimacy in love and love play, at times hilarious and naughty. It concludes by asking for repetition, which would return us to the beginning and start the play all over again.

Christmas 1922 is also the publication date of *Geography and Plays,* the book that was to make Stein's name famous. Her pleasure in reviewing her new collection in print enters *Saints and Singing* and contributes to the burst of creative energy of 1922–23. The new year and the new book are to make her name new.

Saints and Singing is full of names. Saints' names—first names, which move freely, not last names attached to family and world—are adopted and invoked in hymns and prayers. At first, religion appears to dominate the play, but suddenly Stein's words start punning and soon they speak a language as low and worldly as it is high and religious. For while the play is about saints, it is also about lovers, intrigue, impersonation, success, fame—the stuff of Hopwood's work. A twist of a word converts nuns to Hollywood starlets. Canticles "[c]an tickle can tickle." Nuns take saints' names as starlets swap names for a moment in bed or a part in a movie. A collection box turns into a collection of work to make an author famous and wealthy. Admission to heaven is admission to a show.

Near the end Stein explains, "The origin of saints singing is nuns praying. The origin of nuns praying was splendid rehearsing." But next, "The origin of repetition is the Harden admission." What is his admission? It appears to be the admission of Hopwood—become Harden, another friend, since she could not use Hopwood's name. The admission, under Stein's cajoling and teasing interrogation over tea, is to repetition as the key to the success of Hopwood's formula plays. He "recharges the words the music . . . the opera . . . the choice." Stein, herself expert in repetition, cannot simply be critical of what she and Hopwood both rely on. In this play she looks at the nature and use of repetition. She may also have hoped to profit in her work from Hopwood's successful use of it as a gimmick for potboilers.

The language of this play moves from lyrical, rhythmic song of creativity and religious devotion with all the repetitions of ritual, to stiff, hardened, and Latinate discourse whose repetitions fail to sing. The repeats of saints singing are close indeed to the formulas of starlets performing. The lesson of Hopwood's repetition is also the lesson of her own art.

The ending that suggests a return to the beginning includes also a last sentence that warns, "Do not repeat yourself." It is known that Hopwood by 1922 was unhappy about having written much for profit but nothing of lasting value. What Stein learned from commercial theater yielded neither fame nor money.

This play was printed in *Operas and Plays* with substantial errors in the order of scenes. Following notes by Toklas in the manuscript and typescript, the *Reader* restores the correct order.

A List hardly sounds like a title for a play. Yet one look down the left margin shows an astonishing group of characters. Unlike the many different names played with in *Saints and Singing,* these are all nearly uniform names beginning with capital *M,* followed by *a.* They visibly make a list.

In the spring of 1923 Carl Van Vechten showed *A List* to Edmund Wilson, who wanted to publish it in *Vanity Fair* on facing pages with Hopwood's *Our Little Wife* (1916), which Stein had told him was the source. Hopwood's play is an upper-class New York farce about polyandrous wife swapping and couples playing games with hidden letters, names, and addresses of lovers and husbands. To be printed in *Vanity Fair* would have been welcome exposure for Stein; yet when asked for permission to cut her play, she refused, and it was not published.

The relationship between Stein's and Hopwood's disparate plays is puzzling. The most likely link is between the Mabel in the list of *M* names and the situation of Mabel Dodge at that time. Dodge, as an old friend of all four, was the subject of much gossip in the letters of Stein and Van Vechten in 1923 about her fourth marriage, to the Pueblo Indian Antonio Lujan. The innumerable couplings in both *A List* and *Our Little Wife* echo Mabel's many divorces and remarriages.

Stein pieces throughout the years are full of *M* names. First among them is Mary, May Mary, or May May, which puns with "may" and "marry." Their source is undoubtedly Stein's first lover, Mary Bookstaver [Knoblauch], the Helen Thomas of *Q.E.D.* and a source for "Melanctha." Stein's capacity to play with words never neutralized the references of these words.

Martha in *A List* connects no doubt with Martha Hersland in *The Making of Americans.* She also recalls the system of personality types—lists upon lists—that Stein built into that novel. Early in the play Martha appears alone and is "not interesting," but she becomes interesting in relations with others. "How are you known you are known by your name and your share."

Here, with Mabel, Martha, and the others, Stein plays with names, lines of dialogue, and how they look and function on the page. Among the many devices she tries out to connect them are the word *and* as well as the ampersand. In printing *Operas and Plays* the ampersand was not used, but it is found in the manuscript and is therefore restored in the *Reader,* where it most commonly joins Martha and Maryas. As Stein couples and groups names vertically and joins words horizontally, she plays with the configurations of plays, thinking of them as beginning with lists. Throughout *A List* she makes patterns—lists—of names, words, phrases, letters, stage directions, spoken sections, always trying out how things can be grouped. She strings words together like beads or phrases in prayer, putting them in varied sequences. Her insistent sense of order is totally visible in this play.

• • • • •

SAINTS AND SINGING
A Play

Saints and singing. I have mentioned them before. Saints and singing need no door they come before, saints and singing, they adore, saints and singing, or, saints and singing, and this play is about a choice of sentiment. I choose you. And what do you choose. I choose you. We have been baffled by harmony.

ACT ONE. SCENE ONE.

Prelude

And how do you dispose of me.

I dispose of you by being intimate and impersonal. And how do you dispose of me. I don't dispose of you at all.

So many people pray that you will furnish them ribbons and sashes. And do you. No. I furnish them with cakes and little houses. And Christmas trees. We have abandoned Christmas trees.

Not for Christmas.

No for Thanksgiving.

To-morrow is Thanksgiving and what am I giving.

ACT ONE SCENE ONE

I have felt called to call all a revision and I revise Helen Wise, and Beatrice Wise and Henry Wise. I have felt called to call for a decision, and I have decided to abide by religion and all the splendid acts of ministration and administration executed by you and others.

This is so gay.

Herbert. Can you guess why I admire what I admire.

James. For my liberty I am willing to be addicted to ripening.

Arnold. Guess at prayers.

William. I am William.

And what does he say.

He says how readily I can see the day, the day and the night and the protection of his mother. We recall sisters. And a countryman said. When are we up.

End of Scene I

Scene II

A field full of berries and a body of well known and calculating cousins. In America we do not allow for their cousins. In America we do not allow for that, for this, that cousins can wish and do we mean to be allowed very much. We make allowances to those to whom we give it.

Scene II

Feel me.

I feel very well now.

Do you feel very well now. I feel very well now and I feel that I will feel for you, I feel so very well.

All for Hannah.

Hannah is not welcome.

All for Henry.

Henry smiles and when he smiles he feels the need of a recital.

Can we recite with a song.

I sing.

You sing.

We sing.

And now mention me.

I mention you to him and to her.

I mention her.

I mention him. I mention him. I do mention, how frequently we wonder, how often does Jessie how often does Jessie employ, employ those she can mention.

She can mention to me when this you see you are all to me.

It was almost it was mostly thought out by records and moist houses, it was mostly thought out by moist houses that bed-rooms should be heated.

Arnold. How are you Arnold.

How are you Benjamin Arnold and Cora Couperous. How do you do Benjamin and when are you willing to be ready too late. When are you willing to be ready too late. When am I willing to be ready too late.

And Cora what do you think about the loyalty of a section. What do you think about loyalty. What claims have you on Benjamin, and how often do you languish.

How can we be feeble very feeble so feeble, how can we be so feeble now.

I have had every excuse, I have made every excuse, I have given every excuse for men for women and for children. Men women and children make the population.

I do believe in calling. Call me, call me back call me back again, call me by a name. I wonder I do wonder about saints and singing. They sing the same name. Could they sing the same name just the same.

Edward would be a better name. George has the name just the same.

So then.

Coming, I am coming. Yes I am coming. He called me by my name.

And I.

I make a new name, and yet every name is the same, it is always in the name.

It is said that the name is the same name.

Are you coming. Hope is coming. Henry Hope is coming.

Henry Hope is married and Henry Hope is married and he is coming. Henry Hope mentioned me to him.

Do please please please please me.

I have often thought of swimming in water.

Scene III

If there is in between if there is in between the tradition, if there is between that tradition the tradition of laying of laying across the pieces of translations. Translate everybody.

Jennie Charles.

How do you do how do you resume mentioning religion.

Jennie Charles. I am so very well.

I am so very well, and he is my most admiring and startling selection.

And then easily.

And then so easily.

Jennie French.

How have you met Jennie Nightingale.

And please be another Jessie.

When I say Jessie what do I mean.

And now altogether I esteem I esteem the best and the very best and the very best of all of them.

I flatter myself that extra thought, that I give extra thought that I give them, I give to them my extra thinking.

In this way a lesson, in this way they lessen Egyptian and Arabian thinking.

And now do you remember recognition.

A play.

I play.

You play.

Mistinguett can play.

What can we play.

We can play that to-day letters say, Mistinguett have a day.

Oh that way.

I say.

Mistinguett does not get away.

When I wish, veal, when I wish hare when I wish radishes there. When I wish that Paul, Constance, and religion have their place, have their places. I say I play in between their care.

Comes the scene.

In between their, in between their necklaces, in their way of wishes. Can you be rowdier.

I have no wishes.

Gather I gather I gather that you are not teased.

Excite I do excite, excite we excite, how do we excite.

We gather we would rather we would rather gather that we, what can religion sing.

I sing.

You sing.

I sing to you.

You sing.

Now be a flower in May. Now be a flower anyway.

Make names.

Make their names.

Make their names say.

Make their names make sense when they say.

What do they say.

They say speeches.

And what do they say.

They say count to-day, at count to-day.

They say they rapidly say, they say very rapidly just what they say.

How can you be Robert, Robert himself. How can you be so readily filled with the interest of my thoughts.

I have.

You have.

I have my willingness.

And wind sounds like rain, wind when it is turning. How a little nature makes religion, and how a little religion makes creation makes a saint in singing and now rush and hush. We are not going to meeting.

An Interlude

Can tickle can tickle.

Why can he can tickle her.

Can tickle can tickle.

He can tickle her.

Can tickle.

Can tickle.

He can tickle her.

Can tickle.

Can tickle.

He can make her purr.

Where where over there. I do I do love her hair.

Where where over there I do do make a pair.

What What I forgot. I do not forget my dot.

One two Three, One Two Three One Two One Two Holy Holy Gee.

What

What

I forgot

What What

What What

A succession of addresses

She can address him. He can address them. She can dress him. He can dress them. She can dress him. He can he can, She can address him, He can.

He can address them.

Exercise me.

Exercise me I say, I say exercise me. Exercise me I say you may you may exercise with me to-day. Exercise me I say and I say exercise with me and I exercise with her to-day, I say, exercise with me I say exercise with me.

I master pieces of it. Exercise in mastering pieces of it. Exercise in masterpieces. Exercise in her mastering her pieces. I am exercising I am exercised, I am exercised in mastering pieces, I am exercised in masterpieces. Capital. He capitally said, there is the basket of wood and of bread. Capital he said. Capitally he said. I am glad she is able to bring it. And now, wood is gay and bread is gaily and butter is gaily said to be eaten. Mrs. Eaton and Waldemar George, Mrs. Eaton Miss Eaton, Miss Eaton and Waldemar and George.

Miss Eaton and Miss Beaton. Mary why do you remember Mary.

I remember you remember can you remember Carry.

Carry and tea can she carry me.

Carry and tea, Carry the tea, Carry the tea for me and for Mildred and for radium and for X ray. Carry the tea away. Thank you.

Lipschitz Lipschitz Lipschitz and his friend. Lipschitz Lipschitz do you love to blend, Lipschitz Lipschitz how many are there here.

Lipschitz Lipschitz, you can guess it without fear.

They are here.

Thank you.

And interlude in music is an interlude indeed. And interlude in mockery. I do not admit mockery.

ACT II

Scene I

How do you do.

I do not neglect you.

I feel very readily that in these circumstances, Dolly is wild, that in these circumstances, believe me that in these circumstances I see you.

I see you again.

I will see you again.

Come and see me.

I love the moon or dawn.

Jenny. Yes of course certainly and I believe you and as for my husband you know very well that he is not the father of my child. You have known it all. You know he has a child. You know that prayers her prayers, not the child's prayers, but the friend's prayers, she who is sixty nine and capable of praying capable of praying for nine mornings and not singing not even singing not even singing. Prayers do not mix us.

Donald and Dorothy and a collision.

Donald and Dorothy and Antwerp. How many are killed every day by accidents.

Dorothy I say, I say to you Dorothy that you have only stayed a day.

A Scene between a Woman an Egyptian and an Australian.

Hear me speak.

I hear you when you say that you are a wife that you have been worried and that you have placed a cream where it belongs.

A cream.

And not a quarrel.

A cream and not a quarrel.

Forgive me, a cream and not a quarrel.

On the first day of the new year he writes.

And I write too and I say, standard, the standard of yellow and crimson. So historic.

And now please.

Wishes.

I wish for a kiss. I wish for the rest of the day.

And I wish I was a fish. And I wish the most.

Plenty of irritation.

Why do you wash older weddings.

Why do you wash older weddings.

One two three four five six seven. Come again and talk of heaven.

One two three four five six seven.

I come to you so noisily that you astonish me.

Scene II

Why do we stamp.

Don't walk too hard walk gently and continuously and persistently but don't walk too hard.

A compliment. I am a complement to you. You compliment me. I arrange to compliment you. So next to nothing. Why do flashes of older women. Why do flashes of older women compliment him and them.

Why do flashes of older women how can he hear the same name. Dolly. I stretch to Dolly. Nelly I dare to tell her, Nelly is your name. Nelly, a million or three are three or four, and you, you love the remainder of their door.

Nelly why do you wish me.

Nelly why do you wish for me. Nelly why do you wish for me there, Nelly why do you wish me to be there, Nelly.

How realisable are apples and butter. She says apples and potatoes. And we say apples and butter and rapidly diminishing. Who diminishes rapidly.

Sound.

How does it sound.

How do you sound. How do you season. How do you read the reason. How do you How do you How very nearly do you, How do you very nearly breathe.

Books that is paper that is the paper, the paper in books is useful in any army, can be useful in any army, and where can religion tear, where can religion tear away, where can religion tear away from there.

Shout to a man. Men, shout to a man. I shout. Saints who are singing, Saints and singing, I shall keep him from fur. I shall keep fur away from him. I shall not let him. I shall not let her, I shall not let him, I shall not let her use fur. Fur and splendidly willing. Come to the window and sing there.

Saints and singing. Everywhere.

Have you my knife.

He is very sweet to see that he has money readily. And accidentally witness. He can accidentally witness what he can mean.

I mean and you mean.

Remember that I know what I want and I know how to get it. Also remember finishing touches. Also remember me to Emily.

Scene III

I hear that he was rapidly seen.

Rapidly seen to be what.

I hear that he was rapidly seen to be there at all. I hear that he was most subtle most subtly spread with what he was not worthy, not worthy of regulation.

How can chances How can there be chances how can there be chances for him. Oh my dear, cannot you stay, cannot you stay there and feel that yesterday, and to-day are full of all the measure of repetition. Repeat what.

In repeating all in repeating, in repeating all is awaited. They wait they might wait.

A parlor.

A parlor in where nuns are.

Scene IV

Center and enter. I enter to go there.

Five o'clock and nearly all well.

Please press across. Please press across what.

And where.

Nearly everywhere. In an entanglement. How can they spare her to be in an ecstacy. I feel the exact recollection.

Constance Street.

Do come in.

Do come in.

Do come in.

Constance and Elisabeth have not the same name. One is Constance Street and the other is Elisabeth Elkus. It is easy to be three and there they are more often recognized as three.

Thank you for your edition. Thank you very much. And now all walk together and play that silence is restless. I rest so blankly. And you did ask her to send it and did she.

Golden Gate is the second one.

I plan and you plan to meet me. He plans he does not plan at all and he does not call.

A hymn for a whim.

And coffee needs to be wretched and honey needs to be wretched and glasses need to be there.

Come and bear with me.

And now how to be sacred.

Flashlight and bird line and new dollars. If you receive a legacy is the money there. If you receive more do you have to be widowed. Does a widower stare.

I can be here there and everywhere. Does a widower repeat his adjective. Does he say can I harden.

And now something is relatively separate. I separate her from them. And was she aside from this firm and an apple.

Sing to me.

Able to sing to me. Able to sing to them. Able to sing to them of me.

Able to sing to them of me and of them. Able to sing to me. And to them of me and of them.

I sing to them when I sing a second song.

How can I measure threads.

Come together.

They came there and we said I have heard more voices and you have heard more of their voices and we have heard of their voices.

How can you remember that one out of ten. How can you remember that one out of every ten. How can you remember when they were found. Are you bound to remember that they abound.

Are you bound to be a second winter. Can you argue with me. May you live long and prosper.

Scene V

Can you step backward and step on a wooden arrangement of a carving. Can you step backward and step on a round piece of wood which is a part of the arrangement of a wooden carving. Did you. And then he said I hope that you understood me.

He said that he would not be credited with carefulness.

Can you believe in a variety in marbles. I like marble painted. And I like marble imitated.

And I like marble revered.

And as for me I worship reproduction of marble.

And as for me I believe that the coloring the doubling of coloring looks like avarice. Please him by revealing by what has been said and done.

I carefully interrupt and I say Constance go away.

Do be careful of me and do not say again what do I measure again. You measure as a treasure.

Dolly is clearly here. You mean she is clearly not here.

Trouble me please to say if you love a woman you give her money.

And you also say how can I believe in water berries.

I know black currants have religious faces I know that very well and I know that religious faces are very apt to be very well related to corals and fairly acknowledged rounds.

I am around.

Can you mingle vegetable roots with precious herds. Herds of cold cows and herds of good dogs and herds and herds, have you heard of a bird that repeats me.

I can easily follow the cloud about. And about there. Yes about there we stare and we say Harden why do you take offence at the reason you give for everything. Why do you not take offence at the reason that you give for everything. Why do you read lists.

Follow me latterly. That is what I say. Latterly. Follow me.

He is not so expectant, he is not so very splendid, he is not so well intentioned as she is and yet what does she do she annoys every Jew.

How do you know that language I know that language very well. I have faith beside.

And the instant obedience.

And the instant obedience.

When.

Calm yourself Emil, you are not widowed yet. You know very well that you are wedded to your running. You never run away and you never satisfy your librarian.

You never satisfy decidedly you never satisfy, very decidedly do you ever satisfy weddings. Do you ever satisfy their weddings, do you ever satisfy, life and riches. Do you ever satisfy riches. And please do not please her.

Christmas kisses.

Sing to the satisfaction of Monday Wednesday and candlesticks. Can you remember candlesticks. I can remember when the change occurred, I can remember relieving Chinese masterpieces reliving mingled Chinese and European wideness and really asking blessings on San Francisco. Saint Francis, Saint Nicholas Saint Chrysostom and Saint Bartholomew. Saint Bartholomew is nearest to raised eyelashes, eyebrows and columns, and trees begin with a trunk and mountains with meadows. I merrily read I merrily lead I merrily sing to crosses. I believe in respect I believe in relief I believe in actual plenty. I believe in actual plenty in plenty of time. Harden. How are you.

I am very well. Harden what do you think of measuring heat. I feel the cold equally. Harden what are mildewed grapes.

They are to be found in certain seasons.

And what benefit is there in raised pearls.

Raised pearls are beautiful to the eye, and I I like the waiting here. You mean you want the waiting to be here that is to say you wish that the waiting should take place here.

Yes I mean exactly that. I mean to be very exact. I mean to call you, I mean to come, I mean to be especially seen and very nearly established. I mean to cloud the rain and to articulate to articulate very clearly I mean to articulate very clearly and to pronounce myself as aroused. Are you aroused by them or for them. Neither the one nor the other.

Continuation of Scene V

Aunt Louise had once broken her leg as a girl and it was a little sensitive and twenty years later when for the first time she skated again she broke her leg all over again but it did not cause the slightest excitement.

This time a great many people found investigation to be a necessity. Come again Harden. Come again.

I ask questions and he said I have a feeling that he has not been able to answer me.

And what do you ask him.

I ask him about representation. Politically. No neither politically nor numerically but actually. Actually how readily are you how readily do you promise ringing. How readily do you promise to suggest saints and singing saints and then singing. How readily do you promise Harden. Harden, how readily do you promise this threatening this to be threatening. How readily do you vary your caress. How very readily.

How very readily.

Deliberately inclusive.

Pardonably debilitated.

Reserved for them.

Reserved toward them.

And silk for noon. Never silk neither for noon or for morning.

Never any of their silk. Never any of that silk for them neither for them nor before them. Never any mailing never any of silk covering of a silk covering before them in front of them nor behind them. How do you use silk.

Care to go.

Do you care to go.

Do you care to go there.

Feel it restlessly and do not deface stories.

Two stories or three stories.

Six stories are higher. And very much higher. Oh so very much higher.

Harden are you willowy. Are you very famous. Are you famous for these embellishments. Are these embellishments in your occupancy of round ones. Are these recognised embellishments. Are there meagre cuts. Are there very meagre rounds.

How round are rare flowers. How very round are very rare flowers.

How very round are they there. How very rare are they around there.

Not there.

Not where you are when you are privately there.

How famous are the meeting places of religion and law.

How famous are the meeting places of religion and towns. How famous are the meeting places of cousins and exhibitions. How famous are they always, how very famous are they always. How very famous are they always when they are there.

Who can answer and a pardon. Who can answer and pardon faith and reproduction. Who can answer swinging women. Who can answer him there I glance, you glance, you glance at them when they are there.

You recognize that the collection that the collection that the collecting of them that their collecting of them causes them to be there.

Where.

There.

ACT III

Scene I

I have every confidence in their religion and I say nuns every day and I say girls at play and I say she is working all day. She is sixty nine and she has nothing to say except that she will receive her pay. And does she stay.

Harden come in.

Harden come in to tea.

Harden come in to see me.

Harden come in Harden he does not spin nor is he that twin, he is has the right to win he must come in.

Come in again it is always a pleasure to see you.

Scene II

I rapidly read printed matter and I find that nothing at all has been left behind.

Can you believe that he is not there.

Can you believe that he is not here.

Can you believe that brown is one color, that chocolate color and eider down color matter. Oil cloth matters. Can we replace it.

We have replaced and very cheaply and we have not received their good wishes for a pleasant winter. We have received their good wishes.

Converse with me. In a play you converse with me.

They play they partly play this play on the day. On their day.

Scene III

Now read louder. Prayers are not read aloud to be louder, they are louder but not read aloud and saying what are you saying to me Harden can you see.

Say it to me.

Say to me, can you see.

Say can you see to this for me. I can easily see to this and I will see to this and you will see what the result will be.

Harden can you plunge yourself across.

Fight presents, you guess.

You guess that you can fight and read their address. How can you smile bewilderdly. How can you speak to yourself and make of that a principle in repetition.

Reading flowers. How do you read flowers. I read flowers by languages and muttering. How can you resemble that which is heard. How can you.

Speak to me Harden.

Speak to me and tell me what is the cause of the principal relief of retribution. Religion let us. Let us spring. In the spring we make golden butter.

And modesty, modesty ate prettily, modestly he ate very prettily. And what chance have we of meeting again.

What are the chances of our meeting again.

Establish records. He says that he won that before. Thank you.

Thank you for winning.

And now saints and singing and what a scene.

This is the scene.

Scene Four

Open the door.

Scene IV

Before I had begun I was very well arranged for. I had arranged everything very well.

He was not as precious as he had roused himself to be and necessarily very necessarily Roger hums.

To be obliging can he be rapidly be called Harden. Can he be rapidly called by those who love sending saints to do their singing.

Please me.

I please you as a dilatory victory I please you. Do please me. He pleases me connectedly. He pleases me connectedly and usefully regularly. Please me for planting pleasingly the signs of the things I have here. What have you here.

Harden how can you ask. I have here a great many different signs of saintly singing. Saintly singing analysed to me.

Rub it.

When you have a silver lamp rub it.

When you have a silver lamp and you rub it you clean it.

This is equally true of other silver.

When you have other silver and you rub it you clean it. This is true of all the silver.

Now once more Harden, what are your passages. How often have you crossed the ocean. How many people have you met in crossing, toward how many have you incurred the obligation of rejoining them and how very many are you willing to moisten rapid repetition with angular vibration. You are not angular, you do not vibrate nor do you caution men and women as to war and liberation. Run to war and liberation, run to saints and education, run to gardens and elimination run to singing and division, do divide beside do divide beside, do divide saints and singing, do divide beside saints and singing, do divide singing and beside can you ring beside can you ring beside the use and air of elaboration and a vision. Be a vision of the outstanding and nearly impassable religion. Do you read religion. Do you adore singing. Do you blunder to that saint and say I do not pray to-day. What happens next.

He recharges the ship, the steamer, the boat and the color. He recharges the color the meadow the ceiling and the voice. He recharges the words the music and the opera. He recharges the choice.

I choose you, and what do you choose.

I choose the rest.

And what do you depend upon. I depend upon what I need and what I have, and I will undertake to establish a dynasty in this way. A dynasty does not stay. No indeed but neither does it go away. And what are the ample expenditures. They are these. Instruments, pears, hats, and oleanders. How easily oleanders please us. Do not they. Harden do you go away. No not to-day. Read to me while you stay.

Scene V

Everybody sees a saint and yesterday.

Repeat to me about yesterday.

Everybody sees a saint and yesterday, everybody sees a saint.

They serve three years seven months and twelve days.

They considered that the day they were benefited by everything was equal to the willingness those who were willing showed in beatitude in gratitude.

He is acquainted with the recognition that is predicted.

I read of a saint there.

Where.

Reading matters.

I read of a saint having been there.

Where.

In China.

In Savoy.

In despair.

I read of a saint having been where.

Everywhere.

I read of a saint. He reads of the reason that the saint became a saint there.

He reads of the reason that the saints take care. They take care of them there. Saints take care of them everywhere.

And where are saints taken when they are taken away from prayer. They are taken to be made saints to take care of those who love them and who love prayer. Saints are the saints who are the saints who take care of those who take care of prayer and who beware of accrediting to themselves a large share. So then saints and singing seem there, seem to be there, seem to be and are there.

Saints and singing save themselves from the wear and tear of sound in there and they declare, they love to be their indentation there.

Saints and singing and I do care.

How do you care, I care for their care.

Do that nicely, I do that nicely, I do very nicely do that.

And leave me the I leave to you all the rest of the revelation.

The amount of the creation and the question of memory enters into this question readily. I read about calculation recognition and inexperience.

Now cloud the issue. Cloud the issue so that words cause you to tease me.

You are a frightful tease.

You tease me frightfully just as you please. And it pleases you to blunder and when you blunder why do you repeat precious precious you are so precious. Why do you repeat, treasure treasure I love you without measure. Why do you repeat, I repeat what you repeat.

I do not neglect florid graces. I do not neglect torrid races, I do not neglect plenty of places. I do not neglect exaggerated spaces, I do not neglect original traces nor do I neglect absences. Who is absent. Shall I mention Nelly and Harden. Shall I mention Harden again. No I will not mention what I have no intention of corroborating. Witnesses corroborate. I do not have to deny that the reason why I do not deny witnesses witnessing is because the origin the real origin of exhibiting acting is this. Mountains of saints singing. Mountains and mountains of saints singing and singing. Saints witnessing and corroborating. Mountains of saints witnessing and singing. Do sing please.

The origin of mentioning saints singing were nuns praying. The origin of nuns praying was splendid rehearsing. And the origin of repetition is the Harden admission. I admit that he that they that it is not a pause.

Who pauses.

I believe that notwithstanding all of the repetition, all of that repetition makes more imperative what I have just indicated.

What have you indicated.

I have indicated good fortune.

This is the end of the play.

Saints and singing which had a good beginning and now has a very good ending.

Saints and their singing.

Saints and singing do not come to this as an ending. Saints and singing. Read me by repetition. Saints and singing and a mission and an addition.

Saints and singing and the petition. The petition for a repetition.

Saints and singing and their singing.

Saints and singing and winning and.

Do not repeat yourself.

A LIST

Martha. not interesting.

Maryas. Precluded.

Martha. Not interesting.

Marius. challenged.

Martha and Maryas. Included.

Maryas. If we take Marius.

Mabel. And an old window and still.

Mabel Martha and Maryas. Various re-agents make me see victoriously.

Maryas. In as we thrust them trust them trust them thrust them in. In as we brush them, we do not brush them in. In as we trust them in.

Mabel Martha and Susan Mabel Martha and Susan, Mabel and Martha and a father.

Mabel and Martha. There was no sinking there, there where there was no placid carrier.

Martha. not interesting.

Maryas. Not included.

Mabel. And an old window and still.

Marius. Exchange challenges.

Maryas. If added to this speeches are made are speeches played, speeches are included and thrust in and they trust in and they trust in speeches and they brush them in.

Martha. Smiles.

Mabel. And still she did mean to sing-song. We know how to very nearly please her.

Marius. Exchange challenges for challenges and by and by defy, and define by and by Battling Siki and so high. He is higher than they say. You know why beads are broader, in order to be in order to be an order in order to be strung together.

Maryas and Martha. Yes indeed.

Maryas. Can intend to seize her objects seize the objects place the objects, place the objects.

Martha. A list.

Maryas. A list.

Marius. A list.

Martha

Maryas. A list.

Martha

Maryas. A list lost.

Martha. A list lost reminds her of a fire lost. Smoke is not black nor if you turn your back is a fire burned if you are near woods which abundantly supply wood.

Maryas. A list lost does not account for the list which has been lost nor for the inequality of cushions shawls and awls. Nowadays we rarely mention awls and shawls and yet an awl is still used commercially and a shawl is still used is still used and also used commercially. Shawls it may be mentioned depend upon their variety. There is a great variety in calculation and in earning.

Marius. A list.

Mabel. A list.

Martha. A list.

Martha. There is a great variety in the settlement of claims. We claim and you claim and I claim the same.

Martha. A list.

Maryas. And a list.

Mabel. I have also had great pleasure from a capital letter.

Martha. And forget her.

Maryas. And respect him.

Marius. And neglect them.

Mabel. And they collect them as lilies of the valley in this country.

Martha. A list.

Maryas. Sixteen if sixteen carry four, four more, if five more carry four for more, if four more carry four, if four carry fifty more, if four more five hundred and four and for more than that, and four more than eighty four. Four more can carry sixteen if you please if it is acceptable.

Martha. She knows very well that if five are sitting at a table and one leaning upon it, that it makes no difference.

Maryas and Martha. Nearly all of it has made nearly all of it. Nearly all of it has made nearly all of it.

Maryas and Martha. Nearly all of it has made nearly all of it has made nearly all of it has made nearly all of it.

Martha and Maryas. Nearly all of it has made nearly all of it.

Martha. Plenty of time as the pansy is a bird as well as a flower rice is a bird as well as a plant, cuckoo is a flower as well as a bird.

Martha and Marius. A single instance of able to pay any day and as you say we exchange ribbons for ribbons and pictures for pictures successfully.

Marius. Is spelled in this way.

Maryas. They saved it why did they save it they saved it as wire. In this way did you hear me say did they save it in this way, did they save it and will they use it in this way.

Maryas and Martha. Maryas and Martha.

Maryas and Martha. Did you hear me say cloudlessly.

Maryas. Yes.

Maryas and Martha. Yes.

Maryas. May be I do but I doubt it.

Martha. I do but I do doubt it.

Martha and Maryas. May be I do but I doubt, I do but I do doubt it.

Marius and Mabel. Please to please. Pleasure to give pleasure.

Marius. To please and to give pleasure.

Marius and Mabel. To please and please and to give pleasure and to give pleasure.

Marius. To please and to give pleasure.

Marius and Mabel. If you please if you please and if you give pleasure.

Marius. If you give pleasure and if you please.

Marius and Mabel. Please please and pleasure.

Marius. I am very pleased I am indeed very pleased that it is a great pleasure.

Martha. If four are sitting at a table and one of them is lying upon it it does not make any difference. If bread and pomegranates are on a table and four are sitting at the table and one of them is leaning upon it it does not make any difference.

Martha. It does not make any difference if four are seated at a table and one is leaning upon it.

Maryas. If five are seated at a table and there is bread on it and there are pomegranates on it and one of the five is leaning on the table it does not make any difference.

Martha. If on a day that comes again and if we consider a day a week day it does come again if on a day that comes again and we consider every day to be a day that comes again it comes again then when accidentally when very accidentally every other day and every other day every other day and every other day that comes again and every day comes again when accidentally every other day comes again, every other day comes again and every other and every day comes again and accidentally and every day and it comes again, a day comes again and a day in that way comes again.

Maryas. Accidentally in the morning and after that every evening and accidentally every evening and after that every morning and after that accidentally every morning and after that accidentally and after that every morning.

Maryas. After that accidentally. Accidentally after that.

Maryas. Accidentally after that. After that accidentally.

Maryas and Martha. More Maryas and more Martha.

Maryas and Martha. More Martha and more Maryas.

Martha and Maryas. More and more and more Martha and more Maryas.

Marius. It is spoken of in that way.

Mabel. It is spoken of in that way.

Marius and Mabel. It is spoken in that way and it is spoken of in that way.

Marius and Mabel. It is spoken of in that way.

Mabel. I speak of it in that way.

Marius. I have spoken of it in that way and I speak it in that way. I have spoken of it in that way.

Mabel. I speak of it in that way.

Mabel. Spelled in this way.

Marius. Spelled in that way.

Mabel. Spelled in this way and spelled in that way and spoken of in this way and spoken of in that way and spoken in this way.

Martha. In this way. If in a family where some member is devoutly religious another member of the family is ill, other members are not at home and other members have been killed in war, a ball is given for whose benefit is the ball given. For the benefit of the three young ladies who have not as yet left their home.

Martha and Maryas. It was unexpected but intended, it was intended and expected, it was intended.

Maryas. It was intended and in a reasonable degree and not unreasonably she valued it as she was intended to value it as she was expected to value as she expected to value as she intended to value. She did intend to remain. Remember she did intend to remain. She did intend to remain remember she did intend to she intended to remain.

Martha. Not too merrily for me. She had thirty three thirds. Safely. In this way she has a standard, she keeps to it and although she may be although she may be although she will be changed, she will change.

Maryas. Not too long.

Maryas and Martha. Not too long.

Maryas. To long and to long.

Martha. To long.

Maryas. Able to long able to be and to be safely to be safely able to be safely to be safely to be seen to be seen able to long to be safely to safely be here and there to be there. Able to be there. To long. Who is longing now.

Martha. Change songs for safety, change their songs for their safety. Safely change their songs.

Maryas. Change songs and change singing and change singing songs and change singing songs for singing songs.

Martha. Not how do you do.

Maryas. Not yet.

Maryas and Martha. And not yet and not who are you and how are you not how are you.

Martha and Maryas. And not yet not how are you and where are you and how are you and not yet how and where are you and we are here.

Maryas and Martha. Where are you.

Maryas and Martha. How are you.

Martha and Maryas. How do you do and how are you.

Marius. As a change from this.

Marius. In a way to change in that way to change this.

Marius. In this way.

Marius. To change in this way.

Marius. And if they were in various ways differently decided, and if they were delighted, no not delighted, and if they were accidentally relieved and repeatedly received and reservedly deceived, if they were separately announced and deposed and respectfully recalled and regularly preceded, indeed they were there indeed they were there and in the way of it all and why did they ask what do they mean when they say that hay is no more fruitful than fruit and birds no more plentiful than battles. Battles are arranged here and there. Battles are arranged for here and there. Streets have been named so they have, a street might be named Battle Street.

Mabel. And if they were to be here and there and they are very often here, will I be pleased.

Marius and Mabel. If they are very often here and there and they are very often here and they are very often here.

Mabel and Marius. They are here very often.

Martha. Yes and know.

Maryas. Yes.

Martha. Every day by the by every day has a connection between what happened when she kneeled and what she left when she came back to kneel.

Maryas. Every day has a connection by the by every day has a connection between when she went and when she was separately sent.

Martha. Every day has a connection between six and seven in the morning and the disturbances of certainly causing and the disturbance of certainly calling and the disturbance of certainly returning and the disturbance of certainly telling that no address was given. That is a strange story of the address that was found and turned out to be given by her and it was her habit to give her address written down to be written down. We do not color her for that, this does not color her, this does not make lilacs white, they mostly are when they are made in winter.

Maryas. Made in winter, when they are made in winter.

Maryas and Martha. This is not an instance of being polite and perfect.

Maryas. Eighty and eighty pages.

Martha. Eight and eight pages.

Martha and Maryas. Eight pages and eighty pages.

Martha. An instance and for instance, for instance did she leave her key and for instance were we pleased to see that she came to be carefully pleased to be that she came to be carefully that she came to be careful.

Maryas. Contents and intend. I intend to be careful of ashes Tuesdays kneeling and prizes. I intend to be careful of kneeling Tuesdays ashes and prizes.

Martha. We have allowed for it.

Maryas. You do prepare it for me.

Martha & Maryas. We do we will and not forever.

Marius. How do you spell Marius.

Mabel. How do you spell Mabel.

Mabel and Marius. We spell them both correctly.

LIST A

Maryas Martha Marius Mabel.

Maryas Martha Marius Mabel. A list may be taken care of.

Maryas Martha Marius Mabel. If a list is taken care of by five, if five are sitting at a table if four are seated at a table and one is leaning upon it it does not make any difference.

Marius Martha Maryas Mabel. If five are seated at a table and one is leaning upon it it does not make any difference.

Marius Martha Maryas. And if there are four seated at a table and one is leaning upon it it does not make any difference.

Maryas. An instance of this is when we have all meant to be well dressed.

Maryas. An instance of this is when we have all meant to be well dressed.

Maryas. Dress well.

Martha. I know.

Maryas & Martha. We know how.

Maryas Mabel Martha and Maryas. We know how now.

Martha and Maryas. A sector is a piece cut out, a fragment is a piece broken off and an article is all of one piece.

Maryas. Stems and pleasantness.

Maryas. I see I see how creditably and when they stand and she stands and there are stands.

Martha. And how creditably they prepare and she prepares and there are there as there are.

Maryas. And how creditably if they care.

Martha. Very creditable as who can share their thanks for that. Yes that is it and we are not excited.

Martha & Maryas. If you can only tell him so.

Martha & Maryas. If they do and plenty of them would.

Martha. If we do.

Maryas. Can you procure a place for a pillar.

Martha. And he thought of it and saw it.

Martha & Maryas. He thought of it and saw to it.

Martha. That which is lost becomes first comes first to be sent.

Maryas. And might it be predicted by me.

Martha. Extravagantly very extravagantly.

Martha and Maryas. We translate this into that and Mary is so gracious and Mary.

Martha. A second list makes one day, a second list makes some day, a second list makes Monday, a second list makes Sunday, a second list makes more than one day a second list makes one day and makes one day.

Maryas. We never kissed, we have never kissed.

Martha. A second list.

Martha & Maryas. A second list makes a second list.

Marius. If you do prepare to carry olives away from olive trees and rain away from rain and you are necessarily in that case pleased with me are you in earnest when you say that there are plenty of pleasures left.

Mabel. One hundred and one make a second list as naturally one hundred finishes one, probably the first one.

Marius and Mabel. We could be married.

Maryas. One authority.

Martha. No monotony is necessary since I do visit. You do visit, yes I do wisely to visit where my visits are appreciated.

Maryas. Is wisdom perfect.

Martha. And festive.

Marius and Mabel. A Sunday is marked as a Sunday.

Maryas. In this way perfectly.

Martha. In this way not so carefully.

Marius & Mabel. In this way they are allowed to retaliate.

THIRD LIST

Maryas. Texas.

Martha. Mary.

Maryas and Martha. Texas berry.

Maryas. To meet to meet me here.

Martha. To meet me here.

Martha & Maryas. To meet me here.

Maryas. Examples of wool.
Samples of wool.
Samples of silk and wool. Sheep and wool.
Lions and wool.
Lions and sheep and wool. Lions and sheep and wool and silk. Silk and sheep and wool and silk. Silk and sheep, silk and wool, silk and sheep and silk and wool and silk. Sheep and silk and wool and silk and sheep.

Martha. If a feather meant a feather and if a feather meant a feather, we would gather together and it would not matter. What would not matter. My dear it would not matter.

Martha In a minute.

Marius And a third.

Maryas A third of it.

Mabel and Mary. A fourth.
A fourth of it.

Martha. In a minute and a third a third of it.

Marius. A third of it and in a minute a fourth of it.

Mabel. In a minute and a fourth of it in a minute and a fourth of it.

Mary. In a minute and a fourth of it, a third of it and in a minute and a third and a fourth of it.

Maryas. We calm.

Martha. We can call silver silver.

Marius. We can mix silver with silver.

Mabel. We can mix more silver with silver.

Mary. We can mix more than silver with more than silver.

Maryas Martha Marius Mabel and Mary. If there are four seated at a table and one of them is leaning upon it it does not make any difference.

Martha. If I am displeased.

Martha. One may say that one may say that a brother tardily marries.

Maryas. In this way.

Maryas and Martha. Make it selected.

Maryas. We were not confused by separation.

Martha and Marius. If you confuse if you are separated by confusion, if you exchange standing for standing, I often think about exchanging standing for standing.

Martha. Anybody can anybody settle it for me.

Martha. We have met, to be safely arrived. To exchange kneeling for kneeling.

Martha & Maryas. And thoughtful.

Martha. In no great merriment.

Martha and Maryas. I have exactly they have exactly they have called them all in.

Martha. Equally so.

Maryas. It is very well to know this.

Martha. I have no longer any actual reason for this as well.

Maryas. Very evenly.

Martha and Maryas. Can we say we do not.

Martha & Maryas. Fourteen and more are inconsistent.

Martha. Fourteen and more and they are one may believe, they are one may believe liable to abuse.

Martha. Indeed for them and differently preserved pears.

Martha & Maryas. Indeed for them.

Martha & Maryas. In a minute or very nervously or very nervously or in a minute.

Martha. Next to their end.

Martha & Maryas. They left it a half an hour later.

Martha and Maryas. Return it to me.

Martha and Maryas. Two at half past one.
Three at half past two.

Martha and Maryas. Three at half past three.

Martha. I present well.

Maryas. I represent well.

Martha and Maryas. We are pleased to be represented by them for them.

Martha. What was it that was said.

Maryas. No secrets.

Martha and Maryas. No secrets and no secrecy.

Martha Marius Maryas and Mabel. To see and to see.

Martha Marius Maryas Mabel and Mary. To see and to see and to see.

Martha. We are not to see.

Maryas. I am to see where I am to go and what I am to do.

Martha. You do and I do.

Maryas. You do too.

Martha & Maryas. They do believe that no secrets and not secretly will make investigation easy.

LIST FIVE

Martha. This is the way a play fades away.

Martha. You praise me as you say.

Maryas. Ordinarily in this way.

Martha and Maryas. Ordinarily you praise me as you say you say you praise me.

Martha. And a measure. To measure exactly how often six and one, how very often six and one how often is there to be reasonable certainty. How often are they reasonably certain. Six and one and not another more than one.

Maryas. I smile for certainty.

Martha Maryas Mabel and Martin. Martin too was certain to be known. How are you known you are known by your name and your share. Share and share alike.

Mabel Martha and Maryas. Rain mingles with water and a tree can be sweet and can you mingle water with rain and suck at a tree.

Martha. Mentions the place.

Maryas. Yields abundant resemblance.

Mabel. Needs only adequate calls.

Marius. Needs only division of birth.

Martin. Only needs mentioning here.

Mary. Only needs mentioning here.

Martha and Maryas. If they ask me to leave them and they ask them to leave me if they ask me to leave them and they ask them to leave if they ask them to leave and they ask me if they ask me and if they ask them, if they ask them and if they ask them and if they ask them and if they ask me if they ask I say yes that is it.

Maryas. They said he said, he said, two centers, two centers, two surroundings, two surroundings, two centers, and two centers, and they centre, and their center, they centre, they do not centre here.

Mabel. Mabel little Mabel with her face against the pane and it may as can say wistfulness may no wistfulness may, they come again to-day and to-morrow they go to America.

Martin. Exactly Martin, and may useful and preliminary offshoots.

Marius. Recognise it by the name in the way of deliberation and baskets. A great many baskets are made here and there and with some care, that is to say one may give an order to them and indeed they may fulfill. They may even learn to weave and braid officially and not fancifully and in this way they have many certainties and many mountains and a cow, I doubt if they will have a cow. I say they advisedly and speaking entirely in a different sense. You do understand me.

Mary. Mary may no I may say may Mary. So that season is anonymous and indeed easily as they own land in town and country.

A LAST LIST

Marius. Choose to choose you cannot expect me to choose you.

Martha. Carrots and artichokes marguerites and roses. If you can repeat it and somebody chose it, somebody shows it, somebody knows it. If you can repeat and somebody knows it.

Maryas. Half of the marriages, valentines and half of the marriages. I did the valentines and half of the marriages.

Mabel. A little girl is very nearly the same size as she was she was very nearly the same prize and we may say excited.

May. And Mary.

Martha
Mabel
Maryas We may marry.
and
Mary.

CAPITAL CAPITALS

Almost anything that led Stein to "this and that" was a word idea that could become writing. Provence sharpened her eye for geography and led her to the four capital cities, Aix, Arles, Avignon, and Les Beaux. Before the end of 1922, the word *capital* became the lever for play with the four cities that then trailed others—Palma, Barcelona, Marseilles—and bits of regional detail and history. Capital cities, their names capitalized, lead to capital letters. Three of the capitals start with *A* and the fourth with *B*, which yields alphabetical and enumerative order. As nouns, adjectives, and adverbs, capitals allow exercises of grammar and idiom about place, "in the first place," "in the second place," "in sight of," "in the way," "beside," "at my side." The capitals are machines that generate talk and become characters in a play.

This play is assembled like a musical composition. Stein relied loosely on grids of four to place her words and expressions in order. Yet the order never becomes a rigid frame enforcing compositional obeisance. The stiff "Capital One. / Capital Two. / Capital Three. / Capital Four" is offset by the playful "capital wool . . . / Capitally for wool," "Ardently silk," "Camel's hair," "Eider Down." The piece becomes a kind of four-part madrigal whose surprises belie its order. Stein's fascination with the number four is apparent in many pieces of this time, including *A List, Lend a Hand or Four Religions,* and *A Village Are You Ready Yet Not Yet.* She uses "four" as a springboard for punning her way from word to word rather than allowing the great square power of "four" to dominate her movement.

The text is printed here as Stein wrote it and Toklas typed it, including apparent irregularities that are in fact part of the process that is the essence of this text. Stein used centered headings and single and double indentations to make textual distinctions. She made distinctions in meaning with capital and lowercase letters. "The fourth Capital" is not the same as "The fourth capital." *Operas and Plays,* however, eliminated distinctions essential to the writing by regularizing capitalizations and indentations.

Capital Capitals with its formal design was a natural choice for Virgil Thomson to set to music, for four male voices and piano, in the spring of 1927. Thomson always acknowledged that his skill with prosody came from exposure to Stein texts. Yet most studies of his work have treated such Stein texts as *Capital Capitals* as nonsense going nowhere and failed to relate Thomson's scores to Stein's pieces as meaningful designs.

• • • • •

Capitally be.
Capitally see.

It would appear that capital is adapted to this and that. Capitals are capitals here.

Capital very good.
Capital Place where those go when they go.
Capital. He has capital.

We have often been interested in the use of the word capital. A state has a capital a country has a capital. An island has a capital. A main land has a capital. And a portion of France has four capitals and each one of them is necessarily on a river or on a mountain. We were mistaken about one of them.

This is to be distressing.

We now return to ourselves and tell how nearly the world is populated.

First a capital.

Excitement.

Sisters.

First capital.

When we were on an island it was said that there was a capital there. And also that there was a capital on the mainland.

Did he and his wife and his sister expect to eat little birds.

Little birds least of all.

All the capitals that begin with A.

Aix Arles and Avignon.

Those that begin with be Beaux.

That makes four.

These that begin with B.

Barcelona.

Those that begin with m.

Marseilles and Mallorca.

You mean Palma.

Yes P.

Palma de Mallorca.

Do this in painting.

Will you have a strawberry.

Outcropping of the central mountain formation.

Mountain formation and capitals.

Strawberries and capitals.

Letters a b and m and capitals.

Capitals.

First Capital	Capital C.
Second Capital	Capital D.
Third Capital	Capital Y.
Fourth Capital	Capital J.

Fourth Capital. They said that they were safely there.

Third Capital. Safer there than anywhere.

Second Capital. They came there safely.

First Capital. They were said to be safely here and there.

First Capital. Capital wool.

When we say capital wool we mean that all wool pleases us.

Capitally for wool.

First Capital. Egypt.

Second Capital. Rabbit.

Third Capital. Fingering.

Fourth Capital. Ardently silk.

Fourth Capital. Spontaneously married.

Third Capital. Camel's hair.

Second Capital. Eider Down.

First Capital. Chenille.

First Capital. It comes from the caterpillar I think.

Second Capital. If travellers come and a rug comes, if a rug comes and travellers have come everything has come and travellers have come.

Third Capital. The third capital, they have read about the third capital. It has in it many distinguished inventors of electrical conveniences.

Fourth Capital. In how many days can every one display their satisfaction with this and their satisfaction.

Fourth Capital. Let us count the fourth capital. Rome Constantinople Thebes and Authorisation.

Third Capital. There are a great many third capitals.

Second Capital. Surrounding second capitals are third capitals and first capitals.

First Capital. The first capital reminds me of derision.

First Capital. Decide.
Second Capital. To reside.
Third Capital. And what beside.
Fourth Capital. My side.
Fourth Capital. At my side.
Third Capital. And when can they say that there is no room there.
Second Capital. When a great many people filter.
First Capital. In.
First Capital. They play ring around a rosy.
Second Capital. They play London bridges.
Third Capital. They play High Spy.
Fourth Capital. They play horses.
Fourth Capital. We have all forgotten what horses are.
Third Capital. We have all forgotten what horses there are.
Second Capital. We have all forgotten where there are horses.
First Capital. We have all forgotten about the horses.

Capital this and capital that. This is capital and that is capital.

First Capital. Capital One.
Second Capital. Capital Two.
Third Capital. Capital Three.
Fourth Capital. Capital Four.
Capital Four.
Fourth Capital. The fourth capital is the one where we do dream of peppers. It is astonishing how a regular curtain can be made of red peppers. A long curtain and not too high.
Third Capital. The third capital is one in which thousands of apples are red in color and being so they make us in no way angry.
Second Capital. The second capital is one in which butter is sold. Can butter be sold very well.
First Capital. The first capital is the one in which there are many more earrings. Are there many more earrings there than elsewhere.
Capital One. Acclimated. We are acclimated to the climate of the first capital.

Capital Two.	We are acclimated to the climate of the second capital.
Capital Three.	If in regard to climates if we regard the climate, if we are acclimated to the climate of the third capital.
Capital Four.	The climate of capital four is the climate which is not so strange but that we can be acclimated to it. We can be acclimated to the climate of the fourth capital.
Fourth Capital.	If every capital has three or four who lock their door and indeed if we mean to care for their home for them we can complain of lack of water. Water can be bought.
Third Capital.	If in any capital there are three or four who mean to present themselves tenderly then indeed can we silence ourselves by thanking. We can thank then.
Second Capital.	If in any capital they are more seldom seen more and more seldom, if they are more and more seldomly seen what then what of them.
First Capital.	If in every capital there are more than there were before how may a capital continue this preparation. They prepare themselves to say that they will stay.
First Capital.	In the first place the first capital is very well placed.
Second Capital.	In the second place the second capital has more sugared melon.
Third Capital.	In the third place the third capital is aroused.
Fourth Capital.	In the fourth place all four capitals have many shovels.
Fourth Capital.	Except me.
Third Capital.	Accept me.
Second Capital.	Expect me.
First Capital.	Except me.
First Capital.	I do I will.
First Capital.	Very still.
Second Capital.	Catalogue.
Third Capital.	A station.
Fourth Capital.	It is Sunday and beside it is raining.
Fourth Capital.	Spoken.
Third Capital.	Outspoken.
Second Capital.	Presses.

First Capital.	Addresses.
First Capital.	Counting.
Second Capital.	Recounting.
Third Capital.	Extra meals.
Fourth Capital.	Spaces.
Fourth Capital.	Indeed.
Third Capital.	Hearty Kisses.
Second Capital.	In a minute.
First Capital.	Shut the door.
First Capital.	In this way in as they say this way, in this way they say they are as they may say this way. In this way things matter.
First Capital.	Cannot express can express tenderness.
First Capital.	In this way as they say in this way as they say they cannot express tenderness. As they say in the way they say they can express in this way tenderness, they can express tenderness in this way.
Second Capital.	If they are good if they are good to me if I can see that they are good if I can see that they are good to me, if I would if I could I could say that they are good if I would say that they are good to me, if I could if I would, if they could be good if they would be good if they are good, are they good are they good to me do you hear me say that they could be good did they hear me say that they could be good, that they are good that I say that they are good to me.
Third Capital.	If they belong to being more than strong, do they care to be strong do they care to belong do they belong to being strong. If they hear a second day do they say a second day comes before a first day any way. Capitally strong do they belong does it belong to them to be capitally strong. I will say so to-day. They do not answer me in syllables.
Fourth Capital.	To settle and to settle well, to settle very well to settle. Do they settle do we settle do I settle do they settle very well do they settle well do we settle, well do we. Do I settle. Do I settle very well. Very well I do settle. I do settle very well. They do settle very well.

Fourth Capital. Resemble it.

Third Capital. To resemble it.

Second Capital. They resemble it.

First Capital. They resemble.

First Capital. I state that the first capital is the one that has been won to see it settle on itself denial. I deny we deny they deny. I deny what that they are safely there and no one comforted him.

Second Capital. Do not annoy any one needing to feel strongly that if wishes were horses beggars would ride and why are ridden horses still used, why are they still used why are ridden horses still used.

Third Capital. Reasonable wishes do not color reasonable wishes, reasonable wishes are not colored by reasonable wishes, reasonable wishes are rarely colored to be reasonable wishes.

Fourth Capital. Mountains are not merely out croppings they are usefully employed in reasonable association. We reasonably associate with one another and are elaborately aware of waiting. Wait again for me.

Fourth Capital. Capitals are plenty there are plenty of capitals.

Third Capital. Why do they enjoy capitals and why are capitals places rapidly united. We unite ourselves together.

Second Capital. The capital seems to be the capital.

First Capital. A capital is not easily undertaken nor is it easily aroused nor indeed is it impervious.

First Capital. Thoroughly.

Second Capital. And very pleasantly.

Third Capital. Nearer to it than that.

Fourth Capital. Eagerly accepted.

Fourth Capital. They are.

Third Capital. They do.

Second Capital. They will.

First Capital. They are to-night.

First Capital. Paul.

Second Capital. Not Paul.

Third Capital. Paul Cook.

Fourth Capital. Three Capitals in all.

Fourth Capital. I intend to learn to stay away.
Third Capital. I intend to endeavor consolation.
Second Capital. Many win.
First Capital. Many many times in the way.
First Capital. Happily a little calling and covering.
Second Capital. Happily a very little changing and repeating.
Third Capital. Very happily properly placed as a castle.
Fourth Capital. We were very content with the inroad.
Fourth Capital. Inlay.
Third Capital. He mentions me.
Second Capital. Am I in it.
First Capital. He leaves the kitchen as well.
First Capital. In sight of the first capital because of this capital beside this as a capital because of this as their capital and becoming this becoming their possession by way of this and their having the possession, permit to credit you with an excellent reason for remaining here. Permit me to do this and also permit me to assure you that coming again is not as pleasant as coming again and again and coming again and again is very nearly the best way of establishing where there is the most pleasure the most reasonableness the most plenty the most activity, the most sculpture the most liberty the most meditation the most calamity and the most separation. If rose trees are cut down again and again he can be busily engaged and if he is busily engaged can he nourish hope and if he nourishes hope can he converse and if he converses can he say he hopes that some day he will supply the same that he did supply when the sun heated and the sun heated. When the mountains are near by and not high little mountains made at the right angle are not high and yet we can imply that they are neither near by nor high and they are near by and they are near high. The capital was nearly eight hundred miles away. This gives me no idea of its distance of the distance from here to there.
Second Capital. For capitals.

If a second capital has pleased them all if a second

capital is second only in such a way that there is no reason to arouse me, to arouse me, a second capital in all a second capital, does he know that he found it to be so, does he know that he has told us that in walking that in walking he has been more than sufficiently clearly seeing that if a park is green that if a park is green may he be sure of his path may he and may he in association may he in his place may he in such a place may he indeed might he have been employed in such a place and in what way was he employed was it in relation to meat to vegetables to bread to cake to fruit to ices or indeed was it in relation to the homes where all who are religious find themselves crowded. Did he crowd in. No indeed, he meditated in this way, every noon as soon as he was responsible and he was he was responsible to no one, to wife and child and all and he came at their call. Call again.

I often mention what has been seen no no one can say more no one can say any more than that it has been seen that a king has been seen not a king not has been seen not that a king has been seen, not that there has been seen, not that there has been seen not a king not that there has been seen, and when did he wish to waver, waver and waver, and when did he wish to wave it away, wave it away and he will say to-day and January for a day.

Third Capital. I see, say that I see. I see that I say that I see.

Fourth Capital. He went to stay and had his father and his mother been there long. Had his father and his mother been there long and was there no reason for that. Was there no reason for this and he was not found to be splendid. Who was really the manager of the distribution of light. He was not prepared to receive them here and there. Here and there, here and there. Read it again. Here and there.

Fourth Capital. Has a reason.

Third Capital. For this.

Second Capital.	More than all.
First Capital.	The rest.
First Capital.	Did they clear themselves of men and women and did they seem to be able to be especially related.
Second Capital.	Did they seem to be especially related and did they fasten their bamboos as hedges every two years.
Third Capital.	Did they fasten their bamboos as hedges every two years and did they have any objection to their rejection.
Fourth Capital.	Were they really rejected and did they object as it would seem that they did.
The fourth Capital.	If they have to do this and they have to do this, if they have to do this can they attend to their daisies.
The third capital.	And if they attend to their stones and stones are in a way useful can they attend to baggage.
The Second Capital.	In attending to baggage a great many are caught in the rain.
The first capital.	It is Sunday and beside it is raining.
The first capital.	It is too cold to rain.
First Capital.	In the meantime do you see. Yes I see. In the meantime do you see me. Yes I do see you.
Second Capital.	If you went and if you came if they came if you went and came, indeed spring does come before winter that is to say even here. Now understand what I mean. One may say that winter is as winter. They meant to winter.
Third Capital.	Met again or not met.
Fourth Capital.	I see you see he sees me, he can see you can see they can see me.
Fourth Capital.	I meant to say that.
Third Capital.	They meant that beside.
Second Capital.	Ignorant negroes.
First Capital.	Not as ignorant as negroes.
First Capital.	Capital for capital and who knows better than that that capital is mine.

Capital for capital.
Crowd for crowd.
Out loud for out loud.
Crowd for crowd.

Capital for capital.

Second Capital. Capitally.

Capital for Capital.
Question for question.
A caress for a caress.
A river for a river and a spring for a spring. Spring comes very early here, it comes before the days are longer.
Capital for capital.
Candy for candy.
Curtains for curtains and crowds for crowds.
Crowds for crowds.
Curtains for curtains.
Candy for candy and capital for capital.

Third Capital. Capitals for capitals.

Plants for plants.
Bridges for bridges and beds for beds.
Beds for beds.
Bridges for bridges.
Plants for plants and capitals for capitals.

Fourth Capital. Capital Capitals.

Capitally.
Capitally Capable.
Articles for articles.
Buds for buds.
Combs for combs and lilies for lilies.
Lilies for lilies.
Combs for combs.
Buds for buds.
Articles for articles.
And capitals for capitals.
We know how to remove harness and grass.
Capitals for capitals.
Fourth Capital. And capitals for capital.

Third Capital.	And capital and capital.
Second Capital.	And more than capital.
First Capital.	For their capital.
First Capital.	Yes yes.
First Capital.	Able to able to able to go able to go and come able to come and go able to come and go able to do so.

In this way we may date to-day.

What is the date to-day.

What is the date to-day.

I wish to tell all I know about Capitals.

Capitals are the places where every one exactly deprecates the necessity of going away, where every one deprecates the necessity there is to stay where every one utters a welcome that is sufficiently stirring and where every one does know what makes them so, so what so very nearly wider.

Now let me see why capitals are steadily repeated.

I repeat the first Capital.

I repeat I repeat.

I repeat the Second Capital.

You repeat you repeat.

I repeat the third Capital.

We repeat we repeat.

I repeat the fourth Capital.

They repeat they repeat.

I repeat that a capital is a treat.

I repeat that they retreat from the capital and that they retreat.

I repeat that they compete for a capital.

I repeat that they compete.

Do they compete.

I repeat that they defeat that they defeat that they defeat that they deplete that they complete that they seat a great many people in there and it is it is there that they are seated. I know why I say what I do say. I say it because I feel a great deal of pleasure of satisfaction of repetition of indication of separation of direction of preparation of declaration of stability of precaution of accentuation and of attraction. And why do you spare little silver mats. Little silver mats are very useful and silver is very pretty as to color.

CEZANNE

That this portrait was important to Stein is plain from her return to it in her lecture *Pictures* (1934–35), where she comments on Cézanne, Matisse, Picasso, and Juan Gris, the four great painters of her life. She speaks of painting as subject matter, as painting, and of the painter as person. The title *Cezanne* tells nothing about her portrait. Our difficulties in reading arise between what the words name and what they do. To discover what *Cezanne* is, we look at its composition.

The portrait is an intricacy of verbal motifs. There are the Irish lady and Caesar (does Caesar pair with Cézanne by punning on "sees" and "says"?), with their odd sense of the quotidian. To her every day is like the last and the next, and nothing ever changes. To him, all days are his own. "To-day is every day," "Every day is to-day." To the rest of us, every day is as each says, all the same or all different.

Single, small words join in motifs. "Day" moves to "way," "stay," and of course "say." Like the thoughts about every day, the words seem identical, yet different, echoing in eye and ear by repetition, rhyme, alliteration, and end letter. Phrases build by increments—"settled," "settled to stay," "settled to stay Saturday"; "in this way a mouth is a mouth," "if in as a mouth." Linked by variety, words and phrases move about in the piece. Grass that grows nearly four times yearly collapses time and space into one.

Lightly, in the little words, appear hints of a southern landscape—a garden, bees, honey. A mouth for flowing water—Bouches du Rhône—may also become a mouth for speech. Woven into the verbal landscape are words of devotion—*prayer, patient, absolution,* and again, *water*. Three times, almost exactly at the center and supported by *you* and *too,* is the color blue, water color, a precious value for Cézanne, for religious iconography, and for Stein's association with Toklas.

It was the painter on the editorial staff of the *Reader* who in the end spoke to readers of *Cezanne:*

> If I paint or write your portrait, why should *you* be there? How could *you* be *there?* Of course you are not there, I can evoke you with hints. If Stein had not entitled this piece *Cezanne,* would it still stand as a portrait of Cézanne? Cézanne in his settled, unchanging daily routine of visiting the motif, losing himself in its endless subtle manifestations, which after all no one had noticed before. Cézanne's mountain, his chateau, his quarry are each and every one totally absorbing on their own solid terms. Each individual canvas in a series is itself more than a sum of its parts and more than the sum of the series. Perhaps Stein is saying something like this in the "every day is today," "today is every day" series. The universal in the particular.
>
> So the answer to the question, "Is this still a portrait of Cézanne if it is not so titled," is, yes. Or is it a portrait of *a* Cézanne? Render unto Caesar and the Irish lady,

yes, but Stein is again, as in many other portraits, saying, "Thank you" to Cézanne for her rich days with him in Provence.

• • • • •

The Irish lady can say, that to-day is every day. Caesar can say that every day is to-day and they say that every day is as they say.

In this way we have a place to stay and he was not met because he was settled to stay. When I said settled I meant settled to stay. When I said settled to stay I meant settled to stay Saturday. In this way a mouth is a mouth. In this way if in as a mouth if in as a mouth where, if in as a mouth where and there. Believe they have water too. Believe they have that water too and blue when you see blue, is all blue precious too, is all that that is precious too is all that and they meant to absolve you. In this way Cezanne nearly did nearly in this way Cezanne nearly did nearly did and nearly did. And was I surprised. Was I very surprised. Was I surprised. I was surprised and in that patient, are you patient when you find bees. Bees in a garden make a specialty of honey and so does honey. Honey and prayer. Honey and there. There where the grass can grow nearly four times yearly.

AN ELUCIDATION

The title *An Elucidation* sounds philosophical and theoretical. We expect a credo, a statement of method, perhaps the key to meaning. Yet Stein refuses to explain writing and to distinguish theory and practice. To her, real writing comes from inside while theory is imposed from outside, freezing what should remain supple, flexible, and alive. She offers no key, no one-stop shortcut to tell us what she means, except what she says. Writing is its own elucidation. As Alice said in Wonderland, it means what it says and it says what it means.

What does it mean is not only a question asked by readers of Stein but also the prototype question in schoolrooms. Stein becomes a schoolteacher who elucidates step by methodical step. Her schoolroom is a social place, where she picks up anything at hand to show and tell what it is, including what talking about it is. Here she makes us sit down with a paradigm, "May we seat. May we be having a seat. May we be seated. . . ." She quickly adds a differentiating variant, "May we see." Nouns and verbs, varying verb forms, stressed and unstressed syllables, rhyme words and homophones—so many terms, but how much simpler and clearer to follow examples. "I will now give more examples," she says, and sometimes she even numbers them for the sake of order. And more teacher's language, with appropriate gestures, "Suppose or supposing that you had an invitation . . ." and "If I say I stand and pray," then what she is saying is this, not something else paraphrasing this. She asks pupils to listen, readers to follow literally.

A meditation upon elements of writing that are everywhere at hand but not systematized, *An Elucidation* invites us to enter, look, listen, and participate, not to wait for paraphrase and principles. It is the self-portrait of a writer in the act of telling about the world. Everything changes and moves, bit by tiny bit, phrase upon phrase. The teacher puts it in order, "A place for everything and everything in its place." If rivers flow and harbors wash over, can you have them? Can you halve them? Can you make a sentence about having or halving them? Children in schoolrooms fidget when no explanation carries them across a gulf of incomprehension about "principal and secondary." They try or refuse, "I think I won't / I think I will / I think I will / I think I won't." Suddenly Miss Stein asks, "May I see Martha. . . ." Who is Martha?

In February 1923 Carl Van Vechten received Stein's new book, *Geography and Plays* (1922), a collection of work done before and during the war that marked a new start after the war. He wrote that the new volume was a forecast of major recognition and asked about her still-unpublished big book, *The Making of Americans.* By April, he requested a section of the typescript of the novel for submission to his own publisher.

Alfred Knopf. He asked her not to raise her hopes, but Stein foresaw not only getting her book into print but also being taken on by a distinguished publisher.

One impulse for *An Elucidation* in the spring of 1923 was her own review of her work provoked by the publication of *Geography and Plays.* Her style had changed greatly, but her convictions had not. She had composed *The Making of Americans,* including the character of Martha Hersland, who embodied much of herself, by the method of accumulating perceptions that she now followed in new forms. What her writing meant was also bound to come up in reviews of the new book by others. It might also be raised about the long novel. In *An Elucidation,* written partly in St.-Rémy and partly in Paris and extensively revised, she looked at how she wrote. Unlike the rationalizations of method offered three years later in the lecture *Composition as Explanation,* this piece is writing in process. Elucidating it is reading it.

• • • • •

Halve Rivers and Harbors.

Elucidation.
First as Explanation.
Elucidate the problem of halve.
Halve and have.
Halve Rivers and Harbors,
Have rivers and harbors.

You do see that halve rivers and harbors, halve rivers and harbors, you do see that halve rivers and harbors makes halve rivers and harbors and you do see, you do see that you that you do not have rivers and harbors when you halve rivers and harbors, you do see that you can halve rivers and harbors.

I refuse have rivers and harbors I have refused. I do refuse have rivers and harbors. I receive halve rivers and harbors, I accept halve rivers and harbors.

I have elucidated the pretence of halve rivers and harbors and the acceptation of halve rivers and harbors.

This is a new preparation.
Do not share
He will not bestow
They can meditate
I am going to do so.

I have an explanation of this in this way. If we say, Do not share he will not bestow they can meditate I am going to do so, we have organised an irregular commonplace and we have made excess return to rambling. I always like the use of these, but not particularly.

Madrigal and Mardigras.

I do not deny these except in regard to one thing they remind me of Em which is a nickname for Emma. I have always been fond of writing the letter M. and so although Mardigras and Madrigal have more appreciation from me than they might they do not make more questions and more answers passing. He was as if he were going to pass an examination.

I will now give more examples.

She is in and out

It is placed in there

Happily say so

Too happily say so

Very communicative.

I will give other examples to you. I will give the same example to you and to you.

Place. In a place,

A place for everything and everything in its place.

In place in place of everything, in a place.

Again search for me.

She looked for me at me.

May we seat.

May we be having a seat

May we be seated

May I see

May I see

Martha

May I see Martha

May I see.

May I see.

I have written the best example of all before

Able
Idle.
There are four words in all.
There
Why
There
Why
There
Able
Idle.
There are seven in all.
A stall for each.
As tall as each one.

As there are all and four and seven, and seven and four and are four in all and a stall for each one.

We do not think at all of a stall as a box, there used to be a box a loose box and now there are no loose boxes. Boxes are arranged with cement, and so our fancy pleases, and so we may fancy as we please, we may fancy what we please.

There is an excellent example and now I will explain away as if I have been sitting for my portrait every day.

In this way I have made every one understand arithmetic.

To begin elucidating.

If I say I stand and pray.

If I say I stand and I stand and you understand and if I say I pray I pray to-day if you understand me to say I pray to-day you understand prayers and portraits.

You understand portraits and prayers.

You understand.

You do understand.

An introduction and an explanation and I completely introduce as you please.

I completely introduce. Yes you do.

Yes you do.

Yes you do is the longest example and will come at the end.

The longest example.

Yes you do.

Will come at the end.
Disturb
Seated here
I know how to please her.
If I know
If you know how to throw how to throw or to go. I feel that you easily understand that preparation is not everything I understand everything. And now to explain where preparation and preparing show this as an expedition. An expedition is a journey to and for.
Dealing in accelerated authority.
Do not notice this.
Dealing in their delight or daylight.
Do not notice this properly.
Dealing in a regularly arranged decision.
When you wish to diminish.
Let me explain properly.
Properly speaking there is no fear that he will not be prayed for out loud.
Properly speaking there is no fear of neglect. And all words furnish here. I have a great many examples very often.
We do very often,
An explanation of not at all.
Not at all very nearly furnishes us with an illustration. We have mainly added to that.
Now to seriously mean seldom.
It is only seldom that we are selected.
And she knows me.
I will now explain dishes.
I have explained that.
I never do see that I never do see you do see me.
You do see me. A serious explanation.
To explain means to give a reason for in order. He adores her.
You must not be excited before and after. You must make a choice.
I thought perhaps he would not make a choice.
Before and after.
This is an example a very good example or an example.
This is an example or a very good example.
Let me lead you to find this. If in beginning you mention explaining, could he be angry could he really be angry that you had not explained it to him.

Suppose or supposing that you had an invitation, suppose some one had been very inviting supposing some one had given him an invitation supposing you had been inviting him to listen to an explanation suppose there had been an explanation supposing you had given an explanation, I can explain visiting. I can explain how it happened accidentally that fortunately no explanation was necessary.

I explain wording and painting and sealing and closing. I explain opening and reasoning and rolling, I was just rolling. What did he say. He said I was not mistaken and yet I had not when he was not prepared for an explanation I had not begun explaining. It is in a way a cause for congratulation. It is in a way cause for congratulation.

And now to seriously discuss my needing and to discuss very seriously why they have asked for my mediation.

To begin now.

Small examples are preferable.

They are preferred.

And do they stop them. And yet do they stop them.

Preferred as to preference I prefer them.

If you connect them do you connect them.

In this way.

If small examples are preferable and are preferred and they are connected in this way we may say yesterday was nearly seventeen days earlier than to-day, seventeen days earlier in any way. It is connected in this way. Small examples are preferable. They are preferred.

An instance.

Tremble for small examples. I hope you received the three volumes safely.

Tremble for small examples.

It is not easy.

A third part is added to the top and bottom and the middle part is added in between.

Some examples simply

I tire more quickly than you do.

Some examples simply.

Small examples are preferable.

Small examples are preferred.

Brown and white. The nigger and the night and mistaken for mean. I didn't mean to.

I do read better there.

Come on

He consolidated it. That you must not do.

Elucidation.

The sad procession of the unkilled bull. And they stand around.

Two next.

To be next to it.

To be annexed.

To be annexed to it.

We understand that you undertake to overthrow our undertaking.

This is not originally said to frame words this is originally said to underestimate words.

Do you believe in stretches, stretches of time stretches of scenery and stretches of thirds.

Every third time we rhyme, in this way influence is general. Let me recognise copies.

Extra gum.

Gum extra.

Extra gum.

An extra gum.

An extra rubber.

An extra oil.

An extra soap.

And an extra wish.

Wish and White.

Reasons are right.

White and wish.

Reasons for which they have most occasion. They have more occasion for one wish than for another wish.

Do you all understand if you please.

Do you all understand why I explain.

Do you all understand elucidation and extra addresses.

Do you all understand why she sees me.

Do you all understand practice and precept.

Do you all understand principal and secondary.
Do you all understand extraneous memory.
Let me see how earnestly you plead for me.
Let me see.

More beginning.

I begin you begin we begin they begin. They began we began you began I began.

I began you begin we begin they begin. They begin you begin we begin I began.

You began and I began.

I feel the need of a walk in ceremony, of a talk in ceremony of chalk in ceremony. I feel the need of chalk in ceremony.

And it was used too, it was used too.

A settled explanation.

I know the difference between white marble and black marble. White and black marble make a checker board and I never mention either.

Either of them you know very well that I may have said no.

Now to explain.

Did I say explanations mean across and across and carry. Carry me across.

Another Example.

I think I won't
I think I will
I think I will
I think I won't.
I think I won't
I think I will
I think I will
I think I won't.
I think I won't
I think I will
I think I will

I think I won't
I think I will
I think I won't
I think I will
I think I won't.
I think I will
I think I won't
I think I won't
I think I won't
I think I won't
I think I will
I think I won't
Of course
I think I will
I think I won't
I think I won't
I think I will
This is a good example if you do not abuse it.
Where they like.
Can follow where they like.
I think this is a good example.
I think I will.
I am afraid I have been too careful.
I think I will.

Two examples and then an elucidation and a separation of one example from the other one.

I think I will.

Then very certainly we need not repeat.

Can there at this rate can there have been at this rate more and more.

Can at this rate can there have been at this rate can there have been more and more at this rate.

At this rate there can not have been there can not have been at this rate there can not have been more and more at this rate. At this rate there can not have been more and more. There can not have been at this rate, there can not have been more and more at this rate there can not have been more and more at this rate.

What did I say. Full of charms I said.
Full of what. Full of charms I said.
What did I say, full of charms I said.

If in order to see incidentally incidentally I request to see extraordinarily.
If in order to see incidentally I request to see.
I see you I see you too.

A Question.

Should you see me too.

Not a question.

How to combine all this together to make more.
I stopped, I stopped myself.
Combine all these together to make more.

Elucidation.

If in beginning, if in a beginning, I begin to be connectedly and carefully and collectedly if I agree, if in beginning I agree, then I agree you agree and we agree.

If he can recall a boast of victory, I can refuse to be resolutely sure of what he and I both mean to collect.

Now do you see that this is a thing to erase and eradicate.

Do you not see it clearly.

Let me refuse to repair it.

He said that repairs are excellently made.

We have combined to be not at all principally paid. Paid and paid. Do you see halve rivers and harbors and there is no connection.

An example of an event.

If it is an event just by itself is there a question.

Tulips is there a question.

Pets is there a question.

Furs is there a question.

Folds is there a question.

Is there anything in question.

To begin to be told that after she had seen and said she wrote and read.

She read it and she said, she said it and she read it, she wrote and she did indeed change her residence. I have been told that this is an event. If it is an event just by itself is there a question. A great many climates have been quoted. In this way we may expect to see that they have this to see to too. May we quote again.

Should you see me too.

All events, Carrie all events.

All events carry.

In this way researches are easily read.

A short example of stretches of variety.

She made white flowers resemble lilies of the valley and she said do not mean to be prepared to have a goddess of plenty stand in front of a picture.

In this way you see that I have not succeeded.

If at first you don't succeed try try again.

She found china easily adaptable. In using the word china she had in mind porcelain and also painted wood and even painted tin and dishes. She sometimes felt the need of silver and radishes.

Do you measure this by this measure. And altogether what did you say you were to elucidate to-day. By this I mean for this to be seen.

You know how we make it do so and more so, how we make it more so, how we make it even more so.

I lead up to a description of all the birds.

The birds have meant to interest me so have the horses and so indeed have the preparations for cows. So indeed have the preparations so indeed have the preparations, so indeed.

I can see and you can see, you can see and so can I see that I have not made more of it than needs to be made of it. In every way you are satisfied and we have given satisfaction and we have not meant to be swamped by other considerations. And again and once more and frequently from time to time no one has suffered in any way and we are satisfied. It may even be said as if in a joke those who might have to be considered are satisfied. Can you kindly smile.

And now we add that which makes a whole history plainer. What did I say. I said he would tell me the complete history of his life and times. And in this way we recollect perfectly just when he was prepared and just when he was prepared.

Suppose for instance suppose as an instance we mention success. I succeed and you succeed. Yes you succeed very well. You do succeed very well. You do succeed very very well.

Five examples and then the long example entitled Yes you do.

First Example.

How pleasantly I feel contented with that. Contented with the example, content with the example.

As if one example was meant to be succeeded by an example. I remember that he said they can prepare to have it here and to have it there to have it here and there. We have said there to have it there.

First Example.

Suppose, to suppose, suppose a rose is a rose is a rose is a rose.

To suppose, we suppose that there arose here and there that here and there there arose an instance of knowing that there are here and there that there are there that they will prepare, that they do care to come again. Are they to come again.

In this way I have explained that to them and for them that for them alone that to them alone that to them and for them we have no depression. The law covers this, if you say made of fruit or if you say made by the aid of or made with the aid of fruit, or made by using fruit or made with fruit, for the fruit, you see how suddenly if there is in question if there can be any question, what would then compare with their description, with the description of this description. I describe all the time.

The second example is an example of action.

What action.

If you arrange the door, if you arrange the door and the floor. I have lost most of my interest in politics, still it is more interesting than the theater. Brenner says that.

In action.

In every action we can take he knows that if the hair is there and the ears hear and the Caesars share and they linger and if they linger and finger if they finger their pair, if they finger the pair and care to be more hesitant than before if they are to partake in this action, the action is memorable. They can be declared colored by their wish. Wish how can we who are Americans and not credulous remember that there has been written the wished on wish. Do you smile if you do you please you applaud me you say action to take action to behave in action to see their action to dominate their action and their action and do you expect what has been said that some are attempting to hit some one hit some one who was not the one intended to be hit and this is not common this is not common this does not commonly happen in action in their action.

Example third is the one that will show how often every one has cause abundant cause for this and for that.

To explain I will explain. To take the place to take the place of this. In that way. Please help to avail yourself will you please avail yourself of your opportunities.

In this way and in that way they may or they may not, they may avail themselves of their opportunities. We had a long conversation about the way they may and they may not about the way they may avail themselves of their opportunities.

Let us imagine that every one is interested in my wife and children.

One and a million. A million or three. There are three there and here and there there are a hundred and three here and here and there there they are.

How do you do.

We know why we compare we compare this to that, and we share we can share we do share what do they share what do they happen to do what do they to do, what do they do, what do they happen to do why do they do they do it, why do they not do it, why they do they not do this. Do it, oh do do it. Do you do it. How do you do, how do you do it, how do you do it in this way in that way, in the way. They are not in the way. We say they are not there and they say they are here and we say they are here and there. Continue to expect me. I do expect you. You do expect me. We do expect you. We do. We do expect to have you we do expect, do you expect, do you, do you how do you do, how do you do this, how do I do this, how do I do it, how do I do it. How do I do it, I do it, you do it, yes I do do it.

A third example can be too long.

A fourth example shows more plainly what it does show, what does it show, I see you and you see me, I see that you see and you see that I see. A fourth example shows a tendency to declaration.

I declare that they say from Tuesday till Saturday and Friday afternoon too.

I declare I do declare.

And he when we see that they are not as we understood they would be when we see, when we say we see we hear, and when we say we hear we feel and when we say we feel we see and when we say we see we hear.

In this we declare we declare all of us declare what do you declare, declare to me. Declarations rapidly reunited. Action and reaction are equal and opposite. Astonishment means list of persons and places and if she were to be represented there if she were to be represented there. Call me a smiler and fit the fifth exactly.

I fit the fifth exactly.

Yes you do.

This is not an instance. Fit the fifth exactly. Exactly fit the fifth fit it for the fifth. The fifth in this way makes rounding out rounder. If it is round around and rounder if it is around and we tell all we know let me explain directly and indirectly. In the fifth instance there was no coincidence.

Every night generally.

I lead to Yes you do. You lead to yes you do, we lead to yes you do they lead to yes you do.

Yes you do otherwise understood. Otherwise understood. Yes you do. We understand you undertake to overthrow our undertaking. We understand you do understand that we will understand it correctly. Correctly and incorrectly, prepare and prepared, patiently and to prepare, to be prepared and to be particularly not particularly prepared. Do prepare to say Portraits and Prayers, do prepare to say that you have prepared portraits and prayers and that you prepare and that I prepare.

Yes you do.

Organisers.

Yes you do.

Organisation.

Yes you do and you, you do.

To portraits and to prayers.

Yes you do.

PRACTICE OF ORATORY

The practice opens with "four," systematic as a four-part outline. But right away Stein changes the system from numbers to letters, then from capital to lowercase letters. Seven lines into the piece, the outline has become an empty gimmick. The numbers and letters merely make us question what systems of order are good for.

Oratory refers to speech but also to a place of withdrawal for prayer, as in the Latin *orare*, "to pray." Stein withdraws, whether for prayer or from speech. Perhaps "Let us grant to-day . . ." is a prayer for speech. She considers how to begin. "Let us forget to say let us begin as if we were addressing." We need not begin with "Let us begin." Her elaborate attempts to begin are about the difficulty of beginning. She is listening for words, "When I very nearly hear it. . . . I hear it and you hear it." But what she hears is a hailstorm, which leaves her even more insecure "[i]n the practice of orations and the relief of fears." Unrelieved fears become "I have a weakness for exits."

Practice of Oratory is a rehearsal for how to begin a speech, a lecture, an address. One possible occasion for the piece is a letter of 15 May 1923 from Mabel Weeks—a Radcliffe friend who was now a professor at Barnard College—suggesting an American lecture tour. Lecturing was in Stein's mind long before she came to America in 1934 upon the success of the *Autobiography*, and even before the 1926 lectures at Cambridge and Oxford.

Behind Stein lies schooling in the American tradition of public speaking, elocution, lecturing. Consider the *McGuffey Eclectic Readers*. The full title of the fifth edition of 1844 is *McGuffey's Rhetorical Guide or Fifth Reader*. It combines "Elocution" and "Rhetorical Reading." Among the "Principles of Elocution" are articulation, inflection, accent and emphasis, and cultivation and management of the voice. The second and third sections are lessons in reading samples of prose and poetry.

By the end, the four opening letters become headings for examples, often hilariously silly, of what we actually say and how. When we are nervous we beat around the bush, say nothing, or give elaborate, circular openings. Example A defines an "address," to reassure the nervous speaker who does not know how to begin and who will not be helped by a definition. Example B is an example of an example, so involved that the example is emptied of meaning by repetition. Gesture is practiced, effective stance tried out. By the end of Example B, Stein asks Toklas, always her audience, "Dream for me," an impossibility that offers a hope of getting out of the speaking engagement.

Example d shows a mounting sense of success and assurance, "He addresses this to every one." Alice Toklas is "one whose beauty is conceded," and Stein is moved to "pleasure and praise" with one of the great examples of oratory that students memorize in school, Mark Anthony's "I am here in praise of you."

Practice of Oratory was incompletely typed by Alice Toklas. Two pages of the manuscript notebook had stuck together and remained empty when Stein turned the page before concluding. Toklas did not see that the text continued beyond the empty pages and missed the conclusion. The volume *Painted Lace* of the posthumous Yale edition followed Toklas' typescripts and failed to print the conclusion, beginning with "To change it . . . ," which is here restored. After all the hesitation, the piece ends with the wish to escape and a fantasy of success after the speech is given and its advice followed. "Supposing you went to sleep for a minute and everybody did as you said."

• • • • •

PRACTICE OF ORATIONS

Four and their share and where they are.

Practice of Orations.

A.

B.

C.

D.

A. b c and d.

Practice of orations.

A.

ORATORY

I withdraw you drew and he draws, I withdrew neither I nor you neither do I neither do I. It is not as if I spoke, it is not.

Now no more character.

No more character at all.

No more as character.

Let us remember.

Let us say that grant to-day granted any way, let us say grant to-day, he was in cream. In cream and in cream I do not eat cream I do not heat cream I do not heat cream I do not for I do not and yet when you come to think it is not the country for it. Let us forget to say let us begin as if we were addressing, addresses are easily obtained. It is as if in some determination he had dwindled and even so selfishly, can you smile as if it were three long sales. What did we do. If he did do it she was not needed from time to time.

And she wore, and she was and now remember what they will say. Let me ask are you ready yet.

ORATIONS

When I very nearly hear it and I hear it and you hear it when you very nearly hear it, to see is said when you hear, to touch is said when you crowd to fall is said when you call. Call again this can be said when hail, that is a hail storm is mixed with rain. We know very well then that it will not in that case do as much harm.

I do not care if there is no way of expecting all four and knowing them apart. Do you know what do you know. You know you know. Well then.

In the practice of orations and the relief of fears, in the practice of orations and the relief of fears, in the practice of orations and in the relief of fears, he we and they, they and we and he, he and they and we and in the practice of orations and in the relief of fears may we accept that which when sent is not only not acceptable but in a way need not be regarded as a surprise. It is astonishing that nearly in the meantime no one is surprised that that which is sent has been sent and with the choice of sending as if it were to be received. So unequally have astonishment and unalterable recovering astonished the process. I have a weakness for exits, and you, and you and you and you, also you and also you and you also, and also and also you, and as for change of places and as a request come again, as a request. To come again and as a request. I feel this to be oratory.

Let me practice oratory and the practice of orations.

Leaving more to come has it a pointed settlement has it been appointed as a settlement is settlement there something that has been appointed. Have they appointed this as a settlement indeed more so than imagined. You and I indeed you and I you and I may carry pictures to Cahor and in this way a lot we say no one has given or taken away, no one has given and no one has given and give and take, to give and to take.

SPEECH

A speech to him and for him and speech with him. We not to speak and are we to speak. Have you spoken. Do smile to yourself. Do, do. Do and do and if you do, if you do and do, and do, do do.

This is meant to be studies in orations.

Example A.

An address in a simple way of what to say when they come and go away.

And why has there been no declaration of an undertaking and why have they mentioned blue glass and pale yellow glass. In the case of both and also red glass in a summer house the landscape has a different appearance. Why do you smile.

Example B.

An example of how to explain what there is indicated by such examples joined to other examples.

And why have you almost felt the strain why indeed have you and when you are very inclined very nearly inclined to parade packages and certain colored blue colored and very well colored signs, why then indeed it is astounding, they were astonished to learn that there were frequently mounted police at a crossing. In a way it was an announcement. No one felt to blame. No one felt that there would be blame. Not any one certainly would come to be at all blamed and moreover there was representation and addresses. Listen to the addresses.

The first address. If you look to the left and do not see that there is a description below and above and indeed if you hope to be admirably sustained remind me and in so doing remind yourself of the illustrations. The illustration that has been brought to your notice is the following.

They are amazed, no no exchange, they amaze, it is an amazement, and a pretention, no pretention is necessary ruins are ruins and reestablishment, are establishments that have been reestablishment. In this way they are authentic. And allowances. Allowances are made to all and for all and by all and in this way union and celebrations succeed each other in quick succession.

Dream for me.

In dreaming of Mrs. Andrews as you did surprised me.

Example C.

Many many instances of distribution reconstruction and restoration.

If you do do you believe that we have entered after we have mounted the stairway. Indeed not if many are waiting in turn. And what then. Why then we watch something entirely different and do not stay to see it accomplished. And is there no question. Of this there is no question. We do not avoid pressure nor insistence nor even dismay. I do obey. Of course you do.

Example d.

Example d is necessary to show that the emergency if there is an emergency is satisfactorily met.

Meet and met and very well and very well, this may be misread.

To be very kindly reminded by this of Spain, not really of Spain, not really of Spain, not very minutely of sand and strawberries not very minutely of rain and rivers. Have you met with some distraction. Very nearly intentionally and now for an address.

He addresses this to every one.

And mounting, upon this evidence we can decide as we have decided and more beside. And very much more, and very indeed very much more.

I know how linen braided in a certain way enhances the beauty of one whose beauty is conceded. We do not spare pleasure and praise. I am here in praise of you. For this purpose and for this purpose alone I have added this observation. Do not fail to observe the reason of the pleasure we have, you have and we have in corals and colors. Can you find pleasure in such a way. Indeed we can and we do. Do you.

Examples of real oratory.

Allow it, to allow for it, plentifully too the rain will do.

Not not not no

I am making it easy

Not not not.

I am making it easy.

Not not not certainly uncertainly.

Not not not nervously.

Not nervously at all.

Not at all.

Not not at all.

To change it.

I am making it easy.

I can do so.

Practice in oratory makes practice easy.

And then we were impressed by the statement as it was made. It was made in this way. You have said that the best and in the best way in their way they share order and decision. If and I say to you that very suddenly there is transition if peddling makes feeling how easily are prints and people warned. We warned you too.

In this way let us impress this upon ourselves. That never can agreement and disagreement have other than the same opportunity. All opportunities are chosen for their resemblance to land and water. Land and water and south in the south the rain rains at more regular intervals. In the north and by north we frequently mean not more winter. We know very well that winter is not always meant in that way. We mean to go away. Listen and we will come to please you. We listen to you and we listen to you.

The practice of oratory is such that no one hesitates. If you hesitate if you do hesitate and when do you hesitate, indeed and where and why do you hesitate. Plan to hesitate. Hesitation as you may or may not know was a waltz.

Practice of oratory again prepared.

Supposing you went to sleep for a minute and everybody did as you said.

HE AND THEY, HEMINGWAY

This portrait of Hemingway was written in Paris, sometime before the departure of Ernest and Hadley Hemingway for Canada on 16 August 1923. Stein later described it to Sherwood Anderson as "a little skit I presented to him on going away." It also in advance welcomes him back.

Stein starts, as she often does, with the name. She discovers that it rhymes with the occasion, Hemingway/away. In its short form, the name Hem leads to the pronoun "him," the nominative "he" and the plural "they," which can be variously identified. "[H]ead away" is transformed into the characterization "ahead any way" and in turn leads to headhunters, savages, and primitive rituals. Play on "time" also implies *In Our Time*. The portrait requires slow, careful reading, but its elements, while easily overlooked, are methodically assembled and gradually unfold. The verbal transformations may look mechanical but they unmistakably characterize the subject.

Sometimes echoes carry from one piece to another. *An Elucidation,* written not long before this portrait, includes the heading "Madrigal and Mardigras" followed by "they remind me of Em." Stein says Em is Emma, but it has other echoes, perhaps even Hem, especially in a passage that ends with a sentence that may fit Hemingway: "He was as if he were going to pass an examination." There is no way to prove that such details are echoes, but work with sound and rhythm, as in musical composition, is not confined by the boundaries of single pieces. When date and ideas of two pieces connect, as they do here, the ear that picks up echoes is probably right.

It is known that Stein absorbed into this piece, as she did into many others, verbal detail from the illustrations or texts of the French student notebook in which she was writing. This notebook, one in a series on teachers of youth, is about Victor Hugo. The picture shows four of his works, *Quatre-vingt treize, Les châtiments, Lucrèce Borgia,* and *Notre-Dame de Paris.* The four appear in the second to fifth line of the portrait with negatives as "not" connecting with the young Hemingway, who lives in our time and his own way. The reader must determine how and how fully such sources are absorbed into the portrait. Can we read the lines, as Stein surely intended, without knowing their source in the notebook? How Stein in her texts uses the diverse matter of the world, including such notebooks, is a question of great interest, often judged but not well studied.

• • • • •

Among and then young.

Not ninety-three.

Not Lucretia Borgia.

Not in or on a building.

Not a crime not in the time.

Not by this time.

Not in the way.

On their way and to head away. A head any way. What is a head. A head is what every one not in the north of Australia returns for that. In English we know. And is it to their credit that they have nearly finished and claimed, is there any memorial of the failure of civilization to cope with extreme and extremely well begun, to cope with extreme savagedom.

There and we know.

Hemingway.

How do you do and good-bye. Good-bye and how do you do. Well and how do you do.

A BOOK CONCLUDING WITH AS A WIFE HAS A COW

A LOVE STORY

VAN OR TWENTY YEARS AFTER

A SECOND PORTRAIT OF CARL VAN VECHTEN

IF I TOLD HIM A COMPLETED PORTRAIT OF PICASSO

Late in August 1923, Stein and Toklas went to Nice, supposedly to see Picasso, who was in Antibes. Picasso returned to Paris early in September. Stein, who normally kept visits short, stayed on for three full months, until 27 November, working with great intensity and concentration.

In Nice, in close succession, she wrote second portraits of Alice Toklas, Carl Van Vechten, and Pablo Picasso. Though separate works, they are here introduced together as a step in the review of Stein's work and life that began after *Geography and Plays,* continued in *An Elucidation,* and led to a surge of new writing. The three figures are supportive personal friends who are also the subjects of first portraits written between 1910 and 1913. The second portraits appear in sequence in the chronology of her work but appear to be parts of a single process in the mind. *Van or Twenty Years After* is in the same manuscript notebook as *A Book Concluding With As A Wife Has A Cow A Love Story,* and *If I Told Him* is in the same notebook as *Geography.*

Alice Toklas makes writing possible in making living possible. Even in the first portrait *Ada,* the two figures, like lovers everywhere, never tire of telling and listening to love stories. Toklas is inside and outside all stories, inspiring, validating, listening, reciprocating.

The second portrait makes the love story openly and triumphantly erotic. At the center of the enfolding book is the wife who has a cow. In this fact, not in any theory, is the key to the life and work of Gertrude Stein. As making love concludes with the cow, so writing concludes with a book. Sexuality and writing become one. The rhythms of *As A Wife Has A Cow A Love Story* become the surging tides of the Mediterranean and of creativity and sexuality in the second portrait of Picasso.

A Love Story is the subtitle for both *As A Wife Has A Cow* and *A Book.* All Stein's writings become love stories and all her work a single love story. To lift *As A Wife Has A Cow A Love Story* from *A Book* for publication by itself is to violate the integrity of this extraordinary whole.

The *Book* that ends with *As A Wife Has A Cow* differs even visually from the rhapsodic love story. It is written in small sections with headings that become poems or examples, one each on a loose leaf of a pad. Puns open doors just enough to subtexts that are not spelled out but allow us "to read it better a letter and better, to read it and let her it all very well." The book begins with a tiny housekeeping scene of a key to a closet in which she keeps money and candy. The closet opens to a fairy-tale double entendre, "Hands and grateful. This does enjoying this. Hands a very grateful. Go upstairs. . . ." As always, Stein's text absorbs daily life. For example, a Stein gift of ice cream and cake to Julia, the little daughter of Stella Bowen and Ford Madox Ford, is transmuted into a verbal game about color. To pursue the incident distracts from the words that are here.

Late in 1926, six months before he died, Juan Gris did lithographs to illustrate the edition of the portrait published by Daniel-Henry Kahnweiler's Galerie Simon. Stein may well have spoken to Gris about this portrait when she wrote it, while he was working on opera decors in Monte Carlo. The portrait includes apparent references to painting, "Who painted knives first," "How large a mouth has a singer. . . . How much better is one color than another." Gris did not read English but would have understood Stein's comment or translation into French. He had experience with close reading, illustration, collaboration, translation, and writing poetry. His illustrations make visible his comprehension of the enfolding in her portrait. The last illustration, for example, enfolds the guitar—which sings of Spain, courtship, love—in the open pages of the book, with its stories and poems. The two together lie or are propped up on a surface that suggests stylized pansies, a table, or windows opening. Elements of a clef or the scroll of a guitar have anatomical hints. Such interlocked forms, which Stein understood perfectly, perfectly render her interlocked vision.

Among the many reasons Stein had for thinking of Carl Van Vechten in 1923 were his efforts to place *The Making of Americans* with Alfred Knopf for publication; her interest in his new novel, *The Blind Bow Boy;* and his contact with Edmund Wilson, who had reviewed *Geography and Plays* and negotiated with Van Vechten for publication of Stein's *A List.* These details give a sense of the unfailing faith and loyalty of Van Vechten, who became Stein's publicist and in effect her personal agent in America. Whether or not he understood her work, he never deviated in his support of the original gift he perceived Stein to have.

The title of *Van or Twenty Years After,* Stein's second portrait of Van Vechten, begins with the name "Van" in English and goes on to hear its French equivalent, so that Van equals *vingt.* That number reappears translated into English as "twenty" although the friendship was in fact ten years old. When, in a letter sent before she wrote the piece, Stein spoke of doing a portrait with the "twenty years after effect," she also conferred upon Van Vechten literary importance by echoing Alexandre Dumas's *Vingt ans après,* one of the sequels to *The Three Musketeers,* or the twenty-first chapter of *The Education of Henry Adams,* "Twenty Years After (1892)." Such references guarantee the literary weight of Van Vechten and the friendship with Stein.

The portrait opens with punning and often rhyming constructions in paragraphs, first of tiny words, then of longer, denser words and phrases. Some details have identifiable references, for example, "suddenly and at his request. Get up and give it to him" and "Why are the three waiting, there are more than three" come from Van Vechten's request for the typescript of *The Making of Americans* and Stein sending three of the eight typed volumes. Stein always wrote about real things. She did not arbitrarily compose words apart from actuality.

Sometime in August 1923, before Stein left Paris for the Riviera, she wrote a different second portrait, taking off from the first, entitled, *And too / Van Vechten / a sequel to One—*. It was not typed, not sent to Van Vechten, and not published. It is printed in *The Letters of Gertrude Stein and Carl Van Vechten* (864–66).

From 1906 on, Picasso was the great artist and the great friend in Stein's life. His portrait of her and hers of him joined his art to hers and hers to his as both were also joined in friendship. "Portraits and prayers," the phrase first used in *An Elucidation,* speaks of the juncture of the visual and verbal, painting and writing, Picasso and Stein.

In the powerful rhythmic construction of this portrait, the repeated questions and incomplete sentences question completion and refuse to name what history teaches. In the *Autobiography* Stein says that she delighted that summer in the waves on the shore at Antibes, where the portrait was written, as was *Geography.* The waves are more than background. Inside the portrait they become Picasso's creative energy; the conquering armies of the leader, whether Napoleon or Picasso; his power over the empire of art, which might yet, like Napoleon's, crumble; and the fickle sexuality, misogyny, and flattery characteristic of Picasso. Would he like it if she told him all this? Would he like it if she told on him? Would he like what she knows about him? Such questions, with their tone of gossip and threat, flattery and secrecy, are also never answered but persistently and rhythmically repeated.

The manuscript shows an interesting textual discrepancy in the text, which is here restored to the handwritten original. In the section on "exact resemblance," a period before "To exact" in the manuscript makes the difference between an adjective and a verb: "Exact resemblance. To exact resemblance the exact resemblance as exact as resemblance, exactly as resembling, exactly and resembling. . . ." The verb "to exact" adds energy to the creative struggle. Stein explores all possible forms in which "exact" can be joined with "resemblance."

The geography of this portrait is internal, sexual, procreative, in its sucking, pushing, and heaving. It also becomes the actual geography of the coast of the Midi—the waves, the tides, and the land that compose *Geography*.

• • • • •

A BOOK CONCLUDING WITH AS A WIFE HAS A COW.

A LOVE STORY

KEY TO CLOSET.

There is a key.

There is a key to a closet that opens the drawer. And she keeps both so that neither money nor candy will go suddenly, Fancy, baby, new year. She keeps both so that neither money nor candy will go suddenly, Fancy baby New Year, fancy baby mine, fancy.

HAPPEN TO HAVE.

She does happen to have an aunt and in visiting and in taking a flower she shows that she is well supplied with sweet food at home otherwise she would have taken candies to her aunt as it would have been her sister. Her sister did.

RIGHT AWAY.

Active at a glance and said, said it again. Active at a glance and then to change gold right away. Active at a glance and not to change gold right away.

FISH.

Can fish be wives and wives and wives and have as many as that. Can fish be wives and have as many as that.

Ten o'clock or earlier.

PINK.

Pink looks as pink, pink looks as pink, as pink as pink supposes, suppose.

QUICKLY.

She will finish first and come, the second time she will finish first and come. The second time.

DECISION.

He decided when he had a house he would not buy them. By and by. By then.

CHOOSE.

He let it be expected and he let it be expected and she let it be expected and he came and brought them and she did not. Usually she sent them and usually he brought them. They were well-chosen.

HAD A HORSE.

If in place of a nose she had a horse and in place of a flower she had wax and in place of a melon she had a stone and in place of perfume buckles how many days would it be.

JULIA.

She asked for white and it was refused, she asked for pink and it was refused she asked for white and pink and it was agreed, it was agreed it would be pink and it was agreed to.

A COUSIN.

If a mistake as to the other if in mistake as to the brother, if by mistake and it was either if and all of it came and come. To come means partly that.

LOOK LIKE.

Look like look like it and he had twenty and more than twenty of them too. The great question is is it easier to have more than were wanted and in that case what do they do with it.

TO-DAY.

Yesterday not at all. To-day one to each one of four, ten to one two to one fifty to one and none to one. And might be satisfied. So also is the one who not being forgotten had five.

LONGER.

She stayed away longer.

BESIDE.

It can be known that he changed from Friday to Sunday. It can also be known that he changed from year to year. It can also be known that he was worried. It can also be known that his fellow-voyager would not only be attentive but would if necessary forget to come. Everybody would be grateful.

IN QUESTION.

How large a mouth has a good singer. He knows. How much better is one color than another. He knows. How far away is a city from a city. He knows. How often is it delayed. He knows.

MUCH LATER.

Elephants and birds of beauty and a gold-fish. Gold fish or a superstition. They always bring bad luck. He had them and he was not told. Gold fish and he was not old. Gold fish and he was not to scold. Gold fish all told. The result was that the other people never had them and he knew nothing of it.

NEGLECTED AND NEGLECTFUL.

She needed it all very well and pressed her, she needed it all very well and as read, to read it better a letter and better, to read it and let her it all very well.

AND SOUP.

It has always been a test of who made it best, and it has always been a test and who made it best. Who made it best it has always been a test. It has always been a test it has always been a test. Who made it best. Who made it best it has always been a test.

PETER.

Peter said Peter said eyes are always and eyes are always. Peter said Peter said, eyes are always and Peter said eyes are always. Peter said eyes are always.

Peter said eyes are always.

EMILY.

Emily is admitted admittedly, Emily is admittedly Emily is admittedly.

Emily said Emily said, Emily is admittedly Emily. Emily said Emily is admittedly is Emily said Emily is admittedly Emily said Emily is Emily is admittedly.

JULIA AGNES AND EMILY.

Emily is and Julia. Julia is and Agnes. Agnes will entertain Julia. Emily is and Agnes is and will entertain Julia and Agnes will entertain Julia Agnes will entertain Julia.

THERE.

There is an excuse for expecting success there is an excuse. There is an excuse for expecting success and there is an excuse for expecting success. And at once.

IN ENGLISH.

Even in the midst and may be even in the midst and even in the midst and may be. Watched them.

THEY HAD.

They had no children. They had no children but three sister-in-laws a brother which brother and no nephews and no nieces and no other language.

IN ADDITION.

They think that they will they think that they will change their opinion concerning. And it is nearly what they said.

Could and could she be in addition.

THESE.

Three mentioned the three mentioned are too much glass too many hyacinths too many horses. Horses are used at once. Why are horses used at once.

A LITTLE BEGINNING.

She says it is a small beginning, she says that partly this and partly that, she says it is partly this and partly that, she says that it is what she is accustomed to.

INTRODUCTION.

When they introduced not at all when they introduced not at all.

A SLATE.

A long time in which to decide that although it is a slate a slate used to mean a slate pencil.

PLACES.

If he came and was at once inclined inclined to have heard that how many places are there in it. How many places are there in it.

IN ENGLISH.

Longer legs than English. In English longer legs than English.

IN HALF.

Half the size of that. This does not refer to a half or a whole or a piece. Half the size of that refers only to the size.

NOT SURPRISING.

It is not at all surprising. Not at all surprising. If he gets it done at all. It is not at all surprising.

HANDS AND GRATEFUL.

Hands and grateful. This does enjoying this. Hands and grateful very grateful. Go upstairs go upstairs go upstairs go. Hands and grateful.

SUSPICIONS.

He was suspicious of it and he had every reason to be suspicious of it.

AN AID TO MEMORY.

In aid of memory. Mentioned by itself alone. Butter or flattery. Mentioned by itself. In aid of memory mentioned by itself alone.

ALL.

He was the last and best of all not at all. He was the last of all he was the best of all he was the last and best of all not at all.

FANCY.

Fancy looking at it now and if it resembled he made half of it.

A TRAIT.

He met him. It was very difficult to remember who was here alone. This decided us to consider it a trait.

READY.

When I was as ready to like it as ever I was ready to account for the difference between and the flowers.

Are you ready yet, not yet.

KNIVES.

Who painted knives first. Who painted knives first. Who said who painted knives first. Who said who painted knives first. And see the difference.

INSISTED.

I insisted upon it in summer as well as in winter. I insisted upon it I insisted upon it in summer I insisted upon it in summer as well as in winter. To remember in winter that it is winter and in summer that it is summer. I insisted upon it in summer as well as in winter not sentimentally with raspberries.

TO REMIND.

She reminded me that I was as ready as not and I said I will not say that I preferred service to opposition. I will not say what or what is not a pleasure.

SEVEN.

If she follows let her go, one two three four five six seven. She is let go if she follows. If she follows she is let go. If she follows let her go, she is let go if she follows.

A HAT.

It is as pleasant as that to have a hat, to have a hat and it is as pleasant as that. It is as pleasant as that to have a hat. It is as pleasant as that. To have a hat. To have a hat it is as pleasant as that to have a hat. To have had a hat it is as pleasant as that to have a hat.

HOW TO REMEMBER.

A pretty dress and a pretty hat and how to come, leave out two and how to come. A pretty dress and a pretty hat leave out two. How to come and leave out two. A pretty hat and a pretty dress a pretty dress and a pretty hat and leave out two. Leave out two and and how to come.

A WISH.

And always not when absently enough and heard and said. He had a wish.

FIFTY.

Fifty fifty and fifty-one, she said she thought so and she was told that that was about what it was. Not in place considered as places. Julia was used only as cake, Julia cake was used only as Julia. In some countries cake is called candy. The next is as much as that. When do they is not the same as why do they.

AS A WIFE HAS A COW

A LOVE STORY

Nearly all of it to be as a wife has a cow, a love story. All of it to be as a wife has a cow, all of it to be as a wife has a cow, a love story.

As to be all of it as to be a wife as a wife has a cow, a love story, all of it as to be all of it as a wife all of it as to be as a wife has a cow a love story, all of it as a wife has a cow as a wife has a cow a love story.

Has made, as it has made as it has made, has made has to be as a wife has a cow, a love story. Has made as to be as a wife has a cow a love story. As a wife has a cow, as a wife has a cow a love story. Has to be as a wife has a cow a love story. Has made as to be as a wife has a cow a love story.

When he can, and for that when he can, for that. When he can and for that when he can. For that. When he can. For that when he can. For that. And when he can and for that. Or that, and when he can. For that and when he can.

And to in six and another. And to and in and six and another. And to and in and six and another. And to in six and and to and in and six and another. And to and in and six and another. And to and six and in and another and and to and six and another and and to and in and six and and to and six and in and another.

In came in there, came in there come out of there. In came in come out of there. Come out there in came in there. Come out of there and in and come out of there. Came in there. Come out of there.

Feeling or for it, as feeling or for it, came in or come in, or come out of there or feeling as feeling or feeling as for it.

As a wife has a cow.

Came in and come out.

As a wife has a cow a love story.

As a love story, as a wife has a cow, a love story.

Not and now, now and not, not and now, by and by not and now, as not, as soon as not not and now, now as soon now, now as soon, and now as soon as soon as now. Just as soon just now just now just as soon just as soon as now. Just as soon as now.

And in that, as and in that, in that and and in that, so that, so that and in that, and in that and so that and as for that and as for that and that. In that. In that and and for that as for that and in that. Just as soon and in that. In that as that and just as soon. Just as soon as that.

Even now, now and even now and now and even now. Not as even now, therefor, even now and therefor, therefor and even now and even now and therefor even now. So not to and moreover and even now and therefor and moreover and even now and so and even now and therefor even now.

Do they as they do so. And do they do so.

We feel we feel. We feel or if we feel if we feel or if we feel. We feel or if we feel. As it is made made a day made a day or two made a day, as it is made a day or two, as it is made a day. Made a day. Made a day. Not away a day. By day. As it is made a day.

On the fifteenth of October as they say, said anyway, what is it as they expect, as they expect it or as they expected it, as they expect it and as they expected it, expect it or for it, expected it and it is expected of it. As they say said anyway. What is it as they expect for it, what is it and it is as they expect of it. What is it. What is it the fifteenth of October as they say as they expect or as they expected as they expect for it. What is it as they say the fifteenth of October as they say and as expected of it, the fifteenth of October as they say, what is it as expected of it. What is it and the fifteenth of October as they say and expected of it.

And prepare and prepare so prepare to prepare and prepare to prepare and prepare so as to prepare, so to prepare and prepare to prepare to prepare for and to prepare for it to prepare, to prepare for it, in preparation, as preparation in preparation by preparation. They will be too busy afterwards to prepare. As preparation prepare, to prepare, as to preparation and to prepare. Out there.

Have it as having having it as happening, happening to have it as having, having to have it as happening. Happening and have it as happening and having it happen as happening and having to have it happen as happening, and my wife has a cow as now, my wife having a cow as now, my wife having a cow as now and having a cow as now and having a cow and having a cow now, my wife has a cow and now. My wife has a cow.

VAN OR TWENTY YEARS AFTER

A SECOND PORTRAIT OF CARL VAN VECHTEN

Twenty years after, as much as twenty years after in as much as twenty years after, after twenty years and so on. It is it is it is it is.

If it and as if it, if it or as if it, if it is as if it, and it is as if it and as if it. Or as if it. More as if it. As more. As more as if it. And if it. And for and as if it.

If it was to be a prize a surprise if it was to be a surprise to realise, if it was to be if it were to be, was it to be. What was it to be. It was to be what it was. And it was. So it was. As it was. As it is. Is it as it is. It is and as it is and as it is. And so and so as it was.

Keep it in sight alright.

Not to the future but to the fuchsia.

Tied and untied and that is all there is about it. And as tied and as beside, and as beside and tied. Tied and untied and beside and as beside and as untied and as tied and as untied and as beside. As beside as by and as beside. As by as by the day. By their day and as it may, may be they will may be they may. Has it been reestablished as not to weigh. Weigh how. How to weigh. Or weigh. Weight, state, await, state, late state rate state, state await weight state, in state rate at any rate state weight state as stated. In this way as stated. Only as if when the six sat at the table they all looked for those places together. And each one in that direction so as to speak look down and see the same as weight. As weight for weight as state to state as wait to wait as not so. Beside.

For arm absolutely for arm.

They reinstate the act of birth.

Bewildering is a nice word but it is not suitable at present.

They meant to be left as they meant to be left, as they meant to be left left and their center, as they meant to be left and their center. So that in their and do, so that in their and to do. So suddenly and at his request. Get up and give it to him and so suddenly and as his request. Request to request in request, as request, for a request by request, requested, as requested as they requested, or so have it to be nearly there. Why are the three waiting, there are more than three. One two three four five six seven.

As seven.

Seating, regard it as the rapidly increased February.

Seating regard it as the very regard it as their very nearly regard as their very nearly or as the very regard it as the very settled, seating regard it as the very as their very regard it as their very nearly regard it as the very nice, seating regard as their very nearly regard it as the very nice, known and seated, seating regard it, seating and regard it, regard it as the very nearly center left and in the center, regard it as the very left and in the center. And so I say so. So and so. That. For. For that. And for that. So and so and for that. And for that and so and so. And so I say so.

Now to fairly see it have, now to fairly see it have and now to fairly see it have. Have and to have. Now to fairly see it have and to have. Naturally.

As naturally, naturally as, as naturally as. As naturally.

Now to fairly see it have as naturally.

Finis

IF I TOLD HIM
A COMPLETED PORTRAIT OF PICASSO

If I told him would he like it. Would he like it if I told him.

Would he like it would Napoleon would Napoleon would would he like it.

If Napoleon if I told him if I told him if Napoleon. Would he like it if I told him if I told him if Napoleon. Would he like it if Napoleon if Napoleon if I told him. If I told him if Napoleon if Napoleon if I told him. If I told him would he like it would he like it if I told him.

Now.

Not now.

And now.

Now.

Exactly as as kings.

Feeling full for it.

Exactitude as kings.

So to beseech you as full as for it.

Exactly or as kings.

Shutters shut and open so do queens. Shutters shut and shutters and so shutters shut and shutters and so and so shutters and so shutters shut and so shutters shut and shutters and so. And so shutters shut and so and also. And also and so and so and also.

Exact resemblance. To exact resemblance the exact resemblance as exact as a resemblance, exactly as resembling, exactly resembling, exactly in resemblance exactly a resemblance, exactly and resemblance. For this is so. Because.

Now actively repeat at all, now actively repeat at all, now actively repeat at all.

Have hold and hear, actively repeat at all.

I judge judge.

As a resemblance to him.

Who comes first. Napoleon the first.

Who comes too coming coming too, who goes there, as they go they share, who shares all, all is as all as as yet or as yet.

Now to date now to date. Now and now and date and the date.

Who came first Napoleon at first. Who came first Napoleon the first. Who came first, Napoleon first.

Presently.

Exactly do they do.
First exactly.
Exactly do they do too.
First exactly.
And first exactly.
Exactly do they do.
And first exactly and exactly.
And do they do.
At first exactly and first exactly and do they do.
The first exactly.
And do they do.
The first exactly.
At first exactly.
First as exactly.
As first as exactly.
Presently
As presently.
As as presently.

He he he he and he and he and and he and he and he and and as and as he and as he and he. He is and as he is, and as he is and he is, he is and as he and he and as he is and he and he and and he and he.

Can curls rob can curls quote, quotable.
As presently.
As exactitude.
As trains
Has trains.
Has trains.
As trains.
As trains.
Presently.
Proportions.
Presently.
As proportions as presently.
Father and farther.
Was the king or room.
Farther and whether.

Was there was there was there what was there was there what was there was there there was there.

Whether and in there.
As even say so.
One.
I land.
Two.
I land.
Three.
The land.
Three
The land.
Three
The land.
Two
I land.
Two
I land.
One
I land.
Two
I land.
As a so.
They cannot.
A note.
They cannot.
A float.
They cannot
They dote.
They cannot.
They as denote.
Miracles play.
Play fairly.
Play fairly well.
A well.
As well.
As or as presently.
Let me recite what history teaches. History teaches.

GEOGRAPHY

The word *geography* first enters with the book title *Geography and Plays*. It refers not only to new places, from Provence to the Riviera, but also to new ways of writing. Geography is never simply about location, scenery, and the space of the earth, though it includes these. It is about the arrangement of words in compositional space, the disposition of elements from inside. Stein wrote *Geography* in the early fall of 1923 in Nice, at the same time and in the same notebook as the second portrait of Picasso. Later that fall, with geography still in her mind, she wrote pieces about France, Iowa (Van Vechten's home state, already mentioned here), other states, and the directions South and North.

In Nice and Antibes, geography is not a dry school subject but the surging waves, the tide in motion, the seasons, the rhythms of love and of creative activity spreading "geographically" and becoming new writing, new living, or, for Picasso, new painting and new watercolors.

By the thirties, in *Four In America* and *The Geographical History of America*, Stein was thinking about the creative impulse flourishing in an America that was a space of great freedom for the imagination, far beyond that of narrowly delimited countries and regions.

• • • • •

As geography return to geography, return geography. Geography. Comes next. Geography. Comes. Comes geography.

As geography returns to geography comes next geography. Comes. Comes geography.

Geography as nice. Comes next geography. Geography as nice comes next geography comes geography.

Geographically, geographical. Geographically to place, geographically in case in case of it.

Looking up under fairly see fairly looking up under as to movement. The movement described. Sucked in met in, met in set in, sent in sent out sucked in sucked out.

An interval.

If it needs if it needs if it needs to do not move, do not move, do not touch, do not touch, do not if it needs to if it needs. That is what she is looking for. Less. Less threads fairly nearly and geography and water. Descriptive emotion. As it can be.

He was terribly deceived about the Jews about Napoleon and about everything else.

If you do not know the meaning of such things do not use them. That is all. Such phrases.

More geography, more than, more geography. Which bird what bird more geography. Than geography.

Geography pleases me that is to say not easily. Beside it is decided. Geographically quickly. Not geographically but geography.

Geographically not inland not an island and the sea. It is what it is good for to sit by it to eat and to go away. Every time then to come again and so there is an interruption.

Plentifully simply. Napoleon is dimply.

If the water comes into the water if the water as it comes into the water makes as much more as it should can snow melt. If the water as it should does snow melt and could it as it has melted could it melt and does it and does it melt and should it, should it melt and would it melt and does it melt and will it melt and can it and does it melt. As water. I often think about seasonable.

Waterfully when the water waterfully when the water comes to soften when the water comes and to soften when the water and to soften, waterfully and to soften, when the water and to soften, not wetter. When the water and to soften I know noises. As to noises. When the water and to soften as to water as to soften I know I know noises. I have secretly wished altogether. One two three altogether.

Geographically and inundated, geography and inundated, not inundated.

He says that the rain, he says that for rain he says that for snow he says, he says that the rain he says that the snow he says that the rain that the snow he says that is rain he says that is snow he says it is rain he says it is rain he says that it is snow he says it is snow.

He says it is snow.

Paper very well. Paper and water and very well. Paper and water and very well and paper and water and very well and paper and very well and water. Paper and water very well.

Naturally and water color the color of water and naturally. Very naturally the color and very naturally. It is the best yet.

When this you see remember for me remember it for me if you can.

Once again as we can, once again and as we can, once again and as we can and once again and once again and as we can and can.

New to you. New to us. New. I knew. This is a very interesting thing to ask. To ask if it is new if it is new to you. It is a very interesting thing to ask.

It is a very interesting thing to know. That is a very interesting thing to know. Do you know whether it is new whether it is as new whether it is new to you. It is a very interesting thing to know that it is as new as it is to you.

I stands for Iowa and Italy. M stands for Mexico and Monte Carlo. G stands for geographic and geographically. B stands for best and most. It is very nearly decided.

Immeasurably. Immeasurably and frequently. Frequently and invariably. Invariably and contentedly. Contentedly and indefatigably. Indefatigably and circumstances. Circumstances and circumstantially. Initiative and reference. In reference to it. It needs to be added to, in addition. Additionally as in reduction. In geography and in geography.

As it might be said to be as it might be said to be.

As at this was was was as it was was was as it was.

Not to be outdone in kindness.

Can you tell can you really tell it from here, can you really tell it can you tell it can you tell from here. From here to there and from there to there. Put it there. Is he still there.

If to say it if to see it if to say it. If to say it. The point of it, the point is this, that point at that point and twenty at that point and not twenty if you see and if you say it. If you say it and if you see it. As at that point and twenty. Twenty twenty a new figure. And a new finger. As a direction as in a direction. And so in whistling incorrectly. Very near and very near and very nearly and very nearly and very near it was a very near thing, very near to it. Amuse yourself. Vastly.

So much and as much. Much and as much, much and so much. Much and very much, very much and as much. Thank you for it.

Pardon me plainly pardon me. In this and hear. Here. Here at once. Not exactly angry. How exactly angry. Fed as to wheat. Seated by me. Sat and that. If to please. Instead.

Cochin chine as Cochin China Tuesday. What is my delight.

No not that and no not that. And designs and the post, post mark. As dark. We know how to feel British. Saving stamps. Excuse me.

To make no allusion to anybody. Spread as glass is, glass is spread and so are colors, colors and pretty ways.

Able and Mabel. Mabel and able.

As outing. As an outing can it please me.

Leave and leave and leave relieve and relieve and relieve, candy as everywhere, but it is if it is, have happen. I touched it.

As through.

Shipping not shipping shipping not shipping, shipping as shipping shipping in shipping in shipping it. In shipping it as easily. Famous as a sire.

Notably notably reading.

Fasten as lengthily. As one day.

Smell sweetly. Industriously and indeed. It is apt to be.

Is it very apt to be explained.

I know how to wait. This is a joke. It is a pun.

Feasibly. A market as market to market.

In standing in plenty of ways, attending to it in plenty of ways, as opera glasses in plenty of ways as raining and in plenty of ways, hard as a pear run in the way, ran in this way. Ran away. I know the exact size and shape and surface and use and distance. To place it with them.

Any many many any any many many any any many many any any many many any. Any one.

Geography includes inhabitants and vessels.

Plenty of planning.

Geographically not at all.

DESCRIPTIONS OF LITERATURE

This little sampler of descriptions that all start the same way—are they phrases or are they sentences?—is an exercise in how to do descriptions of writing, not descriptions that might be used in writing. It reads like takeoffs on the sort of thing printed in blurbs, publicity notices, book jackets, or even reviews—short statements that highlight the quality of a book. Decontextualized, the descriptions say nothing about the subject matter of books but speak only of their effect or quality. They are pithy, sometimes sharp evaluations of the ambition and the success or failure of writing. Some may refer to Stein's own work. But she must also have looked at what was around her and started describing characteristics she perceived, including, for example, the French school notebook in which she was writing the descriptions, which showed a picture and text about French colonies in West Africa that she incorporated. The little sentences bristle with underplayed feeling, suggested but never named.

By late 1924, when Stein wrote the descriptions, she had two books in print, *Three Lives* (1909) and *Geography and Plays* (1922), published at her own expense. *Tender Buttons* (1914), published by Donald Evans, was out of print. *The Making of Americans,* completed late in 1911, was not printed as a book until the following year, 1925, although selections appeared in nine installments in the *Transatlantic Review* from April to December 1924. One can speculate that writing the descriptions in 1924, when she was thinking about the problematic serialization of her big novel, may have been particularly ironic for Stein, who yearned for publication but faced refusal after refusal from publishers.

• • • • •

A book which shows that the next and best is to be found out when there is pleasure in the reason.

For this reason.

A book in which by nearly all of it finally and an obstruction it is planned as unified and nearly a distinction. To be distinguished is what is desired.

A book where in part there is a description of their attitude and their wishes and their ways.

A book which settles more nearly than has ever been yet done the advantages of following later where they have found that they must go.

A book where nearly everything is prepared.

A book which shows that as it is nearly equally best to say so, as they say and say so.

A book which makes a mention of all the times that even they recognise as important.

A book which following the story the story shows that persons incurring blame and praise make no return for hospitality.

A book which admits that all that has been found to be looked for is of importance to places.

A book which manages to impress it upon the young that those who oppose them follow them and follow them.

A book naturally explains what has been the result of investigation.

A book that marks the manner in which longer and shorter proportionately show measure.

A book which makes no mistake in describing the life of those who can be happy.

The next book to appear is the one in which more emphasis will be given to numbers of them.

A book which when you open it attracts attention by the undoubted denial of photography as an art.

A book which reminds itself that having had a custom it only needs more of it and more.

A book which can not imbue any one with any desire except the one which makes changes come later.

A book explaining why more of them feel as they do.

A book which attracts attention.

A book which is the first book in which some one has been telling why on one side rather than on the other there is a tendency to shorten. Shorten what. Shorten more.

A book which plans homes for any of them.

A book a book telling why when at once and at once.

A book telling why when said that, she answered it as if it were the same.

A book which tells why colonies have nearly as many uses as they are to have now.

A book which makes no difference between one jeweler and another.

A book which mentions all the people who have had individual chances to come again.

A book in translation about eggs and butter.

A book which has great pleasure in describing whether any further attention is to be given to homes where homes have to be homes.

A book has been carefully prepared altogether.

A book and deposited as well.

A book describing fishing exactly.

A book describing six and six and six.

A book describing six and six and six seventy-two.

A book describing Edith and Mary and flowering fire.

A book describing as a man all of the same ages all of the same ages and nearly the same.

A book describing hesitation as exemplified in plenty of ways.

A book which chances to be the one universally described as energetic.

A book which makes no mistakes either in description or in departure or in further arrangements.

A book which has made all who read it think of the hope they have that sometime they will have fairly nearly all of it at once.

A book in which there is no complaint made of forest fires and water.

A book more than ever needed.

A book made to order and the only thing that was forgotten in ordering was what no one objects to. Can it easily be understood. It can and will.

A book which places the interest in those situations which have something to do with recollections and with returns.

A book with more respect for all who have to hear and have heard a book with more respect for all who have heard it.

A book more than ever read.

A book by and by.

A book not nearly so much better than ever.

A book and fourteen. The influence of this book is such that no one has had more than this opportunity.

A book of dates and fears.

A book more than ever a description of happiness and as you were.

A book which makes the end come just as soon as it is intended.

A book which asks questions of everyone.

A book fairly certain of having admirers when at once there are admirers of it.

A book which shows that agreeableness can be a feature of it all.

A book which makes a play of daughter and daughters.

A book which has character and shows that no one need deceive themselves as to the sending of gifts.

A book which has a description of the selection and placing of chairs as an element in Viennese and American life.

A book which standardizes requests and announcements.

A book which urges and reasonably so the attraction of some for others.

A book in which there is no mention of advantages.

A book attaching importance to english and french names.

A book which has to be carefully read in order to be understood and so that the illusion of summer and summer and summer and summer does not remain deceiving. So much so.

A book narrowly placed on the shelf and often added. Added to that.

A book of addresses invented for the sake of themselves.

A book and a bookstore. A book for them. Will they be in it.

SITWELL EDITH SITWELL

By setting and spacing the title in her draft in two lines on a page of a tiny notepad, Stein made it into a sentence inviting the subject into the sitting room of the speaker. In this form the name becomes the command "Sit well," a rising phrase whose accents play against the falling name. The title allows but does not demand the reading of the words as a sentence.

Sit well
Edith Sitwell

"Sit well" is about portraiture, a subject sitting for an artist. It is also about a social occasion, perhaps sitting at tea in Stein's studio. "[T]hey sit around her" may refer to friends and admirers surrounding Sitwell or to Sitwell and other guests sitting around Stein. Among the guests is Mabel Foote Weeks (1872–1964), an old friend of Stein who had been two years ahead of her at Radcliffe College and was now a professor of English at Barnard College. Stein invited Weeks, who in the spring of 1925 was in Europe, to meet Sitwell, a delight for a teacher. The result is the portrait. It contrasts Sitwell and Weeks, marking "a change in time" associated with the time word *weeks*. To Stein, Mabel is the past and an old friendship whereas Sitwell is present friendship, "now altogether different." Friendships change and friends change. Eyes cannot hold both what was and what is, what she knows and what she sees, for they differ radically. "Fill my eyes no no. / It was and held it. / The size of my eyes." Do these eyes hold tears?

The past also returns with the alliterative names Lily [Hansen] and Louise [Hayden], California friends from girlhood, before Toklas and Stein met. The portrait is filled with rhymes and echoes, rhythms and repetitions, contrasting verb forms, present and past, here and there. It ends with five finely modulated ironic lines facing the irreconcilable in looking two ways, "Absently faces and by and by we agree." Does this portrait echo Alice's Mad Tea-Party with its strange sense of time and its riddling conversations?

Stein's first contact with Edith Sitwell came through Sitwell's review in 1923 of *Geography and Plays,* which offered qualified approval. By 1924, after a far more generous review, they met in Paris and quickly became friends. It was Sitwell who arranged the invitation for Stein to lecture at Cambridge and Oxford in June 1926. Stein concluded the lecture with examples of her work, including the portrait of Sitwell, who sat on the stage. The portrait was first published with the lecture *Composition as Explanation* by Leonard and Virginia Woolf's Hogarth Press in November 1926.

• • • • •

In a minute when they sit when they sit around her.

Mixed it with two who. One two two one two two. Mixed it with two who.

Weeks and weeks able and weeks.

No one sees the connection between Lily and Louise, but I do.

After each has had after each has had, after each has had had had had it.

Change in time.

A change in time is this, if a change in time. If a change in time is this. If a change in time.

Did she come to say who.

Not to remember weeks to say and asking, not to remember weeks to-day. Not to remember weeks to say. Not to remember weeks to say and asking.

And now a bow.

When to look when to look up and around when to look down and around when to look down and around when to look around and around and altered.

Just as long as any song.

And now altogether different.

It was in place of places and and it was here.

Supposing she had had a key supposing she had answered, supposing she had had to have a ball supposing she had it fall and she had answered. Supposing she had it and in please, please never see so.

As much even as that, even can be added to by in addition, listen.

Table table to be table to see table to be to see to me, table to me table to be table to table to table to it. Exactly as they did it when when she was not and not and not so. After that perhaps.

She had a way of she had a way of not the name.

Little reaching it away.

As afternoon to borrow.

It made a difference.

This is most.

Introduces.

This is for her and not for Mabel Weeks.

She could not keep it out.

Introduces have and heard.

Miss Edith Sitwell have and heard.

Introduces have and had.

Miss Edith Sitwell have and had.

Introduces have and had introduces have and had and heard.

Miss Edith Sitwell have and had and heard.
Left and right.
Part two of Part one.
If she had a ball at all, if she had a ball at all too.
Fill my eyes no no.
It was and held it.
The size of my eyes.
Why does one want to or to and to, when does one want to and to went to.
To know it as well as all there.
If a little other more not so little as before, now they knew and that and so.
What in execute.
Night is different from bright.
When he was a little sweeter was he.
Part two.
There was a part one.
He did seem a little so.
Half of to mention it at all.
And now to allow literally if and it will if and it does if and it has if and it is.
Never as much as a way.
How does she know it.
She could be as she sleeps and as she wakes all day. She could be as she sleeps and as she wakes all day is it not so.
It leads it off of that.
Please carried at.
Twice at once and carry.
She does and care to and cover and never believe in an and being narrow.
Happily say so.
What is as added.
And opposite.
Now it has to be something entirely different and it is.
Not turned around.
No one knows two two more.
Lose and share all and more.
Very easily arises.
It very easily arises.
Absently faces and by and by we agree.

By and by faces apparently we agree.
Apparently faces by and by we agree.
By and by faces apparently we agree.
Apparently faces by and by we agree.

BUSINESS IN BALTIMORE

"Once upon a time Baltimore was necessary," she says, as if it no longer mattered. Her biting, bitter piece speaks otherwise. Baltimore, the source of the Stein brothers' success and of Stein family pride, never in all the years became neutral for Stein.

Gertrude Stein first came to Baltimore in 1892, after her father's death, to live with an aunt. By the fall of 1893 she went to college in Cambridge and returned four years later, not to family living but to the Johns Hopkins Medical School.

Baltimore spells business and business spells money. Money is about counting, the great skill of Baltimore, which equates quantity with quality, "How many and well." Counting is simple, orderly, and linear. Making money is a function of time, which is nothing more than the road to making money.

To develop these simple ideas the piece uses equally simple literary devices, with devastating effect. A word is followed by one or more jingling rhyme words. "Who finds minds and who lines shines and two kinds finds and two kinds minds." Business arranges life, property, people, marriages. "Business in Baltimore makes a wedding first at first business in Baltimore makes a wedding at first first." In such a palindrome forward and backward are the same. Not only words but phrases and sentences are repeated in parallel forms with only slight variations. Here two rhyme words compose a riddle, "If another married her brother, if another marries their brother, if their brother marries another, if their brother and a brother marry another and the sister how many pairs are there in it." It does not matter how many pairs as we no longer know who is who. Phrases echo in repetition like partners or couples agreeing, "How many papers can make more papers and how many have to have her. Have to have her."

Counting, nonsensically logical, punctuates the whole piece. "The first reason for having seven is six and a half." Counting creates lists of "streets, corners, places, rivers and trees in Baltimore." Daily life is arranged in phrases and sentences so orderly that times and days are indistinguishable. "This is why they have every reason to be arranged and every morning to be morning and every evening to be evening. / This is the reason why they have every Sunday and Tuesday and Monday."

Those who made all the money were individuals, but here nothing is individual. Everything is neutralized and decontextualized. The only name is Julian, either Stein's cousin, the banker who managed her financial affairs, or his young son, aged six and a half and perhaps adept at counting by the summer of 1925. A visit by that family or other relatives may have occasioned this piece. A single dramatic change is visible in the manuscript, in the familiar sentence, "This is the way they make the day they make the day they make the day this is the way they make the day, once a day and it is a reason for having heard of it." The final word "it" is the result of two-step revision.

Stein's original was "Pierpont Morgan." She first replaced the name with the pronoun "him," then reduced "him" to "it," presumably money.

These constructions have an astonishing visual result. The limited vocabulary, parallel phrasing, and equivalent sentences create a visual pattern that fills the page. Take the progress of changing seasons that remain the same, "They can hear winter they can hear summer. . . ." We read this page until the words no longer cumulatively build meanings but make a visual pattern that does not require understanding, like a decorative wallpaper that we see not as details but only as design. Or read aloud and look at the long concluding paragraph, where the comparatives "more" and "better" push toward superlatives "most" and "best" and are driven further forward by approval, "yes" and "yes." The decorative visual regularity creates no rhythmic monotone, for it reads perfectly to the attentive ear.

• • • • •

Nor narrow, long.
Julian is two.
How many and well.
And days and sank.
Thanks to having.
Business in Baltimore thanks to having and days and sank how many and well Julian is two not narrow, long.
Julian is two how many and well thanks to having.
Once upon a time Baltimore was necessary.
How and would it be dressed if they had divided a bank and tan. It connected at once it connected twice it connected doors and floors.
This is in May.
So they say.
How many places for scales are there in it.
Weigh once a day.
In Baltimore there are the ferns the miles the pears the cellars and the coins.
After that the large and small stones or stepping stones.
This is why they have every reason to be arranged and every morning to be morning and every evening to be evening. This is the reason why they have every Sunday and Tuesday and Monday.
Who finds minds and who lines shines and two kinds finds and two kinds minds. Minds it. She never wanted to leave Baltimore anywhere and was it.

Business in Baltimore.
He did and peppers see he did and three.
He did and three he did and see he did and three and see and he did and peppers see and peppers see and three he did.
It is so easy to have felt needed and shielded and succeeded and decided and widened and waited. No waiting for him Saturday Monday and Thursday.
All of them are devoted to it to doing what was done when it was begun and afterwards all sashes are old. Forget wills. The best and finally the first, the first and formerly the rest all of it as they have it to do to do to do already in their house. Suppose in walking up and down they sat around. Imagine vines, vines are not had here imagine vines that are not to be had here and imagine rubbers had here and imagine working working in blue that means over it. Each one of these had to give away had to have to had to give way. How many others brothers and fathers.
He had held him he had held her he had held it for him he had held it for her, he had hold of it, and he had had days. How many days pay, how much of a day pays and how differently from thinking. I think I thought I said I sought I fell I fought I had I ought to have meant to be mine.
Not as funny as yet.
Imagining up and down. How many generations make five.
If another marries her brother, if another marries their brother, if their brother marries another, if their brother and a brother marry another and the sister how many pairs are there of it.
It is easy not to be older than that.
Do you hear me.
It is easier.
How many papers can make more papers and how many have to have her. Have to have her. How many papers can make more papers and how many have to have to have it. How many have to have to have it and how many papers make more papers. It makes a little door to-day.
Put it there for him to see. He knew how and how to have he knew how to have and accepted so much as much or much much of it for it, for it is and in either direction might be saved, saved or so and while it is while it is while it is near near while it is while it is near having monthly in use. To hear them and as it has to be at and for and as it has to be for and mine and as it has to be powder and ice and as it has to be and as it has to be louder and there and as it has to be louder and there and I hear it.
And in there.

When he could not remember that when he could not remember it at all when he could remember it all and when he could remember it all. It started and parted, partly to them and for most. Foremost is a way they have to have used here.

The first time they ever had it, heard it and had it, the first time they ever had it.

In their favor as a favor as a favor or favorable.

Having forgotten how it sounds, have they forgotten all the sound remind them.

The first reason for having seven is six and a half, six and a half and as seldom. After that the real reason for six more than a half and as seldom the real reason for six more and a half and as seldom is six more six more and a half more and six more and a half more and six more and a half more and seldom.

Please put it in paper there.

A little place and for fortunately. Did he and they have a lake to-day. Nearly. Having at it and at once a noise and it, it could be just as much more also. Have a sound of or a sound of or, or Alice. Miss Alice is might it.

The very easy how do red horses have a pair. This makes Arthur and no name. He made him go.

Come near come nearly come nearly come near come near come nearly. Come near. Come near come nearly. He had a haul and I said do you do that and he did and he said not to-day. Anybody can say not to-day.

There was once upon a time a selfish boy and a selfish man, there was once upon a time a selfish man. There was once upon a time a selfish man. There was once upon a time there was once upon a time a selfish man there was once upon a time a selfish boy there was once upon a time a selfish boy there was once upon a time a selfish boy there was once upon a time a selfish man. How selfish. There was once upon a time a selfish man. There was once upon a time a selfish boy, how once upon a time a selfish boy how once upon a time a selfish man.

Nobody knows whose wedding shows it to them. Business in Baltimore makes a wedding first at first business in Baltimore makes a wedding at first first. Business in Baltimore makes a wedding at first at first. Business in Baltimore makes a wedding at first at first first. Business in Baltimore makes a wedding first at first. Business in Baltimore at first makes a wedding first makes a wedding at first. Business in Baltimore makes a wedding at first.

Business in Baltimore makes a wedding at first.

Business in Baltimore at first.

In heights and whites, in whites and lights, in lights in sizes, in sizes in sides and in wise, or as wise or wiser. This not to be the first to know.

To know.

Altogether older, older altogether.

Not following hearing or a son or another. No one spells mother or brother.

To them or then or then by then it was mostly done by them.

Who has had had it had. Had it, he had it and following he had it, he had it.

Following he had it.

Business in Baltimore following he had it. Business in Baltimore following he had it following he had had it. Business in Baltimore following he had had it. Following he had had it following he had had it business in Baltimore following he had had it.

Business in Baltimore.

How easy it is to see voices. How easy it is to see.

How easy it is to see voices and very much of it put as a rug. Supposing a whole floor was covered and on the cover where he stands has a place for it which is attached to them and of this kind. Could it have been made before a boat and no one follows. How many have had hands.

When they were sung to sung to see when they were sung to sung among when they were snugly sung to see, see seeds for that to eat and for and have the size and no more satchels made at all. Satchels may be held loosely. When they are sung and sung and sung and little have to have a hand and hand and two and two hands too, and too and two and handled too to them, handed to them, hand and hands. Hands high. This can be Baltimore and or and Baltimore and for and Baltimore and more and Baltimore and for and Baltimore and or. It does not sound like it.

When he older than that when he older than this when he older than this when he as old as he is, he is as old as he is, he is as old he is as old and would they know that fifty are fairly plenty of later hats. Hats cannot be used as mats not for selling or for much as much. He certainly was amused by it.

Devoted to having a whole a half a half a whole, a whole or told it. Devoted to having a half, a whole a whole or told or it. Devoted to having a whole a half a half a whole a whole or told it. Devoted to having a half a whole a whole a whole a half a whole or told it.

She did see fortunes fade.

Who did see fortunes fade.

Nobody saw fortunes fade. Nobody saw fortunes nobody saw fortunes fade.

A whole a half a half a whole, fortunes fade who never saw fortunes fade he never saw fortunes fade. A half a whole he never saw he never saw fortunes he never saw fortunes fade or faded. He never saw fortunes he never saw fortunes fade.

How much business is there in Baltimore.

And how many are there in business in Baltimore.

And how have they had to have business in Baltimore.

And how has it been how has it been how has he been in business in Baltimore.

He has been in business in Baltimore and before and before he was in business in Baltimore he was not in business he was not in business before he was in business in Baltimore.

He had been in business before he had been in business in Baltimore he had been in business before in Baltimore. How had he been in business in Baltimore. He had been in business before in Baltimore he had not been in business before he was in business in Baltimore.

Business in Baltimore before, before business, before business in Baltimore.

Business in Baltimore is business in Baltimore.

Business in Baltimore in business in Baltimore and business in Baltimore is this business in Baltimore.

How many more are there in business in Baltimore than there were before.

How many more are in business in Baltimore than were in business in Baltimore before.

This business in Baltimore.

That business in Baltimore.

A business in Baltimore.

Business in Baltimore.

Who says business in Baltimore. Who says business in Baltimore and before, and who says business in Baltimore more business in Baltimore more business in Baltimore than before.

Pleases me, and while they have to have eaten eaten it, and eaten eaten it and eaten eaten it eaten eaten eaten eaten eaten it. Then a list is useful. Useful soon, useful as soon. As useful as soon. As useful as soon. Some time and shown. Who has to say so say so. They easily have after and soon.

It was said at once to them that they had it. Afterwards it was said at once to them that they had it. Afterwards it was at once said to them that they had it. It was said to them it was afterwards said to them at once that they had it. It was afterwards said at once said to them afterwards said to them that they had it. It was afterwards said to them that they had it. It was afterwards at once said to them that they had it.

How much easier how much easier, how much easier and how much easier. Forty makes forty and forty-four makes forty-four and forty-four makes four and forty four makes forty-four. Business in Baltimore makes counting easy.

If he had had and had had given and had had given to him what he had had how many more are there to have held it in this way away. One and he was famous not for that nor for provision nor for in addition nothing, nothing too much, not anything more and it was not said to be said. It takes many times more to make many times more and not to make many times more and not to make many times more many times more. Not many times more. Read riches. Anything that begins with r makes read riches and this is as twice and once and once. Once is it once, twice is it twice is it twice once and is it once twice. This is the way they make the day they make the day they make the day this is the way they make the day, once a day and it is a reason for having heard of it. Now at last it is well known that not because he did he did not hurry he did not hurry because he did and did not hurry and who asked him. That is what they say who asked him.

Forgetting a name.

Not to be transferred to Baltimore and so to say so so much. If you do not hear him speak at all louder then not to speak at all louder, not to speak at all louder not to hear him speak at all louder not to hear him speak at all louder and so not to speak at all louder. He does not speak louder and so not to speak louder and so not to speak louder at all.

She was as well as he was as well as he was as well as she was as well as all that.

All that as well as all that and having forgotten all the same having forgotten having forgotten and all the same all the same as having forgotten and to hear it hear it heard it heard it hear heard it heard it, heard it and all the same as forgotten having heard it all the same and all the same and having forgotten and having heard and all the same. Having heard it all the same having heard hear it hear it all the same having forgotten and hear it and having forgotten and hear it and all the same and all the same and hear it and heard it.

So much and so much farther as much and as much farther, and as much farther and so much and hear it and having heard it and all the same and having heard it and all the same and hear it and all the same and hear it and heard and having heard and all the same and hear it. Here and hear it. They are all the same as heard it as hear it all the same as heard it all the same and as heard it. All the same and heard and as heard it and as heard it and as all the same and heard it. All the same. Hear it. All the same hear it all the same.

The same examples are the same and just the same and always the same and the same examples are just the same and are the same and always the same. The same examples are just the same and they are very sorry for it. So is not business in Baltimore. And so it is not and so is it not and as it is not and as it is and as it is not the same more than the same. This sounds as if they said it and it sounds as if they meant it and it sounds as if they meant it and it sounds as if they meant and as if they meant it. Everybody is disappointed in Julian's cousin Julian's cousin too, everybody is also disappointed is disappointed in Julian's cousin too. Julian and everybody is disappointed in Julian's cousin and everybody too is disappointed in Julian's cousin too. How many days are there for it. There are as many days for it as there are ways to see how they do it. Do it too. Julian and a cousin too. Two and two, and two and two and lists and remembered and lists. To commence back further and just as far and as far back and just as far back. Just as far back as that. Just as far back as that and Julian remembers just as far back as that and Julian remembers just as far back and remembers Julian remembers just as far back as that.

Everybody knows that anybody shows shows it as soon as soon and at noon as carefully noon as carefully soon, everybody knows, everybody shows, everybody shows anybody knows carefully as soon carefully and noon carefully at noon everybody knows everybody shows carefully at noon carefully soon carefully soon carefully at noon, everybody knows carefully at noon carefully as soon anybody knows everybody shows everybody shows everybody knows carefully as soon, anybody knows carefully as soon, anybody knows carefully at noon everybody knows carefully as soon everybody knows carefully as soon, anybody knows carefully as soon everybody knows carefully as soon.

Everybody knows carefully as soon, everybody knows carefully at noon everybody knows carefully as soon.

Entirely exposed too.

And how many in passing turn around. Just how many in passing just how many turn around. One can always tell the difference between snowy and cloudy everybody can always tell some difference between cloudy and snowy. Every one can always tell some difference.

Every one can always tell some difference between cloudy and cloudy between snowy and snowy between cloudy and snowy between snowy and cloudy.

Not as to dinner and dinner.

How many are a hundred and how many are two hundred and how many are a million and three. This is for them to answer and in this way more in Baltimore. Business in Baltimore consists of how many and how often and more at once and a half of them there.

Business in Baltimore is always a share a share and care to care and where where in Baltimore. Where in Baltimore. How many kinds are there in it. There are many and as many there are as many as there are streets, corners, places, rivers and trees in Baltimore. Squares can be mentioned too and stones and little and at once to approach. Who changes all changes.

All changes who changes.

Do not hurry to winter and to summer. Do not hurry to winter. Do not hurry to summer. Do not hurry to summer. Not to hurry to winter. Not to hurry to winter and to summer and to winter and not to hurry to summer and not to hurry to winter.

He can hear they can hear they can hear that they do hear her. They can hear that they do hear him. They can hear that they do hear him. They can hear that they do hear her. They can hear that they can hear him.

They can hear winter, they can hear summer they can hear that they do hear summer, they can hear that they do hear that they can hear winter, they can hear summer they can hear winter. They can hear that they hear him they can hear that they can hear her they do hear that they can hear that they do hear her that they do hear winter that they do hear her that they can hear her that they can hear that they do hear him that they do hear him that they can hear that they do hear that they hear that they can hear summer and hear hear her here hear him here that they can hear her that they can hear. They do hear that they can hear winter. They do hear that they can hear summer.

Business in Baltimore for them and with them with them and as a tree is bought. How is a tree bought. Business in Baltimore and for them and by them and is bought how is it to be bought and where is it to be bought. Business in Baltimore and for them and adding it to them and as it has the half of the whole and the whole is more if it is best shown to be more used than it was here and nearly. This and a result. Take it in place, take it to a place take it for a place and places and to place and placed. Placed and placing should a daughter be a mother. Placed and placing should a father be a brother. Placed and placing should a mother be a sister altogether. All this makes it easy that very many say so and very many do so and very many do so and very many say so.

He can so easily amuse himself and so can he so very easily amuse himself and so can he so very easily and so can he so very easily amuse himself and so can he so very easily and so can he so very easily amuse himself and as it were to be they had to have it largely and more and when they needed it all. To begin.

How many houses were there in it. And to go on. And how many houses were there in it.

How to depend upon it. And how many houses were there in it. And how to depend upon it and how many houses were there in it. How many houses are there in it.

There were as many houses as there were in it.

There were as many houses in it as there were as many houses in it. There are as many houses in it. How many houses are there in it. There are as many houses as there are in it. After that streets, corners, connections and ways of walking. There were more houses than there were in it. There were more corners than there were in it. There were more streets than there were in it. How many streets are there in it. How many corners are there in it. How many streets are there in it. How many houses were there in it. Everybody counting. Call somebody Hortense. Please do. And David. Please do.

A little makes it all stop and stopped. A little makes it all stopped and stop. A little makes it all stop. A little makes it all stopped.

It is a great pleasure for Hilda and for William for William and for Hilda. It is a great pleasure for either. If a home and a house and as often as hurry and hurried, they need to and do, they need to do they did need to they did and they did need to and they do and they do and they did need to do it too.

Does she look as much like it as the newspaper would suggest.

Plainly make it mine. Plainly make it plainly make it mine. This is as least not as well said as ever.

Having forgotten to hear, what and having forgotten to hear what had not been forgotten and not forgotten to hear.

They have please they have please they have please. Business in Baltimore they have please.

Did they like five.

Did they like five of five.

Business in Baltimore and more. More seated.

Business in Baltimore need never be finished here when it is there when it is commenced there when it is completed here when it is added to here when it is established there. In this they mean he means to too and two.

Never to be used at last to last and never as it was as if it was a horse. They have no use for horses.

Never as it was as if it was because they had to have a way of counting one to make one.

Could be sitting around faced that way and lean and if he did would he not having been as payed follow to a home. Follow to a home for him.

Two cannot make room for two and two both seated cannot make room for two both seated. Two both seated cannot make room for two both seated.

This is one date.

Two cannot make room for two both seated.

Yes and yes and more and yes and why and yes and yes and why and yes.

A new better and best and yes and yes and better and most and yes and yes and better and best and yes and yes and more and best and better and most and yes and yes. And yes and yes and better and yes and more and yes and better and yes, and yes and yes and more and yes and better and yes and more and yes and yes and yes and more and best and yes and yes and better and most and yes and yes and more and better and best and most and yes and yes and most and better and yes and yes and most and more and yes and yes, and more and yes and yes and better and yes and yes and most and yes and yes and best and yes and yes and better and yes and more and yes and best and yes and better and yes and more and yes and most and yes and more and yes and yes and better and yes and yes and most and yes and yes and best and yes and yes and yes and yes and better and most and yes and yes and better and most and yes and yes and more and most and yes and yes and better and most and yes and yes and more and better and yes and yes and yes and yes and more and best and yes and yes and more and best and yes and yes and more and yes and yes and best and yes and yes and more and yes and yes and better and yes and yes and best and yes and yes and more and yes and yes and better and yes and yes. And yes and yes and and more and better and yes and yes and better and yes and yes and more and yes and yes and better and and yes and yes and better and yes and yes and more and yes and yes and best and better and yes and yes and most and more and yes and yes and yes and yes and better and yes and best and most and better and more and best and better and yes and yes and yes and yes and yes and yes and more and yes and yes and better and yes and yes and more and yes and yes. And more and yes and yes. And more and better and yes and yes and best and more and yes and yes and better and yes and yes and most and yes and yes and best and more and yes and yes and yes and yes and better and more and better and yes and yes and most and better and more and yes and yes and yes and yes. And better and yes and yes and more and yes and yes and yes and yes and more and best and better and most and best and better and most and more and more and most and better and yes and yes.

LIPCHITZ

When Stein wrote this portrait in late 1925, Lipchitz had already done a bust of her, in 1920. Mutual portraiture becomes the thematic and verbal center of her piece. Doing a likeness, making a portrait look or sound like the subject, also involves liking the subject and requires looking with receptiveness and tenderness. The portrait ends with a symmetrical sentence that composes each looking at the other and for the other in mutual regard, "When I know him I look at it for him and I look at him for him and I look at him for him when I know him."

This portrait shows Stein using elements of daily life. Here she appears to refer to Lipchitz standing at or reflected in a window: "When I first knew him he was looking looking through the glass and the chicken." This sentence may connect with an anecdote in the *Autobiography* about Stein meeting Lipchitz as he looked through a shop window at an iron rooster he wanted to buy, which supposedly led to Lipchitz asking her to pose for him. In a different context, she had also noted at this time a dream of young Fritz Peters, the nephew of Margaret Anderson. The boy dreamed "he heard a pheasant calling and very likely a pheasant was calling." Presumably the dream was of interest because the pheasant may have been in the dream or in actuality or both. In the portrait, however, the pheasant appears to connect with the chicken or rooster that Lipchitz looks at in the shop window. Finally, this portrait is in a French student notebook whose cover shows a young soldier in World War I uniform behind a battlement at a lookout post, looking with concentration through a periscope. This illustration may have contributed to "tenderly then standing" and "looking through the glass." Though it is not important to trace such details to their sources, it is important to remember that Stein did not invent details but drew word ideas directly from the world around her. They are not nonsense but fit together and can be understood.

• • • • •

Like and like likely and likely likely and likely like and like.

He had a dream. He dreamed he heard a pheasant calling and very likely a pheasant was calling.

To whom went.

He had a dream he dreamed he heard a pheasant calling and most likely a pheasant was calling.

In time.

This and twenty and forty-two makes every time a hundred and two thirty.

Any time two and too say.

When I knew him first he was looking looking through the glass and the chicken. When I knew him then he was looking looking at the looking at the looking. When I knew him then he was so tenderly then standing. When I knew him then he was then after then to then by then and when I knew him then he was then we then and then for then. When I knew him then he was for then by then as then so then to then in then and so.

He never needs to know.

He never needs he never seeds but so so can they sink settle and rise and apprise and tries. Can at length be long. No indeed and a song. A song of so much so.

When I know him I look at him for him and I look at him for him and I look at him for him when I know him.

I like you very much.

Gertrude Stein.

COMPOSITION AS EXPLANATION

This lecture given in June 1926, Stein's first, differs radically from all other pieces in the *Reader*. Here she addresses the audience personally, as she never does in literary composition. There she may use "I," but not to refer to herself. Stein believed that a serious writer was in the work only as a voice, not as a person, "I am I not any longer when I write." Lecturing violated the principle of impersonality. That violation explains why the context of the lecture, an event that affected her, becomes more biographical than verbal.

The lecture is also a first in explaining her work, but her explanatory voice does not sound at ease. Stein never added introductions or prefaces to compositions. She believed in writing, not in explaining writing. To her, writing that required explanation was deficient. In a lecture, however, she stood on a podium to explain and in effect promote herself.

Many readers think of Stein as a glamorous public figure, painted, photographed, admired, written about. They imagine her in the company of the famous, living the charmed events of *The Autobiography of Alice B. Toklas.* Yet in 1933, when publication of that book launched her into fame and success, she was almost sixty and had wanted readers desperately for over twenty-five years. She was known earlier, of course, but her work was not easily available and she was not widely published or read. Her art collection was better known than the writing she most cared about. At the time of the lecture, when she badly wanted recognition, she was sharply aware of a lack of readers and publications. She wanted an audience and a publisher who would take her on as a major author. But hers was not popular work. She was a financial risk.

With Edith Sitwell she shared the pain of rejection and ridicule. Sitwell, thirteen years younger than Stein, admired her, reviewed her, and was ready to promote her, perhaps thereby enhancing her own reputation. Unlike Stein, Sitwell out of financial necessity reviewed widely and engaged in literary confrontation with dramatic flair. It was Sitwell who arranged and orchestrated the English lecture in the belief that only a personal appearance would win Stein an audience. Since England still represented authority in literary taste in America, they hoped that success in England would lead to acceptance in America, where she most wanted her work known.

An invitation to speak was issued in December 1925 by the Cambridge Literary Club. Stein refused but within a month ended up accepting the invitation, sweetened by Sitwell's promise of a second, at Oxford, to follow. By early February 1926 Stein had written the lecture. There is reason to doubt the veracity of an anecdote in the *Autobiography* that she wrote the lecture at the garage while her car was being repaired.

Material for the lecture and anxious comments anticipating it appear in other works of the winter of 1925–26. Stein and Toklas left Paris on 30 May 1926. On 4 and 7 June she spoke at Cambridge and Oxford. After seeing friends and publishers in London, the women returned to France as quickly as possible; their summer plans included looking for a country house.

Stein faced a generation gap between her audience and herself. In a daring jump, she closes it by likening the artists of the avant-garde—a military term—to her post–World War I audience, including some veterans. As World War I brought warfare from the nineteenth to the twentieth century, so modernism brought art up to date. Nations that did not fight in the war are behind the times, just as those who respond only to ossified ideas of classical beauty in art are behind the times. She places herself on the side of her young English audience, receptive to the modern. As one who has won the battle for the new, she speaks to those who have won on the battlefield.

The second part of the lecture is about Stein's work. To speak about her work was difficult because her printed writing was not well known and much was not even printed. *Three Lives* was available, but *Tender Buttons* was out of print. *The Making of Americans,* recently published, was sold by subscription. Of the pieces in the *Reader,* only the portraits of Picasso and Matisse and the pieces from *Geography and Plays* were available for reading. But major works that showed her changing style were not printed and not known, for example, *Two, A Long Gay Book, Many Many Women,* and *G.M.P.*

She describes her early texts as if they followed a plan when she in fact fumbled and groped for what might work. The sections from *The Making of Americans* in the *Reader* suggest how discontinuous and tentative her efforts were. To compensate for her uncertainty, she coined descriptive terms for her method, though she did not define or illustrate with care since she was impatient with theory. How "prolonged present" and "continuous present" differ is not clear. "Prolonged present" is used once but not distinguished from "continuous present" and not exemplified. "Beginning again and again" and "using everything" create less difficulty. All these have become a part of the terminology of Stein criticism.

The lecture ended with four unpublished pieces, *Preciosilla* (1913), *A Saint In Seven* (1922), *Sitwell Edith Sitwell* (1925), and *Jean Cocteau* (1926). Perhaps to put her audience at ease with familiar designations, she identified them by genre as a poem, a play, and two portraits. Stein chose the samples with great care to make her word work audible and to pay homage to Sitwell and Cocteau.

On 11 June 1926 Leonard Woolf of the Hogarth Press offered to publish the address. For this publication Stein added the title *Composition as Explanation.*

• • • • •

There is singularly nothing that makes a difference a difference in beginning and in the middle and in ending except that each generation has something different at which they are all looking. By this I mean so simply that anybody knows it that composition is the difference which makes each and all of them then different from other generations and this is what makes everything different otherwise they are all alike and everybody knows it because everybody says it.

It is very likely that nearly every one has been very nearly certain that something that is interesting is interesting them. Can they and do they. It is very interesting that nothing inside in them, that is when you consider the very long history of how every one ever acted or has felt, it is very interesting that nothing inside in them in all of them makes it connectedly different. By this I mean this. The only thing that is different from one time to another is what is seen and what is seen depends upon how everybody is doing everything. This makes the thing we are looking at very different and this makes what those who describe it make of it, it makes a composition, it confuses, it shows, it is, it looks, it likes it as it is, and this makes what is seen as it is seen. Nothing changes from generation to generation except the thing seen and that makes a composition. Lord Grey remarked that when the generals before the war talked about the war they talked about it as a nineteenth century war although to be fought with twentieth century weapons. That is because war is a thing that decides how it is to be when it is to be done. It is prepared and to that degree it is like all academies it is not a thing made by being made it is a thing prepared. Writing and painting and all that, is like that, for those who occupy themselves with it and don't make it as it is made. Now the few who make it as it is made, and it is to be remarked that the most decided of them usually are prepared just as the world around them is preparing, do it in this way and so I if you do not mind I will tell you how it happens. Naturally one does not know how it happened until it is well over beginning happening.

To come back to the part that the only thing that is different is what is seen when it seems to be being seen, in other words, composition and time-sense.

No one is ahead of his time, it is only that the particular variety of creating his time is the one that his contemporaries who also are creating their own time refuse to accept. And they refuse to accept it for a very simple reason and that is that they do not have to accept it for any reason. They themselves that is everybody in their entering the modern composition and they do enter it, if they do not enter it they are not so to speak in it they are out of it and so they do enter it. But in as you may say the non-competitive efforts where if you are not in it nothing is lost except nothing at all except what is not had, there are naturally all the refusals, and the things refused are only important if unexpectedly somebody happens to need them. In the case of the arts it is very definite. Those who are creating the modern composition authentically are naturally only of importance when they are dead because by that time the modern composition having become past is classified and the description of it is classical. That is the reason why the creator of the new composition in the arts is an outlaw until he is a classic, there is hardly a moment in between and it is really too bad very much too bad naturally for the creator but also very much too bad for the enjoyer, they all really would enjoy the created so much better just after it has been made than when it is already a classic, but it is perfectly simple that there is no reason why the contemporaries should see, because it would not make any difference as they lead their lives in the new composition anyway, and as every one is naturally indolent why naturally they don't see. For this reason as in quoting Lord Grey it is quite certain that nations not actively threatened are at least several generations behind themselves militarily so æsthetically they are more than several generations behind themselves and it is very much too bad, it is so very much more exciting and satisfactory for everybody if one can have contemporaries, if all one's contemporaries could be one's contemporaries.

There is almost not an interval.

For a very long time everybody refuses and then almost without a pause almost everybody accepts. In the history of the refused in the arts and literature the rapidity of the change is always startling. Now the only difficulty with the *volte-face* concerning the arts is this. When the acceptance comes, by that acceptance the thing created becomes a classic. It is a natural phenomena a rather extraordinary natural phenomena that a thing accepted becomes a classic. And what is the characteristic quality of a classic. The characteristic quality of a classic is that it is beautiful. Now of course it is perfectly true that a more or less first rate work of art is beautiful but the trouble is that when that first rate work of art becomes a classic because it is accepted the only thing that is important from then on to the majority of the acceptors the enormous majority, the most intelligent majority of the acceptors is that it is so wonderfully beautiful. Of course it is wonderfully beautiful, only when it is still a thing irritating annoying stimulating then all quality of beauty is denied to it.

Of course it is beautiful but first all beauty in it is denied and then all the beauty of it is accepted. If every one were not so indolent they would realise that beauty is beauty even when it is irritating and stimulating not only when it is accepted and classic. Of course it is extremely difficult nothing more so than to remember back to its not being beautiful once it has become beautiful. This makes it so much more difficult to realise its beauty when the work is being refused and prevents every one from realising that they were convinced that beauty was denied, once the work is accepted. Automatically with the acceptance of the time-sense comes the recognition of the beauty and once the beauty is accepted the beauty never fails any one.

Beginning again and again is a natural thing even when there is a series.

Beginning again and again and again explaining composition and time is a natural thing.

It is understood by this time that everything is the same except composition and time, composition and the time of the composition and the time in the composition.

Everything is the same except composition and as the composition is different and always going to be different everything is not the same. Everything is not the same as the time when of the composition and the time in the composition is different. The composition is different, that is certain.

The composition is the thing seen by every one living in the living they are doing, they are the composing of the composition that at the time they are living is the composition of the time in which they are living. It is that that makes living a thing they are doing. Nothing else is different, of that almost any one can be certain. The time when and the time of and the time in that composition is the natural phenomena of that composition and of that perhaps every one can be certain.

No one thinks these things when they are making when they are creating what is the composition, naturally no one thinks, that is no one formulates until what is to be formulated has been made.

Composition is not there, it is going to be there and we are here. This is some time ago for us naturally.

The only thing that is different from one time to another is what is seen and what is seen depends upon how everybody is doing everything. This makes the thing we are looking at very different and this makes what those who describe it make of it, it makes a composition, it confuses, it shows, it is, it looks, it likes it as it is, and this makes what is seen as it is seen. Nothing changes from generation to generation except the thing seen and that makes a composition.

Now the few who make writing as it is made and it is to be remarked that the most decided of them are those that are prepared by preparing, are prepared just as the world around them is prepared and is preparing to do it in this way and so if you do not mind I will again tell you how it happens. Naturally one does not know how it happened until it is well over beginning happening.

Each period of living differs from any other period of living not in the way life is but in the way life is conducted and that authentically speaking is composition. After life has been conducted in a certain way everybody knows it but nobody knows it, little by little, nobody knows it as long as nobody knows it. Any one creating the composition in the arts does not know it either, they are conducting life and that makes their composition what it is, it makes their work compose as it does.

Their influence and their influences are the same as that of all of their contemporaries only it must always be remembered that the analogy is not obvious until as I say the composition of a time has become so pronounced that it is past and the artistic composition of it is a classic.

And now to begin as if to begin. Composition is not there, it is going to be there and we are here. This is some time ago for us naturally. There is something to be added afterwards.

Just how much my work is known to you I do not know. I feel that perhaps it would be just as well to tell the whole of it.

In beginning writing I wrote a book called *Three Lives* this was written in 1905. I wrote a negro story called *Melanctha*. In that there was a constant recurring and beginning there was a marked direction in the direction of being in the present although naturally I had been accustomed to past present and future, and why, because the composition forming around me was a prolonged present. A composition of a prolonged present is a natural composition in the world as it has been these thirty years it was more and more a prolonged present. I created then a prolonged present naturally I knew nothing of a continuous present but it came naturally to me to make one, it was simple it was clear to me and nobody knew why it was done like that, I did not myself although naturally to me it was natural.

After that I did a book called *The Making of Americans* it is a long book about a thousand pages.

Here again it was all so natural to me and more and more complicatedly a continuous present. A continuous present is a continuous present. I made almost a thousand pages of a continuous present.

Continuous present is one thing and beginning again and again is another thing. These are both things. And then there is using everything.

This brings us again to composition this the using everything. The using everything brings us to composition and to this composition. A continuous present and using everything and beginning again. In these two books there was elaboration of the complexities of using everything and of a continuous present and of beginning again and again and again.

In the first book there was a groping for a continuous present and for using everything by beginning again and again.

There was a groping for using everything and there was a groping for a continuous present and there was an inevitable beginning of beginning again and again and again.

Having naturally done this I naturally was a little troubled with it when I read it. I became then like the others who read it. One does, you know, excepting that when I reread it myself I lost myself in it again. Then I said to myself this time it will be different and I began. I did not begin again I just began.

In this beginning naturally since I at once went on and on very soon there were pages and pages and pages more and more elaborated creating a more and more continuous present including more and more using of everything and continuing more and more beginning and beginning and beginning.

I went on and on to a thousand pages of it.

In the meantime to naturally begin I commenced making portraits of anybody and anything. In making these portraits I naturally made a continuous present an including everything and a beginning again and again within a very small thing. That started me into composing anything into one thing. So then naturally it was natural that one thing an enormously long thing was not everything an enormously short thing was also not everything nor was it all of it a continuous present thing nor was it always and always beginning again. Naturally I would then begin again. I would begin again I would naturally begin. I did naturally begin. This brings me to a great deal that has been begun.

And after that what changes what changes after that, after that what changes and what changes after that and after that and what changes and after that and what changes after that.

The problem from this time on became more definite.

It was all so nearly alike it must be different and it is different, it is natural that if everything is used and there is a continuous present and a beginning again and again if it is all so alike it must be simply different and everything simply different was the natural way of creating it then.

In this natural way of creating it then that it was simply different everything being alike it was simply different, this kept on leading one to lists. Lists naturally for awhile and by lists I mean a series. More and more in going back over what was done at this time I find that I naturally kept simply different as an intention. Whether there was or whether there was not a continuous present did not then any longer trouble me there was or there was not, and using everything no longer troubled me if everything is alike using everything could no longer trouble me and beginning again and again could no longer trouble me because if lists were inevitable if series were inevitable and the whole of it was inevitable beginning again and again could not trouble me so then with nothing to trouble me I very completely began naturally since everything is alike making it as simply different naturally as simply different as possible. I began doing natural phenomena what I call natural phenomena and natural phenomena naturally everything being alike natural phenomena are making things be naturally simply different. This found its culmination later, in the beginning it began in a center confused with lists with series with geography with returning portraits and with particularly often four and three and often with five and four. It is easy to see that in the beginning such a conception as everything being naturally different would be very inarticulate and very slowly it began to emerge and take the form of anything, and then naturally if anything that is simply different is simply different what follows will follow.

So far then the progress of my conceptions was the natural progress entirely in accordance with my epoch as I am sure is to be quite easily realised if you think over the scene that was before us all from year to year.

As I said in the beginning, there is the long history of how every one ever acted or has felt and that nothing inside in them in all of them makes it connectedly different. By this I mean all this.

The only thing that is different from one time to another is what is seen and what is seen depends upon how everybody is doing everything.

It is understood by this time that everything is the same except composition and time, composition and the time of the composition and the time in the composition.

Everything is the same except composition and as the composition is different and always going to be different everything is not the same. So then I as a contemporary creating the composition in the beginning was groping toward a continuous present, a using everything a beginning again and again and then everything being alike then everything very simply everything was naturally simply different and so I as a contemporary was creating everything being alike was creating everything naturally being naturally simply different, everything being alike. This then was the period that brings me to the period of the beginning of 1914. Everything being alike everything naturally would be simply different and war came and everything being alike and everything being simply different brings everything being simply different brings it to romanticism.

Romanticism is then when everything being alike everything is naturally simply different, and romanticism.

Then for four years this was more and more different even though this was, was everything alike. Everything alike naturally everything was simply different and this is and was romanticism and this is and was war. Everything being alike everything naturally everything is different simply different naturally simply different.

And so there was the natural phenomena that was war, which had been, before war came, several generations behind the contemporary composition, because it became war and so completely needed to be contemporary became completely contemporary and so created the completed recognition of the contemporary composition. Every one but one may say every one became consciously became aware of the existence of the authenticity of the modern composition. This then the contemporary recognition, because of the academic thing known as war having been forced to become contemporary made every one not only contemporary in act not only contemporary in thought but contemporary in self-consciousness made every one contemporary with the modern composition. And so the art creation of the contemporary composition which would have been outlawed normally outlawed several generations more behind even than war, war having been brought so to speak up to date art so to speak was allowed not completely to be up to date, but nearly up to date, in other words we who created the expression of the modern composition were to be recognized before we were dead some of us even quite a long time before we were dead. And so war may be said to have advanced a general recognition of the expression of the contemporary composition by almost thirty years.

And now after that there is no more of that in other words there is peace and something comes then and it follows coming then.

And so now one finds oneself interesting oneself in an equilibration, that of course means words as well as things and distribution as well as between themselves between the words and themselves and the things and themselves, a distribution as distribution. This makes what follows what follows and now there is every reason why there should be an arrangement made. Distribution is interesting and equilibration is interesting when a continuous present and a beginning again and again and using everything and everything alike and everything naturally simply different has been done.

After all this, there is that, there has been that that there is a composition and that nothing changes except composition the composition and the time of and the time in the composition.

The time of the composition is a natural thing and the time in the composition is a natural thing it is a natural thing and it is a contemporary thing.

The time of the composition is the time of the composition. It has been at times a present thing it has been at times a past thing it has been at times a future thing it has been at times an endeavor at parts or all of these things. In my beginning it was a continuous present a beginning again and again and again and again, it was a series it was a list it was a similarity and everything different it was a distribution and an equilibration. That is all of the time some of the time of the composition.

Now there is still something else the time-sense in the composition. This is what is always a fear a doubt and a judgement and a conviction. The quality in the creation of expression the quality in a composition that makes it go dead just after it has been made is very troublesome.

The time in the composition is a thing that is very troublesome. If the time in the composition is very troublesome it is because there must even if there is no time at all in the composition there must be time in the composition which is in its quality of distribution and equilibration. In the beginning there was the time in the composition that naturally was in the composition but time in the composition comes now and this is what is now troubling every one the time in the composition is now a part of distribution and equilibration. In the beginning there was confusion there was a continuous present and later there was romanticism which was not a confusion but an extrication and now there is either succeeding or failing there must be distribution and equilibration there must be time that is distributed and equilibrated. This is the thing that is at present the most troubling and if there is the time that is at present the most troublesome the time-sense that is at present the most troubling is the thing that makes the present the most troubling. There is at present there is distribution, by this I mean expression and time, and in this way at present composition is time that is the reason that at present the time-sense is troubling that is the reason why at present the time-sense in the composition is the composition that is making what there is in composition.

And afterwards.

Now that is all.

AN ACQUAINTANCE WITH DESCRIPTION

The word *acquaintance* in the title makes description sound familiar and intimate, as writing always was to Stein. The most deeply personal way of knowing, writing was never a mere technique for her. She must even as a student have used the word acquaintance as William James defined it in his textbook *Psychology,* where he distinguished "knowledge of acquaintance," the sense of indivisible what-ness based on sensation, from "knowledge-about," the knowledge gathered gradually, by accretion, from perception.

Stein wrote this study of description as one in the explanatory series about writing that had begun with *An Elucidation* of 1923. The series includes not only the pieces she later collected in a book under the title *How To Write* but also the study of description, *More Grammar For A Sentence; More Grammar Genia Berman,* which includes not only grammar but also a portrait of Eugene Berman; and other pieces written separately up to the beginning of 1931.

Even before 1926, in works like *A Third, Natural Phenomena,* and *A Novel of Thank You,* begun the preceding year, description had preoccupied Stein. The study of description was stimulated in part by her trip to England in June 1926. Invited to deliver an address at Cambridge and Oxford, she must have been especially impressed by seeing the countryside. (Much later, in *What Is English Literature,* one of the *Lectures in America* of 1935, the experience returned: "The thing that has made the glory of English literature is description, simple concentrated description.") Her sensitivity to landscape had been sharpened by several summers in the Rhône Valley; by 1926 Stein and Toklas were looking for a country house in France. Stein wrote the study of description after her return to France in the summer of 1926, alongside the family portrait of her friends, *Edith Sitwell And Her Brothers The Sitwells And Also To Osbert Sitwell And To S. Sitwell,* which also recalled England. The piece is an attempt to make a landscape her own, not a theoretical treatise or a travelogue or reminiscence such as Toklas includes in her *Cookbook.* Stein considers how we apprehend what we see and how we compose our perceptions in words. Painting—especially landscape and still life—is never far from her writing.

Since the experience of England had contributed to the study of description, Stein must have been delighted to see it published by Laura Riding and Robert Graves, with whom she had become friends, at their Seizin Press in London in April 1929.

• • • • •

Mouths and Wood.

Queens and from a thousand to a hundred.

Description having succeeded deciding, studying description so that there is describing until it has been adjoined and is in a description. Studies description until in attracting which is a building has been described as an in case of planting. And so studying in description not only but also is not finishing but understood as describing.

To describe it as at all through. Once more. To describe it as not as dew because it is in the trees. To describe it as it is new not because it has come to be for them if it lasts. At last to come to place it where it was not by that time in that way. And what is what is the name. Holly has very little red berries and so have very large fir trees but not at the same time even though in the same place. Not even in houses and gardens not even in woods and why, why because geraniums have one color and to find it high, high and high up, and a little like it was. Once more and more when it was once more and once more when more when it was. When one goes three go and when three go two go. She said she did not believe in there having there having been there having been there having been there before. Refusing to turn away.

A description refusing to turn away a description.

Two older and one very much younger do not make two older and one very much younger. Come again is easily said if they have if they have come back.

A description simply a description.

A sea gull looking at the grain as seen. And then remarkably farming and manufacturing they like wedding and still with horses and it does not matter if you ask they might there might be a choice. This makes that be what a little in the front and not at all what we see. Never having forgotten to be pleased.

What is the difference between not what is the difference between. What is the difference between not what is the difference between. An acquaintance with description or what is the difference between not what is the difference between not an acquaintance in description. An acquaintance in description. First a sea gull looking into the grain in order to look into the grain it must be flying as if it were looking at the grain. A sea gull looking at the grain. Second a sea gull looking into the grain. Any moment at once. Why is the grain that comes again paler so that it is not so high and after awhile there can be very many of a kind to know that kind. Next to find it coming up and down and not when it is directly through around. This comes to be a choice and we are the only choosers. This makes that be what a little in the front and not at all what we see. To have seen very many every time suspended. This can be in black and as grey and surprising. It is not early to be discouraged by their seating. Seating four to a color.

Acquaintance with description if he holds it to him and it falls toward him.

Every little bit different and to ask did he might it be older might it be did it did it have it as suggested it might be older.

Very often not at all. An acquaintance with description and they might be if it were at all needed not by them fortunately. Fortunately is always understood. There is a difference between forests and the cultivation of cattle. In regard to either there is a choice in one a choice of trees in the other a choice.

An acquaintance with description if and acquaintance with description. Making an acquaintance with description does not begin now begin now. In acquaintance with description. Simply describe that they are married as they were married. They married. She the one and she the one and they and none and they and one and she and one and they they were nearly certain that their daughter had a friend who did not resemble either their daughter's father or their daughter's mother and this was not altogether why they had what they had they had it as if they might of if they had asked it of all of all. Meant to be not left to it as if it was not beside that it could be and best. Best and best can be delighted delighted delighted.

It is very inconvenient when there is that by this because because of this being that by then. An acquaintance with description has not been begun. An acquaintance with description to begin three.

Not it is not it is not it is not it is at all as it is. No one should remember anything if it did not make any difference it did not make any difference if it did not make any difference. No one should remember anything and it should not make any difference. No one should remember anything and it should not make any difference. Who makes this carefully. Who makes this carefully that it should not make any difference that not any one should remember anything. When two horses meet both being driven and they have not turned aside they turn aside. They both turn aside.

When it is not remarkable that it takes longer it does not make it more than they could do. It is not more remarkable that it takes longer than that it is more remarkable than that is what they have to do. It is not more remarkable that it takes longer than that it is that they have it to do. It is not more remarkable. After this makes them prepare this. Very well she is very well. I will you will they will he will.

Not finally so much and change it.

They might like it as it is in the sun.

Naming everything every day, this is the way. Naming everything every day. Naming everything every day.

It is a great pleasure to watch it coming.

They might like it, as it is in the sun.

It is a pleasure to watch it coming but it might that she could be unaccustomed to lie down without sleeping it might be that she could be unaccustomed to lie down without sleeping.

What is the difference between three and two in furniture. Three is the third of three and two is the second of two. This makes it as true as a description. And not satisfied. And what is the difference between being on the road and waiting very likely being very likely waiting, a road is connecting and as it is connecting it is intended to be keeping going and waiting everybody can understand puzzling. He said it nicely. This makes it as if they had not been intended and after all who is after all after all it is after all afterwards, as they have left there may be a difference between summer and winter. Everybody makes a part of it part of it and a part of it. If he comes to do it, if he comes to do it and if he comes to do it. He comes to do it. Anybody can be mistaken many times mistaken for it. Turkeys should never be brought any where they belong there where they are turkeys there and this reminds one at once. Acquainted with description is the same as acquainted with turkeys. Acquainted with description is the same as being acquainted with turkeys. Why when the sun is here and there is it here. Acquainted with the sun to be acquainted to be unacquainted and to be unacquainted and to be unacquainted and to be in the sun and to be acquainted to be acquainted with the sun. It can be there.

Look down and see a blue curtain and a white hall. A horse asleep lying surrounded by cows.

There is a great difference not only then but now.

After all after this afterwards it was not only that there had been more than there was differently but it was more often than not recognised there can be instances of difference between recognisable and between recognisable when they had been formidable and in the use of that notwithstanding. Having come along. And not being described as very likely to make it not belong to this at that time and very easily when they were delighted and might it be not only suggested and not only suggested as that could be while they came and after that by nearly very often having when it was that it should be decided. They might not only be very often not more nearly as if they could and should has returned. Not on that account.

Never to be left to add it too. Never to be left to add it to that.

Describing that that trees are as available as they were that trees were as available as they were. And to say that it is not to be more than understood very likely it is very likely to be. To be not only pleased but pleasing and to be not only pleased but to be not only pleased. An acquaintance with description.

What is the difference between a hedge and a tree. A hedge and a tree what is the difference between a hedge and a tree.

Next to that what is there to be more than if it was to be prepared.

In part.

Letting it be not what it is like.

The difference between a small pair and that color and outside. If blue is pale and green is different how many trees are there in it.

Simply a description and sensibly a description and around and a description.

After all who might be who might be influenced by dahlias and roses, pinks and greens white and another color. Who might be careful not to think just as well of what they had when they were there. And never having this by now. A plain description so that anyone would know that pears do grow very well on very good on the very best of pear trees. They made it be theirs yet. After a while they knew the difference after a while they knew that difference after a while they knew this difference after a while they knew the difference after a while they knew the difference after a while they knew the difference. Pleasing them with the description of a pear tree. Pleasing them with the description of a pear tree pleasing them with the description of a pear tree. Pleasing them with the description of a pear tree. And pleasing them by having it not made so much as much differently. They might have been and if by this at once.

Not after all.

An acquaintance with description the difference between by that time and why they went. We have left them now.

An acquaintance with description.

Mary Lake is a pretty name. Two five seven nine eleven. And I was to tell you what, about a window, what was it. She thought it was two four six nine eleven but it was not it was two five five seven nine eleven. Mary Lake is a pretty name she said it was she said she thought it was she said she said it was. Mary Lake is a pretty name all the same she said she said it was. To change to poplar and trees. Mary Lake is a pretty name to change to poplars to change she said it was to change to she said she thought it was to change to she said she she said it was. Mary Lake is a pretty name to change to poplars and to change she said she said it was.

Now then they then they have to have what after all is a difference to be left alone. Nobody needs to be around and gathering the milk. If they have it here and nearly as if they also differently arranged chickens and to calve how do they need to be so sure sure and be certain that they have theirs there and the same. It is astonishing not to please.

Beginning with the poplars as seed. They grow fruit trees just as well. Beginning with the poplars as seed. Is there any difference between Nelson and a Brazilian admiral is there any difference between Nelson and a Brazilian admiral's son and where they chose it. Not as well as he did he is not only the eldest of five but the eldest of eight. In this way he absolutely has not only not but not gone. When they come to say they come and have spoken of an acquaintance with description in describing that there is no intention to distinguish between looking and looking. An acquaintance with description gives a very pleasant programme of fruit and some varieties of carnations. He quotes me. She does not like not only when but how. Not of him but of the time when there is no more relief from irresistible.

How can and how can he climb higher than a house if he can be at that time having had it be as much as that and certain. Never to mention more than never to mention more than that it was like a hat a cardinal can not have a stone hat not have a stone hat a hat and candlesticks of blue green when they are glass and small and a box made at all.

That pleases them and him.

Yes can be mentioned altogether.

Each one can be interested in at a time and added.

There is a difference between whether and leather there is more happening when no one needs to next to a need it for pansies. A watch kept in and three or all the time. Not a mother nor a step-mother but always after all when she did and after all when she did come to be called and they might if they came have it in three different kinds chickens ducks and geese.

Have it in three different kinds before that a sister and a brother and now when at first, at first makes it that they asked him and he said just farther it is a very fearful thing to cross the river Rhone when they might even when they might. They did the second time. The first time they did the second time. Might makes snuff might makes enough enough and snuff. It is very pleasant that a box a little box is just alike.

An acquaintance with description and and an acquaintance with description reconciled.

She is very happy and a farm. She is very happy and a farm. She is very happy and a farm. She is very happy and a farm. She is very happy and a farm.

In and sight if the once and before that could be a hearing heard at most. Might it be needed like it. He can be said if when it might that like it by now. Could he have had a had and have and had a hat. Very every time they were killed for their father. Their father might be their mother. Their mother might be that it might be in their and unison. Unison is not disturbed for their and for their and for their it can be that although they they might if she was here and he was there spoken to by that not alone by slow or snow not alone by snow or slow slowly and snow comes now not by having that it was different from a hollyhock by a chance. He did indeed indeed and might after all his aunt and if she were to be by by and by by and by with the one, they could very often need to select theirs in place. Let it be that his brother was killed altogether his father not his father his mother not his mother the children of his brother and he he was deafened by that and not altogether. He need he need he need he need he need to not to need to be what if it were differently Perrette and Perrine, that makes it said. Safe is when after all they could eat.

Thank you for a description and would have hesitated to ask.

Did you see him fall. Not at all.

If two and two and she likes it and dew was it that it could be not wishing to be left. Not to be respected as it was not to be respected as it was not why it was and she left them and he said I do too and she said do not bother exactly and around they met met if not likely to be nearly where as if looking. This makes it take a place.

Nicely and seated makes it left again left and right makes it regular and because it was not when they wished. They often know that. There is no difference between she not being comfortable and she comfortable. Never again to be signed and resigned and acquaintance with description. If it were not to use we would choose. If we were not Jews we would choose if it were not to use we would choose. They can be as small as that and there reliability there as counted. Never to like it smaller and a lavender color. It might make it added one in green. Not fortunately an alignment. Repeat relate and change three and four to two. This makes it more difficult than fluttering. Not to be argued about. Noon is for nooning.

Do you leave it to be mine and nicely. Out of eight there was one how many are there when there are very many.

Seven and two and nearly awake because snuff is useful in little boxes where there are put metal clippers and no snuff. Anybody can be reasonably satisfied with that exactly.

She liked my description of aunt Fanny, she liked my description of hazel nuts she liked my description of the resemblance between pheasants and peacocks she liked my description of how that would be what was wanted. She liked to have them hear it if it was good not only for theirs but for ours and she would not mind it if they could be what they had at that time and easily no one is ever allowed allowed and aroused around and not the difference between the distance between Brazil and France and the difference between whether they made it be what they liked. It might be changed. They might be not at all easily after all arranged so that they would prefer where it actually is and now as pleases it pleases her to please when it can be fortunately not at all as it might be if they were certain that shells and shells did and did make flowers did and did and easily having examined who they had and when they came they thanked. Now can it be two and Tuesday, leaving it alone.

Leaving it alone. From this time on to borrow to borrow is to reply and to reply is to be useful attentively and might as well as might and might as well as might, might it being the same come to be having it for this and that precisely. An interval between when they had this as well when they had this as well. She said and says that when a higher and not a high hill has it as their left and right how can it be told favorably. It can and will. An acquaintance with description or it can and will.

Will it be that they like when they see why it has not as if when it came leaving that in that round and settled so that if it is described they might be wrong. Not left to it only by what is after all why they like and had it here. This may be otherwise known. If they are sold as they are sold we might as well but not only really not at all reliably placing if it is as it as it is at all very well very well to do so. Yesterday to say.

Describing where they went. Describing when it was like it. They did put a clock face on the telegraph pole.

Eagerly enough they looked to see the difference between a horse and two oxen and they looked eagerly enough to see the difference between poplars at a distance and walnut trees.

Every little while they made it at that time. Not meaning to have lost it when when it had gone away. They saved it in order that it might be had when it was accepted as a large quantity. Not in order to be kind. They liked it fancifully. Might they be placed where they could see. If they were left where they were sent and could be by it when it is fastened and to explain explained that it was that as that had had been theirs too and nearly not while it needed it for it to be arranged by the putting it side by side for them, at least as they had not been very liked and liking that as much as if it had been leaving it near them and coming to have the key put not as now underneath but nearly under all the top so that if when it is not only that he would be releasing sheep releasing sheep they might not only be two who have themselves seated there. Not while it did. Two who have themselves seated there not while it did not come to be four in renown and not be settled to become the next who near and needed did anybody know the difference between their fairly seated and leaving it as seen. Very nearly wrongly so and to be sure and next next can be why they went why they went to stay not as if it was when it is might it be changed changed every day to theirs having if they went and to cross. Back is not why they have called it. She knows what they mean. An acquaintance with description is not earlier and later than they say. They say that they have been as it is why they could. To like it better. I will always describe it where it is at its widest and it will be very well done.

Would it do it any good to be so where they went. To be sure to be so when they leave it to them. And they might have theirs half of the time which is why once and one they make it be that they did not take it then and take it take it apart. Not in this case and would leave it for them to see. Sit is as well as if on top they might have been to change not if it is where where can be separated from while and when it is the same they exchange pleasing it as if very likely when it had not as if she said been heard.

Like and it was if a guinea hen was wild they needed it as well when they had been liked as much if they had need be thought to come as well and it did not. Next to need not be well as well as said need to be seeing it where it is where there is leaving it as very likely well and they might be two having having leaving leaving let it not let it not is nearly around and it did not like that because it was salty because it was salty, not after a very long after a little while after it was there a little while after it was there a little while and might it be theirs for themselves it might. What was it as it said not so what is it as it said and this is why they could be nearly finally theirs in their being nearly when they had it. It need not be so very much. Here I can see it. If it was above and below they could be seen letting it be theirs to think of well why should they when they will be as they were in there and by this with it for the rest they do not need it leaving what it is because if they announced announced readily by the time that it is nearer than that which is very well. Letting it be not leaving it in this way and recommending what they need for it. Letting it be let it alone let it alone and like it. They would never like to let it leave. Continue. They make a mistake it was not that and coming back to it. There is a great difference and when they like it there is a great difference and when they like it. There is a great difference and when they like it. Not taking it away. This is one way to believe their pieces. Very like the water.

There is a difference between the middle and both sides.

They will not be themselves aloud they heard in that with it to leave not when and left, excuse me. If not they wish it.

How can it be left as it will when they know that each one is in some place as if it came to come and leave it likely that it is exactly there. Very often we looked for them. So many ways of forgetting that this is there there where if left to leave it.

Is it likely if it went that it went around it. Is it likely if it did not go and it was in it so that if it was not there it was placed would it be divided. They liked it to be said. Very likely not. It was very encouraging to hear them do it. Not at first it did not at first it did not at first seem to be very likely to be what they would do, to be what they would do it is reasonable that it is more intelligent to see it but not if all at all having not lost it altogether by this time theirs might be easily just as well as if it were. They can be divided between themselves and the others and if they are not only because both sides and pleases but actually when they are identical and left alone it really is too much in a crisis.

There is no difference between what between and at a distance as there is no difference between what between what and at a distance no difference between between and at a distance there is no difference between what between between and at a distance. Next. There is no difference between between and and between at a distance there is no difference between at a distance between and what between there is no difference between what between and at a distance. Next. There is no difference between where and where it is just before never before never between never before never at a distance before, leaving before at a distance between there is no difference between having decided upon thirty, thirty what and having decided upon using both using both how, using both habitably. That makes it different that it is not seen from there.

Example and precept, sitting if in sitting they are there they must as if in crossing two at a time and not bound not bound to be used to as in lead lead to it from their having this in use not to be reaching leaving it as well they might be theirs to connect having to indeed now and and turned around if it were to be prepared as if when this is when it is to be and back need and they need leaving it with a change changed to be could it be remembered and left that it might commandingly so not if as it was said come and across they might if they were third and altogether once more felt and after it was not in place but and beside and a little change and this is if if it was when it was to study study could be could be should it have it round and as could be when there is little to be left when separated not all through when it is shorter than it could and and could not be used as so and it was not to be not when it was that length at length and never yet after all when when is doubtfully repeated in this letting it be as much as if could it be heard coming not in shawl and not in all and after very much after longer not very much shorter and held not very much as held to be coming how often has there been a white one where they could not think to see. It. It is not needing blue having artificially leaves and connecting as stems it is never theirs by right by right winding it later might make not so nearly nearly white and white and while which is just as naturally as every letter. This makes them say delighted. This makes them say delighted. To be liking liked like it like if like like to like like and often often where where is it. It is there just there where I am looking. Very clearly expressed.

Not to leave it be alone and looks like in the way and when it is not left to be themselves have it to say they made it come as if it would be leaving it as fast nicely. One this is to be that it is not here leave it for them by this with whom it is to nicely handle it with what is meant when it is not to be changed what I notice. It is not very nearly that it is not at all it when it is that in the leaving it leave it in not around they might have had it sent it not to come to be theirs when they leave and it was very likely that it had been in that first when it needs to mention how could there in there not so much as that when to be leading it not when it is in front and kept to be sure to be sure. Would it be almost what it is leaving leaving never needs it left because not while it is certainly better than here better than here there.

She would be there if it was very well said that it would be it is would be unsatisfactory it is would be it is would be unsatisfactory and find it from the things as it is done done has been has been it would as it would be is it it as it would be unsatisfactory. Find it as it would be unsatisfactory. She said and as it would it it is as it would be as it is it is in that from this and as it is in this to be and is to be and is to be and is to be unsatisfactory. She said it would be as it is to be unsatisfactory. It is very easily certain that it could happen happen and to be would be would be and to be would be unsatisfactory. Even every thing like in and like and that. In every even like and thing and like and even in and every even in and like and that. There is no difference at all between paper and basket, this has nothing to do with fruit and soap, this has nothing to do with places and bread this has nothing to do with their arrangements. Not to be with it in theirs in hand and now. Now it is open open and liked liked and to-morrow to-morrow when then, the Saone.

Would it be nearly as certain that they would like to have theirs be as much as if when they did by this time if they did make it. Not to mention what it was when they were altogether part of it because because allowing because allowing it to be for this reason leaving it aloud and much of it and never to be what it was when it was opened and very nearly very little ones and as much more as when it was to be sure to be sure erected erected to make islands having it not only that it was sold once and they made it be because of that over and under over and under makes it be nearly that if spoken to spoken of spoken of birds birds and very nearly grass in theirs and to be sure leaving it as an announcement and readily readily makes it be in tufts and when there are two and when there are two and once more it was necessary to buy a piece of ground in order to plant upon it one hundred poplars and to precisely understand plant upon it one hundred poplars and to precisely understand moreover not to be exactly and precisely dated when it is not only to be purchased but also to be purchased planted and very certainly absolutely designed as one hundred poplars when in any event not only having been attached to that but very often very favorably needed needed and needing using using is never adaptable using had and advanced as by and by developed because indeed they might and they might not, because once at once and as this was to be new it was also very nearly needed now. One more observation. It does not need need and necessarily and necessarily and very well understood. And now leave it to be what was as much interrupted like it why is it to be looked looked for it now when it is not altogether where it was where is it. An acquaintance with description and not very good. They planted theirs and have it as it might so that if they and many wider many wider and as if it could not be as a mistake to be in certain certain certain certain that then there there is as not as a mound not as a not as a not as a failing failing that if all at once at once at least and remaining not in right in right in right as if with that and sound sound in a leaf a leaf to be who can be nearly where it was when it was not which needed while it did, telling it as sound as soundly as not by that time to be and when to copy copy which copy which is which is what they could if it could not be in change in change for this at once at once is never nearly why they did not let it be at best at best is what is not when it was change and changed to rest, rest at most thank you. Not an acquaintance with not only with and only with description and only with with it. Is it and and an account of it.

Always wait along never wait so long always wait along always wait along never wait so long never wait as long always wait along always wait along never wait so long never wait so long always wait along always wait as long always wait along never wait so long always wait along. Not to believe it because not to believe it because not to believe that it is here. Come over here now. Left and right white and red and never to be along at all not at all when it is to be nearly left as it was by the time when it shall be so well so well allowed allowed and allowed and leaving it all to that when it is might have been not a little never and a little at all by the time that it is where there is leave it too long have it. Having left it there until there was what seemed to be a little at once like the rest like the rest fairly well finally to be in and in might it have that in change leaving not it not it at last at last differs from the leaving having having never can there not by this about in the way from never there in is they used find it can there is looking at in in comes to let and very well it was not why they did consider it not at all one way.

To find it there yes put it there yes to put it there if to put it there by which not it not it now to see it as it and very adapted to partly leave it there to partly not to partly not put it there it might if a little bit when it is in a corner for the morning so that not to allow allowable around when it is separately not separate to the shore, can a river have a shore or can a little little more before can it be interrupted and not once or twice when too might two be only left to throw it away away from that which was outlined, it was and if wish to wish to a paving it with that. Now to have it in their way when they have it as they will be that they do not mind it.

Why and why often and why often when it is not by the time that there is much much as much as said as said as will because of this and thinning of it out and in this is this that the left is sent by this around and ground and not to leave it in this might it be the change of that to theirs theirs have this leave it very nearly place and might it if it not in this pleased if this when is it in their leave as not all of it can be in this in theirs and interchange in also not to change and china can be sought in this in places in this and places places from this two and uneasy which is why that it must be shown as that in the next never asked to as coming in delight and relight when this is that in theirs left it to be not for this in change near neighbor coming in the last and finding it as can it be that it is right and left so that it is for this and with theirs obligation nearly by this in the instance that it is arranged for that in the most and believe in half and kindly kindly give it to them and away and can it be in theirs and for remaining can and can not left to be in so much as it is in theirs and added not by this which is relieved by none and more to add it more than is not for this openly so seen can in and likely leaving it so nearly with it in this case can find bequeath and needed in regularly to that in those and called and layer of that this below which send sent to the are there why is it as addressed left it as when as or that come to the last which is for that not finally incased but surely where as there is that in an allowed now this and here there most come to be supplied with the whole and share and this and leaves and why and could and some and nestles and no much and come come in and that beside the noise and leave and trust and how to. Following it altogether. She it might be come. Not how is it.

I understand that you do not do much in winter with your land.

Leaving it out when this is seen in the nearest afternoon to there having had left there that is not to do that which is might and might it be and for this as their even left it to be at namely why this is for them considerably liking and like then when it could be after letting and distributed. Now again named whenever it is to that beside by and by can if in the central and why it is not alone nor should it come to theirs be advised leave when shall it reduce to this coming can leave where in the not to be altogether where it is placed to be divided between fish and moths. There to be divided there to be divided divided between find and find out find it in nearly to be sure and more easily if named. When one is what is what is it then it is easier when it is when it is in their name. Leaving out having had it now. They might be while they can if it is can it and they no doubt can leave it leave it at that. There is every day every day every day to be sure to be sure that they can go and have to have very well I thank you. Leave out and account leave it out and account account not to be always to be said that it was there that it was there that it was in there not in there but like in there as it not in there when it was begun begun to be left and left not in that allowance but in that in spite of it being that it was what they could in arrange like it and some to some to some some who have not best at all why not as much as after a while not theirs very well. Remembering everything as seen to like it only is it that it should should come to be what is it when it is no longer theirs at all. To know why we why can it be leave it to be three. There can always be a difference.

If she works then he works but if she reads then he pleads.

If she does knit and he does count how many are then in it. Five in each but unverified and beside beside unverified too and a market two and well left beside the pressure pressure of an earring.

Never deriding anything and then it was not only at a distance but in the distance that it can be many makes it come to be so now. That is not to what it does not have it so to speak that is and said consider it to be theirs aloud.

When it was left. Water was running as large as two fists eighteen. What is when it is of that to be not green and wheat but green and why and green and it can have it to be that it is a third the next of that which when the come for it too leave why which where they announce amuse leave it for in that way come should it have the never changing most now and then in as not have seen the having thought of three as two to be sure from that where they they might could it be curtain and hat not as much as net not only if it were to be wrapped in and for the which it was by this to come to that it is now known. Excuse me.

To change from what was what to that.

Everything that must be as a bed or hedge must when it is to be had where it was must be what is left to be theirs as they wish come to be left when it is found and further could be decided that it was not nearly an arrangement that they had if this was theirs as if it were to be not at least and negligent and so to say so to find it naturally where it was to be if there it was does it really have as much when it is not as much and coming to be not at all nearer nearer than it is to it. Thank you for having been so kind.

There he said he had said that it was where there it was and after all nobody should touch it.

Not more than seldom not more than winning not any having this as that and for it in leaving that is what is when it is at the end of the house which is when it is not an end and it does not look differently because they have seen it otherwise it would look differently because I had seen it otherwise it would look differently because I had seen it otherwise it would look otherwise it would be it would be it would be otherwise it otherwise if it is not

not what is it every little one larger larger and so much smaller when there is no difference between a white carnation and a white lily both are white when they are here when they are here when they are when they are here in this case not as well not as well long as well charcoal as well water as well leaving as well lambs as well why and when with as well leave as well but as but as well why as well a while as well with what as well the piece as well as if as well there more to four as well and as well as well as as well as well as well when if in as and well and see in to be some to cause could in there be from the one that can be in there by the coming to this to be that it is by that in there with it for in in could leave so more this by for it come to be not while it is shall be come to this if it can leave it in this coming talking be as well as the kind at first should left that it was all could can it as rest the rest of it to be that it is not there theirs as it is should the stand fall at once what is it.

That is one way of that to be now nicely see and seen come come to be alike. We are very grateful that it is so large.

Would anybody be allowed would anybody be allowed to come to ask to have it sent in winter.

This is not theirs to be to be to be to be very much very much left as if as if very well knew and known that it should not be again and again and in again and in again and again and again and in again. Peaches should always be eaten over more over as if strawberries as if papers as if printed papers as if printed and papers as if printed and papers as if printed and papers and wool as if printed and papers and peaches as if printed and papers and wool as if printed and papers peaches should always be eaten as if as if papers as if printed and papers as if strawberries as if as if peaches and papers as if as if as if papers as if peaches and papers as if printed papers and wool and strawberries and peaches as if papers as if printed papers as if.

Always the same.

Not as to delight.

An acquaintance with description.

If it is to have the leaving as an obligation to be there and come to to the rest that if there is if there is the next to have it leave to to be in that way four three one leaving it around as it might indeed have it that they not as if it were in opposite around let it might and might be considered as two three three there many there how many there how many three two one leaving it as much behind behind to mind letting letting all in theirs for that most when makes what is why it was as much as much for the having having to be interrupted shall it shall it have the name when there is that in two made which is much the more than theirs for that now leaving it in this to be to be sure let it coming coming to have it given given in place of theirs to have it can it be and fairly well at most in that which which when where and light and come to last last and might and might it be in this and change get it is it not what in their might it come to leave it in this place it could it be that it is when it when it is in theirs to place and to say need it and it was not only why it came to left and calling this is in the way of any other one which is not only why they left they did not have it to fit in when it was that the two were two were to make four places and a little below to say so if it must be just their in that complete why is it only when it is not only if it is in that increase. There can be no difference between a circus a mason and a mechanic between a horse and cooking a blacksmith and his brother and his places altogether and an electrician. In every other way I am disappointed. Yes when it is not only this and having been not prepared to be so much and wonder they had it and they changed it and they made it be very nearly might it be what is it when it is not after all very little of a having not seen it when it came.

It is not well placed if before they had it there and now they put it there and will they place it there and could it be what it was when it might. It is very nearly intended to be a basket made over.

They might do.

If it after all was not what was it when it came and it might do. When could it leave it in this way and say it for this was to be and like it all thank you to say. They went to see it.

Again Albert again write to Albert again basket again changed to have it again have it basket again again as again as a change again basket again basket again it is again as a change again as a basket again at again larger again as many again as a basket again have it a basket again larger again is it again it is it again a basket again as larger again a basket again get it again is it again a basket again it is.

It is is it. A basket.

Basket it is is it.

Very nearly fairly pleased.

Which is why it is that it is looking is it in it as it it is as it is is it as it is there. There it is.

There is always some difference between nine o'clock and eight o'clock.

An acquaintance with description.

There is an arrangement as berries. There is also an arrangement as loop holes. There is also an arrangement as distance. There is also an arrangement as by the way. There is also an arrangement as at first. There is also an arrangement as to be. There is also an arrangement as disappointed. There is also an arrangement as why and let. There is also an arrangement of poplars that give a great deal of pleasure. There is also an arrangement that it can be twice chosen. There is also an arrangement which is advantageous.

Never be left to be that it can have to be if it could leave it all let it be mine while it came shall it have that to see come again like it while it is much to be relied upon as yet and while and awhile and while and it is not that but what if it is by the breaking of it in the place of that nearly by changing that to make it have it be nearly coming as if there is not more than it could be theirs so much not by that time there is between needing needing not by that and if it is in let it let it in light and might it be very well said that if a cloud is light one could read by it. What can be after all the difference between candles and electricity, they go out one after the other they come one one after the other they go on together. Let it be known. It is.

Not to think of any thing which is not what is at least when poplars come to have to be a very little bridge to see at any way if not before when it is well to have a rain bow let alone a wire place and met it. Not easily there chance. After all and met it not easily there chance. An instance of it is as a distance from the come to come and have it had and with it with and leave it let leave it as it must be while then for this as it is not for this for this come to be in their choice come to be this is in an angle if it comes came let it with some not perch come left that not as a very good half to help let it let is is let to be there singular relieve it with it for the not there when why cinnamon and come to have it that it is as a district describe while white not so much as if at first a lake as come to come to pride where fair that it is not so have it from the end to end alright.

Six is more than four how many to a door, who can be so late to see if they wait to be to see if it can to have to meet if it does which is as were and left to right and with it as if when it fell so that he was where it could be and in that as could it by the trace of left and right come to the having as and stands that is as bale that is as hay that is as then that is as if letting be it so much care this to then if for and in case fasten and in most fasten and very likely why it was when it was if they had not had it come to be remembering that to run up hill that to run up hill that to run up hill for the heard it come to be. An actual reasonable time. No one must be very lively about it. It is not at all necessary that it is after this so much as much as much way much for much to much in much left much then much there much those this that the under left might join come leaf and left as if it were not not not not not white.

Anybody could be one. One one one one.

This time not uneasily.

An acquaintance with description above all an acquaintance with description above an acquaintance with description above all an acquaintance with description above an acquaintance with description and above and above an acquaintance with description and an acquaintance with description. Please and an acquaintance with description please an acquaintance with description please an acquaintance with description.

They must be as well as ever to be had to be it when they can if it must as well as if and that is what it can be now that it is if in plainly as much as if what is not come to be had if when it is not that if it is not to have to own and then there scare and scarce and this that in that might which can for most where with in much come to be that this with it left to make to me to mention to the same let if that which in candied let it mean that if then where there this is not that now which is when it is left come to this there come have to be not reconsidered. It meant that it was not kept up.

If if and this is wild from this to the neatness of there being larger left and with it could it might if it not if it as lead it lead it there and incorrectly which is at this time. Once more if refused. Make make it left it with with with not with there may may may not be there though though though if left and the same not only had but will have once more having let it fall altogether.

If in way that should left come by it it not must can near to naturally why do it because it is a pleasure.

What you want to do.

What you want to do.

What you want to do.

Left it what you want to do.

Left it what you want to do.

The regular if all much not could lean well settled plus return more than be lighter for that here.

Very well not in might to ran made with it coat for is need banding when is it sense and send not is it come can for this sure that it change makes it always have the had it could must lean leaning as mine there are in are plain plan must it be trees with be find not lying for this time in and a middle while it is very likely there it is what when not come to this walnut tree if you know that walnut can grow. Say so.

The next which and which to say is how many trees are there in it and what are their ages and their sizes. Who has been counting at a distance. An acquaintance with description is to be used again and again.

And acquaintance with description is to be used again and again. And acquaintance with description is to be used again and again. Always begin an acquaintance with description to be used again and again.

A once in a way makes it at once in a way makes it at once makes it at once once in a way makes it once in a way makes it at once in a way. After this it is left that if it is as wide as less than that as it is as wide as less than that it is as wide as less than that. Never happen to have been in even evenly never to have been in even never to have been in even never even to have happen never to have happen to even to have even have been never even to have happen to have been even as for the point let should not been more as it caught is not the name very easily.

How can there very well be a bell as bell upon as hunting upon as hunting had as there is upon a hunting dog there is.

Pass paper pass please pass pass trees pass trees please pass please pass please pass please as paper as pass as trees. Very likely very nearly likely nearly likely very. Nearly likely very. Nearly very. It is very easy to like to like to pass very likely it is very near nearly to like to pass grass. Farmers or do it. Farmers or do it no one should mix what is heard with what is seen. No one should mix seen and heard. In this way. In this way. Leaves leave it. In this way. Leaves in this way leaves leave it in this way leaves in this way leaves in this way. Not at all to like as alike not at all as this way not troublesome in this way not in this way in this way to have and did it in this way. Different, after having seen one having seen some having seen some. Having seen some. Not having between not having between as long as a field not having between not having seen between as long as a field not having between.

The right was down on the side of the road and the left was on the road. The left was on the road and the right was down on the side of the road. The right was down at the side of the road and the left was on the road. The left was on the road and the right was down by the side of the road.

Let it be for them to know.

Not as much as they could say.

When it is where they have been.

Not to be too much to see that it is so.

There when did it leave to have to come to have given, how did it leave it come to there there there more no. No and acknowledge.

Oh yes of course below.

Because she is because she is Julia because she is Julia because she is and English Julia and Julia Ford.

Never to have been a two one one two one one never to have been a two one one.

To not be surprised if it should rain.

They are to not be surprised if it should rain.

They are to not be surprised if it should rain. There is a difference between rain wind and paper. What is the difference between rain wind and paper. There is a difference between rain wind and paper.

After a little while there is a difference between rain and wind. After a little while there is a difference between wind rain and wind rain and paper and between rain wind and paper and there is after a while there is a difference between rain wind and paper. Thank you very much as much as very much thank you very much as very much as much there is thank you very much there is a difference after a while there is a difference between rain wind and paper thank you very much there is a difference between rain wind and paper thank you very much thank you as much. Let it be that they came there. It was quite as if it was not only not to be not only not to be satisfactory but to be perfectly satisfactory satisfactory satisfactory.

Very well to do it to it to it very well to do it to it to it very well to do it to it very well to do it to it very well to do it to it very well. Why do very small very small marshes very small marshes give pleasure very small marshes give pleasure very small marshes.

Little pieces of that have been where that has made while that is there need it as it can be said to be more and more and more and more and more to be sure come to be what is it for the next and to be sure more and as it is as when they need to be their with their to their be there like might it be come to be mine come to be next when if if it is not might when for spare and let in that come to come with as need it for the have to be nicely near if they consider an acre an acre an acre an acre like much seem when if this let in sign and side two sent which which is a relief if it is sure sure sure surely now how there is a difference in climbing a hill with or without climbing a hill with or without climbing a hill.

Could be a little marsh.

Promise not to be so yet if this is so and this is more and when it is as it was for them if it can and is to be left it alone so that it can if when if it is by that who in that case and can and it is as if it is as if it is as it was to them to them to them to if it was as if it was to them to them and let it come to this for this for this let it as if as if in spite and mean to share let it be come to be beside with them in that in that and could and have and did and like and like and why and in and must and do in do and do leave do leave do leave not without that with with come come come to to to be sure where if if when is when is it when is it all not this to be there and sent when if should have come to be spoken like like like it is alike alike for it is because it is used to it.

There made a mistake.

Do be like it for that which is why when it is not as if in their being made for that in their being to being made to be what is it not as like as if they had had to be when is it that if they could have it be which is as well. He is very certain to be sure to be sure to be sure to be sure not to be sure not to be sure not to be sure to not to be sure to be sure to be sure not to be sure not to be sure not to be sure not to be sure to be sure. Not to be sure. Let it be when it is mine to be sure let it be when it is mine when it is mine let it be to be sure when it is mine to be sure let it be let it be let it be to be sure let it be to be sure when it is mine to be sure let it to be sure when it is mine let it be to be sure let it be to be sure to be sure let it be to be sure let it be to be sure to be sure let it be to be sure let it be to be sure let it be to be sure let it be mine to be sure let it be to be sure to be mine to be sure to be mine to be sure to be mine let it be to be mine let it be to be sure to be mine to be sure let it be to be mine let it be to be sure let it be to be sure to be sure let it to be sure mine to be sure let it be mine to let it be to be sure to let it be mine when to be sure when to be sure to let it to be sure to be mine.

Well there there there very well very well there there there there well there well there there well there and easily counted there there counted easily there there there counted there there there there. Everybody knows everybody knows everybody knows that there there they are easily counted there there there there they are easily there there they are easily counted. Not easily counted as easily seen in between as easily counted not as easily seen counted easily seen there there there easily counted in between as easily seen there. There is no use explaining that melons can be used when melons can be used when melons can be used yellow melons can be used. That if as it might be left to be that if they are as corn as many as corn as many as many as corn as seen as many as corn as seen. There has come a decision that everything and named.

Much as much as if to to be remember that it is to be remember much as much as if to be as much as much as if to be remember that as much as much as if to be remember that as much as much as much as much as if to be remember that as much as much as much as much as much as if to be remember that as much as much as much as much as much as much as much as if to be remember that as if to be as much as much as much as much as much as if to remember that as if to be to be as if to remember that as if to be as much as if to be as much as to remember as much as if to be as much as remember as much as if to be as if to be remember as if as much with wide with wide as much as if to be remember if as much as if as to be as if as much as if to be as much as if as wide as much as if to be to remember as if to be to remember as much to remember as if as much to be as wide as if to be as much. Very naturally they can be if is when last in for be by beside made is in can for that in light and need and made made why can fit this in this and that there leave come easily need why make it be once again to that which is why they can have both grapes and apples and pears. That is might it if when is it in and at a time by which by which by which by which it is very much inclined inclined to inclination which is seized that makes it naturally believe be like and to have it faster than at first. We thought not at all. Go might it be all coming which is why which is why which is which is which is which is a very nearly certain certainly letting and let it much as it does when the moon rises. It is very pleasant to see the moon in daylight.

It was easy to be sure that it looked so far away pansy as the let it be as much which is when it is might be so much as much further which which very wide very well and very not and mount. Pansy. Not having counted the pansies it is impossible to say just how many pansies are in it. Very much let it be last which having it to be worn and where can it be if it can be that there is no difference between ridges and between ridges. There is a difference between ridges and between ridges and between there is a difference between there there and ridges between there there there and ridges there is a difference between there there there there and ridges there is a difference between no difference between pansies and there between pansies and there between not between not telling between not telling the difference between ridges there there there pansies there there there difference there between difference distance there there between distance difference ridges there there there there distance between and very place as much as place as much as place as much how many trees are there place as much as nectarines nectarines is a mixture of vineyard peaches and counted plums and careful very careful very careful of pears. This makes pansies one time at one time at one time pansies not pansies at one time let it at one time two rosy on two rosy in two in two rosy in at one time in and it is true the little pieces are where they are and those that are are a pair a pair of all around it.

An acquaintance with description asking an acquaintance with description asking for an acquaintance with description. All around it asking for an acquaintance with description.

It is very remarkable. Not that. It is very remarkable that that this is after it has been not only that it is when would it be laughed laughed at and about about to do about to do so and about about what where it is by whom by whose after all by whose having had which it for this as this is in a stream a stream can wash celery celery to be sure there there to be certain to be certain there there cultivate to be most to be most and very to be most most which is moistened by their their arranging wool wool which when very much in the meantime greatly greatly influenced by as much as if in this case in each case and arrangement. Let it be not for this when when is it it is not fortunately that they were understood that the same renting relenting buying rebuying referring referring which is it that is not why then and very much an advantage. The situation in respect to what is seen when there is letting it be carefully to-day. It was not not likely that that it was was to be left to them to decide. Let us unify four things principally and pansies, very reasonably and rightly, come to be as much theirs as it was, and left to be not only thirty but thirty trees.

Do not do not what climb the hills hills which are hills and hills which are hills which are strawberry plants and strawberry plants and in and in that when there is none noon there is should shall and might might be an eraser. Very nearly what they did to-day. Should shall be in case of and never be by this this that leave not with this look again.

Find as much.

Not as to bird this year. Let to this why not if it is not as where that is undoubtedly not from to be that this now touch when leaving leaving lay lane much at behold behold for let this inches inches make make please why they can. What happened was this a bee a wasp which tried when there believe behind make that not before when in this into a bank which is made of shrubs which do not grow in California.

Like this.

Once two three.

Once two three again two three two three.

How do you do happily happily with that happily with that. There is a difference between twice one one and leaving it be chosen that they do not any of them always like that. Not only if this is theirs too to have it be that it can send and consent and finally letting letting that if when after that it should be not only recalled but estimated not in case and care for that to be as much as much as much to be sure leaving leaving it for this at once nearly by all. All of it at one time easily.

Might it be that it can be that it can be might it be that it can be that it can be might it be that that it can be might it be that might it be that it can be might it be that it can be might it be that it can be might it be that it can be might it be that that it can be might it be that it can be might it be might it be that might it that it might be might it be that it can be. Very many who have come very many who have come very many who have come who have come very many who have come very many who have come very many who have come. There is to be sure what is there to be sure what there is to be sure that there is what is what is there to be sure there is what there is to be sure. They might be not might be be seated might be not might not might be not might not might be seated not might be not might be not might be not be seated not be seated not might be not might be seated might be not might not might not might not be seated might be. Leading theirs to this and sown sown makes which when when than an indicative nearly an indirectly as satisfied for that as immediately near and lessen too be what is never with it as in minding fairly should it be the carefully resting and left which is it that that let it have it to be fall of the year how is it if the minding minding to be heard let it alone after much leaving so very much to them to them in this how to be sure surely nearly very very well welcome and for that for that. Any one can know that a house which when when it it was was placed having having at that distance distance was not not by that which is what is what is it let it be while at one time. In this way a very large house looks small and so that is true two roofs that is true, not two to three that that is true that is true not why not why not why not why that is true not why that is true it is why must it be what must it be after this is heard heard heard, the daughters can cannot go.

Nevertheless if there is distress and they planted two hundred more when it was certainly not what was needed trees not what was needed vines not what was needed places and not what was needed and now not what was needed and nearly not what was needed and not what was needed and so not what was needed very well in exchange. Did her brother if he was twenty-five years old was he did he like to leave it here. If her sister who was seventeen years old did she need to be left to be here, need to be left to be here need to be left need to be left to be here and if her mother who had been sixteen years or a widow need to be left to be here and if she needed to be left to be here and it was not to be undoubtedly that it was not to be undoubtedly that it was not to be not to be needed to be left to be here. It is certainly very much better that if that would that to be that when and might and make it and this that and that to be with to be with that to be with that to be with to be with that to be with that to be with to be with that very much as if when not and nearly to be nearly which with that there are might to be not for this not because not not because this this and water with with and fruit in in as much and left let it be carried. They might be indifferent. Need it to be left to be their own. With it for them in as much as while while at last neither with nor by and when it is in no way as an estimation which can which can place pleases and coloring collected could it be that they had been waiting. She was very nearly easily seated. Like and like it. Not can it with much left to them now. That which is suited to irresistible irresistibly be very likely need needing needless and needed needed and needed and needed and needed and needed now and now and now and needed needed there is there is there is there is there is there there there will they will they will they hearing made easily made made made come to be making to be made very who is under very well very well. We said the elder he said who is under very well the who is very well who is very well who is very well very well who is under the very who is under the very well the elder who is very well the under the very well. Having five white roses and one having three white roses and very likely two of them were mislaid. Not is to be mean to be to be to be very necessarily that after that after that then and not as well as October after November. Even a wind can be must be could be that and were were not not to come let it be what is not as to a place have this. It never could be nearly when to be when to be when to be would they care to see this now as candles. This now as candles this now as fruit and this now as this now as this now as this now as this now as this.

There to be like alike in here to be like it thank you very much as when do not when do not do more than it is prepare for this and and come to this to the let it shall for this come to this not as much as if letting in in to not nor can it have to be nearly in this come to be in considerable, if it was not for this at that time come to be sure to will and leave and leave and in as if and in are to be come to be in liking let it not when can this and call seen for his and surely to compare it let it not to be near than nearer than this is now what is it come in to when it is not left and left and fairly not to be in when come to be mine. There is when it can to be sure which is left in liking when nearly near come with it welcome for this use and used and very well should it be letting it come to this this this this half of it half of the time they know and now can it be left to them bread and chance to be which is with pears and not to let it come that is when if not coming to in them shut if not as it must at all come to be did it not not to not only left it there. Having watched a further than it is beside. This makes it not which is it nearly nearly never had to be left to them how do they know the difference between bulls and vines and pears and houses and leaves and hares and houses and theirs and by the time it was to be near nearly nearly there there there there can it there there there was it that it was not only in as much as much as not as not at all. It is very easy easily to know to know to do so do so to so so to wish wish wish leave it to need need in case of this which one two cows one two sheep one two ducks one two trees one two not one two not one two not one two not one two not not at once one two one one two not one two one one one two. One two.

Description from the way to have been at the time if not to be certain that it is left to be fallen down there and if it had been then the terrace and it is not by reason of then not only allowed but nevertheless changing not because their nearly having it be like after all shall and by this time. Very readily see see that from the terrace if there is a flooring flooring fixed fixed it so nearly at a while from distance come to be with it in hand. Looking at it last have hand and share. Three plans not three not found there not not much at a time it is easier to rent than to buy than to rent than to buy.

One at a time a meadow at a time a distance at a time and half a house a house at a time and and at a time and then at a time and there there at a time. Who has who had who has who held held it in pieces of theirs beside.

Let leave leant learn line let it make it be it have have have here and might might it try try it try not it as come to be in where they might do it too mix which come there leave and allowance allowance handle handle they make which is it as as likely very likely to be or sure and feeling and faintly faintly there make a mistake useful need a glance shall it be near them the same at once.

There is a great difference between people and places.

Once again have them too all the time night and while to be sure plainly as will not can for this as be shall kind and there. When is it.

When is it that they might see them.

One at a time and a peculiarity of interchanging need it be this to-day to-day clearly which is might it be when if reasonable and liking meaning fortunately exchange by wishes left alone nearly and coming very well to prepare bread.

Bread.

Come to that come to that come to that come to that.

Might it be around. Come to that. Full and feel this place eight days fourteen days really days why will days for the days it need it needed it needed braid it needed braid it needed it is not sound it needed it needed if it needed soldered it needed with it it needed could if it needed with with it with it with it with it with it it with it which is if the difference if this which soldered which which if be and bear and break and be and bear and be and share it find and not at all either not much not as much feel it white make it last.

It is very easy to cook bread in a communal oven. Why because it is prepared in a basket and easily being fluid it remains in place on a pale and the oven being very nearly stone it is longer heated than it was. An hour two an hour too and hour an hour and a half not as very not by the way in standing. Not an acquaintance not an acquaintance with not an acquaintance with description not an acquaintance with with description not an acquaintance with not an acquaintance with description.

Now be by the way. Ellis now be now be by now be by the way Ellis now need now be now be now be now by the way Ellis now be now be now need now be now by now be now be now by the way.

Now Ellis.

Now be now by the way.

To know.

What is there in difference which is what is when it is there most. Like it like it like it for them to them like it very much by which they went.

Fellow follow for fell feel for likely by a stretch of time time to be mostly and usual usually they make make which in strangely let it very likely be which is when there is in January to be there. Who makes might it mountains.

An acquaintance with then with description and leaving which it matters matters very much to them. An acquaintance with description. With then.

Ellis with then.

An acquaintance with their an acquaintance with description which may be which may be pleased and pressed as planted planted it makes it be nearly theirs as choosing choosing and losing who knows. Can we be see. An acquaintance with description nearly very nearly.

Let it be not nearly five which follow cows which follow cows sheep which follow cows let it be not nearly which follow cows sheep. That is one thing. Let it be which when when not for this is like that to theirs allow come satisfaction remount and more over let this come to be to see might it have should it now come this let it for them much it for near now nearly. This is at one time. There is just as much letting it be when is it not to have been nicely recommenced and a lake. Very frequently there is no sunshine very frequently even then it is not very cold even then. Now and now and now roses. Very white and roses very pretty very pretty very pretty large very pretty large very pretty large very pretty roses very pretty very pretty very pretty very pretty very pretty as very pretty roses very pretty large very pretty very pretty very pretty large very pretty. Some some some he did not like to hear it said to him some some some some he did not like to hear it said to him that in place of then to then to then and as in place twenty as in place now could it after which is letting letting letting. A fish where hare where straw where apples where there there any day a way away and kindly. She preferred to have it named after he had he had he had she must five is five so often as often as often one as often, having half and nearly Jenny too, too two two. Jenny is a drop. This is clear clearly. You do leave it here here here here Chambery.

Look up look her up look her up look her up look her look her look her look her up and down. Mr. Pernollet does not supply it yet Mrs. Press does not express lady fingers which are here she was very likely to be really two at most Mr. Baird Mr. Baird makes it better to do so if he likes it which is what what is it it is what very much makes theirs start to finish Mrs. Father has a daughter they do they know they know they do they do they do. Mrs. Middle has a husband really two and two really freshly really freshly freshly really she really very really very very come too, Mr. Bourg is now at peace if he goes if he goes if he goes, can two one of them older and the sister of his mother which is why his wife was is leave it to him, not now that is why liking by it soon. Never to tell well.

What is the difference between a park and a field.

When is a meadow under water when it is a marsh and after which is higher there is always something not might not after this very which is that.

Has it been to be.

If it is when she.

Let it can it be.

If you can and three.

If you see the mountain clearly it means that it will be rainy if you see the mountain it means that it will not be rainy if you see the mountain clearly if you can see the mountain clearly it means that it will not be rainy if you can see the mountain clearly it means it will be rainy if you see the mountain clearly it means that it will be rainy. After this they went to be nearly four nearly five nearly after this they went to be nearly five nearly five nearly four nearly, after this they went away nearly five nearly after this they went away.

Having stopped to gather butter butter can be made to fruiten fruiten can be made to butter having nearly having made to butter having made to fruiten having made to butter fruiten having made to nearly having made to butter fruiten.

Leave which is mine nearly always after it has been the contrary the country nearly which is mine which has been the country which has been the contrary nearly which has been nearly which is mine the country. Leaves which is mine.

Needless to say that it is very needless to say that it is in every way a pleasant month of October as to weather.

There can be flower too flour too flower too there can be corn flour too when there is this and more. There can be this and too when there is corn and too there can be flour too corn flour and this and too. What is the difference between them and grapes grapes are sweeter, what is not what is not ivy what not and ivy which is join and Paulette. Paul and Paulette which is elder older white and next older elder which is left to be now. Does anybody suggest suggest that he can find can find a house with that with that when could eight brothers and their sisters work harder and how. How and how. Could they work harder and how how and how. They kneel knee can it be and see see sat which which is when is this every in the can there make which is why this will this cake if eggs are purchased. Leave it for them to them with them in them and then then like it for its use when this can be nicely left to come to which very little which is not their likely why can it be claimed at once. To like it. Therese can be compared to Therese can be compared to Therese can be compared, very likely very likely which is why it is with that. It is very well very well well enough come to this. Helen has rounder sounder found her found her found her. Think then could it be trout. Trout how. Very likely. Not now not all.

It must be in this little way of placing everything that they believe them it must be as if it is when that it is not as when as when believe it for this which makes nicely not in with and for them this with and for them to be certainly let it be not for this in instance. First they made what is what is let it let it need to be what is meant and unexpectedly have them be theirs. Let us imagine what they do spy what they do spy what they do do what they do with with with spy with spy with with with in what they do. A place which makes when it is not only as high as which can be two see, under like it make and for which is which is why they have to be in pleasing let it be nicely that four houses are mentioned. Four houses are mentioned. Four houses are mentioned. Four houses are mentioned. One for one for one for one for one after that three which may be and not needing it now they cannot them and not needing it now they cannot them and two at once two at once two at once more two at once more more more more two two two more two at once and one to one and to one one and to one to one to one one, have can have one which when a duck two cries makes cannot cannot one can cannot can one can one one, two two which two and one which one. Georgie would like a letter. Not about it. But rather for pleasure. To be sure to be having could it leave it for this might a lieutenant be what is after after all after all small small small after all nicely in decide decide train and nearly which, after this while needs to needs to to needs to needs needs to this next fall as if if water flowing flowing with no flow flowing with no flow flowing need cows cows be fruit and fruit be mentioned mentioned moon as likely as if to intend let it not have it have it in this come it come it and committee and after all never having returned an answer as to the name of that that let it be not to be when to be then to be Xenobie. It is very surprising that a young girl about to be certain that one preparation is better than another is named Marie.

THE LIFE OF JUAN GRIS

THE LIFE AND DEATH OF JUAN GRIS

This lament upon the death of the painter Juan Gris (1887–1927), which is also a portrait, is the only elegy Stein wrote. Gris died of uremia in Paris on 11 May 1927, after months of painful decline. The tone and style make audible how difficult it was for Stein to write about him.

The elegy begins and ends as a traditional narrative, a story, a "life," from "Juan Gris was one of the younger children of a well to do merchant of Madrid" to "This is the history of Juan Gris." It has been said that exposition such as appears here is unusual for Stein. However, in the spring of 1927 she was studying narrative, which may explain the narration here. She follows the linear convention of the obituary with its strong terminal thrust. Perhaps she found it helpful to frame the elegy of a deeply valued friend in a form that promised to make it less painful by keeping it impersonal. Yet her control is unsure. She begins in the past tense but even in the second sentence fails to sustain the past, switches to the present and back again. She also works with jumpy, illogical sentences, such as "In the beginning he did all sorts of things he used to draw for humorous illustrated papers he had a child a boy named George he lived about he was not young and enthusiastic."

Chronological narration of events tells about his early life in Spain. As soon as she speaks of his arrival in France and his art, she gropes for what might render the quality of his vision. In part she relies upon details taken from her own warm, admiring portrait of 1924, *Pictures of Juan Gris,* written for the Juan Gris number of the *Little Review.* Both here and in the elegy she stresses his interest in French art, in proportion, and in the mannerist perfection of the school of Fontainebleau.

In slow and heavy declarative clauses, clipped, discontinuous, and virtually without connecting links, she describes his perfection of cubism. There are small hints about the uneasiness between Picasso and Gris and Stein's own distrust of Picasso. Stein also resented Picasso's failure to produce the promised illustrations for her *Birthday Book,* after Gris, already ill, had completed the lithographs for *A Book Concluding With As A Wife Has A Cow A Love Story,* which Kahnweiler's Galerie Simon published at the end of 1926.

Above all else the life and death of Juan Gris led Stein to Daniel-Henry Kahnweiler, dealer and friend of Gris, Picasso, Braque, supporter of cubism, and friend of Stein since 1907. It was Kahnweiler whose support had given Gris faith and paid his rent through years of hardship and trouble. And it was Kahnweiler who advised Stein when the end was near.

She put the second to last sentence in quotation marks to show that it was spoken by Gris, who said, "Kahnweiler goes on but no one buys anything and I said it to him and he smiled so gently and said I was everything." In *Portraits and Prayers,* the only book that includes the elegy but for which no textual authority has been found, the sentence was printed without quotation marks so that "I" has been misread ever since as referring to Stein bragging that she was everything. Stein's manuscript, Toklas' typescript, and the first printing in *transition* for July 1927 all supply the quotation marks and provide the authority for restoring them in the *Reader.* They are also the authority for minor restorations in paragraphing, spelling, punctuation, and for Stein's misspelling "Bracque."

The elegy, like the portrait of Georges Hugnet, which follows, grows out of other works that Stein was writing at the time. To trace the evolving work, the dates, sequences, and overlapping of compositions must be known. Often a nucleus for a new piece first appears in another and only later becomes a work in its own right. In a sense all of Stein's pieces can also be read as parts of a single continuous work, in which details emerge, shape, reshape and constantly, imperceptibly renew themselves.

• • • • •

Juan Gris was one of the younger children of a well to do merchant of Madrid. The earliest picture he has of himself is at about five years of age dressed in a little lace dress standing beside his mother who was very sweet and pleasantly maternal looking. When he was about seven years old his father failed in business honorably and the family fell upon very hard times but in one way and another two sons and a daughter lived to grow up well educated and on the whole prosperous. Juan went to the school of engineering at Madrid and when about seventeen came to Paris to study. He tells delightful stories of his father and Spanish ways which strangely enough he never liked. He had very early a very great attraction and love for french culture. French culture has always seduced me he was fond of saying. It seduces me and then I am seduced over again. He used to tell how Spaniards love not to resist temptation. In order to please them the better class merchants such as his father would always have to leave many little things about everything else being packages carefully tied up and in the back on shelves. He used to dwell upon the lack of trust and comradeship in Spanish life. Each one is a general or does not fight and if he does not fight each one is a general. No one that is no Spaniard can help any one because no one no Spaniard can help any one. And this being so and it is so Juan Gris was a brother and comrade to every one being one as no one ever had been one. That is the proportion. One to any one number of millions. That is any proportion. Juan Gris was that one. French culture was always a seduction. Bracque who was such a one was always a seduction seducing french culture seducing again and again. Josette equable intelligent faithful spontaneous delicate courageous delightful forethoughtful, the school of Fontainebleau delicate deliberate measured and free all these things seduced. I am seduced and then I am seduced over again he was fond of saying. He had his own Spanish gift of intimacy. We were intimate. Juan knew what he did. In the beginning he did all sorts of things he used to draw for humorous illustrated papers he had a child a boy named George he lived about he was not young and enthusiastic. The first serious exhibition of his pictures was at the Galerie Kahnweiler rue Vignon in 1914. As a Spaniard he knew cubism and had stepped through into it. He had stepped through it. There was beside this perfection. To have it shown you. Then came the war and desertion. There was little aid. Four years partly illness much perfection and rejoining beauty and perfection and then at the end there came a definite creation of something. This is what is to be measured. He made something that is to be measured. And that is that something.

Therein Juan Gris is not anything but more than anything. He made that thing. He made the thing. He made a thing to be measured.

Later having done it he could be sorry it was not why they liked it. And so he made it very well loving and he made it with plainly playing. And he liked a knife and all but reasonably. This is what is made to be and he then did some stage setting. We liked it but nobody else could see that something is everything. It is everything if it is what is it. Nobody can ask about measuring. Unfortunately. Juan could go on living. No one can say that Henry Kahnweiler can be left out of him. I remember he said "Kahnweiler goes on but no one buys anything and I said it to him and he smiled so gently and said I was everything." This is the history of Juan Gris.

GEORGE HUGNET

What strikes eye and ear about this portrait is the astonishing limitation of its means: a small, nearly uniform vocabulary with almost no concrete words (except "azure"); few nouns except four proper names starting with *G* and many words beginning with *w, th;* prominent *ou* dipthongs; insistent half-rhymes, rhymes, and alliteration; single, end-stopped lines; words that become different words, similar in look but unrelated in meaning, by changes in single letters and sounds (out/our/are; "Azure can with our about" makes shifting, unstable combinations audible, e.g., azure/our; as your/as sure/ assure; with/our [lead to] without; out/about).

Stein said in *Portraits and Repetition* that the success of *George Hugnet* came from its being "completely contained within itself and . . . moving." "Self-contained" means that we need not look for information outside the portrait to appreciate it. "It really does not make any difference who George Hugnet was or what he did or what I said. . . ." She had already made Georges Hugnet, a Frenchman in life, into an English or American George in the portrait by lopping off the final *-s* of his name. Yet she retained his last name in the title. In the text, however, George, like Geronimo and Genevieve, is simply a word. Stein is not writing about Genevieve as the patron saint of Paris, though the name carries Parisian echoes into her dance of words, as Geronimo, Spanish in form, carries overtones of Saint Jerome, translator and annotator of texts, and perhaps American Indian echoes.

The linguistic activity in *George Hugnet* centers on bringing "George in our ring," incorporating him in the portrait, the circle of the family or of friendship. The agent that accomplishes the incorporation is not a story, a plot, a description, but Grammar personified, a machine that captures George. Grammar engineers the architecture of the portrait and the inclusion of George in the engineering feat that is the portrait.

Grammar makes meaningful arrangements of forms. Stein does not use standard sentences and does not work with standard grammatical forms of the English language, such as inflection or position. Nor does she rely on phonetic modulations of spoken language such as question and exclamation tones, since hers is writing, not speaking work. To make forms dynamic and meaningful, she modifies words in constantly changing sequences.

The portrait opens with doubts whether George can be incorporated, whether he will be with, remain without, be found out [and] about out[side]. George resists being drawn in. The questions and doubts concern how he can be put inside, within the portrait rather than without, how he can be welcomed as "ours," "in our ring." He is not a person to be represented but a word that Grammar, not to be disappointed, must enclose in the piece. It is as if grammar makes things go round and round in this portrait as in the many singing and dancing games that incorporate players in circles or move them in and out of partnerships.

Stein claims that biography is irrelevant for reading the portrait, but we ask what impelled her to do this portrait and why grammar is its agent. She met the young poet Georges Hugnet (1906–72) in 1927 through Virgil Thomson, the composer. Thomson introduced Stein's work to Hugnet, who knew little English, by translation and by his own musical settings for *Susie Asado* and *Preciosilla.* In April 1928 Hugnet and Thomson offered her a joint tribute of Hugnet poems and a Thomson composition. Early in 1928 Hugnet had begun a small publishing venture to produce his own work and to print books written and illustrated by friends. Soon he and Thomson made plans to translate Stein into French and publish selections from *The Making of Americans* and a group of portraits. For Stein it was a dream come true.

That summer Hugnet wrote a preface about Stein for the new magazine *Orbes* and sent it to her. It portrayed her as a self-created genius born free of parents and described her attempts to free language from the constraints of thought and grammar. In Belley, where Stein summered from 1924 on, she was studying grammar. The portrait *George Hugnet* came directly out of this study and the contact with Hugnet, whose devotion animated her to include him in her circle as he prepared to present her as a French author. She sent him the portrait on 3 October 1928.

• • • • •

George and Genevieve Geronimo with a with whether they thought they were with whether.

Without their finding it out. Without. Their finding it out. With whether.

George whether they were about. With their finding their whether it finding it out whether with their finding about it out.

George with their finding it with out.

George whether their with their it whether.

Redoubt out with about.

With out whether it their whether with out doubt.

Azure can with our about.

It is welcome welcome thing.

George in are ring.

Lain away awake.

George in our ring.

George Genevieve Geronimo straightened it out without their finding it out.

Grammar makes George in our ring which Grammar make George in our ring.

Grammar is as disappointed not is as grammar is as disappointed.

Grammar is not as Grammar is as disappointed.

George is in our ring. Grammar is not is disappointed. In are ring.

George Genevieve in are ring.

EVIDENCE

Evidence of what? Stein does not tell. But this is only one of many questions about this piece, written in Paris in the fall of 1929 and printed in the spring of 1930 in *Blues,* a magazine edited by the young poet Charles Henri Ford. Not until it was checked against the manuscript was it discovered that Stein had withheld major portions from what she submitted to Ford. The five short sections printed in *Blues* and later reprinted in identical form in the collection *Reflection on the Atomic Bomb* (1973) are marked in the manuscript with numbers in Stein's hand and are printed in the *Reader* with the same numbers in parentheses after the subtitle. But the complete piece, far more substantial than the printed version, is preserved uncut in manuscript and typescript and was apparently never submitted for publication. This is most unusual. Stein did not believe in violating the unity of a piece by cutting. The case of *Evidence* provokes questions that the complete text, printed for the first time in the *Reader,* may answer.

On 20 September 1929 Stein sent to the Guggenheim Foundation a recommendation for a fellowship for Bravig Imbs, a young midwesterner who worked in Paris as a journalist and translator while writing poetry and fiction. The statement Stein had received from the foundation about the fellowships pointed to the need for "evidence that candidates [for creative work] are persons of unusual and proved creative ability." This phrase gave her the key word and the title for a piece and made her think about evidence of creative ability beyond the candidate, whose portrait she included in her writing. *Evidence* formulated ideas already latent in her mind.

In the fall of 1929 Stein was working on *Sentences and Paragraphs,* one of the many writing studies she did in those years. In this piece, later printed in *How To Write,* she made sample sentences for study and practice. The sentences were made with the vocabulary of daily life—what went on around her, what she was thinking, what sentences could do. The study has detail that she also used in other pieces of this time, including *Evidence,* and so it becomes a source for them. In the summer of 1929 she thought often about masterpieces, imagination, publication, success, and money.

Hemingway was in Paris on 27 September, the publication date of *A Farewell to Arms,* which immediately became a bestseller. By that time Stein had not seen him regularly for several years. In mid October she had written from the country to a friend in Paris, asking for the new novel and describing herself as "highbrow but not solemn" and Hemingway as "solemn powerful and successful." Late in October she returned to Paris from Bilignin near Belley, where she rented a house from 1929 on.

Meeting Hemingway in Paris, Stein invited him and his wife Pauline; Scott and Zelda Fitzgerald; Allen Tate (a Guggenheim fellow) and his wife, the novelist Caroline Gordon; and Bernard Faÿ for an evening. What happened that evening is variously told in letters, memoirs, autobiographies and biographies of the guests, and particularly in two letters from Hemingway to Fitzgerald of 22 or 29 and 24 or 31 October. The first two sections of *Evidence* are Stein's picture of what happened and how she felt about it. They become a second portrait of Hemingway.

A striking sentence appears both in *Evidence* and in *Sentences and Paragraphs.* In *Evidence,* it reads, "That is the cruelest thing I ever heard is the favorite phrase of Herman." In the sentence study it is the favorite phrase of Gilbert. In both manuscripts these names are revisions of the same crossed-out name, Fitzgerald, and both are followed by a crossed-out subtitle, "Portrait of Fitzgerald." Her man in this sentence is not Hemingway but Fitzgerald, who is one of a pair with Hemingway, as Gilbert is one of a pair with Sullivan. The sentence about the cruelest thing, with its shifting, unidentified antecedents, must have made saving sentences a delight.

In the space of two pages of *The Autobiography of Alice B. Toklas* (267–68), the sentence about the cruelest thing returns, and Stein speaks not of Hemingway but of Sherwood Anderson as "a genius for using the sentence to convey a direct emotion" and not of Hemingway but of Fitzgerald as "the only one of the younger writers who wrote naturally in sentences" and who "created . . . the new generation" in writing. She plays Hemingway off against the others and he does not come off well.

At a moment when Hemingway's success made headlines, Stein may have been wise to suppress this portrait. Perhaps because she had decimated *Evidence,* she added to the submission for *Blues* another, separate piece entitled *Why Willows.* What she had written but submitted only in part was in effect a series of portrayals of creative ability. They were not confined to artists but included a "lady sitting and working at tapestry," plainly Alice Toklas; Basket, the puppy acquired in February 1929; a study of colors and flowers that was named, as an afterthought and perhaps a gift, *Portrait of Madame Langlois;* and by implication the author of all these portraits, Stein herself.

Memoirs like *The Autobiography of Alice B. Toklas* and *A Moveable Feast* are public books written long after the events with distortions of hindsight and an agenda for the future. *Evidence* becomes context for these letters from Hemingway to Fitzgerald, as the letters become context for *Evidence.* Together they also become context for the comments in the *Autobiography.*

Here, then, is the evidence. Of what? Far more, by the end of this piece, than what "creative ability" meant when the Guggenheim documents first gave Stein the impulse to compose it.

• • • • •

American and strange.

There is after with out never having known that he fulfilled.

He was seated after.

Will they till they are efficiently if soon.

Evidence.

A man is a person if he has a reputation to fulfill.

He has a chance to come away if they are waiting to seat him. He is sitting when they are coming.

He will all, add whenever he likes.

This which they like he has heard.

Are they sure that you heard that they ran or rain or a walk.

It is by their reasoning.

Once when he will was indebted he was with anguish. He does not believe in dead letter. He will change to manage finish.

One two three and amen. When they made around.

He mingled with a way.

Three sat when four were agog.

He made a delay of dinner because it was interesting.

Sermon and summon he would like better comfort.

This is it. He told a story. Two stories shorter. This is alright with seamen. Come to our right.

It is always a virtue to be our man.

I could I could I could cough.

How long can you listen with hearers. As long. As they are there. Although he has gotten up twice.

No one who thinks about Wednesday can be revenged.

EVIDENCE II

That is the cruelest thing I ever knew is the favorite phrase of Herman.

Herman and Ernest were sitting where they were willing to be sitting. As they were waiting they met with a disappointment all of a sudden. Their wives had been women. If their wives had been women they would not have been a disappointment or anything.

After a bit there was nothing that would be sudden in a disappointment.

They waited without a chance to sing anything. They were very well payed for singing.

Once in a while they went about and if they met they came to have half of it that could be given.

Ernest and William have exchanges when he tells him something and tells him a thing.

It is the best of their naming that they had as a name in raining.

After a while who met him when he was all but related to him.

Think there is care to be taken in decision.

Herman was never his beside he was her help. He would talk about butter and he would ask about whether it is a matter to them.

Ernest should beware of succeeding to bewildering.

It is very little at a time.

EVIDENCE

A white dog is like a lamb he is stretching. They will wait.

Ernest is a judge. He is with it.

He says and means it.

They will be our example of patience.

He has the money.

EVIDENCE (1)

They come and go. It is the cruelest thing I ever heard is the favorite phrase of Gilbert. And he is right. He has heard many cruel things and it is the cruelest thing that he has heard.

EVIDENCE (2)

A lady sitting and working at tapestry which although it is of to-day in design and color looks ancient. The bell rings and two friends come in they ask may we tell you about it. I have taken the measures but you can measure it yourself. The one who replies is a friend of the other one who has not been in before. They may call each other friends although the one is tired of his mother.

EVIDENCE (3)

Portrait of Bravig Imbs

May Sage has a page who does her errands. He may have dreamed and now to his mother he says see and she knows where they were by their help. If any one is well they make it do.

How do you do is easily said.

He waited.

An old fashioned short story.

EVIDENCE

We may be late. A disappointment does not delay our return but as the streets may. They even do. Disappointment makes no matter when they give it that they have it. We are pleased because we are reasonable. There is no observation of whatever is the cause. Indifference comes before all. Just why. Made that water will fill water. They move about but they do not buy without that water. All hoping of disinterestedness is why they have meant that they are exhibiting patience under distribution and procrastination. Life is such that if we are impatient we are a victim. We are a victim of impatient visiting. We are not visiting and we are patient which is an industry. Undeniably is where they will have what they want if they are willing. Who knows what they are to have. She does because she tells it. Life is the same with everything. It is a permission to visit by invitation. And if she goes and asks her will she come and she refuses nothing is happening because they are coming. Do not disturb me while I write. The men who say to a private individual move a little to the right have nothing to do with anything. The man who was whistling was actually ruminating. Not he but gazing. Gazing and looking without seeing is not the same thing neither is it without being refreshing. A great many things further than mentioning.

EVIDENCE (4)

Cater will be with them as with him. A sentence is annoyed when they mention believe it is not for pleasure that I do it. I was just going on and that dog stopped. Part of it is explained.

How are eggs made of butter.

If they eat.

Eggs and butter.

If they eat eggs and butter.

These are good examples of sentences.

EVIDENCE

I like evidence.

Parlor is a room they will be there.

A name parlor is a name.

They made a parlor.

How are actors made.

It is a disappointment to know that they are beginners.

To get away as usual.

EVIDENCE (5)

We think that the last time is the worst.

EVIDENCE

Portrait of Madame Langlois

Power through repose or how many days are there. That she has. It is a violet which is rose but not rosy. A credit to him that it is a tulip that is violet and red but not rosy. It is a violet that is pink. Hours and violet. Violet and hawthorne. Hawthorne is partly violet. Violet is owned by addition. She is violet. It is amazing. She is violet. Whose is violet which it is. Our announcement comes with its break. With its break is or thought. Are our made with gain cane sugar. How are ours again. Is and again and in better. Finally they govern however. Govern is a gage. Thank you that m is m for may matter. Thank you for may matter.

MORE GRAMMAR FOR A SENTENCE

This is one in the continuing series of what Stein called explanatory works that began with *An Elucidation* of 1923 and went on to *An Acquaintance With Description* and numerous other pieces. Some were eventually collected in *How To Write*. They do not make a unified book nor are they separate essays, but rather a loose series. Stein would complete one and soon find an occasion to begin another. For example, before leaving Paris for the country in the spring of 1930, she completed *Sentences and Paragraphs* and after arrival began a new piece, first drily entitled "Paragraphs" but felicitously retitled *More Grammar For A Sentence*. She completed it before returning to Paris. Since her writing came out of daily life, a change of scene changed the daily life, the perceptions and the sentences. Work done in the country became light, concrete and lyrical in pieces easily identified as country writing. Daily life offered vocabulary for constructing sentences and paragraphs and conceptualizing principles of their making.

More Grammar For A Sentence and the other writing studies ask to be read in two ways at once. One reading follows the events and thoughts of the day, from problems of publication to the observation of a hill on the way to Grenoble to separating heads of lettuce into leaves to watching the growth of Basket, the one-year-old poodle. This reading includes biographical details, such as Stein's waiting for the preface by Pierre de Massot for *Dix Portraits*, translated by Georges Hugnet and Virgil Thomson, or the September wedding party for Florence Tanner, the sister of pianist Allen Tanner, and Georges Maratier. The other reading follows sentences, paragraphs, and thoughts about writing, including the question that comes with country life of whether sentences or paragraphs are natural. Everything in this study becomes personal, immediate, and often hilarious. "A sentence needs help. And she cries." "Now a sentence can come and be no disappointment. She criticizes." "A sentence. Made against. His will." "Think of a natural sentence in religion." Life and sentences or paragraphs interact. The grammar piece offers practice to occupy the mind and keep writing limber. "It is as good as exercise."

The grammar piece is a progressive series of definitions, differentiations, examples. Over and over she tries out how she can say something, or looks at a sentence to see what it tells. Sample sentences become paradigms or illustrative definitions. She gropes for the difference between sentence and paragraph, rejecting the common notion that a paragraph is a group of two or more sentences. To her, sentence and paragraph differ qualitatively, not quantitatively. Unlike the paragraph, the sentence, built of grammar, returns upon itself, coming back in a circle to where it started. A paragraph moves in linear, forward direction. "A sentence is a hope of a paragraph," but a paragraph is not an extended sentence and is not made of grammar. The paragraph with its forward thrust leads Stein by 1930–31 to study movement, rhythm, and poetry.

From the moment this study begins, sentences and paragraphs are in her mind. In the manuscript Stein isolates structural elements of writing to examine them. She begins with "Part One," centered, goes on to "The Almonds," centered, and "Buy me with this," perhaps a sentence, perhaps a subhead, perhaps a subtitle. Then follow two sentences placed flush left; the first of these is actually two sentences repeated, one running into the next. The two look as if by mistake they were not indented, but they are placed as sentences, not indented to mark beginnings of paragraphs. To make us aware of conventions for sentences and paragraphs, she does everything against convention. She leaves a space open or fills it to show that not only grammar and meaning but also placement in space are part of composition. She raises questions, as she so often does, about matters we rarely stop to notice.

• • • • •

PART ONE

The Almonds

Buy me with this.

Will you be well will you be well.

A lily smells as green as when it is annoying that it is right about it.

If for long she had been with or without them. That means that her name had not been changed but not known about. She had been with the and without it making a matter with at all. Why then. She is the mother. Her father. Her brother died a young man so did her husband. He was a young man and the house was bigger. Without it to do. She was very well very well to do very well to do with them. After they are a while. Like that in a sound.

There is no other family with at all.

To go on with going on with it.

It makes it safely with them and who.

Wordly worthy worthy worth were they were or were they with be.

Worth bitter.

It is better or are they better.

It is better or are they bitter.

She had held spend when she was sent.

In and uninvited by the mention of that.

Think of their weeding. They were cutting without it at last.

Not only not it but not it.

Try it out. How do you do. Do they love you. Or curiously. When it is different to be agreeable or agreeably older. There it is not to be mistaken.

They made it a danger to have avoided a door which they meant to have had and a hinge in undividedly an attention.

Remark that a recalled pleasing having for them makes it immediately known which is theirs. They have to be without doubt well known. He likes to have him be hired for that in that with their care named Bradley which made whenever they do more than that deliberately making a mine of use of their acknowledge meant for them a reason assistance made curious and by and nearly which is that. Make without call. It is very beautiful to have the winning language.

This a paragraph in substance.

Of course it looks like it in that shape and they always remind it of it. This may be spoken of why. When they are alike they resume a plant which has that for them that they did which was theirs because of ordinary less than white. Ivy leaves resemble harbors. He harbored added it as in order having had it in detail. This makes a paragraph attached.

What is in amounting. Who is in power with having find. Now or then there never is a need of having nine or mine in a name, a noun with thinking of currants makes it different alright but without their say so they will even will with an account so that there is namely that if they turn they will please do with hesitate. Finally they refuse. All this is how they cannot use the name currants after they were women. This whole paragraph is explanatory.

It is very true that it is of use to after to you. With you they will withdraw with which they have to do with you. After all why will they meet with which.

It is very likely that they tell that they liked when they liked it which was which they have as much as an instance of which it is as well. Known as paragraph.

He fortunately was as playing with him. They need know that he thought with them. With by which it is remain and remained about in by with in having they made it have them with and to do. This is a paragraph that plans of thinking it with as Etienne.

It is at adding in remaking tens. Every little way of calling May away from them. With whom were they careful. They will have been thought well of without. Every little nicely by a paving with when by this in and announced. She let fall something which made a little racket. There is why they need now and know their paragraph. A paragraph is not natural. Who knows how. A noun is nature personified. Alike. A sentence which is in one word is talkative. They like their moon. Red at night sailor's delight a vegetable garden which is when there is a cage wherein they add with add withheld with string. A paragraph is not natural. Peas are natural so are string beans all sausages are natural, butter is natural but not cream paragraphs are not natural, quinces are natural even when they are late and with them they are natural without cherries they are natural. A period is natural a capital with a capital with and with a capital. It is beautiful. A word which makes basket a name. If it is a name will he be confused with whatever with it they make to name. There is no doubt that a mine is natural that always is natural that appointment is natural that nearly is natural that will they have their board is natural. It is natural to remain once again. It is natural. A paragraph is not natural but needful. There are more needful with what they do. Think of everything that is natural. Now. It is very beautiful to have a birthday. In which they invite prefer. With them. A paragraph is not nature. Not unalike.

If I leave with them now if I leave it with them now if I leave it with them. Now. A paragraph is not a division it does not separate. Because if they must go they will not have gone. Not now. Be with a wife. Wifely. Enthusiasm. Natural. They will think about who says. She liked their coffee but she does not like it now.

A paragraph without words. Why are mainly made in comparison.

With having lost. He was not discontented with having lost. By that means he was received without having mine and then it was nearly by the way of fastening. With in union for they made it do. Without them as they could for which they were in an opposite reason of a placement. For their attachment. Which made it be by the time that they could diminish. Upper. And more.

The difference between natural paragraph and moving paragraph.

A little at a time.

It is as good as exercise.

A paragraph of why they will apply theirs to this. In finally acute hire that they can. Appeal that it is very times to be.

A natural paragraph is not waiting.

They will it is not natural to speak of them. It is not natural to speak. It is not natural to have them. They have them come with them. It is natural not to have them come with them. Reduce remaining without them. It is very natural to have returned with them. What has a paragraph to do with it. They are not having it to do it as they wish. Providing they are coming with which they made it anyway. There is no use in a paragraph which is outstanding. A paragraph has no naturally as an encumbrance without which they are with wither a blessing good which is as good. What can a paragraph do eventually. Do without but he minds it. A paragraph is naturally that they are disappointed. A paragraph is made in between continuing which is that they will have it bloom. How can you tell the difference between eat it all and a pea. Which they mean. It is not that they are without equivalent.

To think well of any paragraph they must have affection.

There is no such thing as a natural sentence but there is such a thing as a natural paragraph and it must be found.

It makes no difference whether he gets tired first or whether I do if we continue to go on it is not necessary that we have both went and rested without there after made it be a different in the way. This is not a mistake in wasting which when without theirs as they do needed all alike which if it is a part of inclusive that they make in agreement and after all it was hers I used.

There is no such thing as a natural sentence and why because a sentence is not naturally. A sentence. With them they will detest without whether they will belie it. A paragraph in when there is a little valley in noon or as it is in the way of a little of it as soon as there has been is a moon. That makes it not naturally be a paragraph. When he is afraid he is after afraid and if it is then that it is that it has been might it be in with which it is in return. Rarely afraid. After afraid. A paragraph is naturally after. Afraid. After afraid. To look after. It is after.

There is a difference between after and after afraid. A paragraph is not a sentence after it is a paragraph after.

Supposing three things a will they be having met and at a time with while and after without not at a time with which to trouble with advising why they weeded without grass. Because they prefer separating salad. This and they come alternately again. It cannot be naturally a paragraph because they are there and they have left one shovel so they will be willing which is why two hundred salads are as small and will be larger. A paragraph is an hour.

After every day they think.

About their wheat. Which is coated with bread. And they like grapes. Because a dog looks at it as a ball. Why if they are currants and made it with it.

If a dog looks like it does with them.

It is very nearly a paragraph to cry.

She knew who whose when they lent. It is a basket which they covered with a and with in it. It is very actually fine.

A paragraph made a mention. And Nora or no or a dove which is widen.

Partly Relief.

Nobody knows what I am trying to do but I do and I know when I succeed.

Plainly attaching the string to keep they string beans within. This is nothing.

They know very well how they stand and are thinning but did they. Very likely they always did. It is not a representation of unified attaching to them. Now then she always knew she would be everything. He always knew he was becoming. They are accepted as being in very mainly if intruding. They will accept as well. Well enough alone. They know how they are standing with without moving. I do not think that they never didn't. Well and. Just as very well. In hive in him. Every and one.

Forget how beautifully Marin has his hours. With his hours. She with out him with her son with out him. He may sail. Not with his same as with a name. If he has not asked him she will come and call of him with of her son. He has since been with women and named them attaching inclining for it to be other than their name. A fox which is that it was right basket was a name. There is no need of a paragraph without amounts. This time a paragraph was not natural because he said. If they had three men then they lose it with his good-bye and an offering. There is no use in an unnatural parting. Pears and apart. And will they leave with pillows. With them. This paragraph is not natural. To-morrow is not natural. Without with them. Is not natural.

May full of weights a darkness all in declare.

What is thought about whether with will they go.

Resist having a natural sentence. There are a great many ants in apricots but they can be blown off without very much of an effort.

A natural sentence can not remind one of startling.

It is of very little use to like to walk.

With them.

It is of very little use to like to walk as well as be with them.

A paragraph is why they went where they did.

A sentence made it be all when they were through indeed how are they after all may it be for their sake and ridges. With may if it makes more than at most will be for in for instance. Now a sentence can come and be no disappointment. She criticizes. But which week.

A sentence is natural. He did not come. This is a joke. A sentence is natural. He did. Which is variable and they will offer him liver with and without oil. A sentence. Made against. His will. Will he do it. He will. A sentence made with his meaning.

There is no difference between a paragraph and at once.

If it is better than ever. If it is finished. This is no paragraph. They will remember like that. This is inviting his confidence which is not withdrawn mainly but with it.

A paragraph does need a two by three. Without doubt. Which it does. By the time. They will deliver. With adding. More than they can. In need of a reliance without a difference in their name they have it a name. With them.

A paragraph is mentioned as silly. As silky. As a silky saving that he had.

That is a good paragraph. Thank you. He came. It was so good. Which is that he came. May be he did.

There is no effort in without a paid relief.

What is a trait which they have. They made more.

Forward and back.

Sachey forward and back.

Think quietly of how to do with out a way of which they were well out of it.

Folded wrong.

The salads have been wet.

The salads have been made wet by water. This is as useful as a doll.

Now this is the sort of thing that she would write. I know what a paragraph is after all.

What is he willing to do. For you. As well as for him and they will be asked to come if they answer. They will wave it as many could have made change in a firm hoping for it now. Why are nasturtiums natural which they have as which they are. Awhile at a time. It is our they hope. But they will see. To it.

Did he drink out of his water because of well well. Who can be cured cared while they may. Who while they may. Now do you see how wrong that is.

Leave sizes to paragraphs.

Paragraphs are one two three one two one two one two three paragraphs are sizes.

That is without what paragraphs there are. Paragraphs are sizes.

They began with using me for them. Will they be well and wish.

Paragraphs are named.

They name a paragraph without with this.

Why is a sentence natural if it is not in disuse. A sentence is not natural. Why is a paragraph not natural. A paragraph is not it is not not natural a paragraph is not it is a paragraph and it is not as that that is as a paragraph to tell. Do tell why is a paragraph just as much as ever natural.

A paragraph is natural. They will mend by the time it is mended by the time. A paragraph is natural by the mended that it is by that time. This is not in used. A paragraph if they were occupied which they were there and care. It was foolish to care. Have to take care. Which they have to care.

A paragraph is natural that is it is that it is is very well to know is very well known. Thank you for forgiving with them to with him.

A paragraph is natural with forgotten. That is with may and said.

Think of a paragraph. Reminded and remember. Remembered.

A paragraph is natural. They will be a paragraph will be a paragraph will be as natural. As should never be used for likely.

A paragraph. Which is natural.

They will know that each sat as they lay there. A paragraph is not with drew.

William and who. This is a mistake.

A paragraph is natural.

What can be expected of paragraphs and sentences by the time I am done. With or without. What do we do. We do without. Why is she stout. Because we do do without.

It is perfectly easy to make a paragraph. Without a sentence. Because they like it better. So.

If they do not tell them what they have. That is a natural sentence because it is without this which they finish.

If they do not tell them what they have they will be able to have it as often. This is not a natural sentence. Any more.

Need they be always one of without that. They do have. To like it.

They made it be naturally. Without a place. With theirs.

Think of a natural sentence in religion.

As we went along.

She made it appoint them. They will like which they had being alike.

One of which.

You can have a natural sentence if you look alike.

Reliable they made a bee.

A bee hive is made for once and with is kisses.

Will they cry with their with their with thin with. A sentence made from anxious.

I am thinking a great deal about which sentences are, left over, asked, and leaned, made for it in easy. They made it walked around.

With which do you think me.

That is a natural sentence without Baltimore.

What is the difference between and with made easy, that they came, made why in their amidst with in them, they are tallied, in remainder after soon. That changes it to all of their time. It is very easy to miss a sentence.

But not a paragraph.

It is very wrong to miss a sentence.

If they move they will move with welled and they did not like it for them as fish.

That makes it change readily from Baltimore to Belley. In with when. When announced as added then.

They can refuse paragraphs.

It is.

Baltimore west. Belley east. Boston.

They made it different to have tears.

Let their be paragraphs why or not.

They are no paragraphs. Belley. They are paragraphs. Baltimore.

It is by this wish which is.

What joins which is and which it is. Boston.

There are no paragraphs.

Paragraphs they will bequeath weddings.

Thinking thanking.

A solace.

Natural sentences do exist in arithmetic.

If we both say he threw that tree away.

It does not make any difference how old they all are.

These would be natural sentences if they were at all to call harder than for her.

She does use that which will there oblige it with either at very heard for advent in refer to a sentence.

She does not make it a paragraph.

No nor at all likely.

There is a difference.

There can be natural sentences if they are halting which whichever that is with renown that without that waving that if they or through. This is a sentence.

A sentence is halting with but as a cow gives and is gives it is sent has calves.

The Almonds have women.

A sentence leaves cows out about left where with all it takes.

This sentence is around.

I think naturally not with have their things they like with their shone as add or fancy.

This sentence more and more grows wider without carrots.

A sentence can be natural with wheeling.

With can be natural.

Some say forty. And some say one.

Now make all this into a paragraph without me.

Bend ended wagon. This is no sentence nor a pastime.

A paragraph is natural but not to be amused.

Bend ended wagon here nearby they will paper with comforting in rejoice.

A sentence is without their dear. Dear me with.

A sentence means too much a paragraph doesn't, therefore a paragraph is nature nature we we are averse.

Assent. Recent. Assert. And question. Do stop. When you do. It was a rotation. In regard to their fixing habitual arrange meant.

A sentence needs help. And she cries.

A sentence is why they were folded. Please have it folded.

Who helps whom with help withheld help yourself.

That is or or hour.

A sentence will come.

Chiefly. Will come.

That is a natural sentence. A sentence will come. Chiefly. Will come.

It must be wonderful to hear about these things and then see them.

The difference between not reading and not inviting may do.

It was opposite wholly in directing.

What is a paragraph when they predict rain.

There used ordinary sentences to make it apply.

Really not to care really not to care makes it a hole with a well. A well is not used any more. That is an ordinary sentence and is it satisfactory.

Count again. Fifteen.

This is in a tradition. They will be as careful.

To make it do.

This is a paragraph.

What is it. A paragraph. Grenoble. On the way to Grenoble you pass a hill without a town where you might stop which I see it is used by it in a main while in the way. A usual sentence is placed anywhere. What is a sentence. Without a trouble. They will be just as well aware. Without it. This is a paragraph without delight. They are after it. After awhile. An ordinary paragraph. Which they have.

How is a paragraph. Taken by themselves. Or right away.

What is a sentence. With them a paragraph.

Think carefully about a paragraph. Nobody knows whose is it.

All of which makes how is it. Now think about that. How does it have a help without them they will in relight right away.

A sentence is not in naturally made in part. It is easier.

What is it.

I see what is the trouble with a sentence they will not be two a day. That is the trouble with a sentence. Now try to make a sentence with this experience. Not to care. But with whom by the time they have finished. A sentence by the time. No thank you not to thank you. A sentence by the time who has been named with them. It is nice that they do now.

It is easy to know that a sentence is not a paragraph.

With will with them do. Will they do.

What will they do with them they will want them. They will do what they want to do.

Is this a paragraph or are these sentences. Who will know that about them.

Sentences are not natural paragraphs are natural and I am desperately trying to find out why.

Neither for as turkey which in ended May. She tried to get a sieve in many towns.

It is easy to sound alike and to diminish with their welcome that they state.

What is a paragraph, no place in which to settle. Because they have been moved.

A paragraph is different that is it affects me. That is it it is why they are relished. As for a sentence in what way do they stop. They stop without. And why. With is noon. It is with them it does not make a difference they will wait.

All this leads to me. I can be careful of what I do. That is a sentence. If it is a repeated and for days there can be hopes that Florence will marry which she will. A sentence is a plan. It is never plain. Think of a sentence by its birthday. What is a sentence. With or without an ado. A paragraph is why they will eat with their other brother. And they are hurried. They like the best of all when they made it a part of which they can do. If they feel well. What is a sentence. No. Nobody.

All of it. Content to be obstinate.

What is a sentence. He may mean that he is very nearly his cousin and that he has been made fortunately for him with a tendency to remain thin. That would be a sentence if one did not use anything to have him tell them.

There is this named him. This is a sentence with his name.

Feeling the same.

A sentence is a hope of a paragraph. What is a paragraph that is easy. How can you know better if you say so. A sentence is never an answer. Neither is it. Who answers him. He remains with them. They have to have him because they took him. And they with this are what they are saying.

What is a paragraph. Right off. Write often. What is a paragraph. He drinks as if in wishing. He drinks of if in washing. And so and so they will be out of mind out of hand. This makes no difficulty. Have they thought of that.

A paragraph is naturally without a finish.

A paragraph is alright.

With or without a chicken fish or vegetables she came to pay for a harness. This is what they were taught.

A paragraph always lets it fall or lets it be well and happy or feels it to be so which they never were themselves as worried.

What time is it.

A paragraph has to do with the growth of a dog. They talk about it. She says. No. A paragraph is never finished therefore a paragraph is not natural. A paragraph is with the well acquainted. It languishes in mediocrity. It makes it doubtful if lips are thick and the eyes blue and the blonde which they have it might be cupped and alike which whenever a reliable made to order as plainly. There is nothing troubled with how about them. They are ordered to make it more for them. A paragraph ceases to be naturally with them with cream. With them they are enthused by holding it off. A paragraph is natural if they walk. It is natural if it has not come. In order. Which was given. And no blame. A paragraph reads why do they like where they know why they have gotten all of it back not all of it because a part of it has been missing. This is a paragraph naturally.

There is a difference between natural and emotional.

Who can sing. Sing around and about. If one thinks of a paragraph without thinking one does not think of a paragraph or anything. A sentence is why they like places. He replaces it. She replaces it. She replaces the amount. They place and replace and recorrect their impressions. They do not change. They do not with how do you do. How do you do. How are you. A paragraph never is restless. That is easy. What is a paragraph.

I like to look at it.

What is a paragraph.

She likes it better than Granada.

She likes it.

I like to look at it.

A resolution is a paragraph.

What is a paragraph. I thought a paragraph was naturally a paragraph and now I displease my retaining a paragraph.

What is a paragraph.

She will be with women. She not. She is places where they can hear it which they wherever it is replied. Will she open the gate. She will in spite of an appetite which she has. This is a paragraph and it sounds strange. They may be made to have to have a calf that they feel which that it is for them to sell. They make all of it well will it do. A paragraph need not be a finish. They will be and think with what they said. A paragraph has changed hands. A paragraph made a noun. A noun is the name of anything. How in a paragraph. I like a name use and lose. They will use the name. Some will use the name. A noun is a name. Basket is a name. Will they come for him is a name. What is it is not a name. Why do they like me is why they have it as a name. They change from some.

It is a change for some who come. This is a sentence that is unreliable. A paragraph is of sentences that are reliable. A sentence is very well when it is as if they had sat and waited. Do you see how they sew. This is a sentence of which it is for which in part of the time they will see me. This sentence of which I speak. Made in pairs. Maidens prayers. Made in pairs. With which they are placed. With may which is mainly. This is a mistake. As spelled. It is very beautiful and original.

Now any word made an impression. They will in three make Mrs. Roux. We always speak of her. Mrs. Roux. This is without an opposite with her.

Withdrew, they withdrawn have withdrawn, they withdrew.

It is unbelievable how many sentences have a mistake. Unbelievable. How many have. Very few have. They will do well not to have a mistake. They will do well not to have a mistake in competition. They will be very careful too. Which they are. Whatever they do. Now this is an example of just as well. A sentence is very often more than added. A paragraph is in that case not just a paragraph not at all not without this. What is a paragraph. Who is with to blame. Change meant to mean. A paragraph has been motioned away. And now a sentence is natural if they redivide it.

Redivide. Who will be winning by their half.

It is alright that a sentence and express what is it they will see to it. I know what a sentence is or is not and a paragraph is not a sentence even if it is all one because they shrink from it. Not from it. This is a paragraph for them.

A paragraph is if it is natural that they will change it too. This is a paragraph which is natural. It is a sentence which if it were a paragraph would be natural. If you introduce as natural you do not make it too.

A paragraph is natural because it falls away. A paragraph need not fall away to be natural.

A sentence can not be natural because it is not rounded that is round is natural but rounded is not natural. A sentence is not natural. They will go on. A sentence is not not natural. If a sentence is not natural what should it be. If a paragraph is natural should it be. It should be. A paragraph should not be because to help is to go away, she said he would be busy. This is neither a sentence nor a paragraph the country says no. This is neither a paragraph nor without it. A paragraph is natural because they feel like it. A sentence is not natural without that with that. And now think about damage. It is no trouble to wear green, thank you Len. This is a sentence which they know. If they know. Thank you if they know. This is a sentence. Thank you if they know. What is the difference between rounded.

In other words a paragraph is not naturally a natural thing but it is.

I have suddenly gotten not to care. This is an old sentence. To say so.

She knew she was right by the way that he said so. This is simply that.

There is no distance to come. With them come is came. She came.

No sentence when they were careful. A sentence when they were careful.

It is why they were aware that they were carried away by her. That is a nice sentence but not a natural sentence because they were divided in a sense. They were divided by leaving them about when they were ready. A natural sentence has nothing to do with how do you do. A natural sentence is vainly made by butter. It is in vain.

A natural sentence. A yellow peach may be ripened. There is a kind of a pear that has a rosy center which if felt is not in itself. What is it that made her know with a measure, she said there had been enough.

What is a natural sentence. A natural sentence they need not write. A natural sentence. After all. Who is here. After all who hears him. If they can.

None of that has anything to do with how a sentence is held. A sentence thinks loudly. Why must must is by me. Nearly beside made by then. A sentence cannot be natural. It must be returnable. To be returned. As well. What is a sentence and why cannot it be natural. Because it is a sentence. A sentence is not unnatural. A paragraph is not made of sentences. A paragraph with a precious sweet with eat. A paragraph is not pressed for time. Ever. A sentence if it returns or if it is added or if it is ended or simply in each way they make it do. They always can. Make a sentence do. You see why a sentence is not a part of it. A sentence should be ours. Now listen if he makes believe loving and eats in playing he eats in resumption, this is the same as anything and this is not a margin they make either stopping or not it is a paragraph with how and treasure. A sentence should be within a lope, that is why they had with him. Now think of these things. With them. A same with in all either shawl. Nothing to do with it. What is a sentence. There is no use in telling a whim. Nor in he sews. It is alike. Everything they show is piled alike. There should be a sentence in some arithmetic. But with fair they had it as may fairly hand it our alike. No nor should it be my fish. A fish can be taught as a lake. What is a sentence it used to be that they liked it. Without a notice. That they liked it with that they had to be mine. What is a sentence. Often I will make a paragraph.

It gives all the effect of a mountain but it is on a plain.

Making it have it. It is a part and a part is not where there and have more. A part is not that it is belonging to the same plans.

A sentence if you thin then you thin sauces and sauces have need of Leon and Rosa. Every time you end will you have a refrain. Refrain can only mean that they wind and leave. He has disguised his action by his delight. He is delighted with it. Now these sentences do not make a paragraph. Nor do they make an end without it. Without doubt. That is a sentence but two words cannot make a preface. Is a preface a sentence. Very well. Send it. A sentence is a present which they make. In that way a sentence comes without a paragraph. Do you see. To say, do you see, is finally without employment.

Think of a sentence in two places it is not natural but engaging and very frightened. That is a sentence with waiting for them. It is very disagreeable to be waiting for them. This is a cadence. A cadence does not resemble a sentence it looks like it. A cadence does not resemble a sentence it is partly without a paragraph. Without is vainly made true. Mainly, mainly is the idea. That a paragraph is returned. It is not. It is mire which is not where they used. A paragraph is our, signed William. What is a paragraph, a paragraph is not a partition. A sentence never can be set apart.

A paragraph is this she discovers that the lake which is far away is not absolved in a partition. That is to say the land in between does not belong to them. It is very kindly of them to be back.

This is not completely a paragraph because of hoping that they will hear it alike. If it were a paragraph listen they would be told. How are they. Now a sentence is made by happen to distance.

They will be called anyway. This is neither a paragraph nor a sentence.

After a while.

I feel very differently about it.

Is conversation sentences. Is it paragraphs. Is it seeing them. There is an advantage.

When is it taken the advantage.

By them. Made by them. They will be willing. A conversation changes to paragraphs. With hope. Will, they be pleased. If they go. What is a conversation. They have learned all of it.

A sentence it is so easy to lose what a sentence is. Not so easy with a paragraph it is not so easy to lose what is a paragraph. What is a paragraph. Who loses a hold on him. That is a paragraph. That is not a sentence. Why is it.

What is it.

What is a paragraph.

I can come to know.

I have been known to know and to say so. A paragraph is not varying with the summer or anything.

This is a paragraph because it says so. Do you see. It says so. If you do see and it says so. Yes we do see and it says so. A paragraph says so. A sentence if it could would it say so. Would a sentence say so. If it said so would it have it as if it had it as said so, no. A sentence has not said so. A paragraph has said so. Think of a sentence. Has it said so. Yes it has said so.

Two to a sentence. Yes it has said so. A sentence has not had it. It has not had it to say so. A sentence has not said to say so. A paragraph says so. A paragraph has not to have to have it say so. Easily say so. Too easily say so. A paragraph not too easily to say so. What is a sentence. A paragraph is not a sentence exactly not many more. There have not been sentences whether they say. A sentence always returns if they are happy. A sentence always returns if they were happy. A sentence is a sentence. This may be, but it is not with arrive. Arrival. A Rival Sentence. Will Dan come and meet me. If he is meeting there. Think of a sentence. They will part. A sentence can not exist if it does not come back no not if it does not come back. A paragraph finishes.

This is it.

HOW SHE BOWED TO HER BROTHER

An anecdote told by Alice Toklas in her autobiography, *What Is Remembered* (105–6), describes what may be the occasion for this portrait: the first meeting between Stein and her brother Leo after they separated in 1913, Stein remaining in Paris and her brother moving to Florence. Stein and Toklas are in the car in a traffic jam in Paris. Stein sees Leo, acknowledging him with a bow. The portrait indeed refers to driving. One difficulty with the anecdote is that while it may identify the occasion for the piece, it explains nothing about its composition. Toklas dates meeting and portrait to the post–World War I period. The portrait, however, was written late in 1931, which is consistent with the inclusion of the poodle.

How She Bowed To Her Brother, We Came. A History, Grant or Rutherford B. Hayes, Winning His Way, and other pieces of 1930–31 break up sentences into spoken units moving in pronounced irregular rhythms. The phrases of *How She Bowed To Her Brother* lurch in uncomfortable, jerking, forward and backward movement "like the flickers," full of pauses and hesitations, stuttering in discomfort. It is worth recalling that Leo Stein very early became hard of hearing, as Gertrude Stein also did in later years; deaf people hear not in sentences but in irregular fragments of varying loudness.

To Eugene Jolas, the editor of *transition,* who published the piece in March 1932, Stein spoke of it as "a grammatical experiment." The word *bow* carries many meanings, which she constructs in innumerable different forms and rhythms, from neutral, polite acknowledgement to respect, submission, and hostile formality.

The portrait is here published under the title that appears in the manuscript and reappears in the first sentence, rather than as *She Bowed To Her Brother,* which was used in earlier publications and which ends the piece with a parting nod. The restored title appears to fit the situation more subtly than the simpler one, for she does not in fact bow or submit to her brother but merely nods.

The phrase *She Bowed To Her Brother* recurs in a very personal comment in the Henry James section of *Four In America,* written more than two years later, in 1933, though not published until 1947. William and Henry James, brothers who did not end up in hostile, distant silence, may have reminded Stein of her brother and herself. "It is not necessary never to mention never to have a brother. / Fortunately many foil an instance of that. / She bowed to her brother. / That is coming in here" (153).

• • • • •

The story of how she bowed to her brother.

Who has whom as his.

Did she bow to her brother. When she saw him.

Any long story. Of how she bowed to her brother.

Sometimes not.

She bowed to her brother. Accidentally. When she saw him.

Often as well. As not.

She did not. Bow to her brother. When she. Saw him.

This could happen. Without. Him.

Everybody finds in it a sentence that pleases them.

This is the story included in. How she bowed to her brother.

Could another brother have a grand daughter.

No. But. He could have a grandson.

This has nothing to do with the other brother of whom it is said that we read she bowed to her brother.

There could be a union between reading and learning.

And now everybody. Reads. She bowed. To her brother.

And no one. Thinks.

Thinks that it is clearly. Startling.

She started. By not bowing. To her brother.

And this was not the beginning.

She has forgotten.

How she bowed. To her brother.

And. In mentioning. She did mention. That this was. A recollection.

For fortunately. In detail. Details are given.

Made an expression. Of recollection.

Does whether. They gather. That they heard. Whether. They bowed. To each other. Or not.

If in. They made it. Doubtful. Or double. Of their holding it. A momentary after. That she was never. Readily made rather. That they were. Whether. She asked her. Was she doing anything. Either.

In all this there lay. No description. And so. Whether. They could come to be nearly. More. Than more. Or rather. Did she. Bow to her brother.

PART II

They were a few. And they knew. Not that. She had bowed. To her brother. There were not. A few. Who knew. That she. Had. Bowed to her brother. Because if they knew. They would say. That a few. Knew. That she. Had bowed to her brother. But necessarily. Not a few. Knew. They did. Not know. Because they. Were not there. There are not a few. Who are there. Because. Nobody. Was there. Nor did. She know. That she was there. To help to share. And they can. Be there. To tell. Them. So. That. They know. She bowed. To her brother. More. There. Than. There.

III

It might be easily pointed out. By the chance. Of a. Wish. No wish.

He might. Not wish. Not to. Be easily. Pointed out. By no. Wish.

Which they. Might easily.

Not be pointed. Out. As. A and not. The wish.

It is not. To be. Pointed out. That. There. Is. No wish.

Not. A wish.

She bowed to her brother. Was not easily. Pointed out. And. No wish.

Which it. And easily. Pointed out. And. No. Wish.

She and. No wish. Which is. Not easily pointed out. And. So which. They. And. No wish. Which. And not. Easily pointed out. She bowed to her brother. And no wish. And not. Easily pointed out. And no. Wish.

For them. Which. To wish. Not. Which. Easily. Pointed out. And. No wish. Which. She. No wish. Easily pointed out.

Which. She easily pointed out. Which. She bowed to her brother. And. Which.

If she had been likely to restate that doors which relate an advantage to their advancing. And not at all. As a coincidence.

She bowed to her brother. This was a chance. That might have happened. Minutely.

To interrupt a white dog. Who can occasionally.

In instance

No one counts alike

She bowed to her brother. For. And. Counts alike.

She bowed. To her brother. Could be lost. By their leaving. It as lost. By. The time. In which. They feel. They will. It is. Indebted. That able. Presence. As very much. And idle. If she were walking along. She would be. She would not. Bow to her brother. If she were riding. Along. She would. Be. She would. Be. Not as bowing. To her. Brother.

As she rode along. Easily. By driving. As she rode. Along. She. Bowed. To her brother.

It is. True. As. She drove. Along. She. Bowed. To her brother.

Just like that.

She bowed. To her brother.

They were. There. That is to say. They were. Passing there. They were passing there. But not. On that day. And with this. To say. It was said. She bowed. To her brother. Which was. A fact.

If she bowed. To her brother. Which was. A fact. That is. If she bowed. Which. If she bowed. Which she did. She bowed to her brother.

Which she did. She bowed to her brother. Or rather. Which she did. She bowed to her brother. Or rather which she did she bowed to her brother.

She could think. Of how she was. Not better. Than when. They could say. Not. How do you do. To-day. Because. It is an accident. In suddenness. When there is. No stress. On their. Address. They do not address you. By saying. Rather. That they went by. And came again. Not. As. Or. Why.

It is. What is. Even. Not always occurred. Just by the time. That it. Can happen. To be curious. She bowed. To her brother. And why. Again. In there. Should have been. Not more. Than. That. Which. She bowed. To her brother.

By which. It is. In tendency. To more. By which. It is. In tendency to not. Have had. She in the. Three. She bowed. To her brother.

Would it be. In a way. Not they. Would. Not. They. Be in a way that is. To say. She. Is to say. Did. She bow. To her brother. In. Which way. Did. She come to say. It was. That way.

She bowed to her brother.

If it was. Separately. Not. To separate. Separately. No one. Is there. But there. Was it. With them. As perhaps. Portions. For there. Which. In which. She bowed to her brother.

Not. After. In intention. The same. As mention. She did not mention. Nor was there. Intention. That she. Bowed to her brother.

She bowed to her brother.

STANZAS IN MEDITATION (SELECTIONS)

Between May and November of 1932, at the country house she rented in Bilignin in the Rhône Valley, Stein did an enormous amount of writing—four plays, two short novels, and several works of poetry and prose. In addition, she wrote two book-length works that were diametrically opposed. One was *Stanzas in Meditation,* also called *Meditations in Stanzas,* not published until after her death and still hardly known. Both its title and vocabulary announce a stark, abstract work without reference and context. The other was *The Autobiography of Alice B. Toklas,* which was published as soon as it was written and brought Stein the fame she had always desired, money she wanted, and the lecture tour of 1934–35 that allowed her to return lionized to America. The title identifies its subject and places the book in a narrative tradition as her most concrete, referential work.

In the meditations, consciousness focuses on abstract mental landscapes that do not cohere. Tense wordplay takes place between their elements—two, one of two, two and two, one and one. There is trouble in the quibbles but it is not named and not attached to stories. It is as if in meditation Stein "unhooked" words from events, people, and objects to compose them as efforts of a mind in the act of looking for comprehension. The stanzas are not idyllic summer writing or peaceful summer reading.

The manuscript and one of the two typescripts show revisions in Stein's hand. Almost consistently, the auxiliary verb *may* is changed to *can.* However, it turns out that not only the verb *may* but the word *may* or *May* in all its forms is eliminated. We have no trouble when the month of May is changed to April. On the other hand, we can be in the midst of *May* but not in the midst of *can.* The consistency of the revisions in disregard of sense is astounding.

The elimination of the word *may* turns out to be an attempt to purge the text of the name May following Toklas' discovery of the manuscript of *Q. E. D.* in the spring of 1932. *Q. E. D.,* Stein's first novel, written in 1903, was an autobiographical, lesbian story about a love triangle between three young women. The three were Stein, Adele in the novel; Mabel Haynes, renamed Mabel Neathe; and May Bookstaver [Knoblauch], Stein's lover, renamed Helen Thomas. *Q. E. D.* had not been typed and remained unpublished until well after Stein's death. What enraged Toklas was not the love affair but the fact that when she and Stein, upon falling in love, exchanged "confessions," Stein had not told her about it. What further enraged Toklas was to discover the verbal presence of May in many Stein works. That presence is mentioned in the headnote for *A List,* but a careful reader will discover the word *may,* the name May, and the person May, or May May, May Mary, and M.M. in innumerable passages.

It must have been as if a ghost, buried for years, stepped out of the abstract word constructions into the women's daily life. The revisions were executed by Stein but no doubt initiated by Toklas, who also destroyed or made Stein destroy May Bookstaver's letters. In the texts of the summer of 1932 and in others that were being reviewed for the publication of *Operas and Plays,* what looks like innocent wordplay is made to stand out angrily by underlining, retracing of words, and insertion of letters, like an *n* that makes "may" into "many."

Both the sixth volume of the posthumous Yale edition, *Stanzas in Meditation and Other Poems (1929–1933)* and *The Yale Gertrude Stein* print this revised, corrupt text. The stanzas included in the *Reader* restore Stein's original text. Given the length of *Stanzas,* only a selection of poems could be included in the *Reader.* However, the text of each stanza included is complete.

The *Autobiography* is a brilliant invention but not an invention of language. Her first "public book," it presents none of the challenges of Stein's experimental writing and is not included in the *Reader.*

The stanzas must be read as word constructions, not as concealed pieces of autobiography. Their impulse is not to tell stories or to explain but to meditate upon what she perceived and, as she said, to achieve in their disembodied form an "exactitude of abstract thought." Only one poem, Stanza LXXI of Part V, includes a proper name. Stein identifies it as "an introduction to Picabia" because it was used, in a translation by Marcel Duchamp, to preface Picabia's exhibition of drawings in Paris in December 1932.

• • • • •

PART I

Stanza VI

I have not heard from him but they ask more
If with all which they merit with as well
If it is not an ounce of which they measure
He has increased in weight by losing two
Namely they name as much.
Often they are obliged as it is by their way
Left more than they can add acknowledge
Come with the person that they do attach
They like neither best by them altogether
For which it is no virtue fortune all
Ours on account theirs with the best of all
Made it be in no sense other than exchange

By which they cause me to think the same
In finally alighting where they may have at one time
Made it best for themselves in their behalf.
Let me think well of a great many
But not express two so.
It is just neither why they like it
Because it is by them in as they like
They do not see for which they refuse names
Articles which they like and once they hope
Hope and hop can be as neatly known
Theirs in delight or rather may they not
Ever if shone guessing in which they have
All may be glory may be may be glory
For not as ladling marguerites out.
It is best to know their share.
Just why they joined for which they knelt
They can call that they were fortunate.
They may be after it is all given away.
They may. Have it in mine.
And so it is a better chance to come
With which they know theirs to undo
Getting it better more than once alike
For which fortune favors me.
It is the day when we remember two.
We two remember two two who are thin
Who are fat with glory too with two
With it with which I have thought twenty fair
If I name names if I name names with them,
I have not hesitated to ask a likely block
Of which they are attributed in all security
As not only why but also where they may
Not be unclouded just as yes to-day
They call peas beans and raspberries strawberries or two
They forget well and change it as a last
That they could like all that they ever get
As many fancies for which they have asked no one.
Might any one be what they liked before
Just may they come to be not only fastened
It should be should be just what they like

This May in unison
All out of cloud. Come hither. Neither
Aimless and with a pointedly rested displeasure
She may be glad to be either in their resigning
That they have this plan I remember.
Well welcome in fancy.
Or just need to better that they call
All have been known in name as call
They will call this day one for all
I know it can be shared by Tuesday
Gathered and gathered yes.
All who come will will come or come to be
Come to be coming that is in and see
See elegantly not without enjoin
See there there where there is no share
Shall we be three I wonder now

Stanza XV

Should they may be they might if they delight
In why they must see it be there not only necessarily
But which they might in which they might
For which they might delight if they look there
And they see there that they look there
To see it be there which it is if it is
Which may be where where it is
If they do not occasion it to be different
From what it is.
In one direction there is the sun and the moon
In the other direction there are cumulous clouds and the sky
In the other direction there is why
They look at what they see
They look very long while they talk along
And they may be said to see that at which they look
Whenever there is no chance of its not being warmer
Than if they wish which they were.
They see that they have what is there may there
Be there also what is to be there if they may care
They care for it of course they care for it.

Now only think three times roses green and blue
And vegetables and pumpkins and pansies too
She knew she grew all these through to you
And she may be there did he mind learning how now
All this cannot be mixed.
Once again I think I am reflecting
And they may be patient in not why now
And more than if which they are reflecting
That if they with which they will be near now
Or not at all in the same better
Not for which they will be all called
By which they will may be as much as if wishing
But which each one has seen each one
Not at all now
Nor if they like as if with them well or ordinarily
Should they be more enjoined of which they like
It is very well to have seen what they have seen
But which they will not only be alike.
They are very evenly tired with more of this
For they will happen to be in which resolve
Always made by which they prepare that no one
Is more able to be sure of which
They will not will they compel
Not only where they see which they see
But will they be willing for needing
Only which they could call not by it
If they have come again to do it not at all
As very much made in once by their own saying
Yes of course which they will not be at all
Not only not for them in which they like
I lead all may be caught by fattening
Or not either sent all which may positively say so
In their own pleasure neither which they like
It is mine when they need to accept add me
For which they mind one at a time
It is at one time no different between how many hills
And they look like that caught in I mean
For which they will add not when I look
Or they make it plain by their own time.

This which they see by
They turn not their back to the scenery
What does it amount to.
Not only with or better most and best
For I think well of meaning.
It is not only why they might stare to change
Or feel crops well as he has promised, he said.
That there would be several days not of rain
And there would then be plenty of good weather
Probably the crops would be good.
Alright they think in wishes
And some superstitions and some
Beginning and fortunately with places of ditches
And also formidably of which when
When they find the clouds white and the sky blue
The hills green and different in shape too
And the next to what followed when the other bird flew
And what he did when he dug out what he was told to
And which way they will differ if they tell them too
And what they do if they do not cover the vine too
They do it by hand and they carry it all too
Up the way they did still have it to do
And so they think well of well wishers.
I have my well-wishers thank you.

PART II

Stanza VII

What do I care or how do I know
Which they prepare for them
Or more than they like which they continue
Or they may go there but which they mind
Because of often without care that they increase aloud
Or for them fortunately they manage this
But not only what they like but who they like.
There may be said to be all history in this.
They may be often opposite to not knowing him
Or they may be open to any impression

Or even if they are not often worried
They may be just bothered
By wondering do they often make it be alike afterward
Or to continue afterward as if they came
It is useless to introduce two words between one
And so they must conceal where they run
For they can claim nothing
Nor are they willing to change which they have
Oh yes I organise this. But not a victory
They will spend or spell space
For which they have no share
And so to succeed following.
This is what there is to say.
Once upon a time they meant to go together
They were foolish not to think well of themselves
Which they did not were they willing
As they often were to go around
When they were asked as they were well aware
That they could think well of them
Remember this once they knew that the way to give
Was to go more than they went
For which they meant immediately faster
It is always what they will out loud
May they like me oh may they like me.
No one can know who can like me.
This is their hope in wishing however
When they were not only laden with best wishes
But indeed not inclined for them to be careless
Might they be often more than ever especially
Made to be thought carelessly a vacation
That they will like this less.
Let me listen to me and not to them
May I be very well and happy
May I be whichever they can thrive
Or just may they not.
They do not think not only only
But always with prefer
And therefore I like what is mine
For which not only willing but willingly

Because which it matters.
They find it one in union.
In union there is strength

Stanza IX

Just why they could not ask them to come here
Or may they press them to relieve delight
Should they be planned or may they cause them then
To have it only lost they do not care to leave
Should they come when and will they forward it back
Or neither when they care just when they change
May they not leave or will they not allow
More than they wish it is often that it is a disappointment
To find white turkeys white and little ones the same
Should they be pleased or should they rather not be pleased
Or more than they do should they rather keep it for them
Or more than this should they not infrequently
Or now when they see the difference between round and about
Or not only why they change but what they change
One for one another.
It is often a very best need that they have
To come to see that after all
It was after all when they came back
Or need they not be provoked
By thinking that they will manage to please them.
How often very often do they go
Not which they wish or not which they wish
However it is better not to like it at all
I find it suddenly very warm and this may easily be
Because after all may be it is
In which case do they need any more explanation
Or indeed will they bother
Or after all can there be any difference
Between once in a while and very often
And not at all and why not and will they
Should they be pleased with everything just the same
So that they will think how well they like
What they will do which they do

For them at all.
It is often no matter and a difference
That they see this when they look here
And they may very well be ready
To see this when they look where they do
Nor or may they be there where they are
But not there where they are when
They are at once pleased with what they have
As they do not wish not only but also
To have it better where they like.
It is often no purpose not to have disgrace
Said that they will wait.
All often change all of it so.
It may be decided or not at all
That it is meant should they use
Or would they care to think well long
Of what they think well.
And thank you
It is why they ask everything of them.
Should it be equally well planned
Made to carry or please it for them too
As they may often care or the difference
Between care and carry and recall
Should they find it theirs may they
Will they not be thought well of them.
Or not at all differently at once.
She may have no illusions
Nor be prepared not to be baffled
Or think well of them for which awhile
They chose.
It is for this that they come there and stay.
Should it be well done or should it be well done
Or may they be very likely or not at all
Not only known but well known.
I often think I would like this for that
Or not as likely
Not only this they do
But for which not for which for which
This they do.

Should it be mine as pause it is mine
That should be satisfying

Stanza XIX

She may think the thought that they will wish
And they will hold that they will spell anguish
And they will not be thought perverse
If they angle and the will for which they wish as verse
And so may be they may be asked
That they will answer this.
Let me see let me go let me be not only determined
But for which they will mind
That they are often as inclined
To have them add more than they could
She will be certainly seen if not as much
They will be left to be determined
As much as if they pleased they pleased
Not only theirs but only theirs
For them as much as known and not only
Not repeated because they will be seen
Partly and for less for which they are not very clearly
Made to be better than often as serviceable
Is it as much as why they like
For which they are often as much mistaken
Anything astonishes a mother or any other.
A stanza in between shows restlessly that any queen
Any not a stanza in between for which before which
Any stanza for which in between
They will be for which in between
Any stanza in between as like and they are likely
To have no use in cherishing.
They could be not alone consoled
They could be they may may they
Finally relieve.
It is often eight that they relinquish a stanza
Just when they feel that they are nearly
That they may could and do color
For which they will not only be inconvenient

For which they all for a forest
Come in as soon as our allowed
They prepare nor do they double
Or do they add prefer to before and call
She may be ours in allusion not only to
But why they will as much encourage
Readily for instance or may for instance
Come with not only as much as they tell
They tell it because if not why not
Such should be called their glory or their make
Of angling with and for around
May it be wading for which they wade
Theirs once again the same
All which they said it said it in and answered
May be they like
Might it be uncontained likely
That they should as much joined with ease
But not by this for once once is not only one
They presume once alike not by their own present.
They present well. It followed once more
Only theirs in case. For which.
They add conditionally to not previously adding
More than they gave to one.
One is not one for one but two
Two two three one and any one.
Why they out tired Byron

PART III

Stanza V

It is not a range of a mountain
Of average of a range of a average mountain
Nor may they of which of which of arrange
To have been not which they which
May add a mountain to this.
Upper an add it then maintain
That if they were busy so to speak
Add it to and

It not only why they could not add ask
Or when just when more each other
There is no each other as they like
They add why then emerge an add in
It is of absolutely no importance how often they add it.

Stanza VII

By it by which by it
As not which not which by it
For it it is in an accessible with it
But which will but which will not it
Come to be not made not made one of it
By that all can tell all call for in it
That they can better call add
Can in add none add it.
It is not why she asked that anger
In an anger may they be frightened
Because for it they will be which in not
Not now.
Who only is not now.
I can look at a landscape without describing it.

Stanza IX

Tell me darling tell me true
Am I all the world to you
And the world of what does it consist
May they be a chance to may they be desist
This come to a difference in confusion
Or do they measure this with resist with
Not more which.
Than a conclusion.
May they come with may they in with
For which they may need needing
It is often by the time that not only
Which waiting as an considerable
And not only is it in importance
That they could for an instance

Of made not engaged in rebound
They could indeed care
For which they may not only
Be very often rested in as much
Would they count when they do
Is which which when they do
Making it do.
For this all made because of near
No name is nearly here
Gathering it.
Or gathering it.
Might it in no way be a ruse
For it which in it they an obligation
Fell nearly well.

Stanza XIX

Not what they do with not
Not only will they wish what
What they do with what they like
But they will also very well state
Not only which they prefer by themselves
And now add it in aging ingenuity
But which they will as soon as ever they can
But which they tell indeed may they or may they not proudly
Not only theirs in eight but which they meant
They will all old declare
That believing it is a patent pleasure in their care
Nor where where will they go older than not
Nor will they furnish not only which they had but when they went
In reason.
It is often that they allow a cloud to be white
Or not only patently white but also just as green
Not only theirs in pleasure but theirs in case
Not only however but not only however
Or not at all in wishes that they had chickens
Which may be alternately well or ducks
Or will they spread for them alone
To be not only their care.

This which and whatever I think
I not only do but make it be my care
To endanger no one by hearing how often I place
Theirs not only why they are best not
Not by it as they like.
I have thought while I was awakening
That I might address them
And then I thought not at all
Not while I am feeling that I will give it to them
For them
Not at all only in collision not at all only in mistaken
But which will not at all.
I thought that I would welcome
And so I could be seen.
I then thought would I think one and welcome
Or would I not.
I then concluded that I might be deceived
And it was a white butterfly
Which flew not only not but also
The white dog which ran
And they they were accomplished
And once in a while I would rather gather
Mushrooms even than roses if they were edible
Or at least what not.
I do not wish to say what I think
I concluded I would not name those.
Very often I could feel that a change in cares
Is a change in chairs and not only can and cares
But places
I felt that I could welcome in anticipation wishes
Not only which they do but where they do
How are our changes.
When they could fix titles or affix titles.
When this you see hear clearly what you hear.
Now just like that not just like that
Or they will enjoin and endanger
Damage or delight but which they crow
They have threatened us with crowing
Oh yes not yet.

I cannot think with indifference
Nor will they not want me
Do will they add but which is not
Where they could add would or they would or not
For which they for which fortunately
Make it be mine.
I have often thought of make it be mine.
Now I ask any one to hear me.
This is what I say.
A poem is torn in two
And a broom grows as well
And which came first
Grows as well or a broom
Of course any one can know which of two
This makes it no accident to be taught
And either taught and either fight or fought
Or either not either which either
May they be either one not one only alone.
Should it be thought gracious to be a dish
Of little only as they might mean curiously
That we heard them too
And this I mean by this I mean.
When I thought this morning to keep them so they will not tell
How many which went well
Not as a conclusion to anxious
Anxious to please not only why but when
So then anxious to mean. I will not now

PART IV

Stanza II

I come back to think everything of one
One and one
Or not which they were won
I won.
They will be called I win I won
Nor which they call not which one or one
I won.

I will be winning I won.
Nor not which one won for this is one.
I will not think one and one remember not.
Not I won I won to win win I one won
And so they declare or they declare
To declare I declare I declare I win I won one
I win in which way they manage they manage to win I won
In I one won in which I in which won I won
And so they might come to a stanza three
One or two or one two or one or two or one
Or one two three all out but one two three
One of one two three or three of one two and one

PART V

Stanza X

I have tried earnestly to express
Just what I guess will not distress
Nor even oppress or yet caress
Beside which tried which well beside
They will not only will not be tried.
It is not trying not to know what they mean
By which they come to be welcome as they heard
I have been interrupted by myself by this.
This may be which is not an occasion
To compel this to feel that that is so
I do not dearly love to liven it as much
As when they meant to either change it or not
I do not change it either or not.
This is how they like to do what they like to do.
I have thought often of how however our change
That is to say the sun is warm to-day because
Yesterday it was also warm
And the day before it was not warm
The sun as it shone was not warm
And so moreover as when the sun shone it was not warm
So yesterday as well as to-day
The sun when it shone was warm

And so they do not include our a cloud
Not at all it had nothing to do with a cloud
It had not to do with the wind
It had not to do with the sun
Nor had it to do with the pleasure of the weather either.
It had to do with that this is what there had been.
It is very pleasant that it is this that it should have been
And now that it is not only that it is warmer
Now very well there is often that they will
Have what they look when they look there or there
To make a mistake and change to make a mistake and change
To have not changed a mistake and to make a mistake and change.
Change the prophecy to the weather
Change the care to their whether they will
Nothing now to allow
It is very strange that very often
The beginning makes it truly be
That they will rather have it be
So that to return to be will they be
There will they be there with them.
I should often know that it makes a difference not to look about
Because if to do they that is is it
Not which it makes any difference or
But just what with containing
They need or made so surrounded
In spite of in a delay of delayed
It is often very changed to churn
Now no one churns butter any more.
That is why that is where they are here.
I wish I had not mentioned it either.
This whole stanza is to be about how it does not make any difference.
I have meant this.
Might it be yes yes will it
Might it not be as much as once having it
Might it not only be allowed
And if not does not it bring back
Or bring back what is it
If they bring it back not for me
And if it brings it back for me

Or if it brings it back for me
So and so further than if.
It is easy to be often told and moved
Moved may be mad of sun and sun of rain
Or if not not at all.
Just when they should be thought of so forth.
What they say and what they do
One is one and two is two
Or if not two who.

Stanza LXXI

There was once upon a time a place where they went from time to time.
I think better of this than of that.
They met just as they should.
This is my could I be excited.
And well he wished that she wished.
All of which I know is this.
Once often as I say yes all of it a day.
This is not a day to be away.
Oh dear no.
I have found it why will he.
This which I wish to say is this.
Something that satisfies refuses.
I refuse to be ought or caught.
I like it to be caught or ought.
Or not if I like it to be ought or caught.
This is whatever is that they could be not there.
This is an introduction to Picabia.
When I first knew him I said
Which was it that I did not say I said.
I said what I said which was not in him.
Now who wishes that said is said.
Not him or women.
Or sigh or said.
I did not say I wished it was in him.
Not at all I said forget men and women.
Oh yes I said forget men or women.
Oh yes I said I said to forget men and women.

And I was not melancholy when I thought of everything.
Nor why I thought.
Of course nor why I thought.
That is enough not to have given.
And now if why might I.
The thing I wish to say is this.
It might have been.
There are two things that are different.
One and one.
And two and two.
Three and three are not in winning.
Three and three if not in winning.
I see this.
I would have liked to be the only one.
One is one.
If I am would I have liked to be the only one.
Yes just this.
If I am one I would have liked to be the only one
Which I am.
But we know that I know.
That if this has come
To be one
Of this too
This one
Not only now but how
This I know now.

Stanza LXXVI

I could not be in doubt
About.
The beauty of San Remy.
That is to say
The hills small hills
Beside or rather really all behind.
Where the Roman arches stay
One of the Roman arches
Is not an arch
But a monument

To which they mean
Yes I mean I mean.
Not only when but before.
I can often remember to be surprised
By what I see and saw.
It is not only wonderfully
But like before.

Stanza LXXXI

The whole of this last end is to say which of two.

Stanza LXXXII

Thank you for hurrying through.

Stanza LXXXIII

Why am I if I am uncertain reasons may inclose.
Remain remain propose repose chose.
I call carelessly that the door is open
Which if they may refuse to open
No one can rush to close.
Let them be mine therefor.
Everybody knows that I chose.
Therefore if therefor before I close.
I will therefor offer therefore I offer this.
Which if I refuse to miss may be miss is mine.
I will be well welcome when I come.
Because I am coming.
Certainly I come having come.
These stanzas are done.

IDENTITY A POEM

One of several pieces about identity, this short play is stitched together almost completely, with only minor links added, from passages in *The Geographical History of America Or The Relations Of Human Nature To The Human Mind,* which Stein wrote after her return to France from her American lecture tour. She began the history in June and completed it in the early fall of 1935; it was published in October 1936.

The puppeteer Donald Vestal had not heard Stein lecture when on 30 November 1934 he met her on the street in Chicago and they had a short exchange about puppets. In the summer of 1935 he wrote to ask her for a play for the marionettes he manipulated. As a result, as Stein wrote to Carl Van Vechten, she "put together the plays in [*The Geographical History of America*]" for Vestal. The reference to "the plays" explains the many subtitles, "Play," "Play 2," "Another Play," "Scene II" in *Identity.* On 9 July 1936 Vestal produced *Identity* at the National Puppetry Conference in Detroit.

The problem of identity preoccupied Stein from the moment *The Autobiography of Alice B. Toklas* was published in the spring of 1933, propelling her into fame and into the admiration of an audience that left her not knowing who she was. For a while after the success she was altogether unable to write. Most of her work from the summer of 1933 on shows traces of the temptations of "audience writing"—for fame and applause rather than for substance and truth. The success struck her with the fear of obliteration of her art and with the worry about selling out for popularity, which she loved and therefore needed to fear. Her distinction, in *The Geographical History,* between the human mind, which is the source of creation, and human nature, which is merely the source of personality, is one result of the preoccupation with fame. The question of identity also lies behind *Four In America,* the novel *Ida,* and other late works.

What Stein calls human nature is always self-conscious. The human mind, however, is free of time, memory, identity, and free of the need for applause. That freedom is what allows it to play.

• • • • •

PLAY I

I am I because my little dog knows me. The figure wanders on alone.

The little dog does not appear because if it did then there would be nothing to fear.

It is not known that anybody who is anybody is not alone and if alone then how can the dog be there and if the little dog is not there is it alone.

The little dog is not alone because no little dog could be alone. If it were alone it would not be there.

So then the play has to be like this.

The person and the dog are there and the dog is there and the person is there and where oh where is their identity, is the identity there anywhere.

I say two dogs but say a dog and a dog.

The human mind.	The human mind does play.
The human mind.	Plays because it plays.
Human nature.	Does not play because it does not play again.

It might desire something but it does not play again.

And so to make excitement and not nervousness into a play.

And then to make a play with just the human mind.

Let us try.

To make a play with human nature and not anything of the human mind.

Pivoines smell like magnolias
Dogs smell like dogs
Men smell like men
And gardens smell differently at different seasons of the year.

PLAY 2

Try a play again.
Every little play helps.
Another play.

There is any difference between resting and waiting.
Does a little dog rest.
Does a little dog wait.
What does the human mind do.
What does human nature do.

A PLAY

There is no in between in a play.
A play could just as well only mean two.
Then it could do
It could really have to do.

The dog.	What could it do.
The human mind.	The human mind too

Human nature. Human nature does not have it to do.

What can a dog do and with waiting too.

Yes there is when you have been told not to cry.

Nobody knows what the human mind is when they are drunk.

Everybody who has a grandfather has had a great grandfather and that great grandfather has had a father. This actually is true of a grandmother who was a granddaughter and grandfather had a father.

Any dog too.

Any time any one who knows how to write can write to any brother.

Not a dog too.

A dog does not write too.

ANOTHER PLAY

But. But is a place where they can cease to distress her.

ANOTHER PLAY

It does not make any difference what happens to anybody if it does not make a difference what happens to them.

This no dog can say.

Not any dog can say not ever when he is at play.

And so dogs and human nature have no identity.

It is extraordinary that when you are acquainted with a whole family you can forget about them.

ANOTHER PLAY

A man coming.

Yes there is a great deal of use in a man coming but will he come at all if he does come will he come here.

How do you like it if he comes and looks like that. Not at all later. Well any way he does come and if he likes it he will come again.

Later when another man comes

He does not come.

Girls coming. There is no use in girls coming.

Well any way he does come and if he likes it he will come again.

PART IV

THE QUESTION OF IDENTITY.

A PLAY

I am I because my little dog knows me.
Which is he.
No which is he.
Say it with tears, no which is he.
I am I why.
So there.
I am I where.

ACT I SCENE III

I am I because my little dog knows me.

ACT I SCENE

Now this is the way I had played that play.
But not at all not as one is one.

ACT I SCENE I

Which one is there I am I or another one.
Who is one and one or one is one.
I like a play of acting so and so and a dog my dog is any one of not one.
But we we in America are not displaced by a dog oh no no not at all not at all at all displaced by a dog.

SCENE I

A dog chokes over a ball because it is a ball that choked any one.

PART I SCENE I

He has forgotten that he has been choked by a ball no not forgotten because this one the same one is not the one that can choke any one.

SCENE I ACT I

I am I because my little dog knows me, but perhaps he does not and if he did I would not be I. Oh no oh no.

ACT I SCENE

When a dog is young he seems to be a very intelligent one.

But later well later the dog is older.

And so the dog roams around he knows the one he knows but does that make any difference.

A play is exactly like that.

Chorus There is no left or right without remembering.

And remembering.

They say there is no left and right without remembering.

Chorus But there is no remembering in the human mind.

Tears There is no chorus in the human mind.

The land is flat from on high and when they wander.

Chorus Nobody who has a dog forgets him. They may leave him behind. Oh yes they may leave him behind.

Chorus There is no memory in the human mind.

And the result

May be and the result

If I am I then my little dog knows me.

The dog listens while they prepare food.

Food might be connected with the human mind but it is not.

SCENE II

And how do you like what you are

And how are you what you are

And has this to do with the human mind.

Chorus And has this to do with the human mind.

Chorus And is human nature not at all interesting. It is not.

SCENE II

I am I because my little dog knows me.

Chorus That does not prove anything about you it only proves something about the dog.

Chorus Of course nobody can be interested in human nature.

Chorus Nobody is.

Chorus Nobody is interested in human nature.

Chorus Not even a dog

Chorus It has nothing to do human nature has nothing to do with anything.

Chorus No not with a dog

Tears No not with a dog.

Chorus I am I because my little dog knows

Chorus Yes there I told you human nature is not at all interesting.

SCENE III

And the human mind.

Chorus And the human mind

Tears And the human mind

Chorus Yes and the human mind.

Of course the human mind

Has that anything to do with I am I because my little dog knows me.

What is the chorus.

Chorus What is the chorus.

Anyway there is the question of identity.

What is the use of being a little boy if you are to grow up to be a man.

Chorus No the dog is not the chorus.

SCENE II

Any scene may be scene II

Chorus And act II

No any act can be act one and two.

SCENE II

I am I because my little dog knows me even if the little dog is a big one and yet a little dog knowing me does not really make me be I no not really because after all being I I am I has really nothing to do with the little dog knowing me, he is my audience, but an audience never does prove to you that you are you.

And does a little dog making a noise make the same noise.

He can almost say the b in bow wow.

I have not been mistaken.

Chorus Some kinds of things not and some kinds of things.

SCENE I

I am I yes sir I am I.

I am I yes madame am I I.

When I am I am I I.

And my little dog is not the same thing as I am I.

Chorus Oh is it.

With tears in my eyes oh is it.

Yes madame or am I I.

And there we have the whole thing

Am I I.

And if I am I because my little dog knows me am I I.

Yes sir am I I.

The dog answers without asking because the dog is the answer to anything that is that dog.

But not I.

Without tears but not I.

ACT I SCENE I

The necessity of ending is not the necessity of beginning.

Chorus   How finely that is said.

SCENE II

An end of a play is not the end of a day.

SCENE IV

After giving.

DOCTOR FAUSTUS LIGHTS THE LIGHTS

It is astonishing that Gertrude Stein, who explored not great themes and figures but words, should have written a *Faust.* Nor did she set out to do a *Faust.* Between May and December of 1937 she started the novel *Ida,* a study of a public personality moving about in idle activity and going nowhere. But the novel gave her trouble, even after revisions and reviews of its difficulties with Thornton Wilder. In December she wrote him she had a "scheme" for it, but by May 1938 she announced, "Ida has become an opera, and it is a beauty, really is, an opera about Faust." The libretto *Doctor Faustus Lights The Lights* was finished by June 1938. Late that summer, she returned to *Ida.* She finally completed the novel by the summer of 1940.

We can only speculate about the mysterious process of transmutation that must have taken place to start *Faustus,* for Stein said nothing about it. Ida does not become Faustus, but she undergoes a change and is transformed, the traditional Marguerite becoming Marguerite Ida and Helena Annabel, a protean figure from a charmed, demonic world who summons Faustus as Faustus summons Mephisto.

These transforming figures and relations may be the culmination of Stein's meditation upon who she was. That meditation began with the private events that precipitated *The Autobiography of Alice B. Toklas* and *Stanzas in Meditation* and was followed as in a chain by further events, all public: the success of the *Autobiography;* the American lecture tour; the return to Baltimore with her fame; the reception in Hollywood; the further book contracts; the performance of *Four Saints in Three Acts* in Hartford, New York, and Chicago; the publication of *Everybody's Autobiography;* and the production of *A Wedding Bouquet* by Sadlers Wells in London.

By the alchemy of Stein's writing what became *Doctor Faustus Lights The Lights* absorbed and compounded her experience. In his brilliant invention of electric light the opera comes to embody light itself. It took up the glitter of publicity, the footlights of the theater, the stars of Hollywood. Stein did not grow up taking electric light for granted. Until the second decade, Paris apartments had no electric light, and gas lamps and street lights had to be lit every evening. During the Great War she experienced blackouts. The new work also gathers up the experience of light in painting that Cézanne had illuminated for her. It dramatizes Stein's doubts about technology and progress in the world of industrial America, where electric power makes daylight unnecessary, defeating time, age, and experience until we can finally see it all in moving pictures without living and suffering it.

With the *Autobiography* Stein for the first time had the power to make money—or to sell her soul for pieces of silver. The first of her *Lectures in America, What Is English*

Literature, written in the summer of 1934, speaks of the temptation to abandon God for Mammon, alternately capitalized and decapitalized since it is not theological. Over and over, the lecture says that writing to serve mammon is done for effect but writing that serves god is visionary art. If the *Autobiography* served mammon, it was her pact with the devil.

In this *Faust* there is a natural world of mountains and woods, time, stars, daylight, seasons, and even snakes. Marguerite Ida and Helena Annabel is bitten by a snake as Stein herself had been bitten in the summer of 1933. Stein said that the snakebite made her feel biblical. The snake of the Garden of Eden appears further transformed in the artifical viper, in Mr. Viper, and in the death of the boy and the dog. The natural world returns in *The World Is Round,* written in the summer of 1938. Here the wild woods that Marguerite Ida and Helena Annabel sees everywhere surround Rose climbing the mountain in the night. Here too, in the searchlight that locates Rose, light returns, reassuring her and allowing her to see color in the world again.

Yet the power of this astonishing *Faust* is in its words. It is not the language of ideas and high rhetoric but the most ordinary, colloquial words and phrases that make this play reverberate. Stein uses her verbal skill to build an enormous inventory of primitive incantations, riddles, jingles, chants, and echoes of popular songs. She writes a spell that sounds familiar though we do not know where it originates. "Butter better very well / Butcher whether it will tell / Well is well and silver sell / Sell a salted almond to Nell. . . ." The dog, who had earlier conferred identity in the tag "I am I because my little dog knows me," now receives identity from his master and utters the refrain, "Thank you." Faust and Mephisto confront each other in the most everyday language. On the page their exchanges often look like unrelieved blocks of short words strung together. Heard aloud, they range from poetry to prose, from the insistently vulgar to the insinuatingly endearing, from the patterned lines we see to the repeating anger and terror we hear. In this language a primitive power makes audible the stark scheme of *Faust* with a lucidity that opens the mind's presence to itself.

• • • • •

ACT I

Faust standing at the door of his room, with his arms up at the door lintel looking out, behind him a blaze of electric light.

Just then Mephisto approaches and appears at the door.

Faustus growls out. The devil what the devil what do I care if the devil is there.

Mephisto says. But Doctor Faustus dear yes I am here.

Doctor Faustus. What do I care there is no here nor there. What am I. I am Doctor Faustus who knows everything can do everything and you say it was through you but not at all, if I had not been in a hurry and if I had taken my time I would have known how to make white electric light and day-light and night light and what did I do I saw you miserable devil I saw you and I was deceived and I believed miserable devil I thought I needed you, and I thought I was tempted by the devil and I know no temptation is tempting unless the devil tells you so. And you wanted my soul what the hell did you want my soul for, how do you know I have a soul, who says so nobody says so but you the devil and everybody knows the devil is all lies, so how do you know how do I know that I have a soul to sell how do you know Mr. Devil oh Mr. Devil how can you tell you can not tell anything and I I who know everything I keep on having so much light that light is not bright and what after all is the use of light, you can see just as well without it, you can go around just as well without it you can get up and go to bed just as well without it, and I I wanted to make it and the devil take it yes you devil you do not even want it and I sold my soul to make it. I have made it but have I a soul to pay for it.

Mephisto coming nearer and trying to pat his arm.

Yes dear Doctor Faustus you of course you have a soul of course you have, do not believe them when they say the devil lies, you know the devil never lies, he deceives oh yes he deceives but that is not lying no dear please dear Doctor Faustus do not say the devil lies.

Doctor Faustus. Who cares if you lie if you steal, there is no snake to grind under one's heel, there is no hope there is no death there is no life there is no breath, there just is every day all day and when there is no day there is no day, and anyway of what use is a devil unless he goes away, go away old devil go away, there is no use in a devil unless he goes away, how can you remember a devil unless he goes away, oh devil there is no use in your coming to stay and now you are red at night which is not a delight and you are red in the morning which is not a warning go away devil go away or stay after all what can a devil say.

Mephisto. A devil can smile a devil can while away whatever there is to give away, and now are you not proud Doctor Faustus yes you are you know you are you are the only one who knows what you know and it is I the devil who tells you so.

Faustus. You fool you devil how can you know, how can you tell me so, if I am the only one who can know what I know then no devil can know what I know and no devil can tell me so and I could know without any soul to sell, without there being anything in hell. What I know I know, I know how I do what I do when I see the way through and always any day I will see another day and you old devil you know very well you never see any other way than just the way to hell, you only know one way. You only know one thing, you are never ready for anything, and I everything is always new and now and now perhaps through you I begin to know that it is all just so, that light however bright will never be other than light, and any light is just a light and now there is nothing more either by day or by night but just a light. Oh you devil go to hell, that is all you know to tell, and who is interested in hell just a devil is interested in hell because that is all he can tell, whether I stamp or whether I cry whether I live or whether I die, I can know that all a devil can say is just about going to hell the same way, get out of here devil, it does not interest me whether you can buy or I can sell, get out of here devil just you go to hell.

Faustus gives him an awful kick, and Mephisto runs away and the electric lights just then begin to get very gay.

Alright then

The Ballet

Doctor Faustus sitting alone surrounded by electric lights.

His dog comes in and says

Thank you.

One of the electric lights goes out and again the dog says

Thank you.

The electric light that went out is replaced by a glow.

The dog murmurs.

My my what a sky.

And then he says

Thank you.

Doctor Faustus' song.

If I do it
If you do it
What is it.

Once again the dog says

Thank you.

A duet between Doctor Faustus and the dog about the electric light about the electric lights.

Bathe me

says Doctor Faustus

Bathe me
In the electric light

During this time the electric lights come and go

What is it

says Doctor Faustus

Thank you

said the dog.

Just at this moment the electric lights get brighter and nothing comes

Was it it

says Doctor Faustus

Faustus meditates he does not see the dog.

Will it
Will it
Will it be
Will it be it.

Faustus sighs and repeats

Will it be it.

A duet between the dog and Faustus

Will it be it
Just it.

At that moment the electric light gets pale again and in that moment Faustus shocked says

It is it

A little boy comes in and plays with the dog, the dog says

Thank you.

Doctor Faustus looks away from the electric lights and then he sings a song.

Let me Alone

Let me alone
Oh let me alone
Dog and boy let me alone oh let me alone
Leave me alone
Let me be alone
little boy and dog
let let me alone

He sighs
And as he sighs
He says

Dog and boy boy and dog leave me alone let me let me be alone.

The dog says

Thank you

but does not look at Faustus
A pause
No words
The dog says

Thank you
I say thank you

Thank you
The little boy
The day begins to-day
The day
The moon begins the day
Doctor Faustus
There is no moon to-day
Dark silence
You obey I obey
There is no moon to-day.
Silence
and the dog says
I obey I say
Thank you any day
The little boy says
Once in a while they get up.
Doctor Faustus says
I shall not think
I shall not
No I shall not.
Faustus addresses little boy and dog
Night is better than day so please go away
The boy says
But say
When the hay has to be cut every day then there is the devil to pay
The dog starts and then he shrinks and says
Thank you
Faustus half turns and starts
I hear her
he says
I hear her say
Call to her to sing
To sing all about
to sing a song
All about
day-light and night light.
Moonlight and star-light
electric light and twilight
every light as well.

The electric lights glow and a chorus in the distance sings

Her name is her name is her name is Marguerite Ida and Helena Annabel.

Faustus sings

I knew it I knew it the electric lights they told me so no dog can know no boy can know I cannot know they cannot know the electric lights they told me so I would not know I could not know who can know who can tell me so I know you know they can know her name is Marguerite Ida and Helena Annabel and when I tell oh when I tell oh when I when I when I tell, oh go away and go away and tell and tell and tell and tell and tell, oh hell.

The electric lights commence to dance and one by one they go out and come in and the boy and the dog begin to sing.

Oh very well oh Doctor Faustus very very well oh very well, thank you says the dog oh very well says the boy her name her name is Marguerite Ida and Helena Annabel, I know says the dog I know says the boy I know says Doctor Faustus no no no no no nobody can know what I know I know her name is not Marguerite Ida and Helena Annabel, very well says the boy it is says the boy her name is Marguerite Ida and Helena Annabel, no no no says Doctor Faustus, yes yes yes says the dog, no says the boy yes says the dog, her name is not Marguerite Ida and Helena Annabel and she is not ready yet to sing about day-light and night light, moonlight and star-light electric light and twilight she is not she is not but she will be. She will not be says Doctor Faustus never never never, never will her name be Marguerite Ida and Helena Annabel never never never never well as well never Marguerite Ida and Helena Annabel never Marguerite Ida and Helena Annabel.

There is a sudden hush and the distant chorus says

It might be it might be her name her name might be Marguerite Ida and Helena Annabel it might be.

And Doctor Faustus says in a loud whisper

It might be but it is not, and the little boy says how do you know and Faustus says it might be it might not be not be not be, and as he says the last not be the dog says

Thank you.

Scene II

I am I and my name is Marguerite Ida and Helena Annabel, and then oh then I could yes I could I could begin to cry but why why could I begin to cry.

And I am I and I am here and how do I know how wild the wild world is how wild the wild woods are the wood they call the woods the poor man's overcoat but do they cover me and if they do how wild they are wild and wild and wild they are, how do I know how wild woods are when I have never ever seen a wood before.

I wish, (she whispered) I knew why woods are wild why animals are wild why I am I, why I can cry, I wish I wish I knew, I wish oh how I wish I knew. Once I am in I will never be through the woods are there and I am here and am I here or am I there, oh where oh where is here oh where oh where is there and animals wild animals are everywhere.

She sits down.

I wish (says she conversationally) I wish if I had a wish that when I sat down it would not be here but there there where I could have a chair there where I would not have to look around fearfully everywhere there where a chair and a carpet underneath the chair would make me know that there is there, but here here everywhere there is nothing nothing like a carpet nothing like a chair, here it is wild everywhere I hear I hear everywhere that the woods are wild and I am here and here is here and here I am sitting without a chair without a carpet, oh help me to a carpet with a chair save me from the woods the wild woods everywhere where everything is wild wild and I I am not there I am here oh dear I am not there.

She stands up with her hands at her sides she opens and closes her eyes and opens them again.

If my eyes are open and my eyes are closed I see I see, I see no carpet I see no chair I see the wild woods everywhere, what good does it do me to close my eyes no good at all the woods the woods are there I close my eyes but the green is there and I open my eyes and I have to stare to be sure the green is there the green of the woods, I saw it when my eyes were closed I saw the wild woods everywhere and now I open my eyes and there there is the wild wood everywhere.

Would it do as well if my name was not Marguerite Ida and Helena Annabel would it do as well I would give up even that for a carpet and a chair and to be not here but there, but (and she lets out a shriek,) I am here I am not there and I am Marguerite Ida and Helena Annabel and it is not well that I could tell what there is to tell what there is to see and what do I see and do I see it at all oh yes I do I call and call but yes I do I see it all oh dear oh dear oh dear yes I am here.

She says

In the distance there is daylight and near to there is none.

There is something under the leaves and Marguerite Ida and Helena

Annabel makes a quick turn and she sees that a viper has stung her. She sees it and she says and what is it. There is no answer. Does it hurt she says and then she says no not really and she says was it a viper and she says how can I tell I never saw one before but is it she says and she stands up again and sits down and pulls down her stocking and says well it was not a bee not a busy bee no not, nor a mosquito nor a sting it was a bite and serpents bite yes they do perhaps it was one.

Marguerite Ida and Helena Annabel sits thinking and then she sees a country woman with a sickle coming. Have I she says have I been bitten, the woman comes nearer, have I says Marguerite Ida and Helena Annabel have I have I been bitten. Have you been bitten answers the country woman, why yes it can happen, then I have been bitten says Marguerite Ida and Helena Annabel why not if you have been is the answer.

They stand repeating have I and yes it does happen and then Marguerite Ida and Helena Annabel says let me show you and the woman says oh yes but I have never seen any one who has been bitten but let me see no I cannot tell she says but go away and do something, what shall I do said Marguerite Ida and Helena Annabel do something to kill the poison, but what said Marguerite Ida and Helena Annabel, a doctor can do it said the woman but what doctor said Marguerite Ida and Helena Annabel, Doctor Faustus can do it said the woman, do you know him said Marguerite Ida and Helena Annabel no of course I do not know him nobody does there is a dog, he says thank you said the woman and go and see him go go go said the woman and Marguerite Ida and Helena Annabel went.

As she went she began to sing.

Do vipers sting do vipers bite
If they bite with all their might
Do they do they sting
Or do they do they bite
Alright they bite if they bite with all their might.
And I am I Marguerite Ida or am I Helena Annabel
Oh well
Am I Marguerite Ida or am I Helena Annabel
Very well oh very well
Am I Marguerite Ida very well am I Helena Annabel.

She stops she remembers the viper and in a whisper she says was it a sting was it a bite am I alright, was it a sting was it a bite, alright was it a sting, oh or was it a bite.

She moves away and then suddenly she stops.

Will he tell
Will he tell that I am Marguerite Ida that I am Helena Annabel.
Will he tell.
And then she stops again
And the bite might he make it a bite.
Doctor Faustus a queer name
Might he make it a bite
And so she disappears.

Scene III

Doctor Faustus the dog and the boy all sleeping, the dog dreaming says thickly
Thank you, thank you thank you thank you thank you, thank you.
Doctor Faustus turns and murmurs
Man and dog dog and man each one can tell it all like a ball with a caress no tenderness, man and dog just the same each one can take the blame each one can well as well tell it all as they can, man and dog, well well man and dog what is the difference between a man and a dog when I say none do I go away does he go away go away to stay no nobody goes away the dog the boy they can stay I can go away go away where where there there where, dog and boy can annoy I can go say I go where do I go I go where I go, where is there there is where and all the day and all the night too it grew and grew and there is no way to say I and a dog and a boy, if a boy is to grow to be a man am I a boy am I a dog is a dog a boy is a boy a dog and what am I I cannot cry what am I oh what am I
And then he waits a moment and he says
Oh what am I.
Just then in the distance there is a call
Doctor Faustus Doctor Faustus are you there Doctor Faustus I am here Doctor Faustus I am coming there Doctor Faustus, there is where Doctor Faustus oh where is there Doctor Faustus say it Doctor Faustus are you there Doctor Faustus are you there.
The dog murmurs
Thank you thank you
and the boy says
There is somebody of course there is somebody just there there is somebody somebody is there oh yes somebody is there.
and all together they say

Where is there nobody says nobody is there. Somebody is there and nobody says that somebody is not there. Somebody somebody is there somebody somebody somebody somebody says there is where where is it where is it where is it where, here is here here is there somebody somebody says where is where.

Outside the voice says

Doctor Faustus are you there Doctor Faustus say where, Doctor Faustus are you there.

And then there is a knock at the door.

The electric lights glow softly and Marguerite Ida and Helena Annabel comes in.

Well and yes well, and this is yes this is Doctor Faustus doctor doctor Faustus and he can and he can change a bite hold it tight make it not kill not kill Marguerite Ida not kill Helena Annabel and hell oh hell not a hell not well yes well Doctor Faustus can he can make it all well.

And then she says in a quiet voice.

Doctor Faustus have you ever been to hell.

Of course not she says of course you have not how could you sell your soul if you had ever been to hell of course not, no of course not.

Doctor Faustus tell me what did they give you when you sold your soul, not hell no of course not not hell.

And then she goes on.

I I am Marguerite Ida and Helena Annabel and a viper bit or stung it is very well begun and if it is so then oh oh I will die and as my soul has not been sold I Marguerite Ida and Helena Annabel perhaps I will go to hell.

The dog sighs and says

Thank you

and the little boy coming nearer says

what is a viper, tell me Marguerite Ida and Helena Annabel I like you being Marguerite Ida and Helena Annabel what is a viper do I know it very well or do I not know it very well please tell you are Marguerite Ida and Helena Annabel what is a viper.

Doctor Faustus says

Little boy and dog can be killed by a viper but Marguerite Ida and Helena Annabel not very well no not very well

(He bursts out)

Leave me alone

Let me be alone

Little boy and dog let me be alone, Marguerite Ida and Helena Annabel let me be alone, I have no soul I had no soul I sold it sold it here there and everywhere.

What did I do I knew

I knew that there could be light not moon-light star-light day-light and candle light, I knew I knew I saw the lightening light, I saw it light, I said I I I must have that light, and what did I do oh what did I too I said I would sell my soul all through but I knew I knew that electric light was all true, and true oh yes it is true they took it that it was true that I sold my soul to them as well and so never never could I go to hell never never as well. Go away dog and boy go away Marguerite Ida and Helena Annabel go away all who can die and go to heaven or hell go away oh go away go away leave me alone oh leave me alone. I said it I said it was the light I said I have the light I said the lights are right and the day is bright little boy and dog leave me alone let me be alone.

The country woman with the sickle looks in at the window and sings Well well this is the Doctor Faustus and he has not gone to hell he has pretty lights and they light so very well and there is a dog and he says thank you and there is a little boy oh yes little boy there you are you just are there yes little boy you are and there is Marguerite Ida and Helena Annabel and a viper did bite her, oh cure her Doctor Faustus cure her what is the use of your having been to hell if Marguerite Ida and Helena Annabel is not to be all well.

And the chorus sings

What is the use Doctor Faustus what is the use what is the use of having been to hell if you cannot cure if you cannot cure this only only this Marguerite Ida and Helena Annabel.

Doctor Faustus says

I think I have thought thought is not bought oh no thought is not bought I think I have thought and what have I bought I have bought thought, to think is not bought but I I have bought thought and so you come here you come you come here and here and here where can I say that not to-day not any day can I look and see, no no I cannot look no no I cannot see and you you say you are Marguerite Ida and Helena Annabel and I I cannot see I cannot see Marguerite Ida and I cannot see Helena Annabel and you you are the two and I cannot cannot see you.

Marguerite Ida and Helena Annabel

Do not see me Doctor Faustus do not see me it would terrify me if you did see me do not see me no no do not see me I am Marguerite Ida and Helena Annabel but do not see me cure me Doctor Faustus does the viper bite does the viper sting his sting was a bite and you you have the light cure me Doctor Faustus cure me do but do not see me, I see you but do not see me cure me do but do not see me I implore you.

Doctor Faustus

A dog says thank you but you you say do not see me cure me do but do not see me what shall I do.

He turns to the dog

The dog says

Thank you

and the boy says

What difference does it make to you if you do what difference oh what difference does it make to you if you do, whatever you do do whatever you do do what difference does it make to you if you do.

Marguerite Ida and Helena Annabel

What difference does it make to you if you do what difference does it make to you but I a viper has had his bite and I I will die but you you cannot die you have sold your soul but I I have mine and a viper has come and he has bitten me and see see how the poison works see see how I must die, see how little by little it is coming to be high, higher and higher I must die oh Doctor Faustus what difference does it make to you what difference oh what difference but to me to me to me to me a viper has bitten me a bitter viper a viper has bitten me.

The dog

Oh Thank you thank you all all of you thank you thank you oh thank you everybody thank you he and we thank you, a viper has bitten you thank you thank you.

The boy

A viper has bitten her she knows it too a viper has bitten her believe it or not it is true, a viper has bitten her and if Doctor Faustus does not cure her it will be all through her a viper has bitten her a viper a viper.

Dog

Thank you

Woman at the window

A viper has bitten her and if Doctor Faustus does not cure her it will be all through her.

Chorus in the distance

Who is she
She has not gone to hell
Very well

Very well
She has not gone to hell
Who is she
Marguerite Ida and Helena Annabel
And what has happened to her
A viper has bitten her
And if Doctor Faustus does not cure her
It will go all through her
And he what does he say
He says he cannot see her
Why cannot he see her
Because he cannot look at her
He cannot look at Marguerite Ida and Helena Annabel
But he cannot cure her without seeing her
They say yes yes
And he says there is no witness
And he says
He can but he will not
And she says he must and he will
And the dog says thank you
And the boy says very well
And the woman says well cure her and she says she is Marguerite Ida and Helena Annabel.

There is silence the lights flicker and flicker, and Marguerite Ida and Helena Annabel gets weaker and weaker and the poison stronger and stronger and suddenly the dog says startlingly

Thank you

Doctor Faustus says

I cannot see you
The viper has forgotten you.
The dog has said thank you.
The boy has said will you
The woman has said
Can you
And you, you have said you are you.
Enough said.
You are not dead.
Enough said
Enough said.

You are not dead.
No you are not dead
Enough said
Enough said
You are not dead.

All join in enough said you are not dead you are not dead enough said yes enough said no you are not dead yes enough said, thank you yes enough said no you are not dead.

And at the last
In a low whisper
She says
I am Marguerite Ida and Helena Annabel and enough said I am not dead.

Curtain

ACT II

Some one comes and sings
Very
Very
Butter better very well
Butcher whether it will tell
Well is well and silver sell
Sell a salted almond to Nell
Which she will accept
And then
What does a fatty do
She does not pay for it.
No she does not
Does not pay for it.
By this time they know how to spell very
Very likely the whole thing is really extraordinary
Which is a great relief
All the time her name is Marguerite Ida Marguerite Ida

They drift in and they sing
Very likely the whole thing is extraordinary
Which is a great relief
All the time her name is Marguerite Ida

Marguerite Ida.

Then they converse about it.

Marguerite Ida is her name Marguerite Ida Marguerite Ida and Helena Annabel who can tell if her name is Marguerite Ida or Helena Annabel Sillies all that is what makes you tall.

To be tall means to say that everything else is layed away.

Of course her names is Marguerite Ida too and Helena Annabel as well.

A full chorus

Of course her name is Marguerite Ida too and Helena Annabel as well.

A deep voice asks

Would a viper have stung her if she had only had one name would he would he.

How do you know how do you know that a viper did sting her.

How could Doctor Faustus have cured her if there had not been something the matter with her.

Marguerite Ida and Helena Annabel it is true her name is Marguerite Ida and Helena Annabel as well and a viper has stung her and Doctor Faustus has cured her, cured her cured her, he has sold his soul to hell cured her cured her cured her he has sold his soul to hell and her name is Marguerite Ida and Helena Annabel and a viper had to bite her and Doctor Faustus had to cure her cure her cure her cure her.

The curtain at the corner raises and there she is Marguerite Ida and Helena Annabel and she has an artificial viper there beside her and a halo is around her not of electric light but of candle light, and she sits there and waits.

The chorus sings

There she is
Is she there
Look and see
Is she there
Is she there
Anywhere
Look and see
Is she there
Yes she is there
There is there
She is there
Look and see
She is there.

There she is
There there
Where
Why there
Look and see there
There she is
And what is there
A viper is there
The viper that bit her
No silly no
How could he be there
This is not a viper
This is what is like a viper
She is there
And a viper did bite her
And Doctor Faustus did cure her
And now
And now
And now she is there
Where
Why there
Oh yes there.
Yes oh yes yes there.
There she is
Look and see
And the viper is there
And the light is there.
Who gave her the light
Nobody did
Doctor Faustus sold his soul
And so the light came there
And did she sell her soul.
No silly he sold his soul
She had a viper bite her
She is there
Oh yes she is there
Look there
Yes there
She is there.

Marguerite Ida begins to sing

I sit and sit with my back to the sun I sat and sat with my back to the sun.
Marguerite Ida sat and sat with her back to the sun.
The sun oh the sun the lights are bright like the sun set and she sat with her back to the sun sat and sat.

She sits.

A very grand ballet of lights.

Nobody can know that it is so
They come from everywhere
By land by sea by air
They come from everywhere
To look at her there.
See how she sits
See how she eats
See how she lights,
The candle lights.
See how the viper there,
Cannot hurt her.
No indeed he cannot.
Nothing can touch her,
She has everything
And her soul,
Nothing can lose her,
See how they come
See how they come
To see her.
See how they come.
Watch
They come by sea
They come by land
They come by air
And she sits
With her back to the sun
One sun
And she is one
Marguerite Ida and Helena Annabel as well.

They commence to come and more and more come and they come from the sea from the land and from the air.

And she sits.

A man comes from over the seas and a great many are around him

He sees her as she sits.

And he says

Pretty pretty dear
She is all my love and always here
And I am hers and she is mine
And I love her all the time
Pretty pretty pretty dear.
No says the chorus no.
She is she and the viper bit her
And Doctor Faustus cured her.
The man from over seas repeats
Pretty pretty pretty dear
She is all my love and always here
And I am hers and she is mine
And I love her all the time.

Marguerite Ida and Helena Annabel suddenly hears something and says What is it.

He comes forward and says again

Pretty pretty pretty dear she is all my love and she is always here.

She sings slowly

You do or you do not.

He

Pretty pretty dear she is all my love and she is always here.

Well well he says well well and her name is Marguerite Ida and Helena Annabel and they all say it was a viper, what is a viper, a viper is a serpent and anybody has been bitten and not everybody dies and cries, and so why why say it all the time, I have been bitten I I I have been bitten by her bitten by her there she sits with her back to the sun and I have won I have won her I have won her.

She sings a song

You do or you do not
You are or you are not
I am there is no not
But you you you
You are as you are not

He says

Do you do what you do because you knew all the way through that I I was coming to you answer me that.

She turns her back on him.

And he says

I am your sun oh very very well begun, you turn your back on your sun, I am your sun, I have won I have won I am your sun.

Marguerite Ida and Helena Annabel rises. She holds the viper she says

Is it you Doctor Faustus is it you, tell me man from over the sea are you he.

He laughs.

Are you afraid now afraid of me.

She says

Are you he.

He says

I am the only he and you are the only she and we are the only we. Come come do you hear me come come, you must come to me, throw away the viper throw away the sun throw away the lights until there are none. I am not any one I am the only one, you have to have me because I am that one.

She looks very troubled and drops the viper but she instantly stoops and picks it up and some of the lights go out and she fusses about it.

And then suddenly she starts,

No one is one when there are two, look behind you look behind you you are not one you are two.

She faints.

And indeed behind the man of the seas is Mephistopheles and with him is a boy and a girl.

Together they sing the song the boy and the girl.

Mr. Viper think of me. He says you do she says you do and if you do dear Mr. Viper if you do then it is all true he is a boy I am a girl it is all true dear dear Mr. Viper think of me.

The chorus says in the back,

Dear dear Mr. Viper think of them one is a boy one is a girl dear dear viper dear dear viper think of them.

Marguerite Ida and Helena Annabel still staring at the man from over the seas and Mephisto behind them.

She whispers

They two I two they two that makes six it should be seven they two I two they two five is heaven.

Mephisto says

And what if I ask what answer me what, I have a will of iron yes a will to do what I do. I do what I do what I do, I do I do.

And he strides forward,

Where where where are you, what a to do, when a light is bright there is moon light, when a light is not so bright then it is day light, and when a light is no light than it is electric light, but you you have candle light, who are you.

The ballet rushes in and out.

Marguerite Ida and Helena Annabel lifts the viper and says

Lights are all right but the viper is my might.

Pooh says Mephisto, I despise a viper, the viper tries but the viper lies. Me they cannot touch no not any such, a viper, ha ha a viper, a viper, ha ha, no the lights the lights the candle lights, I know a light when I see a light, I work I work all day and all night, I am the devil and day and night, I never sleep by any light by any dark by any might, I never sleep not by day not by night, you cannot fool me by candle light, where is the real electric light woman answer me.

The little boy and girl creep closer, they sing.

Mr. Viper dear Mr. Viper, he is a boy I am a girl she is a girl I am a boy we do not want to annoy but we do oh we do oh Mr. Viper yes we do we want you to know that she is a girl that I am boy, oh yes Mr. Viper please Mr. Viper here we are Mr. Viper listen to us Mr. Viper, oh please Mr. Viper it is not true Mr. Viper what the devil says Mr. Viper that there is no Mr. Viper, please Mr. Viper please Mr. Viper, she is a girl he is a boy please Mr. Viper you are Mr. Viper please Mr. Viper please tell us so.

The man from over the seas smiles at them all, and says

It is lovely to be at ease.

Mephisto says

What you know I am the devil and you do not listen to me I work and I work by day and by night and you do not listen to me he and she she and he do not listen to me you will see you will see, if I work day and night and I do I do I work day and night, then you will see what you will see, look out look out for me.

He rushes away

And Helena Annabel and Marguerite Ida shrinks back, and says to them all

What does he say

And the man from over the seas says

Pretty pretty dear she is all my love and she is always here.

and then more slowly

I am the only he you are the only she and we are the only we,

and the chorus sings softly

And the viper did bite her and Doctor Faustus did cure her.

And the boy and girl sing softly.

Yes Mr. Viper he is a boy she is a girl yes Mr. Viper.

And the ballet of lights fades away.

Curtain

ACT III

Scene I

In Faust's house

Faust in his chair, the dog and the boy, the electric lights are bright but the room is dark.

Faust

Yes they shine
They shine all the time.
I know they shine
I see them shine
And I am here
I have no fear
But what shall I do
I am all through
I cannot bear
To have no care
I like it bright
I do like it bright
Alright I like it bright,
But is it white
Or is it bright.
Dear dear
I do care
That nobody can share.
What if they do
It is all to me
Ah I do not like that word me,

Why not even if it does rhyme with she. I know all the words that rhyme with bright with light with might with alright, I know them so that I cannot tell I can spell but I cannot tell how much I need to not have that, not light not sight, not bright not night not alright, not night not sight not bright, no no not night not sight not bright no no not bright.

There is a moment's silence and then the dog says

Thank you.

He turns around and then he says

Yes thank you.

And then he says

Not bright not night dear Doctor Faustus you are right, I am a dog yes I am just that I am I am a dog and I bay at the moon, I did yes I did I used to do it I used to bay at the moon I always used to do it and now now not any more, I cannot, of course I cannot, the electric lights they make it be that there is no night and if there is no night then there is no moon and if there is no moon I do not see it and if I do not see it I cannot bay at it.

The dog sighs and settles down to rest
and as he settles down he says

Thank you.

The little boy cuddles up close to him and says

Yes there is no moon and if there is a moon then we do not bay at the moon and if there is no moon then no one is crazy any more because it is the moon of course it is the moon that always made them be like that, say thank you doggie and I too I too with you will say thank you.

They softly murmur

Thank you thank you thank you too.

They all sleep in the dark with the electric light all bright, and then at the window comes something.

Is it the moon says the dog is it the moon says the boy is it the moon do not wake me is it the moon says Faustus.

No says a woman no it is not it is not the moon, I am not the moon I am at the window Doctor Faustus do not you know what it is that is happening.

No answer.

Doctor Faustus do not you know what is happening.

Back of her a chorus

Doctor Faustus do not you know what is happening.

Still no answer
All together louder

Doctor Faustus do not you know do not you know what it is that is happening.

Doctor Faustus.

Go away woman and men, children and dogs moon and stars go away let me alone let me be alone no light is bright, I have no sight, go away woman and let me boy and dog let me be alone I need no light to tell me it is bright, go away go away, go away go away.

No says the woman no I am at the window and here I remain till you hear it all. Here we know because Doctor Faustus tells us so, that he only he can turn night into day but now they say, they say, (her voice rises to a screech) they say a woman can turn night into day, they say a woman and a viper bit her and did not hurt her and he showed her how and now she can turn night into day, Doctor Faustus oh Doctor Faustus say you are the only one who can turn night into day, oh Doctor Faustus yes do say that you are the only one who can turn night into day.

The chorus behind says

Oh Doctor Faustus oh Doctor Faustus do say that you are the only one who can turn night into day.

Faustus starts up confused he faces the woman, he says,

What is it you say.

And she says imploringly,

Oh Doctor Faustus do say you are the only one who can turn night into day.

Faustus slowly draws himself erect and says

Yes I do say I am the only one who can turn night into day.

And the woman and the chorus say,

He is the only one who can turn night into day.

And the dog says

He is the only one who can turn night into day, there is no moon any night or any day he is the only one to turn night into day,

and the little boy says

Yes he is the only one to turn night into day.

And the woman then says

But come Doctor Faustus come away come and see whether they say that they can turn night into day.

Who says it

says Doctor Faustus

She says it

says the woman

Who is she

says Doctor Faustus

They answer
Marguerite Ida or Helena Annabel
She
says Doctor Faustus
Who said I could not go to hell.
She she
says the woman
She she
says the chorus
Thank you
said the dog
Well
said Doctor Faustus
Well then I can go to hell, if she can turn night into day then I can go to hell, come on then come on we will go and see her and I will show her that I can go to hell, if she can turn night into day as they say then I am not the only one very well I am not the only one so Marguerite Ida and Helena Annabel listen well you cannot but I I can go to hell. Come on every one never again will I be alone come on come on every one.

They all leave.

Scene II

The scene as before, Marguerite Ida and Helena Annabel sitting with the man from over the seas their backs to the sun, the music to express a noon-day hush.

Everybody dreamily saying
Mr. Viper please Mr. Viper,
some saying
Is he is he Doctor Faustus no he isn't no he isn't, is he is he is he all he loves her is he is he all she loves him, no one can remember anything but him, which is she and which is he sweetly after all there is no bee there is a viper such a nice sweet quiet one, nobody anybody knows how to run, come any one come, see any one, some, come viper sun, we know no other any one, any one can forget a light, even an electric one but no one no no one can forget a viper even a stuffed one no no one and no one can forget the sun and no one can forget Doctor Faustus no no one and and no one can forget Thank you and the dog and no one can forget a little boy and no one can forget any one no no one.

(These words to be distributed among the chorus)

and the man from over seas murmurs dreamily

Pretty pretty pretty dear here I am and you are here and yet and yet it would be better yet if you had more names and not only four in one let it be begun, forget it oh forget it pretty one, and if not I will forget that you are one yes I will yes I will pretty pretty one yes I will.

Marguerite Ida and Helena Annabel stiffens a little.

Well will you yes I will, no one can know when I do not tell them so that they cannot know anything they know, yes I know, I do know just what I can know, it is not there well anywhere, I cannot come not for any one I cannot say what is night and day but I am the only one who can know anything about any one, am I one dear dear am I one, who hears me hears me I am here and here I am, yes here I am.

The chorus gets more lively and says

Yes there she is

Dear me

says the man from over the seas.

Just then out of the gloom appears at the other end of the stage Faust and the boy and the dog, nobody sees them, just then in front of every one appears Mephisto, very excited and sings

Which of you can dare to deceive me which of you he or she can dare to deceive me, I who have a will of iron I who make what will be happen I who can win men or women I who can be wherever I am which of you has been deceiving which of you she or he which of you have been deceiving me.

He shouts louder

If there is a light who has the right, I say I gave it to him, she says he gave it to her or she does not say anything, I say I am Mephisto and what I have I do not give no not to any one, who has been in her who has been in him, I will win.

The boy and girl shrilly sing

She is she and he is he and we are we Mr. Viper do not forget to be. Please Mr. Viper do not forget to be, do not forget that she is she and that he is he please Mr. Viper do not forget me.

Faustus murmurs in a low voice

I sold my soul to make it bright with electric light and now no one not I not she not they not he are interested in that thing and I and I I cannot go to hell I have sold my soul to make a light and the light is bright but not interesting in my sight and I would oh yes I would I would rather go to hell be I with all my might and then go to hell oh yes alright.

Mephisto strides up to him and says

You deceived me.

I did not

says Faust

Mephisto.

You deceived me and I am never deceived

Faust

You deceived me and I am always deceived

Mephisto

You deceived me and I am never deceived.

Faust

Well well let us forget it is not ready yet let us forget and now oh how how I want to be me myself all now, I do not care for light let it be however light, I do not care anything but to be well and to go to hell. Tell me oh devil tell me will she will Marguerite Ida and Helena Annabel will she will she really will she go to hell.

Mephisto

I suppose so.

Faust

Well then how dear devil how how can I who have no soul I sold it for a light how can I be I again alright and go to hell.

Mephisto

Commit a sin

Faust

What sin, how can I without a soul commit a sin.

Mephisto

Kill anything

Faust

Kill

Mephisto

Yes kill something oh yes kill anything.

Yes it is I who have been deceived I the devil who no one can deceive yes it is I I who have been deceived.

Faust

But if I kill what then will.

Mephisto

It is I who have an iron will.

Faust

But if I kill what will happen then.

Mephisto

Oh go to hell.

Faust

I will

He turns he sees the boy and dog he says

I will kill I will I will.

He whispers

I will kill I will I will.

He turns to the boy and dog and he says

Boy and dog I will kill you two I will kill I will I will boy and dog I will kill you kill you, the viper will kill you but it will be I who did it, you will die.

The dog says

Thank you, the light is so bright there is no moon to-night I cannot bay at the moon the viper will kill me. Thank you,

and the boy says

And I too, there is no day and night there is no dog to-night to say thank you the viper will kill me too, good-bye to you.

In the distance the voices of the boy and girl are heard saying Mr. Viper please listen to me he is a boy she is a girl.

There is a rustle the viper appears and the dog and the boy die.

Faust

They are dead yes they are dead, dear dog dear boy yes you are dead you are forever ever ever dead and I I can because you die nobody can deny later I will go to hell very well very well I will go to hell Marguerite Ida Helena Annabel I come to tell to tell you that I can go to hell.

Mephisto

And I, while you cry I who do not deny that now you can go to hell have I nothing to do with you.

Faustus

No I am through with you I do not need the devil I can go to hell all alone. Leave me alone let me be alone I can go to hell all alone.

Mephisto

No listen to me now take her with you do I will make you young take her with you do Marguerite Ida and Helena Annabel take her with you do.

Faust

Is it true that I can be young.

Mephisto

Yes.

Faust

Alright.

He is young he approaches Marguerite Ida and Helena Annabel who wakes up and looks at him. He says

Look well I am Doctor Faustus and I can go to hell.

Marguerite Ida and Helena Annabel

You Doctor Faustus never never Doctor Faustus is old I was told and I saw it with my eyes he was old and could not go to hell and you are young and can go to hell, very well you are not Doctor Faustus never never.

Faustus

I am I am I killed the boy and dog when I was an old man and now I am a young man and you Marguerite Ida and Helena Annabel and you know it well and you know I can go to hell and I can take some one too and that some one will be you.

Marguerite Ida and Helena Annabel

Never never, never never, you think you are so clever you think you can deceive, you think you can be old and you are young and old like any one but never never, I am Marguerite Ida and Helena Annabel and I know no man or devil no viper and no light I can be anything and everything and it is always always alright. No one can deceive me not a young man not an old man not a devil not a viper I am Marguerite Ida and Helena Annabel and never never will a young man be an old man and an old man be a young man, you are not Doctor Faustus no not ever never never

and she falls back fainting into the arms of the man from over the seas who sings

Pretty pretty pretty dear I am he and she is she and we are we, pretty pretty dear I am here yes I am here pretty pretty pretty dear.

Mephisto strides up

Always deceived always deceived I have a will of iron and I am always deceived always deceived come Doctor Faustus I have a will of iron and you will go to hell.

Faustus sings

Leave me alone let me be alone, dog and boy boy and dog leave me alone let me be alone

and he sinks into the darkness and it is all dark and the little boy and little girl sing

Please Mr. Viper listen to me he is he and she is she and we are we please Mr. Viper listen to me.

Curtain